A CASEBOOK ON **Roman Family Law**

AMERICAN PHILOLOGICAL ASSOCIATION

CLASSICAL RESOURCES SERIES

Joel Lidov, Series Editor

NUMBER 5
A CASEBOOK ON ROMAN FAMILY LAW

Bruce W. Frier and Thomas A.J. McGinn

A CASEBOOK ON
Roman Family Law

Bruce W. Frier and Thomas A.J. McGinn

OXFORD
UNIVERSITY PRESS

2004

OXFORD
UNIVERSITY PRESS

Oxford   New York
Auckland   Bangkok   Buenos Aires   Cape Town   Chennai
Dar es Salaam   Delhi   Hong Kong   Istanbul   Karachi   Kolkata
Kuala Lumpur   Madrid   Melbourne   Mexico City   Mumbai   Nairobi
São Paulo   Shanghai   Taipei   Tokyo   Toronto

Copyright © 2004 by The American Philological Association

Published by Oxford University Press, Inc.
198 Madison Avenue, New York, New York 10016

www.oup.com

Oxford is a registered trademark of Oxford University Press

Library of Congress Cataloging-in-Publication Data
Frier, Bruce W., 1943–
A casebook on Roman family law / Bruce W. Frier and Thomas A.J. McGinn
  p. cm.—(Classical resources series / American Philological Association ; no. 5)
Includes bibliographical references and index.
ISBN 978-0-19-516186-1
1. Domestic relations (Roman law) I. McGinn, Thomas A. II. Title.
III. Classical resources series ; no. 5.
KJA2227 .F75 2003
346.45'632015—dc21   2002013989

Printed in the United States of America
on acid-free paper

Preface

This Casebook introduces the area of Roman law governing the most personal and urgent problems that free Romans normally confronted: the marital relationship, the power of fathers over their children, and the devolution of property within the family. This area of law is interesting even today because, although many parts of it seem at least generally familiar, Roman family law was organized and developed on lines that are radically, and at times almost breathtakingly, different from any modern legal system. On one level, then, students are invited to think about a set of legal rules that are unlike anything they have ever seen before but that nonetheless are distinctly "legal" in a way that any modern lawyer can understand; but on another level students are also encouraged to think about how these rules are likely to have affected the actual lives of Romans.

A casebook relies on direct use of primary sources in order to convey a clear understanding of what legal sources are like and how lawyers work. For Roman law, the primary sources are above all the writings of the early imperial jurists. Almost all their writings date to what is commonly called the classical period of Roman law, from approximately 31 B.C. to A.D. 235. Justinian's *Digest,* promulgated at Constantinople in A.D. 533, collects more than nine thousand lightly edited excerpts (totaling over eight hundred thousand words) that derive mainly from classical juristic writings. The excerpts vary in length from a few words to several pages. Modern knowledge of classical Roman law rests chiefly on the *Digest* and a few other sources: most prominent among them being the *Institutes* of Gaius, an elementary textbook written about A.D. 160, which is the sole work of the classical jurists that has survived to us more or less intact; and also the *Institutes* of Justinian, an elementary textbook loosely based on Gaius.

Roman family law was also the subject of considerable legislation, which is frequently referred to and interpreted by the jurists. The most important of this legislation takes the form of laws (*leges*) passed by the Roman legislative assemblies especially during the early Empire; and decrees of the Senate (*senatusconsulta,* abbreviated SC) passed by the Roman Senate, usually after they had been moved by the emperor or his agent. A large amount of imperial lawmaking also takes the form of rescripts, answers to questions of law addressed by officials or private citizens to the emperor. These rescripts, which become increasingly numerous starting in the second century A.D., are somewhat haphazardly collected, but many can be found in the *Codex* of Justinian, promulgated at Constantinople in A.D. 534.

For the most part, however, the 235 Cases in this book derive from the writings of preclassical and classical jurists. The Roman jurists were not judges in our sense, nor were they like modern lawyers or law professors. They were, instead, a tiny elite of legal professionals who were charged with conserving and developing the law, especially the private law that Romans used in lawsuits between themselves. Although the Cases often describe fact situations at least loosely drawn from real life, they are, with very few exceptions, not judicial opinions on real legal cases. Rather, the jurists write about hypothetical but realistic situations as part of their effort to discuss and develop law. The jurists' writings were originally intended, in the main, for reading by their fellow jurists or other skilled legal scholars, not by laypersons. However, the legal rules that the jurists created through their writings were then applied directly to actual cases that arose in Roman courts, in order to settle questions of law.

During the classical period of Roman law, private lawsuits in the city of Rome were normally brought in the court of the urban praetor, a magistrate of the Roman state. So that potential plaintiffs could know which lawsuits he was willing to grant, the praetor, at the start of his year in office, issued an Edict listing all the causes of action that he recognized as available. The praetor used his Edict both to implement existing law and to create new actions. By the classical period, the contents of this Edict were usually carried over mechanically from praetor to praetor, although changes remained possible until the Edict was given its final form in the early second century A.D.

Actual trials took place in two stages. A plaintiff first came before the praetor and asked him to grant a lawsuit. If the plaintiff stated an acceptable cause of action, the praetor granted a trial and assigned the case for decision by a "judge" (*iudex*), who was normally a layperson lacking any deep familiarity with law. The praetor and the two parties to the lawsuit also prepared a special *formula*; this *formula* (which gives its name to Roman "formulary procedure") appointed the *iudex,* instructed him on the general nature of the dispute, and ordered him to decide it. During the second stage of the trial, the *iudex* listened to arguments from advocates for both sides and then decided the outcome of the case in accordance with the *formula*. Normally, this verdict could not be appealed or reviewed.

When important questions of law arose either before the praetor or during the actual trial before the *iudex,* they were usually settled through reference to the opinions of jurists. Thus, the Roman jurists, although they were not formally a part of the judicial system, played a pivotal role in determining law within Roman courts.

The "Case-Law" Approach

In this Casebook, students are exposed to the working methods of the Roman jurists, to their internal controversies, and to the principles and values that underlay their law. One important area, family law, has been chosen to illustrate these points. The basic framework of Roman family law derives from two sources: statutes (legislation in various forms) and the Edict of the urban praetor. Some Cases involve juristic interpretation of these fundamental sources. But in most Cases the jurists range well beyond the basic framework into broader legal issues associated with the life of the family; and most of Roman family law is in fact the jurists' own creation, not the result of straightforward statutory or edictal interpretation.

At our respective universities, we use this Casebook as the basic text for a semester-long undergraduate course in Roman law. The course is organized around classroom discussion of the individual Cases—usually about four to six Cases each hour. By delving into the Cases, students develop their own ability to examine legal rules and to assess them critically. Over a semester, the improvement in their legal skills is usually remarkable. Further, all law is to a large extent a seamless cloth, and this is no less true of Roman law; so students soon pick up a good deal of Roman law in areas besides family law, as well as some of the rules in their own legal system.

In order to encourage a deeper understanding of the Cases, we require students to purchase a general handbook on Roman law (e.g., Barry Nicholas, *An Introduction to Roman Law*, 1962). We also recommend that they purchase Edward Levi's *An Introduction to Legal Reasoning* (1949) or some comparable book introducing the process of legal reasoning. Students who not only participate in classroom discussion but also read these assigned books come away from the course with a good grasp of the nature of legal thinking in general, as well as an appreciation of the general content of both Roman and modern family law.

This Casebook is modeled after the format of Herbert Hausmaninger's highly successful German casebooks on Roman contract and property law, as well as Bruce Frier's *Casebook on the Roman Law of Delict* (1989). To our mind, this format offers the best available method to communicate to modern students the content and character of classical Roman law. Direct exposure to original sources is far more intellectually stimulating than lectures or a superficial reading of modern synthetic accounts; students also learn much more about law from the original sources than they could possibly learn from a mere summary. We believe that students are best advised to avoid the crabbed formalism of elementary works such as the *Institutes* of Gaius or of Justinian and instead to plunge as soon as possible into the actual working texts of the jurists.

How to Use This Casebook

The presentation of the Cases is invariable: first, the Latin text with the appropriate citation; second, an English translation of the text; third, for some Cases, a brief restatement of the main hypothetical problem in the Case; fourth, discussion of the elements of the Case to orient students regarding the main legal problems raised, and questions to encourage deeper reflection on the Case and its ramifications.

The Cases are grouped by subject matter and presented in a definite order, usually so that legal questions can be explored on a progressively deeper basis. It is important to think about the interrelationship between the Cases and the various approaches that the jurists take within them.

The discussion questions have several forms. Some encourage accurate understanding of the Case itself, others involve application of the Case to different situations, and still others raise open-ended problems that invite a response based on broader considerations, including morality and public policy. For this reason, not all of the questions have clear and specific answers. Some, in fact, are intended mainly to stimulate thought and classroom discussion, and these questions may have no "correct" answer at all. Roman law, like all law, tends to raise difficulties on several levels simultaneously; students should learn to think about the connection between broad and narrow legal issues.

Frequent reference is made to other legal texts, including many not quoted in this Casebook. Although it is not necessary to look up these references in order to understand the discussion, students who wish to learn more about Roman law are urged to consult these texts and the works mentioned in the "Suggested Further Reading" at the end of the book. To assist readers in becoming familiar with some of the more common technical terms of Roman law, a Glossary has been provided that contains definitions of key Latin words and some unfamiliar English words.

Finally, students should remember that the writings of the Roman jurists span more than three centuries and accordingly display a development in legal ideas. The chronological list of jurists presented following the table of contents should make it easier to observe this development. An Appendix to the Casebook contains short biographies of the major Roman jurists. Fortunately, they are few in number, and students who look up the biographies will soon become familiar with their names.

In reading this Casebook, students should think about not only the particular problems raised by the Cases but also the larger issues they concern. On what principles does a civil society attempt to structure an institution as fundamental as the family? How, and to what extent, is law used to protect not only the existence of the family but also the independent interests of the various persons who participate in families? The jurists' thought on these matters is in some respects similar to our own and in other respects sharply different. What explains the differences? Do they result chiefly from the relative social and economic "underdevelopment" of the Roman world or from deeper disagreements about the way in which societies should be organized and governed? To what extent is the development of Roman law affected by accidents of its history or the conservatism of the jurists, and to what extent by the conscious or unconscious efforts of the jurists to achieve a socially beneficial body of rules? How close is the "fit" between Roman law and the social needs of Roman society? These are difficult questions, concerning which modern scholars still often disagree.

A Note on Translation

Throughout this Casebook, "D." stands for the *Digest* (*Digesta*) of Justinian, "C." for the *Codex* of Justinian, and "*Inst.*" for the *Institutes* (*Institutiones*) of Gaius or Justinian, as indicated. Many Cases also come from several postclassical epitomes of juristic sources: the *Collatio* (a "comparison" of Roman with Mosaic law); the *Sentences* (*Sententiae*) attributed to the jurist Paul but actually of considerably later date; and the *Excerpts from Ulpian's Writings* (*Tituli ex Corpore Ulpiani;* also sometimes called *Ulpiani Regularum Epitome*), which probably has only a loose connection to Ulpian. Although these late imperial sources all derive their substance in large part from earlier classical sources, all have been subjected to post-classical abbreviation. A few Cases are also taken from nonlegal works by Cicero, Quintilian, Aulus Gellius, and other Roman authors.

In handling texts, we have adopted a few special editorial conventions: square brackets ([ ]) indicate letters or words in the standard transmitted Latin text that we believe are not authentic and that we therefore do not translate, while angle brackets (< >) indicate letters or words that we have inserted into the Latin text. Within the English translations (whether or not a Latin text is also printed), parentheses always indicate our editorial insertions intended to clarify or explain the translation. Finally, readers unfamiliar with the Latin originals of Justinianic sources may wish to know that "pr." in a citation (e.g., Case 2: D.1.5.4 pr.–1) refers to the *principium*, or "beginning," of the Latin fragment, before the numbered subsections; this rather awkward numbering system originated in the Renaissance.

The translations in this Casebook are intended to render the original Latin into clear and comprehensible English, even at the cost of wordiness. Where the Latin text is disputed or its meaning ambiguous, we have opted for what we feel is the best solution; and this has also often meant making small changes in the transmitted text. All translations are our own, although we have often been influenced by the renderings in *The Digest of Justinian* (a four-volume English translation edited by Alan Watson, 1985), *The Institutes of Gaius* (an English translation by Francis de Zulueta, 1946–1953), and other standard translations.

For reasons that should become clear, we have usually left untranslated some important technical terms, since any English translation of these terms might fatally prejudice understanding of them. It is preferable that students learn the meaning of these words from the contexts in which they appear. However, the Glossary at the end of the volume should help with unfamiliar vocabulary.

Acknowledgments

Thomas McGinn would like to thank Eileen McGinn for helping to make this project possible; the Vanderbilt University Research Council for its generous support during a leave in 1999, when the bulk of his work on the book was completed; and also the Interlibrary Loan staff of Vanderbilt's Jean and Alexander Heard Library: James Toplon, Marilyn Pilley, and Rachel Adams. Bruce Frier wishes to thank the Cook Research Fund of the University of Michigan Law School, which supported his work on the book over several summers; as well as Kendra Eschleman, who assisted in his research.

Both authors are grateful to Judith Evans Grubbs for her extremely insightful comments on the text. We also appreciate the care with which our manuscript was reviewed by the American Philological Association and its two anonymous readers; we especially thank Joel Lidov and Jeffrey Rusten, who oversaw the approval process. At Oxford University Press, the manuscript was skillfully and speedily edited by Jessica Ryan and Pamela Bruton.

We have dedicated this book to our families.

B. W. F. and T. A. J. McG.

Contents

Chapter III: *Patria Potestas*

Chapter V. Tutelage and the Status of Children and Women

Classroom Notes

The authors have prepared a set of teaching notes to accompany this book. Teachers may obtain a copy, free of charge, by sending a request on departmental stationery to Prof. Bruce W. Frier, Law School, The University of Michigan, Ann Arbor, MI 48109-1215, USA.

Major Jurists Cited in This Casebook
(in Rough Chronological Order)

Jurist	*Roman Emperor*

Preclassical (100–30 B.C.)

Q. MUCIUS Scaevola
G. Aquilius GALLUS
SERVIUS Sulpicius Rufus
P. ALFENUS Varus

Early Classical (30 B.C. to A.D. 90)

M. Antistius LABEO	Augustus (31 B.C. to A.D. 14)
Masurius SABINUS	Tiberius (14–37)
G. CASSIUS Longinus	Claudius (41–54)
PROCULUS	Nero (54–68)
PLAUTIUS	Vespasian (69–79)
	Domitian (81–96)

High Classical (A.D. 90–190)

L. JAVOLENUS Priscus	Trajan (98–117)
L. NERATIUS Priscus	Hadrian (117–138)
P. Juventius CELSUS	
P. Salvius JULIANUS (JULIAN)	Antoninus Pius (138–161)
Ulpius MARCELLUS	
VENULEIUS Saturninus	
Sextus Caecilius AFRICANUS	Marcus Aurelius (161–180)
GAIUS	
Sextus POMPONIUS	
Q. Cervidius SCAEVOLA	Commodus (180–192)

Late Classical (A.D. 190–235)

Aemilius PAPINIANUS (PAPINIAN)	Septimius Severus (193–211)
CALLISTRATUS	
Julius PAULUS (PAUL)	Caracalla (211–217)
Domitius ULPIANUS (ULPIAN)	
Aelius MARCIANUS (MARCIAN)	Alexander Severus (222–235)
Herennius MODESTINUS	

Note: The Latin name by which each jurist is referred to in the text and listed in the Appendix is capitalized. The Appendix contains further biographical information on these and other jurists mentioned in the text.

Introduction to Roman Family Law

Family law concerns legal aspects of the domestic relationships between persons who are grouped together within a household understood as a social, political, and economic unit. Usually these persons are close kin to one another: spouses, parents, children, siblings.

Plainly the family is of great legal interest because of the decisive role it has historically played in the raising and socialization of children and in the mutual economic support of its members. But justification for the family has also frequently been located in the incentives to benevolence and in the psychological satisfaction that its intense intimacy produces in its members. In other words, the remarkable resilience of the family unit over the ages is not solely a matter of its instrumental role in promoting social welfare and demographic reproduction. Since at least the time of Aristotle, family life has been understood as essential to a complete human life; and family law, in turn, fosters this human good by reducing the uncertainties and inequities that are frequently associated with more unstructured conjugal relationships.

In the modern world, the legal prototype of the family has long been the nuclear family in its various stages, from the initial establishment of a household by a newly married couple, through the birth and rearing of their children, until the eventual dissolution of the family as children depart and the marriage ends through the death of one spouse or by divorce. During recent decades, however, legal attention has increasingly turned to "nontraditional" families, especially those headed by unmarried single persons or unmarried couples, including same-sex couples. Further, the legal aspects of family relationships have become increasingly intertwined with numerous other branches of law, including not just the traditionally important areas of property law but also contract and tort law, statutory and administrative regulations, and even constitutional law. This is an area of modern law that is rapidly expanding and changing.

But in the more extended view of history, it is surely unwise to regard any particular family formation as authentically "traditional." To be sure, the biological requirements for reproduction have, until quite recently, imposed some irreducible elements of pattern on families. But this biological substratum hardly explains by itself the wide variety of manifestations that the family has had in historical cultures. The tacit presumptions of modern family life are so deeply instilled in all of us that at least initially it may be difficult to comprehend the range of meanings that past societies have given to such rudimentary concepts as marriage, parenting, kinship, household, coresidence, and so on. Continuities of vocabulary over long periods of time may, in fact, conceal enormous differences.

Roman legal sources introduce a system of family law that, on its face, diverges sharply from anything we know in the modern industrialized world. These sources describe a legal regime that prevailed during the first three centuries of the Roman Empire (roughly, 31 B.C. to A.D. 235), especially in Rome, the capital city of the Empire. Roman "families" (*familiae,* more accurately translated as "households") were fundamental units of this legal regime. In some respects, it is true, the Roman household looks not entirely unlike many modern households. Indeed, literary sources describing Roman domestic life frequently induce in modern readers a sense of "familiarity" and recognition across two millennia of history: deeply affective interactions, warmth and abiding love between spouses and between parents and children.

But the legal sources suggest another, rather darker perspective. The main cast of characters that will move through the Cases in this book is small and easily assembled:

- the *pater familias,* male head of the household, sole owner of all property belonging to the household, and endowed by law with considerable power over all his descendants through the male line no matter their age;
- his wife, joined to him by astonishingly fragile bonds of matrimony but sharing with him neither in the control nor in the ultimate disposition of the household's wealth except as concerns her own property and her dowry (a fund that is, however, managed largely at his discretion so long as the marriage lasts);
- and his descendants, captured within a household structure that allows them little true social or economic independence until they are finally freed from his mastery not by their own adulthood but by his death.

In short, the legal sources suggest a household regime that is described mainly through the exercise of power. Even *pietas,* which the jurists often mention as the emotional glue of the Roman household, is a distinctly frosty virtue: a traditional sense of the duty that is owed to other family members, rather than a sentiment believed to stem from genuine affection.

Two features of Roman family law may particularly surprise a contemporary viewer. First, this law reflects the values of a world still largely dominated by males, in which, therefore, the public role of adult women is considerably restricted by custom and by law (see especially Cases 228–235). Much of this male domination is emphatically reinforced within family law, where, in the centuries just before the classical era, the Romans had actually moved from an "archaic" model of marriage in which the wife was a full member of the household (albeit in principle subordinated to her husband, Cases 37–40) to a "classical" model in which the wife's presence is legally so tenuous that she seems at times only to be tolerated as an unavoidable prerequisite for the bearing and raising of children.

Second, the overriding concern of Roman family law is not with setting standards for a family's life and internal governance but rather with the implications of family structure for the holding and disposition of property. That is, Roman family law is primarily directed toward economic issues. Spousal and child abuse, for example, can hardly have been altogether missing from the Roman world, but they are rarely even alluded to in Roman legal sources; and in general the Roman lawyers seem, if not blind, then at least myopic when it comes to the possibility that the *pater familias* might misuse his considerable power over people and things. In truth, for every juristic ruling on child custody or parental discipline, there are a hundred or more rulings on dowry. Even though, in recent decades, the theory and practice of modern American family law have been gradually shifting from moral to economic issues, Roman law still remains extreme from our vantage point.

From the state's perspective, Roman family law is generally antipaternalistic, cautious about intruding on the autonomy that in principle surrounds the household. Therefore, such intrusions as do occur—and there are some, particularly toward the end of the classical period—merit close attention. Most of the more meaningful instances are imperial initiatives: requiring a *pater familias* to facilitate the marriage of his children (Cases 32, 103); deterring divorce when it originates, not from a husband or wife, but from the *pater familias* of one spouse (Case 104); averting exercise of the *pater's* ultimate power to kill or harshly discipline descendants in his power (Cases 91–93, 158); forcing linear relations to provide material support to the destitute (Case 112); and so on. And even before these initiatives, Roman magistrates had, for instance, substantially altered the law of intestate succession so as to recognize blood ties running beyond the archaic family structure; these praetorian reforms were furthered by early imperial legislation (Cases 161–170). Many later efforts had also been anticipated in the writings of the Roman jurists, as they explored the "wiggle room" in traditional rules.

The sum of these various changes is substantial but not huge, more a matter of amelioration than of fundamental transformation. Softening the details was perhaps less a matter of imperial benevolence than an imperative in an era when Roman citizenship was gradually being extended from its original Italian core to the upper classes of the provinces, and finally (in A.D. 212) to almost the entire free population of the Empire. In this process, perhaps as many as fifty million persons became subject to Roman private law. To large numbers of these newly enfranchised peoples, the institutions of Roman family law doubtless seemed as exotic as they do to us today; and the subtle but unremitting clamor for revision and reform is not difficult to detect beneath the prosaic surface of legal sources.

But what did not change was the iron core of the law. In order to understand Roman family law more fully, therefore, we need to broaden our focus still further and see this law in relation to its historical context, particularly its social and economic context. To be sure, such an approach is not easy, since we are, in general, far better informed about Roman legal rules than about the actual process of their application and effect within the Roman world. Therefore, it is often hard to determine how much consequence rules had in such a relatively primitive society. But in this instance the exercise is worth the effort.

There is today no real doubt that resources were chronically maldistributed in the Roman Empire: a tiny urbanized elite, essentially a governing class, enjoyed a vastly disproportionate share of the Empire's income and wealth. Although Roman private law itself was nominally egalitarian and seldom based upon overt differentiations of social class and wealth, and although the law is likely to have had some impact on the lives of persons well below the ranks of the elite, nonetheless there are solid reasons to believe that the outlook, values, and interests of the upper classes (from whose ranks the Roman jurists were overwhelmingly drawn) were crucially important in shaping both the overall texture and the specific rules of classical Roman family law. Above all, this elite enjoyed easy access to law; and the wealth and privilege in which the elite traded were far more readily susceptible to the application of legal norms.

Directly or indirectly, the Roman elite drew much of its income from landed investments and much of its prestige from tradition, and accordingly it laid great stress on familial continuity from generation to generation. The elite of the Roman Empire had, by modern or even premodern standards, little enthusiasm for risky entrepreneurial activities in the realm of manufacturing and commerce, and entrepreneurship was therefore undervalued as a social asset. On the other hand, strategies of succession—the conveyance of family wealth to succeeding generations—were integral to Roman family law to a far greater degree than is true of modern family law. (For this reason, our Casebook includes a chapter briefly introducing this complex area of Roman law.) As you read the Cases below, you should constantly bear all this in mind. When the jurists conceive the brief fact situations that serve as the basis of their rulings, are they thinking primarily in terms of the well-to-do? Is it reasonable to think of their law as most directly intended to serve the needs of a landed aristocracy?

In short, then, Roman family law was designed not only for a world much different from our own but also for a world in which law may have operated differently than it does today. There are two further aspects of this world that bear directly on the Roman household. First, such evidence as we have (it is poor in quality) strongly suggests that even upper-class Romans had to confront very high levels of mortality, a demographic regime in which the real possibility of imminent death was more or less a constant. Because of high infant mortality, more than half of newborn children may have died before their fifth birthday; and those who survived still faced continuous perils of disease or deadly accident. All this is certain to have significantly influenced the landscape within which family law was articulated. To give just one obvious example, it cannot have been at all unusual for Roman children to be orphaned at a very tender age, so that for a great many Romans the awesome power of the *pater familias* ended well before they reached full adulthood. Furthermore, large numbers of orphans meant that legal institutions of guardianship (Cases 213–222) had considerable social importance.

Second, any account of Roman family law would be imperfect if it ignored the constant presence, within upper-class households, of fairly large numbers of slaves, who, in the urban settings often presupposed by the Roman jurists, performed many domestic services. A good, if perhaps rather horrifying, example is Case 56, a legal problem resulting from the amalgamation of a husband's and a wife's slaves within a single dwelling. But Roman masters also commonly freed their urban slaves, which led to fresh problems; for instance, an ex-master might wish to marry his freedwoman (Case 14). The presence of slaves is not always obvious in the sources; still, it repays the effort to bear their presence in mind, since slaves were a major capital asset in the Roman world. Further, slaves are often more subtly present in the consciousness of the jurists, as a basis of comparison when considering the legal position of children, for instance; the sources on the *peculium* (Cases 125–128) illustrate this point nicely. Unfortunately, however, Roman slave law is extremely intricate, and we therefore considered it impossible to deal with this subject more than obliquely within the present Casebook.

During the past three decades, the Roman family has been the subject of many stimulating and very fruitful scholarly studies, some of which we refer to in the introductions to the chapters; see also the concise bibliography at the end of this volume. It is true that the field had long been rather neglected, so that it was ripe for sophisticated new approaches. But its revival is also related to a larger scholarly debate among historians about the nature of the premodern family.

Briefly, the problem is this. We have reliable historical evidence that in crucial respects the European family underwent a major transformation during the period from approximately 1750 to 1900: a transformation, let us say, from the family's premodern to its modern form, which then spread to European colonies and is today rapidly becoming worldwide. A demographic key to this transformation is that, in the general population of Europe, married couples came to regard procreation as a matter for their own personal determination, something they could regulate for themselves without overzealous regard for the moral strictures of tradition or of their governments or churches. The final consequence of this change in attitude was a drastic break from previous patterns of behavior: newly married couples now tended to think first in terms of how many children they themselves wished to have, and to stop reproducing when they felt they had achieved that number; further, they increasingly concentrated childbirth within the first five or ten years of marriage. These developments lie at the core of what is called the fertility transition, a dramatic overall lowering of the fertility rates that had previously prevailed. There is no firm evidence that any earlier general population (including the population of the Roman Empire) had ever behaved in this way.

The transfer of basic reproductive decisions to the forum of marital conscience is one of the most significant events in modern social history, an event with consequences, particularly in the realm of female empowerment, that even today have not yet been completely worked out. So much is not in serious dispute. But because this change in the general population's behavior transpired "subhistorically," beneath the level of most historical records, it is hard to understand exactly why and how it occurred.

One powerful attempt to explain the change has underscored what may be thought of as an "ideological" transformation in the European concept of the family, a transformation that hypothetically occurred more or less simultaneously with the observed change in reproductive behavior. Many distinguished social historians, including Philippe Ariès and Lawrence Stone, have vigorously championed this view, and it now enjoys widespread scholarly approval despite stout resistance from other historians, including Stephen Ozment.

According to the prevailing viewpoint, the premodern European family (in Ozment's words) "adopted a rigid internal organization for its own protection—one that is said to have been hostile to democracy, the emancipation of women, and the gratification of children." The premodern family was "an impersonal household, ruled over by an imperious patriarch to whom all members were subordinate and subject." When this model of the premodern family is caricatured in such stark terms, its contrast with "sentimental" models of modern family life is apparent. Ozment's critique of this model, however, tends to stress the continuity of European family life from premodern to modern and in particular any indications that premodern families were by no means so austere and autocratic as historians have commonly asserted.

The deeper issue in this debate is whether we should think of "the family" as an inaccurate covering name for what is really a series of distinct social formations over time or whether we should view it as a single and essentially continuous social institution that has only mutated in some of its outward and inward manifestations. Historical questions of this type are hard to answer in large part because so much can depend on the character of the particular sources that historians are interrogating. Nonetheless, on the whole the nature of family life does seem to have altered appreciably with the onset of the modern period. This does not mean, of course, that affective relationships were missing from premodern families, or even that they could not be conspicuous to some observers. Perhaps it is more helpful to think of the historical "family" as mixing numerous social ingredients, of which some that were once dominant have now receded in significance, while others have come to the fore; but such a variation in ingredients may quite possibly have led to institutional formations that are paradigmatically distinct and therefore historically incommensurable.

Almost inevitably, in any case, the debate about the European family has lapped over into scholarly discussions of the Roman family. Some ancient historians (most notably Richard Saller and Suzanne Dixon) have recently sought to portray the Roman family, and particularly the upper-class family, in softer colors than historians have traditionally used: still hardly "modern," to be sure, but not nearly so unremittingly harsh. Other historians have been more hesitant in departing from the traditional model. Almost every conceivable type of evidence has been brought into this discussion, from literary and subliterary texts to artistic representations and archaeological data. But beyond all doubt, Roman law has remained the chief sticking point.

On any fair accounting, so we believe, the legal sources for family law are a formidable impediment for historians wishing to reconstruct the Roman family on modernist lines. It should be apparent, for instance, that the prevailing scholarly view of the premodern European family bears an uncanny resemblance to the Roman family as it is depicted in the rulings of the Roman jurists. Nor is this resemblance entirely coincidental, since the premodern period was precisely the high point of Roman law's direct influence on European law and institutions. The web of legal logic that the Roman jurists wove around the family was so intricate and hardened that subsequent centuries found it difficult to break free.

Still, certain promising avenues of research may yet permit us to circumvent the barrier of Roman law. Even if we leave to one side the obvious open texture of its legal rules, it remains today quite controversial how deeply Roman private law penetrated into the social structure of the Roman Empire. This is a question you should continually think about as you read the materials in this Casebook, but it is worth the effort to set down here some preliminary observations and concerns.

First, it is hard for a modern reader to escape the feeling that the Roman institution of marriage was far too weak to be socially viable. Case 76, for instance, describes an actual trial during the late Republic. The trial concerned a man who left his pregnant wife in a province of the Roman Empire and moved to Rome, where, without informing his first wife, he married another woman, who bore him a second child. Was the second child legitimate? This depends, in turn, on whether his second marriage could be enough in itself to constitute an effective divorce from his first wife—that is, whether, in certain circumstances, remarriage by itself, with nothing further, brings about divorce. How can we deal with a legal system in which divorce might be achieved so easily, on the initiative of either spouse at any time, without direct notice to or control by the state, and perhaps even without notice to an affected spouse? Should we look for countervailing social factors that might have acted to promote marital stability or for indirect legal obstacles to divorce (such as dowry encumbrances, Cases 81–89)? Or are we better advised to accept the possibility that free divorce may not be such a threat to social order as many of us have thought?

Second, *patria potestas,* the enormous power over descendants that Roman law vested in a *pater familias,* remains an enigma. For instance, in Case 93, the Emperor Alexander Severus apparently tells a man named Artemidorus that if he encounters difficulty in applying corporal punishment to his adult son, he can ask for assistance from a magistrate; and other legal sources suggest that thrashing adult children was a legally acceptable, if not a regular, part of a father's exercise of parental dominion. However, after carefully surveying the nonlegal sources on this issue, Richard Saller concludes: "[T]he law granting the *paterfamilias* powers of nearly limitless coercion over his children is an inadequate guide to Roman family relations. . . . [T]here is no strong evidence for holding up Roman fathers as a paradigm of brutal severity. In all likelihood the Romans, in drawing the line between punishment and abuse, accepted more severe physical punishment than we would today, but no more severe than later Europeans." But if this view is correct (as it certainly appears to be), then how should we read the legal sources on *patria potestas*? Was such a weapon ever forged to lie rusting in its sheath? Was the mere potential of violence sufficient for Roman fathers? Or is it conceivable that some defect clouds the vision of the nonlegal sources?

Lurking behind these two problems is a larger and considerably more important question. Roman family law was constructed around a certain mental image of what a "typical" Roman household was like. The jurists did try to define *familia* (see Case 4), but in general, and quite wisely, they put little trust in such definitions; for, as one jurist famously remarked (Javolenus, D. 50.17.202), "In the civil law every definition is dangerous, since it is rare that one cannot be undermined." In general, the Roman jurists allowed their conception of the household and its operation to emerge implicitly from their rules, and so one must constantly be on the alert for clues to the jurists' broader understanding.

But one should also recognize that even this legal conception was contrived for a specific and rather constricted purpose: to permit the development and application of intellectually coherent legal rules. Therefore, it is at best only a highly stylized representation of what was inevitably a far more complex social reality, some traces of which also occasionally peep through in the legal sources. Be on the watch for these layers of historical meaning and particularly for any indications that the jurists were evaluating and revising their conceptions and rules on the basis of how well they performed socially. Social performance is the key. Roman law was not everywhere successful, but then neither is any legal system. In your thinking about this body of law, it is critical to develop a more general sense for when law succeeds in achieving its ends and when it fails and, in either case, why.

One final caution: Ambiguity and misdirection are common features of law and legal thinking, and Roman law is no exception. In Case 177, the jurist Paul nails down a subtle legal point by casually observing that, after all, Roman fathers had once been permitted to kill their own children. Should Paul's words be understood as nostalgia or as irony?

CHAPTER I

Basic Concepts

This brief chapter introduces some central legal concepts that underlie Roman family law. Most of them are related to the legal idea of "family" itself.

As it turns out, the Latin word *familia* is usually better translated into English as "household" rather than "family"—and even this translation is none too accurate. It is easier, perhaps, to begin with the importance that Roman private law attached to the *familia* as the basic building block of the Roman state, since, metaphorically, the *familia* is often understood as the state in miniature. It has a form of governance that is theoretically vested in one person, a "head of the household" (*pater familias*, literally "father of the *familia*"). This person has extensive and virtually exclusive power over all property belonging to the household, including any slaves. But his power also extends to controlling the lives of those of his descendants related to him through males (sons and daughters, grandchildren through sons, and so on), that is, through what the Romans call an agnatic relationship; and in principle the power of the *pater familias* continues no matter how old these descendants are, unless the *pater* himself has released them from his power.

Further, the power of the *pater familias* could be exercised over other free persons, including adopted children and also, in the archaic form of Roman marriage, his wife; but in the standard classical form of marriage the wife remained under the power of her own father (if he was still alive), and despite her marriage, she did not fall under her husband's power.

The Roman *familia* was thus, at least in legal theory, a little monarchy, with strict rules as to who was subject to the monarch's power and who was not. This monarchy dissipated only on the death of a *pater familias*, to be replaced by new *familiae* governed by the father's offspring.

All this takes some getting used to, since it is so alien to modern understandings of the family. The work of the Roman jurists, as they developed these basic concepts during the first three centuries of the Roman Empire (roughly, 31 B.C. to A.D. 235), is intricate and fascinating, but it must always be appreciated as a set of primarily legal institutions, not as an anthropological description of actual Roman family life—which, as it turns out, was in many ways not all that different from modern family life. The relationship of legal abstractions to real life is a fascinating subject in its own right, but one that is not directly treated in the present book. However, it is important, in reading the pages that follow, to bear in mind that the real-world functioning of social institutions is often not directly determined by law, even though law may linger persistently in the background of daily life.

The following concepts are introduced in this chapter: freedom as contrasted with slavery; Roman citizenship; the Roman *familia* (household); the *pater familias*; agnatic relationship; and, among free persons, the distinction between full legal capacity (*sui iuris* status) and dependency (*alieni iuris* status). Don't move on until you have mastered these concepts, since all of them will be important in the chapters that follow.

CASE 1: Freedom, Citizenship, and Household

D. 4.5.11 (Paulus libro secundo ad Sabinum)

Capitis deminutionis tria genera sunt, maxima media minima: tria enim sunt quae habemus, libertatem civitatem familiam. igitur cum omnia haec amittimus, hoc est libertatem et civitatem et familiam, maximam esse capitis deminutionem: cum vero amittimus civitatem, libertatem retinemus, mediam esse capitis deminutionem: cum et libertas et civitas retinetur, familia tantum mutatur, minimam esse capitis deminutionem constat.

(Paul in the second book on Sabinus)

There are three kinds of change for the worse in civil status: greatest, middle, and least, corresponding to the three things that we have: freedom, citizenship, and household (*familia*). When we lose all of these, that is, freedom and citizenship and household, this is the greatest change in status. But when we lose citizenship and retain freedom, this is the middle change in status. When both freedom and citizenship are retained and only the household is changed, clearly this is the least change in status.

1. Change in Civil Status. This Case pertains to the Roman "law of persons" (*ius personarum*), an area of law defining the legal status of individuals for purposes of private law: for example, their capacity to own property, write wills, make contracts, bring private lawsuits, and so on. This law of personal status was highly developed in Rome, in large measure because the institution of slavery was widespread but also because, even among free persons residing in the Roman Empire, many were not Roman citizens until the nearly universal grant of Roman citizenship in A.D. 212. A change in civil status could occur when, for instance, a free person became a slave (perhaps because of criminal condemnation or enemy capture) or when a slave became a free person (perhaps through manumission by a master); or when a free person changed citizenship (perhaps when a free noncitizen received Roman citizenship from the emperor). Such changes in status gave rise to legal complexities that often affected not just the person himself but also those around him. For example, what happened to a man's family and property if he was enslaved? Was his will still valid? What if his children wished to marry? And so on. The Roman jurists necessarily spent much time discussing such questions, but they are of more modest concern to us, since we will ordinarily assume, simplistically, that we are dealing only with Roman citizens.

2. "The Three Things That We Have." The jurist Paul identifies the three basic constituents of civil status. For many purposes, clearly the most important are freedom (*libertas*) and citizenship (*civitas*). Still, private law lays equal, if not greater, emphasis on a person's position within a "household," the Latin word for which is *familia*. If, as this and the following Case suggest, the Romans

think of freedom as the most fundamental "divide" in determining the legal status of an individual, and of citizenship (in particular, Roman citizenship) as the next most fundamental, the third layer of status involves one's *familia*. Although our word "family" obviously derives from *familia,* the Latin word means something rather different, and that difference in meaning has consequences that deeply affect the Roman law of personal status. We usually think of a "family" as primarily established by kinship and coresidence; thus, a "nuclear family" consists of parents and their children residing in the same house. The Roman *familia* is also influenced by kinship and coresidence, but its framework is much more emphatically determined by a nexus of legal relationships, which are explored in the materials within this Casebook. Especially important among these legal relationships are the marriage bond between husband and wife and the power that the male head of a household (the *pater familias*) exercises over household property and over his descendants. Both these relationships are conceived very differently from their modern counterparts; they are the subject of Chapters II and III.

3. Omitted Factors. "The three things that we have" identify very significant aspects of civil status, but this list omits other personal characteristics that have considerable impact. Foremost among these are age (see below, Case 6; also Chapter V.A.1–2) and sex (Chapter V.B). Generally speaking, adult males are accorded the highest civil status, and they also predominate in legal sources, reflecting, obviously, a society that is largely male dominated. But other factors, such as sanity, can also influence civil status (Chapter V.A.3). By contrast, wealth and social status are not, in themselves, major determiners of civil status in classical Roman private law, though they gradually become important in some areas of later classical law; by the second century A.D., for instance, barriers were erected to some marriages where the parties were of different statuses (see Case 10). The legal weight that is attached to social stratification increases significantly in the late Empire.

CASE 2: Slavery and Freedom

D. 1.5.3 (= Gaius, *Institutiones* 1.9)

Summa itaque de iure personarum divisio haec est, quod omnes homines aut liberi sunt aut servi.

D. 1.5.4 pr.–1 (Florentinus libro nono Institutionum)

(pr.) Libertas est naturalis facultas eius quod cuique facere libet, nisi si quid vi aut iure prohibetur. (1) Servitus est constitutio iuris gentium, qua quis dominio alieno contra naturam subicitur.

(Gaius in the first book of his *Institutes*)

The foremost distinction in the law of personal status is this, that all human beings are either free or slaves.

(Florentinus in the ninth book of his *Institutes*)

(pr.) Freedom is the natural ability to do what one wishes, except if it is prevented by coercion or by law. (1) Slavery is an institution of the law of nations, whereby, contrary to nature, a person is made subject to another's ownership.

1. "The Foremost Distinction." No division is more stark in the Roman world than that which divides free persons (including Roman citizens, but also free noncitizens) from those who are slaves. As a matter of basic legal principle, free persons cannot be owned, while, as Florentinus emphasizes, ownership is the very essence of slavery. Slaves are thought to have constituted about a sixth of the population of Roman Italy and perhaps a tenth of the Empire's total population of fifty to sixty million persons. Although Roman slaves were encouraged to reproduce, and although for this purpose they often formed family-like entities, for the most part Roman family law does not extend to slaves.

2. "Contrary to Nature." Florentinus, in defining slavery, observes that it arises as a result of a widely prevailing human law (the "law of nations"), but that this law is contrary to a more fundamental law of "nature" whereby all persons are naturally free; see also Case 5 below, and also Ulpian, D. 50.17.32: "Insofar as civil law is concerned, slaves are deemed nonpersons; but not so in natural law, since, insofar as natural law is concerned, all men are equal." (Sound vaguely familiar?) Do observations of this type necessarily amount to a moral condemnation of slavery? Are any legal consequences likely to result from what Florentinus and Ulpian say?

3. "The Natural Ability to Do What One Wishes." How plausible is Florentinus's definition of freedom, especially in the context of a slaveholding society? From a legal perspective, it may seem reasonable to hold that "natural" free-

dom is inevitably limited by legal constraints; but does it also make sense to hold that freedom may be limited by nonlegal or even illegal coercion? Do you think that this could be simply the jurist's recognition of a grim underlying social reality, in which members of a social elite often prevailed simply because of their money, power, or influence?

4. How Bright Is the Line? Florentinus writes as if the distinction between free person and slave was defined by a "bright line." This may well have been true for ideological purposes, but within the Roman world it is more questionable as a matter of fact. One of the issues that you should be sensitive to as you read these Roman legal sources is whether ordinary Romans would have experienced the legal distinction as a material one affecting their lives. For example, we know that press gangs occasionally seized free Romans and sold them into slavery, often to buyers who were unaware of the truth about their condition; a Roman citizen, caught in such a situation, was legally unable to establish his own liberty and had to rely upon help from a third party who was willing to undertake the arduous burden of proving his free status. More generally, many Romans, particularly those massed at the bottom of the social and economic pyramid, lived lives of desperate poverty that may actually have been worse, in material terms, than those lived by all but the lowliest of agricultural slaves. However, in part because Roman slavery was not constructed on a racial basis, individual slaves within a household were more easily able to rise to positions of considerable trust and power, exercising influence that even threatened the independence of free persons. It is a good idea always to be alert to these possible complexities, even when the Roman sources seem to ignore them or take them for granted.

CASE 3: Agnatic Relationship

Gaius, *Institutiones* 1.156

Sunt autem agnati per virilis sexus personas cognatione iuncti, quasi a patre cognati, veluti frater eodem patre natus, fratris filius neposve ex eo, item patruus et patrui filius et nepos ex eo. at hi, qui per feminini sexus personas cognatione coniunguntur, non sunt agnati, sed alias naturali iure cognati. itaque inter avunculum et sororis filium non agnatio est, sed cognatio. item amitae, materterae filius non est mihi agnatus, sed cognatus, et invicem scilicet ego illi eodem iure coniungor, quia qui nascuntur, patris, non matris familiam sequuntur.

(Gaius in the first book of his *Institutes*)

Agnates (*agnati*) are persons related (solely) through males, roughly relatives through the father: for instance, a brother born from the same father, this brother's son, or a grandson from him; likewise, an uncle on the father's side, this uncle's son, or a grandson from him.

But persons who are related through females are not agnates but are otherwise relatives (*cognati*, "cognates") by natural law. Thus, the relationship between an uncle and the son of his sister is not agnate but cognate. Likewise, the son of an aunt on my father's or mother's side is not my agnate but my cognate; and in turn, of course, I am related to him by the same rule.

For newborns fall into the household (*familia*) of their father, not of their mother.

1. Agnates. Blood relationship is expressed in Latin by the word *cognatio* (kinship), which is broad enough to include all those whom we would normally regard today as our relatives. However, the Latin language and Roman law draw a distinction, which we usually do not draw, between blood relatives who are related only through males and those related through either males or females. The members of the first group are described as "agnates." Between any two individuals, an agnate relationship exists if they are descended in the male line from a common male ancestor. Thus, a brother and sister are agnates to each other; and each of them, in turn, is an agnate to the sister or brother of their father (a paternal aunt or uncle) and to a paternal uncle's sons and daughters (cousins), and so on. Agnate relationship is crucial in constituting the *familia;* and especially in early law agnates were also important in family law more generally. Relatives through females are sometimes called "enates," but this term is not important for law.

2. Classifying Relatives. Try sorting out your own blood relatives based on whether or not they are your agnates. One of the most surprising results, which, however, flows straightforwardly from the definition of agnatic relationship, is that your father is your agnate, but your mother is not; similarly,

your paternal grandfather is an agnate, but your paternal grandmother and maternal grandparents are not. What social or political factors might have prompted early Romans to have made such a distinction? As this Case indicates, Latin even differentiates between uncles and aunts: paternal (*patruus, amita*) and maternal (*avunculus, matertera*).

CASE 4: The Household (*Familia*) and the *Pater Familias*

D. 50.16.195.1–5 (Ulpianus libro quadragensimo sexto ad Edictum)

(1) "Familiae" appellatio qualiter accipiatur, videamus. Et quidem varie accepta est. . . . (2) Familiae appellatio refertur et ad corporis cuiusdam significationem, quod aut iure proprio ipsorum aut communi universae cognationis continetur. iure proprio familiam dicimus plures personas, quae sunt sub unius potestate aut natura aut iure subiectae, ut puta patrem familias, matrem familias, filium familias, filiam familias quique deinceps vicem eorum sequuntur, ut puta nepotes et neptes et deinceps. pater autem familias appellatur, qui in domo dominium habet, recteque hoc nomine appellatur, quamvis filium non habeat: non enim solam personam eius, sed et ius demonstramus: denique et pupillum patrem familias appellamus. et cum pater familias moritur, quotquot capita ei subiecta fuerint, singulas familias incipiunt habere: singuli enim patrum familiarum nomen subeunt. . . . communi iure familiam dicimus omnium adgnatorum: nam etsi patre familias mortuo singuli singulas familias habent, tamen omnes, qui sub unius potestate fuerunt, recte eiusdem familiae appellabuntur, qui ex eadem domo et gente proditi sunt. (3) Servitutium quoque solemus appellare familias, ut in edicto praetoris ostendimus sub titulo de furtis, ubi praetor loquitur de familia publicanorum. . . . (4) Item appellatur familia plurium personarum, quae ab eiusdem ultimi genitoris sanguine proficiscuntur (sicuti dicimus familiam Iuliam), quasi a fonte quodam memoriae. (5) Mulier autem familiae suae et caput et finis est.

(Ulpian in the forty-sixth book on the Edict)

(1) Let us examine how the word *familia* is used. It has various usages. . . .

(2) The word *familia* is also employed to signify a sort of body (*corpus*) defined either by a rule particular to its members or by the common rule of general relationship.

By a particular rule, we describe a *familia* as a number of persons who, either by nature or by law, are subjected to the power (*potestas*) of one person: for example, a *pater familias* (male head of a household), a *mater familias* (here, a wife if she is subject to her husband's *manus*), a son or daughter in their father's power, and those who then follow them in turn, for example, grandsons and granddaughters (from sons), and so on. The person called the *pater familias* has mastery (*dominium*) in the home, and he is correctly so called even if (in fact) he has no son; for we refer not only to his person but to his legal right. And so even a young ward (*pupillus*) is called a *pater familias*. And when the *pater familias* dies, all the individuals who were subject to him start to have their own households; for they each assume the status of *pater familias*. . . .

By a common rule, we use *familia* for all agnates. For although, when the *pater familias* dies, they each have their own *familiae*, still all those who were once under one person's power are properly described as belonging to the same *familia*, since they stem from the same home and lineage.

(3) We also customarily describe slaves as *familiae*. We see this in the praetor's Edict in the title on theft, where the praetor speaks of the *familia* of public contractors. . . .

(4) Likewise, *familia* is used of many persons who descend from the blood of the same original ancestor; for example, we speak of the Julian *familia*, as it were, from some wellspring of memory.

(5) But a woman is both the beginning and the end of her *familia*.

1. *Familia*. This is an exceptionally important Case, which you should not leave until you understand it fully. As Ulpian states, the Latin word *familia* is used in several different senses. For instance, it can describe a "family relationship" between free persons who share a common, even if ultimately untraceable, descent from a single ancestor (a "clan"); and it can also designate all the slaves in a single household or under a single owner. But by far the most significant usage for our purposes is the one described in section 2: the *familia* as household.

2. The Household. Ulpian describes the household as a kind of collective, a *corpus*, over which one person (prototypically a male, the *pater familias*) has "mastery" (*dominium*) in the home. What this means is that the *pater familias* owns all the property (including slaves) belonging to the household. All other free persons in the household are "subjected to the power of one person," the *pater familias*. With some exceptions, these persons are all agnatically related descendants of the *pater familias*, no matter how old they may be. Thus, in Roman law it is possible (although demographically unlikely) for a *familia* to consist of a *pater familias* aged seventy-five; his son aged fifty; his son's son aged twenty-five; and his son's son's newborn son. These last three could own nothing independently of the *pater familias*, and the advanced age of the son would not distinguish him, in this respect, from the newborn great-grandson. Further, all these descendants were alike in being subject to the "paternal power," the *patria potestas*, of the *pater familias* (see Chapter III). It is well to pause for a moment and absorb the full implications of this household structure. What social causes might have led to its creation in this form?

3. Daughters and Wives. The hypothetical family described above consists solely of males. What about women? Within the household structure of the early Roman Empire, the daughter of a *pater familias* is in much the same legal position as a son; and so too for his agnatically related female descendants generally. What may seem truly extraordinary is that this legal position does not change when the daughter marries; that is, in a classical marriage, she remains within the *familia* of her *pater familias* and subject to his *patria potestas* so long as he lives, even though, as would normally be the case, she is now residing in her husband's house. By the early Empire, this classical form of mar-

riage had largely replaced an earlier form of marriage, called *manus* marriage, in which a bride passed from her father's household to that of her husband; in *manus* marriage, she became subject to the power of her husband, although to a lesser extent than his children (see Case 37). By contrast, classical marriage is "free" in the sense that a wife does not enter into her husband's *familia*, nor does he have any legal power over her actions. As we shall see, however, this simplified legal portrait does not entirely correspond to social reality.

4. Exceptions. The *familia* usually comprises blood kin, but there are some exceptions: the *pater familias* may adopt children (Chapter III.C.2) or may eject them from the *familia* by emancipating them (Chapter III.C.3) or by giving them in adoption.

CASE 5: *Sui Iuris* and *Alieni Iuris*

Gaius, *Institutiones* 1.48, 52, 55 (= D. 1.6.1 pr.–1; 1.6.3)

(48) Sequitur de iure personarum alia divisio. nam quaedam personae sui iuris sunt, quaedam alieno iuri sunt subiectae. . . . (52) In potestate itaque sunt servi dominorum. quae quidem potestas iuris gentium est: nam apud omnes peraeque gentes animadvertere possumus dominis in servos vitae necisque potestatem esse, et quodcumque per servum adquiritur, id domino adquiritur. . . . (55) Item in potestate nostra sunt liberi nostri, quos iustis nuptiis procreavimus. quod ius proprium civium Romanorum est. fere enim nulli alii sunt homines, qui talem in filios suos habent potestatem, qualem nos habemus, idque divus Hadrianus edicto, quod proposuit de his, qui sibi liberisque suis ab eo civitatem Romanam petebant, significavit.

(Gaius in the first book of his *Institutes*)

(48) There follows another distinction in the law of personal status: some persons are *sui iuris*, some are subjected to another's legal right (*alieno iuri*). . . .

(52) So, slaves are in the power (*in potestate*) of their owners. This power comes from the law of nations; for uniformly among all peoples we can observe that owners have the power of life and death over their slaves, and whatever is acquired through a slave is acquired for the owner. . . .

(55) Likewise in our power (*in potestate nostra*) are our children whom we have sired in a legitimate marriage. This right (called *patria potestas*) is unique to Roman citizens, for virtually no other peoples have power over their children that is as great as ours; and the deified Emperor Hadrian (reign: A.D. 117–138) noted this fact in the edict he issued concerning persons who were petitioning him for Roman citizenship for themselves and their children.

1. When the Old Man Dies. "And when the *pater familias* dies, all the individuals who were subject to him start to have their own households; for they each assume the status of *pater familias*." So says Ulpian in Case 4, but not quite correctly. Suppose, for instance, that a *pater familias* dies and leaves behind only a son and a daughter; the son then becomes a *pater familias* even though he does not have any children (and may not even be old enough to procreate), and the daughter also becomes head of her own *familia*. But because she can have no agnatic descendants of her own (be sure you understand why; see Case 3), she is, as Ulpian puts it in section 5 of Case 4, "both the beginning and the end of her *familia*," in the sense that her independent household will die with her. This general situation would be unaffected if either the son or the daughter were married with children prior to their father's decease, nor would it matter if either one was no longer resident in the father's home. But what if, for instance, the son had married, had children, and then predeceased his father? His children (unlike those of his sister) would remain in the

household of his *pater familias;* and even if they were still infants when their grandfather died, each of them would begin to have a separate household. That is to say, as a general rule, upon the death of a *pater familias,* all the free persons who were directly in his power, without any surviving intermediary, at once became heads of their own households. This consequence is immediately reflected in the Roman law governing intestate succession, which determines how the household property is split up among the intestate heirs (see Chapter IV, esp. Part A).

2. *Sui Iuris.* A person who is head of a household, whether male or female, is described in Roman law as *sui iuris,* that is, "under his own legal power." *Sui iuris* persons are, in principle, the only completely free individuals in Roman private law. Some of them may, however, be unable to function fully because of their youth or mental incapacity; for these persons there are various kinds of guardians (see Chapter V.A). All other free persons are "subjected to another's legal right (*alieno iuri*)"; they are usually referred to as *alieni iuris,* "under another's power," although this is not a technical term.

3. Back to the Real World. In this chapter, particularly in Cases 4 and 5, many strange concepts are introduced within a fairly brief space of time. Don't worry if it doesn't all make sense at first. What is important is to absorb a basic idea of the very different legal framework within which Roman family law was conceived, even if this framework seems, at first, simply impossible to believe. As anthropologists have shown, household structures are in fact extremely malleable; and the Roman one endured, with only limited modifications, for more than a millennium. Nevertheless, as you will also have occasion to observe in the following chapters, many of the differences between the Roman household and our own are more matters of legal emphasis than of substance. This Case, for instance, appears to draw a direct comparison between slaves and children-in-power. But free children are not slaves (that would violate the fundamental principle of Case 2), and in many respects actual Roman family life does not appear to depart profoundly from the behavioral norm for premodern societies (see Chapter III). Correspondingly, the peculiar fact that in Roman law a wife does not join the household of her husband but remains in that of her *pater familias* does not undermine the considerable importance of marriage as a Roman social institution (see Chapter II).

CASE 6: The Age of Majority

Gaius, *Institutiones* 1.196

Masculi autem cum puberes esse coeperint, tutela liberantur. puberem autem Sabinus quidem et Cassius ceterique nostri praeceptores eum esse putant, qui habitu corporis pubertatem ostendit, id est eum qui generare potest; sed in his qui pubescere non possunt, quales sunt spadones, eam aetatem esse spectandam, cuius aetatis puberes fiunt. sed diversae scholae auctores annis putant pubertatem aestimandam, id est eum puberem esse existimant, qui XIIII annos explevit. . . .

(Gaius in the first book of his *Institutions*)

When males reach puberty, they are freed from guardianship (*tutela*). Sabinus, Cassius, and the rest of our teachers think that a male reaches puberty when he displays this physically, that is, when he is able to procreate. But for those persons, like eunuchs (*spadones*), who cannot undergo puberty, the age at which they become adults should be used. By contrast, the authors of the other (Proculian) school think that puberty should be reckoned in years; that is, they judge that a male reaches puberty if he has completed fourteen years. . . .

1. Guardianship. Through the premature death of a father, a person can become *sui iuris* even though he or she is still far too young to be capable of adult decision making. Such young people require considerable supervision. Among the Romans, supervision was achieved by appointing a guardian, called a *tutor* (see Chapter V.A.1).

2. Reaching Adulthood. When does a person cease being a child and become an adult? In determining this, the Romans made use of the physical changes associated with the onset of puberty. Unfortunately, however, these changes are often difficult to observe without an embarrassing inspection. For girls, the age of majority was therefore simply set at twelve, which was taken as the normal time of puberty. Boys, by contrast, mature more slowly. This Case reflects a controversy between two groups of early imperial jurists: the Sabinians (Gaius's school), who in general required a boy to have the actual physical ability to procreate and who therefore presumably required physical inspection; and the Proculians, who set an age of fourteen for boys. Which approach is preferable? The issue was not finally settled until A.D. 529, when Emperor Justinian upheld the Proculian view (C. 5.60.3). On eunuchs, see Case 8.

3. The Consequences of Adulthood. As this text indicates, an adult is no longer subject to the close supervision of a *tutor,* although even adult *sui iuris* women still were required to have a *tutor* (with considerably reduced powers), and both male and female youths often also had a sort of business advisor, called

a *curator,* to help them with business affairs until they reached age twenty-five; on all this, see Chapter V.A.2. In addition, males and females who reached adulthood were able to marry (Case 7) and to write wills for themselves (Case 173). Does the Roman age of adulthood strike you as too early? What social conditions can help determine what age is best?

CHAPTER II

Marriage

In a famous and much debated fragment, the late classical jurist Modestinus describes Roman marriage as "the union of a male and a female in a complete life partnership, the sharing of divine and human law" (D. 23.2.1: *Nuptiae sunt coniunctio maris et feminae et consortium omnis vitae, divini et humani iuris communicatio*). This august description, however, scarcely isolates Roman marriage as a distinct historical phenomenon. At best, Modestinus may be thought to identify an abiding cultural ideal rather than the real Roman marriage that emerges from legal and literary sources.

Marriage is usually considered the most fundamental building block of human societies, and it is certainly the most persistent. But its configuration, and in particular its legal configuration, has varied extremely widely through the ages. Modestinus emphasizes above all the alliance between husband and wife, and their subsequent companionship. But even a quick glance at Roman literary sources will suggest that close spousal interrelationships were only one part of the picture, and in some respects not even the most important part. In the Roman world, as in human societies generally, marriage as an institution was deeply saturated with numerous social meanings and uses, which potentially conflict with one another in particular circumstances. First, a wedding between two individuals often served to create a link between their families; and if one or both of the new spouses were in the power of *patres familias*, a father's heavy presence is also often detectable in the immediate background of a marriage ceremony. Second, the arrangements leading to a marriage could have major property implications for the two families, since a bride usually required a dowry; and more generally the issue of a couple's maintenance was important to their marriage's ultimate success. Third, the two families, as well as the public at large, might take an active interest in the marriage at least to the extent that procreation, and hence the renewal of a population, was regarded as an intrinsic and important aspect of marriage.

As we shall see, these and other considerations influence not only Roman marriage as a social institution but also its structure within Roman law. In the end, marriage is one of Rome's most interesting and distinctive institutions, quite unlike anything to be found in the modern world.

It is impossible now to write on this subject without acknowledging the influence of Susan Treggiari's monumental study, *Roman Marriage*, published in 1991. Treggiari seeks to integrate literary and legal sources within a detailed study of all aspects of the Roman institution. The focus in this chapter is different in that our primary interest is narrower: how legal sources describe and develop the institution. But for a fuller picture, Treggiari's book is very highly recommended.

PART A

Getting Married

In modern legal systems, the requirements for marriage typically fall into three broad categories. First, there are capacity requirements, answering the question: "Who can marry whom?" Such capacity requirements regularly specify minimum ages and appropriate conditions of mental and physical health, and they also often prohibit, for instance, incestuous marriages or polygamy. Second are consent requirements, which establish the basis of a marriage in the free will and honest intention of the parties who enter into it, and in some instances also in the required assent of their parents or guardians. Third are process requirements, which set up certain formalities whereby parties who are eligible to marry, and who have the necessary agreements, can then go about marrying. The process of marriage typically falls into two stages: the couple must first obtain a marriage license (the government uses licensing mainly to implement its capacity requirements for marriage); and then they must solemnize their marriage through a formal ceremony conducted by a designated civil or religious authority.

As we shall see, Roman marriage law has rules in all three categories, but they are organized in a distinctive and (to us) somewhat joltingly idiosyncratic way. Most developed are the capacity requirements, which involve not only the sorts of rules familiar to us but also legal restrictions resulting ultimately from social prejudices (bans on marriage with certain social groups) or from public policy (encouragements to marry and procreate). The greatest differences, however, are in the consent and process requirements, where the Romans seemingly pared the marriage process down to a bare minimum (the Roman government did not license or even register marriages, nor did it prescribe any specific ceremony for marriage) and instead used agreement (*consensus*) as a sort of a litmus test for both the inception and the continued existence of marriage. Such extreme legal simplicity has both advantages and disadvantages: limited regulation of the marriage process eliminates the need for a large government bureaucracy but risks insecurity within a critically important social institution.

For present purposes, we will generally assume that marriage is occurring between two *sui iuris* Roman citizens. For the most part, therefore, we will ignore here the potential influence of the *pater familias* on the marriage process, since this influence is better considered in relation to *patria potestas* (see Cases 98–107); but it is important to stress that a father's approval—or at least the absence of his disapproval—was often decisive in the marriage process.

As you read the Cases in this part, consider both the advantages and disadvantages of the Roman approach to marriage. It has often been argued that the Roman legal model of marriage was constructed entirely, or nearly entirely, on a "contractual" framework, in which, provided that the couple met certain formal capacity requirements, their mental agreement to marry created the marriage in essentially the same way that their agreement on the terms of a contract of sale would create a sale, with no further act required. The Cases below should give you ample opportunity to consider whether this argument is correct.

CASE 7: Less Than Minimum Age

D. 48.5.14.8 (Ulpianus libro secundo de Adulteriis)

Si minor duodecim annis in domum deducta adulterium commiserit, mox apud eum aetatem excesserit coeperitque esse uxor, non poterit iure viri accusari ex eo adulterio, quod ante aetatem nupta commisit, sed [vel] quasi sponsa poterit accusari ex rescripto divi Severi, quod supra relatum est.

(Ulpian in the second book *On Adulteries*)

A girl less than twelve years old was led into the home (of her prospective husband) and (then) committed adultery; soon thereafter she passed the age (of marriage) in his house and began to be his wife. He cannot use a husband's right to accuse her of an adultery which she committed when married before the (legal) age; but she can be accused as a betrothed woman (*sponsa*), in accord with the rescript of the deified Emperor Severus that was set out above.

Hypothetical Situation

Sempronia, aged ten, is "married" to her fiancé Titius; in a wedding ceremony, she leaves her own home and moves into his. Before she reaches the age of twelve, she has sexual relations with a man other than Titius. After she reaches twelve and becomes legally married to Titius, can he accuse her of adultery?

1. The Minimum Age. This rather sensational Case proceeds from the Roman definition of minimum age at marriage. Although the jurists frequently define the minimum female age in terms of physical maturity (she must be "capable of sexual relations," *viripotens;* see Case 13 and also, e.g., Labeo, D. 24.1.65, 36.2.30), many sources, like this one, point clearly to age twelve as the conventionally set minimum. For the minimum male age at marriage, see Case 6 (usually age fourteen or so). These ages are bound to seem young in a modern setting. What are the likely social implications?

2. Prepubescent "Marriage." A surprisingly large number of Roman legal sources suggest that in the case of women the minimum age was not always observed; see also, for instance, Case 26 below. In the present Case, a girl younger than twelve has been "led" (*deducta*) in a wedding procession to the home of a man; such a "leading" from the home of the girl's father into her husband's is one common form of marriage ceremony (see Case 20). It is not impossible that in this Case, as in Case 26, the man thought of himself as an actual husband; but such a view is firmly resisted by the jurists (e.g., Pomponius, D. 23.2.4: "A woman married when less than twelve years old will be a legitimate wife when she has reached age twelve in her husband's house"). So how is her status in the meantime to be legally described? The Case hinges on the answer to this question.

3. Adultery. Under the *lex Iulia de adulteriis* of 18 or 17 B.C. (a law promulgated by the Emperor Augustus; see Cases 50–55 and 95–96), a husband who discovered that his wife had committed adultery was strongly encouraged to divorce her and then to bring criminal charges against her for adultery; this is the "husband's right" to which Ulpian refers. In Case 7, however, the "wife" has committed adultery before reaching the age of twelve (!); hence, by the ordinary rules of Roman law, she was not yet a legitimate wife and could not be accused under the *lex Iulia*. Ulpian solves this problem by using a rescript of Emperors Septimius Severus and Caracalla (see D. 48.5.14.3), who ruled that the law of adultery should apply not just to wives but also to betrothed women (*sponsae*), "because it is impermissible to violate, not just every kind of marriage, but also the hope of marriage (*spem matrimonii*)." On betrothal, a formal engagement prior to marriage, see Section 2 below. Does this sort of extension seem sensible to you? But in this Case Ulpian's solution requires a legal construction that the man's "wife" was actually his betrothed prior to her reaching the required age for marriage. Ulpian accepts this construction here and also, for example, at D. 42.5.17.1 (where much less controversial issues are involved than here) but emphatically rejects it in Case 26. Given what you already know about Roman social conventions, does the outcome in Case 7 seem unfair? If so, to whom? On the assimilation of betrothal and marriage, see also Case 27.

4. Actual Age at Marriage. The sources on age at marriage among ordinary Romans, although poor in quality, suggest that women ordinarily entered their first marriage in their middle to late teens, but men only in their mid- to late twenties; and Augustus's marriage legislation favored individuals who had children by about these ages (Case 12: age twenty for women, twenty-five for men, reporting late classical law). However, in the upper classes young girls were often used as dynastic pawns between powerful families, and for this and other reasons, they were often given in marriage at an extremely tender age. Do the jurists seem to have utilized law as a means to resist pressures for early marriage? Ulpian (D. 27.6.11.3–4, citing Julian) discusses the possible reasons a father might have for arranging an early marriage: among others, an affectionate desire "to introduce his daughter more swiftly into her betrothed's household." Is this line of thinking fanciful?

5. Why Set an Age? What general legal purposes are served by setting a minimum age for marriage? A modern lawmaker might aim to set an age that will prevent unwise marriages of immature persons, as part of an effort to reduce the divorce rate and promote marital stability; or that will encourage young people (and especially young women) to complete their educations and become economically independent, perhaps as part of a larger effort to restrain population growth. What policy aims might the Romans have had in setting the age where they did?

CASE 8: The Ability to Procreate

D. 23.3.39.1 (Ulpianus libro trigesimo tertio ad edictum)

Si spadoni mulier nupserit, distinguendum arbitror, castratus fuerit necne, ut in castrato dicas dotem non esse: in eo qui castratus non est, quia est matrimonium, et dos et dotis actio est.

(Ulpian in the thirty-third book on the Edict)

If a woman marries a eunuch (*spado*), I think a distinction should be drawn as to whether or not he was castrated. In the case of a castrated man, you should hold that there is no dowry; (but) in the case of someone who was not castrated, since there is a marriage, there is both a dowry and an action for the dowry.

1. Eunuchs. In Case 6, Gaius describes eunuchs (*spadones*) as those "who cannot undergo puberty"; the age of majority for such men is set at the normal age of male puberty, probably meaning that they could marry at age fourteen. A eunuch lacks testicles either naturally or because of castration (Ulpian, D. 21.1.6.2, 50.16.128). What is odd about the present Case is the distinction Ulpian draws between eunuchs who had been castrated and those who had not been. As Ulpian holds, a castrated male lacks the capacity to marry, and so a dowry is impossible since there can be no valid marriage (see Part B.2 below); but a male who is otherwise physically unable to sire children can both marry and receive a dowry from his wife. What is the point of this distinction? In Case 184, Ulpian uses the same distinction in ruling that a castrated male cannot institute a posthumous child as an heir, although otherwise infertile males can; see also Justinian, *Inst.* 1.11.9, cited in the Discussion of Case 150 on adoption. Does this suggest that Ulpian's primary objection was moral? Does Ulpian presume that the eunuch's castration was deliberate, not accidental? And if deliberate, who bears the blame? What if, for instance, a slave was castrated by his owner and subsequently freed; why should the freedman have no right to marry?

2. Procreation. In the Roman world, as in many other past and present societies, a strong tradition linked marriage to the procreation of children; for instance, it was commonly said (as in Case 16) that marriages were concluded "in order to beget children" (*liberorum procreandorum causa*); and this tradition was considerably reinforced by imperial legislation devised to encourage childbirth (see Case 12). Nonetheless, as this Case shows, inability to beget children was not in itself necessarily a bar to marriage. The elderly can also enter valid marriages even though they are no longer able to procreate (Case 12). See also Case 184.

3. Marriage and Procreation. Does the legal capacity of the impotent or infertile to marry undermine the rationale behind allowing men and women to marry as soon as they reach puberty (see Case 7)?

4. Same-Sex Marriage. No classical legal source expressly prohibits marriage between two persons of the same sex, but neither does any source indicate that same-sex marriage could be legitimate. Modestinus (D. 23.2.1), quoted more fully in the introduction to this chapter, describes marriage as "the union of a male and a female." Does this description rule out same-sex marriage by definition? Are Roman policies linking marriage and procreation enough to make same-sex marriage impossible?

CASE 9: *Conubium*

Tituli ex Corpore Ulpiani 5.3–5, 8–10

(3) Conubium est uxoris iure ducendae facultas. (4) Conubium habent cives Romani cum civibus Romanis: cum Latinis autem et peregrinis ita, si concessum sit. (5) Cum servis nullum est conubium. . . . (8) Conubio interveniente liberi semper patrem sequuntur: non interveniente conubio matris condicioni accedent, excepto eo qui ex peregrino et cive Romana peregrinus nascitur, quoniam lex Minicia ex alterutro peregrino natum deterioris parentis condicionem sequi iubet. (9) Ex cive Romano et Latina Latinus nascitur et ex libero et ancilla servus, quoniam, cum his casibus conubia non sint, partus sequitur matrem. (10) In his, qui iure contracto matrimonio nascuntur, conceptionis tempus spectatur: in his autem, qui non legitime concipiuntur, editionis. veluti si ancilla conceperit, deinde manumissa pariat, liberum parit: nam quoniam non legitime concepit, cum editionis tempore libera sit, partus quoque liber est.

(Excerpts from Ulpian's Writings)

(3) *Conubium* is the capacity to take a wife legitimately. (4) Roman citizens have *conubium* with Roman citizens and (also) with persons of Latin status and peregrines (*peregrini*) if this (right) has been granted. (5) With slaves there is no *conubium*. . . .

(8) When *conubium* is present, children always follow (the status of) their father. When *conubium* is not present, they accede to their mother's (legal) status, except for a person born from a male peregrine and a female Roman citizen; for the *lex Minicia* orders that the child of a foreign mother or father follows the condition of the parent of lower status. (9) From a male Roman citizen and a female Latin, a Latin is born; and from a free male and a slave woman, a slave. The reason is that there is no *conubium* in these cases, so the offspring follows the mother.

(10) In the case of children born in a legally contracted marriage, the time of conception is observed (in determining the children's status); in the case of children not legitimately conceived, that of birth. For instance, if a slave woman conceives and then gives birth after being manumitted, she bears a free child; for since she conceived illegitimately but was free at the time of birth, her offspring is also free.

1. Status in the Roman World. This Case gives a hasty introduction to the complex issue of legal status. At the beginning of the Roman Empire, its free subjects included a relatively small proportion of Roman citizens, those to whom Roman private law was directly applicable. Other free persons included the "Latins" (*Latini*), who were accorded a sort of half-citizenship; and "peregrines" (*peregrini*, "foreigners"), permanent resident aliens who were usually the descendants of conquered peoples. All three groups (Roman citizens,

Latins, and peregrines) were further subdivided. As time passed, more and more of those in the nonprivileged groups were accorded Roman citizenship, until in A.D. 212 Emperor Caracalla extended Roman citizenship to virtually all free subjects of Rome.

2. Interstatus Marriage. As this Case indicates, *conubium* is a legal concept describing the capacity of a man or woman to conclude a valid marriage with a given individual. It is also used, for instance, to proscribe incestuous marriage (Case 11). The Roman rules on *conubium* are, however, complicated by the intricacies of legal status in the Roman world. In principle, there is always *conubium* between two Roman citizens, although their marriage may sometimes be barred by other legal impediments (Case 10). When a Roman wished to marry a Latin or a peregrine, however, *conubium* was present only when this right had been granted as a favor by the Roman state; the grant might be either to individuals or to cities or peoples. For example, Gaius (*Inst.* 1.57) notes that Roman emperors granted some veteran soldiers *conubium* to marry Latin or peregrine women after their term of military service; this meant that the children of such marriages were Roman citizens in the power of their fathers. Marriage to a person with whom one does not have *conubium* effectively invalidates the marriage from the perspective of Roman law, although the marriage may be recognized by non-Roman legal systems within the Empire. Why might the Romans have been so grudging about marital rights? Do you see a relationship to the Roman principle of "divide and conquer"?

3. Following the Status of the Mother. Where a couple did not have *conubium*, the general result in Roman law (with some exceptions, one of which is noted in this Case) was that children acquired their mother's status and that their father did not have *patria potestas* over them; that is, the children were treated, to some extent, like bastards for purposes of Roman law (although the word "bastard" carries moral baggage that is not always appropriate in a Roman context). In the case of two free persons, the result in Roman law was often harsh. What explains the exception introduced by the *lex Minicia*? Consider the following paradox: under the previously prevailing rule, if a Roman citizen woman married a peregrine with *conubium*, her children would be peregrines as well; but if she married a peregrine without *conubium*, then her children would be Roman citizens! Where the mother is a slave, the rule given in this Case allows an exception, perhaps as a result of imperial intervention: a child is freeborn if its mother was free at any point in time from the conception of the child to its birth (Paul, *Sent.* 2.24.1–3, who justifies this change on the basis of *favor libertatis*). What policy reasons might have motivated this exception?

4. **Marriages with Slaves.** Slaves have no *conubium* and so are unable to marry free persons, although they can enter a sort of informal (and legally inconsequential) union called *contubernium* (Paul, *Sent.* 2.19.6). Paul (D. 16.3.27) reports an interesting case in which a free Roman gave his daughter-in-power as wife to another man's slave, even supplying a "dowry." Paul rules that since there is no valid marriage, there is also no true dowry (see Case 29), but the money can be reclaimed as a "deposit." Marriages between slaves are also invalid at law, but they are sometimes recognized in fact. A poignant example is mentioned by Ulpian (D. 23.3.39 pr.): A female slave, upon entering a long-term relationship with a fellow slave, provided him a dowry that passed from her *peculium* (a fund that her master allows her to administer) into his; later the couple were both freed and their relationship continued as marriage. If the dowry property still survives, Ulpian holds that it has been converted tacitly into a real dowry. The original "dowry" had, of course, no legal validity.

CASE 10: Legal Impediments

D. 23.2.44 pr. (Paulus libro primo ad legem Iuliam et Papiam)

Lege Iulia ita cavetur: "Qui senator est quive filius neposve ex filio proneposve ex <nepote> filio nato cuius eorum est erit, ne quis eorum sponsam uxoremve sciens dolo malo habeto libertinam aut eam, quae ipsa cuiusve pater materve artem ludicram facit fecerit. neve senatoris filia neptisve ex filio proneptisve ex nepote filio nato libertino eive, qui ipse cuiusve pater materve artem ludicram facit fecerit, sponsa nuptave sciens dolo malo esto neve quis eorum dolo malo sciens sponsam uxoremve eam habeto."

Tituli ex Corpore Ulpiani 13.2

Ceteri autem ingenui prohibentur ducere <corpore quaestum facientem et> lenam et a lenone lenave manumissam et in adulterio deprehensam et iudicio publico damnatam et quae artem ludicram fecerit: adicit Mauricianus et a senatu damnatam.

(Paul in the first book on the *lex Iulia et Papia*)

The *lex Iulia* provides: "Now and in the future, let no one who is a senator, or who is or will be a senator's son or a grandson from a son or a great-grandson from a grandson born to a son, knowingly and intentionally take as his betrothed or his wife a freedwoman or a woman who herself or whose father or mother acts or will act on the stage. And let no senator's daughter, or a granddaughter from a son or a great-granddaughter from a grandson born to a son, knowingly and intentionally be betrothed or married to a freedman or to a man who himself or whose father or mother acts or will act on the stage; and let none of these persons intentionally and knowingly have her as his betrothed or wife."

(*Excerpts from Ulpian's Writings*)

But other freeborn males are forbidden to take (as wife) a prostitute, a procuress, a woman manumitted by a pimp or procuress, a woman taken in adultery, a woman condemned in a public trial, and one who acts on the stage. Mauricianus added also a woman condemned by the Senate.

1. The Augustan Marriage Legislation. In his effort to reestablish Roman morality, the Emperor Augustus (reign: 31 B.C. to A.D. 14) had a series of laws enacted that created additional legal barriers to marriage, barriers that were based on social prejudice; and these barriers were much elaborated by later emperors. The details are controversial in part because our sources are contradictory; but you should be able to make out the main lines of prohibitions, as well as the likely reasons for them. Marriages in contravention of these laws were not at first void (at least for senatorial marriages; that hap-

pened later, under Marcus Aurelius: Paul, D. 23.2.16 pr.), but the couple did not enjoy the benefits that the Augustan legislation assigned to married couples (see *Tit. Ulp.* 16.2: no right to inherit from one another). On the benefits, see also Case 12.

CASE 11: Incestuous Marriage

Tituli ex Corpore Ulpiani 5.6–7

(6) Inter parentes et liberos infinite cuiuscumque gradus sint conubium non est. inter cognatos autem ex transverso gradu olim quidem usque ad quartum gradum matrimonia contrahi non poterant: nunc autem etiam ex tertio gradu licet uxorem ducere, sed tantum fratris filiam, non etiam sororis filiam aut amitam vel materteram, quamvis eodem gradu sint. eam, quae noverca vel privigna vel nurus vel socrus nostra fuit, uxorem ducere non possumus. (7) Si quis eam quam non licet uxorem duxerit, incestum matrimonium contrahit: ideoque liberi in potestate eius non fiunt, sed quasi vulgo concepti spurii sunt.

(Excerpts from Ulpian's Writings)

(6) There is no *conubium* between ascendants and descendants no matter how far removed. Between collateral relatives, at one time marriages could not be contracted up to the fourth degree. But now it is permitted to take a wife also from the third degree—but only a brother's daughter, not a sister's daughter or a paternal or maternal aunt, although they are of the same degree. We cannot take as wife a woman who was our stepmother or stepdaughter or daughter-in-law or mother-in-law.

(7) If someone takes a wife who is not permitted, he contracts an incestuous marriage; so the children (of this marriage) are not in his power but are bastards, as if promiscuously conceived.

1. Degrees of Kinship. All this is explained in great detail by Justinian (*Inst.* 3.6). Your parents and children are related to you in the first degree (*primus gradus*); your siblings, grandparents, and grandchildren, in the second degree (*secundus gradus*); and so on. You can figure this out by looking at a family tree; if you count persons back from yourself to the closest ancestor that a relative shares with you, and then forward to the relative, you establish the degree of that person's kinship. The Roman rules barring incestuous marriage are established, in principle, on the basis of actual blood relationship, not on the basis of agnation or the usual family structure; thus, for instance, a male ex-slave cannot marry his biological sister (Pomponius, D. 23.2.8: "this rule is derived from morality, not statutes").

2. Endogamy and Exogamy. In most societies, marriage is typically thought of as exogamous, meaning that, at least in principle, the bride and groom come from different social groups and their marriage establishes a link between the groups (group A is linked to group B). In many historical Mediterranean societies, by contrast, marriage seems often to be regarded as endogamous: the primary aim of marriage is to cement a bond within a recognized social group (group A is linked to group A). Where this phenomenon occurs, the boundaries for incestuous marriage tend to be drawn fairly narrowly, and there is

frequently an inward pressure on them (i.e., a tendency for relaxed restrictions). At Rome, marriage between ascendants and descendants (e.g., a father or grandfather and a daughter) was probably always forbidden, as this Case indicates. As for collateral relatives, some evidence suggests that the boundary was originally the sixth degree (so that second cousins could not marry), but by the classical period it was drawn at the fourth degree (so that first cousins could marry; for an example, see Case 98) and, as this Case indicates, sometimes even closer. (The exception in this Case was introduced when Emperor Claudius married Agrippina, his fraternal niece; see Gaius, *Inst.* 1.62. According to the historian Dio Cassius, 68.2.4, it was later repealed.) In your opinion, is the Roman tolerance for close-kin marriage too extreme? Although the evidence is not very good, close-kin marriages were apparently uncommon among at least the Roman upper classes. In Egypt of the early Roman Empire, by contrast, even full brother-sister marriages were frequent; these marriages were illegal in Roman law.

3. Non–Blood Relations. The incest rules tend to be applied more laxly to non–blood relations. Thus, for instance, where there is no blood relationship, a man can marry his adopted sister's daughter (Ulpian, D. 23.2.12.4), but not his adopted sister unless either the bride or the groom is no longer under the father's power (Gaius, D. 23.2.17 pr.–1). A relation by a terminated marriage is forbidden only in the direct line; so a man cannot marry his stepmother after the end of her marriage with his father (Gaius, *Inst.* 1.63). However, Gaius (D. 23.2.17.2) states that marriage between a man and his father's sister is forbidden even when the two are related only as a result of adoption. Should adopted relatives be treated as natural for purposes of incest law?

4. Ignoring the Rules. Does the penalty described in this Case seem to you too harsh? Essentially, the marriage is null and any children are treated as illegitimate, which means that they have no claim on their natural father's estate; further, criminal penalties were applied at least in the later Empire (e.g., Paul, *Sent.* 2.26.15: deportation to an island). Still, jurists and even emperors often show some leniency, especially to women who enter such marriages through ignorance of the law, particularly where the law is not obvious. A spectacular example is given by the jurist Marcian (D. 23.2.57a), who cites a rescript of Marcus Aurelius writing to a woman: "I am swayed both by the length of time that, through ignorance of the law, you have lived in marriage with your maternal uncle, and by the fact that your grandmother arranged the marriage, and by your many children. Taking these things together, I confirm the status of your children issuing from this marriage contracted forty years ago, just as if they had been legitimately conceived." This signal instance of imperial clemency also clearly indicates the sort of circumstances in which such a marriage might arise.

5. Bigamy. In A.D. 258, the emperors Valerian and Gallienus wrote (C. 9.9.18): "Official disgrace (*infamia*) undoubtedly attends a man who has two wives. In this matter we consider, not (just) the enforcement of the law forbidding our citizens to contract multiple marriages, but their mental intent. (1) Nevertheless, in the case of the man who sought to marry you by pretending to be unmarried when he had another wife in a province, a lawful accuser may also charge him with criminal debauchery (*stuprum*), from which you are insulated because you thought yourself to be a wife." Note that bigamy is not a crime in itself, although it does lead to praetorian disgrace (*infamia*, D. 3.2.1); but it is criminal to have sexual relations with the second wife when she is unaware of the bigamy. Why does it make sense under Roman law not to criminalize bigamy? Is the second marriage necessarily invalid? See Case 76. As the rescript indicates, the second wife, had she known of her husband's bigamy, would also be guilty of *stuprum*.

CASE 12: Incentives to Marry and Reproduce

Tituli ex Corpore Ulpiani 16.1

Aliquando vir et uxor inter se solidum capere possunt: velut si uterque vel alteruter eorum nondum eius aetatis sint, a qua lex liberos exigit, id est si vir minor annorum XXV sit aut uxor annorum XX minor: item si utrique lege Papia finitos annos in matrimonio excesserint, id est vir LX annos, uxor L: item si cognati inter se coierint usque ad sextum gradum: aut si vir absit, et donec abest et intra annum, postquam abesse desierit. libera inter eos testamenti factio est, si ius liberorum a principe impetraverint, aut si filium filiamve communem habeant, aut quattuordecim annorum filium vel filiam duodecim amiserint, vel si duos trimos vel tres post nominum diem amiserint, ut intra annum tamen et sex menses etiam unus cuiuscumque aetatis impubes amissus solidi capiendi ius praestet. item si post mortem viri intra decem menses uxor ex eo pepererit, solidum ex bonis eius capit.

(Excerpts from Ulpian's Writings)

Sometimes a husband and wife can each take in full under each other's wills: for instance, if either or both of them have not yet reached the age when the law requires (them to have) children, that is, if the husband is less than twenty-five or the wife less than twenty; likewise if in their marriage both have reached the age set by the Papian law, that is, the husband is sixty and the wife fifty; likewise, if the pair are relatives within the sixth degree; or if the husband is away (from the couple's home), both while he is away and for a year after he ceases to be away.

They have an unrestricted right of testation between themselves if they have the "right of children" (*ius liberorum*) received from the emperor or, if they have a common son or daughter, they have lost a son aged (at least) fourteen or a daughter aged (at least) twelve, or if they have lost two children aged (at least) three or three children after their name day. But when even one child is lost of whatever age prior to puberty, they have the right of taking the estate in full for the next eighteen months. Likewise, if after her husband's death a wife bears his child within ten months, she takes the estate in full (if it is left to her).

1. Once More the Augustan Marriage Legislation. Besides legally restricting the freedom to marry socially as one wished (Case 10), the Emperor Augustus also introduced an elaborate system of civil penalties and benefits that were intended to induce marriage and childbearing. The *lex Iulia et Papia* (actually two laws, from 18 B.C. and A.D. 9) imposed sanctions especially on persons who did not marry (as a rule, they could not inherit) or who married but had no children (they could take only half the benefits they inherited). This Case describes further testamentary penalties and benefits pertaining to the couple themselves; if the couple do not fall within the intricate excep-

tions, a spouse can inherit only a tenth of the other's estate, plus further tenths for children from this and other marriages (*Tit. Ulp.* 15.1–2). How well do you think that laws such as these would work in achieving their desired purpose?

SECTION 2. Agreement and Marital Affection

CASE 13: The Requirement of Agreement

Tituli ex Corpore Ulpiani 5.2

Iustum matrimonium est, si inter eos qui nuptias contrahunt conubium sit, et tam masculus pubes quam femina potens sit, et utrique consentiant, si sui iuris sunt, aut etiam parentes eorum, si in potestate sunt.

(*Excerpts from Ulpian's Writings*)

A marriage is legitimate (*iustum*) if (the following three conditions are met:) there is *conubium* between the parties who contract the marriage; the male has reached puberty and the female is capable (of sexual relations); and both parties agree (*consentiant*) if they are *sui iuris*, or also if they are in (a father's) power, their parents (agree).

1. What Is Agreement? This Case gives a standard list of the requirements for Roman marriage: *conubium*; adulthood; and the agreement (*consensus*) of all relevant parties, which includes not just the bride and groom but also their *patres familias* if they are in power (see Cases 98–103; the requirement of parental consent is important!). But even between the couple, what is meant by "agreement"? If we say that the parties must "agree" to the marriage, we may mean one of two things: either they must actually (inwardly) agree, even though an outside observer might not realize that they do (this is called subjective agreement); or they must appear to agree even though they may really not, so that an outside observer would conclude they agree (objective agreement). Or is some intermediate position preferable? As you read the following Cases, try to decide which view the Romans adopt. Note that the author of this Case says nothing about public licensing or registration of the marriage (the Romans had neither); and he also does not list a wedding ceremony among the essential requirements.

2. Insanity. Paul, D. 23.2.16.2: "Since agreement (*consensus*) is required, insanity (*furor*) prevents a marriage from being contracted; but it does not invalidate one that has been validly contracted." So an insane person cannot marry initially; but if a spouse goes mad after marrying, this does not by itself dissolve the marriage. The jurists often hold that the insane are by definition unable to function in civil society; they cannot make contracts, write wills, or marry. As to marriage, does this rule help to decide between a subjective and an objective concept of agreement? Suppose, for instance, that a bride is unaware that she is marrying a man who is legally insane; is their marriage valid? On the guardianship of the insane, see Case 223.

3. Legal Exactitude. As you read the Cases that follow, try to decide whether it is always important that legal rules be absolutely clear and unequivocal in their application. Should room be deliberately left for judicial discretion in individual cases? If so, how much room?

CASE 14: A Freedwoman's Agreement

D. 23.2.28 (Marcianus libro decimo Institutionum)

Invitam libertam uxorem ducere patronus non potest:

D. 23.2.29 (Ulpianus libro tertio ad legem Iuliam et Papiam)

quod et Ateius Capito consulatu suo fertur decrevisse. hoc tamen ita observandum est, nisi patronus ideo eam manumisit, ut uxorem eam ducat.

(Marcian in the tenth book of his *Institutes*)

A patron cannot take his freedwoman as his wife if she is unwilling,

(Ulpian in his third book on the *lex Iulia et Papia*)

which (the jurist) Ateius Capito is also said to have decided during his consulate (A.D. 5). But this rule should be observed unless the patron manumitted her precisely to take her as a wife.

1. Marrying One's Freedwoman. This seems not to have been unusual; for instance, Gaius (*Inst.* 1.19) states that freeing a slave woman in order to marry her is "a legitimate reason for manumission" (*iusta causa manumissionis*). As this Case indicates, if the slave woman was manumitted without the master indicating his intent to marry her, she could not then be forced against her will to marry him. Is this a straightforward application of the usual rule requiring agreement (Case 13)? By contrast, when during manumission the master's intent to marry was unambiguous, the freedwoman could not marry anyone else even if her patron then changed his mind about the marriage, unless he actually renounced his right to marry (Licinius Rufinus, D. 23.2.51 pr.). Still, in practice these rules were liberally interpreted to favor the slave woman; for details, see Ulpian, D. 24.2.11.

2. Can She Divorce Him? A provision of the Augustan marriage legislation held that "a freedwoman who married her patron cannot then marry someone else if he is unwilling" (Ulpian, D. 23.2.45 pr.). "If he is unwilling" was interpreted to mean that he would not agree to a divorce; that is to say, she could not unilaterally escape from her marriage to her patron. (She could, however, separate permanently; see Case 75.) If her patron-husband went mad and so became mentally incapable of agreeing to divorce, she was stuck with him (ibid. 5).

3. Social Decency. It is hard to recapture the intricate Roman sense of social propriety. As Modestinus remarks in passing (D. 23.2.42 pr.): "In marriages we should consider not just what is permitted but also what is decent (*hones-*

tum)." Thus, a free woman is not legally barred from manumitting a male slave in order to marry him; however, Ulpian (D. 23.2.13) flatly describes such a woman as "degraded" (*ignobilis*). A social judgment, amounting to a double standard, is thus not "reflected" in the law. Why?

CASE 15: Not Standing on Ceremony

Quintilianus, *Institutio Oratoria* 5.11.32

Nihil obstat quominus iustum matrimonium sit mente coeuntium, etiamsi tabulae signatae non fuerint: nihil enim proderit signasse tabulas, si mentem matrimonii non fuisse constabit.

(Quintilian in the fifth book of his *Rhetorical Institutes*)

Nothing prevents a marriage from being legitimate (solely) through the will of the partners, even if no (marriage) documents are signed, since (conversely) the fact that they signed documents will be of no use if it (later) emerges that they had no will to marry.

1. An Argument *ex Contrario*. Quintilian, a renowned late-first-century A.D. teacher of rhetoric, was not a jurist, although he often argued civil cases in Roman courts. He uses this particular example to illustrate what he calls an *argumentum ex contrario iure*. Do you follow his reasoning? The second half of this sentence (from "since" on) seems correct: going through the form of a marriage does not lead to a marriage if the parties do not actually want to marry. (Compare Papinian, D. 39.5.31 pr.: "Documents don't make a marriage.") But does it necessarily or even reasonably follow that a marriage can arise "through the will of the partners" alone, without any further objective evidence? That is, if the parties' intent (what Quintilian calls their "will," *mens*) is always required for a valid marriage, does that mean that there is not, or that there should not be, any further requirement of form? Think about this question in relation to marriage in modern law as well.

2. "A Sham Marriage." With the second part of this Case, compare Gaius, D. 23.2.30: "A sham marriage (*simulatae nuptiae*) has no effect." What does Gaius mean by "sham marriage"? Consider the following examples: a marriage ceremony performed onstage during a play; or as a joke at a party; or simply to escape the effects of laws penalizing failure to marry (Case 12), by two persons who do not intend to have sexual relations or to raise children; or between two persons who know that, under Roman law, they cannot be married even if they wish to be (e.g., two persons of the same sex). Are these four situations entirely equivalent? What about a marriage that arises as a result of fraud (e.g., the groom has lied about his solvency or his ability to sire children; the bride has lied about being pregnant), duress (e.g., a shotgun wedding), or mistake (the groom believes he is marrying a different woman)? Since divorce was so easy in Roman law, the jurists rarely worry about problems stemming from defective agreement to marriage.

3. Unequal Marriages. Although this was evidently not the position of classical Roman law, in the later Empire a view arose, perhaps under Greek influence, that a marriage between persons of unequal social rank was valid only if confirmed by dowry documents; Justinian (C. 5.4.23.7; A.D. 520–523) repeals this "law." Why would marriages of this kind seem to call for more than usual proof?

CASE 16: What the Neighbors Know

C. 5.4.9 (Imp. Probus A. Fortunato)

Si vicinis vel aliis scientibus uxorem liberorum procreandorum causa domi habuisti et ex eo matrimonio filia suscepta est, quamvis neque nuptiales tabulae neque ad natam filiam pertinentes factae sunt, non ideo minus veritas matrimonii aut susceptae filiae suam habet potestatem.

(The Emperor Probus to Fortunatus; A.D. 276–282)

If your neighbors or others knew that you had in your home a wife in order to sire children (*liberorum procreandorum causa*) and (also) that a daughter from this marriage was accepted (by you as your legitimate offspring), then although no documents were drawn up relating to the marriage or to the daughter's birth, nonetheless the truth of the marriage and of the accepted daughter has force on its own.

1. Rescripts. In this Case, the Emperor Probus authoritatively answers a legal question from a petitioner named Fortunatus. Though most such rescripts are not legislative, rescripts were the most common means that emperors used to declare private law from about A.D. 120 on.

2. Proving Marriage. What was it that primarily concerned Fortunatus: the validity of his marriage or the legitimacy of his daughter? The emperor points to two conventional means of showing that a marriage existed: private "marriage documents" (usually relating to a dowry and confirmed during or soon after the marriage ceremony) and a public document registering a child as a legitimate offspring (see Case 147); but Fortunatus had evidently used neither. Was he taking a risk, and if so, how great a risk? In apparently holding the marriage valid, was the emperor moved mainly by the fact that Fortunatus had a wife "in order to sire children" (a common phrase in relation to legal marriage) and that the couple did then have a daughter? In any case, why should it make any difference what the neighbors claim to "know"? Is it because the couple seem to have held themselves out as married to third parties?

3. "Their Agreement and the Belief of Friends." A century and a half later, the Emperors Theodosius and Valentinian consider a case in which there had been no marriage settlement and no marriage ceremony, but the couple are of equal social status (why is that relevant?), have *conubium*, and had produced children. The marriage is held legitimate "because it is confirmed by their agreement (*consensu*) and the belief (*fide*) of their friends" (C. 5.4.22 = *C.Th.* 3.7.3; A.D. 428). Compare C. 5.17.8 pr. (A.D. 449): "We hold that lawful marriages can be contracted by agreement." Is this rule identical to the one in the present Case? In general, consider the observation of Gaius (D. 20.1.4 =

22.4.4): "Writings are made so that what was transacted can more easily be proved; but even without them what was transacted is valid if there is proof. Thus, marriages are valid even though there is no written witness." Is Gaius right about why people commonly document important transactions, or is this just a lawyer speaking?

CASE 17: Marital Affection

D. 24.1.32.13 (Ulpianus libro trigesimo tertio ad Sabinum)

Si mulier et maritus diu seorsum quidem habitaverint, sed honorem invicem matrimonii habebant (quod scimus interdum et inter consulares personas subsecutum), puto donationes non valere, quasi duraverint nuptiae: non enim coitus matrimonium facit, sed maritalis affectio: si tamen donator prior decesserit, tunc donatio valebit.

(Ulpian in the thirty-third book on Sabinus)

If a wife and her husband have for a long time lived apart, but they reciprocally continued to honor the marriage—something that we know sometimes occurs even among persons of consular rank—, I think gifts between them are invalid since their marriage continues. For it is not sexual intercourse that makes a marriage but rather marital affection (*maritalis affectio*). But if the donor dies first, then the gift is valid.

1. Living Apart. As we have seen, the issue of a marriage's existence is often important in determining the legitimacy of children. Another area where the issue can arise involves gifts between a man and a woman, since Roman law held, in principle, that a husband and wife could not make valid gifts to one another; and therefore, such a gift could be reclaimed by the giver (see Case 61). In this Case, the couple were living apart and had exchanged gifts. The question, then, is whether they were still married, since, if so, the gifts were invalid. How does Ulpian suggest that this problem should be solved? How is "marital affection," as Ulpian uses the term, different from the *consensus* required for marriage?

2. Deportation. For a more extreme example, see Case 74, in which a wife has been deported, thereby losing her citizenship but not her freedom. Ulpian says her marriage is not necessarily dissolved by deportation, since "nothing stops both the man from keeping a husband's affection (*mariti affectionem*) and the woman from her intent to remain a wife (*uxoris animum*)." How long could the couple remain separated before there is a presumption of divorce? If her absent husband began having sex with other women, would that indicate that he no longer had "a husband's affection"? If not that, then what?

3. Continued Reaffirmation? Does Roman law require, if a marriage is to endure, that the parties must not only consent at its outset but also constantly renew that agreement? Or is it enough that neither actively repudiates their initial agreement? The same ambiguity crops up in legal sources on the contract of partnership (*societas*), where Gaius (*Inst.* 3.151) asserts: "Partnership

lasts as long as they (the partners) persist in the same agreement (*consensus*). But when one renounces the partnership, it is dissolved." In Gaius's view, is their agreement presumed to continue unless and until one party makes an open renunciation?

CASE 18: A Wife or a Concubine?

D. 25.7.1 pr. (Ulpianus libro secundo ad legem Iuliam et Papiam)

Quae in concubinatu est, a<n> invito patrono poterit discedere et alteri se aut in matrimonium aut in concubinatum dare? ego quidem probo in concubina adimendum ei conubium, si patronum invitum deserat, quippe cum honestius sit patrono libertam concubinam quam matrem familias habere.

D. 25.7.3 pr. (Marcianus libro duodecimo Institutionum)

In concubinatu potest esse et aliena liberta et ingenua, [et] maxime ea quae obscuro loco nata est vel quaestum corpore fecit. alioquin si honestae vitae et ingenuam mulierem in concubinatum habere maluerit, sine testatione hoc manifestum faciente non conceditur. sed necesse est ei vel uxorem eam habere vel hoc recusantem stuprum cum ea committere.

(Ulpian in the second book on the *lex Iulia et Papia*)

Can a woman who is living in concubinage leave her patron against his will and either marry someone else or be his concubine? I think that in the case of a concubine, *conubium* should be taken away from her if she leaves her patron against his will, since it is obviously more respectable for a patron to have a freedwoman as a concubine than as a wife.

(Marcian in the twelfth book of his *Institutes*)

A concubine can be another person's freedwoman, as also a freeborn woman can, especially one who is of low birth or who was a prostitute. However, if a man wishes to have as his concubine a freeborn woman of respectable background, this is not allowed unless a sworn statement makes the situation clear. But his choice is either to take her as his wife or, if he declines (to marry her), to commit debauchery (*stuprum*) with her.

1. Concubines. A concubine (*concubina*) is, in the commonest usage, a free woman who lives with a man as his long-term sexual partner but does not become his wife. Concubinage is a sort of quasi-legal relationship that is not adulterous (that would be a crime) but also does not entitle the concubine to anything; any children follow her status. As this Case indicates, men normally took as concubines women of a lower social class than themselves—often, their ex-slaves. Respectable women were not supposed to enter concubinage. The problem, then, is how to determine whether a given relationship is marriage or concubinage. Paul says (D. 25.7.4): "A woman should be considered a concubine on the basis of intent alone." But how helpful is such a rule in practice? Here are some examples of the jurists wrestling with the problem:

   • Modestinus, D. 23.2.24: "Living with a free woman is interpreted as marriage, not concubinage, unless she is a prostitute." Compare Marcellus, D.

23.2.41.1: "I hold that a woman who is the concubine of someone other than her master lacks a matron's respectability."

- Ulpian, D. 24.1.3.1: "Let us see between whom gifts are invalid. If a marriage occurs in accord with our customs and laws, a gift will be invalid. But if some (legal) obstacle intrudes to prevent marriage altogether, the gift will be valid. So if a senator's daughter marries a freedman in contravention of the decree of the Senate [see Case 10], . . . the gift will be valid since there is no marriage. But it is not proper that such gifts be affirmed, since then offenders are better off (than those who marry in accord with the law). However, the deified Emperor Severus decided the opposite in the case of a freedwoman of the Senator Pontius Paulinus, since she was treated with the affection due a concubine, not that due a wife." Does Ulpian appear to favor reversing the general rule?

- Papinian, D. 39.5.31 pr.: "It is agreed that gifts to a concubine cannot be revoked; nor, if the two parties afterward marry, does what was before legally valid become invalid. I responded that whether marital honor and affection (*maritalis honor et affectio*) preceded (the giving of the gift) should be determined by comparing the persons involved and examining the nature of their life together."

In this last passage, Papinian apparently examines a case in which the issue is whether a relationship with a concubine had "ripened," so to speak, into a marriage by virtue of the "marital affection" between the couple. How well could that sort of thing ever be determined?

2. Ulpian's Logic. Regarding the end of D. 25.7.1 pr., Jane F. Gardner (in *Women in Roman Law and Society*) has argued: "The logic is doubtful. Since the patron is . . . acquiring more honour for himself by *not* marrying her, *she* is penalised for taking advantage of this; if he sacrifices some honour and marries her, she is the loser, if the marriage is unhappy; yet it is unlikely that Ulpian meant that it was more honourable for a freedwoman to be her patron's concubine than his wife." Do you agree?

3. Debauchery. Marcian indicates that men must be cautious when living with "respectable" Roman women. In their case, only three alternatives are available: marriage (which law will normally construe as existing; see Modestinus's observation above), concubinage (but this must be very carefully established), or debauchery (*stuprum*), a criminal sexual relationship. Ulpian also warns (D. 25.7.1.1): "the only women who can be held in concubinage without fear of a criminal charge are those against whom debauchery is not committed." The exception to this remorseless reasoning is where the woman had previously socially degraded herself, for example, by becoming a prostitute or being convicted as an adulteress. Is Roman law excessively moralistic?

4. **What Does Paul Mean?** Paul, *Sent.* 2.20.1: "From the moment that someone takes a wife, he cannot have a concubine. Therefore, a concubine is distinguished from a wife by intent alone (*solo dilectu*)." Does Paul mean that a woman cannot simultaneously be a wife and a concubine, or that a man cannot simultaneously have both a wife and a concubine? In any case, it appears that Roman men rarely kept both a wife and a concubine (or at least, if they did, they almost never talked openly about it). Is there any reason to believe that such a course would have been, if not illegal, then perhaps at least legally impossible?

CASE 19: An Archaic Wedding Ceremony

Gaius, *Institutiones* 1.110, 112

(110) Olim itaque tribus modis in manum conveniebant: usu, farreo, coemptione. . . . (112) Farreo in manum conveniunt per quoddam genus sacrificii, quod Iovi Farreo fit: in quo farreus panis adhibetur, unde etiam confarreatio dicitur: conplura praeterea huius iuris ordinandi gratia cum certis et sollemnibus verbis praesentibus decem testibus aguntur et fiunt. quod ius etiam nostris temporibus in usu est: nam flamines maiores, id est Diales, Martiales, Quirinales, item reges sacrorum, nisi ex farreatis nati non leguntur: ac ne ipsi quidem sine confarreatione sacerdotium habere possunt.

(Gaius in the first book of his *Institutes*)

(110) At one time women entered into the *manus* (of their husbands) in three ways: by usage, by sacrificial cake (*farreum*), or by formal purchase. . . . (112) They entered into *manus* by *farreum* through a kind of sacrifice made to Jupiter Farreus. In this, a loaf of emmer bread is used, hence it is called *confarreatio*. In carrying out this procedure, many things are enacted and done with prescribed and ceremonial words, in the presence of ten witnesses. This procedure is still in use today. For the greater priests (*flamines*), that is, those of Jupiter, Mars, and Quirinus, along with the King of Sacrifices (*rex sacrorum*), are chosen only from the sons of couples married by *confarreatio;* and they themselves cannot hold the priesthood unless married by *confarreatio.*

1. *Manus* Marriage. In the earliest forms of Roman marriage usually the bride left the *familia* of her father (his *patria potestas* ended) and entered into the *manus*—literally, the "hand," or the control—of her husband. Gaius describes three ways in which this occurred, but he plainly regards *manus* as a historical relic; in classical marriage, a married woman remains in the control of her *pater familias* and becomes *sui iuris* upon his death, and her husband exercises only very limited power over her (see below, Part C). On *manus*, see further Part C.1 below. Although classical jurists still occasionally speak of *manus* marriages as a living possibility, in fact it seems to have virtually disappeared by the end of the Roman Republic.

2. The Role of Ceremony. *Confarreatio*, described in this Case, is a typical archaic Roman ceremony. It emphasizes a precise ritual leading to marriage, and the ritual is witnessed. Gaius's description should lead you to think a little about the role of ceremony in relation to marriage, since ceremony continues to be a very common part of modern weddings. What different purposes do such ceremonies serve, both as marking a distinct stage in the personal lives of the marrying couple and as advertising to the world the transformation of their relationship? The ceremony of *confarreatio* was, as Gaius suggests, originally associated with the elite of the archaic Roman state; perhaps

it was even reserved for patricians. In the classical period, the ceremony seems to have survived only because the incumbents of certain ancient priesthoods had to be the issue of marriages formed by *confarreatio*. But because the ceremony moved the wife into the burdensome *manus* relationship, it became increasingly unpopular; and the Romans, who found it difficult to locate candidates for these priesthoods, eventually were forced to limit this particular *manus* to the sacred sphere alone (Gaius, *Inst.* 1.136; see Tacitus, *Annales* 4.16).

3. *Coemptio* and *Usus*. Gaius describes two other means for creating a *manus* marriage:

- *Coemptio* (purchase) is an imaginary sale, with prescribed words, in which the bride's *pater familias* hands her over to the groom in the presence of witnesses (*Inst.* 1.113); the legal result is the same as with *confarreatio*. The ceremony used for this purpose is an adapted form of mancipation, an almost infinitely flexible ritual that the Romans used also for adopting and emancipating children (see Case 149) and for making wills (Case 171, where the procedure is described); no money actually changes hands, although the parties may separately arrange for a dowry. Gaius strongly implies that *coemptio* was still a living institution in his day (the mid–second century A.D.), but there is little other evidence for its survival that late. Although in form *coemptio* resembles the sale of the bride to the groom or his family, this sale was unreal in historical times (i.e., no actual money was paid to the bride's family). We have no clear evidence that the sale had ever been a true one, although the practice of paying a brideprice (the reverse of dowry) was widely found among the Roman Empire's Celtic and Germanic neighbors.
- The other means for entering a *manus* marriage is through "usage" (*usus*), which is not a ceremony but a sort of right that arises from long-term cohabitation: if the husband and wife live together for one continuous year, she becomes subject to her husband's *manus*, but she can escape this outcome by absenting herself from the household for three nights each year (*Inst.* 1.111). Originally, *usus* was perhaps thought of as a catchall that would bring every married woman into *manus* eventually, even if there was some formal defect in a marriage ceremony; but the ability of women to escape from *manus* clearly raises the possibility of non–*manus* marriage as an alternative to traditional *manus* marriage. Gaius says that by his own day *usus* had been undermined by statutes and had fallen into disuse.

CASE 20: Leading a Bride into the Home

D. 23.2.5 (Pomponius libro <decimo> quarto ad Sabinum)

Mulierem absenti per litteras eius vel per nuntium posse nubere placet, si in domum eius deduceretur: eam vero quae abesset ex litteris vel nuntio suo duci a marito non posse: deductione enim opus esse in mariti, non in uxoris domum, quasi in domicilium matrimonii.

(Pomponius in the fourteenth book on Sabinus)

The prevailing view is that a woman can marry an absent man through a letter from him or by messenger if she is led into his house. But if she is absent, she cannot be married by a husband through a letter or by her messenger; for there must be a "leading" (*deductio*), not into the wife's house, but into the husband's, as into the marriage domicile.

1. *Deductio* and the Marriage Procession. Although early imperial Rome knew no prescribed ceremony for weddings, literary sources frequently describe an extremely colorful nighttime procession in which a rowdy band of revelers lead the bride from her home to that of the groom, where she enters to considerable clamor. Apart from welcoming the bride into his house, the groom plays little part in this procession; apparently no formal vows are exchanged, although dowry documents are often executed during or soon after this ceremony (see Case 21). In this Case Pomponius probably uses the word *deductio* ("leading" or "escorting") to refer to the ceremonial procession or at least to ceremonies of this general sort.

2. The Marriage Domicile. Does Pomponius simply assume that a married couple will always live in the husband's home? Would the couple be married if the groom were to move into the bride's home in her absence? When the couple come from different cities, the jurists regularly hold that their legal domicile will be the husband's (e.g., Papirius Justus, D. 50.1.38.3, paraphrasing an imperial rescript). Can this be regarded as a hard and fast rule? Ulpian (D. 25.2.11 pr.) appears to describe a divorce occurring when a wife expels her husband from her home. Were they presumably married without a *deductio*?

3. Was *Deductio* Required? In this Case, what does Pomponius require in order for a woman to marry a man in his absence? Clearly, there must be some objective sign of his agreement to the marriage (the letter or the messenger bearing his agreement). But must there also be an actual procession, a *deductio*? Suppose, for instance, that he sent her a letter proposing marriage and enclosing the key to his house. If she then used the key and began to live in his house with the professed intention of marrying him, would the couple be already married, or would something additional be required? If Pomponius does require an actual *deductio*, could this simply be because of the ambiguity

caused by the groom's absence in this particular situation? In any event, a postclassical imperial rescript states explicitly that no procession (*pompa*) is required if other evidence for a valid marriage can be found: Theodosius and Valentinian, C. 5.4.22 (= *C.Th.* 3.7.3; A.D. 428). With this Case, compare also Paul, *Sent.* 2.19.8: "An absent man can take a wife, but an absent woman cannot marry"; Paul omits the requirement of a *deductio.*

4. Terminology. In Latin, the bride is said to "marry" the groom (*nubere*), and the word "marry" is reserved for women; by contrast, the groom "takes a wife" (*ducere uxorem*), where the verb *ducere* provides the root of *deductio.* How likely do you think it is that the Roman rules on marriage were only a straightforward inference from this linguistic fact?

5. The Husband's Control. Does this Case at least support the view that "the only form required [for contracting a valid Roman marriage] was the placing of the wife in the husband's control" (W. W. Buckland)? Should we regard *deductio* (or its equivalent), not as a form at all, but rather simply as objective evidence of the parties' agreement? If the latter, is *deductio* best understood primarily as a means for publicizing the existence of marriage, a means that was legally encouraged, but not quite required, in order to protect the legitimacy of children?

6. Agreement Alone? P. E. Corbett, one of the great experts on Roman marriage law, firmly rejected the view that form was of no significance in classical law. His argument ran as follows: "If the consent of the consorts—and of course of their *patresfamilias* if they were *alieni iuris*—was all that was necessary to make them man and wife, then the marriage must date from the last necessary consent, and there should have been no obstacle to celebration between *absentes*. It is precisely on these two points—date of completion and celebration *inter absentes*—that the view which rejects all form leads to serious difficulty." What is this difficulty, and should it be regarded as insurmountable? Was it important to the Romans that they be able to determine with some precision the exact moment at which a marriage began? What actually depended on this determination?

CASE 21: The Significance of Ceremony

D. 24.1.66 pr. (Scaevola libro nono Digestorum)

Seia Sempronio cum certa die nuptura esset, antequam domum deduceretur tabulaeque dotis signarentur, donavit tot aureos: quaero, an ea donatio rata sit. non attinuisse [tempus], an antequam domum deduceretur, donatio facta esset, aut <tempus> tabularum consignatarum, quae plerumque et post contractum matrimonium fierent, in quaerendo exprimi: itaque nisi ante matrimonium contractum, quod consensu intellegitur, donatio facta esset, non valere.

C. 5.3.6 (Imp. Aurelianus A. Donatae)

Cum in te simplicem donationem dicas factam esse die nuptiarum et in ambiguo possit venire, utrum a sponso an marito donatum sit, sic distinguendum est, ut, si in tua domo donum acceptum est, ante nuptias videatur facta esse donatio, quod si penes se dedit sponsus, retrahi possit: uxor enim fuisti.

(Scaevola in the ninth book of his *Digests*)

Seia was about to marry Sempronius on a preset day. Before she was led into his house and the dowry documents were signed, she gave him a sum of gold coins. I ask whether this gift is valid.

    (Scaevola responded:) It is irrelevant whether the gift was made before she was led into his house, or that an inquiry has established the (exact) time when the documents were signed, since this often occurs even after a marriage is contracted. So the gift is invalid unless it was made before the marriage was contracted, a time established on the basis of their agreement (*consensus*).

(The Emperor Aurelian to Donata; A.D. 270–274)

You say that on your marriage day an outright gift was made to you, and that it could be uncertain whether it was given by (him as) your betrothed or as your husband. This distinction should be drawn: if the gift was received in your house, the gift was apparently made before the marriage (and thus cannot be recovered by him); but if your betrothed gave it in his house, it is recoverable, since you were his wife.

    1. An Uncertain Gift. In both these texts, the same problem is raised: On their marriage day, one party has given the other a gift. If the gift was received prior to the couple's marriage, then the gift is irrevocable; but if after the marriage, then it is revocable, since husbands and wives usually could not exchange gifts (see Case 61). The issue, then, concerns when they were married. To what extent do the jurist Scaevola and the Emperor Aurelian approach this issue differently? What do their differences indicate about the interrelationship between the couple's agreement and the ceremony through which they execute their agreement?

2. Responses. Scaevola's opinion has the literary form of a juristic response (*responsum*): fact situation; question; answer. This text may or may not be based on an actual inquiry, but the names are typical "John Doe" names and the situation is deliberately kept hypothetical.

CASE 22: Cohabitation and Marriage

D. 24.1.66.1 (Scaevola libro nono Digestorum)

Virgini in hortos deductae ante diem tertium quam ibi nuptiae fierent, cum in separata diaeta ab eo esset, die nuptiarum, priusquam ad eum transiret et priusquam aqua et igni acciperetur, id est nuptiae celebrentur, optulit decem aureos dono: quaesitum est, post nuptias contractas divortio facto an summa donata repeti possit. respondit id, quod ante nuptias donatum proponeretur, non posse de dote deduci.

(Scaevola in the ninth book of his *Digests*)

A virgin (bride-to-be) was led into (her future husband's) suburban estate two days before the marriage took place there; she stayed in a separate chamber from him. On the day of the marriage, before she crossed to him and before she was received with water and fire, that is, before the wedding celebration, he provided her with ten gold coins as a gift. It was asked whether, when they divorced after having contracted the marriage, the sum that was given can be reclaimed (by him).

   He (Scaevola) responded that in this hypothetical case the gift was made before the wedding and (so) cannot be deducted from the dowry (as an invalid gift).

1. Living in the Same Property prior to Marriage. In this Case, the bride-to-be, evidently for reasons of personal convenience, was led (*deductae*) into her husband's estate and took up residence there a few days before the marriage ceremony was scheduled to occur; but she lived apart from him during the intervening period. On the day of the marriage ceremony, he gave her some money, and she then "crossed to him and . . . was received with water and fire," in a variant of the traditional *deductio*. "Crossing to him" apparently means moving into his quarters within the estate. How easy is it to reconcile Scaevola's response here with the one he gives in Case 21? For Scaevola, would it have changed the outcome if, prior to their scheduled wedding ceremony, the couple had lived together in the same apartment? If they had had sexual relations?

2. Prior Residence in the Same Property. With this Case, compare Ulpian, D. 35.1.15 (= D. 50.17.30 in part): "A legacy was left to a woman under the condition: 'if she had married within the *familia*.' The condition is regarded as fulfilled as soon as she is taken as a wife, even though she has not yet entered her husband's bedroom. For it is not sleeping together, but rather agreement, that makes a marriage." The woman is a freedwoman who can receive the legacy once she has married a fellow freedman. She and her intended are, however, already living in the same household, even though they have not yet slept together. According to Ulpian, when do they become married?

3. Virginity. The Latin word *virgo*, frequently used to describe a woman (especially one of respectable status) prior to her first marriage, is hard to translate; but at times (as in the following Case) it clearly does refer to physical virginity, which in any case was a culturally valued quality.

CASE 23: The Man Who Died beside the Tiber

D. 23.2.6 (Ulpianus libro trigesimo quinto ad Sabinum)

Denique Cinna scribit: eum, qui absen<s> accepit uxorem, deinde rediens a cena iuxta Tiberim perisset, ab uxore lugendum responsum est.

D. 23.2.7 (Paulus libro singulari ad legem Falcidiam)

Ideoque potest fieri, ut in hoc casu aliqua virgo et dotem et de dote habeat actionem.

(Ulpian in the thirty-fifth book on Sabinus)

Finally, (the jurist) Cinna writes: "It was responded that when in his absence a man received a wife, and then, while returning from a dinner, he had died beside the Tiber, he must be mourned by his wife."

(Paul in his monograph on the *lex Falcidia*)

And so, in this instance, it can come about that a woman, (while still) a virgin, has both a dowry and an action for dowry.

1. What Happened? The facts are given in such abbreviated form that it is hard to determine exactly what happened. Apparently, while the man was away from Rome, he "received" his wife; this presumably means that she moved into his house (see Case 20). (The transmitted Latin text, however, is not *absens* but *absentem*, meaning that *she* is absent; but that reading seems to make no sense.) Ulpian does not expressly mention a *deductio*, but perhaps one can be inferred from "received" (*accepit*). Subsequently, as the man was "returning" (presumably, returning to his home) "from dinner" (a marriage dinner?), he "died beside the Tiber" in circumstances that are not further specified. Was his death natural or accidental? Was he waylaid? Does it matter?

2. Must She Mourn? Roman law prescribed a period of time during which close family members were required to mourn their relatives. Wives, in particular, were expected to mourn a deceased husband for ten months, a period of time that was understood mainly as clarifying the paternity of a posthumous child; thus, for instance, the widow could end her mourning and remarry at once if she gave birth before the end of the ten-month period (Ulpian, D. 3.2.11.2). In this Case, however, as it seems, the bride never had sex with her husband; indeed, given the Roman penchant for arranged marriages (see Case 24), she may not even have met him previously. Still, Ulpian holds that she is married and must mourn her husband. Does this view follow straightforwardly from what you have already learned about Roman marriage law?

3. So Where Do We Stand? Try at this point to summarize what was required to become married in Roman law. How clear are the requirements?

Further Aspects of the Marriage Process

As the sources in Part A have indicated, the Romans thought of marriage, not as an event, but as a process, one that might take a considerable period of time even when it culminated in a ceremony. Perhaps for this reason, we have no evidence that Roman couples celebrated the anniversary of their marriage, doubtless because they did not conceive of marriage as occurring at a distinct moment in time (a wedding day). Two additional aspects of marrying frequently served to reinforce this concept of marriage as entered through a process, although neither was required in order to contract a valid marriage.

The first is betrothal (*sponsalia*), the formal engagement of a couple. This was, as Case 24 shows, frequently arranged by intermediaries rather than resulting entirely from the initiative of the couple themselves; and Gaius (D. 23.1.17) indicates that betrothals might last for several years owing to the poor health of either betrothed party, the death of one of their parents, or other circumstances. Betrothal may have originally been somewhat similar to the modern institution of engagement, a purely informal act without specific legal consequences in itself; but it was often accompanied by formal promises that could give rise to litigation for "breach of promise." Gradually betrothal was "legalized" as a sort of initial stage for marriage, and the betrothed parties acquired some of the rights and duties associated with marriage. Nevertheless, in classical law it was no longer possible for one party to sue for damages if the other withdrew, because of the principle that marriage should be "free."

Still more significant is the second institution, dowry (*dos*), a contribution from the bride or her family to the marital household. Dowry was often the subject of protracted premarital negotiations between the woman's side and the man's: either their families or the parties themselves if they were *sui iuris*. Within wide limits, the dowry could take whatever form and amount the parties wished, and accordingly the discussion of its amount and form could be extremely delicate; see, for instance, Terentius Clemens, in D. 23.3.61.1, who describes talks about whether or not the dowry is to be paid in cash.

Dowry is therefore one of the more elaborate Roman legal institutions, and the Cases in Section 2 below offer only a brief introduction to some important points that are likely to have been brought up often in negotiations. What these Cases do not clearly indicate, however, is that the dowry was pivotal to the Roman institution of marriage. The size of a dowry was a significant marker of social prestige for both parties. Further, a dowry was often substantial enough to constitute a significant problem for the bride or her family; but once it had been transferred to the husband and the marriage had begun, he could then face major difficulties in repaying it— one good reason, it appears, for his being circumspect in seeking a divorce. Granted the extremely limited state regulation of both marriage and divorce, dowry served as a social and legal institution that deterred the couple from entering and exiting marriage too hastily. Further, the dowry often provided the wife with maintenance during marriage and some hope of economic independence if the marriage were to end through divorce or her husband's death. For further details as to how dowries were managed during a marriage and what happened to them when the marriage ended, see Cases 66–72 and 81–89.

SECTION 1. Betrothal

CASE 24: Arranging a Betrothal

D. 23.1.4 (Ulpianus libro trigesimo quinto ad Sabinum)

(pr.) Sufficit nudus consensus ad constituenda sponsalia. (1) Denique constat et absenti absentem desponderi posse, et hoc cottidie fieri:

D. 23.1.5 (Pomponius libro sexto decimo ad Sabinum)

haec ita, si scientibus his qui absint sponsalia fiant aut si postea ratum habuerint.

D. 23.1.18 (Ulpianus libro sexto ad edictum)

In sponsalibus constituendis parvi refert, per se (et coram an per internuntium vel per epistulam) an per alium hoc factum est: et fere plerumque condiciones interpositis personis expediuntur.

(Ulpian in the thirty-fifth book on Sabinus)

(pr.) Bare agreement (*nudus consensus*) is enough to bring about a betrothal. (1) So it is settled that an absent person can become betrothed to an absent person, something that occurs every day,

(Pomponius in the sixteenth book on Sabinus)

provided that the absent parties know the betrothal is being arranged, or that they ratify it later.

(Ulpian in the sixth book on the Edict)

It matters little whether betrothal is arranged through the parties themselves—in their presence or by messenger or by letter—or through someone else. Quite frequently the conditions (of the betrothal) are settled by intermediaries.

1. Betrothal. Betrothal (*sponsalia*) is a formal kind of engagement. In D. 23.1.1–3, the jurists Florentinus and Ulpian define it as "the proposal and the mutual promise of a future marriage" and derive the word *sponsalia* from an earlier custom of exchanging formal promises (*sponsiones*); if one party then called off the marriage, these promises may once have made possible an action for "breach of promise." In classical law this is no longer true (see Case 28).

2. Bare Agreement. The concept of agreement (*consensus*), explored previously in relation to marriage, returns for betrothal. If marriage is impossible when the bride is absent (Case 20), why then can betrothal be arranged between absent parties? Could it be that the amount of objective evidence required for establishing the existence of agreement varies depending on the importance and finality of the act in question? No witnesses are required, nor is any oral formality or written proof of the betrothal (Paul, D. 23.1.7 pr.). However, Paul (D. 24.1.36.1) describes a betrothal in which a man gave his intended a ring, a common practice among the Romans (as with us) to symbolize their

agreement; the ring actually belonged to someone else, but he then gave her his own ring after their marriage. Quite exceptionally, this second gift is held not to contravene the prohibition on gifts between spouses, since it merely "confirms" the earlier ring.

3. Intermediaries. As Case 103 suggests, the *pater familias* of a woman was regarded as having a duty to find a husband for his daughter; and in general, as Case 25 shows, the older generation, where it survived, is likely to have had an especially large influence on a woman's first marriage. However, the Romans may also have made use of marriage brokers. In C. 5.1.6 (an imperial rescript of unknown authorship and date but probably from the sixth century A.D.) the maximum fee a broker can charge for arranging a marriage is discussed: 5 percent of the dowry, provided this fee is agreed to in advance. Is the bride's family or the groom's likelier to have paid this fee?

CASE 25: Agreement to Betrothal

D. 23.1.11 (Iulianus libro sexto decimo Digestorum)

Sponsalia sicut nuptiae consensu contrahentium fiunt: et ideo sicut nuptiis, ita sponsalibus filiam familias consentire oportet:

D. 23.1.12 (Ulpianus libro singulari de Sponsalibus)

(pr.) sed quae patris voluntati non repugnat, consentire intellegitur. (1) Tunc autem solum dissentiendi a patre licentia filiae conceditur, si indignum moribus vel turpem sponsum ei pater eligat.

D. 23.1.14 (Modestinus libro quarto Differentiarum)

In sponsalibus contrahendis aetas contrahentium definita non est ut in matrimoniis. quapropter et a primordio aetatis sponsalia effici possunt, si modo id fieri ab utraque persona intellegatur, id est, si non sint minores quam septem annis.

(Julian in the sixteenth book of his *Digests*)

Like marriage, betrothal occurs by the agreement (*consensus*) of the contracting parties; and, as in marriage, so too in betrothal a daughter-in-power must agree.

(Ulpian in his monograph *On Betrothals*)

(pr.) But if she does not resist her father's wish, she is understood to agree. (1) Still, a daughter is granted the privilege (*licentia*) of dissenting from her father only if he chooses for her a betrothed who is morally unfit or degraded.

(Modestinus in the fourth book of his *Distinctions*)

In arranging betrothal, the (minimum) age of the contracting parties is not defined, as it is in marriage. Therefore, betrothal can be brought about from a very early age, provided each party understands what is happening, that is, if they are not less than seven years old.

1. The Reality of Agreement. The jurists insist that the betrothed couple must both agree to the betrothal (for males, see Paul, D. 23.1.13), and, as with marriage, insanity makes agreement impossible (Gaius, D. 23.1.8). This Case, however, suggests that at least the agreement of a daughter-in-power could often be implied, and her right to refuse might even be understood as a "privilege" she could exercise only in extreme circumstances. As to the minimum age for agreement to betrothal, the ending of this Case may be a Justinianic addition to the original text. Paul (*Sent.* 2.19.1) states: "Betrothal can be contracted between adults (*puberes*) as well as among children (*impuberes*)"; this text gives no minimum age, and we learn elsewhere that some girls were betrothed almost at birth. What justifies a degree of casualness in handling agreement to betrothal?

CASE 26: Betrothal and Marriage

D. 24.1.32.27 (Ulpianus libro trigesimo tertio ad Sabinum)

Si quis sponsam habuerit, deinde eandem uxorem duxerit cum non liceret, an donationes quasi in sponsalibus factae valeant, videamus. et Iulianus tractat hanc quaestionem in minore duodecim annis, si in domum quasi mariti inmatura sit deducta: ait enim hanc sponsam esse, etsi uxor non sit. sed est verius, quod Labeoni videtur et a nobis et a Papiniano libro decimo Quaestionum probatum est, ut, si quidem praecesserint sponsalia, durent, quamvis iam uxorem esse putet qui duxit, si vero non praecesserint, neque sponsalia esse, quoniam non fuerunt, neque nuptias, quod nuptiae esse non potuerunt. ideoque si sponsalia antecesserint, valet donatio: si minus, nulla est, quia non quasi ad extraneam, sed quasi ad uxorem fecit et ideo nec oratio locum habebit.

(Ulpian in the thirty-third book on Sabinus)

If a man has a fiancée and then takes her as his wife at an age when this was not permitted, let us examine the validity of gifts made during this "betrothal." Julian discusses this question in the case of a woman less than twelve years old who had been led into her "husband's" home before maturity. He says that she is betrothed, even though she is not a wife.

But the more correct view, the one that seemed preferable to Labeo and was approved by me and by Papinian in the tenth book of his *Questions*, is that if a betrothal actually preceded, it continues even though the man who led her in thinks she is already his wife. But if it did not precede, there is no betrothal since one did not occur; nor is there a marriage, because marriage was impossible. And so if a betrothal preceded, the gift is valid; (but) if not, it is invalid, since he made it as if to his wife and not to a stranger; and thus the legislative proposal (of the Emperor Septimius Severus) will be inapplicable.

1. Is a "Marriage" Actually a Betrothal? The problem here proceeds from the situation in Case 7. A girl below the minimum age for marriage has undergone a marriage ceremony and is now living with her "husband." At law, she cannot be a wife yet. But, in the interim, is she at least his betrothed? Julian answers yes, apparently understanding the situation as a "constructive" betrothal (a purely legal fiction); but Ulpian, following the lead of Labeo and Papinian, holds that an actual betrothal must take place. Which position seems better to you? If the girl is not betrothed, what is she? Ulpian uses the phrase *loco nuptae* (in the position of a wife) to describe her situation (D. 23.1.9). In any event, the underage girl's relationship with her "husband" has some legal validity. For instance, money given for her dowry cannot be recovered unless a "divorce" intervenes before she reaches legal age (Neratius, D. 12.4.8), but like an ordinary betrothed woman, she enjoys privileged status against other

creditors when it comes to recovering any property offered as a dowry (Ulpian, D. 42.5.17.1).

2. Validity of the Gift. Betrothed couples or their families often exchanged gifts, and these gifts were presumably most often made in anticipation of the impending marriage. Roman law holds that when these gifts are made simply out of generosity, they are irrecoverable; but if they are made with the express or implicit condition of marriage, they are often recoverable if the marriage does not take place. For example, Papinian (*Frag. Vat.* 262) holds: "Property given outright to a betrothed woman is not recovered if the marriage does not ensue. But if gifts are made for the purpose of contracting a marriage relationship (*adfinitatis contrahendae causa*) and the betrothed man is at fault for sending a repudiation, they are also not recovered. But the situation should be understood in this way unless, for recalling the gifts, a condition is included of not executing the contract if the marriage is not joined." What might the purpose of such premarital gifts be? The "proposal" (*oratio*) referred to in the last sentence of this Case is a famous initiative of Septimius Severus in A.D. 206; the emperor allowed an invalid gift between spouses to become valid if the donor died before revoking it (see Case 65).

3. *Donatio ante Nuptias.* Dowry, bestowed by the bride's family, was normal in classical Roman marriages; see below, Section 2. However, out of the custom of exchanging betrothal gifts there gradually developed an institution that in the later Empire had considerable importance: *donatio ante nuptias*, a "prenuptial gift" made by the husband to the wife, who then incorporated it within her dowry; it was intended mainly for the support of her and her children during marriage. The earliest clear reference is in a rescript of Septimius Severus (C. 5.3.1; A.D. 193–211), but a roughly contemporary fragment of Paul (D. 6.2.12 pr.) cites an earlier rescript of Antoninus (reign: A.D. 138–161) that may be relevant. Does the rise of this institution suggest a shift in the balance of power during the delicate interfamily negotiations preceding marriage? *Donatio ante nuptias* eventually became a requirement for marriage in the eastern half of the Roman Empire, although it existed alongside dowry.

CASE 27: An Affront to the Fiancée

D. 47.10.1.9 (Ulpianus libro quinquagensimo sexto ad edictum)
Idem ait Neratius ex una iniuria interdum tribus oriri iniuriarum actionem neque ullius actionem per alium consumi. ut puta uxori meae filiae familias iniuria facta est: et mihi et patri eius et ipsi iniuriarum actio incipiet competere.

D. 47.10.15.24 (Ulpianus libro <quinquagesimo> septimo ad edictum)

Sponsum quoque ad iniuriarum actionem admittendum puto: etenim spectat ad contumeliam eius iniuria, quaecumque sponsae eius fiat.

(Ulpian in the fifty-sixth book on the Edict)

Neratius likewise says that sometimes a single affront (*iniuria*) results in three persons having the action on affront; nor is one person's action lost through another person (bringing suit). If, for example, an affront is inflicted on my wife who is (also) a daughter-in-power, the action on outrage becomes available to me, to her father, and to her.

(Ulpian in the fifty-seventh book on the Edict)

In my view, a betrothed man should also be allowed an action on affront. For any affront to his fiancée results in insult to him (as well).

1. Affront. An affront (*iniuria*) is a deliberate affront to one's personal standing, for example, a physical assault or a defamation; in the case of a respectable woman, it can arise from indecent sexual suggestions. Normally not only the affronted woman but also her father or husband or both are allowed to sue on the affront (Gaius, *Inst.* 3.221). In this Case, the privilege is extended also to betrothed men. What is the rationale? See also Case 44.

2. Assimilating Betrothal to Marriage. Many sources suggest that the jurists came to regard betrothal as a quasi-legal institution subject to many of the same rules as marriage. Thus, for instance, just as a husband could not be involuntarily compelled to testify against his wife's father, so also a betrothed man could not be compelled to testify against his intended's father (Gaius, D. 22.5.5); and just as it was "parricide," not ordinary murder, for a man to slay his father-in-law, so too if he slew his intended's father (Marcian, D. 48.9.3–4). Incest rules came to be applied within the context of betrothal (e.g., a man cannot marry his son's intended bride: Ulpian, D. 23.2.12.2); and so too did rules forbidding certain types of marriage (e.g., the mere betrothal of a senator to a freedwoman is void: Ulpian, D. 23.1.16). See also Case 7, on the application of the adultery law to fiancées. What might explain this legalization of an essentially informal relationship? One factor to consider is that a betrothed man was treated as married for purposes of escaping the penalties on celibacy in the Augustan marriage legislation, although under the law such an engagement was allowed to run for no more than two years.

CASE 28: Jilting Your Intended

C. 5.1.1 (Impp. Diocletianus et Maximianus AA. et CC. Bianori)

Alii desponsata renuntiare condicioni ac nubere alii non prohibetur.

D. 23.1.10 (Ulpianus libro tertio Disputationum)

In potestate manente filia pater sponso nuntium remittere potest et sponsalia dissolvere. enimvero si emancipata est, non potest neque nuntium remittere neque quae dotis causa data sunt condicere: ipsa enim filia nubendo efficiet dotem esse condictionemque extinguet, quae causa non secuta nasci poterit. nisi forte quis proponat ita dotem patrem pro emancipata filia dedisse, ut, si nuptiis non consentiret, vel contractis vel non contractis repeteret quae dederat: tunc enim habebit repetitionem.

(The Emperors Diocletian and Maximian to Bianor; A.D. 293)

A woman betrothed to one man is not forbidden from calling off the proposal and marrying another man.

(Ulpian in the third book of his *Disputations*)

As long as a daughter remains in (her father's) power, the father can give notice to the betrothed and end the betrothal. If she was emancipated, however, he cannot give notice nor reclaim what was given (by him) for her dowry. For the daughter herself, by marrying, will bring it about that this is a dowry and (so) will eliminate a recovery claim that could arise if the cause (for giving a dowry) were not carried out. But now suppose that the father gave a dowry for his emancipated daughter on the condition that if he did not agree to the marriage, he might reclaim what he had given whether or not the marriage was contracted. In this case he will have a claim for recovery.

1. No Form Required. A betrothal is usually repudiated by giving notice (literally, "sending back a message," *remittere nuntium*), as here. There is no formality, but some care is necessary, since official disgrace (*infamia*) is inflicted on anyone who, while betrothed to one person, becomes engaged to or marries another: D. 3.2.1 (quoting the Edict). As this Case indicates, a daughter-in-power, but not an emancipated daughter, can have her impending marriage called off by her father (see also Cases 100, 105; on emancipation, Cases 155–159); but the guardians of a *sui iuris* adult woman do not have this power (see Ulpian, D. 23.1.6). Unless specially so arranged, a dowry given for a *sui iuris* woman cannot be reclaimed before the marriage ends.

2. No Penalty. Breach of promise to marry is not actionable. Attempts to create actionability by stipulating penalties if the marriage does not take place are void; as Paul (D. 45.1.134 pr.), explains, such a stipulation is "contrary to good morals (*non secundum bonos mores*), since it has seemed dishonest that a present or future marriage be constrained by the bond of a penalty." Why do you think this rule was created?

SECTION 2. Dowry

CASE 29: Marriage, Dowry, and Public Policy

D. 23.3.1 (Paulus libro quarto decimo ad Sabinum)

Dotis causa perpetua est, et cum voto eius qui dat ita contrahitur, ut semper apud maritum sit.

D. 23.3.2 (Paulus libro sexagesimo ad edictum) (= Paulus, D. 42.5.18)

Rei publicae interest mulieres dotes salvas habere, propter quas nubere possunt.

D. 23.3.3 (Ulpianus libro sexagesimo tertio ad edictum)

Dotis appellatio non refertur ad ea matrimonia, quae consistere non possunt: neque enim dos sine matrimonio esse potest. ubicumque igitur matrimonii nomen non est, nec dos est.

(Paul in the fourteenth book on Sabinus)

A dowry's purpose is permanent, and in accord with the giver's wishes, it is so arranged that it remain forever with the husband.

(Paul in the sixtieth book on the Edict)

It is in the public interest that women's dowries are secure, since they can marry because of them.

(Ulpian in the sixty-third book on the Edict)

The term "dowry" is not used for marriages that cannot arise (because they are illegal), since there can be no dowry without (legal) marriage. So whenever the word "marriage" is not applicable, neither is "dowry."

1. The Nature of Dowry. Dowries are unfamiliar in the modern Western world, but these three fragments, which begin the *Digest* title on dowries, make some fundamental points that should help you to understand them. A dowry is a contribution from the wife's side to the husband. It is given with the expectation that it will (or at least may) remain permanently with the husband, but it is also commonly intended in some sense to benefit the wife. Finally, dowries are integrally associated with marriages: they are almost always created during the marriage process, and they depend on the marriage for their validity. These principles will play out in the Cases that follow. Why would the custom of giving a dowry arise in the first place?

2. "Since They Can Marry Because of Them." What does Paul mean by saying that dowries must be secure because women need them in order to marry? Does he mean that a dowry helps a woman to enter her first marriage, or does he mean that it may help her in the future to enter subsequent marriages? In either case, why is there a public interest in this? What other benefits might the wife hope to receive from a dowry? With this Case, compare Pomponius,

D. 24.3.1: "It is in the public interest that dowries be preserved for women, since for the procreation of offspring and the replenishment of the state with children, it is emphatically necessary that women have dowries." How evident is the link between dowry and procreation?

3. **Limits on the Freedom of the Parties.** One reason the law of dowry is so complicated is that the parties had wide-ranging, though by no means unlimited, freedom to shape details of the dowry as they wished. Only when arrangements challenged the basic nature and purposes of dowry did their validity come into question. Here are some examples of invalid agreements:

- When the marriage ends, the dowry will not be returned under any circumstances to the wife (Paul, D. 23.4.16; see ibid. 12.1).
- In returning the dowry, the husband can delay beyond the usual legal time limits for its return (D. 23.4.14–18).
- If there are children, then no matter how the marriage ends, the entire dowry will remain with the husband; this is invalid if the marriage ends through the husband's death (Ulpian, D. 23.4.2).
- The land that the wife has placed in her dowry is subject to the condition that her husband will return any fruits from the land to the dowry; this is invalid in most circumstances (Ulpian, D. 23.4.4, because it infringes on the purpose of dowry; why?).
- The husband, in administering the dowry, is liable for nothing but his deliberate misconduct, *dolus* (Ulpian, D. 23.4.6).
- The husband cannot retain a portion of the dowry in the event of his wife's marital misconduct (Paul, D. 23.4.5 pr.).
- The husband cannot sue for necessary expenses in maintaining the dowry, "because by operation of law such expenses reduce the dowry" (Paul, D. 23.4.5.2; see Case 85).

In each instance, try to figure out what it is about the particular agreement that is legally offensive. How closely regulated was the dowry relationship? Could individual parties have had good reasons for wishing to depart from some of the set guidelines?

4. **How Much?** As we will see, the jurists often associate dowry with the wife's maintenance during marriage. Hence, depending on her social status, a dowry could be quite hefty, though the exact amount was subject to negotiation and depended on the relative power of the two families; but legal and other sources indicate that the practice of giving dowries occurred even when the couple's families were relatively poor. Dowries, although regarded as burdensome, seem typically to have amounted to only about one year's household income for the bride's family, rather than the three to five years' income

that was common in early modern Europe. Still, a dowry often represented a substantial transfer of assets from one family to another, and because it usually required dipping into capital, givers often found it difficult to raise the sums involved; cash payments, for instance, were normally allocated over a number of years in order to ease the hardship. The same problem also arose, naturally enough, when a husband later had to return the dowry to the giver, and much the same solution was adopted (*Tit. Ulp.* 6.8).

CASE 30: Giving the Dowry

Tituli ex Corpore Ulpiani 6.2

Dotem dicere potest mulier quae nuptura est et debitor mulieris, si iussu eius dicat: item parens mulieris virilis sexus per virilem sexum cognatione iunctus, velut pater avus paternus. Dare promittere dotem omnes possunt.

D. 23.3.5 pr.–4 (Ulpianus libro trigesimo primo ad Sabinum)

(pr.) Profecticia dos est, quae a patre vel parente profecta est de bonis vel facto eius. (1) Sive igitur parens dedit dotem sive procurator eius sive iussit alium dare sive, cum quis dedisset negotium eius gerens, parens ratum habuerit, profecticia dos est. (2) Quod si quis patri donaturus dedit, Marcellus libro sexto Digestorum scripsit hanc quoque a patre profectam esse: et est verum. (3) Sed et si curator furiosi vel prodigi vel cuiusvis alterius dotem dederit, similiter dicemus dotem profecticiam esse. (4) Sed et si proponas praetorem vel praesidem decrevisse, quantum ex bonis patris vel ab hostibus capti aut a latronibus oppressi filiae in dotem detur, haec quoque profecticia videtur.

(Excerpts from Ulpian's Writings)

A woman who is about to marry can unilaterally promise a dowry (*dicere dotem*), and (so too can) the woman's debtor if she orders him to promise; likewise, the woman's male ascendant who is related in the male line, for example, a father or paternal grandfather; (but) all persons can give or formally promise a dowry (for a woman).

(Ulpian in the thirty-first book on Sabinus)

(pr.) A dowry is "profectitious" (*profecticia*) when it has "traveled" (*profecta est*) from the property or from a transaction of a (wife's) father or (other) male ascendant. (1) So the dowry is profectitious if the ascendant gave the dowry or if his *procurator* (did so) or if he ordered a third party to give it or if the ascendant ratified the gift of someone who was managing his affairs. (2) So if the giver wished to make a gift to the (bride's) father, Marcellus in the sixth book of his *Digests* wrote that this too "traveled" from the father, a view that is correct. (3) Again, if the *curator* of a lunatic or a prodigal or of anyone else gives the dowry, we will similarly term this a profectitious dowry. (4) But suppose that a praetor or (provincial) governor judicially ruled on how much should be given as a dowry from the property of a father who had been either captured by the enemy or kidnapped by bandits; this too seems profectitious.

1. Who Can Create a Dowry, and How? In part, this Case deals with some technical details that are important to Roman law but of scant modern interest. The first fragment describes three ways to make a dowry: first, by a unilateral declaration (*dictio dotis*), which could be given only by the woman (or her

debtor on her order) or by an agnate ascendant; second, by handover of property; or third, by a formal promise, a contract called a stipulation, in which, typically, the promisee asks, "Do you promise to give me 50,000 sesterces as a dowry?" and the promisor answers, "I promise." The second two forms can be used by anyone, and dowries were sometimes created for poor women by wealthy relatives, friends, or patrons. However, by far the most common source of a dowry was the bride herself (if she was *sui iuris*) or her *pater familias*. Does this fact help to explain why a slightly less formal procedure was permitted in their case?

2. **"Profectitious" and "Adventitious" Dowries.** For reasons that have to do less with the form or content of the dowry than with what happens to it when the marriage ends (see Cases 81–82), the jurists distinguish between two main types of dowry. A "profectitious" dowry (*dos profecticia*) comes from a woman's paternal ascendant (usually her father and *pater familias*, but the same rules would apply even if she were emancipated); its main characteristic is that it can be reclaimed if a wife predeceases her husband. An "adventitious" dowry (*dos adventicia*) comes from any other source (including the woman herself), and upon the wife's death the giver can reclaim it only if this had been specified at the time of the dowry's creation; otherwise, it remains with the husband. Why should male ascendants have been privileged in this way? Pomponius (D. 23.3.6 pr.) tries to explain: "Legal help is given to the father to comfort him for his lost daughter by returning the dowry that came from him, so that he not suffer the loss of both his daughter and his money." Convinced?

3. **"Traveling."** Dowries were often the subject of protracted negotiation, and they took an almost infinite variety of forms. Almost any form of property could be in a dowry, but cash and land (particularly farms) were probably the most common. The profectitious dowry is interesting because it had to "travel" (derive) from the male ascendant's substance (his property or his transaction); that is, he had to be financially worse off because of the dowry. This Case illustrates some of the possibilities. Where the *pater familias* ordered someone else to give the dowry, he obligated himself to pay the third party; hence the dowry derives from his substance. Does the same logic apply in the case of the redirected gift (section 2)? In section 4, the *pater* does not even know that the dowry was created. Applying the logic of this Case, in which of the following situations does the dowry derive from the giver's substance?

- The bride's father inherits an estate but declines it so that the estate can go to the groom, who has been named as substitute heir (Ulpian, D. 23.3.5.5).
- A father provides a dowry for his adopted daughter (ibid. 13).

- A third party gives money to the father with instructions that it is to be used for the dowry (ibid. 9).

4. Suing Your Father-in-Law. If a bride's father has promised a dowry, can her husband sue for it? And if so, must the father pay the full amount or only what he is financially able to pay? Does it matter whether the couple are still married? All this was the subject of an unusually lively controversy among the jurists: Labeo/Paul, D. 23.3.84; Pomponius, D. 42.1.22 pr.; Paul (citing Neratius and Proculus), D. 24.3.17 pr.; Paul (citing Neratius), D. 42.1.21. Why might such questions have caused dissension? Can it be argued that the bride's father should enjoy special privileges?

CASE 31: The Bride Gets Cold Feet

D. 23.3.21 (Ulpianus libro trigesimo quinto ad Sabinum)

Stipulationem, quae propter causam dotis fiat, constat habere in se condicionem hanc "si nuptiae fuerint secutae," et ita demum ex ea agi posse (quamvis non sit expressa condicio), si nuptiae <fuerint secutae>, constat: quare si nuntius remittatur, defecisse condicio stipulationis videtur

D. 23.3.22 (Paulus libro septimo ad Sabinum)

et licet postea eidem nupserit, non convalescit stipulatio.

(Ulpian in the thirty-fifth book on Sabinus)

It is settled that a stipulation made for dowry purposes contains the implicit condition "if the marriage occurs," and so it is also settled that although the condition was not expressed, a lawsuit can be brought on it only if the marriage occurs. So if the messenger is sent back (and the marriage thereby called off), the stipulation's condition clearly failed,

(Paul in the seventh book on Sabinus)

and although she afterward marries the same man, the stipulation does not revive.

1. Stipulating for a Dowry. In this Case, someone—most likely, the bride-to-be's father—has formally promised a dowry to the groom before the marriage. Obviously the givers of a dowry usually prefer a promise rather than an immediate transfer, since they can then wait until the marriage actually takes place before fulfilling the promise. However, a premarriage transfer of dowry property can be reclaimed if the wedding is called off (see, e.g., Ulpian, D. 12.4.6). The general rule on enforcing the stipulation is stated by Paul (D. 2.14.4.2): "Prior to the marriage, a lawsuit on it fails, as if this had been expressly provided; and the stipulation is automatically void if the marriage doesn't ensue."

2. A Change of Mind. As it seems, the woman in this Case first called off the wedding and then decided to go through with it. Do you agree with the legal outcome? Contrast the following situation described by Papinian (D. 23.3.68): A dowry is promised, and a wedding then takes place; but the marriage is not immediately valid either because the bride's father has not agreed to it or because she is too young. Some time later, the deficiency is remedied and the marriage becomes valid. Can the promise now be sued upon? Papinian holds that it can be; but is this holding easily reconciled with the present Case? In any event, as Papinian observes, the promise definitely fails if the woman marries someone else first; and it does not revive if she later marries her original suitor.

CASE 32: The Duty to Provide a Dowry

D. 12.6.32.2 (Iulianus libro decimo Digestorum)

Mulier si in ea opinione sit, ut credat se pro dote obligatam, quidquid dotis nomine dederit, non repetit: sublata enim falsa opinione relinquitur pietatis causa, ex qua solutum repeti non potest.

(Julian in the tenth book of his *Digests*)

If a woman's state of mind is such that she believes herself obligated (to pay something) for a dowry, whatever she gives on account of the dowry she does not reclaim (as not being owed). For after her false belief is removed, there (still) remains the ground of family respect (*pietas*), because of which she cannot reclaim what she paid.

1. A Social Obligation. In this Case, a woman mistakenly thought she was obligated to pay something as a dowry to her husband, and she made the payment. Normally, amounts paid in error can be recovered through a legal device called the *condictio indebiti;* so, for example, Ulpian, D. 12.6.1.1: "If someone mistakenly pays an unowed debt, he can sue for it through this action." Here, however, it is held that the woman, despite her mistake, cannot reclaim the money (at least not before the end of her marriage). Julian explains this outcome by referring to the *pietas* that she owes her husband. Does this argument make his holding any clearer? Literary sources clearly indicate that dowry was a socially expected part of marriage, and some legal sources seem to suggest the same idea. For example, Venuleius (D. 42.8.25.1) indicates that undowered women would simply not find husbands; and Celsus (D. 37.6.6) says that male antecedents have a "duty," *officium,* to find them one. A nice example is Ulpian, D. 23.3.5.8: A son-in-power borrowed money and used it as a dowry for his daughter; although his *pater familias* was unaware of what had happened, the dowry is still held to be profectitious up to the amount that the grandfather would have given, "for the arrangement appears to have benefited him." How was he benefited? See also Cases 123, 217.

2. A Legal Obligation? Marcian (D. 23.2.19 = Case 103; very poorly preserved) may indicate that in the late classical period, under some circumstances, a *pater familias* could be legally compelled to provide his daughter with a dowry. The Emperor Justianian refers to earlier, "well-known" laws to the same effect (C. 5.11.7.2; A.D. 531). How this came about is impossible now to determine, but some form of imperial intervention (probably by the Emperor Septimius Severus; reign: A.D. 193–211) is not unlikely. A rescript of Diocletian (C. 5.12.14; A.D. 293) holds: "A mother is not forced to give a dowry for her daughter except when the cause is great, clear, and specially provided for by law; but a father lacks the capacity to provide a dowry from the property of

his unwilling wife." This rescript suggests that by the late third century A.D. fathers had some legal duty themselves to provide dowries.

3. An Early Inheritance? In many historical societies where dowry has been prevalent, fathers have tended to see the settlement of a dowry on a daughter as, in effect, the allocation to her of her future inheritance; that is, the daughter cannot anticipate a further distribution after her father's death. Roman legal sources provide some evidence for this view. For instance, Modestinus (D. 28.5.62) reports on a man who, in his will, disinherited his daughter, saying that she should be "content with the dowry." (Compare Papinian, D. 6.1.65.1, 31.77.9, 38.16.16; Modestinus, D. 31.34.5.) Still, such legal and literary evidence is, on the whole, rather thin for Rome. What legal and social considerations might have deterred the Romans from understanding dowry as an early estate distribution to the woman? You should keep this question in mind as you read further about dowry in the remainder of the present chapter.

4. Family Relations. "The provision of dowry was . . . one of the mechanisms by which Roman families, like those in many other preindustrial societies, maintained their social status relative to each other, and so there was a strong social if not, for most of the classical period at any rate, legal obligation to provide dowries for daughters" (Jane F. Gardner, *Women in Roman Law and Society*). Assess the cogency of this theory.

CASE 33: Appropriate Dowries

D. 32.43 (Celsus libro quinto decimo Digestorum)

Si filiae pater dotem arbitratu tutorum dari iussisset, Tubero perinde hoc habendum ait ac si viri boni arbitratu legatum sit. Labeo quaerit, quemadmodum apparet, quantam dotem cuiusque filiae boni viri arbitratu constitui oportet: ait id non esse difficile ex dignitate, ex facultatibus, ex numero liberorum testamentum facientis aestimare.

(Celsus in the fifteenth book of his *Digests*)

If (in his will) a father had ordered that his daughter (when she marries) is to be given a dowry "at her tutors' discretion," Tubero says this should be interpreted as if the legacy were made "at the discretion of a good man" (*viri boni arbitratu*).

Labeo asks how to determine the amount of a dowry that should be established for each daughter "at the discretion of a good man." He says it is not hard to assess this in accord with the testator's standing (*dignitas*), his means, and the number of his children.

1. How Much Is Enough? In this Case, a father left all or part of his estate to his minor daughter but ordered her guardians (on tutelage, see Chapter V.A.1) to provide her with a dowry at their discretion, from her property. This instruction might seem to give them sweeping powers, but the Roman jurists hold that such discretion must be exercised in accord with objective good faith (the amount that a "good man," a *vir bonus*, would have given by way of dowry), consideration being paid to the deceased's social standing, his means, and competing demands on those means (i.e., other dowries that must be paid). Is it clear how much the girl's guardians should provide to the woman? Elsewhere, Celsus states that the husband's *dignitas* also deserves consideration (D. 23.3.60; see Papinian, D. 23.3.69.4); does that seem reasonable?

2. An Objective Standard. If the guardians do not provide a proper dowry, can they be sued? If so, by whom and on what legal theory? What would be the most common complaint: that the girl's dowry was too much or too little?

3. Giving Too Much. The pressure on the bride's side to come up with a respectable dowry could sometimes be crushing. A poorly preserved fragment of Paul (*Frag. Vat.* 115) describes a *sui iuris* woman who married a man of appreciably higher *dignitas* than her own; she gave him her entire property as a dowry, and the jurists accept this as legal (so too Alexander Severus, C. 5.12.4; A.D. 223). Still, such extravagance was considered something an older woman would never engage in (Paul, D. 4.4.48.2). Perhaps for this reason, the jurists are especially cautious when it comes to younger women, below

the age of twenty-five. Ulpian, D. 4.4.9.1: "Also as regards the dowry's amount, the woman (less than twenty-five) should be helped if through trickery she gave a dowry exceeding the means of her estate, or (if she gave) the entire estate." (The legal help that Ulpian mentions took the form of allowing her to apply for rescission of the dowry; see Case 220.)

CASE 34: The "Dowered" Wife

D. 48.5.12.3 (Papinianus libro singulari de Adulteriis)

Socer cum nurum adulterii accusaturum se libellis praesidi datis testatus fuisset, maluit accusatione desistere et lucrum ex dote magis petere. quaeritur, an huiusmodi commentum eius admitti existimes. respondit: turpissimo exemplo is, qui nurum suam accusare instituisset, postea desistere maluit contentus lucrum ex dote retinere tamquam culpa mulieris dirempto matrimonio: quare non inique repelletur, qui commodum dotis vindictae domus suae praeponere non erubuit.

(Papinian in his monograph *On Adulteries*)

By filing a criminal complaint with the (provincial) governor, a father-in-law gave notice that he would accuse his daughter-in-law of adultery. But he subsequently preferred to abandon the accusation and instead to seek to profit from the dowry. It is asked whether you think this sort of chicanery is permissible.

He (Papinian) responded: It sets a dreadful precedent that a man, after he had begun to accuse his daughter-in-law, preferred (instead) to profit from the dowry on the theory that the woman was at fault (*culpa*) for the marriage's breakup. So he will not unfairly be repulsed (i.e., his claim to a portion of the dowry should be refused), since he did not blush to prefer benefit from the dowry over revenging his own home.

1. The Temptations of Money. This is a fascinating Case, the psychological complexity of which runs deep. The father-in-law officially accused his son's wife of adultery, but then withdrew his accusation in favor of an "amicable" divorce in which he would retain a portion of the dowry, evidently on the grounds that her misconduct had caused the marriage's breakup (see Case 83). Is Papinian suggesting that the father-in-law was in effect bribed, or just that he saw an opportunity and seized it? Is the father-in-law being treated as constructively a pimp (*leno*)? The recommended penalty is that he lose his claim to a dowry portion. Would the outcome probably have been different if he had not already filed notice of his intent to accuse his daughter-in-law? In any event, the more basic problem here is one that literary sources often allude to: a woman's dowry could be so large as to effectively grant her immunity from ordinary social responsibilities. From this perspective, although the husband's side would normally bargain for a high dowry, too high a dowry presented them with some offsetting risks. One of these risks was that her husband could find repayment extremely difficult, thus substantially weakening his negotiating position if a whisper of divorce was in the air.

CASE 35: The Burdens of Marriage

D. 23.3.56.1–2 (Paulus libro sexto ad Plautium)

(1) Ibi dos esse debet, ubi onera matrimonii sunt. (2) Post mortem patris statim onera matrimonii filium sequuntur, sicut liberi, sicut uxor.

D. 23.3.7 pr. (Ulpianus libro trigesimo primo ad Sabinum)

Dotis fructum ad maritum pertinere debere aequitas suggerit: cum enim ipse onera matrimoniii subeat, aequum est eum etiam fructus percipere.

(Paul in the sixth book on Plautius)

(1) The dowry should be where the burdens of marriage (*onera matrimonii*) are. (2) After a father's death, the burdens of marriage fall to the son instantly, along with his wife and children.

(Ulpian in the thirty-first book on Sabinus)

Fairness requires that the "fruits" of the dowry (*fructus dotis*) should accrue to the husband. Since he bears the burdens of the marriage (*onera matrimonii*), it is fair that he also receive the fruits.

1. Marriage Burdens. The "burdens of marriage" (*onera matrimonii*) are, as it seems, the additional expenses of maintaining a marital household, particularly food, clothing, and shelter for the wife, her attendant slaves, and perhaps the couple's children as well. In the case of a married son-in-power, these expenses are in principle borne by his father, who accordingly controls his daughter-in-law's dowry up until his death; but the dowry immediately reverts to the son after the father's death. Ulpian, D. 10.2.20.2: "Further, (in settling an estate of a deceased *pater familias*) his son-in-power, who is named as heir, has a preferential claim to his wife's dowry, and rightly so since he assumes the burdens of marriage." The jurists describe the link between a dowry and household expenses as a fundamental principle of law; for example, Paul, D. 23.4.28: "[T]he fruits of a dowry should relieve the burdens of marriage." Why is this such a problem for the Romans? (For one answer, see Case 60.)

2. Fruits of the Dowry. "Fruits" (*fructus*) is a technical term referring to the direct or indirect income that property produces. In general, fruits arise from capital through cultivation (e.g., crops, wool, milk), but the jurists extend the term to include minerals excavated from mines, the value of work done by slaves, and even the proceeds from a lease of property. It is these fruits, usually converted into cash, that are supposed to compensate the husband for his sustaining the burdens of marriage, although no exact accounting is ever required. On the general problem of linking dowry income to the actual costs of maintenance, see below, Part C. 4 and C.5.

CASE 36: Appraising the Dowry

D. 23.3.10 pr. (Ulpianus libro trigesimo quarto ad Sabinum)

Plerumque interest viri res non esse aestimatas idcirco, ne periculum rerum ad eum pertineat, maxime si animalia in dotem acceperit vel vestem, qua mulier utitur: eveniet enim, si aestimata sit et eam mulier adtrivit, ut nihilo minus maritus aestimationem eorum praestet. quotiens igitur non aestimatae res in dotem dantur, et meliores et deteriores mulieri fiunt.

D. 23.3.42 (Gaius libro undecimo ad edictum provinciale)

Res in dotem datae, quae pondere numero mensura constant, mariti periculo sunt, quia in hoc dantur, ut eas maritus ad arbitrium suum distrahat et quandoque soluto matrimonio eiusdem generis et qualitatis alias restituat vel ipse vel heres eius.

(Ulpian in the thirty-fourth book on Sabinus)

Usually it is in the husband's interest that the property (in the dowry) not be appraised, so that the risk for it not fall on him, especially if he receives as dowry the animals or the clothing his wife uses. For if it was appraised and his wife (then) wore it out, the result will be that the husband is still liable for its appraised value. So, whenever unappraised property is given as dowry, both an increase and a decrease in value fall on the wife.

(Gaius in the eleventh book on the Provincial Edict)

When items in the dowry can be weighed, counted, or measured, they are at the husband's risk, since they are given so that the husband may alienate them at his discretion; and when the marriage ends, he or his heir is to restore other property of the same kind and character.

    1. Appraisal. In the bargaining before marriage, one weapon on the bride's side is appraisal (*aestimatio*), an agreement that sets a fixed value on an object in the dowry. As Ulpian points out (D. 23.3.10.4), once the marriage has taken place, the effect of this agreement is somewhat like a sale: if the object is destroyed, even without the husband's fault, he is liable for its appraised value. (There are some exceptions to this liability, of minor concern here.) In this Case, Ulpian points out a potential trap for the husband. Why should he bear the cost when his wife wears out her dowry clothing, or when dowry animals die? In general, the appraisal must be honest at least on the husband's part (ibid. 12.1). The husband might also provide security for the dowry's return (Gaius, *Inst.* 3.125).

    2. Risk. This Case introduces the problem of risk (*periculum*) in dowry, the potential liabilities associated with the destruction or deterioration of dowry property. As Gaius observes, fungibles (things normally thought of as re-

placeable by substitutes; e.g., a sack of wheat or a sum of money) are not appraised because the husband is expected to return their replacements; hence they are held at his risk. What if they are accidentally destroyed before he can make use of them?

PART C

The Marital Regime

The older form of Roman marriage involved the subjection of the wife to the control (*manus*) of her husband. This form of marriage was fast becoming obsolete already by the beginning of the classical period of Roman private law, and accordingly we know less about it than we would like. Gaius preserves a relatively full description of how *manus* marriages were entered (see Case 19), but he indicates that two of the three traditional methods were no longer in use by the mid–second century A.D.; the third (*coemptio*) seems to have survived only marginally at that date.

The four Cases in this section were selected to introduce the main features of *manus* marriage, particularly because these features stand in sharp contrast to the "free" marriage of classical Roman law. One of the most remarkable features of Roman family law is that the Romans went through a transition from an archaic form of marriage featuring the wife's legal subjection to her husband to a form of marriage resting almost entirely upon voluntary cooperation between the spouses, without, as it seems, passing through any intermediate stage.

CASE 37: *Filiae Loco*

Collatio 16.2.1–3 (Gaius, *Institutiones* 3.1–3)

(1) Intestatorum hereditates lege duodecim tabularum primum ad suos heredes pertinent. (2) Sui autem heredes existimantur liberi qui in potestate morientis fuerunt. . . . (3) Uxor quoque, quae in manu est, ei cuius in manu est sua heres est, quia filiae loco est: item nurus quae in filii manu est, nam et haec neptis loco est. sed ita demum erit sua heres, si filius, cuius in manu sit cum pater moritur, in potestate eius non sit. idemque dicimus et de ea, quae in nepotis manu matrimonii causa sit, quia proneptis loco est.

(Gaius in the third book of his *Institutes*)

(1) By the Law of the Twelve Tables, the inheritances of those who die intestate fall first to their *sui heredes* (privileged heirs).

(2) By *sui heredes* are meant descendants who were in the dying man's *potestas*. . . .

(3) A wife in *manus* is also a *sua heres* to the man in whose *manus* she is, since she is in the position of a daughter (*filiae loco*). Likewise for a daughter-in-law who is in a son's *manus,* since she is in the position of a granddaughter; but she will be a *sua heres* only if she is in the *manus* of a son who is not in his father's power when the father dies. And we say the same about a woman who is in a grandson's *manus* for marriage purposes, since she is in the position of a great-granddaughter.

1. Intestate Succession and Women in *Manus*. This Case relates not to family law as such but rather to rights of succession when a *pater familias* dies without leaving a will. In very early Roman law (the Twelve Tables date from 449 B.C.), the estate of the *pater* falls first to those persons directly under his control, the *sui heredes* (roughly, "his privileged heirs"); for details, see Case 159. These include his children-in-power but also his wife in *manus,* who is treated, for this purpose, like a daughter; that is, the wife shares the inheritance with her children, on an equal basis. Not only is a wife in *manus* a *sua heres* to her husband, but she can also inherit from her children and vice versa (Gaius, *Inst.* 3.14), something that was frequently untrue of a wife in free marriage. See Case 167.

2. "The Position of a Daughter." On the various means for creating a *manus* marriage, see Case 19. Its main consequence is, as Gaius says (*Inst.* 1.111), that "she crossed into the *familia* of her husband and took on the position of a daughter." That is, she leaves the *familia* of her *pater familias* (or, if she is already *sui iuris,* her *familia* comes to an end), and instead she becomes a part of her husband's. This is one example of a change in civil status with respect to the family (see Case 1). As a consequence, her agnate relationship (see Case 3) with her prior relations is sundered; but in its place she acquires an agnate

relationship with her husband and with his agnates, including his children (whether by her or by a previous wife) and his other descendants through males (see *Tit. Ulp.* 23.3). That said, it is still potentially misleading to describe her as actually assuming "the position of a daughter" if this is taken to mean that she enters into the *patria potestas* of her husband. We know very little about *manus,* which was passing out of existence during the later Roman Republic; but it is at least clear that *manus* was conceived as a much less one-sided relationship than *potestas*. A wife in *manus* was protected by certain social conventions, which were transformed into legal norms at a very early time; thus, it was apparently illegal for a husband to sell his wife, to give her in adoption, or to execute her even for serious misconduct without first consulting a *consilium* of relatives (compare Cases 52, 95–96). Further, the wife acceded to the responsible and socially honored position of *mater familias*. Although there is no denying that her position was weak in law, it was not entirely abject.

CASE 38: The Wife's Property

Gaius, *Institutiones* 2.98

Si cui heredes facti sumus, sive cuius bonorum possessionem petierimus, sive cuius bona emerimus, sive quem adoptaverimus, sive quam in manum ut uxorem receperimus, eius res ad nos transeunt.

Cicero, *Topica* 23

Cum mulier viro in manum convenit, omnia quae mulieris fuerunt viri fiunt dotis nomine.

(Gaius in the second book of his *Institutes*)

If we are made heirs to someone or sue to acquire a (deceased) person's estate or buy an (insolvent) person's estate or adopt someone or take a woman into *manus* as a wife, that person's property passes to us.

(Cicero in his *Topics*)

When a woman comes into her husband's *manus*, everything that belonged to the woman becomes her husband's as a dowry.

1. "All Her Property." Gaius is firm in stating that when a *sui iuris* woman enters into a *manus* marriage, all her property becomes her husband's. More precise is Gaius, *Inst.* 3.83: "For when . . . a woman enters into *manus*, all her property both incorporeal and corporeal, as well as what is owed to her, . . . is acquired for (her husband), except for those things lost through her change of (family) status"; see also 3.84 and 4.38 (creditor protections preventing her marriage from discharging her prior obligations). This would seem to indicate that she loses the property utterly. By contrast, Cicero, writing in the late Roman Republic, speaks of this property becoming her dowry; this should mean that she can recover the property if, for instance, the marriage ends through her husband's death. Is this possibly a historical development related to the decline of *manus* marriage? If so, why would Gaius (writing ca. A.D. 150) retain the older view?

2. Dowry for Women in *Manus* Marriages. The historical process whereby dowry developed is poorly known, although most of the basic elements were probably in place by the mid–second century B.C. In 230 B.C. a Roman senator named Sp. Carvilius Ruga divorced his wife because she had not born him a child and was apparently sterile. The marriage evidently was with *manus*. It was hotly disputed whether Ruga's excuse was acceptable; but the more important point is that he seems to have succeeded in retaining his wife's dowry. This should indicate that in *manus* marriages the dowry belonged outright to the husband unless the giver (the wife's family) had received a specific prom-

ise of its return, a point that was made two centuries later by the jurist Servius (whose views are reported in Gellius, *Noctes Atticae* 4.3.2). Eventually the return of dowry became a right that the woman (or her family) could sue for (see Case 82).

CASE 39: Acquisitions by a Wife in *Manus*

Tituli ex Corpore Ulpiani 19.18–19

(18) Adquiritur autem nobis etiam per eas personas quas in potestate manu mancipiove habemus. itaque si quid mancipio puta acceperint aut traditum eis sit vel stipulati fuerint, ad nos pertinet. (19) Item si heredes instituti sint legatumve eis sit, et hereditatem iussu nostro adeuntes nobis adquirunt et legatum ad nos pertinet.

(*Excerpts from Ulpian's Writings*)

(18) We acquire (property) through those persons whom we have in our *potestas*, our *manus*, or our charge (*mancipium*). So if, for instance, something is mancipated or handed over to them or a formal promise is made to them, it comes to us. (19) Likewise, if they are named heirs or a legacy is made to them, they acquire an inheritance for us by entering it on our orders, and the legacy comes to us.

1. Acquisitions. Again in this Case, the similarity between the position of a wife in *manus* and that of children-in-power is emphasized. During her marriage, the wife in *manus* owns nothing of her own and therefore cannot bring any lawsuit based on her ownership (Gaius, *Inst.* 2.96). She cannot make a binding promise to anyone (ibid. 3.104, 114); and, as this Case indicates, anything that she acquires goes automatically to her husband, including, for instance, an inheritance or a legacy that she receives from a third party. Quite apart from the moral objections one will certainly have to this legal arrangement, what are its likely practical disadvantages?

2. Can Your Wife Be Stolen? A third party who abducted someone's son-in-power interfered with the rights of the *pater familias*. One line of legal thinking, probably old, allows the *pater familias* to avenge his loss by bringing a claim on the delict of theft against the abductor; how damages would be reckoned is impossible to say, but they would presumably be thought of as a multiple of the value of the son's "worth" to the *pater familias*—as measured, perhaps, by his work. In any case, not surprisingly, the *pater* was also allowed to sue if his wife in *manus* was "stolen" (Gaius, *Inst.* 3.199 = Case 108). In calculating damages, how would a judge measure her worth?

CASE 40: Can a Wife in *Manus* Divorce?

Gaius, *Institutiones* 1.137–137a

(137) <In manu autem esse mulieres desinunt iisdem modis, quibus filiae familias potestate patris liberantur: sicut igitur filiae familias una mancipatione de potestate patris exeunt, ita eae, quae in manu sunt, una mancipatione> desinunt in manu esse, et si ex ea mancipatione manumissae fuerint, sui iuris efficiuntur. (137a) <. . . [Q]uae cum viro suo coemptionem fecerit, . . . haec autem virum suum> nihilo magis potest cogere, quam et filia patrem. sed filia quidem nullo modo patrem potest cogere, etiam si adoptiva sit: haec autem <virum> repudio misso proinde compellere potest, atque si ei numquam nupta fuisset.

(Gaius in the first book of his *Institutes*)

(137) <Women cease being in *manus* in the same ways as daughters-in-power are freed from a father's *potestas*. Just as daughters-in-power depart from a father's *potestas* through one mancipation, so through one mancipation women in *manus*> cease being in *manus*, and if they are manumitted after this mancipation, they are made *sui iuris*. (137a) <. . . [A] woman who makes a *coemptio* with her husband . . .> can no more force <her husband> (to emancipate her) than a daughter can force her father. But there is no way that a daughter can force a father, even if she is adopted; while the woman can force her husband after giving notice of divorce, just as if she had never been married to him.

1. Emancipation and Divorce. Children are released from the *potestas* of their father through a formal process called emancipation (see Cases 155–158). As this Case indicates, a *pater familias* could use the same process of emancipation in order to free his wife from *manus* (see also Gaius, *Inst.* 1.118). Is this equivalent to divorcing her? The text of this Case has been heavily restored, and many of its details are of modest concern to us; but Gaius mainly refers to *manus* marriage by the ceremony of *coemptio*, which he regards as the only surviving form of *manus* marriage (see Case 19). The issue in section 137a is whether a wife can force her husband to release her by going through a counter-ceremony that undoes the effects of *coemptio*. Gaius first states that she cannot but then holds that she can if she first sends notice that she is divorcing him. Is this likely to have been the original rule? Note that in any case the former *pater familias* of the wife had no power to force a divorce after she entered into *manus*, since his *patria potestas* has already been broken through the marriage.

The remaining sections of this part deal with the "free" marriage of classical Roman law. The Cases in this section concern general issues of marital relations. The Roman jurists fairly rarely deal with such issues, for obvious reasons: Roman marriage was so easily formed and dissolved that, in general, many of the problems that arise in our society were rare. For example, one major problem in modern marriage centers on spousal abuse, particularly of wives, abuse that is often thought to be concealed by the "cover" of marriage. But since a Roman woman was able to leave a marriage more or less at will, this problem is never so much as mentioned by the jurists. No classical source indicates that a Roman husband had any legal right to discipline his wife physically or to require her to have sex with him.

In certain respects, therefore, the liberality of the Roman marriage regime may seem attractive—like the latest thing from California! Before accepting such a judgment, however, you should consider all the social ramifications, including above all the issue of whether Roman marriage is sufficiently stable as a social and legal institution. That is, does it provide too much encouragement to individualism? Should the state have intervened more strongly to keep marriages together? These are complex questions not only because they raise difficulties across the entire spectrum of legal rules that govern marriage but also because they seem to imply the possibility of regulatory and dispute-settling institutions (such as marriage courts) that the Romans, with their limited bureaucratic capacity, would have been hard-pressed to supply. Still, even admitting this latter aspect, the Roman tolerance for unregulated marriage seems quite extraordinary by the standards of premodern societies in general; and we are therefore obliged to ask, among other things, whether Roman law's liberalism may have been compensated for, in practice, by social pressures that promoted long-term marital stability.

We begin, in any case, with a small group of sources that suggest something of how the Romans looked upon marriage.

CASE 41: Free Marriage: The Principle of Noninterference

C. 5.4.14 (Impp. Diocletianus et Maximianus AA. et CC. Titio)

Neque ab initio matrimonium contrahere neque dissociatum reconciliare quisquam cogi potest. unde intellegis liberam facultatem contrahendi atque distrahendi matrimonii transferri ad necessitatem non oportere.

(Emperors Diocletian and Maximian to Titius; A.D. 284–305)

No one can initially be forced to contract a marriage nor to restore one that has broken apart. Therefore, you understand that the free power of contracting and breaking up a marriage must not be subjected to coercion.

1. Noninterference. The emperors here state one of the bedrock principles of Roman marriage law. What sort of inquiry might have triggered this statement? For example, what might Titius have been seeking permission to do? Some sixty years earlier, the Emperor Alexander had applied the same principle in order to invalidate a penalty agreement that would have prevented divorce (Case 75). To be sure, there is need to be cautious in interpreting the word "forced" in this Case, since sometimes the consent of the parties may approach the illusory, as we have seen. But the general principle remains a powerful one: as a rule, the state will encourage couples to marry, but it will not force them either to marry or to remain married, nor will it permit the parties to use private arrangements for this purpose. A postclassical Greek commentary on Roman law notes: "For it is preposterous that marriage, which needs unending harmony, exist because of a penalty and not from the intent (of the parties)" (*Scholia Sinaitica* 6). Why did Roman law take this extremely inhibited position, granted the widely conceded significance of marriage as a social institution? Is it in fact so clear that other views are "preposterous"?

2. Forcing Marriage? Titia married Gaius Seius. By prior marriages, she had a son and he had a daughter. After marrying, Titia and Gaius Seius agreed that the son would marry the daughter; and they arranged a penalty payable if either of them obstructed the marriage. Gaius Seius then died while still married to Titia, and his daughter refused to marry Titia's son. Can Titia claim the penalty from the heirs of Gaius Seius? The jurist Paul's response (D. 45.1.134 pr.) is that the stipulated penalty is "not in accord with sound morals (*non secundum bonos mores*) . . . , since it seems improper that a marriage, whether in the future or already contracted, be constrained by the bond of a penalty." Probably the children were both minors when their parents arranged the marriage for them. Is it important to this decision that his daughter refused to go through with the ceremony only after Gaius Seius died? Do you think there is any likelihood that the penalty would have been valid if Gaius Seius were still alive? Do you think such an agreement should be enforceable?

CASE 42: Sharing Status

D. 1.9.8 (Ulpianus libro sexto Fideicommissorum)

Feminae nuptae clarissimis personis clarissimarum personarum appellatione continentur. clarissimarum feminarum nomine senatorum filiae, nisi quae viros clarissimos sortitae sunt, non habentur: feminis enim dignitatem clarissimam mariti tribuunt, parentes vero, donec plebeii nuptiis fuerint copulatae: tamdiu igitur clarissima femina erit, quamdiu senatori nupta est vel clarissimo aut separata ab eo alii inferioris dignitatis non nupsit.

(Ulpian in the sixth book *On Trusts*)

Women married to *clarissimi* (most eminent persons) are included in the designation *clarissimi*. But the daughters of senators are not included in the term *clarissimi* unless they have received *clarissimi* as their husbands, for husbands confer this status on their wives, but parents (confer status on their children) previous to the time when they are joined in marriage to a person of lower status. So a woman will be *clarissima* for as long as she is married to a senator or another *clarissimus*, or, after separating from him, (for as long as) she has not married another man of lesser status.

1. Eminence. The *clarissimi,* Roman senators and their immediate families, are the Empire's elite. As time passed, formal distinctions of status became more and more important at Rome, above all because they brought privileged treatment in some areas of law. Struggles over status were almost inevitable. Here are some examples:

   - "Women previously married to a man of consular rank (i.e., an ex-consul or someone awarded this rank as an honor) commonly petition the emperor, although seldom (with success?), that they retain consular rank when they remarry a man of lesser status" (Ulpian, D. 1.9.12 pr.).
   - "The wives of men of consular rank we call consular. The jurist Saturninus adds their mothers, an unprecedented notion that has not been accepted" (Ulpian, D. 1.9.1.1).
   - "When a senator's daughter pursues marriage with a freedman (in contravention of Roman law, see Case 10), her father's fall (from senatorial rank) does not make her a wife, since the rank attained for children should not be removed because their father fell by being removed from the Senate" (Papinian, D. 1.9.9).
   - "You say you were not born from a senatorial father but attained the name of a *clarissima* by marrying a senator. Senatorial status (*claritas*), which was granted to you to benefit your husband, is forfeited if by marrying a man of

lesser rank you have returned to the level of your former status" (Diocletian and Maximian, C. 5.4.10; A.D. 284–305).

2. No Name Change. Roman women did not usually change their surnames as a consequence of marriage. What might explain this?

CASE 43: Showing Reverence

D. 24.3.14.1 (Ulpianus libro trigensimo sexto ad Sabinum)

Eleganter quaerit Pomponius libro quinto decimo ex Sabino, si paciscatur maritus, ne in id quod facere possit condemnetur, sed in solidum, an hoc pactum servandum sit? et negat servari oportere, quod quidem et mihi videtur verum: namque contra bonos mores id pactum esse melius est dicere, quippe cum contra receptam reverentiam, quae maritis exhibenda est, id esse apparet.

(Ulpian in the thirty-sixth book on Sabinus)

In the fifteenth book from Sabinus, Pomponius poses an ingenious question: should the agreement be upheld if a husband agrees (with his wife) that he be condemned (in an action for recovery of dowry) not for what he can provide but for the entire amount? And he denies it ought to be upheld, a view that seems correct to me as well; for the better holding is to say that this agreement is contrary to sound morals (*contra bonos mores*), since it appears to be clearly at odds with the traditional reverence (*reverentia*) that must be shown to husbands.

1. The Problem. If a wife sues her husband to recover her dowry (see Part D.2 below), a long-standing tradition limited the judgment to "what he can provide," that is, the extent of his resources; see the Discussion on Case 81. This rule obviously places limits on his liability if repayment of the dowry is financially oppressive. In this Case, the couple sought to evade the rule. Try to explain the rationale that Ulpian uses in rejecting their agreement. Why was the agreement "contrary to sound morals"? It should be noted that at least a portion of the Case (beginning with "since it appears") has usually been regarded as a later addition, not part of Ulpian's original opinion. Does this clause look like a clumsy attempt to explain why the agreement is against sound morals, by someone who doesn't really understand why? Would eliminating the clause substantially change the holding?

2. Reverence. *Reverentia* is a sense of restraint or deference that one exhibits in the presence of one's superiors. This Case, if its last clause was actually written by Ulpian, suggests that the wife owes reverence to her husband. By contrast, Paul (D. 25.2.3.2) uses the same word in explaining why a husband cannot bring an action of theft against his wife for a theft she committed against him before the couple were married: *propter reverentiam personarum*, "because of the reverence toward them." Should "reverence" then be understood as a reciprocal obligation between spouses? Many literary sources suggest that this is correct, but jurists tend to avoid the word, perhaps because of its religious overtones. Is *affectio maritalis* (Case 17) a secular equivalent of *reverentia*? In a portion of a will quoted by the jurist Scaevola (D. 32.41 pr.), the testator speaks of "the love and familial respect" (*affectio et pietas*) that he owes to his wife.

CASE 44: An Affront to a Spouse

Gaius, *Institutiones* 3.221

Pati autem iniuriam videmur non solum per nosmet ipsos, sed etiam per liberos nostros quos in potestate habemus; item per uxores nostras, quamvis in manu nostra <non> sint. itaque si filiae meae quae Titio nupta est iniuriam feceris, non solum filiae nomine tecum agi iniuriarum potest, verum etiam meo quoque et Titii nomine.

D. 47.10.2 (Paulus libro quinquagensimo <quinto> ad edictum)

Quod si viro iniuria facta sit, uxor non agit, quia defendi uxores a viris, non viros ab uxoribus aequum est.

(Gaius in the third book of his *Institutes*)

But we seem to suffer an affront (*iniuria*) not only when it is inflicted on us but also through our children whom we have in our power and also through our wives even if they are not in our *manus*. And so, if you inflict an affront on my daughter who is married to Titius, you can be sued for affront not only in the daughter's name but also in my name and that of Titius.

(Paul in the fifty-fifth book on the Edict)

But if an affront is given to a man, his wife does not sue (on it), since it is fair that wives be protected by husbands, not husbands by wives.

1. Vicarious Insult. Compare Case 27, on betrothal. The Gaius fragment summarizes the chief free persons through whom one can be affronted. The affront (*iniuria*), though actually delivered to the intended victim, is held to be indirectly aimed at her father and/or husband as well. What is the logic? If it makes sense to hold that a *pater familias*, as the head of the *familia*, can avenge affronts directed to children in his power and to a wife in *manus*, should such a claim also be extended to a husband whose wife is not in *manus*? Is the nature of the marriage bond here overcoming the traditional agnatic limits on the *familia*? (The emendation in this text seems certain.)

2. Why the Double Standard? Paul argues that it is "fair" (*aequum*) for husbands to protect their wives, but not the reverse. What presumptions underlie his argument? Can you think of a better explanation for the Roman rule?

CASE 45: No Infamy

D. 25.2.1 (Paulus libro septimo ad Sabinum)

Rerum amotarum iudicium singulare introductum est adversus eam quae uxor fuit, quia non placuit cum ea furti agere posse: quibusdam existimantibus ne quidem furtum eam facere, ut Nerva Cassio, quia societas vitae quodammodo dominam eam faceret: aliis, ut Sabino et Proculo, furtum quidem eam facere, sicuti filia patri faciat, sed furti non esse actionem constituto iure, in qua sententia et Iulianus rectissime est:

D. 25.2.2 (Gaius libro <decimo> ad edictum praetoris titulo de re iudicata)

nam in honorem matrimonii turpis actio adversus uxorem negatur.

(Paul in the seventh book on Sabinus)

The special lawsuit concerning removal of property (*rerum amotarum iudicium*) was introduced against an ex-wife, since it was unacceptable to be able to sue her for theft. Some jurists, like Nerva and Cassius, think that she does not commit theft at all, since a partnership for life (in marriage) makes her in a sense an owner (of her husband's property). Others, like Sabinus and Proculus, (think) that she does commit theft, like a daughter does to her father, but that by established law there is no action on theft. Julian is quite rightly of this (second) view,

(Gaius in the tenth book on the praetor's Edict, the title on Judicial Decisions)

for a degrading lawsuit against a wife is dismissed in order to respect the marriage.

1. Can a Wife Steal from her Husband? The problem here might most commonly have arisen when a couple divorced and the departing wife took with her property that the husband believed to be his own. A defendant who was found liable in a private action for the delict of theft (*furtum*) was compelled to pay a penalty that was a multiple of the value of the object stolen; but a convicted defendant was also labeled with *infamia,* a public label of shame with some adverse consequences in private law. For ex-wives, however, Roman law used the much milder action described here. The issue that divides the jurists is how to explain the exception: is it that she cannot steal during and after the marriage, or that she can steal but the infaming action of theft is inappropriate in her case? Which view seems likelier? Ulpian (D. 25.2.19) holds there is no action on theft even if she hired professional thieves to help her remove the property.

2. Infaming Lawsuits. In classical law, no broad rule prevented spouses from bringing infaming lawsuits against one another, but such suits were increasingly discouraged. See, for example, Marcian, D. 11.3.17 (a reduction in the penalty for corrupting a spouse's slave); Septimius Severus and Caracalla, C.

5.12.1.2 (A.D. 201; no action on deceit, *dolus*). The Emperors Diocletian and Maximian (C. 5.21.2; A.D. 290 or 293) generalized the rule. What considerations are likely to have motivated this trend?

Inevitably, issues relating to sex and procreation play a large role in the law of marriage. Roman law originally left this matter largely in the control of the household itself. But this situation changed with the moral legislation of the Emperor Augustus, one main focus of which was to encourage both marriage and procreation, particularly among the upper classes, who, there is reason to believe, may well have been attracted by nontraditional, more individualistic life styles. In 18 B.C. Augustus passed two laws that fundamentally altered many aspects of marriage law. The *lex Iulia de maritandis ordinibus* established an elaborate series of civil penalties and benefits that were intended to foster marriage and procreation especially among the well-to-do (see Cases 10, 12). In that same year or the next, the *lex Iulia de adulteriis coercendis* established a new sexual regime by criminalizing various forms of sexual misconduct, but above all marital infidelity.

This section examines the centrality of childbirth within marriage as it relates to the origin of *patria potestas,* the father's power over children, a topic examined at greater length in Chapter III. These two topics were doubtless linked in the Roman mind, although the connection is not always salient; for example, Papinian (D. 48.5.6.1), in a piece of folk etymology, derives the word *adulterium* from "offspring engendered by another" (*partum ex altero conceptum*), pointing to the adulterer as a genetic interloper. The whole point of Augustus's law, it seems, was to strengthen the social perception of adultery as a misdeed that warranted criminal penalty and thereby to strengthen the concept of marriage as an exclusive sexual union. Modern scholars are strongly divided, however, on whether this law was successful in achieving its aims.

In most legal systems of the modern Western world, adultery is no longer treated as a crime. It is well worth thinking about why this is so, and whether those reasons should affect our evaluation of the Roman legislation.

CASE 46: An Unknown Son

D. 40.4.29 (Scaevola libro vicensimo tertio Digestorum)

Uxorem praegnatem repudiaverat et aliam duxerat: prior enixa filium exposuit: hic sublatus ab alio educatus est <nec> nomine patris vocitatus: usque ad vitae tempus patris tam ab eo quam a matre, an vivorum numero esset, ignorabatur: mortuo patre testamentoque eius, quo filius neque exheredatus neque heres institutus sit, recitato filius et a matre et ab avia paterna adgnitus hereditatem patris ab intestato quasi legitimus possidet. quaesitum est, hi qui testamento libertatem acceperunt utrum liberi an servi sint. respondit filium quidem nihil praeiudicii passum fuisse, si pater eum ignoravit, et ideo, cum in potestate et ignorantis patris esset, testamentum non valere. servi autem manumissi si per quinquennium in libertate morati sunt, semel datam libertatem infirmari contrarium studi<o> [favore] libertatis est.

(Scaevola in the twenty-third book of his *Digests*)

A man divorced his pregnant wife and married another woman. The first wife bore a son and exposed (i.e., physically abandoned) him. The boy was taken up and raised by a third party, and he was not called by his (true) father's name. Up to his father's death, his father and mother were both unaware whether the boy was alive. After the father died, his will was read, in which the son was neither disinherited nor named an heir. But the son was then acknowledged by both his mother and his paternal grandmother, and he took possession of his father's inheritance as the legitimate heir upon intestacy. A question arose as to whether those (slaves) who received freedom under the will are (now) free or slaves.

He answered that the son clearly suffered no prejudicial disadvantage if his father was unaware of him, and so, since he was in the power even of an unknowing father, the will is invalid. But if the manumitted slaves had spent five years in freedom, it is contrary to the interest in freedom that this be annulled after it was once given.

1. The Power of Paternity. The legal question Scaevola faces is simple: if slaves are manumitted under the terms of a will that later turns out to be invalid, is the manumission revoked? (The answer is a qualified yes.) Much more remarkable are the circumstances that led to this will being invalid. Here, the father failed to provide in his will for a son of whose very existence he was uncertain and perhaps even unaware, but who was nonetheless in his power (exactly what does this "power" amount to here?); this omission leads to the invalidity of the entire will. Why does Scaevola recount the family drama in such detail? What does he mean by saying that the son "clearly suffered no prejudicial disadvantage"? Does Scaevola think that the father was somehow negligent in not either instituting the son as heir or disinheriting him? (See Cases 178–179.) In any event, this Case nicely sets a background to those that follow, by indicating why the Romans were often concerned about a possible pregnancy when a marriage ended.

CASE 47: Notice of Pregnancy

D. 25.3.1.3–4, 16 (Ulpianus libro trigesimo quarto ad edictum)

(3) Denuntiare autem hoc tantum esse mulierem ex eo praegnantem. non ergo hoc denuntiat, ut mittat custodes maritus: sufficit enim mulieri hoc notum facere, quod sit praegnas. mariti est iam aut mittere custodes aut ei denuntiare, quod non sit ex se praegnas: hoc autem vel ipsi marito vel alii nomine eius facere permittitur. (4) Poena autem mariti ea est, ut, nisi aut custodes praemiserit aut contra denuntiaverit non esse ex se praegnatem, cogatur maritus partum agnoscere: et, si non agnoverit, extra ordinem coercetur. debebit igitur respondere non esse ex se praegnatam aut nomine eius responderi: quod si factum fuerit, non alias necesse habebit agnoscere, nisi vere filius fuerit. . . . (16) Plane si denuntiante muliere negaverit ex se esse praegnatem, tametsi custodes non miserit, non evitabit, quominus quaeratur, an ex eo mulier praegnas sit. . . .

(Ulpian in the thirty-fourth book on the Edict)

(3) The wife needs to do no more than give notice (to her husband) that she is pregnant by him. So she does not give notice to her husband to send guards; for it is enough for the woman to make it known she is pregnant. The husband's role is then either to send guards or to give notice to her that she is not pregnant by him; but either the husband himself or someone acting in his name is allowed to do this. (4) The penalty for the husband is this: unless he sends guards or replies giving her notice she is not pregnant by him, the husband is compelled to acknowledge the offspring; if he does not acknowledge it, he is forced by extraordinary judicial measures. So he will have to answer that she is not pregnant by him, or response must be made in his name. If this is done, he will not otherwise have to acknowledge it unless it really is his son. . . . (16) Obviously, if the woman gives notice to him and he denies she is pregnant by him, then, even if he does not send guards, he will not avoid an inquiry as to whether the woman is pregnant by him. . . .

1. Guarding the Pregnant Woman. Under the Senatusconsultum (SC) Plancianum (a senatorial decree probably of the early second century A.D.), a divorced woman was allowed to notify her husband within thirty days of the divorce that she was pregnant by him (Ulpian, D. 25.3.1 pr.–1). The ex-husband then has the range of choices spelled out in this Case. His failure to answer concedes paternity of the subsequently born child, and so he may be held liable for the child's support. However, if he answers by denying that the child is his, a later inquiry may still establish his paternity. To our eyes, the strangest of the responses is sending guards; what is their purpose? Probably, they were meant to prevent a changeling child from being passed off as the ex-husband's child; see, e.g., Paul, D. 48.10.19.1: "An accusation that a child was substituted is not defeated by the passage of time; nor does it matter

whether or not the woman alleged to have made the substitution has died." If a woman gives notice of her pregnancy and then refuses to accept judicially appointed guards, the ex-husband is free not to acknowledge the offspring as his own (Ulpian, D. 25.3.1.6).

2. The Ex-Husband's Failure to Act. If the ex-husband does nothing, he is liable to support the child; but does that make him automatically the father as well? Not necessarily. Ulpian, in D. 25.3.1.12 (a troubled text), wrestles with a case in which a man neither sends guards nor denies paternity and is thus forced by the decree to acknowledge the child; still, he can argue that someone else was actually the father, although his "admission creates great prejudice in favor of the son." Does this outcome seem about right?

3. Failure to Give Notice. The jurists hold that the rights of the child are not jeopardized if the woman fails to notify her ex-husband of her pregnancy (so Julian, cited by Ulpian, D. 25.3.1.8, see 15). But why shouldn't they be, at least to some extent, since the husband loses the opportunity to deny paternity at an early stage or to guard against a changeling? Should the outcome depend on whether it was difficult to give the required notice?

4. The Husband Dies. Somewhat similar rules govern the case where a marriage ends through the death of a man who leaves a pregnant wife. Here a posthumous child may render the father's will invalid, or at least the estate settlement may be complicated (see Cases 182–185). In such a situation, the Romans use a device called *bonorum possessio ventris nomine,* whereby the praetor allows the dead father's estate to be possessed by a guardian "in the name of the womb" (i.e., on behalf of the fetus). This arrangement is provisional until the child is born and its legitimacy established. See D. 25.5; 37.9. The praetor's Edict, which probably antedates the SC Plancianum, also set out elaborate rules to safeguard the child's delivery. It suffices to quote a few of them (from Ulpian, D. 25.4.1.10): "Let the chamber in which the woman will give birth have no more than one entrance; if there will be more, let them be boarded up on either side. Before this room's door, let three free men and women keep guard with two companions. Whenever the woman goes into this room or elsewhere or into a bath, let the guards, if they wish, examine it beforehand and search those who enter. . . . Let there be at least three lamps" (since, notes Ulpian, darkness helps a substitution). What danger is feared?

5. Judicial Determination of Paternity. A paternity case comes to court, and a *iudex* decides that a man is the father of a child; but subsequently discovered evidence establishes that this verdict is erroneous. Can the matter be reopened? No; see Ulpian and Julian, D. 25.3.1.16–3.1. Why is this so? Does the outcome seem to you harsh or unfair?

6. The Social Adequacy of Law. These rules are all very complex, but they invite some thought about the underlying social issues. Are the interests of all the parties sufficiently protected? What are the costs of being so specific about competing rights? Are elaborate rules such as these inevitable in a time when paternity is important to personal standing but cannot be decisively established through scientific means?

CASE 48: Protecting the Unborn Child

D. 25.4.1 pr. (Ulpianus libro <tricesimo> quarto ad edictum)

Temporibus Divorum Fratrum cum hoc incidisset, ut maritus quidem praegnatem mulierem diceret, uxor negaret, consulti Valerio Prisciano praetori urbano rescripserunt in haec verba: "Novam rem desiderare Rutilius Severus videtur, ut uxori, quae ab eo diverterat et se non esse praegnatem profiteatur, custodem apponat, et ideo nemo mirabitur, si nos quoque novum consilium et remedium suggeramus. igitur si perstat in eadem postulatione, commodissimum est eligi honestissimae feminae domum, in qua<m> Domitia veniat, et ibi tres obstetrices probatae et artis et fidei, quae a te adsumptae fuerint, eam inspiciant. et si quidem vel omnes vel duae renuntiaverint praegnatem videri, tunc persuadendum mulieri erit, ut perinde custodem admittat atque si ipsa hoc desiderasset: quod si enixa non fuerit, sciat maritus ad invidiam existimationemque suam pertinere, ut non immerito possit videri captasse hoc ad aliquam mulieris iniuriam. si autem vel omnes vel plures non esse gravidam renuntiaverint, nulla causa custodiendi erit."

(Ulpian in the thirty-fourth book on the Edict)

During the reign of the deified brothers (Marcus Aurelius and Lucius Verus, A.D. 161–169), it happened that a husband asserted his wife was pregnant, but she denied it. When consulted, they (the coemperors) sent a rescript to Valerius Priscianus, the urban praetor, as follows:

"Rutilius Severus patently seeks a novel remedy, that he (be permitted to) appoint a guard for his wife, who had divorced him and insists she is not pregnant. Thus, no one will be surprised if we furnish a new plan and remedy. So if he persists in this demand, the easiest solution is to choose the home of a most respectable woman, into which Domitia may come and there be inspected by three midwives of proven skill and trustworthiness, to be chosen by you. If all or two of them report that she seems pregnant, then the woman must be persuaded to allow a guard just as if she had wanted this herself; but if she does not give birth, the husband should know that this involves ill will and his own reputation, since he cannot implausibly be held to have seized on this to cause some affront to his wife. But if all or most (of the midwives) report she is not pregnant, there will be no further need for guards."

1. Denying Pregnancy. This situation is the opposite of that in Case 47. Under what appears to be an older procedure, the woman was summoned to appear in the praetor's court and then forced to answer, under threat of fine or property forfeiture, whether she was pregnant (Ulpian, D. 25.4.1.2–4). What circumstances might have led Marcus Aurelius and Lucius Verus to devise a new procedure? Do procedures such as these seem unduly obtrusive?

CASE 49: Custody of Children

D. 43.30.3.5 (Ulpianus libro septuagensimo primo ad edictum)

Etiamsi maxime autem probet filium pater in sua potestate esse, tamen causa cognita mater in retinendo eo potior erit, idque decretis divi Pii quibusdam continetur: optinuit enim mater ob nequitiam patris, ut sine deminutione patriae potestatis apud eam filius moretur.

(Ulpian in the seventy-first book on the Edict)

Even if a father fully proves that a son is in his power, still, after an inquiry, the mother will (at times) prevail in keeping him, as is held by some judicial decisions of the deified Emperor Antoninus Pius (reign: A.D. 138–161). For because of the father's depravity the mother obtained custody of the son in her home, (though) without decrease in *patria potestas*.

1. Presumption of Custody. One of the most important points that emerge from this Case and other legal texts is that the usual modern legal presumption on custody (favorable to the mother) is exactly reversed in Roman law. The Roman presumption is stated, for example, by Ulpian (D. 25.4.1.1), with regard to a child born to a divorced wife: "Clearly, after the child is born, the husband can rightfully claim the boy through an interdict, either that it be produced or he be allowed to lead it away." (Compare Chapter III.A.3, where the issue of custody is considered in more detail.) Even in later classical law, this presumption is overcome only if the husband is shown to be of unusually bad character: depraved, as in this Case. Finally, in the early postclassical period, the Emperor Diocletian reached a more balanced position (C. 5.24.1; A.D. 294): "Although no constitution of ours or of our deified ancestors provides that the division of children among parents be carried out on the basis of sex, still a competent judge will assess whether after a divorce children should stay with and be raised by the father or the mother." In this Case, Ulpian stresses the continuance of *patria potestas*; is that realistic, do you think?

2. Child Support. When the child remains with the mother, she can sue the father for what she is required to spend in raising the child. Ulpian, in D. 25.3.5.14, quotes a rescript of Marcus Aurelius: "But the judges will assess how much her father must provide you for the provisions you necessarily furnished to your daughter; nor should you receive what you would have spent on your daughter on the basis of your maternal love, even if she had been raised by her father." How much guidance does this rescript provide to the judges?

CASE 50: Adultery and Marriage

D. 48.5.2.8 (Ulpianus libro octavo Disputationum)

Si simul ad accusationem veniant maritus et pater mulieris, quem praeferri oportet, quaeritur. et magis est, ut maritus praeferatur: nam et propensiore ira et maiore dolore executurum eum accusationem credendum est, in tantum, ut et si pater praevenerit et libellos inscriptionum deposuerit, marito non negligente nec retardante, sec accusationem parante et probationibus inst<r>uente et muniente, ut facilius iudicantibus de adulterio probetur, idem erit dicendum.

(Ulpian in the eighth book of his *Disputations*)

If a woman's husband and father simultaneously accuse her (of adultery), it is asked who should be preferred (as the accuser). The better view is that the husband is preferred, since it must be assumed that he will carry out the accusation with both sharper rage and greater anger. So much so is this true that the same should be held even if the father is the first to lodge the claims of indictment, (at any rate) if the husband was not careless or slow but was instead readying an accusation and preparing and strengthening it with proofs so that the adultery might be more easily proved to the judges.

1. How Should the Husband React? As this Case indicates, the Romans took a sour view of adultery by married women. The husband is usually presumed to react with rage (*ira* or *calor*) and anger (*dolor*), particularly when he has discovered his wife *in flagrante delicto*. Papinian (*Coll.* 4.11.1) relates this reaction to outrage over the invasion of his house (*iniuria laesae domus*); still, fears about the compromised paternity of offspring are probably not irrelevant.

2. The Augustan Law on Adultery. The following Cases largely derive from the elaborate juristic commentaries on the *lex Iulia* on adultery, a statute passed on the initiative of the Emperor Augustus in 18 B.C. This statute has wide implications for Roman criminal law, and so the materials below necessarily offer only a general introduction to its intricacies. What is clear, in any event, is that the statute greatly sharpened the penalties while also providing, at least in a general way, a new legal structure for evaluating sexual misconduct, particularly by women.

3. Evaluation. In reading the Cases below, try to evaluate the desirability of a law such as this one. Will it be effective in curbing adultery? What is the public interest in doing so, and how urgent is that interest? What are the negative consequences? Modern scholarly assessments of the Augustan legislation have varied widely, from enthusiasm ("an outstanding piece of legislation": Hugh Last) to resigned pessimism ("a brake, though a feeble one, upon one sort of ethical decline": John Buchan); but more typical of recent reactions is

this: "By introducing such a structure of charge and countercharge, Augustus can hardly be thought to have raised the tone of conjugal life. He had merely made wife, husband, and their slaves and friends more insecure" (Susan Treggiari, *Roman Marriage*). Decide for yourself.

CASE 51: Killing the Adulterer . . .

D. 48.5.25 pr.–1 (Macer libro primo Publicorum <Iudiciorum>)

(pr.) Marito quoque adulterum uxoris suae occidere permittitur, sed non quemlibet, ut patri: nam hac lege cavetur, ut liceat viro deprehensum domi suae (non etiam soceri) in adulterio uxoris occidere eum, qui leno fuerit quive artem ludicram ante fecerit in<ve> scaenam saltandi cantandive causa prodierit iudiciove publico damnatus neque in integrum restitutus erit, quive libertus eius mariti uxorisve, patris matris, filii filiae utrius eorum fuerit (nec interest, proprius cuius eorum an cum alio communis fuerit) quive servus erit. (1) Et praecipitur, ut is maritus, qui horum quem occiderit, uxorem sine mora dimittat.

(Macer in the first book of his *On Public Trials*)

(pr.) A husband is also allowed to kill his wife's adulterer, but, unlike with her father, not just any (adulterer). For the statute (the *lex Iulia* on adultery) provides that the husband is permitted to kill a man taken in his home—but not in his father-in-law's home—while in the act of adultery with his wife, provided that this man is a pimp or was previously an actor or went on the stage to dance or sing or was condemned in a public (criminal) trial and has not been restored to his former state or is the freedman of the husband or wife or of one of their parents or children—nor does it matter whether the slave was entirely theirs or held in common with another—or is a slave. (1) And it orders a husband who kills any of these persons to divorce his wife promptly.

1. Legal Murder? It had long been customary at Rome for the husband to take some form of vengeance on an adulterer, but the *lex Iulia* made this a matter of law. As this Case shows, the right is severely restricted: the adulterer must be caught in the act, and in the husband's home; further, the adulterer must fall into one of the unprotected classes. Why were these limitations imposed? Does the right to kill granted by the *lex Iulia* presuppose that the husband was actually provoked by outrage into a retaliatory killing? What if he was not angry but just wanted to kill the adulterer? Paul (*Coll.* 4.12.5) reports two additional requirements of the law: "After killing the adulterer, he should immediately divorce his wife and within three days notify (the authorities) where and with which adulterer he found his wife"; and failure to do this made the killing criminal (Paul, *Coll.* 4.3.5). What was the purpose of these two requirements?

2. Outside the Rules. If the killing violated the rules, it was homicide; the Emperor Alexander (reign: A.D. 222–235; C. 9.9.4.1), however, adds with regard to a particular case: "If, exceeding the law's authorization, he killed the adulterer out of unthinking anger, although he committed homicide, still because both the night and his legitimate anger mitigated his act, he can be sent into

exile" instead of suffering capital punishment. For similar leniency from Marcus Aurelius, see Paul, *Coll.* 4.3.6. In situations where the husband was not allowed or did not wish to kill the adulterer, the *lex Iulia* permitted him to forcibly detain the adulterer for up to twenty hours in order to coerce a confession (Ulpian, D. 48.5.26 pr.).

CASE 52: . . . But Not His Own Wife

D. 48.5.39.8 (Papinianus libro trigensimo sexto Quaestionum)

Imperator Marcus Antoninus et Commodus filius rescripserunt: "Si maritus uxorem in adulterio deprehensam impetu tractus doloris interfecerit, non utique legis Corneliae de sicariis poenam excipiet." nam et divus Pius in haec verba rescripsit Apollonio: "Ei, qui uxorem suam in adulterio deprehensam occidisse se non negat, ultimum supplicium remitti potest, cum sit difficillimum iustum dolorem temperare et quia plus fecerit, quam quia vindicare se non debuerit, puniendus sit. sufficiet igitur, si humilis loci sit, in opus perpetuum eum tradi, si qui honestior, in insulam relegari."

(Papinian in the thirty-sixth book of his *Questions of Law*)

The Emperor Marcus Aurelius and his son Commodus (coreign: A.D. 175–180) sent this rescript: "If a husband, borne on a flood of anger, kills his wife whom he catches in adultery, he will at least not receive the penalty of the *lex Cornelia* on murderers."

For the deified Emperor Antoninus Pius (reign: A.D. 138–161) sent a rescript to Apollonius, as follows: "When a man does not deny that he killed his wife whom he caught in adultery, capital punishment can be remitted, since it is very hard to restrain legitimate anger, and his punishment should result from his doing more (than he should have) rather than from his having no duty to take revenge. So it will suffice, if he is of modest rank, that he be handed over to a life of hard labor; and if of more respectable rank, that he be relegated to an island."

1. Killing Your Wife Is Wrong. Although the *lex Iulia* may not have specifically stated this, it granted no right to kill a wife. Thus, Papinian (*Coll.* 4.10.1) remarks: "In no section of the statute is a husband allowed to kill his wife; so it is clearly and unambiguously against the law for him to have done this." Still, as in this Case, our sources tend to regard the crime as less serious than ordinary murder, although the penalties are still substantial; Papinian suggests a maximum punishment of exile, which does not entail loss of citizenship. Was it simply presumed that the husband had killed his wife out of anger? (Suppose, for instance, it can be shown that he was not angry.) It should be noted that, with respect both to the adulterer and to the wife, the husband's self-help rights are considerably narrower than those of a father with a daughter (Cases 95–96). What might explain this difference, granted that husbands were supposed to react with greater anger than fathers (Case 50)? For instance, Ulpian (D. 48.5.30 pr.) remarks of a man who caught his wife in adultery that he "ought to vent his rage on his wife, who has dishonored his marriage." Of course, he could also "vent his rage" by prosecuting her for adultery.

2. Extending the Statute to Nonwives. The provisions of the *lex Iulia* concerning a husband's rights when his wife commits adultery came to be applied widely: to betrothed women (Case 7) and wives not in valid Roman marriages (e.g., Ulpian, D. 48.5.14.1), although not to concubines (ibid. pr., 6). In extended applications, the affected male partner can prosecute the adulteress but not kill her (see Paul, *Coll.* 4.6.1, citing a rescript, on betrothed women).

CASE 53: Pandering

D. 48.5.2.2–4 (Ulpianus libro octavo Disputationum)

(2) Lenocinii quidem crimen lege Iulia de adulteris praescriptum est, cum sit in eum maritum poena statuta, qui de adulterio uxoris suae quid ceperit, item in eum, qui in adulterio deprehensam retinuerit. (3) Ceterum qui patitur uxorem suam delinquere matrimoniumque suum contemnit quique contaminationi non indignatur, poena adulter<i in e>um non infligitur. (4) Qui hoc dicit lenocinio mariti se fecisse, relevare quidem vult crimen suum, sed non est huiusmodi compensatio admissa. ideo si maritum velit reus adulterii lenocinii reum facere, semel delatus non audietur.

(Ulpian in the eighth book of his *Disputations*)

(2) The crime of pandering (*lenocinium*) is set out in the *lex Iulia* on adulterers, where a penalty is established against a husband who receives anything from his wife's adultery or who retains her after she is caught in adultery. (3) But if a man allows his wife to misbehave and (thus) despises his own marriage and is not outraged at the contamination, the penalty for adultery is not inflicted on him. (4) A man who says he acted (as an adulterer) because of the husband's pandering wants to lighten his own offense, but an offset of this sort is not permitted. So if an adultery defendant wishes to accuse the husband of pandering, he will not be listened to after he is accused.

> 1. What Is Pandering? The derivation of the word *lenocinium* indicates that it means acting like a pimp (*leno*) who prostitutes women for money; and this is certainly one major form of the offense, which also is committed by an initially unknowing husband who receives "hush money" from an adulterer (Ulpian, D. 48.5.30.4). But pandering took on a much broader meaning in this statute. For instance, Ulpian (D. 48.5.30 pr.) uses the term for a husband who caught his wife in adultery and chose to keep her while letting the adulterer go. Ulpian adds: "The husband should be punished when he cannot excuse his ignorance (of his wife's adultery) nor hide his indulgence by claiming disbelief." So, is a husband, if he merely suspects that his wife may be having an affair, obliged to act on his suspicions and investigate further? Ulpian gives a sort of answer (ibid. 4): "But if he allows his wife to misbehave, not for profit, but because of his carelessness or fault or some indulgence or excessive trust, it seems that he does not fall within the statute." Similarly, the Emperors Severus and Caracalla (C. 9.9.2; A.D. 199) explain: "The crime of *lenocinium* is committed by those who have retained in marriage a wife caught in adultery, not those who had a suspected adulteress." Can the husband therefore just turn a blind eye unless he has actually walked in on his wife *in flagrante delicto*? Suppose, for instance, he receives an anonymous letter alleging her

adultery, or he discovers incriminating physical evidence. What might have made the jurists hesitant to require extreme diligence from the husband?

2. Pandering Equals Adultery. A number of sources say this, but the clearest is Tryphoninus, D. 4.4.37.1, quoted below in the discussion of Case 54. Does this mean that the pandering husband *is* an adulterer or just that the punishment is the same?

CASE 54: The Necessity of Divorce

D. 48.5.27 pr.–1 (Ulpianus libro tertio Disputationum)

(pr.) Constante matrimonio ab iis, qui extra maritum ad accusationem admittuntur, accusari mulier adulterii non potest: probatam enim a marito uxorem et quiescens matrimonium non debet alius turbare atque inquietare, nisi prius lenocinii maritum accusaverit. (1) Derelictam vero a marito accusationem etiam ab alio excitari utile est.

(Ulpian in the third book of his *Disputations*)

(pr.) So long as her marriage endures, a woman cannot be accused of adultery by those persons who, apart from her husband, are allowed to bring an accusation (once the marriage ends). For a third party, unless he first accuses the husband of pandering, should not disturb a wife of whom her husband approves and trouble a tranquil marriage. (1) But it is (publicly) useful that an accusation abandoned by the husband be revived by a third party.

1. No Prosecution While Married. In this Case, the rule is clear: a wife cannot be prosecuted for adultery unless her husband first divorces her, and he is not compelled to do this; however, by failing to divorce her, he may run the risk of being accused of pandering by some third party. This helps to explain why he must divorce his wife immediately after killing an adulterer (Case 51). What legal advice would you give to a husband who found himself in this situation?

2. Prosecution. A criminal accusation of adultery can be lodged by third parties, although the law required accusation within five years of the alleged offense (Ulpian, D. 48.5.30.5–7). However, the husband (or, failing the husband, the wife's father) is preferred as a prosecutor of the woman for the first sixty days following a divorce (Papinian, D. 48.5.12.6); and it seems clear that the statute was encouraging an aggrieved ex-husband to act in this capacity. What might the reason be? The husband could also accuse the adulterer (Paul, *Sent.* 2.26.10).

3. A Convenient Checklist. At the end of the classical period, Tryphoninus (D. 4.4.37.1) lists the major cases in which a man can be convicted of "adultery" (i.e., as though he were an adulterer) without actually being an adulterer: "for example, if he knowingly takes as his wife a woman condemned for adultery or does not divorce a wife caught in adultery or makes a profit from his wife's adultery or receives money to conceal criminal debauchery (*stuprum*) or offers his home for the commission of *stuprum* or adultery within it." As this list makes evident, the range of the offense stretches also to third parties who aid and abet adultery. The first item on this checklist has the effect of condemn-

ing a convicted adulteress to a sort of permanent social exile, over and above any criminal penalty she suffers; the *lex Iulia* was responsible for this extra punishment as well (Ulpian, D. 48.5.30.1). At most, the convicted adulteress could be kept as a concubine (Ulpian, D. 25.7.1.2). Does this strike you as overkill?

CASE 55: A Double Standard?

C. 9.9.1 (Impp. Severus et Antoninus AA. Cassiae)

Publico iudicio non habere mulieres adulterii accusationem, quamvis de matrimonio suo violato queri velint, lex Iulia declarat, quae, cum masculis iure mariti facultatem accusandi detulisset, non idem feminis privilegium detulit.

(Emperors Septimius Severus and Caracalla to Cassia; A.D. 197)

The *lex Iulia* states that in a public trial women cannot bring an accusation of adultery even if they wish to complain about a violation of their own marriage. Although it (the statute) conferred on males the capacity to accuse (an ex-wife of adultery) by (using) a husband's right, it did not confer the same privilege on females.

1. Why Can't Women Accuse? The statutory prohibition, as stated in this rescript, prevents women from accusing anyone else, including their husbands, of adultery. What reason might the legislator have had for such a prohibition? What circumstances may have led Cassia to raise the question?

2. Debauchery (*Stuprum*). Although the jurists spend far more time discussing adultery because it intrudes directly on the private institution of marriage, Roman law also knew the criminal offense of "debauchery" (a loose translation of *stuprum*). As Papinian observes (D. 48.5.6.1), the *lex Iulia de adulteriis* used the terms *stuprum* and *adulterium* indiscriminately; but technically adultery was committed only in the case of married women, while "*stuprum* is committed against a virgin (a never-married woman) or a widow or divorcee (*vidua*)." The statute expressly forbade both: "Let no one hereafter knowingly and intentionally commit *stuprum* and adultery" (Ulpian, D. 48.5.13). It therefore appears that the *lex Iulia* was meant to regulate all consensual heterosexual relations in which at least one of the partners was free; and a few sources indicate that some illicit homosexual relations may also have been covered by the statute (e.g., Paul, *Sent.* 2.26.12: "A person who debauches an unwilling free male is capitally punished"; Papinian, D. 48.5.9 pr.). For males, *stuprum* was a potentially serious charge, and we have already seen some implications of it: a man must be very cautious if he lives in a long-term nonmarital union with a respectable freeborn woman (Case 18). In general, however, males were legally permitted to have extramarital affairs with slaves or disgraced women, while "respectable" females were not allowed any sex outside marriage. Further, charges of adultery seem to have been in fact far more common than those of *stuprum*. To what extent did the Emperor Augustus enact a genuine double standard? To what extent is this double standard likely to have been rather the result of law's inevitable operation within a male-dominated society?

SECTION 4. The Property of the Spouses

One issue that marriage always raises centers on property: if two persons from different families form a household, what effect will that have not only on the property they each own at the time the marriage is contracted but also on what they acquire during the marriage? Here Roman law accepts a radical analysis: marriage has virtually no effect on the individual property rights of the two parties, both when they marry and afterward. In principle, both husband and wife retain their separate estates. The result is a remarkable simplicity, an institution that one of our students once described as "the pre-nup from hell." The analogy here is apt, for the chief purpose of modern prenuptial agreements is to prevent one party (usually the economically weaker) from obtaining access to the present and future assets of the other. Roman law seems to achieve this result through law itself, and with such thoroughness that husband and wife are even prevented, at least as a general rule, from exchanging gifts that would tend to alter their relative wealth.

It is possible to object to this arrangement on many grounds. First, it often seems impractical to anticipate that husband and wife will live together, in the same house, like roommates, without shared ownership of the property they tend to use in common. Even the jurists seem to recognize the difficulties here, although they still cling to the notion that it will eventually be possible to separate the couple's property. But second, the very effort to preserve the barrier between the estates of the two spouses may seem to defeat the core purpose of marriage, by making it altogether too easy to end marriages at will; however, the Roman insistence on separate estates at least meant that many of the ugly scenes associated with modern divorce courts could be largely (although not entirely) avoided.

In the end, though, the most substantial problem with the Roman system is that it seems to extend unduly narrow protection to the economically weaker partner, who, it can be assumed, was usually the wife. In the modern world, women have access to opportunities that were unheard of in the Roman world, and accordingly they may, in some instances, be willing to forgo a share of their husbands' income and wealth—and today, in many cases, vice versa as well. By contrast, Roman women had sharply limited career chances; and, as we shall see, within marriage they could not even legally require their husbands to maintain them. Much, then, came to depend on the leverage that their dowries provided them—a question to which we turn in Section 5.

CASE 56: Separate Estates

D. 29.5.1.15 (Ulpianus libro quinquagesimo ad edictum)

Si vir aut uxor occisi esse proponantur, de servis eorum quaestio habetur, quamquam neque viri servi proprie uxoris dicantur neque uxoris proprie viri: sed quia commixta familia est et una domus est, ita vindicandum atque in propriis servis senatus censuit.

(Ulpian in the fiftieth book on the Edict)

In the event that a husband or wife is killed, their slaves are questioned (under torture), even though the husband's slaves are not properly described as the wife's, nor the wife's as the husband's. But because their slave household (*familia*) is intermingled and they have a single home, the Senate voted the same punishment as for their own slaves.

1. Murder Most Foul. This Case relates to the SC Silanianum, a decree that the Senate passed in A.D. 10. This decree, along with some subsequent legislation, provided that when a master or mistress was killed, this person's coresident slaves—all of them!—were to be subjected to torture and eventually executed, without regard to their actual guilt, so long as they *could* have prevented the murder. Ulpian (D. 29.5.1 pr.) explains the purpose of the legislation: "Since otherwise no home can be safe unless slaves are forced, upon peril of their lives, to protect their masters from both internal and external threats, *senatusconsulta* were introduced as to public questioning of the slave household of murder victims." Should measures such as these be regarded as an indication that Roman slave owners lived in constant terror of their slaves? In this Case, Ulpian points to a problem that arose from the actual character of many upper-class households; how was the problem solved?

2. The Intermixed Household. The importance of this Case for our immediate purposes is that it points up two fundamental aspects of Roman marriage. First, unlike in modern law, there is no automatic or even normal community of property between husband and wife. Instead, to the extent that they have any property of their own, the husband retains both ownership and control over his property, and the wife over hers, throughout the marriage. (The dowry is an important exception here, to which we will come in Section 5.) Second, in practice their personal property, in particular, was not infrequently intermingled within a single home, creating large sources of potential confusion if and when the time came to separate the two estates. With regard to larger holdings, such as real estate, this confusion was considerably less likely to arise; and doubtless the Roman law on the subject would have been much simpler if their insistence on separate estates had been limited to larger or more expensive assets. Instead, as we shall see, the Romans tried to preserve the separation even down to relatively insignificant items, with results that

can, on occasion, be somewhat unsettling. As you read the Cases that follow, try to figure out the Romans' reasons for setting up the marital property regime in this way.

3. Obligations. From the separation of their property, it follows that Roman spouses are, as a rule, not liable for each other's debts to third parties, whether these arise from contracts or from civil wrongs (delicts). With respect to one another, obligations arise much as they would between any two Romans; marriage has relatively little effect on this aspect of their legal relationship. Thus, for instance, a wife is liable if she borrows pearls from her husband and then damages them (Ulpian, D. 9.2.27.30); however, out of respect for marriage, infaming actions are generally disallowed (Case 45). As to contracts, legal sources frequently mention loans of money between spouses; for example, Scaevola (D. 34.3.28.13) describes a large business loan by a wife to her husband. (If this loan was interest free, would it be a gift?) Less frequent are references to other transactions, such as sales (e.g., Proculus, D. 19.5.12: a man sells farms to his wife, with an option to repurchase them if they divorce).

4. A Shared Household. In modern law, couples often try to keep their estates separate, at least to some extent, through prenuptial agreements that prevent mingling. In Roman law, agreements between husband and wife might be used for exactly the opposite purpose. Scaevola (D. 34.1.16.3) reports on a household in which husband and wife had preserved a total partnership of property (*societas omnium bonorum*) for more than forty years. Upon his death, the husband left half to each of his heirs: his wife and his grandson. Most probably the wife was entitled to receive, in the settlement, half of whatever belonged to her and her husband (this was her share of the partnership), plus, under the will, half of her deceased husband's share. This agreement, which in some respects actually looks more modern than ordinary Roman law, was a purely contractual arrangement between husband and wife, which either party was free to dissolve even while their marriage persisted. Our sources give no sign that arrangements of this type were ever other than exceptional.

CASE 57: Managing His Wife's Property

D. 35.2.95 pr. (Scaevola libro vicesimo primo Digestorum)

Maritus uxoris res extra dotem constitutas administravit eaque decedens ante rationem sibi redditam administrationis ex asse eundem maritum heredem reliquit eiusque fidei commisit, ut decem uncias filio communi cum moreretur restitueret, duas autem uncias nepoti. quaesitum est, an id quoque, quod ex administratione rerum apud maritum resedisse constiterit, cum ceteris bonis pro rata decem unciarum filio restitui debeat. respondit id, quod debuisset hereditati, in rationem venire debere.

(Scaevola in the twenty-first book of his *Digests*)

A husband administered his wife's nondowry property. She died before receiving an accounting (from him) of his administration. She left her husband as heir to everything, but (in her will) entrusted it to his faith (*fidei commisit*) that on his death he restore five-sixths (of the estate) to their common son and one-sixth to their grandson.

Question was raised whether the five-sixths share that must be restored to the son includes not only the rest of the estate but also the amount that the husband is discovered to have retained from his administration of her property. He (Scaevola) responded that what he had owed to her estate must be taken account of.

1. Maladministration? Here, the wife apparently entered marriage with considerable property of her own, "outside the dowry" (*extra dotem*). Although she was not obliged to (see Chapter III.A.3 on the ability of *sui iuris* women to conduct their own business affairs), she allowed her husband to administer her property; and he did so, without accounting to her for his administration. When she died leaving him as heir, he might have avoided an accounting; but her additional request created a "trust" (*fideicommissum;* see Chapter IV.C.2) in favor of her son and grandson, meaning that they acquired what we would call a future interest in her estate. Accordingly, as Scaevola holds, what her husband may have owed to the wife's estate (presumably as a result of his commingling his own assets with his wife's) must be paid. How easy will it be to determine the amount that is due? The husband's position here is not substantially different, in Roman law, from that of any third-party administrator of another's property.

2. Wives as Administrators. Legal sources also mention the reverse arrangement. Papinian (D. 3.5.32) discusses a situation in which, during their marriage, the wife had her husband's property "in her power" (*in sua potestate*); after the husband died, his heir, suspecting mismanagement, sought an accounting.

CASE 58: What the Woman Brings with Her

D. 23.3.9.2–3 (Ulpianus libro trigesimo primo ad Sabinum)

(2) Dotis autem causa data accipere debemus ea, quae in dotem dantur. (3) Ceterum si res dentur in ea, quae Graeci *parapherna* dicunt quaeque Galli peculium appellant, videamus, an statim efficiuntur mariti. et putem, si sic dentur ut fiant, effici mariti, et cum distractum fuerit matrimonium, non vindicari oportet, sed condici, nec dotis actione peti, ut divus Marcus et imperator noster cum patre rescripserunt. plane si rerum libellus marito detur, ut Romae volgo fieri videmus (nam mulier res, quas solet in usu habere in domo mariti neque in dotem dat, in libellum solet conferre eumque libellum marito offerre, ut is subscribat, quasi res acceperit, et velut chirographum eius uxor retinet res quae libello continentur in domum eius se intulisse): hae igitur res an mariti fiant, videamus. et non puto, non quod non ei traduntur (quid enim interest, inferantur volente eo in domum eius an ei tradantur?), sed quia non puto hoc agi inter virum et uxorem, ut dominium ad eum transferatur, sed magis ut certum sit in domum eius illata, ne, si quandoque separatio fiat, negetur: et plerumque custodiam earum maritus repromittit, nisi mulieri commissae sint. videbimus harum rerum nomine, si non reddantur, utrum rerum amotarum an depositi an mandati mulier agere possit. et si custodia marito committitur, depositi vel mandati agi poterit: si minus, agetur rerum amotarum, si animo amoventis maritus eas retineat, aut ad exhibendum, si non amovere eas connisus est.

(Ulpian in the thirty-first book on Sabinus)

(2) The term "property given because of the dowry" we should take to mean the property placed into the dowry. (3) But if the property is placed into what is called *parapherna* (supplemental property) by the Greeks and a *peculium* by the Gauls, let us see whether it belongs to the husband at once. I would think that if it was given for this purpose, then it does belong to the husband. And (so) when the marriage has broken up, she should claim it not as owned by her but as owed to her, nor should an action on dowry be brought; this is held in rescripts from the deified Emperor Marcus Aurelius (reign: A.D. 161–180) and our Emperor Caracalla with his father Septimius Severus (coreign: A.D. 197–211).

Clearly, if the husband is given an inventory of the property, as we often see occurring at Rome—for the wife usually writes out the things that she commonly uses in her husband's home and that she does not put into the dowry, and she provides the list to her husband for his signature, on the basis that he received the property; and the wife (then) retains, as it were, his signed document that she bore into his house the things listed—let us see whether these things belong to the husband. I think they don't, not because they weren't handed over to him—for what difference does it make whether they are handed over to him or carried into his house with his consent?—but because I think husband and wife arranged, not the transfer of ownership to him, but (only) that it be certain what was brought into his house, so there is no denial if a separation (of their property) ever occurs. Frequently the husband guarantees safekeeping (*custodia*) of such property, unless it was entrusted (on a day-to-day basis) to the wife.

As to this property, we will (now) examine whether, if it is not returned, the wife can sue on removal of property or on deposit or on mandate. If its safekeeping (*custodia*) is entrusted to the husband, she can sue on deposit or mandate. If not, suit lies on removal of property if the husband kept it with the intent to remove it, or for production if he did not attempt to remove it.

1. Supplemental Property. This extended passage begins to suggest some of the practical difficulties that might intrude in Roman marriage. Over and above her dowry, a wife could bring personal property of her own into her husband's house. This Case indicates that she could, if she wished, consign ownership of this property to him for the duration of the marriage, in which case she would have to reclaim it as "owed" to her at the end of the marriage—rather as though it had been loaned to him for his use. But more frequently, it seems, a wife chose to retain ownership and control—hence the signed documents that Roman women used to prevent these items from "inadvertently" becoming part of their husbands' property. Still, as the last paragraph of the Case shows, even where the wife retained ownership, her husband might still "receive" the property and promise to safeguard it. What does all of this suggest about the realism of Roman law in insisting on separate property for the spouses? In any case, as a postclassical rescript states (Theodosius and Valentinian, C. 5.14.8; A.D. 450), the husband was not allowed to have dealings with this property unless his wife permitted. On the wife's supplemental property, Papinian (D. 39.5.31.1 = *Frag. Vat.* 254) discusses nondowry property contributed by a husband's mother-in-law; by a legal fiction, ownership of the property is treated as passing to the wife, who then hands it over to her husband. A wife who was still in her father's power could also have a *peculium* given to her by her father, distinct from her dowry (Papinian, D. 6.1.65.1); on the *peculium*, see Chapter III.B.3. How likely is it that these various categories of property will remain distinguishable?

2. The Wife's "Property." Correspondingly, certain items that belong to the husband may, during the marriage, be effectively under the wife's control. We learn about such property mainly from legal sources interpreting wills in which husbands leave their wives some or all of this property, sometimes described as "things acquired for the wife's use" (*uxoris causa parata*). Other sources discuss toiletries (*mundus*; see Ulpian, D. 34.2.25.10, who mentions mirrors, jars, perfumes, perfume bottles, and other items associated with the bath or the dresser), jewelry, clothing, furniture (*supellex*; see D. 33.10), kitchen stores (*penus*; see Ulpian, D. 33.9.3 pr.: "things for eating and drinking"), and so on. Separating out such property from the testator's estate was often difficult and rather arbitrary. For an example, see Case 202.

CASE 59: Q. Mucius's Presumption

D. 24.1.51 (Pomponius libro quinto ad Quintum Mucium)

Quintus Mucius ait, cum in controversiam venit, unde ad mulierem quid per-venerit, et verius et honestius est quod non demonstratur unde habeat existimari a viro aut qui in potestate eius esset ad eam pervenisse. evitand<ae> autem turpis quaestus <quaestionis> gratia circa uxorem hoc videtur Quintus Mucius probasse.

(Pomponius in the fifth book on Quintus Mucius)

Quintus Mucius says: "When dispute arises about the source of property that came to a wife, the more accurate and respectable course is that when its origin is unclear, it be held to have come to her from her husband or a person in his power." Quintus Mucius apparently approved this so as to avoid an inquiry regarding a wife's unseemly profit.

1. A Demeaning Inquiry. The problem discussed in this Case might come up in a variety of circumstances, wherever it is necessary to separate the wife's property from her husband's. Some of this property may be of indeterminate origin, perhaps because no one alive remembers. The "bright line" rule proposed by Q. Mucius Scaevola (consul in 95 B.C.), the earliest major Roman jurist, merely establishes a legal presumption for dealing with such property; it appears that, for example, the woman could still prove that she had purchased the property herself or been given it by a third party, but in any case the burden of proof is on whoever alleges an origin other than her husband (so Alexander Severus, C. 5.16.6.1; A.D. 229). Why did Q. Mucius feel that this presumption was "more accurate and respectable"? What is the "inquiry" that Pomponius thinks the earlier jurist feared? See also Case 202.

2. Danger to the Wife. "[T]he presumption might be a source of danger to a woman, for it would mean that she risked losing her property if she could not prove where she had got it from" (H. F. Jolowicz). What could a wife do to lessen this difficulty?

CASE 60: Maintenance

D. 24.3.22.8 (Ulpianus libro trigesimo tertio ad edictum)

Sin autem in saevissimo furore muliere constituta maritus dirimere quidem matrimonium calliditate non vult, spernit autem infelicitatem uxoris et non ad eam flectitur nullamque ei competentem curam inferre manifestissimus est, sed abutitur dote[m]: tunc licentiam habeat vel curator furiosae vel cognati adire iudicem competentem, quatenus necessitas imponatur marito omnem talem mulieris sustentationem sufferre et alimenta praestare et medicinae eius succurrere et nihil praetermittere eorum, quae maritum uxori adferre decet secundum dotis quantitatem. sin vero dotem ita dissipaturus [ita] manifestus est, ut non hominem frugi oportet, tunc dotem sequestrari, quatenus ex ea mulier competens habeat solacium una cum sua familia, pactis videlicet dotalibus, quae inter eos ab initio nuptiarum inita fuerint, in suo statu durantibus et alterius exspectantibus sanitatem <au>t mortis eventum.

(Ulpian in the thirty-third book on the Edict)

But if, after a wife becomes violently insane, her husband cunningly declines to end the marriage but instead ignores his wife's distress and does not attend to her and clearly provides her no adequate care, but misuses her dowry, then the mad woman's *curator* or her relatives have leave to approach a competent court to the extent that her husband is required to provide all such subsistence of the woman and to furnish maintenance and to provide medical aid and (generally) to omit nothing that a husband ought to provide his wife, in accord with the size of her dowry.

But if it is clear that he will waste the dowry as a provident man would not, then (they can force) the dowry to be sequestered up to the extent that a (mentally) competent woman and her household would be indemnified from it; but of course the dowry agreements that the parties entered between themselves at the start of the marriage remain in their (former) condition and await the other person's recovery or eventual death.

1. A Desperate Situation. This Case illustrates one extraordinary aspect of Roman marital law: a husband had no legal duty to provide maintenance to his wife, even though he did eventually have a duty to maintain other close relatives (see Case 112). Here a wife, who is *sui iuris,* went mad and therefore lacked the mental capacity to initiate a divorce (Case 77); but her husband declined to divorce her because he wanted continued control of her dowry. Internal evidence of language and law shows that the compilers of Justinian's *Digest* rewrote this entire text, with the result that we cannot know in what way Ulpian would have solved the problem of how the husband could be forced to maintain his insane wife; but it seems reasonable to assume that the

compilers, at least, found the traditional solution inadequate. Why might the classical jurists have been cautious?

2. The Dowry? As this Case suggests, the dowry was normally linked to the wife's maintenance, although this link was mainly traditional. As you read the following Cases, try to decide how well the link would have worked in practice.

CASE 61: No Gifts

D. 24.1.1 (Ulpianus libro trigesimo secundo ad Sabinum)

Moribus apud nos receptum est, ne inter virum et uxorem donationes valerent. hoc autem receptum est, ne mutuo amore invicem spoliarentur donationibus non temperantes, sed profusa erga se facilitate:

D. 24.1.2 (Paulus libro septimo ad Sabinum)

ne cesset eis studium liberos potius educendi. Sextus Caecilius et illam causam adiciebat, quia saepe futurum esset, ut discuterentur matrimonia, si non donaret is qui posset, atque ea ratione eventurum, ut venalicia essent matrimonia.

D. 24.1.3 pr. (Ulpianus libro trigesimo secundo ad Sabinum)

Haec ratio et oratione imperatoris nostri Antonini Augusti electa est: nam ita ait: "Maiores nostri inter virum et uxorem donationes prohibuerunt, amorem honestum solis animis aestimantes, famae etiam coniunctorum consulentes, ne concordia pretio conciliari viderentur neve melior in paupertatem incideret, deterior ditior fieret."

(Ulpian in the thirty-second book on Sabinus)

We have received the customary rule that gifts between husband and wife are invalid. This rule was received so that they not each be ruined by mutual love, not sparing on gifts but with extravagance toward themselves,

(Paul in the seventh book on Sabinus)

(and) so that they not lose interest in further raising children. Sextus Caecilius (Africanus) adds also this cause: that it would come about that if he did not give when he could, marriages would break down, and so it would turn out that marriages were for sale.

(Ulpian in the thirty-second book on Sabinus)

This rationale is also derived from the legislative proposal (*oratio*) of our Emperor Caracalla (reign: A.D. 211–217), who says the following: "Our ancestors forbade gifts between husband and wife, thinking that love was respectable when purely psychological (but) also looking to the reputation of spouses, so that they not seem harmoniously reconciled for a price, with the better (spouse) becoming impoverished while the worse one grows richer."

1. Where Did the Rule against Gifts Come From? Ulpian describes the rule as of customary origin, but it cannot be very old (since it is inapplicable to *manus* marriages; you see why, don't you?). Possibly it arose as a response to the decline of *manus*, when the Romans came to realize that a wife not in the

legal power of her husband might constitute a drain on the resources of the *familia;* for although the rule is applicable to both spouses, the legal sources speak much more often of gifts from husband to wife. If a scenario something like this is correct, there still remains the question of whether this rule is wise as policy. What principle is being protected?

2. Why? In this Case, the jurists offer several explanations: that gifts motivated by love would drain the spouses' estates, distract the couple's attention from procreation, introduce a venal element into the continuation of marriage, and operate to the benefit of the morally unscrupulous. Is any of this convincing? The legal sources repeatedly stress that the rule is not meant to deemphasize the significance of abiding marital affection. Is love purer if material exchange is discouraged? Septimius Severus later extended the rule to ban most gifts between relatives by marriage (Ulpian, D. 24.1.3.1–9).

3. All Gifts? The intricacy of everyday life in a household meant that the policy against gifts could not be applied overly rigorously. Here are a few examples:

   • "If a husband gave his wife an excessive present on Mother's Day or on her birthday, this is a (prohibited) gift" (Pomponius, D. 24.1.31.8). Therefore, it seems that less lavish gifts were acceptable.
   • "A wife is held not to be enriched if she is given money that she spends on provisions or on perfumes or on food for the slaves" (Pomponius, D. 24.1.31.9); but see Scaevola, D. 24.1.58.1, for a somewhat harsher view (only if slaves are used by both parties).
   • "If the husband or wife uses slaves or clothing belonging to the other, or lives for free in the other's house, the gift is valid" (Pomponius, D. 24.1.18).
   • "If the husband's slaves do some work for the wife or vice versa, the better view is that no account be taken of it (i.e., it is not a gift). And indeed the rule on prohibited gifts should not be applied harshly nor as between enemies, but as between those joined by the highest love and fearing poverty alone" (Paul, D. 24.1.28.2).
   • "When a man owes his wife money payable on a certain day, he can pay it now without danger of this being a gift, even if he could gain some time advantage by keeping the money" (Pomponius, D. 24.1.31.6). What about the interest on the money?
   • "Between husband and wife a gift (of a slave) for manumission is allowed, either because freedom is favored or at any rate because no one is enriched by this" (Paul, *Sent.* 2.23.2). A freed slave owes services to a manumitter; isn't that a gift?
   • "You were about to leave a legacy or an estate to me. At my request, you can leave it to my wife, and this is evidently not a gift since nothing is lost from my property. Proculus says that our ancestors helped the donor mainly to

prevent one party being despoiled by love of the other, not from ill will to prevent one becoming richer" (Pomponius, D. 24.1.31.7).

There are other more important exceptions, some of which are examined below.

4. What Happens to Improper Gifts? The jurists usually describe them as void, and it seems plain that ownership does not pass (since the giver can demand return of the gift, if it still exists, on the basis of ownership: e.g., Ulpian, D. 24.1.5.18). But gifts (or their value) are more usually reclaimed during a divorce, as part of the property settlement (see Case 83).

CASE 62: A Fake Sale

D. 24.1.5.5 (Ulpianus libro trigesimo secundo ad Sabinum)

Circa venditionem quoque Iulianus quidem minoris factam venditionem nullius esse momenti ait: Neratius autem (cuius opinionem Pomponius non improbat) venditionem donationis causa inter virum et uxorem factam nullius esse momenti, si modo, cum animum maritus vendendi non haberet, idcirco venditionem commentus sit, ut donaret: enimvero si, cum animum vendendi haberet, ex pretio ei remisit, venditionem quidem valere, remissionem autem hactenus non valere, quatenus facta est locupletior: itaque si res quindecim venit quinque, nunc autem sit decem, quinque tantum praestanda sunt, quia in hoc locupletior videtur facta.

(Ulpian in the thirty-second book on Sabinus)

Also as regards sale (by one spouse to the other), Julian says that a sale at a lower price is void. But Neratius, whose view Pomponius does not reject, (said) that a sale between husband and wife is void only if the husband, without the intent to sell, faked a sale in order to give a gift. But if he had the intent to sell but forgave her a part of the price, the sale is quite valid, but the remission is invalid to the extent she was (actually) enriched. So if a thing worth fifteen was sold for five but is now worth ten, only five should be furnished because she was evidently enriched (only) to this extent.

1. A Difference of Opinion? To what extent do Julian and Neratius disagree? Consider the following example: A wife's slave is worth fifteen on the open market; she sells the slave to her husband for five. Julian appears to hold the sale void under all circumstances. But Neratius makes a distinction between whether the wife actually wished to sell the slave or simply to make a gift to her husband. How can this be determined? (Suppose, for instance, that the husband immediately resells the slave to his wife for fifteen. Would it be different if he resells for fifteen to a third party? Or if he simply keeps the slave?) If the wife actually wished to sell, then the sale is valid, but the difference between the price and current value can be recovered, presumably usually during divorce proceedings. Is this distinction too cumbersome to implement?

2. Imaginary Sales. Paul, *Sent.* 2.23.4: "Husband and wife cannot contract an imaginary sale with a view to making a gift." Is an imaginary sale one in which an excessively low price is set, or one in which the price is just but the seller later declines to collect some or all of it? Ulpian (D. 24.1.32.26) indicates that the Romans usually drew no distinction between these two situations; is Neratius's view in this Case different? In general, it should be noted, classical Roman law, with forthright liberalism, permits the parties to set prices as they wish, nor is an element of express gift giving excluded; the husband/wife situation is in this respect unique (see Ulpian, D. 18.1.38).

CASE 63: Making Clothes

D. 24.1.31 pr.–1 (Pomponius libro quarto decimo ad Sabinum)

(pr.) Sed si vir lana sua vestimentum mulieri confecerit, quamvis id uxori confectum fuerit et uxoris cura, tamen viri esse neque <id> impedire, quod in ea re uxor tamquam lanipendia fuerit et viri negotium procurarit. (1) Si uxor lana sua, operis ancillarum viri, vestimenta sui nomine confecit muliebria, et vestimenta mulieris esse et pro operis ancillarum viro praestare nihil debere: sed viri nomine vestimenta confecta virilia viri esse, ut is lanae uxori praestet pretium: sed si non virilia vestimenta suo nomine mulier confecit, sed ea viro donavit, non valere donationem, cum illa valeat, cum viri nomine confecit: nec umquam operas viri ancillarum aestimari convenit.

(Pomponius in the fourteenth book on Sabinus)

(pr.) But if from his own wool a man makes clothing for his wife, although it was made for the wife and under her supervision, (a jurist holds that) it is still the husband's, nor is it an obstacle (to this outcome) that the wife served as a spinner in this matter and oversaw her husband's business.

(1) If with her own wool, but using her husband's slave women, a wife makes women's clothing on her own behalf, (a jurist holds that) the clothing is the wife's and she should give her husband nothing for the services of the slave women. But male clothing made in her husband's name is the husband's, provided he pays his wife the price of the wool. But if the wife did not make men's clothing in her own name but gave them to her husband, the gift is invalid, since it is valid (only) when she makes it in her husband's name. But it is never appropriate that the work of the husband's slave women be appraised.

1. Making Clothes. According to Gaius (*Inst.* 2.79), the jurists disagreed on the issue of manufacture, when, for instance, one person takes wool that belongs to another person and, without the owner's consent, makes clothing from it. Some jurists held that the manufactured item belonged to the owner of its materials; others held that it belonged to the maker. Which view does Pomponius follow? Which view seems more sensible—or does it depend? See if you can work out the rules of this Case. Which of the hypothetical situations that Pomponius describes strikes you as the most difficult?

2. An Apartment Building. A husband gives a vacant lot to his wife, who erects an apartment house on it. Who owns the building? In general, when a nonowner builds permanent structures on another person's land, they belong to the owner of the land; does that help you to answer? See Pomponius, D. 24.1.31.2, who awards the building to the husband but lets the wife hold the building until he pays compensation for her expenses; is that sufficient?

CASE 64: Exceptions

D. 24.1.14 (Paulus libro septuagesimo primo ad edictum)

Quod si vir uxori, cuius aedes incendio consumptae sunt, ad refectionem earum pecuniam donaverit, valet donatio in tantum, in quantum aedificii extructio postulat.

D. 24.1.42 (Gaius libro undecimo ad edictum provinciale)

Nuper ex indulgentia principis Antonini recepta est alia causa donationis, quam dicimus honoris causa: ut ecce si uxor viro lati clavii peten<d>i gratia donet vel ut equestris ordinis fiat vel ludorum gratia.

(Paul in the seventy-first book on the Edict)

If a wife's house has burned down and her husband gives her money for rebuilding it, the gift is valid for as much money as the building's construction requires.

(Gaius in the eleventh book on the Provincial Edict)

Recently, through the kindness of the Emperor Antoninus Pius (reign: A.D. 138–161), another basis for a gift has been introduced, which we call "for the sake of honor": for example, if a wife gives to her husband to enable him to seek senatorial or equestrian status or for games.

1. A Slippery Rule. Particularly as the emperors assumed a more active legislative role in Roman private law, the rule against spousal gifts gradually became riddled with exceptions. Try to decipher the logic that motivates each exception, and then decide whether any overall pattern unites these exceptions. Financial emergencies, such as the wife's house burning down, almost invite a bit of flexibility; see Paul, D. 24.3.20, on emergency return of dowry to the wife. Such rulings are generalized in Ulpian, D. 24.1.21 pr.: "It is not a gift for a man to meet the necessary expenditures (of his wife)." Why not?

2. Gifts Anticipating the End of Marriage. One situation in which gifts were permitted from a fairly early date was when the end of marriage was directly foreseeable. A good example is a gift a spouse makes *mortis causa*, in anticipation of death; the validity of the gift is contingent on the spouse then actually dying (see, e.g., Ulpian and Gaius, D. 24.1.9.2, 10; also Cases 211–212). Analogously, one spouse may provide the other with a tomb, the gift becoming irrevocable when the donee or someone else is buried there (Ulpian, D. 24.1.5.8–11). The exception was then extended to gifts made *divortii causa*, in anticipation of an impending divorce; see Case 80 on the plausibility of this extension. Perhaps falling into the same category are gifts *exilii causa*, in anticipation of one spouse's impending exile for a criminal offense (Paul, D. 24.1.43).

3. A Meaningless Rule? "With all these exceptions, little substance was left to the prohibition. It might still serve a useful purpose as a check, to be judiciously applied, upon excessive generosity" (P. E. Corbett). Do you agree?

CASE 65: Severan Reforms

Fragmenta Vaticana 276 (Divi Diocletianus et Constantius . . . iae)

Si pater tuus nomine matris tuae de sua pecunia fundum comparavit donationis causa eique tradidit et decedens non revocavit id quod in eam contulisse videtur, intellegis frustra te velle experiri, cum oratione divi Severi huiusmodi donationes post obitum eorum, qui donaverunt, confirmentur.

(The Deified Diocletian and Constantius, to a woman; A.D. 290)

If, in the name of your mother but using his own money, your father bought a farm as a gift and handed it over to her, and before his death he did not revoke that which had evidently been bestowed on her, you do understand that your wish to sue (for recovery of the farm) is ineffectual, since by the legislative proposal (*oratio*) of the deified Emperor Septimius Severus such gifts are confirmed after the death of the donors.

1. Why the Reform? This late classical change in the law dates to A.D. 206 and is widely reported, usually with references to the emperor's oration proposing the legislation to the Senate (a portion of this oration is quoted in Case 61). The essence of the change is summarized by Diocletian: when one spouse gives another a gift that is normally impermissible, that gift becomes irrevocable if the donor subsequently dies while still married and without a change of mind. Explaining the reform, Ulpian (D. 24.1.32.2) quotes the emperor: Revocation "is proper if the donor changes his mind; but it is harsh and stingy that an heir (of the donor) seize (the gift) perhaps against the donor's last wishes." What is the policy argument here? That since the gift is effective only on the donor's death, it should be considered as a sort of gift *mortis causa*? (So Ulpian, ibid. 3.) If the donee dies first, the gift can be reclaimed. What if both die at the same time or in circumstances where priority of death cannot be established? Ulpian considers this problem too (ibid. 14): the donor is construed as having died first; and this is true even if they had exchanged gifts! This decision suggests a legal policy in favor of upholding gifts.

2. Divorce. Under the reform, the gift becomes ineffective if the couple divorce before the donor's death (Ulpian, D. 24.1.32.10–13, a part of which is quoted as Case 17). Why should divorce be treated differently from death?

3. Change of Intention. Of course, the Severan reform contains a major loophole: the gift is confirmed only if the donor's mind did not change. How can this be known? Ulpian (D. 24.1.32.5) suggests an indirect proof: a husband gives his wife some land and then uses the land as collateral for a loan. Is the gift thereby rescinded? (Yes.)

4. Promise of Gift. The sources divide as to whether the Severan reform validates a stipulation to give a gift in the future, where the promisor dies before fulfilling the promise: see Ulpian, D. 24.1.23, as against Ulpian, ibid. 33 (Ulpian v. Ulpian!).

As we have seen, the legal structure of Roman marriage was fragile, in the sense that it was far from creating the family as a real partnership with respect to property; the wife appears, at times, almost as an intruder within a household structure still centered on the *pater familias*. In practice, it seems, the jurists relied on the institution of dowry to provide this delicate union with a degree of stability. As we have also seen (Cases 29–36), creating the dowry was a customary part of the marriage process at Rome, even though it was not required for marriage. With the decline of *manus* marriage (Cases 37–40), the importance of dowry greatly increased, not only because providing for the wife was considerably more problematic in "free" marriage, but also because the inevitable reluctance of the husband to surrender the dowry became a prime deterrent to his precipitate ending of their marriage.

To be sure, it was not a legal presumption that Roman marriages were lacking in love or at least in affection—quite the contrary (see Cases 43–45). But the real issue is whether, when inevitable conflicts arose between the spouses, the marital regime of Roman law tended indirectly to exacerbate these conflicts and thus to prove counterproductive, at any rate if one long-term goal of marriage law was to encourage stable unions. So, in approaching dowry law, you should ask, above all, whether the Roman rules were fair to all parties and gave sufficiently clear guidance, so that the day-to-day management of dowries was unlikely to occasion quarrels between husband and wife or to inflame their preexisting quarrels. Did legal rules adequately protect the interests of the wife, both during the marriage and when it eventually ended?

Other issues are also important. Dowry places substantial property in the hands of one party, who holds it (or at least part of it) for the benefit of another, in what we tend to think of as a trust relationship (although the Romans avoid this line of analysis). In such situations, one major problem centers on the management of the property: is the holder required, or at least encouraged, to invest and develop the property, or is he allowed to let it deteriorate? How are incentives to proper behavior built into the structure of the dowry institution? Much here depends on the extent to which the husband's expenditure on the property can be reclaimed. To what extent is he encouraged to manage the property prudently, not only in his own interests but in those of his wife?

More broadly still, you should think about whether the Roman jurists may have expected too much from dowry as an institution. Was dowry, even when operating in its ideal form, likely to provide Roman marriage with adequate stability? Did the jurists do everything they could to develop this controversial institution in a rational way? How might it have been improved?

CASE 66: Equitable Ownership?

D. 23.3.75 (Tryphoninus libro sexto Disputationum)

Quamvis in bonis mariti dos sit, mulieris tamen est, et merito placuit, ut, si in dotem fundum inaestimatum dedit, cuius nomine duplae stipulatione cautum habuit, isque marito evictus sit, statim eam ex stipulatione agere posse. porro cuius interest non esse evictum quod in dote fuit quodque ipsa evictionem pati creditur ob id, quod eum in dotem habere desiit, huius etiam constante matrimonio, quamvis apud maritum dominium sit, emolumenti potestatem esse creditur, cu<m e>ius etiam matrimonii onera maritus sustinet.

(Tryphoninus in the sixth book of his *Disputations*)

Although the dowry is part of the husband's property, it is still the wife's. It was (thus) correctly held that if she placed into the dowry an unappraised farm, with regard to which she was protected by a stipulation for double its price, and this (farm) was then taken away from her husband (by its true owner), she can immediately sue on the stipulation. Further, it was in her interest that there be no eviction from dowry property; and since she is considered to suffer the eviction herself because she ceases to have it in the dowry, while the marriage lasts the husband has ownership but she is regarded as having the power of receiving financial advantage, even when her husband bears the burdens of the marriage itself.

1. The Problem. The woman purchased a farm. Because of concern about its title (a frequent problem in Roman law, since there was no adequate land registry), she took a stipulation from the seller that he would pay her double the purchase price if a true owner appeared and took the farm away. She then placed the farm in her dowry. Sure enough, the true owner showed up and evicted the husband from the farm. The issue is: can she sue the seller for double even though the farm was in her dowry? Tryphoninus holds that she can. Why might this decision be doubted? (The same outcome is specified in Paul, D. 21.2.71, a slightly more complicated case.)

2. "Part of the Husband's Property." Tryphoninus begins by holding that the dowry is part of the husband's property (in the technical Roman expression, the dowry is in his *bona*, "goods"). Does he also own the dowry, at least for as long as the marriage lasts? The jurists occasionally write as though he did; a good example is Ulpian's discussion of the precise moment when dowry property "becomes the husband's," *fiunt mariti*, in D. 23.3.7.3 and 9 pr. Usually, this means a transfer of title to the husband (see Case 72). Further, he has very extensive powers of disposition with respect to the dowry property, although he always remains accountable for the dowry's overall value (see Cases 84–89). Within wide limits, he can sell items from the dowry as he

wishes or use dowry money for purchases, although the proceeds from such transactions remain in the dowry (see, e.g., Gaius, D. 23.3.54: "Property purchased with dowry money is regarded as dowry"); his wife, by contrast, cannot sell or give away items in the dowry (Diocletian and Maximian, C. 5.12.23, 8.53.21; A.D. 294). The husband can also manumit dowry slaves (Gordian, C. 7.8.7; A.D. 238–244). At the end of the marriage, if he is obliged to return all or part of the dowry, this does not occur automatically; his ex-wife or another entitled party (such as her *pater familias*) must sue for it (see Case 82). Above all, the jurists do not describe a husband's relationship to the dowry as fiduciary, in the sense that he is holding the dowry as a sort of trustee on her behalf; for example, even if a wife suspects that her husband is squandering or abusing her dowry, she cannot demand an immediate accounting from him but at best can only threaten divorce. (The language of trusts does not appear until Justinian: C. 5.12.30 pr.; A.D. 529.) All of this is consistent with the husband's having a strong property interest that is as good as outright ownership during the marriage.

3. "Still the Wife's." Nevertheless, the jurists also recognize that the wife had a real stake in the dowry, even if she could not examine her husband's stewardship until the marriage had ended. A good example is Pomponius, D. 24.3.10 pr.: "a daughter who was married and had a dowry that came from her father" (*filia, quae nupta erat et dotem a patre profectam habebat*); "have" (*habere*) is the usual Latin word for "own." Ulpian refers to the dowry as her "quasi property" (*quasi patrimonium:* D. 11.7.16) or even "her own property" (*proprium patrimonium:* D. 4.4.3.5); and Paul (*Sent.* 4.1.1) states that a woman who receives her dowry after a marriage's end "is held to recover her own property" (*proprium recipere videtur*). Nor, in fact, was the wife's dowry counted when assessing the husband's wealth (Paul, D. 50.1.21.4). In classical Roman law, there is a gradually growing recognition of the importance of the dowry to the wife both during and after a marriage. As Paul observes in Case 29, "It is in the public interest that women's dowries are secure, since they can marry because of them." At issue, in this Case and in those that follow, is the extent to which Roman law successfully reconciled the wife's interests with the husband's.

4. What If the Husband Goes Broke? One occasion when conflict between the interests of the two spouses can arise is when the wife has reason to believe that her husband is becoming insolvent and so may be unable to repay her dowry. She has no right to demand an accounting; but if the cause of her distress is clear, she can demand that her husband provide security for return of the dowry, and if it becomes evident that his funds are insufficient, she can also sue for return of the dowry even while the marriage continues: Ulpian,

D. 24.3.24 pr.–2 (with Scaevola, D. 24.3.65). Are her interests adequately protected?

5. Back to the Problem. In light of the discussion above, does Tryphoninus's decision in this Case seem any clearer? Why is it that the wife, while her marriage continues, can sue the seller over the eviction?

CASE 67: Fruits and Capital Gains

D. 23.3.10.1–3 (Ulpianus libro trigesimo quarto ad Sabinum)

(1) Si praediis inaestimatis aliquid accessit, hoc ad compendium mulieris pertinet: si aliquid decessit, mulieris damnum est. (2) Si servi subolem ediderunt, mariti lucrum non est. (3) Sed fetus dotalium pecorum ad maritum pertinent, quia fructibus computantur, sic tamen, ut suppleri proprietatem prius oporteat et summissis in locum mortuorum capitum ex adgnatis residuum in fructum maritus habeat, quia fructus dotis ad eum pertineat.

(Ulpian in the thirty-fourth book on Sabinus)

(1) If there was some increase to unappraised land (in the dowry), this goes to the wife's benefit; if some decrease, the loss is the wife's. (2) If slaves bear offspring, the profit is not the husband's. (3) But the young of dowry animals go to the husband because they are counted as fruits (*fructus*), although his prior obligation is to make good the property; after substituting offspring in place of dead animals, the husband has the remainder as fruit, since the *fructus* of the dowry goes to him.

1. Fruits (*Fructus*). We briefly examined the concept of *fructus* in Case 35. If the dowry is thought of as capital, the *fructus* is the "interest" generated from this capital—not necessarily in direct monetary form, however. For example, as section 3 of this Case indicates, if the dowry includes a herd of cattle, newborn calves are the "fruits" of the herd, to the extent that they are not required to maintain the herd; they can be sold, for instance. Many other examples are given in D. 22.1; the ordinary agricultural produce of a farm is a fairly obvious one, or the wood from a forest or the ore from a mine or the fleece from a sheep or the milk from a cow, but so too is the money obtained from leasing out a slave or a building. Why are the offspring of slaves an exception to this pattern? This was a very old anomaly in Roman law (Ulpian, D. 7.1.68, citing many early sources). In any case, anything legally classified as fruits goes to the husband, in theory as compensation for the expenses of marriage (Case 35).

2. Capital Gains. Contrasted with the *fructus* are changes in the value of the underlying capital, whether through market forces or otherwise; unless the dowry property was appraised (Case 36), the husband does not take the risk of these changes. Thus, if an unappraised slave in the dowry dies of natural causes, the wife's dowry is decreased by the slave's value; and conversely, if a sudden surge in land prices sends the value of a dowry farm soaring, the dowry is enriched. But the line between *fructus* and capital gains is often difficult to draw.

3. **A Legacy.** Suppose a third party leaves a legacy to a dowry slave; does the husband acquire the legacy? Pomponius (D. 23.3.65) seems to decide that he does unless the testator did not wish him to receive it, in which case it accrues to the dowry. Is this ruling consistent with the general principles of Roman dowry law?

CASE 68: A Dowry Allowance to the Wife

D. 24.1.15 (Ulpianus libro trigesimo secundo ad Sabinum)

(pr.) Ex annuo vel menstruo, quod uxori maritus praestat, tunc quod superest revocabitur, si satis immodicum est, id est supra vires dotis. (1) Si maritus uxori pecuniam donaverit eaque usuras ex donata pecunia perceperit, lucrabitur. haec ita Iulianus in marito libro octavo decimo Digestorum scribit.

(Ulpian in the thirty-second book on Sabinus)

(pr.) From an annual or monthly sum provided by the husband to the wife, any surplus will be revoked if its amount is inordinate, that is, beyond the dowry's capacity. (1) If the husband gives money to his wife and she receives interest on this money gift, she will be enriched. So Julian writes with regard to a husband, in the eighteenth book of his *Digests*.

1. Maintenance and the Dowry. As Case 35 shows, the jurists often associate the dowry with "the burdens of matrimony," including maintenance of the wife. However, this association is informal and not legally mandated (see Case 60). The husband was not required to use any of the proceeds of the dowry for this purpose, nor was the amount of the dowry tied to the level of the wife's maintenance. In this Case, the husband has voluntarily given his wife an allowance out of which she was evidently to pay at least her own expenses; and, as it seems, the allowance was fairly loosely coordinated with income from the dowry. Paul (D. 23.3.73.1) indicates that it would also be acceptable if during marriage he restored to her the entire dowry so that she could maintain herself and her slaves—so long as she was the thrifty type! In some cases, a husband apparently supported his wife without drawing on the dowry income at all. Papinian (D. 24.1.54) reports a husband who was promised the interest from a dowry but never claimed it, preferring instead to maintain his wife and her slaves at his own expense during their marriage. Why is it, do you think, that such arrangements seem never to have become common?

2. Another Allowance. Something of the complexity of these arrangements can be gleaned from Julian (D. 23.4.22): "A man received a farm as dowry from his wife and they agreed that he would give her the rent from this farm as an annual payment. He then leased the cultivation of this farm to his wife's mother for a fixed rent. She died still owing the farm's rent, but left her daughter as her sole heir. The couple divorced, and the husband then claimed from his wife the rent her mother had owed." Will he win his lawsuit? The answer may depend on whether the annual payment should be regarded as a gift to her. If so, the gift is void and so he can claim the unpaid rent from his ex-wife; but if not (presumably because the money was intended for her maintenance), the rent and maintenance payments should offset each another.

3. **Can a Wife Give Her Husband an Allowance?** This is held to be an improper gift and, furthermore, "inconsistent with and contrary to the nature of her sex" (Ulpian, D. 24.1.33.1). Why this sudden outburst of sexism? Was Ulpian a misogynist?

CASE 69: Tying the Dowry to the Wife's Maintenance

D. 24.1.21.1 (Ulpianus libro trigesimo secundo ad Sabinum)

Si uxor viro dotem promiserit et dotis usuras, sine dubio dicendum est peti usuras posse, quia non est ista donatio, cum pro oneribus matrimonii petantur. quid tamen, si maritus uxori petitionem earum remiserit? eadem erit quaestio, an donatio sit illicita: et Iulianus hoc diceret: quod verum est. plane si convenerat, uti se mulier pasceret suosque homines <et> idcirco passus est eam dote sua frui, ut se suosque aleret, expeditum erit: puto enim non posse ab ea peti quasi donatum, quod compensatum est.

(Ulpian in the thirty-second book on Sabinus)

If a wife promised to her husband a dowry along with the interest on it, it must undoubtedly be held that he can claim the interest, since this is no gift because it is claimed in compensation for the burdens of marriage.

But what if the husband remits to his wife the claim for this? The same question will arise about whether it is an impermissible gift. Julian says that it is, correctly.

Obviously, if they had agreed that the wife support herself and her slaves, and he allowed her to use her dowry for the purpose of maintaining herself and her slaves, there will be no difficulty; for I do not think that a compensatory payment can be reclaimed from her as a gift.

1. Promises, Promises. At first sight, this Case is a bit confusing: the wife promises a dowry and the interest, but the husband wants to claim only the interest; why? In fact, arrangements of this sort are described as common and, at times, even implied by law (Papinian, D. 23.3.69 pr.). Paul (D. 23.4.12.1; a troubled text) states that in one form of these agreements, a woman promises to support herself with her own dowry, which her husband is not to claim from her while the marriage continues. This promise creates a dowry (e.g., if the marriage ends through the wife's death, the husband can then claim the dowry from her estate; see Case 81), but during the marriage the wife keeps the dowry capital in her own hands and uses it to maintain herself, independent of her husband. Is such an arrangement likely to solve some of the problems with the traditional law of dowry? In the present Case, a similar outcome is achieved: the husband is entitled to claim the interest on the dowry but can then remit the claim to his wife, and this remission is not regarded as a gift if, by prior agreement, the interest is to be used for her maintenance. Do you follow Ulpian's logic? Is it convincing? It is also possible for the wife's side to deliver only part of the dowry (Papinian, D. 24.3.42.2; Paul, D. 23.4.12.2).

2. Controversy. A woman promised a dowry to her husband-to-be in the following way: "When I die, a sum of money is owed to you as a dowry." Is this

promise valid? Julian says yes, noting that agreements of this type are common. Paul (D. 23.3.20), citing several other jurists, disagrees. He argues: "It is one thing to delay collection but quite another to stipulate from the outset for (collection at) a time when the marriage will not exist." What is it that the woman was probably trying to accomplish by promising her dowry in this way? Is it simply presupposed that she would retain the dowry and support herself from its income? How serious is the objection that Paul raises?

3. A Tangled Case. Lucius Titius promised to Gaius Seius a dowry of 100,000 for his daughter, but Titius and Seius agreed that Seius would not demand payment of the dowry during Titius's lifetime. Some time later, Seius was at fault for divorcing his wife, as a result of which he was obliged to repay her dowry to her (Case 83). Shortly thereafter, Titius died; his will appointed other persons as heirs and disinherited his daughter. Can Seius collect the dowry from Titius's heirs? What remedies does Seius's ex-wife have? This case is handled by Paul (D. 24.3.44.1).

4. Broken Promises. A father promised a dowry and agreed that he would support his daughter, evidently by retaining the dowry but paying her support out of it; but he then failed to carry out his agreement. Her husband, reasonably believing that his wife's father would pay for her support, lent her money to spend on necessities for herself and her slaves; and she also dipped into some household funds that had been entrusted to her. She then died. Because the dowry came from his wife's father, the husband is not entitled to claim it now (see Cases 30, 81). But can her husband at least demand that his father-in-law repay the money spent on his wife's support? For the answer, see Scaevola, D. 15.3.20 pr. and 21.

CASE 70: Diligence

D. 23.3.17 pr. (Paulus libro septimo ad Sabinum)

In rebus dotalibus virum praestare oportet tam dolum quam culpam, quia causa sua dotem accipit: sed etiam diligentiam praestabit, quam in suis rebus exhibet.

D. 24.3.24.5 (Ulpianus libro trigesimo tertio ad edictum)

Si maritus saevus in servos dotales fuit, videndum, an de hoc possit conveniri. et si quidem tantum in servos uxoris saevus fuit, constat eum teneri hoc nomine: si vero et in suos est natura talis, adhuc dicendum est immoderatam eius saevitiam hoc iudicio coercendam: quamvis enim diligentiam uxor eam demum ab eo exigat, quam rebus suis <adhib>et, nec plus possit, attamen saevitia, quae in propriis culpanda est, in alienis coercenda est, hoc est in dotalibus.

(Paul in the seventh book on Sabinus)

As to dowry property, the husband should be responsible for both his deliberate misconduct (*dolus*) and his fault (*culpa*), since he received the dowry for his own benefit; but he will also be responsible for the (level of) carefulness (*diligentia*) that he exercises for his own property.

(Ulpian in the thirty-third book on Sabinus)

If a husband acted brutally toward dowry slaves, let us examine whether he can be sued for this. If, indeed, he was cruel only to the wife's slaves, clearly he is liable on this account. But if he is naturally this way also to his own (slaves), it should still be held that his excessive brutality should be curbed by this legal remedy. For although his wife may require of him only the carefulness (*diligentia*) he uses for his own property, and no more, nonetheless a brutality that is blameworthy as to his own property must be curbed as to that of others, that is, the dowry.

1. Standards of Care. With regard to the dowry, the husband must exercise a fairly high level of care: not to harm it deliberately (through *dolus*) or carelessly (through *culpa*); the second standard is objective and requires him to exert the care of a reasonable person in preventing harm to the property. Paul justifies this level of care by claiming that "he received the dowry for his own benefit"; in what sense and to what extent is that true? On *culpa*, see also Case 89. This standard applies only to nonfungible property that is not received under appraisal (Case 36).

2. Pursuing a Promised Dowry. Forming a dowry often requires a husband-to-be to collect promises from potential dowry givers. What if the promisors renege? Is the husband liable to his wife if he does not bring suit against them? Ulpian, in a long discussion citing earlier juristic opinions and rescripts (D.

23.3.33), makes a distinction: If the promise came from the woman herself or from her father, the husband is not liable for failing to sue; "for no *iudex* will listen patiently to a woman's explanation of why he did not press her father to pay the dowry he promised from his own property, much less why her husband did not sue her." But if the promise came from a third party, the husband is liable for failing to collect from a promisor whose motives were not purely altruistic (e.g., if the third party promised money that he owes to the wife); but the husband need not press an altruistic promisor even when by doing so he could collect the amount promised. If the husband is bound to avoid fault and thus to exercise reasonable care in collecting the dowry, what do Ulpian's rules suggest about the extent to which he must go? What considerations must he balance? See also Julian, D. 24.3.30.1.

3. Carefulness. *Diligentia*, by contrast, is a subjective standard that requires the husband to protect the dowry property just as scrupulously as he does his own. This still higher standard was probably introduced in the early second century A.D. Is it based on the premise that a husband would normally be very careful with his own property? How successful is Ulpian's attempt to fend off the possible objection concerning a brutal husband? To what extent does Ulpian's application of the *diligentia* standard suggest that the dotal slaves are, or are not, the husband's property?

CASE 71: Necessary Expenses

D. 25.1.4 (Paulus libro trigesimo sexto ad edictum)

Et in totum id videtur necessariis impensis contineri, quod si a marito omissum sit, iudex tanti eum damnabit, quanti mulieris interfuerit eas impensas fieri. sed hoc differt, quod factarum ratio habetur, etsi res male gesta est, non factarum ita, si ob id res male gesta est: itaque si fulserit insulam ruentem eaque exusta sit, impensas consequitur, si non fecerit, deusta ea nihil praestabit.

(Paul in the thirty-sixth book on the Edict)

Necessary expenses are held to include everything for which, if the husband failed to do it, a judge will condemn him to pay the extent of his wife's interest in these expenses being made. But there is this difference: account is taken of outlays even if the matter turned out badly, but account is taken of outlays not made only if the matter turned out badly for this reason (i.e., because of the failure to make them). Thus, if he propped up a collapsing apartment block and it (then) burned down, he is compensated (for the attempted repair); (but) if he did not do this and it burned down, he will not be responsible.

Hypothetical Situation.

In Sempronia's dowry, there is an apartment building that is in dire need of structural support. Can Seius, Sempronia's husband, recover his expenses if he pays for the support and (a) the building remains standing; (b) the building collapses anyway; (c) the building remains standing but is then consumed by a catastrophic fire? Conversely, if Seius does not pay for the building's support, is he liable for his wife's interest if (a) the building remains standing; (b) the building then collapses because of the lack of support; (c) the building is then consumed by a catastrophic fire?

1. What's Necessary? On the basis of this passage, formulate a rule defining when the husband must spend money on the dowry property. Propping up a collapsing building was probably a traditional example of a necessary expense; compare *Tit. Ulp.* 6.15: "Necessary expenses are those where the dowry will lose value unless they are made, for example, if someone repairs a dilapidated building." What if the cost of propping up the building was more than the building was worth? From Cases 84 and 85, where necessary expenses are further discussed, we learn that the husband can offset necessary expenses against the value of the dowry; is he expected to use judgment about making such expenses, or can he just shift them all onto his wife?

2. Catastrophic Fire. The Case speaks of the building burning down. The Romans often treat fires as catastrophic events that human planning and effort cannot prevent. In Latin, this is *vis maior*, "higher force," similar to an "act of God": for example, "events to which resistance is impossible, such as the

deaths of slaves occurring without a person's intent or fault, incursions of brigands or enemies, ambushes of pirates, shipwreck, catastrophic fire (*incendium*), and flight by slaves not normally confined" (Gaius, D. 13.6.18 pr.). Even if the husband does not make necessary expenses on dowry property, he is not liable for the loss if the property is then destroyed by *vis maior;* the jurists apparently reason that the property would have been destroyed in any case. Is this position entirely convincing?

3. Cultivation and Preservation. Neratius, D. 25.1.16: "Above all, whatever expenses are incurred in order to harvest the fruits, although they are made also to cultivate and so are necessary not only to gather the fruits but also to preserve the property itself, (nonetheless) the husband pays them, and he has no deduction from the dowry on this account." Why was this exception made? On the fruits (*fructus*), see Case 67. Elsewhere Neratius explains (ibid. 15): "[A] husband should look after dowry property at his own expense. If it were otherwise, then the board given to dowry slaves, modest repairs of dowry buildings, and even the cultivation of land would lessen the dowry, since all these appear to be necessary expenses. But they are held to arise from the property itself, in such a way that you do not so much spend money on the property as you are held to profit less from it after these expenses are subtracted. It is not so easily determined in the abstract what expenses should be deducted from the dowry according to this distinction; but on a case-by-case basis they can be assessed from the kind and the extent of the expenses." How sharply can the usual expenses of operating a farm be distinguished from deductible necessary expenses? Does it seem likely, for instance, that the husband would be allowed to deduct payment of taxes on dowry property? See Paul, D. 25.1.13 (no).

CASE 72: Statutory Limits on a Husband's Power

Gaius, *Institutiones* 2.62–63

(62) Accidit aliquando, ut qui dominus sit, alienandae rei potestatem non habeat, et qui dominus non sit, alienare possit. (63) Nam dotale praedium maritus invita muliere per legem Iuliam prohibetur alienare, quamvis ipsius sit vel mancipatum ei dotis causa vel in iure cessum vel usucaptum. Quod quidem ius utrum ad Italica tantum praedia an etiam ad provincialia pertineat, dubitatur.

(Gaius in the second book of his *Institutes*)

(62) It sometimes happens that the owner of property does not have the power to alienate it, while a nonowner can alienate it. (63) For by the *lex Iulia* (on adultery), a husband is forbidden to alienate dowry land if his wife is unwilling, even though the property is his own either through mancipation to him for the dowry or through cession in court or usucapion. It is disputed whether this rule applies only to Italian land or also to provincial (land).

1. Alienating Land. For reasons that are not entirely clear, this exception was introduced by Augustus's adultery law of 18 B.C.; see also Paul, *Sent.* 2.21b.2. The exception is significant as the first major statutory restraint on the husband's free disposition of the dowry. The husband was not only forbidden to alienate Italian dowry land without his wife's consent but also could not use it as security even with her consent (Justinian, *Inst.* 2.8 pr., citing C. 5.13.1.15, from A.D. 530). What do you think was the likeliest reason for the original law? Justinian, in imposing even more sweeping restrictions on the husband's power (and thereby ending the dispute that Gaius mentions by including the provinces), says that Augustus had feared that female weakness (*sexus muliebris fragilitas*) would be played upon in order to waste their property. Misogyny aside (on which, see Chapter V.B.1–2), what point is he getting at? Papinian (D. 41.3.42) indicates that if, in contravention of the statute, a husband tried to sell dowry land, the sale was void.

2. Manumitting Slaves. Augustus's marriage legislation also prohibited the husband from manumitting dowry slaves without his wife's consent (D. 24.3.61–64). However, a nonconforming manumission is not void but only exposes him to liability if his wife continues to object. One aim of these statutes was evidently to encourage the husband to consult with his wife about important decisions concerning the dowry; see also Case 86. Why might this have been regarded as desirable?

3. Ownership of the Dowry. Incidentally, in this Case, Gaius makes clear what, for the most part, Justinianic sources leave obscure: that the husband usually acquires ownership of the dowry either through formal transfer of title from the bride's side (mancipation or cession in court) or through long-term possession (usucapion). See Case 66.

PART D

The End of Marriage

"Marriage is ended by divorce, death, captivity, or the enslavement otherwise occurring of either party." So writes Paul (D. 24.2.1). Divorce and the death of the husband or wife were in the Roman world, as they are today, far and away the most common reasons for a marriage ending. Captivity or enslavement, by contrast, are odd to us, but they cause the end of marriage because of the Roman theory of change of status (Case 1).

Divorce, as the Romans conceived it, is in some respects the reciprocal of marriage. The state did not intervene to regulate or even to register divorce, and there were no divorce courts as such because there was relatively little to settle. The spouses' property had remained separate during marriage, and so its division upon divorce was, in theory, easy. Further, custody of children was not an issue since as a rule they remained in their father's control (Case 49), although he could arrange for them to be brought up by their mother.

Under these circumstances, the law was able to tolerate what may seem to us an extraordinary casualness about divorce. Just as entering marriage was chiefly a matter of an objectively manifested agreement between husband and wife, so too, without much formality, divorce could be accomplished by either spouse at any time, through a simple process of terminating the "marital affection" upon which the continuity of the marriage depended. Still, practicality dictated that divorce require more than a mere mental act of renunciation; and the jurists toy with a requirement that the divorcing spouse must notify, or at least try to notify, the other party.

Although divorce itself was a simple process, major complications were introduced by dowries, which husbands (or their heirs) frequently had to surrender when marriages ended. Literary evidence suggests that the burden of returning a dowry was often oppressive, mainly because husbands found it hard to gather up and transfer appreciable capital. Further, the return of the dowry was complicated by the Roman tendency to treat this as an appropriate occasion for a complete financial settling between husband and wife. The consequence was the creation of numerous legal bases whereby the husband could "retain" portions of the dowry. For the most part, there is no evidence that such retentions are of statutory origin, and the jurists seem generally to have crystallized them out of long-standing judicial practice; doubtless, lawsuits over retentions were not uncommon. The retentions based on the husband's prior expenditures on the dowry raise particularly important questions about how Roman law preferred that husbands administer dowries.

CASE 73: Captured

D. 24.2.6 (Iulianus libro sexagesimo secundo Digestorum)

Uxores eorum, qui in hostium potestate<m> pervenerunt, possunt videri nuptarum locum retinere eo solo, quod alii temere nubere non possunt. et generaliter definiendum est, donec certum est maritum vivere in captivitate constitutum, nullam habere licentiam uxores eorum migrare ad aliud matrimonium, nisi mallent ipsae mulieres causam repudii praestare. sin autem in incerto est, an vivus apud hostes teneatur vel morte praeventus <sit>, tunc, si quinquennium a tempore captivitatis excesserit, licentiam habet mulier ad alias migrare nuptias, ita tamen, ut bona gratia dissolutum videatur pristinum matrimonium et unusquisque suum ius habeat imminutum: eodem iure et in marito in civitate degente et uxore captiva observando.

(Julian in the sixty-second book of his *Digests*)

Wives of men who fall into enemy hands can be deemed to remain married simply because they cannot rashly marry another man. And in general, so long as it is known that the husband survives in captivity, it should be ruled that their wives have no freedom to move to another marriage, unless the women themselves prefer to be responsible for the divorce.

But if it is uncertain whether he is held alive with enemies or has died, then if five years have elapsed from the start of captivity, the wife is free to move to another marriage, but in such a way that the first marriage is held to have been dissolved with goodwill on either side (*bona gratia*) and each party retains their rights unimpaired.

The same rule should be observed when the husband remains within our sovereignty and his wife is captive.

1. The Classical Rule? Paul (D. 24.2.1) states flatly that a marriage ends when a husband or wife is captured. Elsewhere, Paul holds that if a promise is made conditional on the promisee's wife "for some reason" no longer being married to him, this condition is met if she is captured by enemies (D. 24.3.56); and vice versa, "the wife of a captive, even if she devoutly wishes otherwise and lives in his house, is still not married" (Tryphoninus, D. 49.15.12.4). Therefore, if the captive returns, the marriage must be renewed by mutual consent (Pomponius, D. 49.15.14.1). This Case, however, imposes a five-year period during which, so long as it is uncertain that a captured spouse is still alive, the other spouse cannot remarry without being responsible for the end of the marriage (see Case 83). Very probably, however, Julian's original text has been rewritten by the compilers of Justinian's *Digest,* since we happen to know that Justinian enacted this rule himself (*Novellae* 22.7; A.D. 535-536). In all likelihood, the classical jurists held that the other spouse could remarry more or less immediately after a capture. Did Justinian improve on the classical rule?

2. **A Freedwoman's Plight.** When, as here, we have strong reason to believe that the text of a classical jurist has been altered by later editors, naturally it is impossible to say exactly what the original rule might have been. Still, sometimes we have a clue in other texts. For example, Ulpian (D. 23.2.45.6) reports on the situation where a freedwoman marries her patron, who is then captured. Can she remarry? As you will recall (Case 14), Roman law placed sharp limits on the ability of a freedwoman, once married to her patron, to remarry without the patron's consent. In the case of a captured patron, Ulpian takes the probable classical view that she can remarry, just as she could if her patron had died. But he also reports Julian's dissenting view that "a freedwoman's marriage continues even in (his) captivity because of the respect she owes a patron." Perhaps a text of this sort formed the basis for the rewriting that the compilers of the *Digest* undertook in this Case.

3. **When Both Spouses Are Captured.** The Roman Empire was surrounded by other peoples with whom the Romans interacted, often peacefully through trade but sometimes violently; and capture of free Romans was common enough that a substantial body of law developed around the problems of return from captivity (*postliminium*). Would former legal rights revive with the restoration of the captive to freedom? What about what had happened in the meantime? One particular problem arose from a situation in which both husband and wife were captured, and the wife then bore her husband a child; if the child later returned to the Empire (with or without the parents), was the child legitimate? Septimius Severus and Caracalla ruled in favor of the child's legitimacy, provided that he or she returned with at least the father (C. 8.50.1; A.D. 197-211; with Marcian, D. 49.15.25).

CASE 74: A Daughter Is Deported

D. 48.20.5.1 (Ulpianus libro trigensimo tertio ad edictum)

Quod si deportata sit filia familias, Marcellus ait, quae sententia et vera est, non utique deportatione dissolvi matrimonium: nam cum libera mulier remaneat, nihil prohibet et virum mariti affectionem et mulierem uxoris animum retinere. si igitur eo animo mulier fuerit, ut discedere a marito velit, ait Marcellus tunc patrem de dote acturum. sed si mater familias sit et interim constante matrimonio fuerit deportata, dotem penes maritum remanere: postea vero dissoluto matrimonio posse eam agere, quasi humanitatis intuitu hodie nata actione.

(Ulpian in the thirty-third book on the Edict)

But if a daughter-in-power is deported, Marcellus says, and his view is also correct, that the marriage is not at once dissolved by the deportation. For since the woman remains free, nothing stops both the man from retaining a husband's affection (*mariti affectio*) and the woman from intending to remain a wife (*uxoris animus*). So if the woman is of the view that she wishes to divorce her husband, Marcellus says that her father can then sue on the dowry. But if she is a *mater familias* and is deported while the marriage continues, the dowry stays with the husband; but afterward, when the marriage is dissolved, she can sue (for return of the dowry), and on grounds of kindness the action is treated as arising today.

1. Deportation. This criminal penalty involves perpetual banishment accompanied by seizure of all property, loss of Roman citizenship, and confinement to a definite place, but not loss of freedom. Deportees could hope only for imperial amnesty. Does it make sense to hold that a marriage can continue despite the near obliteration of a spouse's legal personality? Paul (D. 24.3.56) states that marriage ends with deportation, just as it would with captivity or enslavement. But others may have believed that the slim chance of amnesty made it worth holding that the marriage was not automatically dissolved—so, for instance, Ulpian, D. 24.1.13.1 (quite probably interpolated, however). Thus, a rescript attributed to the Emperor Alexander Severus (C. 5.17.1; A.D. 229) states: "Marriage is not dissolved by deportation . . . if the circumstances into which the husband fell do not alter the wife's affection (*uxoris adfectio*)." Which is the better solution? Does the answer depend, at least in part, on the importance that law attaches to the continuation of marriage as socially desirable?

2. "Grounds of Kindness." The meaning of the last sentence is not entirely clear, and later alteration of the wording is suspected; but evidently a *sui iuris* wife would have difficulty exercising her right to divorce while in captivity. The issue here is whether her rights to the dowry are protected until she re-

turns. In the wording as preserved, why does the fact that a woman is a *mater familias* result in her maintaining this much of her status after she is deported? Deportation is a serious punishment; women convicted of adultery, for instance, were not deported but only "relegated" (internally exiled), usually to an unpleasant place.

CASE 75: Free Divorce

C. 8.38.2 (Imp. Alexander A. Menophilo)

Libera matrimonia esse antiquitus placuit. ideoque pacta, ne liceret divertere, non valere et stipulationes, quibus poenae inrogarentur ei qui divortium fecisset, ratas non haberi constat.

(The Emperor Alexander to Menophilus; A.D. 223)

Long-standing tradition holds that marriages are free. So it is settled that agreements preventing divorce are invalid, and stipulations imposing penalties on the party who divorced are not considered licit.

1. The Freedom to Be Alone. Roman law continually emphasizes the right of parties to make and break marriages as they wish; compare Case 41 ("The Principle of Noninterference"). The parties are also not allowed to try to prevent divorce by obligating themselves for the future through penalty clauses. Why should this be so? Could it be argued that even if the state itself has no strong interest in keeping couples together against the will of one or both of them, individual couples should still be allowed to create and enforce lasting unions between themselves? More broadly, as a matter of logic or of public policy, does it necessarily follow that if marriage is "free" in the sense that its formation rests on a consensual basis, divorce must also be "free" in the sense that either party can end the marriage more or less at will? Do you agree with the following point (from Mireille Corbier, in Beryl Rawson, *Marriage, Divorce, and Children*): "The principle of the dissolubility of the matrimonial bond is a consequence of the consensual nature of marriage." Does the Emperor Alexander agree?

2. Capacity to Divorce. Under the Augustan marriage legislation, a freedwoman who married her ex-master was unable to marry someone else unless her patron first renounced his right to remain married to her (Case 14). The statute, however, did not prevent her, if she wished, from separating herself permanently from him, and thereby effectively divorcing him (Ulpian, D. 24.2.11 pr.). On the other hand, a spouse who goes mad is incapable of divorce (see ibid. 4, with Case 60), obviously because the required will is missing.

3. Fault. Although both parties have virtually unrestricted power to divorce, the notion of fault (*culpa*) is not missing from Roman law. A party who repudiates a marriage without cause, or who furnishes a just occasion for divorce by the other party, may lose valuable rights in relation to the dowry; see Case 83.

CASE 76: Divorce by Remarriage?

Cicero, *De Oratore* 1.183

Quid? quod usu memoria patrum venit, ut pater familias, qui ex Hispania Romam venisset, cum uxorem praegnantem in provincia reliquisset, Romaeque alteram duxisset neque nuntium priori remisisset, mortuusque esset intestato et ex utraque filius natus esset, mediocrisne res in contentionem adducta est, cum quaereretur de duobus civium capitibus et de puero, qui ex posteriore natus erat, et de eius matre, quae, si iudicaretur certis quibusdam verbis, non novis nuptiis fieri cum superiore divortium, in concubinae locum duceretur?

(Cicero in the first book of his *On the Public Speaker*)

In the memory of our fathers it happened that a *pater familias* left a pregnant wife in the province of Spain and moved from there to Rome, where he married another woman without sending notice (of divorce) to his first wife. He died intestate, leaving a son born from each woman. Was the matter at issue trivial when question (subsequently) arose about the civil standing of two persons: not only the boy born from the second woman but also his mother, who, if the verdict was that divorce from an earlier wife takes place (only) through some fixed form of words and not by means of a new marriage, was transformed into the equivalent of a concubine?

1. Is She His Wife? Cicero, the foremost orator of the late Roman Republic, is here recounting an actual legal case that arose probably during the second half of the second century B.C. The two sides can be imagined: as plaintiff, the son by the second wife (if she is a wife), seeking legitimacy and half his father's estate; as defendant, the son by the first wife, trying to succeed his father as sole heir. Is it fair to deduce from the tone of Cicero's narrative that the son of the second wife probably won his lawsuit? What was the legal issue in this trial? Cicero says that the lawsuit caused intense debate among the jurists (*De Or.* 1.238). Presumably, some jurists believed that the man could not divorce his Spanish wife without "some fixed form of words," which would have formalized his intent to divorce and also, in most cases, have given notice to his spouse. But what did the opposing jurists believe? That there were no formal requirements whatsoever for divorce? Or, more moderately, that a unilateral act or declaration clearly inconsistent with a marriage is sufficient to end that marriage even when no attempt is made to notify the affected spouse (see Case 78)? Or what? In their view, was the new marriage only a proof that divorce had occurred, or did it actually bring about the divorce?

2. Bigamy? Would the situation be different if the man had shuttled back and forth between his two households in Rome and Spain? Yes, since that would clearly be bigamy (see the Discussion on Case 11), and the second marriage would then be void.

3. Is She an Adulteress? A woman heard that her absent husband had died. She married another man, and her first husband then returned. This case, which again appears to be a real one, is discussed by Papinian (D. 48.5.12.12), who says that if the woman was genuinely deceived, something that should be determined from her behavior, then she did nothing wrong; but if she simply took advantage of a rumor because she wanted to remarry, then she should be punished, apparently as an adulteress. This decision would seem to indicate that, in the eyes of the law, she remained married to her first husband both before and after she remarried. Papinian was active in the late second century A.D., at least three centuries after the lawsuit described by Cicero. How much had Roman law changed in the intervening period? Does it seem likely to you that the *lex Iulia* on adultery could have caused some of this change?

4. A Home Wrecker. A married woman was on a trip when she met a man who took her into his house as his wife and then sent a repudiation (notice of divorce) to her husband. According to Papinian (D. 24.2.8), the Emperor Hadrian (reign: A.D. 117-138) condemned the man to relegation for three years. What was his offense: bigamy, adultery, neither, or both?

CASE 77: The Mental Element

D. 24.2.3 (Paulus libro trigesimo quinto ad edictum) (= D. 50.17.48 in part)

Divortium non est nisi verum, quod animo perpetuam constituendi dis<c>ensionem fit. itaque quidquid in calore iracundiae vel fit vel dicitur, non prius ratum est, quam si perseverantia apparuit iudicium animi fuisse: ideoque per calorem misso repudio si brevi reversa uxor est, nec divortisse videtur.

(Paul in the thirty-fifth book on the Edict)

Divorce does not take place unless it is genuine, made with the intent of establishing a permanent separation. So something that is either done or said in the heat of anger is not confirmed until, because of its persistence, it was clear that a mental judgment occurred. Therefore, if a wife sent a repudiation in anger but soon thereafter returned (to her husband), she is held not to have divorced.

1. Is It Final This Time? This Case, like many others, insists on the importance of at least one spouse having a deeply felt intent to divorce. In Paul's opinion, is the intent to establish "a permanent separation" only a necessary condition for divorce or also a sufficient one? That is, once a spouse manifests such an intent, does the divorce occur automatically or is something more, such as actual physical separation, also required? The jurists have some difficulty distinguishing transient quarrels from genuine repudiations. Where a couple separates and then reunites, Marcellus (D. 23.2.33) rules that this is "the same marriage" if not too much time has elapsed, if neither party has remarried someone else, and above all if the dowry has not been returned. Does this suggest that he is trying to measure depth of intent from subsequent acts? If so, would even the most absolute and harshly worded repudiation necessarily be enough in itself to bring about a divorce?

2. Reconciliation Gifts. A man gave gifts to his divorced wife in order to induce her to return; she did so but then divorced him again. Can she keep the gifts? According to Javolenus (D. 24.1.64; disputed text), early imperial jurists were divided. Some thought that the gifts were valid if the first divorce was genuine but invalid if it was a sham (why might this be suspected?). Others thought that the first divorce was valid and the gifts unreclaimable only if she did not marry a third party or if she remained unmarried for long enough that it was clear that her first marriage had been dissolved; otherwise, the gifts were ineffectual. How do these two approaches differ in interpreting the situation? Which approach seems more plausible? On either approach, does it seem likely that in some situations it would be unclear to external observers, and perhaps also to one or both of the spouses, whether a divorce had actually occurred?

3. Maecenas and Terentia. The rule in this Case was invoked in a famous instance of suspected false divorce, that between Maecenas (a wealthy advisor to the Emperor Augustus) and his wife Terentia; see Javolenus, D. 24.1.64.

CASE 78: Formal Requirements?

D. 24.2.2.1, 3 (Gaius libro undecimo ad edictum provinciale)

(1) In repudiis autem, id est <in> renuntiatione comprobata sunt haec verba: "tuas res tibi habeto," item haec: "tuas res tibi agito." . . . (3) Sive autem ipsi praesenti renuntietur sive absenti per eum, qui in potestate eius sit cuiusve is eave in potestate sit, nihil interest.

D. 24.2.9 (Paulus libro secundo de Adulteriis)

Nullum divortium ratum est nisi septem civibus Romanis puberibus adhibitis praeter libertum eius qui divortium faciet. libertum accipiemus etiam eum, qui a patre avo proavo et ceteris susum versum manumissus sit.

(Gaius in the eleventh book on the Provincial Edict)

(1) In repudiations, that is, in the renunciation (of marriage), these are the accepted words: "Have your own property." Likewise, "Take care of your own property." . . .
   (3) It makes no difference whether renunciation is made to the other party while he or she is present or while absent through a person who is in that party's power or in whose power he or she is.

(Paul in the second book *On Adulteries*)

No divorce is confirmed unless seven adult Roman citizens have been summoned, as well as a freedman of the person who is going to divorce. By "freedman," we will understand also a person manumitted by his father, grandfather, great-grandfather, and other male descendants or ascendants.

1. "Some Fixed Form of Words." In Case 76, the second son of the man from Spain was in legal hot water because his father had not used a specific formula to repudiate his first wife. The phrases that Gaius recommends in this Case are widely attested elsewhere and were traditional. Gaius says these phrases are "accepted"; does he also mean that they, or some close variant, were required for a valid divorce? Legal sources apparently do not go that far. When the two parties are apart, it was usually enough for one to send to the other an unambiguous repudiation: *remittere nuntium* or the like. Although sometimes it appears that a messenger carried the repudiation orally, more often it is fairly obvious that it was written. But when the couple are living together in the husband's house, the husband is frequently described as simply "expelling his wife from the house" (*expellere uxorem domo:* Ulpian, D. 25.2.11 pr., who also envisages the reverse situation) or "sending his wife away" (*dimittere uxorem:* e.g., Paul, *Coll.* 4.3.5, 4.12.5 and 7), without any indication that a specific formula was first used or indeed that anything whatsoever was done beyond the application of raw force. Even in a society where divorce

does not involve oversight by governmental institutions, what factors militate for and against requiring some sort of specific formula?

2. **Seven Witnesses.** This passage from Paul is the only classical source describing a considerably more formal process: the summoning of seven qualified witnesses, before whom a declaration of intent to divorce is evidently recited. Despite the universal language in which Paul's rule is couched ("No divorce is confirmed unless . . ."), he is writing about the *lex Iulia de adulteriis*, the adultery law, and this may be significant. The adultery law, it will be recalled, very strongly encouraged a husband who discovered his wife in adultery to divorce her (Case 53), and in consequence a clear, legally conclusive mechanism for effecting divorce was urgently required; it may well be that the ceremony described by Paul was statutorily created to serve such a purpose. Is a narrow interpretation of the passage supported by the requirement that a freedman of the divorcing party be present? (The freedman was presumably charged to deliver news of the renunciation to the other spouse.) See also Ulpian, D. 38.11.1.1: "The *lex Iulia de adulteriis* treats a divorce as ineffective unless it was made in a specific way." Does this refer to all divorces or (perhaps more plausibly) just to those occurring in the immediate context of the adultery statute? A few other sources mention required ceremonies; of these, the strongest is Ulpian, D. 24.1.35: "If a divorce was not made in accord with the statutory protocol (*secundum legitimam observationem*), gifts made after such a divorce are void since the marriage is not held to be dissolved." However, it is unclear what "protocol" Ulpian refers to.

3. **Must Notice Be Served?** Must the other party receive, or at least know of, the repudiation? The Gaius fragment suggests not, at least to the extent that a divorce seems to occur when just the affected party's *pater familias* is notified. Still more to the point is Ulpian, D. 24.2.4: in dealing with the case of a wife who goes mad, Ulpian follows Julian in holding that "a mad woman can be repudiated because her position is analogous to that of a person unaware (of the repudiation)." But if the other party does not need to receive the repudiation, what purpose would it serve? Simply to indicate the firm intent of the divorcing spouse? See also Ulpian, D. 23.2.45.5; Diocletian and Maximian, C. 5.17.6 (A.D. 294): "Even though the repudiation document is neither handed over nor known to the husband, the marriage is dissolved." Is this related to the Roman principle of unilateral divorce?

4. **At Least Try to Give Notice?** In the parallel case of renouncing a betrothal (see Case 28), the Emperors Valerian and Gallienus held (C. 5.17.2; A.D. 259): "If your daughter's betrothed has been away traveling for three years, and she thinks there is no point in waiting longer, she is free to abandon hope of this union and to marry (another man) so as not to lose the opportunity of mar-

riage; for while he was present, she could have given him notice if she had wished to change her mind." Are the emperors saying that notice would normally be given? If this is true in the case of betrothal, would it also be true for marriage?

5. Changing Your Mind. Papinian (D. 24.2.7) describes a man who sent a written repudiation but then changed his mind before the letter was delivered. What is the outcome? The marriage continues, holds Papinian, "unless the recipient knew of the change of mind and (nonetheless) wished to dissolve the marriage; for then the marriage was dissolved by the recipient." What does this suggest about the legal nature of a written repudiation? If the recipient did not know of the sender's change of mind but went forward on the assumption that the marriage was over, would the recipient then be responsible for causing a divorce?

CASE 79: Free-Form Divorce

Fragmenta Vaticana 106-107 (Paulus libro octavo Responsorum)

(106) Convenit in pacto dotali, ut divortio facto sextae liberorum nomine retiner-
entur: quaero, an discidio interveniente sextae retineri possint. Paulus respondit
secundum ea quae proponuntur posse. (107) Item quaesitum est, si vir repudium
misit et eandem reduxit eaque mulier absente viro de domo eius discesserit, an
aeque sextae retineri possint ex priore pacto. Paulus respondit, si verum divortium
intercessit et ad eundem rursum reversa non renovato pacto manente dote divortit,
sextas liberorum nomine ita demum retineri posse, si culpa mulieris divortium
intercessit.

(Paul in the eighth book of his *Responses*)

(106) In a dowry agreement the parties arranged that in the event of divorce, a
sixth (of the dowry) be retained for each child. I ask whether sixths can be retained when a separation (*discidium*) has occurred. Paul responded that on the
facts proposed, they can.

(107) Again, it was asked whether sixths can be retained on the basis of the
earlier agreement if a man sent a repudiation and (then) remarried the same
woman, and this woman, while her husband was away, departed from his home.
Paul responded that if, after a true divorce, she returned again to the same man
without renewing the agreement but leaving the dowry (itself) still in place, and
she (then) divorced (a second time), sixths can be retained for each child only if
the divorce occurred because of the wife's fault (*culpa*).

1. Is Separation Divorce? In section 106, the specific legal problem is the en-
forceability of the dowry agreement. One issue that may be relevant is
whether a separation (*discidium*) amounts to the "divorce" required in the
agreement; but Paul seems to have no difficulty on this score, and in other
legal texts *discidium* is commonly treated as a synonym for "divorce" (e.g., Papinian, D. 48.5.12.13; Paul, D. 49.15.8). But are we then to conclude that in
Roman law divorce is essentially identical with a prolonged separation, so
long as the requisite mental intent to divorce is present? Reread Case 17,
which deals with a husband and wife who have long been separated but ex-
hibit reciprocal marital affection; they are held to be still married. But in their
case, why would the question of divorce have even come up, unless separation itself was regarded as one leading indicator that a divorce had occurred?
That is, could separation play much the same role in proving divorce that *deductio* might play in proving marriage (Case 20)? In sum, are we perhaps justified in thinking of Roman divorce, like Roman marriage, as less an event
than a process? (In the end, the separation issue is probably not of great significance in section 106 of this Case; Paul's main concern is that the agree-

ment provides for surrender of one-sixth of the dowry for each child, without regard to which party is at fault for causing the divorce. See below.)

2. Departing from the Home. In section 107, the legal problem changes: the husband sent a repudiation, but the couple were then reconciled and remarried, and the dowry from the first marriage was brought over into the second (quite common, and favored by law: Paul, D. 23.3.30). There were two distinct marriages (Paul rules out the possibility of a sham divorce; see Case 77), so the remaining issue is whether, when the wife subsequently leaves her husband, her agreement from the first marriage also survived into the second. Paul concludes that since the agreement was not independently renewed, it does not survive, and that the husband can therefore retain sixths for the children only if his wife was responsible for the second divorce (see Case 82). But what is extraordinary about section 107 is not this relatively perfunctory legal analysis but the description of the second divorce: while the husband is absent, the wife simply packs her bags and leaves, apparently without any effort to notify her husband of her intentions. Yet Paul unhesitatingly describes this as a divorce, and he does not seem troubled by this aspect of the Case. Should he be?

3. Where Do We Go from Here? Try to sum up the position of the classical jurists on the issue of divorce. If you were a lawyer in Rome, how would you advise a client who inquired about the most effective way to go about divorcing a spouse? What difficulties would you warn the client of? It was not until the mid–fifth century A.D. that written notice of a repudiation clearly came to be required in Roman law. See, for instance, C. 5.17.8 pr. (Theodosius and Valentinian; A.D. 449): "We ordain that while lawful marriages can be formed by agreement (*consensus*), once contracted they are not dissolved unless a repudiation is sent. Because we favor the children, dissolution of marriage should be more difficult (than entry into marriage)." Is Christian influence necessarily the only, or even the best, explanation for such an innovation? Apart from Christian views of marriage, does it seem reasonable to hold that more is at stake in a divorce than just the immediate desires of husband and wife? In general, postclassical law, starting with Constantine (*C. Th.* 3.16.1; A.D. 331), is extremely hostile to unilateral divorce but is far more tolerant of consensual divorce. To what extent is there a different societal stake in these two ways of divorcing?

CASE 80: Amicable Divorce

D. 24.1.60.1 (Hermogenianus libro secundo Iuris Epitomarum)

Divortii causa donationes inter virum et uxorem concessae sunt: saepe enim evenit, uti propter sacerdotium vel etiam sterilitatem

D. 24.1.61 (Gaius libro undecimo ad edictum provinciale)

vel senectutem aut valetudinem aut militiam satis commode retineri matrimonium non possit:

D. 24.1.62 pr. (Hermogenianus libro secundo Iuris Epitomarum)

et ideo bona gratia matrimonium dissolvitur.

(Hermogenianus in the second book of his *Epitome of Law*)

Gifts are permitted between husband and wife on account of divorce (*divortii causa*). For it often happens that because of a priesthood or also infertility

(Gaius in the eleventh book on the Provincial Edict)

or old age or health or military service, a marriage is just too hard to continue;

(Hermogenianus in the second book of his *Epitome of Law*)

and so the marriage is dissolved with goodwill on either side (*bona gratia*).

1. Divorce Gifts?! As the jurists recognized (Ulpian, D. 24.1.32.10), not all marriages end in bitterness. Hermogenianus (an early postclassical jurist) and Gaius list several reasons why couples might amicably agree to divorce. Incompatibility, a favorite modern theme, does not figure on their list but perhaps underlies some items on the list. The decision by the jurists to permit gifts *divortii causa* is not so innocent as it seems, since such gifts might often be made to induce the other party to consent to a friendly divorce; that way, neither husband nor wife ran the risk of being held at fault for the divorce, a finding that could have consequences for the return of the wife's dowry (Case 83). Perhaps considering this possibility, Paul (D. 24.1.12) holds that gifts in consideration of divorce are valid only when made at the time of the divorce, not in contemplation of a future divorce. Is this enough to prevent the potential bad effects of such gifts?

2. Was the Roman Law Moral? Evaluate the following: "Conscious of the true limits of law as were the Roman lawyers, . . . they realized that it is beyond the strength of law to preserve matrimony against the will of the spouses, since law can never compel them to live peacefully together. Law can maintain matrimony in the legal sense, but neither morality nor the community is in the least interested in the existence of a mere legal marriage" (Fritz Schulz).

CASE 81: A Wife Dies

Tituli ex Corpore Ulpiani 6.4-5

(4) Mortua in matrimonio muliere dos a patre profecta ad patrem revertitur, quintis in singulos liberos in infinitum relictis penes virum. quod si pater non sit, apud maritum remanet. (5) Adventicia autem dos semper penes maritum remanet, praeterquam si is qui dedit, ut sibi redderetur, stipulatus fuerit: quae dos specialiter recepticia dicitur.

(*Excerpts from Ulpian's Writings*)

(4) When a wife dies during marriage, a dowry that came from her father returns to her father, but her husband keeps one-fifth for each child no matter how many. If the father is no longer alive, it (all) stays with the husband. (5) An "adventitious" dowry (*adventicia dos*) always stays with the husband unless the giver stipulated that it be returned to him; this form of dowry has the technical name "retained" (*recepticia*).

1. Profectitious versus Adventitious. Reread Case 30. Though the vocabulary is unfamiliar, the basic distinction here is not difficult. (1) In the typical case, a profectitious dowry deriving from the wife's father or paternal grandfather (whether or not she was still in his power) is given special treatment in that the giver can reclaim it when the marriage ends through the wife's death; the husband can, however, deduct a fifth for each (surviving?) child (with possible deductions as well for other things; see below). (2) In all other cases, including when the wife gave her own dowry, the dowry is adventitious, and the wife's death results in the entire dowry remaining with the husband, unless the giver had expressly arranged for its return. If the giver of a profectitious dowry dies before the wife, the dowry is treated as adventitious.

2. Why the Distinction? These are the rules. Much harder to explain is the reason for them. The default rule, as it appears (although this could be varied by agreement: *Tit. Ulp.* 6.5), is that the husband keeps the dowry when the marriage ends through his wife's death. First of all, why should this be true? Second, if the exception from the default rule in favor of the wife's present or former *pater familias* can be explained as an effort to encourage dowry giving within the household, what is the significance of the husband's deductions for their children? The most important problem here is to determine what legal or social functions the dowry is serving, or being made to serve, beyond its somewhat feeble role in providing the wife with maintenance during the marriage.

3. Uxoricide. Do the rules in this Case apply if a husband murders his wife? Most emphatically not! See Pomponius, D. 24.3.10.1: "It is not fair that the husband should expect to profit from the dowry through his crime." And so

too, it should be said, for the reverse situation. This is not a trivial issue; in some parts of the modern world where dowry is still common, husbands have allegedly killed their wives, or vice versa, to gain control of the dowry.

4. And If the Husband Dies First? Here the default rule is the exact reverse: in principle, the entire dowry returns to the wife (or to her *pater familias*) when the marriage ends through the husband's death. The claim lies against the husband's heir, who can make many of the normal retentions from the dowry but not that for immorality on the part of the wife (Paul, D. 24.3.15.1; why?). There is also no retention for children, and agreements between the parties to modify that rule are void (see, e.g., Ulpian, D. 23.4.2, 33.4.1.1). Do these rules help to clarify the general pattern?

5. Reclaiming the Dowry. It is important to note that even where the husband is obliged, at the end of marriage, to surrender the dowry, the dowry property does not automatically revert from his ownership. Instead, in the typical case, the couple had to reach agreement on his voluntary surrender of the dowry; and if this failed, then the wife had to sue for it. The relevant lawsuit is called "the action on a wife's property" (*actio rei uxoriae*). The model formula for this action—the instructions to the *iudex* in the case—has been reconstructed as follows: "If it appears that the defendant ought to return the dowry or a part of it to the plaintiff, let the *iudex* condemn the defendant to pay the plaintiff the portion of it that is better and fairer; if this does not appear, let him absolve him." Of particular importance is the phrase "better and fairer" (*aequius melius*), meaning that it is found to be "better and fairer" that the wife receive this portion rather than that her husband keep it. The jurists describe this action as a *bona fides* trial: in arriving at a judgment, the *iudex* can take into account all legitimate claims and counterclaims of the two parties (Gaius, *Inst.* 4.62-63). Such an open-ended format provides the legal basis for granting the various retentions discussed in the following Cases and also for many other rules governing how husbands administered dowries. In suing for recovery of dowry, an ex-wife enjoys privileged status over other unsecured creditors of her husband or of his estate; see Ulpian and Paul, D. 42.5.17.1-19 pr.

6. "What He Can Provide." Husbands often found it difficult to return dowries, presumably because they had a hard time laying their hands on so much capital. If the dowry was in money, they were usually permitted to repay in three annual installments rather than all at once (*Tit. Ulp.* 6.8). One unexpected implication that the jurists drew from the phrase "better and fairer" is that, even ignoring retentions, a husband was not necessarily obliged to return the entire dowry. As Ulpian puts it (D. 24.3.12): "The recognized rule is that a husband is condemned for what he can provide," meaning that if the husband has limited means, a *iudex* should lower the amount he has to return. This

rule points to the difficulties many husbands had in returning a large sum of dowry capital; but is it fair to the wife? What if the husband's own actions have rendered him insolvent? Pomponius (D. 24.3.18.1) holds that even if the husband was careless, the award should still be lowered unless he acted with malicious intent (*dolus*) to squander the dowry.

CASE 82: Divorce and the Dowry

Tituli ex Corpore Ulpiani 6.6-7

(6) Divortio facto, si quidem sui iuris sit mulier, ipsa habet rei uxoriae actionem, id est dotis repetitionem. quod si in potestate patris sit, pater adiuncta filiae persona habet actionem rei uxoriae: nec interest, adventicia sit dos an profecticia. (7) Post divortium defuncta muliere heredi eius actio non aliter datur, quam si moram in dote mulieri reddenda maritus fecerit.

(*Excerpts from Ulpian's Writings*)

(6) After a divorce, a wife herself, if she is *sui iuris,* has the action on a wife's property (*actio rei uxoriae*), that is, a claim for return of the dowry. But if she is in a father's power, the father, accompanied by the daughter, has the action on a wife's property; it does not matter whether the dowry is adventitious or profectitious. (7) If the wife dies after the divorce, her heir is given the action only if her husband has delayed in returning the dowry to the wife.

1. The Wife Sues. Although this Case states the law correctly, one thing it does not adequately emphasize is that, no matter the form of the dowry, after a divorce the wife is the primary plaintiff. This point is explained by Ulpian (D. 24.3.2.1): where the woman is in the power of a *pater familias,* the dowry is thought of as belonging to them jointly, so that her father cannot sue for it without obtaining her consent. However, by a rescript of Caracalla, it was decided that her consent should be presumed unless she knew of the lawsuit and actively opposed it. As Ulpian says (ibid. 2): "If the daughter is not present, we must hold that this (the lawsuit) is not brought in accord with her will, and the father must provide security that she will ratify it; for if she is sane, we require that she know (of the proceeding) so that she not appear to oppose it." Why might a wife be unwilling to sue her ex-husband over the dowry?

2. The Wife Delays in Suing. Pomponius, D. 24.3.9: "If the wife has delayed in recovering the dowry, her husband should be liable only for deliberate misconduct (*dolus malus*), not also for (unintentional) fault (*culpa*), so that he not be forced by his wife's act to cultivate her land in perpetuity. But the fruits that he acquires are returned (to her)." Here the husband is holding dowry property to which his former wife is now entitled; her failure to act in a timely fashion (called *mora,* "delay," in Roman law) results, not in her losing her rights through waiver, but rather in her suffering the "penalty" of his reduced duty of care for the property. Is this the best way to handle a situation of this kind? Does it make sense that the husband should no longer be liable for carelessness that results in harm to the property? Does the rule provide sufficient incentive for a woman to act quickly in reclaiming her dowry?

CASE 83: Retention on Moral Grounds

Tituli ex Corpore Ulpiani 6.9-10, 12-13

(9) Retentiones ex dote fiunt aut propter liberos aut propter mores aut propter impensas aut propter res donatas aut propter res amotas. (10) Propter liberos retentio fit, si culpa mulieris aut patris cuius in potestate est divortium factum sit: tunc enim singulorum liberorum nomine sextae retinentur ex dote, non plures tamen quam tres. . . . (12) Morum nomine graviorum quidem sexta retinetur, leviorum autem octava. graviores mores sunt adulteria tantum, leviores omnes reliqui. (13) Mariti mores puniuntur in ea quidem dote, quae a die reddi debet, ita ut propter maiores mores praesentem dotem reddat, propter minores senum mensum die. in ea autem, quae praesens reddi solet, tantum ex fructibus iubetur reddere, quantum in illa dote quae triennio redditur repraesentatio facit.

(Excerpts from Ulpian's Writings)

(9) Retentions from a dowry occur (for five reasons:) either because of children, because of morality, because of expenses, because of gifts, or because of removal of property. (10) Retention occurs because of children if the divorce came about through the wife's fault (*culpa*) or that of the father in whose power she was; for then a sixth is retained from the dowry for each child up to a maximum of three. . . .

(12) On the basis of serious immorality a sixth is retained, but an eighth for less serious instances. Only adultery counts as serious immorality; all the rest is less serious. (13) The husband's immorality is punished in the case of a dowry that must be returned from a (given) day, as follows: for serious immorality he returns the dowry at once; for less serious, in six months' time. In the case of a dowry that should be returned at once, he is ordered to return from the fruits as much as the payment made for a dowry returned over three years.

1. Fault (*Culpa*). Classical divorce itself was fault free, in the sense that no allegation of misconduct was required in order to effect a divorce. Things were different when it came to reclaiming the dowry, at any rate if there were children. The rule stated in (10) somewhat resembles that in Case 79: if the divorce occurs because of the wife's fault (*culpa*), the husband is allowed to retain a sixth of the dowry for each child; but this Case sets an upper limit of one-half the dowry (so also Paul, in Boethius's commentary *Ad Ciceronis Topica* 19). These sources do not refer to the husband's fault, which was evidently irrelevant in this context, except perhaps if both parties were held to be at fault. The reason for the rule is hard to make out, although it seems unconnected to the welfare of the children (who would normally remain under the husband's power in any case; see Case 49); a parallel rule is used for a dowry coming from the wife's *pater familias* (see Case 81). Perhaps the rationale was that the wife, in seeking return of her dowry, had "dirty hands" if she was re-

sponsible for the marriage ending. Can you see other possible explanations for shifting the costs of child rearing onto the ex-wife? In general, to what extent are the rules on dowry retentions likely to limit the unrestricted freedom to divorce?

2. **What Is Fault?** Classical sources are unclear on this point, although the spouse who initiates the divorce is not necessarily the one at fault (see, on this, Cicero, *Top.* 19, who otherwise misstates the rule); but perhaps this spouse usually bore the burden of proof. Doubtless, neither party is at fault when a divorce is amicable (Case 80). Some clue as to possible legitimate grounds for divorce may be had from late imperial legislation, which, under Christian influence, restricted divorce itself. According to the most complete list (Theodosius and Valentinian, C. 5.17.8; A.D. 449), one spouse could justify divorce if the other was convicted of a major crime (treason, kidnapping, etc.) or had betrayed the marriage in a specified way (adultery and attempted murder for both spouses; for a husband, wife beating or openly consorting with prostitutes; for a wife, licentious behavior). This list may at least suggest the flavor of classical law. Remarkable is the absence of alleged financial misconduct, especially by the husband with regard to the dowry. Further, desertion, mental cruelty, and mutual incompatibility, those familiar modern standbys, are also missing, unless perhaps they are implicit in other categories. On the other hand, Ulpian (D. 24.3.22.7) holds that a husband who divorces an insane wife is at fault for ending the marriage unless her insanity is "so savage and dangerous that there is no chance of recovery."

3. **Retention for Immorality.** At least serious immorality would surely be a justification for the other spouse to initiate divorce. However, as this Case makes clear, retention on the basis of immorality was separate and cumulative (since otherwise a childless but offending wife would escape without penalty); that is, the husband retained separate fractions on the basis of the wife's immorality and because of children if she had caused the divorce. By contrast, the wife who proves her husband's immorality receives only accelerated repayment. Where both spouses have grounds for repudiation because of each other's immoral conduct, their offenses are offset (Papinian, D. 24.3.39) and no retention is allowed; and so too, if the husband instigates his wife's adultery (Scaevola, D. 24.3.47). Are these legal proceedings likely to be messy? Only the husband or his *pater familias* is entitled to a retention for immorality; his heirs are not (Paul, D. 24.3.15.1). Further, the retention was probably available only while the wife was still alive (Constantius and Constans, *C.Th.* 3.13.1; A.D. 349). What might explain these limitations?

4. **The Action on Immorality.** In classical law, when a husband was sued for return of the dowry, he could assert his right to retain because of his wife's im-

morality. An older procedural form, called the *iudicium de moribus* (trial on morality), allowed the husband to sue his wife directly on a charge of immorality. Justinian (C. 5.17.11.2b; A.D. 533), describing the procedure as uncommon, abolished it; for this reason it is poorly known, although it could result in a woman's forfeiting part or all of her dowry.

5. Other Retentions. This Case also mentions retentions from the dowry to offset improper gifts (see Cases 61-65) and "removal of property" (see Case 45). In both instances separate lawsuits were also available, even where there was no dowry (Pomponius, D. 25.2.8 pr.). Of course, the wife could use these lawsuits against her husband as well.

CASE 84: Retaining Necessary Expenses

D. 25.1.1.3 (Ulpianus libro trigesimo sexto ad Sabinum)

Inter necessarias impensas esse Labeo ait moles in mare vel flumen proiectas. sed et si pistrinum vel horreum necessario factum sit, in necessariis impensis habendum ait. proinde Fulcinius inquit, si aedificium ruens quod habere mulieri utile erat refecerit, aut si oliveta reiecta restauraverit, vel ex stipulatione damni infecti ne committatur praestiterit,

D. 25.1.2 (Paulus libro septimo ad Sabinum)

vel in valetudinem servorum impenderit,

D. 25.1.3 pr. (Ulpianus libro trigesimo sexto ad Sabinum)

vel si vites propagaverit vel arbores curaverit vel seminaria pro utilitate agri fecerit, necessarias inpensas fecisse videbitur.

(Ulpian in the thirty-sixth book on Sabinus)

Labeo says that necessary expenses include jetties built out into the sea or a river. But also if it was necessary to build a mill or a storehouse, he says this should be treated as a necessary expense. So Fulcinius says that if he repairs a collapsing building that it was useful for his wife to have, or if he brought abandoned olive orchards back into cultivation, or he paid (something) on the basis of a stipulation against causing threatened loss,

(Paul in the seventh book on Sabinus)

or he spent (money) on the health of slaves,

(Ulpian in the thirty-sixth book on Sabinus)

or if he planted vines or cared for trees or made plant nurseries of use to the farm, he is held to have made necessary expenses.

1. What's Necessary? In Case 71, necessary expenses were described as those that the husband had to make in order to prevent the dowry from losing value. Do all the examples that are mentioned in this Case strike you as falling into that category? For example, when is it "necessary to build a mill or a storehouse" or to bring "abandoned olive orchards back into cultivation"? Wouldn't these normally be thought of as long-term capital improvements rather than emergency expenses? With this Case, compare Paul, D. 25.1.12: "An arbiter (in settling a lawsuit over return of dowry) should not bother about moderate expenses on constructing buildings, on replanting and cultivating vines, and on the health of slaves. Otherwise, the trial will seem to be on administration of affairs rather than on dowry." Paul's point is that the husband is not accurately described as administering the dowry on behalf of his

wife, since he himself derives a profit from it and hence must pay for its up-keep. Can a rule be devised for separating ordinary operating expenses from "necessary" ones?

2. Ransoming the Wife's Relatives. If a husband uses dowry money in order to pay ransom to bandits who are holding one of his wife's relations, is this payment a necessary expense? See Ulpian, D. 24.3.21 (yes). "Relations" are *necessarii*, persons closely connected by ties of friendship or family. Would you have expected Ulpian's ruling, granted the definition of "necessary expense" used in this Case? What if the ransom payment is as large as the entire value of the dowry?

3. Paying for the Wife's Funeral. Proculus (D. 24.3.60) considers the following case: A wife was still in the power of her father, who had provided her with a dowry. She died, and her father paid for her funeral. Can he seek compensation from her husband? Proculus says yes; indeed, he can sue immediately, even though the husband still has time left before he has to repay the dowry to the father. This source clearly indicates that the husband was legally obliged to pay for his wife's funeral; but why? If the husband had no duty to maintain his wife during her lifetime (Case 60), why should he have an obligation to bury her? Should the funeral expenses be thought of as "necessary expenses," such that the husband is liable via the dowry if he fails to make them (Case 71)? (Paul, *Sent.* 1.21.11, seems to take this line: "A husband can retain from the dowry what he spends on his wife's funeral.") What if the husband objects that his father-in-law's outlays were extravagant? Eventually, a fairly elaborate law developed around this subject (D. 11.7.16-20, 22-30, 46.1). If the wife had no dowry, or if her husband had already returned it, he had no obligation to pay for her funeral except as a last resort; and under no circumstances was she ever obligated to pay for his. Would a husband also be liable for his wife's emergency medical expenses, if she survived?

CASE 85: Reducing the Dowry by Law

D. 25.1.5 pr., 2 (Ulpianus libro trigesimo sexto ad Sabinum)

(pr.) Quod dicitur necessarias impensas dotem minuere, sic erit accipiendum, ut et Pomponius ait, non ut ipsae res corporaliter deminuantur, ut puta fundus vel quod-cumque aliud corpus: etenim absurdum est deminutionem corporis fieri propter pecuniam. ceterum haec res faciet desinere esse fundum dotalem vel partem eius. manebit igitur maritus in rerum detentationem, donec ei satisfiat: non enim ipso iure corporum, sed dotis fit deminutio. ubi ergo admittimus deminutionem dotis ipso iure fieri? ubi non sunt corpora <in dote>, sed pecunia: nam in pecunia ratio admittit deminutionem fieri. proinde si aestimata corpora in dotem data sint, ipso iure dos deminuetur per inpensas necessarias. hoc de inpensis dictum est, quae in dotem ipsam factae sint: ceterum si exstrinsecus, non imminuent dotem. . . . (2) Si dos tota soluta sit non habita ratione inpensarum, videndum est, an condici possit id, quod pro impensis necessariis compensari solet. et Marcellus admittit condic-tioni esse locum: sed etsi plerique negent, tamen propter aequitatem Marcelli sen-tentia admittenda est.

(Ulpian in the thirty-sixth book on Sabinus)

(pr.) As for the saying that necessary expenses reduce the dowry, this should not be interpreted to mean, as Pomponius also says, that the property is physically reduced, for instance, a farm or some other physical object; for it is ludicrous that physical loss occur because of money. But this will make the farm, or part of it, cease to be in the dowry. So the husband will continue to detain the property until he is satisfied (by receiving compensation for his necessary expenses), and the reduction that occurs by operation of law is not of the physical objects but of the dowry (itself).

Therefore, when do we concede that the dowry is (actually) reduced by op-eration of law? When the dowry consists not of physical objects but of money; for, in the case of money, reason permits a reduction. Hence, if appraised objects are given as dowry, by operation of law the dowry will be reduced through nec-essary expenses. This rule applies to expenses made on the dowry itself; but those made outside (the dowry) do not reduce the dowry. . . .

(2) If the entire dowry has been repaid without taking expenses into ac-count, we must examine whether a claim can be brought for what should be off-set for necessary expenses. Marcellus concedes that a claim is appropriate. Al-though many deny this, the view of Marcellus should be allowed because of fairness.

1. How to Reclaim Necessary Expenses. The problem dealt with in the first part of this Case stems from a venerable rule: "necessary expenses reduce the dowry by operation of law (*ipso iure*)." What this rule apparently means is that these expenses are, at least in principle, immediately offset against the value

of the dowry, even though this offset may not be realized until years later when the marriage ends. Where the wife's dowry consists entirely or partly of money, this rule meant that necessary expenses automatically reduced the dowry; that is, even though the money originally handed over had not been spent, the husband was entitled to take the appropriate amount as his own. The problem arose when the dowry consisted entirely of land or other physical objects, or when the money in the dowry ran out. How does Ulpian think this problem should be handled? Suppose, for instance, that the necessary expenses on a dowry farm had gradually grown until they equaled the total value of the farm; would the husband be obliged to wait until the marriage's end before reclaiming these expenses? This specific problem is dealt with by Paul, D. 23.3.56.3, where the text, as preserved, seems to say that the property would cease to be in the dowry if the wife failed to pay off the expenses within one year; but scholars widely believe that this text was subsequently altered to give a nonclassical solution.

2. Final Settlement? At the marriage's end, the husband (or his heir) is in a strong legal position in that he holds the dowry, while the wife is obliged to sue if the parties cannot settle amicably. In the course of this lawsuit, the husband's various retentions come into play, mainly as counterclaims. Normally, however, the husband also has available a separate action if he fails to raise one of his counterclaims. As the last part of this Case shows, this could well be untrue for necessary expenses, so that if the husband fails to raise them in the action for recovery of dowry, he may lose them as claims altogether. Marcellus and Ulpian believe, as a matter of equity, that he should be able to sue separately; but Ulpian notes that most jurists reject this view. What might their reasoning have been? Were they concerned that husbands might try to reclaim necessary expenses even before the dowry was being returned? If so, what reasons can be given for this not being permitted?

CASE 86: Useful Expenses

D. 25.1.5.3 (Ulpianus libro trigesimo sexto ad Sabinum)

Utiles autem impensae sunt, quas maritus utiliter fecit, <quae> meliorem <rem> uxoris feceri<n>t, hoc est dotem,

D. 25.1.6 (Paulus libro septimo ad Sabinum)

veluti si novelletum in fundo factum sit, aut si in domo pistrinum aut tabernam adiecerit, si servos artes docuerit.

D. 25.1.8 (Paulus libro septimo ad Sabinum)

Utilium nomine ita faciendam deductionem quidam dicunt, si voluntate mulieris factae sint: iniquum enim esse compelli mulierem rem vendere, ut impensas in eam factas solveret, si aliunde solvere non potest: quod summam habet aequitatis rationem.

(Ulpian in the thirty-sixth book on Sabinus)

Useful expenses are those the husband made usefully, that improve the wife's property, that is, the dowry,

(Paul in the seventh book on Sabinus)

for instance, if a plant nursery is constructed on a farm or if he adds a bakery or a shop in a house or if he teaches skills to slaves.

(Paul in the seventh book on Sabinus)

Some say that a deduction (from the dowry) should be made for useful expenses only if his wife was willing to have them made. For it is unfair that the wife be forced to sell property to pay expenses made on it if she cannot otherwise pay. This reasoning is eminently fair.

1. What's Useful? How clear is the conception of useful expenses that underlies this Case? Can they be readily distinguished from necessary expenses? Other sources state that, unlike necessary expenses (which only keep up the property's value), useful expenses lead to an increase in the property's profitability. So, Paul, D. 50.16.79.1: "Fulcinius says that useful expenses are those that make the dowry better, not those that do not allow it to worsen; (that is, they are expenses) from which return is acquired for his wife" (compare *Tit. Ulp.* 6.16). Other examples, besides those given in this Case, are bringing forestland under cultivation, planting new vineyards or olive orchards, or constructing a storehouse. Can these all be characterized as long-term capital investments? How about educating or teaching skills to a slave? Ulpian (D. 25.1.14.1) gives the strangest example: placing cows on property in order to fertilize it; what might he be thinking of?

2. Compensation for Useful Expenses. Paul, in the fragment quoted in the previous paragraph, describes useful expenses as those "from which return is acquired for his wife." This observation raises an important point: many such expenses should result in an increased income stream from the property, at least eventually. Under the rules of dowry, the husband acquires this income as "fruits" from the dowry (Case 67), but the wife has both a future interest in the increased income (since under many circumstances she will recover the dowry) and a present interest (to the rather limited extent that her maintenance is legally tied to the dowry income). Under these conditions, should the husband be compensated for expenses that seem likely to increase the dowry income? In this Case, Paul agrees with "some" jurists (perhaps a minority) who hold that the wife should pay for these expenses only if she had been consulted and was willing to have them made; this obviously means that if her husband wants compensation, he must first obtain her approval. In D. 50.16.79.1, Paul uses the same argument for this restriction: "It is wrong that a wife who is unaware or unwilling be burdened on their account, lest she be forced to lose her farm or slaves." Why is Paul fearful that the wife might lose her property? Does this rule presuppose a novel theory of a husband's control over his wife's dowry?

3. Dissent? This Case gives the rule preferred by Justinian (C. 5.13.1.5e; A.D. 530). As Paul indicates, during the classical period other jurists may have felt that the wife should usually, or perhaps even invariably, compensate her husband for useful, as well as necessary, expenses. One such jurist may have been Ulpian, who holds (D. 24.3.7.16): "Plainly, if he necessarily constructs a new farmhouse or repairs an old one that has totally collapsed through no fault of his, he will have a claim for this expense; and likewise if he brings land under cultivation. For these expenses are either necessary or useful, and they give rise to the husband's lawsuit." (See also Javolenus, in Case 87.) If Ulpian and Paul are in fact disagreeing (some scholars think that Ulpian's text was reworked by the *Digest* compilers), try to decide who has the better position. Among the things you should consider are the desirability of the wife's consent to any long-term improvements in her dowry property; the instability of the Roman marriage structure (high death rates and the ease of divorce), which may mean that the husband will not profit from long-term improvements; the husband's capacity to engage in embezzlement and other forms of opportunism, and the wife's limited means to prevent such misconduct during the marriage; and the perspective of public policy on all these issues. Should it matter whether the husband's "useful expenses" were reasonable, and whether they led in fact to increased income? How might the economic interests of husband and wife diverge when it comes to improvement of dowry property?

CASE 87: Opening a Quarry

D. 24.3.8 pr. (Paulus libro septimo ad Sabinum)

Si fundus in dotem datus sit, in quo lapis caeditur, lapidicinarum commodum ad maritum pertinere constat, quia palam sit eo animo dedisse mulierem fundum, ut iste fructus ad maritum pertineat, nisi si contrariam voluntatem in dote danda declaraverit mulier.

D. 23.5.18 pr. (Iavolenus libro sexto ex Posterioribus Labeonis)

Vir in fundo dotali lapidicinas marmoreas aperuerat: divortio facto quaeritur, marmor quod caesum neque exportatum esset cuius esset et impensam in lapidicinas factam mulier an vir praestare deberet. Labeo marmor viri esse ait: ceterum viro negat quidquam praestandum esse a muliere, quia nec necessaria ea impensa esset et fundus deterior esset factus. ego non tantum necessarias, sed etiam utiles impensas praestandas a muliere existimo nec puto fundum deteriorem esse, si tales sunt lapidicinae, in quibus lapis crescere possit.

D. 24.3.7.13-14 (Ulpianus libro trigesimo primo ad Sabinum)

(13) Si vir in fundo mulieris dotali lapidicinas marmoreas invenerit et fundum fructuosiorem fecerit, marmor, quod caesum neque exportatum est, <est> mariti et impensa non est ei praestanda, quia nec in fructu est marmor: nisi tale sit, ut lapis ibi renascatur, quales sunt in Gallia, sunt et in Asia. (14) Sed si cretifodinae, argenti fodinae vel auri vel cuius alterius materiae sint vel harenae, utique in fructu habebuntur.

(Paul in the seventh book on Sabinus)

If the dowry includes a farm on which stone is cut, it is settled that the husband takes the profit from the quarry, since his wife obviously gave him the farm intending that its fruits go to the husband, except if the wife states a contrary aim in giving the dowry.

(Javolenus in the sixth book from Labeo's *Posthumous Writings*)

A man had opened marble quarries on a dowry farm. After a divorce, it was asked who owned the marble that was cut but not removed, and whether the husband or wife should pay for expenses on the quarry. Labeo says the marble is the husband's; but he denies that the wife must pay anything to her husband, since these expenses were not necessary and the farm became worse. I think that the wife must pay not only necessary but also useful expenses, nor do I think the farm worse if the quarries are such that the stone in them can increase.

(Ulpian in the thirty-first book on Sabinus)

(13) If a man discovered marble quarries on his wife's dowry farm and he made the farm more profitable, the marble that was cut but not removed is the husband's, nor must his expenses be paid (by the wife) since marble is not included

in fruits unless it is such that the stone there is renewed, like some in Gaul and Asia. (14) But if there are clay beds, mines for silver or gold or any other substance, or sand pits, they will certainly be regarded as fruits.

1. A Babble of Sources? The juristic sources on marble quarries are not easy to follow, so don't worry if they seem contradictory. A number of questions are raised in these sources:

   • Should quarried stone be considered part of the fruits of the dowry?
   • Can a husband profit by extracting and selling stone from an already opened quarry on dowry land?
   • May he open a new quarry and profit in a similar manner?
   • Even if he is allowed to open a quarry, is he obliged to compensate his wife if the overall value of the land is lowered because of the quarry?
   • Must his wife compensate him for his expenses in opening a new quarry?
   • When stone is being extracted from the quarry, at what point does it become the husband's: when it is separated from the surrounding rock, or when it is actually removed?

   As to each question, how much real disagreement is there between the various jurists? Why does Ulpian believe that there is a difference between marble quarries and such other extractions as clay from a clay bed, gold or silver from a mine, or sand from a sand pit? More generally, what kinds of legal problems do extractions of this type raise, and how are they different from the legal problems associated with ordinary agricultural production? If quarries seem a little remote to your experience, consider a husband who wishes to strip-mine a farm belonging to his wife. Can he both capture the profits from the mine and force his wife to repay him for the expense of opening it? Would that just rub salt in the wound?

2. A Red Herring? Pomponius, D. 23.3.32: "If, with his wife's approval, a husband sold stone from the quarries on a dowry farm or trees which were not fruits or the right to construct a building atop land (*superficies*), the money from this sale is received for the dowry." This evidently means that proceeds from the sale go to increase the dowry. Is the ruling consistent with our other sources on quarries?

3. Another Red Herring? Alfenus, D. 23.5.8: "At his wife's request, a man cut down an olive orchard on a dowry farm in order to establish a new one. Later he died and left the dowry to his wife as a legacy. He (the jurist Servius) responded that the wood that was cut from the olive orchard must be returned to the wife." If he had not died, would the wood have belonged to him? How, if at all, is the wood different from the quarried stone in this Case?

4. Living Rock? The jurists were evidently the victims of a hoax.

CASE 88: Luxury Expenses

D. 25.1.9 (Ulpianus libro trigesimo sexto ad Sabinum)

Pro voluptariis impensis, nisi parata sit mulier pati maritum tollentem, exactionem patitur. nam si vult habere mulier, reddere ea quae impensa sunt debet marito: aut si non vult, pati debet tollentem, si modo recipiant separationem: ceterum si non recipiant, relinquendae sunt: ita enim permittendum est marito auferre ornatum quem posuit, si futurum est eius quod abstulit.

(Ulpian in the thirty-sixth book on Sabinus)

For luxury expenses, unless the wife is ready to permit their removal by her husband, she faces a demand for repayment (of their cost). For if the wife wishes to have them, she should return to her husband what was spent (on them); but if she does not want them, she should allow their removal, provided their separation is feasible. But if this is not feasible, they must be left; for the husband is allowed to take away the decoration he put up only if what he took will be his.

1. What's Luxury? The final category of expenses are those that, as *Tit. Ulp.* 6.17 puts it, neither worsen the dowry nor make it more profitable but only make the dowry property more pleasing. Paul (D. 50.16.79.2) gives as examples the installation of gardens, fountains, wall paneling and revetments, and pictures; Ulpian (D. 25.1.14.2) adds the construction of baths. All these were normal amenities of upper-class dwellings.

2. The Right to Remove. As a general rule, the husband cannot receive compensation for luxury expenses, even if his wife consents to them. Ulpian, D. 25.1.11 pr.: "Aristo writes that even if they are made with the wife's approval, repayment of luxury expenses cannot be demanded." Why should this be true, if the wife wanted the decorations and will enjoy them after the marriage has ended and the dowry has been returned to her? In this Case, Ulpian describes an exception: the husband may insist that his wife permit removal of the decorations; and she must then either permit removal or pay their cost. This remedy will work only if they are removable without damage to the structure and are usable after removal (compare Paul, D. 24.1.63: on the wife's removing her property that has become attached to that of her husband). Is this exception sufficient to protect the husband?

3. Saleability. If a house is redecorated in order to make it more saleable, is that a luxury expense? See Paul, D. 25.1.10 (no; it's useful). Explain the result.

CASE 89: Gaius Gracchus and Licinia's Dowry

D. 24.3.66 pr. (Iavolenus libro sexto ex Posterioribus Labeonis)

In his rebus, quas praeter numeratam pecuniam doti vir habet, dolum malum et culpam eum praestare oportere Servius ait. ea sententia Publii Mucii est: nam is in Licin[n]ia Gracchi uxore [statuit], quod res dotales in ea seditione, qua Gracchus occisus erat, perissent, ait, quia Gracchi culpa ea seditio facta esset, Licin[n]iae praestari oportere.

(Javolenus in the sixth book from Labeo's *Posthumous Writings*)

With regard to property (other than counted-out money) that the husband has as a dowry, Servius says he must be liable for intentional harm and for fault (*dolus malus* and *culpa*). This is the view of Publius Mucius Scaevola; for in the case of Licinia, the wife of (C.) Gracchus, because (her) dowry property had perished during the uprising in which Gracchus was killed, he says that Licinia should be compensated because Gracchus was at fault for the uprising.

1. Liability for Harming the Property. As you will recall from Case 70, a husband who harms property in the dowry is liable if the harm results from his deliberate misconduct (*dolus*) or from his negligent fault (*culpa*); the jurists eventually also required him to exercise a degree of diligence comparable to that he showed for his own property. This Case refers to a very early juristic decision related to the death of the popular politician Gaius Gracchus in 121 B.C. The Roman Senate had condemned Gracchus's political maneuvers as seditious, and on this basis his death at the hands of a mob was justified; but in their zeal the mob had also destroyed dowry property belonging to his wife, Licinia, who now wishes to receive compensation from Gracchus's estate. Does it seem fair to hold that Gracchus should be held responsible for causing this loss? Is this what you would normally think of as negligence?

2. Publius Mucius Scaevola. Would it surprise you to learn that P. Mucius Scaevola, the jurist who issued this opinion, was a political enemy of Gracchus? Gracchus's wife, Licinia, came from a wealthy and well-connected family. P. Mucius is the father of Q. Mucius Scaevola (consul in 95 B.C.), a much better known jurist.

3. A Final Assessment of Dowry. On the basis of what you have read so far, evaluate the following statement: "[T]he existence of dowry . . . was a central aspect of the family system, related to class differences that were relevant to women as well as to men. It structures the whole problem not simply of choice of partner but of the position of women throughout the marriage, especially after the death of the husband when widows often came to control

what, in gross, was considerable wealth. . . . Wealth of course is not to be translated directly into authority and even power, but it makes an important contribution. In general dowry represented an empowerment of women" (Jack Goody, in *The Development of the Family and Marriage in Europe*, 1983, writing of dowry "in Eurasia generally").

CHAPTER III

Patria Potestas

Marriage, the first linchpin of the Roman family, may seem, from a modern perspective, surprisingly poorly developed and supported in Roman law. By contrast, *patria potestas* (paternal power), the second linchpin, is forcefully constructed, so forcefully, in fact, that it is one of the most distinctive aspects of the Roman legal tradition.

Common to almost all legal systems is a recognition that, during their youth, children require close control by, if possible, their parents, who through social and legal norms have extensive powers to discipline their children and control their property; nor, in premodern legal systems, is it at all unusual for these powers to be concentrated chiefly in the father as representative of a traditional patriarchy. But what is unusual about Roman law is that paternal dominance did not end when children attained maturity or adulthood. On the contrary, with limited exceptions, this dominance continued as long as the child had any living antecedent in the direct male line (father, paternal grandfather, and so on).

The jurists recognize *patria potestas* as a distinctive cultural marker, a determinant of national identity. As Gaius observes: "This is a right peculiar to Roman citizens, since generally speaking no other people have such power over their children" (*Inst.* 1.55). In legal theory, at least, the right was not only lifelong but virtually unlimited; *patres familias,* as the wielders of *patria potestas,* could decide whether those in their power lived or died, whether and whom they could marry and for how long, whether they could treat any property as their own (even though the *pater* always remained the true owner), and so on.

In practice, however, *patria potestas* was limited in various ways. Perhaps most significantly, as Richard Saller and other historians have recently shown, high Roman mortality levels meant that most adults (past the age of twenty-five) were released from *patria potestas* because they no longer had any living male antecedents. Furthermore, even for those who still had *patres,* social institutions sprang up that discouraged at least the more extreme abuses of paternal power, though these institutions might not be effective against a determined father.

More interesting for us is the gradual process whereby unconstrained *patria potestas* was undermined in Roman law. The process was not completed during the classical period, nor could it be, since the Romans were evidently determined to leave the *familia* in place as a more or less inviolable domain of the *pater's* personal autonomy. Still, in reading the Cases that follow, stay alert to the tensions in juristic rulings and imperial decrees on *patria potestas*. Seen from this perspective, legal sources suggest a conflict between a cultural identity connected with an idealized past and broad social changes as Rome became a wealthy, powerful, and "world-embracing" empire. Tradition collided, at times forcefully, with individualism, in an exchange where the stakes could occasionally be high enough to require the intervention of the state. Public policy does make an occasionally dramatic entrance into the law of *patria potestas* in order to preserve a balance between these and other competing interests. The results of such interventions, however, are not uniformly or unambiguously successful.

PART A

Powers

Unquestionably, the starkest of the rights that Roman law gave to the *pater familias* was "the power of life and death" (*vitae necisque potestas*) over those descendants who were in his paternal power. This is thought to be a very old institution and is sometimes associated with the kings of Rome (e.g., Papinian, *Coll.* 4.8.1); it also may have been mentioned in Rome's earliest legal code, the Twelve Tables of 449 B.C. (4.2). Other sources (esp. Aulus Gellius, 5.19.9) indicate that the power of life and death was regarded in early law as the essential element of *patria potestas*. The Greek antiquarian Dionysius of Halicarnassus describes the original power this way: "a virtually total right over a son during his entire life, whether he chose to imprison him, scourge him, place him in chains and set him to work in the fields, or kill him" (2.26.4).

The father's right to kill a child, though perhaps never formally rescinded in classical Roman law, is apparently treated as void in A.D. 318/319 by the Christian emperor Constantine (C. 9.17.1 = C.Th. 9.15.1). However, by that date the right to kill one's children was, as it seems, long since obsolete. Actual instances of a *pater familias* using the right in order to kill a juvenile or an adult child are rare and mainly associated with early Rome, prior to the emergence of a contemporary historical record in the late third century B.C. It is therefore difficult to be sure about the historicity of these incidents, though Roman authors do appear to believe that there was a time when the father's power was virtually unrestricted by law.

In classical law, the power of life and death may have survived more as a symbolic indicator of the father's general authority and control over his descendants. In practice, the right was hedged round with social restrictions that had grown up to prevent its arbitrary use; above all, the *pater* was expected not to act without first consulting a *consilium,* an informal council made up of relatives and close friends, whose function seems often to have been to delay action until cooler heads prevailed. But even if the father's right to kill or maim survived only in theory, law did support his right to use corporal punishment against disobedient children, sometimes to the extent of letting public officials administer the actual punishment.

Further, not until the later Empire did Roman law restrict the right of the *pater familias* to cause the abandonment of, or even to kill, newborn infants in his power. It is hard to say with certainty how frequent this practice was, though clearly it was far more common than the killing of children past the stage of infancy. Most modern scholars believe that the Romans used infanticide preferentially against female newborns.

Finally, there is the "right of killing" (*ius occidendi*) introduced by the Emperor Augustus in a statute of 18 or 17 B.C. that criminalized adultery. One provision of this law allowed a *pater familias* to kill his daughter and her lover when they were taken in adultery; but this right, which the jurists sometimes treat as related to the *vitae necisque potestas,* is so restricted by legal, practical, and psychological limitations as to cast doubt on its real utility.

Even from an early date, limits on *patria potestas* were already enforced when it came into conflict with the state and the civic responsibilities required of Roman citizens. Then the interests of the family yielded to the greater interests of the Roman citizen body.

CASE 90: The *Consilium* I: Almost the Entire Senate

Valerius Maximus, *Facta et Dicta Memorabilia* 5.9.1

L. Gellius, omnibus honoribus ad censuram defunctus, cum gravissima crimina de filio, in novercam commissum stuprum et parricidium cogitatum, propemodum explorata haberet, non tamen ad vindictam continuo procucurrit, sed paene universo senatu adhibito in consilium expositis suspicionibus defendendi se adulescenti potestatem fecit inspectaque diligentissime causa absolvit eum cum consilii tum etiam sua sententia. quod si impetu irae abstractus saevire festinasset, admisisset magis scelus quam vindicasset.

(Valerius Maximus in the fifth book of *Memorable Deeds and Sayings*)

Lucius Gellius, a man who had held all public offices up through that of censor, possessed near certainty that his son was guilty of very serious offenses, namely committing adultery with his stepmother and plotting the murder of his father. Still, he did not rush at once to vengeance but (instead) summoned almost the entire Senate to his *consilium,* set forth his suspicions, and offered the young man the chance to defend himself. And when he had very carefully examined the case, he acquitted him not only by the verdict of the *consilium* but also by his own. Now if, carried away by the force of anger, he had hastened to vent his cruelty, he would more have committed a wrong than avenged one.

1. The Senate as *Consilium.* Why did Lucius Gellius, a prominent politician of his day (consul in 72 B.C., censor in 70 B.C.), summon "almost the entire Senate" to sit as his *consilium* in determining the fate of his son? Was he required to do so by law? Was he looking for political cover? Or was he concerned with adverse public reaction if he did not act in this way? In any case, does this move suggest that Gellius felt he did not enjoy full freedom to exercise the *vitae necisque potestas,* despite a case that appeared, at least to him, to be one of manifest guilt? Could he have reserved the right to disagree with his *consilium?* On the basis of this Case, what can be said with certainty about the late Republican law on the subject?

2. The Verdict Rules. Is Valerius Maximus more impressed by the procedure that Gellius follows or by the verdict that he issues? Suppose Gellius had found his son guilty. From the Roman perspective, would the charges have justified his killing his son? Does it seem likely that he would have been officially prosecuted or sanctioned? Note that this incident occurred before the adoption of the Augustan adultery legislation (Cases 50–55, 95–96).

3. Death without Due Process. What if a father ignored the advice of a *consilium?* In the late second century B.C., Q. Fabius Maximus Eburnus, like Gellius a senator and a former consul and censor, was convicted and forced into exile for killing his son. The main sources (Valerius Maximus, 6.1.5; [Quintilian],

Declamationes Maiores 3.17; Orosius, 5.16.8) are difficult to reconcile, but the following story seems likely. Eburnus suspected his adolescent son of improper sexual conduct (probably homosexuality). After "an investigation at home" (*cognita domi causa*) that presumably involved a *consilium*, the son was sent off to live in the country, away from temptation. But Eburnus subsequently dispatched two slaves who killed the son in return for a promise of freedom. This use of the slaves may indicate an attempt at concealment. We do not know exactly why Eburnus was convicted of murder; but does his conviction necessarily mean that the jury rejected the *vitae necisque potestas* as a defense? Is it possible that the son's offense was deemed insufficiently serious to warrant death, or that the jury condemned the father's implicit rejection of his *consilium*'s advice? A fragmentary late Roman commentary on Gaius (*Gaius Augustodunensis* 86) appears to indicate that a son could not be killed "without just cause" (*sine iusta causa*), a rule ascribed to the Twelve Tables of 449 B.C. How would the verdict of a *consilium* help in establishing the existence of just cause?

4. **Killing a Thief.** Most reported instances of fathers killing sons for domestic offenses involve sexual misconduct. However, Orosius (4.13.18) reports a late-third-century B.C. incident in which a father (an ex-censor) put his son to death for committing a theft. The correctness of this report has been doubted, but it raises the issue of how wide a father's authority was to govern a son's conduct. Did it include misconduct toward persons outside the *familia*?

5. **A Political Conspirator.** In 63 B.C., evidently just a few years after the incident in this Case, Aulus Fulvius, another senator, killed his son for setting out to join Catiline in his coup against the Roman state. The sources (Sallust, *Bellum Catilinae* 39.5; Valerius Maximus, 5.8.5; Dio, 37.36.4) present the killing as fairly impetuous and apparently undertaken without consulting a *consilium*; yet it seems Fulvius escaped both legal consequences and serious public criticism. What is the essential difference between this case and those of Gellius and Eburnus? In other sources from the later Republic, we hear of sons condemned by their fathers for extorting money during a provincial governorship or for running away in a battle.

6. **Daughters.** Though fathers usually act against sons, they could also kill their daughters (see, e.g., Valerius Maximus, 6.1.6: a daughter put to death for sexual turpitude, *stuprum*).

7. **Newborns.** It is clear (from sources such as Case 46) that *patria potestas* arises when a legitimate child is born; no special act of parental recognition or legitimation is required (see below, Part C.1). The one time during which a *pater familias* has an apparently unfettered legal right to kill his child (or to abandon it through exposure) is shortly after its birth. This right was not

substantially limited until the fourth century A.D., evidently under Christian influence.

8. Contraception and Abortion. Classical Roman law did little to restrict private attempts to curb fertility, and abortion was permitted if the husband consented; for example, Marcian (D. 47.11.4) observes that Septimius Severus exiled a woman who "defrauded her husband of children" by obtaining an abortion. The primary legal interest, then, is protecting the husband's expectation of children; how does this differ from modern law? The husband's rights could last beyond the marriage; Severus also exiled a woman who, after a divorce, aborted her fetus "to avoid bearing a son for her now hateful husband" (see Tryphoninus, D. 48.19.39). See also Cases 47–48.

CASE 91: The *Consilium* II: The Quality of Mercy

Seneca, *De Clementia* 1.15.1–6, 16.1

(15.1) Trichonem equitem Romanum memoria nostra, quia filium suum flagellis occiderat, populus graphiis in foro confodit; vix illum Augusti Caesaris auctoritas infestis tam patrum quam filiorum manibus eripuit. (15.2) Tarium, qui filium deprensum in parricidii consilio damnavit causa cognita, nemo non suspexit, quod contentus exilio et exilio delicato Massiliae parricidam continuit et annua illi praestitit, quanta praestare integro solebat; haec liberalitas effecit, ut, in qua civitate numquam deest patronus peioribus, nemo dubitaret, quin reus merito damnatus esset, quem is pater damnare potuisset, qui odisse non poterat. (15.3) Hoc ipso exemplo dabo, quem compares bono patri, bonum principem. cogniturus de filio Tarius advocavit in consilium Caesarem Augustum; venit in privatos penates, adsedit, pars alieni consilii fuit, non dixit: "Immo in meam domum veniat"; quod si factum esset, Caesaris futura erat cognitio, non patris. (15.4) Audita causa excussisque omnibus, et his quae adulescens pro se dixerat, et his, quibus arguebatur, petit, ut sententiam suam quisque scriberet, ne ea omnium fieret, quae Caesaris fuisset; deinde, priusquam aperirentur codicilli, iuravit se Tarii, hominis locupletis, hereditatem non aditurum. (15.5) Dicet aliquis: "Pusillo animo timuit, ne videretur locum spei suae aperire velle filii damnatione." ego contra sentio; quilibet nostrum debuisset adversus opiniones malignas satis fiduciae habere in bona conscientia, principes multa debent etiam famae dare. iuravit se non aditurum hereditatem. (15.6) Tarius quidem eodem die et alterum heredem perdidit, sed Caesar libertatem sententiae suae redemit; et postquam approbavit gratuitam esse severitatem suam, quod principi semper curandum est, dixit relegandum, quo patri videretur. . . . (16.1) O dignum, quem in consilium patres advocarent! o dignum, quem coheredem innocentibus liberis scriberent! haec clementia principem decet; quocumque venerit, mansuetiora omnia faciat.

(Seneca the Younger in the first book *On Mercy*)

(15.1) I can remember when the people in the Forum used pens to stab an equestrian named Tricho because he had flogged his son to death; the authority of Caesar Augustus barely rescued him from the hostile hands no less of fathers than of sons.

(15.2) There is (however) no one who did not admire Tarius. He caught his son plotting against his life and condemned him after a full hearing; but content with a sentence of exile, and a very comfortable exile at that, he confined the parricide at Marseilles and paid him the same allowance he had been accustomed to pay before the offense. His generosity had the result that, in a society where the worst sort never lack a defender, no one doubted that the defendant had been rightly condemned, since the father could find him guilty but (obviously) could not hate him.

(15.3) I will use this very case to illustrate a good emperor, whom you can compare to a good father. When he was about to hold the hearing on his son, Tarius invited Caesar Augustus to participate in his *consilium*. He (the emperor) came to a private household, took his seat, and joined in a *consilium* led by another; he did not say: "Rather, let him come to my house." Had he done so, it would have been an emperor's inquest, not that of a father.

(15.4) When the case had been heard and all the evidence reviewed, what the young man had said in his own defense as well as the accusations against him, Augustus asked each member of the *consilium* to deliver his verdict in writing, so that *he* not prejudice everyone's vote with his own. Then, before the tablets were opened, he solemnly swore that he would not accept an inheritance from Tarius, who was a wealthy man.

(15.5) Someone will say (of Augustus), "He was acting like a coward, worried that he would seem to want to make room for his own interests by condemning the son." I have a different view: any one of us should have had enough confidence in his own good conscience in the face of malicious criticism, (but) emperors must concede a great deal even to appearances. He swore an oath that he would not accept an inheritance.

(15.6) To be sure, Tarius (thereby) lost two heirs on the same day, but Augustus preserved the integrity of his own vote and, after he showed that his strictness was disinterested—a factor that always should be of concern for an emperor—he said that the son ought to be exiled to a place chosen by the father. . . .

(16.1) How worthy he was of fathers inviting him to join a *consilium*! How worthy that they make him coheir to children innocent of fault! This sort of mercy becomes an emperor: wherever he goes, he should make everything more humane.

1. The Unfortunate Mr. Tricho. Similar acts of "street justice" are not uncommon in Roman sources; they often indicate popular moral reactions. Seneca's account was written around A.D. 54 but refers to events a half century earlier. In Seneca's presentation, what did the crowd object to? That Tricho killed his son, that he did not afford him due process, or that he killed him in such a cruel way? Why does Seneca stress that Tricho's conduct was offensive not only to sons but also to their fathers? (Tricho is otherwise unknown. The "pens" used by the crowd are the sharp implements used on wax-covered writing tablets.)

2. The *Consilium* of Tarius. Seneca vividly describes a domestic council at work during the reign of Augustus (31 B.C. to A.D. 14). The protagonist is L. Tarius Rufus, suffect consul in 16 B.C. and a fabulously wealthy parvenu; the son was presumably after his money. As you can see, this *consilium* has somewhat the trappings of a public criminal trial: it is summoned by the *pater familias*, who presents his evidence as to his son's wrongdoing; the members of the *consil-*

ium listen to both sides and then cast votes; if a majority find the son guilty, the father issues a condemnation; after consultation on the punishment, there follows a sentence. At this point, before considering the intervention of Augustus in this particular case, you should weigh the advantages and disadvantages, from a legal perspective, of permitting such a domestic trial to occur at all. For instance, how much of a problem is it that Tarius acts as both prosecutor and judge (summoning a *consilium* of his own choosing and then issuing a verdict)? Is such a proceeding likely to be harsher or more lenient than a criminal trial?

3. The 800-Pound Gorilla. Why did Tarius invite Augustus to participate in his *consilium?* Could his motives be similar to those of Gellius in summoning "almost the entire Senate"? How did Augustus's presence affect the proceeding? For instance, why did Augustus insist that the verdicts be delivered in written form and not orally? And what is the point of his oath denying any interest in Tarius's estate? Seneca suggests a possible criticism of this move; is his defense against that criticism entirely convincing? Does the presence of Augustus seem quite so innocent as Seneca suggests?

4. The Envelope, Please. The written verdict of the *consilium* was clearly a vote of guilty. On Seneca's account, Augustus then suggested exile as an appropriate penalty, and Tarius followed through on this suggestion. As Seneca concludes: "This sort of mercy becomes an emperor: wherever he goes, he should make everything more humane." What does Seneca mean? Does he regard the penalty as disproportionately lenient, by then prevailing standards, in relation to the son's crime? Is he implying that Tarius had little choice in accepting the emperor's suggestion?

5. "I'm Going to Disneyworld!" The father continued the son's allowance as before and selected for his exile the ancient Greek city of Massilia, modern Marseilles, a sort of combination resort and college town with a reputation for excellent seafood. As the parties well knew, there were far less inviting places of exile. Did this defeat the purpose of Augustus's suggestion? Or was Tarius's choice also influenced by the emperor in some way? Is the result optimal for all parties concerned?

6. The Dust Settles. What was left of the *vitae necisque potestas* in the wake of this case? When similar episodes arose subsequently, would other fathers correctly interpret the emperor as having rejected harsher penalties such as putting the son to death? That is, would an event like this set a precedent? And if it did, would that undermine the function of the domestic trial? Might Augustus conceivably have wanted such an outcome? In any case, we seem to have no subsequent evidence of a domestic *consilium* resulting in the death of a child-in-power.

CASE 92: A Hunting Accident?

D. 48.9.5 (Marcianus libro quarto decimo Institutionum)

Divus Hadrianus fertur, cum in venatione filium suum quidam necaverat, qui novercam adulterabat, in insulam eum deportasse, quod latronis magis quam patris iure eum interfecit: nam patria potestas in pietate debet, non atrocitate consistere.

D. 48.8.2 (Ulpianus libro primo de Adulteriis)

Inauditum filium pater occidere non potest, sed accusare eum apud praefectum praesidemve provinciae debet.

(Marcian in the fourteenth book of his *Institutes*)

While hunting, a man had killed his son, who (at the time) was committing adultery with his stepmother. The deified Hadrian (reign: A.D. 117–138) is said to have exiled him to an island, because in killing him he used more a brigand's right than a father's. For a father's power (*patria potestas*) ought to be founded upon *pietas* not cruelty.

(Ulpian in the first book *On Adulteries*)

A father cannot kill his son without a hearing but should bring an accusation against him before the prefect (of Rome) or the provincial governor.

1. What Did the Father Do Wrong? Marcian appears to assume, at any rate for purposes of argument, that the son had been committing adultery, and that, in retaliation, his father staged the hunting accident. What is it that Hadrian found unacceptable in the father's conduct: that the father had acted without semblance of due process or that the punishment (death) was excessive in relation to the crime of adultery? Or some combination of both? What clues does the text offer as to the emperor's reaction? Would Hadrian have accepted the son's death if it had been preceded by a hearing in a domestic *consilium*? Or if the son's offense had been, not just adultery, but a plot to kill his father, as in the preceding Case?

2. The Gravity of the Offense. Is it relevant that adultery was not ordinarily a capital crime? Can you imagine a similar situation in which a father killed his son but might not be guilty of murder? What if he had walked in on his son and wife during sex? The Augustan *ius occidendi,* discussed below in Cases 95–96, allowed fathers to kill their daughters in certain circumstances, but there is no mention of sons; and there are strict limitations on the social class of males whom a husband can kill when they are taken in adultery with his wife (Case 51).

3. What Crime Did the Father Commit? He suffered deportation, a criminal penalty involving capital exile accompanied by loss of citizenship and confis-

cation of property—a punishment just short of execution. But what was his crime? Marcian's fragment comes from his remarks on the *lex Pompeia de parricidiis,* a statute (probably of 52 B.C.) dealing with *parricidium,* the murder of close relatives. At D. 48.9.1, Marcian summarizes the statute: it concerns anyone who kills or brings about the killing of "a father or mother, a grandfather or grandmother, a brother or sister, a first cousin from a father's or a mother's brother, a paternal or maternal uncle, a paternal or maternal aunt, a first cousin from one's maternal aunt, a wife or husband, a betrothed man, a father-in-law, a son-in-law, a mother-in-law, a daughter-in-law, a stepfather, a stepson or stepdaughter, a patron or patroness." A long list, but notice any glaring omissions? (Not only are children and grandchildren left out, but also a stepmother and a betrothed woman. However, these latter two were soon covered "by the spirit of the law"; Marcian, D. 48.9.3.) As Marcian goes on to say, the statute was extended by interpretation to include a mother who killed her child. Did Hadrian's decision effectively stretch the statute still further to include a father who does the same? The sanction under this statute was exceedingly severe for the killing of a parent or grandparent (by long-standing tradition, the parricide was flogged, then sewn into a sack with a dog, cock, viper, and monkey; next, the sack was thrown into the sea); but for other killings the standard murder punishment was used. See Modestinus, D. 48.9.9. The sack punishment, after falling into disuse, was actually revived (see Paul, *Sent.* 5.24). The Emperor Constantine (C. 9.17.1 = C.Th. 9.15.1; A.D. 318/319) extended it to parents who killed their children; see also C.Th. 11.27.1 (A.D. 315).

4. *Pietas.* Marcian's justification for Hadrian's decision ties paternal power to *pietas,* an untranslatable word conveying a sense of the devotion and duty that Romans considered an ideal aspect of relations between close family members. What constraints do you think invocation of this concept placed on exercising the *vitae necisque potestas?*

5. Generalization. Ulpian wrote about a century after Hadrian's decision. What is the relationship between Marcian's report of this decision and Ulpian's rule? Note that the Ulpian fragment derives from his commentary on the adultery statute; can it be regarded as generalizing Hadrian's decision only with respect to charges of adultery, or should it be understood more broadly? When Ulpian states that a father cannot kill his son "without a hearing," does he preclude the possibility that the father might use a domestic *consilium* for this purpose?

6. How Much Survived? Our sources on this aspect of *patria potestas* are not very full. Still, does it seem that, in the late classical period, a *pater familias*

could still kill his child, whether after consulting a *consilium* or not? Do the sources give any clear clues as to the reasons for such legal change as did occur? In Case 177, the jurist Paul (a contemporary of Marcian and Ulpian) observes that "it was (once) permitted to kill" sons. Does this suggest a living right in his time?

CASE 93: Disciplining a Troublesome Son

C. 8.46.3 (Imp. Alexander A. Artemidoro)

Si filius tuus in potestate tua est, res adquisitas tibi alienare non potuit: quem, si pietatem patri debitam non agnoscit, castigare iure patriae potestatis non prohiberis, artiore remedio usurus, si in pari contumacia perseveraverit, eumque praesidi provinciae oblaturus dicturo sententiam, quam tu quoque dici volueris.

(The Emperor Alexander Severus to Artemidorus; A.D. 227)

If your son is in your power, he could not alienate (i.e., transfer ownership of) property that he had (previously) acquired for you. If he (now) fails to display the *pietas* that is owed to a father, you are not prevented from punishing him by exercising the right of a father's power (*ius patriae potestatis*). You may resort to a harsher remedy if he persists in such defiance, and you may hand him over to the provincial governor for issuance of the verdict that you also wish to be issued.

1. The Dispute. The first sentence suggests a dispute between father and son over the ownership of property. Sons-in-power cannot own property (see below, Part B.1), and a *pater familias* owns any property that they acquire; further, only in limited circumstances can sons alienate their father's property (see Part B.2 below). Try to reconstruct the dispute, to the extent that this brief allusion allows. It may center on alienation of property the father owns indirectly, through the son's management of a *peculium* (see below, Part B.3). On this theory, does the son have a legitimate claim? What exactly is the father, Artemidorus, requesting from the emperor? What role does *pietas* play in Alexander's decision? Is it similar to that in Case 92?

2. Paternal Discretion. What punishments may Artemidorus inflict on his son and for what must he rely on the provincial governor? Does this Case suggest that corporal punishment short of killing could be routinely visited by fathers upon children, even adult children, with the express sanction of the state and without consultation of a *consilium*? What inferences can be drawn from the enforcement of paternal discretion by the Roman government? According to Ulpian (D. 1.16.9.3), among the matters a provincial governor can dispose of routinely and without a formal hearing (!) are the issuance of orders that proper respect be shown to parents and the admonishment and instilling of fear in a son whose misbehavior is reported by his father. This seems to indicate that the magistrate's power is largely supplemental to the father's and deployed only when the father seeks help. Is that consistent with the present Case? No classical source indicates that magistrates ordinarily monitored corporal punishment by fathers, much less that they had to approve it in advance.

3. Judicial Discretion. How broad is the governor's discretion in terms of assessing the nature of the offense? Must the son be found guilty of an actual criminal law offense before the governor imposes a penalty?

4. A Nonassertive Father. Is it clear what the emperor is threatening at the end of this Case? Does his language suggest that Artemidorus himself had asked about the capital penalty? If it does not, what does this allow us to conclude about Roman attitudes toward the exercise of the *vitae necisque potestas*? Is there a development traceable over time?

5. Excessive Punishment. How bright is the line between ordinary discipline and child abuse? According to Papinian (Case 158), the Emperor Trajan compelled a father who had maltreated his son "contrary to family duty" (*contra pietatem*) to emancipate the boy, thereby releasing him from the father's power. This suggests a degree of governmental oversight at least in extreme cases of cruelty. How do you suppose that such a case would come to the emperor's attention?

6. "Honey, I Sold the Kids." If discipline doesn't work, can you at least sell your son into slavery? Some evidence suggests that this may have been possible in archaic law; but except in peculiar circumstances (e.g., see below, Part B.4) it is missing from classical law, which usually treats the sale of free persons as void (e.g., Paul, D. 18.1.34.2). The Emperor Caracalla (reign: 211–217) describes a father's sale of freeborn sons as "an illicit and dishonest act" (C. 7.16.1); and a postclassical source takes a similar view of a father who gave his son as security for a debt (Paul, *Sent.* 5.1.1 = D. 20.3.5). As this source observes: "No price can be put on a free person." Is this a purely formal objection, or does it reflect a deeper principle of public policy?

7. What about Mothers? In a rescript of A.D. 259 (C. 8.46.4), the Emperors Valerian and Gallienus write to a woman who is disputing with her sons. The emperors prefer the quarrel to stay "within the home" (*intra domum*); but if it becomes necessary, she is allowed to approach a provincial governor, who "will force the sons to display the reverence owed to their mother and, if he discovers that their wickedness has reached the point of more brutal indignities, will more strictly punish this breach of *pietas*." What do you make of the extension of help to mothers? How does it change the character of earlier remedies?

CASE 94: An Offense Related to Public *Pietas*

D. 37.15.1.2 (Ulpianus libro primo Opinionum)

Si filius matrem aut patrem, quos venerari oportet, contumeliis adficit vel impias manus eis infert, praefectus urbis delictum ad publicam pietatem pertinens pro modo eius vindicat.

(Ulpian in the first book of his *Opinions*)

If a son uses vituperative language against the mother or father, whom he ought to honor, or lays irreverent hands upon them, the prefect of the city punishes, in proportion to its severity, an offense related to public *pietas*.

1. A Postclassical Source. Although Ulpian's name is attached to the *Opinions,* this work is widely believed to be from some later legal author, writing after the classical period and perhaps in the late third century A.D. The *Opinions* are important because they may shed some light on legal developments after the great Roman jurists had stopped writing. To judge from this fragment, did the prefect (an imperial appointee) require a parent's request before intervening? What sort of offense would cause him to act? What do "vituperative language" (*contumeliae*) and battery have in common? Is it important that the Case makes no distinction between a mother and a father? In short, to what extent does this ruling represent an innovation from classical Roman law, and in this respect is the ruling "progressive"?

2. Public *Pietas.* What role is played by *pietas* in this holding? *Publica pietas* may mean something like "legally protected *pietas*." How does this differ from the *pietas* found in classical legal sources?

3. Correction of Morals in the Late Empire. In A.D. 365, the Emperors Valentinian and Valens allow "older kinsmen" to use corporal punishment in disciplining wayward juveniles, "in proportion to their offense" (*pro qualitate delicti:* C. 9.15.1 = C.Th. 9.13.1). This ruling seems to assume that the juveniles are *sui iuris*, that is, that they have no *pater familias* of their own; the emperors are thus extending the ambit of those who can use corporal punishment. Punishment for more serious offenses is, however, reserved for criminal courts. Does this represent a further step in the decay of *patria potestas?*

4. Revoking Emancipation. Two years later, in A.D. 367, the emperors issue a rescript (C. 8.49.1 = C.Th. 8.14.1) concerning sons who, after being emancipated by their father from his power (see below, Part C.3), then engage in grossly insulting behavior toward him; their emancipation can be revoked. Revoking emancipation for ingratitude was not possible in classical law. Is the rescript a major novelty? Does it imply a further change in the relationship between the state and the family?

CASE 95: An Adulterous Daughter

D. 48.5.21 (Papinianus, libro primo de Adulteriis)

Patri datur ius occidendi adulterum cum filia quam in potestate habet. itaque nemo alius ex patribus idem iure faciet, sed nec filius familias pater:

D. 48.5.22 (Ulpianus, libro primo de Adulteriis)

(sic eveniet, ut nec pater nec avus possint occidere) nec immerito: in sua enim potestate non videtur habere, qui non est suae potestatis.

(Papinian in the first book *On Adulteries*)

The right of killing an adulterer along with a daughter is granted to her *pater* if he has her in his power. Therefore, no other type of father may lawfully do this, including a father who is himself a son-in-power.

(Ulpian in the first book *On Adulteries*)

And thus it will happen that neither a father nor a grandfather is able to kill. This result is quite right, since a person who is himself not legally independent is not held to have another in his power.

1. The Statute. The *lex Iulia de adulteriis coercendis*, promulgated by the Emperor Augustus in 18 or 17 B.C., granted the right of killing (*ius occidendi*) to fathers as well as to outraged husbands, but with this difference: the husband was permitted to kill only certain types of adulterers (this group included pimps, gladiators, actors, condemned criminals, freedmen of the husband, of the wife, or of close family members, and slaves), and he was not allowed to kill his wife under any circumstances. The purpose of this provision was presumably to deter and punish adulterers, though it seems to have been narrowly construed by the jurists; see Cases 51–52 on the husband's *ius*.

2. *Potestas* and *Manus*. Papinian (D. 48.5.23 pr.) states that the law did not distinguish between biological and adoptive fathers, which makes sense, given how the statute connects the *ius occidendi* with *patria potestas*. Other texts show, however, that fathers who had given their daughters in marriage with *manus* were also entitled to the *ius*: Paul, *Coll.* 4.2.3; Papinian, *Coll.* 4.7.1. What is the rationale for this extension? Why, on the other hand, were grandfathers who held *potestas* not granted the right of killing an adulterous woman with her lover?

3. Father versus Husband. Both the statute and the jurists tend to draw a connection between the *ius occidendi* and *patria potestas*. Does this make sense? What is the motive for making such a connection? Does it help explain why the father's "self-help" powers are more extensive than those of the husband? Which of these two parties was thought to care more deeply about a woman's

adultery? Ulpian (D. 48.5.2.8 = Case 50) states that when a husband and father appear simultaneously as prosecutors in a case of adultery, the husband should be preferred, because his "sharper rage and greater anger" will make him more effective in this role. Why not apply the same logic to the *ius occidendi*? Compare also Papinian's explanation (D. 48.5.23.4): "The reason it is the father and not the husband who is permitted to kill the woman and any adulterer is that for the most part the *pietas* natural to a father's role intercedes on behalf of his children, but a husband's heat and impulsiveness of a husband leaps easily to a decision and ought to be held in check." Convinced?

4. Son-in-Power. Are you persuaded by Ulpian's justification for denying the right to a father who happens to be a son-in-power? Is the statute being interpreted narrowly, and, if so, why?

5. Emancipated Daughters. Could fathers also kill their daughters (along with their lovers) once the daughters had been emancipated, that is, were of independent legal status (*sui iuris*)? Some jurists did permit this: Marcellus and Paul, *Coll.* 4.2.4. Does their view seem consistent with the statute as paraphrased by Papinian? If such a view is correct, would it follow that the right to kill is legally determined less by *patria potestas* than by the self-help enforcement of marital fidelity?

6. Is This Right Superfluous? In the late classical period, Papinian (*Coll.* 4.8.1) reports an inquiry: "Since ancestral law gives to a father the power of life and death over a child, please answer me this, for I want to know: what was accomplished by including in the statute that there is also a power of killing a daughter?" That is, doesn't the *vitae necisque potestas* already allow the father to kill his daughter? And if so, why should he need additional legislative support? In response, Papinian takes an indirect approach: "Does this addition provide us with an argument *ex contrario* that the statute be held not to have given (a right) to one who did not have it (i.e., the father), but (rather) to have ordered that she be killed along with the adulterer, so that he seem to have killed the adulterer from larger motives of fairness, since he also did not spare his daughter?" Why didn't Papinian answer by saying that the *vitae necisque potestas* no longer exists, or that this power cannot be extended from sons to daughters?

CASE 96: Limitations on Killing a Daughter

D. 48.5.24 pr., 4 (Ulpianus libro primo de Adulteriis)

(pr.) Quod ait lex "in filia adulterum deprehenderit," non otiosum videtur: voluit enim ita demum hanc potestatem patri competere, si in ipsa turpitudine filiam de adulterio deprehendat. Labeo quoque ita probat, et Pomponius scripsit in ipsis rebus Veneris deprehensum occidi: et hoc est quod Solo et Draco dicunt *en ergō*. . . . (4) Quod ait lex "in continenti filiam occidat," sic erit accipiendum, ne occiso hodie adultero reservet et post dies filiam occidat, vel contra: debet enim prope uno ictu et uno impetu utrumque occidere, aequali ira adversus utrumque sumpta. quod non si affectavit, sed, dum adulterum occidit, profugit filia et interpositis horis adprehensa est a patre qui persequebatur, in continenti videbitur occidisse.

(Ulpian in the first book *On Adulteries*)

(pr.) The law says: "he shall have caught the adulterer inside his daughter." This (wording) does not seem without point, for it (the law) intended that the father have this privilege if and only if he should catch his daughter in adultery, while she was actually engaged in the shameful act. Labeo too accepts this, and Pomponius has written that (only) a person caught in the very act of lovemaking is killed; and this is (also) what (the Athenian lawgivers) Solon and Draco mean by "in the act." . . .

(4) When the law says "he should kill his daughter immediately," this must be understood as follows: when the lover is killed on one day, he should not spare his daughter and then kill her several days later, or vice versa. This is because he should kill both of them with virtually the same blow and the same assault, with an equal amount of rage directed against each. But if he has not laid hold of her, and, while he is killing the lover, his daughter has made her escape and is (then) caught by her father a few hours later while he was in hot pursuit, he will be considered to have killed her "immediately."

1. Statutory Interpretation. How do Ulpian and his predecessors interpret the statutory phrase "shall have caught the adulterer inside his daughter"? Was this interpretation inevitable? Why invoke the early Athenian lawgivers Solon and Draco? What motives might there be for this restriction in the first place?

2. Statutory Limits. Both the statute and the jurist appear to assume that most fathers would be readier to kill the lover than the daughter. Why then require the father to kill both? Remember that the husband is strictly forbidden to kill both parties, even where he is permitted to kill the lover. Why insist on killing both immediately rather than, for example, allowing the father to call a *consilium* of friends and family members to determine guilt?

3. Die Harder. If the father does not obey the rules, he may be guilty of homicide. Suppose the daughter survives her wounds. Macer (D. 48.5.33 pr.) writes: "It makes no difference whether or not the father kills his adulterous daughter first, provided he kills them both. For if he kills (only) one, he will be a defendant under the *lex Cornelia* (for homicide). But if one is killed and the other wounded, he is not, to be sure, freed from liability according to the wording of the statute; but the deified Marcus and Commodus have laid down in a rescript that freedom from liability is granted to him, because, although after the lover was killed the woman survived such serious wounds as her father had inflicted on her, she was preserved more by chance than by his will—since the law demands an equal measure of anger and expects similar drastic action against those who have been caught in the act." Does this mean that a good-faith effort counts?

4. Wrongful Intent. Do you see how a father who kills both parties may be guilty of a double homicide if he merely hesitates over the second victim? This emerges clearly from Paul. *Coll.* 4.2.6–7: "And if he did not kill the daughter but only her lover, he is liable to a charge of homicide. (7) Even if he killed the daughter after a space of time, the same point holds true, unless he killed her in hot pursuit; for he appears (in the second case) to have acted under the authority of the statute through his unbroken state of mind." This suggests that the jurists developed an objective test for evaluating the legal propriety of the father's action. What precisely is required to justify the father's action? How do you reconcile this requirement with the requirement of homicide law that murder be committed with wrongful intent (*dolo malo*)? And how is it determined that the requirement is met?

5. Just Anger. Is it reasonable or fair to insist that the murderous rage of the father exercising the *ius* be somehow distinguishable from intent to commit homicide? And suppose outward manifestations of such rage are lacking. At what point is the *ius occidendi* not an independent "right" but simply an affirmative defense against a charge of murder?

6. Killing at Home. The statute also required the father to have discovered the adultery either in his own home (whether or not the daughter resided there) or in that of his son-in-law; and if the father owned more than one house, only his main residence qualified. See Papinian and Ulpian, D. 48.5.23.2, 24.2–3. Ulpian (24.2) explains: "The reason the father is not permitted to slay his daughter wherever he catches her but only in his own house or that of his son-in-law is thought to be that the legislator deemed it a greater affront (*iniuria*) should a daughter dare to admit a lover into her father's house or that of her husband." Do these limitations suggest that the right to kill a daughter is

less aimed at directly deterring or punishing adulterers than at legitimizing a father's violent reaction to the invasion of his home?

7. Narrow Interpretation? One way to get rid of an awkward legal rule is to interpret it in such a way that it is rarely applicable. Do the jurists seem to have done this with the *ius occidendi*?

CASE 97: A Son and the State

D. 1.6.9 (Pomponius libro sexto decimo ad Quintum Mucium)

Filius familias in publicis causis loco patris familias habetur, veluti ut magistratum gerat, ut tutor detur.

(Pomponius in the sixteenth book on Quintus Mucius)

In public matters a son-in-power is treated as a *pater familias*, for example, in order that he hold a magistracy or be named a *tutor*.

1. Clashes between the Family and the State. This brief fragment states a principle of great significance: that a father's power over a son (in particular) normally comes to an abrupt end when the son attempts to act, or is called upon to act, in his capacity as a citizen. At issue here are questions such as these: can a father prevent a son from joining the army or running for public office, can he order him to vote for a particular candidate in a public election, can he prevent him from undertaking a public duty such as acting as a guardian (*tutor*) to a ward, and so on? Although the answer to these questions is almost always no, it is fair to ask whether a father might use his powers to influence an adult son's public actions through means more indirect than outright command or prohibition. In any event, despite the considerable powers of *patres familias,* sons-in-power are not slaves and are never conceived of as such in Roman law.

2. A Son Is Dragged from the Dais. A good example of the conflicts that gave rise to the rule in this Case is the anecdote recounted by Valerius Maximus (5.4.5). In 232 B.C., the plebeian tribune C. Flaminius proposed a radical measure allotting newly conquered land to landless Romans. The conservative Roman Senate resisted this measure and threatened armed force if Flaminius persisted. But the tribune persevered, and just as he was putting the law to a popular vote, his father seized him and pulled him down from the Rostra while the crowd of voters looked meekly on. Supposing that this anecdote is basically true, what does it suggest about the depth of the roots of *patria potestas* in archaic Roman society?

3. My Son the Governor. You are a *pater familias.* Your son has just become a provincial governor, and since then he has been insufferable to you. Can you humiliate him by giving him in adoption to somebody else, using your son's own court for the final stage of the adoption process? (On the procedure, see Case 149.) See Paul, D. 1.7.3 (yes). Is there any problem with such a procedure?

4. Sons-in-Power and Women. Adult Roman males, even while still in the power of a *pater familias,* participated in civic life as equals. Adult women were quite differently treated: they were excluded in principle from participation whether or not they were *sui iuris.* See Chapter V.B.1–2.

Control over descendants meant that the *pater familias* also enjoyed considerable power to arrange and dissolve their marriages. As the jurists stress, in principle the consent of the bride and groom is essential to Roman marriage. But as we saw in Chapter II (esp. Cases 13 and 24), in practice this requirement was often formalistic, and perhaps particularly so in the case of a daughter just past the minimum age for marriage (Case 7). Similarly, as Case 98 shows, the *pater familias* of a bride or groom must also consent to the marriage; but again this consent might often be interpreted rather broadly, as implied from the circumstances of a wedding (the father has not raised an objection), or even as presumptively present.

In this way, the stark authority of the *pater familias* was accommodated to the realities of social life, which often required, or at least made desirable, a level of participation in these decisions not only by the affected child but also by the mother and other close relatives who had no legal standing. However, when a father actively found a marriage to be objectionable, his power to stop it, or even to dissolve it after it had been contracted, for a long time remained unassailable.

But this was an area in which the Roman government also had a well-recognized interest, especially in the wake of the marriage legislation of Augustus, which sought to promote marriage and childbirth as matters of public policy. To some extent, therefore, emperors and jurists alike were inclined to interfere with the father's power when it was used to prevent a marriage from occurring; and their inclination could become even stronger when the father tried to break up a marriage that, at least in the view of the husband and wife themselves, was established and successful. The resulting collision between public policy and the traditional autonomy of the *pater familias* was not entirely resolved in classical Roman law. But in practice the clash was somewhat eased by the Roman demographic regime, in which high mortality rates meant that Roman men and women often no longer had a *pater familias* by the time they reached their thirties.

One point that emerges clearly from the juxtaposition of Case 97 with the Cases that follow is that Roman marriage, while subject to some indirect legal regulation, was not thought of as a "public" or "civic" act, similar to voting or holding public office. Accordingly, *patria potestas* is only sporadically trumped by public policy in favor of marriage and procreation.

CASE 98: Who Consents

D. 23.2.2 (Paulus libro trigesimo quinto ad edictum)

Nuptiae consistere non possunt nisi consentiant omnes, id est qui coeunt quorumque in potestate sunt.

D. 23.2.3 (Paulus libro primo ad Sabinum)

Si nepotem ex filio et neptem ex altero filio in potestate habeam, nuptias inter eos me solo auctore contrahi posse Pomponius scribit et verum est.

D. 23.2.16.1 (Paulus libro trigesimo quinto ad edictum)

Nepote uxorem ducente et filius consentire debet: neptis vero si nubat, voluntas et auctoritas avi sufficiet.

(Paul in the thirty-fifth book on the Edict)

A marriage is not valid unless everyone agrees, that is, (both) those who marry and those in whose power they are.

(Paul in the first book on Sabinus)

If I have a grandson by one son and a granddaughter by another, (and both these grandchildren are) in my power, Pomponius says that they can marry each other on my authority alone; and this view is correct.

(Paul in the thirty-fifth book on the Edict)

When a grandson marries, his father ought also to agree; but should a granddaughter marry, the consent and authority of the grandfather will be enough.

1. Controversy. Compare Case 13 (*Tit. Ulp.* 5.2), which states the general rule in slightly less exact language. The general rule requires not only consent from both parties to the marriage but also consent from a *pater familias* if either one happens to be in his power. Paul's citation of Pomponius in the second text and the phrase "this view is correct" suggest that some jurists may have disagreed with an aspect of this rule. What problem might they have seen?

2. Legal Logic. The issue in the third text is this: A grandfather has in his power both his son and a grandson by that son. If the grandson marries, which of the two antecedents must consent: the grandfather or the father or both? Given the general rule as stated in the first text, which of the following two texts gives the most logical statement of the law? As you consider this question, should it matter that both the first and third texts are from the same book of Paul's commentary on the urban praetor's Edict?

3. Double Consent. With regard to the third text, why should the consent of the father (himself a son-in-power), as well as that of the grandfather holding *potestas,* be required for marriage of the grandson but not for that of the granddaughter? How independent is the son's consent going to be in any case?

4. Paul versus Paul. Is it possible to reconcile the apparently divergent views of Paul on whether a son-in-power must consent to his son's marriage? The second text states that the grandson and granddaughter stemmed from different sons of the grandfather, and that these first cousins were marrying each other. (Marriage between first cousins was legal if not especially common: see Case 11.) Is such a close-kin marriage the crux of the matter? Can the third text be read to imply only that, at least in Paul's view, under any other circumstances a son-in-power would have had to consent to his son's marriage?

5. Freedom of Choice. Lawrence Stone, the noted historian of the English family, suggests four basic models for matchmaking: "The first is that the choice is made entirely by parents, kin and family 'friends,' without the advice or consent of the bride or groom. The second option is that the choice is made as before, but the children are granted the right of veto. . . . The third option, made necessary by the rise of individualism, is that the choice is made by the children themselves, . . . with the parents retaining the right of veto. The fourth option, which has only emerged in [the twentieth] century, is that children make their own choice and merely inform their parents of what they have decided" (Stone, *The Family, Sex and Marriage in England, 1500–1800* [rev. ed. 1979]). Which of these patterns seems most closely to resemble the one presumed by Roman law? No matter which pattern was theoretically prescribed at Rome, what sort of psychological interplay can you imagine in its implementation?

CASE 99: Compelling a Child's Consent

D. 23.2.21 (Terentius Clemens libro tertio ad legem Iuliam et Papiam)

Non cogitur filius familias uxorem ducere.

D. 23.2.22 (Celsus libro quinto decimo Digestorum)

Si patre cogente ducit uxorem, quam non duceret, si sui arbitrii esset, contraxit tamen matrimonium, quod inter invitos non contrahitur: maluisse hoc videtur.

(Terentius Clemens in the third book on the *lex Iulia et Papia*)

A son-in-power cannot be compelled to marry.

(Celsus in the fifteenth book of *Digests*)

If a man is compelled by his father to marry a woman whom he would not have married were it up to him, he has nonetheless contracted a (valid) marriage since the parties to it were not unwilling; he (the son) is held to have preferred this course.

1. Contradiction or Construction? In these two texts, the issue is the reality of the consent that a child gives while he or she is in the power of a *pater familias*. Do Terentius Clemens and Celsus contradict each other? Or does Celsus accept the circumstances he describes as a case of constructive consent? On the requirement that the couple agree to their marriage, see also Cases 13–18.

2. Rationale for the Holding. In any case, does the wording of Celsus's holding seem peculiar to you? What do you think is the motive for his decision? Does it seem to arise from a practical concern or is he simply following a legal policy of favoring marriage (*favor matrimonii*)?

3. Can You Marry Off an Insane Daughter? Suppose that a *pater familias* has a mad daughter. Plainly, she cannot herself give a valid consent to marriage (see Discussion 2 on Case 13); but can her father assent on her behalf? Ulpian (D. 24.3.2.2) discusses a somewhat comparable situation where a father is suing for recovery of dowry after the dissolution of his daughter's marriage; ordinarily her consent to his lawsuit would be required (Case 82), but in this instance she is insane and obviously unable to consent. The jurists therefore resort to a legal fiction: "when, because of madness, she cannot object, we correctly regard her as agreeing." Is it likely that a similar fiction would have been applied also in the case of a marriage? What crucial factor makes these two situations different?

CASE 100: A Father's Consent

D. 23.2.34 pr. (Papinianus libro quarto Responsorum)

Generali mandato quaerendi mariti filiae familias non fieri nuptias rationis est: itaque personam eius patri demonstrari, qui matrimonio consenserit, ut nuptiae contrahantur, necesse est.

(Papinian in the fourth book of his *Responses*)

For the making of a marriage, it is not an acceptable legal basis that a general commission was given (to a third party) to find a husband for a daughter in her father's power. Therefore, it is necessary to the contracting of a marriage that he (the husband) be personally presented to her father for his consent to their marrying.

Hypothetical Situation.

A father commissioned a marriage broker to find an acceptable husband for his daughter; the broker then located a prospective husband who met the father's criteria and was acceptable to the daughter. Is anything further required from the father in order for the marriage to be valid?

1. Meeting Her Old Man. As Papinian makes clear, in ordinary circumstances the father is not construed as consenting to his daughter's marriage unless he at least knows her prospective husband. (For the use of marriage brokers, see Discussion 3 on Case 24.) How much more is required? Must there be a formal presentation? Must the father clearly assent to the marriage, or is it enough if he simply "takes notice" of the prospective husband? What if he had met him some time ago but not recently? Must he express consent at the wedding as well? Assess this reconstruction of the law (from P. E. Corbett): "It would merely be necessary, if any question arose, to show that the *pater*, knowing the man and aware of the marriage, had raised no objection." In any event, manifestation of parental consent could be very casual; for instance, no signed document was required (Severus and Caracalla, C. 5.4.2).

2. A Son Wishes to Marry. This Case concerns a daughter. Would you anticipate greater or lesser rigor in the case of a son in his father's power? An adult son might be expected to enjoy more independence; on the other hand, his marriage and eventual offspring have potential consequences for the household of the *pater familias*. Roman sources do not make clear what the classical rule was for sons, but their discussion of what happens when the *pater familias* is insane (Case 101) implies that parental consent was more or less strictly required for sons, at least by fairly clear inference from the father's conduct. This is also consistent with an early postclassical decision of Diocletian (C.

5.4.12; A.D. 285) reaffirming a son's right to marry whom he wishes "provided that in contracting marriage your father consents."

3. **What If Parental Consent Was Not Given?** The consequences could be dire. Paul (D. 1.5.11) gives the following example: A woman was in her father's power; she entered into a marriage without his knowledge and conceived a child; her father then died still unaware of the putative marriage. The child is held to be illegitimate even if it was born only after her father's death; and so the marriage is also plainly invalid before then. In the materials that follow, examine how the jurists found ways to mitigate this harsh rule.

4. **Consent after the Event.** While his father was away, Lucius Titius, a son in his father's power, married Septicia and received a dowry from her father. Titius's father later returned and lived in proximity to his son, evidently without expressing either approval or disapproval of the marriage, until his son died. Is this enough to validate the marriage? Paul (in *Frag. Vat.* 102) says that a father who agrees to a marriage "even after the event" (*etiam postea*) makes the marriage valid and the dowry binding; and the father in this case, by not objecting, had apparently agreed. As it seems, this marriage is validated retroactively, back to when it was contracted and the dowry given. Would the outcome have been different if the couple had married while Titius's father was present? Probably not. The Emperor Alexander Severus (C. 5.4.5; A.D. 222–235) addresses a woman petitioner who had married a man in his father's power, but obviously without obtaining her father-in-law's clear consent; after her husband's death, the woman need not be concerned about a challenge to her child's legitimacy so long as her father-in-law had known of the marriage and had not expressly objected.

5. **A Father's Consent to Betrothal.** According to Paul (D. 23.1.7.1), betrothal requires consent from the same persons as does marriage; that is, a father's agreement is required for the engagement of a child in his power. But betrothal is not a binding arrangement (see Chapter II.B.1), and accordingly the requirements are interpreted laxly. Thus, a daughter's consent to betrothal is often presumed from her failure to object (Case 25). Conversely, says Paul (citing Julian): "a father is always held to grant consent to (the engagement of) his daughter unless he should openly refuse it." Why is the jurist so ready to presume the consent of the *pater familias*? Is the father's interest adequately protected?

6. **Consent of Relatives.** A *sui iuris* woman of legal age, no longer in the power of her father, could marry as she pleased (see Paul, D. 23.2.20). Still, it is likely that, especially for young women, older adults often played a role in choosing a husband; thus, for instance, the Emperor Septimius Severus (C. 5.4.1; A.D. 199) refers to a quarrel between a woman's guardian, her mother,

and her relatives over the best choice. The woman's guardian (see Chapter V.B.1) was probably involved because his consent was required to constitute a dowry from her property. More interesting is the participation of relatives, which apparently became formalized during the later Empire for women under twenty-five (C. 5.4.18, 20; A.D. 371, 408–409). Earlier, a letter of Pliny the Younger (*Epistulae* 1.14) vividly illustrates the intervention of relatives to find a suitable spouse for a woman.

CASE 101: Impaired Consent: Madness

D. 23.2.9 pr. (Ulpianus libro vicesimo sexto ad Sabinum)

Si nepos uxorem velit ducere avo furente, omnimodo patris auctoritas erit necessaria: sed si pater furit, avus sapiat, sufficit avi voluntas.

(Ulpian in the twenty-sixth book on Sabinus)

If a grandson wishes to marry and his grandfather is insane, his father's authorization will be absolutely necessary. But if his father is insane and his grandfather sane, the grandfather's consent is enough.

1. No Consent. Insanity of a prospective spouse was a bar to marriage because it negated consent, an essential requirement (see Paul, D. 23.2.16.2, quoted in the Discussion on Case 13). Here the same problem arises over the insanity of a *pater familias*. With which of the two positions stated by Paul in Case 98 does Ulpian agree?

2. The Whole Family's Crazy. Suppose both father and grandfather were insane; could the son go ahead with the marriage? Does the following Case suggest a possible answer to this question?

3. Justinian's Solution. In a constitution of A.D. 530 (C. 5.4.25; see Justinian, *Inst.* 1.10 pr.), Justinian weighed in on the more general problem. As he acknowledges, the classical jurists had debated whether the children of an insane father could marry. Virtually all the jurists had agreed that a daughter could marry; they held it sufficient if the father did not object. But there was much more doubt in the case of a son. Why would this case be more difficult? Finally, in the mid–second century A.D., imperial intervention allowed sons of senile fathers to marry, an outcome that Justinian confirms and extends. To what extent do you think it likely that Justinian's solution has influenced the way in which Justinian's *Digest* reports on controversies among the classical jurists?

CASE 102: Impaired Consent: Captivity

D. 23.2.9.1 (Ulpianus libro vicesimo sexto ad Sabinum)

Is cuius pater ab hostibus captus est, si non intra triennium revertatur, uxorem ducere potest.

D. 23.2.10 (Paulus libro trigesimo quinto ad edictum)

Si ita pater absit, ut ignoretur ubi sit et an sit, quid faciendum est, merito dubitatur. et si triennium effluxerit, postquam apertissime fuerit pater ignotus, ubi degit et an superstes sit, non prohibentur liberi eius utriusque sexus matrimonium vel nuptias legitimas contrahere.

D. 23.2.11 (Iulianus libro sexagesimo secundo Digestorum)

Si filius eius qui apud hostes est vel absit ante triennium captivitatis vel absentiae patris uxorem duxit vel si filia nupserit, puto recte matrimonium vel nuptias contrahi, dummodo eam filius ducat uxorem vel filia tali nubat, cuius condicionem certum sit patrem non repudiaturum.

(Ulpian in the twenty-sixth book on Sabinus)

If a man's father has been captured by the enemy and should not return home within three years, he can marry.

(Paul in the thirty-fifth book on the Edict)

If a father should be absent and it is unknown where he is or whether he is still alive, it is rightly doubted what should be done. If three years have passed from the time when it became very clear that the father's whereabouts or survival was unknown, his children of either sex are not prevented from contracting a lawful marriage.

(Julian in the sixty-second book of his *Digests*)

If the son or daughter of a man who is in enemy hands or (otherwise) absent marries before the end of a three-year period of the father's captivity or absence, I think that the marriage in either case is validly contracted, provided the son or daughter marry someone whose status the father is certain not to repudiate.

1. *Postliminium*. The Romans developed a body of rules, known collectively as *postliminium*, that dealt with the problem of citizens who had been captured by the enemy and actually or at least putatively enslaved. The legal relationships of such persons were a prime concern. The rule for those in the *potestas* of a captive was that, if he died in enemy hands, they were deemed to have been freed from his power retroactively to the date of his capture, whereas, if he returned, they were considered never to have left his power. If certain conditions were met, they could marry while their *pater familias* was in captivity,

which meant that not only they but, if they were sons, their children came under his *potestas* immediately upon his return. The jurist Tryphoninus justifies this somewhat odd result with the assertion that "it's not strange, since the situation and requirements of the occasion, plus the public good of marriage, call for this" (D. 49.15.12.3). What does he mean? How does "the public good of marriage" (*publica nuptiarum utilitas*) figure into his analysis?

2. The Three-Year Rule. Ulpian and Paul do not permit marriage until three years have passed since the father's disappearance or capture; but Julian apparently allows it at once, provided the spouse is suitable. Although these rules are formally compatible, do they seem to imply a different policy with regard to marriage? Do you think that the three-year rule cited by the jurists in these texts arose first in the context of *postliminium* or rather in that of simple absence? To which is it better suited?

3. A Suitable Spouse. What does Julian mean by "provided the son or daughter marry someone whose status the father is certain not to repudiate"? If it turns out that, contrary to reasonable expectation, the returning father does in fact disapprove of the spouse, will his disapproval be enough to end the marriage from that time forward, if not retroactively? (Remember that children may have been born in the interim.) In Julian's view, would it make any difference whether the three years had elapsed before the father's return? It should perhaps be noted that Julian uses "repudiate" (*repudiare*), the usual word for notification of divorce; can it be assumed that he regards the marriage as valid until the father ends it?

4. Dowry. One problem is that Roman marriage often involved a dowry, which was awkward to conclude while the status of a father was uncertain. Paul (D. 23.4.8) solves the problem this way: "Whenever a child-in-power marries while his or her father is insane or has been captured by enemies, a pact will also necessarily be made with them just for the dowry." Is this text entirely consistent with the present Case? See also Paul, *Frag. Vat.* 102.

CASE 103: Parental Consent and Public Policy

D. 23.2.19 (Marcianus libro sexto decimo Institutionum)

Capite trigesimo quinto legis Iuliae qui liberos quos habent in potestate iniuria prohibuerint ducere uxores vel nubere, vel qui dotem dare non volunt ex constitutione divorum Severi et Antonini, per proconsules praesidesque provinciarum coguntur in matrimonium collocare et dotare. prohibere autem videtur et qui condicionem non quaerit.

(Marcian in the sixteenth book of his *Institutes*)

In Chapter 35 of the *lex Iulia,* those who wrongfully prevent children in their power from marrying or, in accordance with the decree of the deified Emperors Severus and Caracalla, those who refuse to provide a dowry for them, are compelled by provincial governors to arrange marriages and provide dowries for them. Further, a person who does not (actively) seek to arrange this is deemed to prevent it.

1. Augustan Marriage Law. The *lex Iulia (et Papia)* in this text is the Augustan marriage legislation (see Case 12), the goal of which was to foster marriage and the rearing of children. What was the law on consent before Augustus? His law, at least as it is reported in this text, effectively required a father to arrange a marriage for his children; did it also require him to consent to a particular marriage of which he disapproved? And does the statute still allow him to force a marriage on his children?

2. New Rules. What is the contribution of Severus and Caracalla (joint reign: A.D. 197–211) to these rules? The Latin text is almost as convoluted as the translation given here, and many scholars have supposed that the preserved version is actually Justinian's generalization and consolidation of more gradual developments in classical law. See also the Discussion on Case 32.

3. Social Role. What does the last sentence suggest about the social role of the *pater familias* in the formation of his children's marriages?

4. Dowry. The Augustan law also provided that a *sui iuris* woman could apply to the urban praetor for the assignment of a *tutor* to constitute her dowry if her own *tutor* were under age and so unable to do this (*Tit. Ulp.* 11.20). What is the significance of the dowry here? Does this anticipate the rule enacted by Severus and Caracalla in any way?

CASE 104: Divorce: The Emperor Pius Intervenes

Paulus, *Sententiae* 5.6.15

Bene concordans matrimonium separari a patre divus Pius prohibuit . . . nisi forte quaeratur, ubi utilius morari debeat.

(Paul in the fifth book of his *Sentences*)

The deified Emperor Pius prohibited a father from breaking up a happy marriage, . . . unless perhaps question should arise as to where the person might with greater advantage reside.

1. Limits on *Potestas*. The Case evidently refers to the assertion of *potestas* through one of two interdicts granted by the praetor, whereby a *pater familias* could reclaim a child held by a third party (see Cases 107–108). It appears that the Emperor Antoninus Pius (reign: A.D. 138–161) was the first to restrict this paternal claim. Why might this change have been considered desirable? The legal texts suggest that in classical law a child-in-power could divorce without explicit permission from his or her *pater familias*. How does that square with the rule given here?

2. Residual Right. The last portion of this Case suggests that the father might still act if it was in the child's best interest. Who made that determination? Would another, more advantageous marriage be enough to satisfy the exception?

3. A Different Rule? Paul (*Frag. Vat.* 116) discusses a case in which a father, against his daughter's wishes, sends a declaration of divorce to his son-in-law; the father then reclaims the dowry that he had provided for the marriage (see Case 30). Paul responds: "The marriage, indeed, is legally dissolved by this very act (of sending the declaration); but if she is unwilling, the father cannot separate his daughter from her husband, nor can he reclaim the dowry unless his daughter (also) agrees." Can this decision be reconciled with the one above? Is it possible that Paul might distinguish between divorce and the physical separation of the couple? Or is the crucial issue whether the father has good cause for his declaration? As to the daughter, if her marriage has ended, what is her status if she remains with her spouse?

4. Yet Another Rule? Finally, consider Paul, *Sent.* 2.19.2: "For persons in the power of a *pater,* marriage cannot be legally contracted without his will (*sine voluntate eius*), but a marriage once contracted is not dissolved; for consideration of the public good outweighs the convenience of private individuals." Is Paul presuming here that the father does not have good cause? How is Paul attempting to balance "the public good" and "the convenience of private individuals"? What weighs on either side of this balance?

CASE 105: A Father Changes His Mind

C. 5.17.5 (Impp. Diocletianus et Maximianus AA. et CC. Scyrioni)

(pr.) Dissentientis patris, qui initio consensit matrimonio, cum marito concordante uxore filia familias ratam non haberi voluntatem divus Marcus pater noster religiosissimus imperator constituit, nisi magna et iusta causa interveniente hoc pater fecerit. (1) Invitam autem ad maritum redire nulla iuris praecepit constitutio. (2) Emancipatae vero filiae divortium in arbitrio suo non habet.

(The Emperors Diocletian and Maximian to Scyrio; A.D. 294)

(pr.) The deified Marcus, our predecessor and a most scrupulous emperor, established that if a father initially granted consent to a marriage and (then after the marriage) changed his mind, his will (*voluntas*) is deemed legally ineffective when his daughter-in-power is living in harmony with her husband. But (the outcome is) otherwise if the father acted on the basis of a great and just reason.

(1) Still, no provision of law requires that an unwilling woman return to her husband.

(2) He (the father), to be sure, does not have it within his discretion to bring about the divorce of a daughter who is freed from his power.

1. Reason. Diocletian relies on a statutory pronouncement (*constitutio*) of Marcus Aurelius (A.D. 161–180). What might qualify as a "great and just reason" validating a father's breakup of a marriage? Consider the following possibilities:

   • he learns that his son-in-law lied about his status;
   • his son-in-law lied about his wealth and is bankrupt;
   • his son-in-law is far less wealthy than he made himself out to be;
   • he learns that his son-in-law is cheating on his daughter;
   • the son-in-law or his close relative has become a political enemy.

   To what extent does Marcus Aurelius's *constitutio* seem like a logical development from the prohibition of his immediate predecessor, Antoninus Pius (Case 104)? It is conceivable that Marcus Aurelius was broadening a rather narrow ruling by Pius.

2. Father's Discretion. What do sections 1 and 2 contribute to an understanding of the father's discretion in the main Case under discussion? (Note that under no circumstances does a mother have a right to interfere with her children's marriages: Diocletian, C. 5.17.4; A.D. 294.)

CASE 106: Disposition of Gifts

D. 24.1.32.19–21 (Ulpianus libro trigesimo tertio ad Sabinum)

(19) Si socer nurui nuntium miserit, donatio erit irrita, quamvis matrimonium concordantibus viro et uxore secundum rescriptum imperatoris nostri cum patre comprobatum est: sed quod ad ipsos, inter quos donatio facta est, finitum est matrimonium. (20) Proinde et si duo consoceri invicem donaverint, idem erit dicendum, si invitis filiis nuntium remiserint, inter ipsos irritam esse donationem. in hac autem donatione inter soceros facta mors desideranda est eius qui donavit constante matrimonio et iure potestatis durante: idemque et in his qui sunt in eorum potestate. (21) Si consocer consocero donaverit et alter eorum vel uterque copulatos emancipaverit, debet dici donationem ad orationem non pertinere et ideo infirmari donationem.

(Ulpian in the thirty-third book on Sabinus)

(19) If a father-in-law has taken formal steps to break up his daughter-in-law's marriage, a (previous) gift (from her to him) will be invalid, even though the emperor (Caracalla) and his father have affirmed the (continuing) validity of a marriage where husband and wife are in harmony. But as far as the parties to the gift are concerned, the marriage has ended.

(20) Similarly, if two fellow fathers-in-law make gifts to one another, the same rule will apply if they take formal steps to end the marriage even though their children are unwilling; so gifts made between them are invalid. Moreover, in this gift giving between fathers-in-law, the one who made the gift must die while the marriage is still current and his *potestas* over his child remains (for the gift to be valid). The same holds for those in their power.

(21) If one father-in-law makes a gift to another and one or both of them emancipate the children united in marriage, the gift must be classed as irrelevant in terms of the legislative initiative (*oratio*) and so is invalid.

1. No Gifting. An old rule held that spouses could not make valuable gifts to each other or, if they were in a father's power, since they themselves could own no property, to the holders of *potestas* over each: see Cases 61–65. The motives were both idealistic and practical, effectively protecting patrimony for transmission to their children. This rule was amended by a legislative proposal (*oratio*) of Severus and Caracalla, subsequently ratified by the Senate, that permitted gifts, if made during a marriage and never rescinded, to remain valid if the giver died while still married; see Case 65. What is the point of this change in law? In the event of divorce, the old rule still held, so that, in order to be valid, the gift had to be confirmed by the giver after the divorce. Does this seem likely for a daughter-in-law whose father has tried to break up her marriage? •

2. Rescript. The text mentions a rescript of Severus and Caracalla that affirmed the validity of a harmonious marriage against the attempt by the *pater familias* to break it up. Is this rule consistent with those attributed to Pius and Marcus in the previous two Cases? Note that here the holder of *potestas* simply takes formal steps, by sending a notification of divorce, rather than relying on the interdicts mentioned in Case 107. Does this matter? If the marriage is still on, why is the daughter-in-law's gift to her father-in-law invalid? Can her marriage continue even though, as between her and her father-in-law, it has ended? Can the invalidity of her prior gift be correctly interpreted as a penalty assessed on the father-in-law?

3. Meddling In-Laws. The next paragraph (20) extends the rule to two meddling fathers-in-law. Was the intent aimed at discouraging such behavior in the case of a happy marriage?

4. Emancipation. In the context of release of one or both children from *potestas* (21), why does this make the gift irrelevant to the *oratio* and thus invalid?

CASE 107: Breaking Up Is Hard to Do

D. 43.30.1.5 (Ulpianus libro septuagensimo primo ad edictum)

Si quis filiam suam, quae mihi nupta sit, velit abducere vel exhiberi sibi desideret, an adversus interdictum exceptio danda sit, si forte pater concordans matrimonium, forte et liberis subnixum, velit dissolvere? et certo iure utimur, ne bene concordantia matrimonia iure patriae potestatis turbentur. quod tamen sic erit adhibendum, ut patri persuadeatur, ne acerbe patriam potestatem exerceat.

D. 43.30.2 (Hermogenianus libro sexto Iuris Epitomarum)

Immo magis de uxore exhibenda ac ducenda pater, etiam qui filiam in potestate habet, a marito recte convenitur.

(Ulpian in the seventy-first book on the Edict)

If a man's daughter is married to me, and he wishes to lead her away with him or should seek to have her produced for him, must an affirmative defense be raised against the interdict if, for instance, the father wishes to break up a happy marriage, perhaps even one enhanced by children?

We follow the fixed principle that truly happy marriages are not to be disturbed by the exercise of a father's power. Nevertheless, this rule is to be carried out by persuading the father not to employ his *patria potestas* harshly.

(Hermogenianus in the sixth book of his *Epitome of the Law*)

Indeed, as to producing and leading away a wife, it is more proper that a father, even one who has a daughter in his power, be sued by her husband.

1. Interdicts. As with the ruling of Pius (Case 104 above), this case concerns the praetor's grant of two interdicts, one to have children produced that a person claims are in his *potestas* and a second effectively granting custody upon his proof of the claim: see the Discussion on Case 108. We learn here that an affirmative defense (*exceptio*) was allowed to defeat the assertion of *potestas* in the case of a happy marriage, where the father evidently had no good grounds for demanding its dissolution. Why does it matter if there were children from the marriage?

2. Persuasion. From the Cases just examined, would you have predicted Ulpian's final point about persuading the holder of *potestas*? Why do you think the jurist insists on this? Suppose the father refused to be persuaded?

3. The Husband Sues. Hermogenianus is an early postclassical jurist active in the reign of Diocletian (A.D. 284–305). The right of a husband to sue his father-in-law for recovery of his wife is first attested in this period (see also Diocletian, C. 5.4.11). How big a change is this from classical law?

In modern family law, issues relating to the custody of children loom large, particularly in the aftermath of divorce. In Roman law, as in most legal systems prior to the modern period, custody is often thought of in a way that seems strange to us; the primary issue is, more or less, to whom do the children "belong"? At Rome, the strongly patriarchal ideology represented by *patria potestas* meant that, more or less inevitably, questions of custody were normally resolved in favor of the *pater familias*. Accordingly, the praetor's Edict provided a *pater familias* with means whereby he could compel third parties to produce and hand over children in his power (see the Discussion on Case 108). We have already seen these legal mechanisms at work against a son-in-law when a father wished to break up his daughter's marriage (Cases 104, 107), but, as this section shows, they could also be used against a wife or other relative. If, during these proceedings, a question arose about whether a child was in fact in the plaintiff's power, it was settled by a preliminary trial on this issue alone (see esp. Ulpian, D. 6.1.1.2).

Although this patriarchal regime generally prevailed throughout the long history of Roman law, problems with it inevitably arose. From a modern perspective, the problems are not hard to understand. They stem from realization that children, particularly those of "tender years," are often best raised by their mothers; that some parents may be unfit to act as custodians for their children; that children themselves may have a strong preference in the matter; and, above all, that the "best interests of the child" should be closely observed and are at times not satisfied by automatic preference of one parent over another—a powerful concept that refocuses attention on the child rather than the parents. These and other competing considerations make the modern law of custody complex and controversial. But even when Roman legal sources acknowledge difficulties with the traditional Roman household regime, they allude to the underlying sources of the difficulties only in passing—and this despite the fact that such difficulties must have been considerably exacerbated by the continuance of paternal control into adulthood. Visitation rights for the noncustodial parent are not mentioned in legal sources, nor are arrangements for joint custody, though presumably informal agreements to this effect were not unknown.

Closely related to custody is the issue of maintenance. As we have seen (Case 60), a husband normally had no legal duty to maintain his wife, although her dowry was often used for this purpose (e.g., Case 69). Originally, fathers also probably had no duty to maintain their children by providing food, shelter, and so on; nor, as it seems, were children obligated to support their parents. This changed, however, in the mid–second century A.D., when the emperors began to enforce duties of maintenance between linear ascendants and descendants; these duties were imposed, furthermore, without regard to the traditional boundaries and kinship ties of the agnatic *familia,* so that, for instance, not just fathers but mothers as well could now be ordered to support their children, and vice versa, regardless of whether the children had been released from *patria potestas* through emancipation (Cases 155–158). No doubt the creation of a civil duty of maintenance substituted for the absence of governmental social programs; we have no real way of assessing how well the duty of maintenance worked in practice, and also no reason to be optimistic on this score.

CASE 108: Stealing a Child

Gaius, *Institutiones* 3.199

Interdum autem etiam liberorum hominum furtum fit, veluti si quis liberorum nostrorum qui in potestate nostra sint, sive etiam uxor quae in manu nostra sit, sive etiam iudicatus vel auctoratus meus subreptus fuerit.

(Gaius in the third book of his *Institutes*)

What is more, sometimes there can even be theft of free persons, for example, if one of our children who is in our power is stolen, or also a wife in our *manus* or also my judgment-debtor or sworn gladiator.

1. Just Like a Slave. Gaius makes this striking extension of the delict of theft (*furtum*) in the context of his discussion of stealing slaves. Children-in-power are here ranked with wives married with *manus,* who with regard to their husbands are in a legal position somewhat analogous to that of a child (see Case 37). So are judgment-debtors, who have been condemned in a lawsuit and bound over to the plaintiff in order to work off their debt; and gladiators who, though nominally free, take a solemn oath (*auctoramentum*) that places them entirely at the disposal of their employer. Can you determine what these types have in common with each other? In what sense is it possible to "steal" such persons from someone? Does this rule effectively reduce them to the status of property, like slaves?

2. The Suit for Theft. In Roman law, the victim of a theft is permitted to sue the thief not only for return of the stolen object or its value (by what is called a *condictio furtiva*) but also for a multiple of the value of the object, presumably in order to punish the thief and assuage the victim's outrage. How would the value of a "stolen" child be measured?

3. Procedure. Paul (D. 47.2.38.1) observes that although it is possible to sue on *furtum* for the theft of free persons, it is not permitted to bring the action for recovery of property (*condictio furtiva*). Does this make sense? In practice, however, it was more common for the father to ask for one or both of the two interdicts (orders issued by a praetor or other authorized official, such as a provincial governor) that require a defendant, who is allegedly detaining a child in the plaintiff father's power, to produce that child and not to take the child away. For the wording of these interdicts, see Ulpian, D. 43.30.1 pr. and 3 pr. The child who is the subject of such an interdict might, of course, be an adult; see Case 107 for an example, where a father attempts to use the interdict in order to break up his daughter's marriage. Custody of a child is claimed on the basis of *patria potestas.* But the actuality of the *patria potestas* could, of course, be contested by the defendant, in which case a trial would ensue to determine this (see Case 110).

CASE 109: Mother versus Father

D. 43.30.1.3 (Ulpianus libro septuagensimo primo ad edictum)

Si vero mater sit, quae retinet, apud quam interdum magis quam apud patrem morari filium debere (ex iustissima scilicet causa) et divus Pius decrevit et a Marco et a Severo rescriptum est, aeque subveniendum ei erit per exceptionem.

(Ulpian in the seventy-first book on the Edict)

If indeed it is the mother who retains custody—for the deified Pius has decided in a court case, and (the Emperors) Marcus and Severus have determined in rescripts, that sometimes a child should better remain with her rather than with the father, provided there is a very convincing reason—(then) it is fair that she be assisted by (being given) an affirmative defense (against her husband's claim of custody).

Hypothetical Situation.

After a divorce, a father uses an interdict to sue his former wife in order to force her to surrender custody of their child to him. Under what circumstances can she resist his claim?

1. Maternal Custody. What would Ulpian regard as "a very convincing reason" for granting the mother custody? Is this issue clarified by the reference in Case 49 to the father's "depravity"? Does either case seem to permit the mother to challenge a father who already has custody of a child? Probably not; compare Paul, D. 47.2.38 pr., who does not permit the mother to sue on theft of her child (see Case 108). Does this follow logically from general principles of Roman family law?

2. Losing Custody. Does the denial of custody mean that the father loses *patria potestas* over the child? In Case 49, Ulpian says no: the mother obtains custody "without decrease in *patria potestas*." Is this any more than a legal fiction in deference to tradition?

3. Rule Change. What was the law before Pius? What do you think this emperor's motive was in making this change? This Case is an especially nice example of how legal change often occurred in classical Roman law: an imperial decision in a particular lawsuit (perhaps a "hard case") is gradually extended by subsequent imperial rescripts, until the jurists finally generalize it as a legal rule.

4. Postclassical Law. After the classical period, judges acquired much greater power to allocate custody of children after a divorce; see, for instance, the rescript of Diocletian (C. 5.24.1; A.D. 294) quoted in the Discussion on Case 49. It is likely that this later law has influenced the reporting of earlier law in sources such as Justinian's *Digest*.

CASE 110: Deciding on Custody

D. 43.30.3.4 (Ulpianus septuagensimo primo ad edictum)

Iulianus ait, quotiens id interdictum movetur de filio ducendo vel cognitio et is de quo agitur impubes est, alias differri oportere rem in tempus pubertatis, alias repraesentari: idque ex persona eorum, inter quos controversia erit, et ex genere causae constituendum est. nam si is, qui se patrem dicit, auctoritatis prudentiae fidei exploratae esset, usque in diem litis impuberem apud se habebit: is vero, qui controversiam facit, humilis calumniator notae nequitiae, repraesentanda cognitio est. item si is, qui impuberem negat in aliena potestate esse, vir omnibus modis probatus, tutor vel testamento vel a praetore datus pupillum, quem in diem litis apud se habuit, tuetur, is vero, qui patrem se dicit, suspectus est quasi calumniator, differri litem non oportebit. si vero utraque persona suspecta est aut tamquam infirma aut tamquam turpis, non erit alienum, inquit, disponi, apud quem interim puer educeretur et controversiam in tempus pubertatis differri, ne per collusionem vel imperitiam alterutrius contendentium aut alienae potestati pater familias addicatur aut filius alienus patris familiae loco constituatur.

(Ulpian in the seventy-first book on the Edict)

Julian says that whenever this interdict granting custody is at issue, or when a judicial investigation is under way, and the person whose status is in dispute is a child (*impubes*), sometimes the matter should be deferred until the child becomes an adult, and at other times it ought to be dealt with right away; this issue must be determined on the basis of the nature of the parties to the dispute and the character of the case. For if the person claiming to be a *pater familias* is someone of proven respect, judgment, and trustworthiness, he will keep the child in his custody until the day the lawsuit is decided; but if the man challenging his claim is a lower-class false accuser of known worthlessness, a hearing ought to be held at once.

Likewise, if the man who denies that the child is actually in someone else's power is a man upright in every way, for example, a guardian appointed by will or by the praetor, he will keep his ward in his custody until the day of the lawsuit; but if, however, the person who claims to be a *pater* is thought to be making a false accusation, the suit ought not to be postponed.

If, to be sure, both parties are deemed to be of unsound or bad character, it will not be inappropriate, he (Julian) says, for an arrangement to be made that the child be brought up in the custody of a third party and that the dispute be postponed until his or her adulthood, so that a person of independent status (a *pater familias*) not be bound over to the power of another person, nor someone else's son-in-power be granted independent status through collusion or the inexperience of either of the litigants.

Hypothetical Situation

A ten-year-old boy who feels that he is being abused by his father takes refuge with a relative. The father attempts to retrieve the boy by applying for an interdict. Will the father succeed?

1. Legal Majority. This Case does not concern a custody battle between a husband and wife after their divorce but rather deals with a more fundamental issue: the efficacy of the father's claim to custody and how this claim was handled by Roman law when what we refer to as the best interests of the child may be fairly directly involved. What is surprising is the degree of flexibility that this Case permits. According to the jurist Julian, a contemporary of the Emperor Antoninus Pius, it was possible to defer a grant of custody under the edict *de liberis ducendis* until the child reached the age of majority, which was fourteen for boys, twelve for girls (see Case 6). At this age a child without a *pater familias* achieved in principle the same rights over his or her property that adults enjoyed (although until age twenty-five boys and girls often made use of a different form of guardian, called a *curator,* with responsibilities only for the child's property; see Chapter V.A.2), and they also might legally marry. Why is this an opportune time for deciding the issue of custody?

2. Haste. According to the text, if the man claiming to be the father is a well-respected person, he may retain custody until the issue is decided at the time of the child's majority. But if not, and particularly if the man is thought to be making a false claim, the hearing should be held at once. On this set of facts, what outcome would you expect from an accelerated hearing? Why the need for haste?

3. Usual Scenario. Ulpian posits a scenario where a claim of *potestas* is countered by a man who is acting as guardian (*tutor*) of the child. How likely a situation is this?

4. *Tutor.* If the man acting as *tutor* is well respected, Ulpian says the child can stay with him until majority; but if the man asserting *potestas* is thought to be making a false claim, the matter should be decided at once. Does this make sense?

5. Third Party. If both parties are deemed unsuitable for reasons of character, a third party must be found who will raise the child until determination of the matter at the child's majority. The justification for the delay is a concern that an erroneous decision on *potestas* might be made "through collusion or the inexperience of either of the litigants." What does this suggest about the practical limits on the magistrate's ability to acquire good information about a case

before him? How does this justify the outcome? Are the child's interests adequately protected? It is unusual for the jurists to acknowledge frankly shortcomings in Roman judicial procedure. What influence might these shortcomings have had both on this and on other decisions you have read?

CASE 111: Self-Custody

D. 43.30.5 (Venuleius libro quarto Interdictorum)

Si filius sua sponte apud aliquem est, inutile hoc interdictum erit, quia filius magis apud se quam apud eum est, in quem interdicetur, cum liberam facultatem abeundi vel remanendi haberet: nisi si inter duos, qui se patres dicerent, controversia esset et alter ab altero exhiberi eum desideraret.

(Venuleius in the fourth book *On Interdicts*)

If of his own accord a child is living in a third party's house, this interdict will have no place, because the child is more in his own custody than in that of the person against whom the interdict will lie, since he has a free choice of going or staying. An exception occurs if a dispute arises between two men who assert *potestas,* and one of them wishes the child to be produced in court by the other.

1. Age Limit. The interdicts for producing and leading away a child-in-power can be used only against third parties, not against the children themselves (Ulpian, D. 43.30.3.3). What minimum age must children have reached to be able to decide the issue of custody on their own? Does this Case seem to presume a fact situation somewhat like the following: because of a quarrel with his father, an adult child has gone to live with a friend?

2. Character. Is the character of the father relevant to the child's ability to decide?

3. Two Claims of *Potestas.* Under the exceptional situation canvassed by the jurist, is the true holder of *potestas* guaranteed custody?

4. Custody without *Potestas.* Where *potestas* was not an issue, for example, when the *pater familias* was deceased, the praetor or provincial governor had great latitude in awarding custody, even to the point of disregarding the deceased father's instructions as expressed in his will (see Ulpian, D. 27.2.1 and 5). Ulpian indicates that the magistrate in making his decision should be concerned to shield the child from possible sexual abuse. Why is there no mention of possible physical abuse by corporal punishment? See Case 94 above.

5. Coresidence. Do the Cases you have read on custody establish conclusively that coresidence is not important to the Roman legal concept of a *familia?* That is, in Roman law is the "family" (as we recognize it) fundamentally distinct from the *familia?*

CASE 112: Maintenance of Relatives

D. 25.3.5 pr.–4 (Ulpianus libro secundo de Officio Consulis)

(pr.) Si quis a liberis ali desideret vel si liberi, ut a parente exhibeantur, iudex de ea re cognoscet. (1) Sed utrum eos tantum liberos qui sunt in potestate cogatur quis exhibere, an vero etiam emancipatos vel ex alia causa sui iuris constitutos, videndum est. et magis puto, etiamsi non sunt liberi in potestate, alendos a parentibus et vice mutua alere parentes debere. (2) Utrum autem tantum patrem avumve paternum proavumve paterni avi patrem ceterosque virilis sexus parentes alere cogamur, an vero etiam matrem ceterosque parentes et per illum sexum contigentes cogamur alere, videndum. et magis est, ut utrubique se iudex interponat, quorundam necessitatibus facilius succursurus, quorundam aegritudini: et cum ex aequitate haec res descendat caritateque sanguinis, singulorum desideria perpendere iudicem oportet. (3) Idem in liberis quoque exhibendis a parentibus dicendum est. (4) Ergo et matrem cogemus praesertim volgo quaesitos liberos alere nec non ipsos eam.

(Ulpian in the second book *On the Duties of the Consul*)

(pr.) If someone seeks support from (his or her) children, or if children (ask) that they be maintained by a parent, a judge will investigate the matter. (1) But we must examine whether a person is compelled to support only children who are in his power or rather also emancipated (children) or those who became *sui iuris* for some other reason. The better view, I think, is that even if children are not in power, they must be supported by their parents, and conversely they should support their parents.

(2) But let us examine whether we are compelled to support only a father or a paternal grandfather or a great-grandfather on the paternal side and other male antecedents or rather also a mother and other antecedents and relatives through that (female) sex. The better view is that the judge should intervene generally, so as to relieve the financial needs of some and the infirmity of others; and since this matter derives from fairness and from affection for blood relatives, the judge must weigh the claims of (all) individuals.

(3) The same should be said also for the maintenance of children by their parents.

(4) Therefore, we also compel a mother to support especially her illegitimate children; and (conversely) them (to support) her.

1. Descent and the Duty of Maintenance. This text is from Ulpian's commentary on the duties of the consul, a magistrate charged by the emperors with a variety of judicial duties in areas related to private law. Here, he is evidently directed to determine whether one family member is obliged to maintain another. This duty was established in a series of imperial enactments that begin in the reign of Antoninus Pius (A.D. 138–161); C. 5.25.1 quotes one of these ("It is right that children provide for the needs of their parents"). Gradually

the duty was enlarged, but as the present text shows, its exact extent remained controversial. The following points should be noted: (1) The duty extends only to linear ascendants and descendants, not to collateral relatives; hence a parent or a child may have this duty to one another but not, for example, to siblings or first cousins, to say nothing of spouses (see Case 60). (2) The duty runs in both directions, from ascendants to descendants and vice versa. (3) Jurists disputed whether the duty included only agnates or all blood relatives; in section 2, Ulpian opts for the more generous interpretation, which, it should be noted, oversteps the ancient insistence on agnatic kinship as the basic organizing principle of family duties. (4) A closely related issue arose over whether the duty was limited only to persons linked by *patria potestas* or extended also to legitimate children released from their father's power through emancipation (on which, see below, Part C.3), or even further to illegitimate children; in section 1 and 4, Ulpian opts for the more generous interpretation. What arguments might other jurists have made in favor of a more restrictive view? Does it make any sense to include an emancipated child but exclude a brother?

2. Illegitimacy. The duty of maintenance, says Ulpian in section 2, "derives from fairness (*aequitate*) and from affection for blood relatives"; and a rescript of Septimius Severus (C. 5.25.4; A.D. 197) indicates that the law only provides what family members normally do of their free will. How compelling is this justification? Is it wise to use legal sanctions to enforce ordinary family obligations? In any case, one of the most striking applications of the duty concerns illegitimate children. In section 4, Ulpian holds the mother responsible for maintenance, but a rescript of Marcus Aurelius (C. 5.25.3; A.D. 162), addressed to a woman named Tatiana, indicates that the father, if he could be identified, was also responsible: "If you prove to a competent judge that this boy, whom you allege you gave birth to from Claudius, is (in fact) his son, he (the judge) will order that maintenance be provided to him in proportion to his (the father's) means. He will also assess whether he should be raised in his (the father's) house." The boy is fairly clearly illegitimate and hence not subject to the father's *potestas;* but the law requires only that the father's parentage be proven (Ulpian, D. 25.3.5.8), not also legitimacy. Which prevails in this rescript, fairness or affection for blood relatives?

3. Measuring Maintenance. The formula used over and over again is that maintenance is owed "in proportion to (the defendant's) means" (*pro modo facultatium*). This is a flexible standard; however, as the rescript quoted in the previous note makes clear, not only physical sustenance but also other needs are covered (compare Ulpian, D. 25.3.5.12). (However, a son need not pay his father's debts: ibid. 16.) Maintenance was only awarded when the relative was in actual need, for instance, because he could not practice a trade owing to

illness (ibid. 7); and though past practice might help determine the amount, it need not be lavish (ibid. 14). A rescript of Septimius Severus (C. 5.25.4; A.D. 197) indicates that a son-in-power whose father had declined him basic support could apply for maintenance like any other entitled relative. Do these sources indicate that maintenance involves more than providing subsistence? On enforcement, see Ulpian, D. 25.3.5.10: if the relative refuses, his property is sold at public auction.

4. Ingratitude. A judge was also expected to assess whether a relative might have good reason for not providing support. Thus, a father can properly refuse support if his son has informed on him to the authorities (Ulpian, D. 25.3.5.11).

PART B

Property and Obligations

The Roman institution of *patria potestas* seems odd enough today even if we look only at the father's direct control over the lives of his children. However, this is scarcely the extent of the institution. In this part we examine the effects of *patria potestas* on the interactions of the household with the external world. As we shall see, paternal power has the potential consequence of bottling up much entrepreneurial energy within the household. In modern societies, children, as they reach adulthood, tend to leave the family domicile and establish themselves elsewhere, earning money and keeping the profits for themselves. This usually renders them independent, or largely so, of their parents, and so they are able to make their own contribution to society. Children retain the rewards of their labor, so the theory runs, and society benefits from increased wealth.

The Roman arrangement, though considerably mitigated by high mortality rates, tended to contain youthful energy and discourage individual initiative. However, as we shall see, the arrangement was not without certain advantages. In particular, the household tended to operate within society and the economy as a sort of protocorporation, an economic unit; and the Roman jurists were ingenious in figuring out ways to facilitate this function. Children were an important part of the corporate nature of the household, but the Romans also made extensive use of slaves to the same effect.

We begin with the issue of acquisitions. We are used to the idea that even young children can have an independent estate. A ten-year-old boy who receives a large legacy from an aunt takes the money for himself, even if it is managed by others until he reaches adulthood; a four-year-old movie star earns residuals on her own behalf. By contrast, the children in a Roman household had no independent estates. With only modest exceptions, at law they owned and possessed no property of their own, and this was true no matter how old they were, so long as they remained in the power of a *pater familias*.

What, then, if third parties transferred property to children or promised to pay them money as a gift or in return for services? The short answer is that the *pater familias* acquired everything. But this also meant that he was able to use his children (as well as his slaves) as extensions of himself in the amassing of wealth for his household.

In the end, though, one issue you may wish to consider is whether a legal regime such as the Roman one would have been socially tolerable except under conditions of very high mortality. But even if only a fairly restricted number of adults were encumbered with a living *pater familias*, why wouldn't their plight have led to legal change?

CASE 113: Owning and Possessing Nothing

D. 41.2.49.1 (Papinianus libro secundo Definitionum)

Qui in aliena potestate sunt, rem peculiarem tenere possunt, habere possidere non possunt, quia possessio non tantum corporis, sed et iuris est.

(Papinian in the second book of his *Definitions*)

Those who are in another person's power can hold (i.e., physically possess) the property in a *peculium,* (but) they cannot own or (legally) possess it, since possession is a matter not just of physicality but also of law.

1. The *Peculium.* Papinian states the fundamental rule in this Case clearly but somewhat obliquely. Although a child-in-power (like a slave) had no property of his or her own, the *pater familias* frequently granted the child effective control over some property, in a way broadly similar to a modern allowance but, at least among the upper classes, often on a much larger scale; and this control was recognized at law as the *peculium* (literally, as it seems, "petty cash fund"), with legal implications examined more fully below in section 3. Nonetheless, as Papinian says, the child does not legally own or possess this property. Rather, it is owned and possessed by the *pater familias* and so forms part of the household. Is it fair to conclude that, since children-in-power do not even own or possess their *peculia,* they will therefore also not own or possess any other property within the household?

2. Two Kinds of Possession. What is the difference between physical possession ("holding"; the Latin verb is *tenere*) and legal possession (*possidere*)? The latter is, as Papinian says, a legal relationship that is defined by law and protected by legal remedies if it is violated. A son may physically control property in the sense of having it with him and using it; but precisely because he is in his father's power, he is still not in legal possession of it, and if a third party interferes with property held by the son, it is only his father who has the remedies.

3. *Patria Potestas.* It is obviously consistent with the nature of *patria potestas* that children-in-power are denied the capacity to own property. But does *patria potestas* actually entail the child's lack of capacity? For instance, could a *pater familias* grant his children the right to own and possess property for themselves, in a way that would then be legally enforceable against third parties or even against himself? Why or why not?

4. Can Children-in-Power Write Wills? A postclassical text (*Tit. Ulp.* 20.10 = Case 138) gives an emphatic answer: "A son-in-power cannot make a will since he has nothing of his own that he can make a will for." Soldiers were a partial exception; see Case 138.

CASE 114: Through Whom Do We Acquire?

Gaius, *Institutiones* 2.86–87

(86) Adquiritur autem nobis non solum per nosmet ipsos, sed etiam per eos quos in potestate manu mancipiove habemus; item per eos servos, in quibus usumfructum habemus; item per homines liberos et servos alienos quos bona fide possidemus. . . . (87) Igitur <quod> liberi nostri quos in potestate habemus, item quod servi nostri mancipio accipiunt vel ex traditione nanciscuntur, sive quid stipulentur, vel ex aliqualibet causa adquirunt, id nobis adquiritur; ipse enim, qui in potestate nostra est, nihil suum habere potest. et ideo si heres institutus sit, nisi nostro iussu hereditatem adire non potest; et si iubentibus nobis adierit, hereditas nobis adquiritur proinde atque si nos ipsi heredes instituti essemus; et convenienter scilicet legatum per eos nobis adquiritur.

(Gaius in the second book of his *Institutes*)

(86) Moreover, we acquire (ownership of property) not only through ourselves but also through those whom we have in our *potestas, manus,* or charge (*mancipium*). The same is true for those slaves whose usufruct we have, as well as for free persons and slaves belonging to others if we possess them in good faith. . . . (87) So whatever our children-in-power and slaves take through formal conveyance or handover, or whatever they stipulate for or acquire on any basis whatsoever, becomes our property. For a person in our power can own no property of his own.

For this reason, if he (our son-in-power or slave) is appointed heir (by a third party), he cannot accept the inheritance unless we order him to do so, and if he accepts an inheritance upon our order, the inheritance becomes our property just as if we had been appointed heirs ourselves. In consequence, a legacy of course also accrues to us through them.

1. The Household Circle. In section 86 Gaius attempts an exhaustive list of the persons through whom a *pater familias* can acquire property. They fall into two broad classes. The first class consists of free family members, of which natural descendants (but also adopted children; see below, Part C.2) are the major examples; but the class also includes a wife in *manus* (Chapter II.C.1; virtually obsolete in classical law) and free persons held in a state of civil bondage called *mancipium* (see the introduction to section 4 below). The second class consists of the slaves of the *pater familias,* including not only his own slaves (held in his *potestas*) but also slaves who are owned by a third party but whose labor he profits from under a property arrangement called usufruct. Finally, and by analogy (as it seems), the head of the household also acquires through persons (whether actually freemen or slaves belonging to another) whom he holds in the honest but mistaken belief that they are his own slaves; the freeman may successfully assert his free status, or the true

owner may reclaim the slave, but in the meantime the holder in good faith can acquire through them. Despite the complexity of these various classes (some of which were controversial among the jurists), the two essential groups are the children and the slaves of the *pater familias*.

2. Agency? Agency is a legal relationship in which one person acts for or represents another by the latter's authority. In its most fully developed form, the agent becomes effectively an extension of the principal, who alone acquires legal rights and duties as a result of the agent's transaction. Agency is today one of the most common legal phenomena, a building block of modern commercial enterprises. In Roman law, however, as the next Case shows, agency is rarely permitted outside the immediate legal context of the household. If children and slaves can acquire for a *pater familias,* can they be correctly described as his agents? What distinguishes them from modern agents is that they were entitled to act on another's behalf by reason of a separate and preexisting legal relationship. A *pater familias* has children in his power, just as he owns slaves, and it is *because* of *patria potestas* or ownership (and not because of an authorization) that his children and slaves can acquire for him. Is this difference crucial? As we shall see, children-in-power and slaves are much less than full agents in the modern sense.

3. Three Kinds of Acquisition. Papinian mentions three distinct ways in which the *pater familias* can acquire. The first is mancipation, a formal ceremony whereby the ownership of property of certain kinds (*res mancipi:* principally land, slaves, and large farm animals) is transferred from one person to another. The second is physical handover (*traditio*), whereby the possession of property is transferred; in the case of property other than *res mancipi,* handover also usually transfers ownership if this is what the parties intend. The third is stipulation, whereby one person (called in Roman usage the stipulator) receives another person's formal promise that he or she will act, usually to the stipulator's benefit; see further Case 117. Thus, a *pater familias* can acquire both property and contractual claims through his children and slaves.

4. Acquiring and Owning. The persons who acquire for another cannot own property of their own. Is this necessarily true? Consider the following example: A son-in-power, while plowing his father's field, uncovers a treasure trove buried long ago by an unknown party. Does his *pater* acquire the treasure? See Tryphoninus, D. 41.1.63 pr. (yes). Why shouldn't the son be allowed to keep the treasure for himself? Does the Roman rule encourage deception or slacking on the part of the son?

5. Bequests. The last portion of this Case deals with a situation in which a third party dies and leaves his or her estate, or a legacy from that estate, to someone else's child-in-power or slave. This seems to have been common; why might

it have occurred? Gaius indicates that the heir or legatee is allowed to "approach" (*adire;* i.e., accept) the bequest only after receiving the "order" (*iussum*) of the *pater familias* (see also *Tit. Ulp.* 19.19). The bequest then becomes the property of the *pater*. Why must the child-in-power receive the permission of the *pater*? As we shall see (in Case 116), a father's knowledge, at least, may also be required in the case of other acquisitions; but inheritances are arguably more delicate. Why?

CASE 115: Ownership and Possession

Gaius, *Institutiones* 2.89, 95

(89) Non solum autem proprietas per eos, quos in potestate habemus, adquiritur nobis, sed etiam possessio; cuius enim rei possessionem adepti fuerint, id nos possidere videmur; unde etiam per eos usucapio procedit. . . . (95) Ex his apparet per liberos homines quos neque iuri nostro subiectos habemus neque bona fide possidemus, item per alienos servos in quibus neque usumfructum habemus neque iustam possessionem, nulla ex causa nobis adquiri posse. et hoc est, quod vulgo dicitur per extraneam personam nobis adquiri non posse; tantum de possessione quaeritur, an per <procuratorem> nobis adquiratur.

(Gaius in the second book of his *Institutes*)

(89) Through those whom we have in our power, we acquire not only ownership but also possession; for when they take possession of anything, we are held to possess it. So also usucapion runs through them. . . .

(95) From these considerations it seems that on no basis can we acquire (ownership or possession) through free persons whom we do not hold subject to our power and whom we do not possess in good faith, nor through slaves whom we neither have in usufruct nor have legal possession of. And it is for this reason that it is commonly said that ownership cannot be acquired through an outside person.

A question arises only concerning possession, as to whether we acquire it through a general manager (*procurator*).

1. Usucapion. Section 89 basically reaffirms the rule of Case 114. It adds, however, one new wrinkle. Suppose that possession of a slave (a *res mancipi*) is handed over to a son-in-power, and that the transferrer intends to transfer ownership as well; nevertheless, ownership does not pass, because title to a *res mancipi* must be conveyed by a formal ceremony. But in Roman law, under ordinary circumstances, the possessor still is protected as if he or she were the owner; the possessor becomes, in the technical phrase, a "bonitary owner." After one year in the case of a movable *res mancipi* (two years for land), the bonitary owner becomes the full owner. Gaius is saying that the *pater familias* can become a bonitary owner through his child-in-power or a slave.

2. The Exclusive Household and the *Procurator*. It is section 95 that is really important here. Why is it that, although acquisition can occur through subordinates within the household, it cannot occur through "outsiders" (*extranei*, "strangers" or "foreigners")? Gaius notes a possible exception only for a *procurator*, a free person whom a principal appoints to manage his or her affairs. (The text of Gaius is restored on the basis of Neratius, D. 41.1.13 pr.) At most, on Gaius's view, the *procurator* can acquire for the principal only possession,

not ownership; however, in most instances, by taking possession the principal would also acquire ownership either immediately or through usucapion (see, e.g., Ulpian, D. 41.1.20.2). Why might the Romans have resisted the concept of "outside" agency even in the case of beneficial acquisitions? In other words, why are they so reliant on their household circle?

CASE 116: The Father's Knowledge

D. 41.2.1.5 (Paulus libro quinquagensimo quarto ad edictum)

Item adquirimus possessionem per servum aut filium, qui in potestate est, et quidem earum rerum, quas peculiariter tenent, etiam ignorantes, sicut Sabino et Cassio et Iuliano placuit, quia nostra voluntate intellegantur possidere, qui eis peculium permiserimus. igitur ex causa peculiari et infans et furiosus adquirunt possessionem et usucapiunt, et here<dita>s, si hereditarius servus emat.

(Paul in the fifty-fourth book on the Edict)

Likewise we acquire possession through a slave or a son who is in (our) power; and indeed, (we acquire possession) of those things that they hold in a *peculium* even though (we are) unaware (that we do so), since, according to Sabinus and Cassius and Julian, they are understood to possess by our will (*nostra voluntate*) since we allowed them to have a *peculium*. So on the basis of a *peculium*, even an infant and a madman acquire possession and usucapt, as does an inheritance if a slave in the inheritance makes a purchase.

1. Is Knowledge Required? Look back at the text of Cases 114–115. Does Gaius seem to require that the *pater familias* know of the acquisition by the son or slave? In this Case, by contrast, Paul strongly implies that knowledge is required (except in the case of a *peculium*); if so, that would significantly limit the role of a child-in-power or slave as an agent. Our sources are not clear, and classical jurists themselves may have disputed the issue; but some scholars believe that Justinian's compilers altered classical texts to produce the result here. In any case, why might acquisition outside the *peculium* have made some Roman lawyers uneasy?

2. Is Knowledge Required Only for Usucapion? Compare this fragment of Paul, D. 41.4.2.11: "Celsus writes that if my slave takes possession on the basis of a *peculium*, I usucapt even though unaware of this action; but if not on the basis of a *peculium*, (I do) not (usucapt) unless I know." If this text is taken at face value, the slave's action, if not on the basis of a *peculium*, would result in the master possessing but not yet being able to usucapt (acquire ownership of a *res mancipi* through passage of time). (Compare Papinian, D. 41.3.44.7; Paul, D. 41.3.47.) Is this position preferable to the one suggested by the present Case?

3. The Slave's Knowledge. Paul, D. 41.2.1.9–10: "However, the person through whom we wish to possess must have an understanding of possession. (10) So if you send an insane slave to take possession, you are not regarded as taking possession." Does this mean only that the slave or child-in-power must understand that possession is being taken, or is an intent to take possession

specifically for the *pater* also required? Possibly the latter; see Paul, D. 41.2.1.19 ("[I]f you order your slave to take possession and he enters possession with the intent that he does not wish to acquire for you but rather for Titius, you have not acquired possession"). But this text may have been altered by the compilers of the *Digest*.

CASE 117: Acquiring a Debt

D. 45.1.38.17 (Ulpianus libro quadragensimo nono ad Sabinum)

Alteri stipulari nemo potest, praeterquam si servus domino, filius patri stipuletur: inventae sunt enim huiusmodi obligationes ad hoc, ut unusquisque sibi adquirat quod sua interest: ceterum ut alii detur, nihil interest mea. . . .

(Ulpian in the forty-ninth book on Sabinus)

No one can make a stipulation to the benefit of someone else except where a slave makes a stipulation on behalf of his master, or a son-in-power on behalf of his *pater* (*familias*). Obligations of this kind were devised so that each man should acquire for himself what is of benefit to him; but it is of no benefit to me that something be given to another person. . . .

1. Stipulation to the Benefit of Third Parties. A stipulation is a formal oral contract in which one party, the stipulator, puts a question ("Do you promise to pay me 50?"), and the other party, the promissor, responds ("I promise"). Such a promise is legally binding because it accords with the formal requirements for this contract (see Gaius, *Inst.* 3.92–109). Ordinarily, however, a stipulation in favor of a third party ("Do you promise to pay 50 to Titius?") is entirely void, meaning that neither Titius nor the stipulator can sue if the promissor fails to pay. Why is this so, do you think? However, as this Case indicates, children-in-power and slaves can make binding stipulations in favor of a *pater familias* ("Do you promise to pay 50 to my father?"); the *pater* can then sue to enforce the promise. Does this follow logically from the more general right to acquire through a child or slave? Is the knowledge of the *pater* apparently required?

2. Nobody Turns Down Free Money. Can a son stipulate to his father's benefit even if his father forbids this? The answer is yes; see Julian, D. 45.1.62 (a slave). Is this rule problematic? Are there persons from whom you would be unwilling to receive gifts or the promise of gifts, even indirectly? If a son entered into a contract, such as a sale, giving rights and duties to both parties, the father could enforce the rights only if he was willing to fulfill the duties; see Paul, D. 21.1.57 pr. (of a slave). Does this suggest some dangers with unwanted contractual "entanglements"?

3. A Disabled *Pater Familias*. Since a stipulation is an oral contract, a *pater familias* cannot conclude one if he is mentally or physically disabled, for instance, if he is insane or deaf. The solution was to use his son or slave to make the stipulation (Gaius, *Inst.* 3.105–106; Ulpian, D. 27.8.1.15, 45.1.1 pr.).

4. Can a Son Also Sue in His Own Name? Ulpian (D. 5.1.18.1) discusses the issue. Basically, for situations where the father was entitled to sue as a result of his son's act, the son could sue in his own name only if, for some reason, the father was unavailable (e.g., "if the father happens to be in the provinces"). See also Paul, D. 44.7.9, who lists a small number of exceptions.

In the previous section we saw how a child-in-power (like a slave) can acquire both property and obligations for a *pater familias*. We turn now to examine the reverse: the extent to which a child-in-power or other person subject to the power of a *pater* can either transfer to a third party the ownership of property belonging to the *pater* or make him liable to an obligation to a third party, particularly if the *pater* is unwilling that this occur. As might be anticipated, a child-in-power has only a limited ability to do so. The major exception to this pattern concerns the *peculium,* which we will examine below in section 3.

In general, those in the power of another were not able to alienate that person's property unless he or she agreed to this (see, e.g., Ulpian, D. 6.1.41.1: *domini voluntate*). This means that without his father's consent a son-in-power could not directly make a third party its owner by handover or otherwise. What might the reason be? One simple way to think of it is that since children own nothing (Case 113), they have no transferable property rights of their own. However, once the *pater* has consented to the alienation, children-in-power operate as virtually full extensions of him. They can transfer ownership in almost all of the ways that he could; and, indeed, it suffices if after the fact he ratifies their transfer of ownership (Paul, D. 13.7.20 pr.).

The situation with regard to contractual obligations is considerably more complex. In principle, neither children nor slaves could obligate a *pater familias* without his consent or at least his profit. But could they at least obligate themselves, granted that the objection to alienation, raised above, is not applicable in this context? Here Roman law drew a distinction between male and female children-in-power; females, like slaves, were unable to obligate themselves, but males, provided they were of age and otherwise competent (see, e.g., Gaius, D. 45.1.141.2), had full contractual capacity. In theory, though, this was of little advantage, since (in the absence of a *peculium*) they had no assets with which to satisfy their creditors.

This situation meant that a great deal of potential economic energy was bottled up within the legal boundaries of the agnatic *familia*. However, Roman praetors, in close alliance with the jurists, developed a number of ingenious ways to mitigate the resulting difficulty. One major task they faced, which is dealt with in this section, was to find ways whereby the *pater* could be made contractually liable through a child-in-power or a slave. Three major ways are discussed in this section: the *pater* was liable because (1) he had ordered the transaction, (2) he had profited from it, or (3) at least by implication he had held himself out as willing to be bound within a narrow business setting.

These three ways all have their importance, but the subject of section 3, namely the *peculium,* is still more important in freeing up the potential economic independence of children and slaves.

CASE 118: The Uniqueness of the Son-in-Power

Gaius, *Institutiones* 3.104

Praeterea inutilis est stipulatio, si ab eo stipuler, qui iuri meo subiectus est, item si is a me stipuletur. servus quidem et qui in mancipio est et filia familias et quae in manu est, non solum ipsi, cuius iuri subiecti subiectaeve sunt, obligari non possunt, sed ne alii quidem ulli.

(Gaius in the third book of his *Institutes*)

Further, a stipulation is ineffective if I stipulate from a person who is subject to my power; and likewise, if he stipulates from me. But in the case of a slave, a person who is in *mancipium*, a daughter-in-power, and a wife in *manus*, they cannot be (legally) obligated not only to the person to whose power they are subject but also to anyone else.

1. No Obligations within the *Familia*. The principle in the first sentence applies more broadly than just to stipulations, and it runs in both directions. For example, Pomponius, D. 44.7.7: "Actions cannot be provided to a son against his father while the son is in his power." What this means, in part, is that promises made within the *familia*, between a *pater* and his children, cannot be enforced by law. Is this consistent with the general nature of the Roman household?

2. Sons and Daughters. Gaius's list in the second sentence is notable for its pointed omission of sons-in-power; for, as we shall see, if sons are otherwise qualified (of adult age, sane, and so on), they possess full capacity to contract with a third party. By contrast, as Gaius says, daughters-in-power (and also wives in archaic *manus* marriages) cannot be obligated to anyone; that is, they lack the capacity to make a contract that is binding upon themselves. What is the reason for this rule, and what inconveniences does it cause? Suppose that a daughter-in-power borrows from a neighbor a piece of jewelry which she then carelessly damages. According to Ulpian (D. 13.6.3.4), she herself cannot be sued on the contract for damaging the jewelry, and her *pater familias* can be sued only up to the value of her *peculium*, if she has one. Would this make third parties reluctant to deal with daughters? What safeguards might they take?

3. Slaves. It may seem more logical that slaves cannot themselves be direct parties to obligations either within or without the *familia*. However, as it turns out, this is not entirely accurate even as to relationships between a slave and his owner, since, for instance, slaves could sometimes make valid contracts with a view to their future manumission (e.g., Ulpian, D. 4.3.7.8).

4. Natural Obligations. Even if the contracts of slaves or daughters were not legally enforceable when made, they were not entirely without legal effect. They are referred to as *obligationes naturales,* with the result, for instance, that if the daughter or slave performs as promised, the value of that performance cannot be reclaimed as not having been originally owed. See, for example, Paul, D. 12.6.13 pr. (a slave).

CASE 119: As Though He Were a *Pater Familias*

D. 44.7.39 (Gaius libro tertio ad edictum provinciale)

Filius familias ex omnibus causis tamquam pater familias obligatur et ob id agi cum eo tamquam cum patre familias potest.

(Gaius in the third book on the Provincial Edict)

A son-in-power is bound in all matters as though he were a *pater familias,* and for this reason an action can be brought against him as though he were a *pater familias.*

1. A Legal Fiction. What does Gaius mean by "as though he were a *pater familias*"? Does he really intend to grant the son-in-power the rights and privileges of a *pater familias*? Or is he simply employing a legal fiction for the purpose at hand?

2. Suing a Son-in-Power. A son is liable for his contracts. Is the father also liable? Ulpian, D. 15.1.44: "A person who contracts with a son-in-power has two debtors, the son for the entire amount and the father for up to the value of the (son's) *peculium.*" (See the following Case.) That is, both the father and the son can be sued separately on the same contractual obligation, though the plaintiff's recovery would ultimately be limited to the value of the obligation. But this brings up the central problem with the son-in-power's liability: if the son is sued for the entire amount (*in solidum*), he has no assets with which to satisfy a judgment, and so the plaintiff must rely on the father's generosity (which may, in fact, often have been forthcoming). Otherwise, the plaintiff has to wait until the son comes into his inheritance. (If the son was emancipated or disinherited, the praetor provided the plaintiff with a more modest remedy: D. 14.5.2 pr.)

3. The SC Macedonianum. This decree of the Senate (*senatusconsultum,* SC), which dates to the reign of Vespasian (A.D. 69–79), displays something of the tensions in the Roman legal regime. According to the decree's preamble (D. 14.6.1 pr.), Macedo, an upper-class son-in-power, borrowed heavily from moneylenders, who pressed him for repayment; he then murdered his father in order to obtain his inheritance. The Senate, seeking to ease such tensions, decreed that a person who lent money to a son-in-power could not sue on the debt even after the death of the *pater familias.* How effective is this likely to have been as a remedy? What problems would you anticipate? The jurists tend to interpret the decree fairly narrowly. For an example of the decree's application, see Case 132.

CASE 120: Suing the Son

D. 5.1.57 (Ulpianus libro quadragensimo primo ad Sabinum)

Tam ex contractibus quam ex delictis in filium familias competit actio: sed mortuo filio post litis contestationem transfertur iudicium in patrem dumtaxat de peculio et quod in rem eius versum est. certe si quasi procurator alicuius filius familias iudicium acceperit, mortuo eo in eum quem defenderit trans<latio vel actio> iudicati datur.

(Ulpian in the forty-first book on Sabinus)

An action can be brought against a son-in-power from both contracts and delicts. But if a son-in-power dies after the joinder of issue (*litis contestatio*), the trial is transferred to his *pater* (*familias*), with liability limited to the amount of the *peculium* and to the benefit he derived from this.

Obviously, if a son-in-power accepted a lawsuit as someone's legal representative (*procurator*), upon his death the person whom he defended is subject to a transfer of the trial or an action on the judgment.

1. Limits on the Father's Liability. This Case fills out the picture in Case 119. As Ulpian indicates, a son-in-power is liable to third parties both for his contracts and for his delicts (civil wrongs, somewhat similar to Common Law torts; see section 4 below), despite having no assets of his own. If a plaintiff brings suit against the son and the praetor grants the action, there follows in Roman civil procedure what is called the "joinder of issue," meaning essentially that the first phase of the trial is over, the plaintiff's right to sue is exhausted (so that normally, if the defendant died after this point, the plaintiff would have no recourse), and the actual case will now be heard by a *iudex*, who will decide it. Ulpian is describing what happens if a son dies between joinder and a verdict. Why is the *pater* substituted for his son in most circumstances? The *pater* will only be liable if he had granted a *peculium* to his son, and then only up to its value at the time of the lawsuit; see section 3 below. What does this Case suggest about the legal relationship between the *pater familias* and the son-in-power?

2. *Procurator*. The second portion of the Case deals with an exception: the son has undertaken to represent someone in court (as a *procurator* for the lawsuit) and so has assumed responsibility for seeing the lawsuit through to its end and paying any judgment. Typically, he would protect himself against an adverse result in or out of court by making an agreement for indemnification with the principal. Does the jurist assume such an agreement was made? What would be the outcome if the son-in-power had not died? That is, would his *pater familias* assume responsibility for any liability he had incurred?

CASE 121: The Father's Order

Gaius, *Institutiones* 4.70

Inprimis itaque si iussu patris dominive negotium gestum erit, in solidum praetor actionem in patrem dominumve comparavit, et recte, quia qui ita negotium gerit, magis patris dominive quam filii servive fidem sequitur.

D. 15.4.2.1 (Paulus libro trigensimo ad edictum)

Si iussu domini ancillae vel iussu patris filiae creditum sit, danda est in eos quod iussu actio.

(Gaius in the fourth book of his *Institutes*)

First of all, therefore, if business is conducted on the order (*iussum*) of a father or master, the praetor provides an action against the father or master for the entire amount, and rightly so. For one who conducts business in this manner relies more on the credit (*fides*) of the father or master than on that of the son or slave.

(Paul in the thirtieth book on the Edict)

If credit is extended to a slave woman on the order (*iussum*) of her master, or to a daughter on the order of her father, the action on the order (*actio quod iussu*) should be granted against them (the master or father).

1. What Is an Order? To circumvent the legal regime described in the previous three Cases, a person who enters into a contract or other transaction with a son-in-power (or a slave) must have a basis for establishing the liability of the *pater.* Roman law provides several such bases. We look first at the situation in which the transaction occurred because the *pater* gave an "order" (*iussum*) for it to occur. Why should this be an exception? The order can be entirely informal and very general (e.g., Ulpian, D. 15.4.1.1: "Do whatever business you want with my slave Stichus, at my risk"); but it can also be more restricted in its terms, and in any case may be revoked at any time prior to an actual transaction (ibid. 2). More important is a broader issue: can this action be brought if the order is given just to the son or slave, or just to the other party, or does it make no difference? Does Gaius's reference to reliance on the father's credit suggest an answer? Is the father's "order" really better described as an authorization?

2. Ratification. Ulpian, D. 15.4.1.6: "If someone ratifies what his slave or son did, an action on the order is given against them." A ratification occurs after the transaction, when it is brought to the attention of the *pater.* Is this ruling consistent with your answer to the previous question?

3. Orders and Agency. In the second text, Paul apparently presumes that the slave woman or the daughter would not herself be liable (see Case 118). If a son had concluded the transaction on his father's order, would he be liable, separately from his father? (The answer is yes; why?)

CASE 122: Turned to the Father's Benefit

D. 15.3.1 pr. (Ulpianus libro vicensimo nono ad edictum)

Si hi qui in potestate aliena sunt nihil in peculio habent, vel habeant, non in solidum tamen, tenentur qui eos habent in potestate, si in rem eorum quod acceptum est conversum sit, quasi cum ipsis potius contractum videatur.

D. 15.3.15 (Ulpianus libro secundo Disputationum)

Si filius familias constituerit quod pater debuit, videndum est, an de in rem verso actio dari debeat. atquin non liberavit patrem: nam qui constituit, se quidem obligat, patrem vero non liberat. plane si solvat post constitutum, licet pro se videatur solvisse, hoc est ob id quod constituit, in rem tamen vertisse patris merito dicetur.

(Ulpian in the twenty-ninth book on the Edict)

If those in another person's power have nothing in their *peculium* or have not enough for the entire amount (of their debt), the persons who have them in their power are liable if what was received was turned to their benefit (*in rem conversum*), on the theory that the contract was really with them.

(Ulpian in the second book of *Disputations*)

When a son has promised to pay a debt his father owed, we must examine whether the action on benefit received (*actio de in rem verso*) should be granted. But he did not (thereby) free his father (from the debt); for (merely) by promising to pay he obligates himself but does not free his father. Clearly, if he should (actually) pay after having promised, (then) even though he is held to have paid on his own behalf, that is, because he promised, nonetheless he is correctly held to have benefited his father.

1. The Father's Benefit. What is the theory behind the rule that if the *pater* benefits from the transaction of a child-in-power or a slave, he must pay for the benefit? The basic rules are set out by Ulpian, D. 15.3.5.2, 7.1: If a child or slave contracts an obligation with the consent of the *pater*, then the action on an order lies (Case 121); but if without consent, then the action on benefit will lie if *either* the *pater* ratifies the transaction (contrast Discussion 2 to Case 121; is this a better way to handle the problem?) *or* the expenditure was "necessary or useful" (*necessaria vel utilis*) to the *pater*, that is, insofar as his estate had materially profited. In the latter case, it makes no difference that the *pater* did not know of the transaction and did not want the benefit. For example, if the son or slave uses borrowed money to maintain or improve the *pater's* house, this is recoverable from the *pater* even if he did not want the improvement; but luxurious decorations are not recoverable (Ulpian, D. 15.3.3.2, 4). Why is this justified?

2. **Paying Off the Old Man's Debts**. How does the second passage illustrate the general rule? Compare also Ulpian, D. 15.3.10.2, where it is observed that there is no recovery if the son intended to make a gift to the *pater*. Does that make sense?

CASE 123: Obtaining a Daughter's Dowry

D. 15.3.7.5 (Ulpianus libro vicensimo nono ad edictum)

Si filius familias pecuniam mutuatus pro filia sua dotem dederit, in rem versum patris videtur, quatenus avus pro nepte daturus fuit. quae sententia ita demum mihi vera videtur, si hoc animo dedit ut patris negotium gerens.

D. 15.3.8 (Paulus libro trigensimo ad edictum)

Et nihil interesse Pomponius ait, filiae suae nomine an sororis vel neptis ex altero filio natae dederit. idem ergo dicemus et si servus mutuatus fuerit et domini sui filiae nomine in dotem dederit.

D. 15.3.9 (Iavolenus libro duodecimo ex Cassio)

Si vero pater dotem daturus non fuit, in rem patris versum esse non videtur.

(Ulpian in the twenty-ninth book on the Edict)

If a son-in-power borrowed money and gave a dowry for his daughter, (then) to the extent that the grandfather would have given (a dowry) for his granddaughter, this is held to benefit his (the son's) father. This view seems to me correct only if he gave it with the intent to conduct his father's business.

(Paul in the thirtieth book on the Edict)

And Pomponius says it makes no difference whether he gives (a dowry) in the name of his daughter or sister or in the name of a granddaughter (of the *pater familias*) from another son. So we will rule the same if a slave borrowed money and gave a dowry for the daughter of his master.

(Javolenus in the twelfth book from Cassius)

But if the father would not have given a dowry, it is not held to have benefited the father.

1. Constitution of Dowry by Son-in-Power. How does it benefit a *pater familias* if his son-in-power uses borrowed money to create a dowry for his daughter? Do the jurists presume a strong social expectation that the grandfather would supply a dowry, to the extent that he is legally presumed to have planned to do so with his own money? On the social background, see also Case 32 and above all Ulpian, D. 23.3.5.8, cited in the Discussion there.

2. Limit on Borrowed Money. Ulpian in the first passage places a limit on how much borrowed money can be used for this purpose ("to the extent that . . ."). Is he suggesting that the woman's father might also be expected to contribute to the dowry? Note the last sentence in the first passage. If the son was acting for his own sake in constituting the dowry, where does that leave the creditor and his claim?

3. Extension of Principle. Paul, citing Pomponius, extends the principle to cover dowries for several other female relatives. Does this extension seem correct? How much further would the jurists be willing to go, do you think?

4. Slave Borrowing Money. Paul also applies the rule to the case of a slave who uses borrowed money to constitute a dowry for his master's daughter. Does this application seem easier or more difficult than the ones that precede?

5. Javolenus's Comment. What does the comment of Javolenus in the third passage seem to imply? That is, would we expect a specific declaration from the grandfather that he did not intend to furnish a dowry? Would it have to be earlier in date than the son's actions?

CASE 124: Business Managers

Gaius, *Institutiones* 4.71

. . . Institoria vero formula tum locum habet, cum quis tabernae aut cuilibet negoti-ationi filium servumve aut quemlibet extraneum, sive servum sive liberum, praepo-suerit et quid cum eo eius rei gratia, cui praepositus est, contractum fuerit. ideo autem institoria vocatur, quia qui tabernae praeponitur, institor appellatur. quae et ipsa formula in solidum est.

D. 14.3.19.2 (Papinianus libro tertio Responsorum)

Tabernae praepositus a patre filius mercium causa mutuam pecuniam accepit: pro eo pater fideiussit: etiam institoria ab eo petetur, cum acceptae pecuniae speciem fideiubendo negotio tabernae miscuerit.

(Gaius in the fourth book of his *Institutes*)

. . . The procedure for the managerial action (*actio institoria*) is relevant when someone places his son or slave, or (indeed) any outsider whether slave or free, in charge of a shop or some other business, and a contract is (then) made with him in relation to what he was placed in charge of. It is called the managerial ac-tion because a person placed in charge of a shop is called a "manager" (*institor*). This procedure is also for the entire amount.

(Papinian in the third book of his *Responses*)

A son placed in charge of a shop by his father took money on loan for (the pur-chase of) goods; his father acted as personal guarantor (*fideiussor*) for him. Here too he (the father) is liable in a managerial action because, by guaranteeing it, he made the receipt of the loan into shop business.

1. The *Institor*. The theory here is quite different from that in the action on an order (*quod iussu*) and the action for benefit (*de in rem verso*), in which the *pater* is liable because he either authorized or benefited from a transaction by a slave or son-in-power. This action, which increased steadily in scope during the classical period, makes the *pater* liable on transactions by anyone (includ-ing persons not within his power) whom he places in operational charge of a business belonging to him; as Paul's *Sententiae* argues (2.8.1), just as the *pater* reaps the potential benefits, so should he accept the losses. Virtually any form of enterprise qualifies. The *Sententiae* (ibid. 2) mentions moneylending, oper-ating a farm, and storing or selling crops; Ulpian (D. 14.3.5.7–9) instances overseas trading in commodities, undertaking, and a bakery.

2. Is the *Institor* an Agent? No. The transaction of the *institor* makes the princi-pal liable to a third party; for instance, if the *institor* as manager sells a slave, the third party can sue the principal on sale if the slave is not delivered. But the reverse is not true; the principal does not automatically acquire the action

against the third party, although this action is usually available through some other legal theory. Thus, for instance, if the third party refuses to pay for the slave, and if the *institor* is a slave or a son-in-power, the *pater* acquires the right of action on the theory of Case 117. If the *institor* is a free person (e.g., an employee hired to run a shop), the principal can use the action of mandate; and so on. See Ulpian and Gaius, D. 14.3.1–2. Finally, if this is legally possible (as it would be in the case of a son-in-power), the *institor* also remains personally liable on the transaction; that is, his transactions as an *institor* are not treated as, in effect, transactions by the principal. What concrete difference does all this make?

3. Scope of Authorization. As Gaius observes, a transaction binds the principal only if it is connected with the business ("made with him in relation to what he was placed in charge of"). The second passage, from Papinian, illustrates how elusive that concept can be. The son was placed in charge of a shop and then borrowed money in order to purchase merchandise; why would there be any question that such a loan is connected with the business? How does the father's personal guarantee of the loan affect Papinian's decision? Can the following examples, all developed by analogy from Ulpian, D. 14.3.5.12–15, be reconciled with each other?

- The father places his son in charge of buying goods; the father is liable on the son's contract if the son buys but not if he sells.
- The father places his son in charge of buying goods and paying for the lease on a shop; the father is liable if the son borrows money in order to pay for the goods or to pay the rent, even though he had no specific authorization to borrow money.
- The father places his son in charge of buying and selling olive oil; the father is liable if a third party lends olive oil to the son in the expectation of repayment without interest.
- The father places a son in charge of selling olive oil; the father is liable if the son sells olive oil on credit, unless the son was ordered to sell only for ready cash.

4. Notice to Third Parties. The sources are unclear about whether the third party must realize that he or she is dealing with a manager rather than with the principal, but it is likely that this was not necessary. Usually a customer could reasonably presume that the person managing a shop did not own the business; and it would be cumbersome to have to inquire further as to the identity of the principal. For this reason, the jurists emphasize that if the principal, seeking to limit his liability, does not want customers to contract directly with the person placed in charge of the shop, he must post a clear notice to this effect. Ulpian (D. 14.3.11.2–4) lays down some requirements: the

notice must be in plain letters, clearly visible, and in the local language; the principal bears the risk if someone takes down the notice or it is destroyed by rain; and so on. As Ulpian says (ibid. 2): "It is not that permission must be given to contract with an *institor*, but that he who wishes no contracts must forbid this; and otherwise a person who put someone in charge will be liable as a result of this act." Does this suggest that the jurists regarded customer reliance as justified? Even if notice was posted against doing business with a manager who was a slave or son-in-power, someone who did business anyway could still sue for up to the value of the manager's *peculium* (Paul, D. 15.1.47 pr., and see also Case 137).

There is no more remarkable institution in all of Roman law than the *peculium,* the principal device whereby some of the entrepreneurship of children-in-power and slaves was released from the constrictions of the *familia.* The *peculium* seems to have begun life as a small assemblage of property allocated by the *pater familias* to his subordinate, whom the *pater* then let deal with the property as he or she wished; it may have resembled the allowance that modern parents give to children in order to teach them the value of money. However, by the early Empire, *peculia,* often of very large size, had become a ubiquitous feature of Roman economic life; a *peculium* could include an entire farm or a business operation. Particularly slaves, but also children, actively traded with their *peculia,* in effect operating as managers of quasi-independent "firms" although still within the ambit of the *familia.*

In principle, children, like slaves, could own and possess nothing (Case 113); and the fact that a person held a *peculium* did not alter that person's legal position as a subordinate to a *pater familias.* Thus, for instance, a son-in-power remained subject to his father's *potestas,* and any power that the son possessed was still derivative from that of his father. The *peculium* itself was granted by the father, who theoretically could withdraw it at will; but in practice the fund tended to be regarded as the son's "quasi property," which the father was socially (and to some extent also legally) discouraged from rescinding.

The *peculium* came into its own when the child or slave dealt with third parties on the basis of it. Usually the *pater* accorded its holder "free administration" (*libera administratio*) in such dealings, meaning that the holder could enter into contracts and conduct other business as he or she wished, without consulting the *pater* or seeking his subsequent approval. Any property or debts acquired on the basis of these dealings became effectively part of the *peculium,* and so they indirectly were acquired by the *pater* even though he was unaware of them (see Case 116). In furtherance of *peculium* business, the holder of a *peculium* was also usually able to alienate (transfer ownership of) property. And when the *peculium* became indebted to a third party, this person was able to sue the *pater* on the debt, although only up to the value of the *peculium* at the time of the lawsuit. Thus, by more or less formally ceding the *peculium* to a subordinate, the *pater* achieved a limited liability in its regard, while his children and slaves were permitted to demonstrate and develop their independent commercial skills.

The jurists richly developed the basic legal institution of the *peculium,* and the Cases in this section represent only a sampling of their legal rules. Even so, you should be able to appreciate the novelty of the *peculium.* In many respects, it looks like a distant prototype of a modern corporation, in which a stockholder (the *pater familias*) owns a separately incorporated firm (the *peculium*) but, in return for limited liability, leaves the direction of the firm in the hands of a manager (the child or slave). Indeed, many of the problems we associate with modern corporate law arise also in relation to the Roman *peculium,* although the *peculium* seems to have had no direct historical influence on modern corporations. However, in some respects the *peculium* is distinctly different from a modern corporation. As these similarities and differences emerge below, you should ask yourself how they can be explained.

CASE 125: The Nature of the Fund

Iustinianus, *Institutiones* 4.6.10

Actiones autem de peculio ideo adversus patrem dominumve comparavit Praetor, quia licet ex contractu filiorum servorumve ipso iure non teneantur, aequum tamen esset peculio tenus, quod veluti patrimonium est filiorum filiarumque, item servorum, condemnari eos.

(Justinian in the fourth book of his *Institutes*)

The praetor provided actions on the *peculium* against a father or an owner (of a slave) because, although by (civil) law itself they are not liable on the contract of sons or slaves, nonetheless it is fair that they be condemned up to the value of the *peculium*, which is like the property (*patrimonium*) of sons and daughters or of slaves.

1. The *Institutes* of Justinian. This elementary textbook of Roman law was published in Constantinople in A.D. 533 under the general authority (and putative authorship) of the Emperor Justinian, who was also responsible for the compilation of the *Digest* and the *Codex,* our two most important sources for classical Roman law. Justinian's *Institutes* is based heavily on the *Institutes* of the classical jurist Gaius, which was written nearly four centuries earlier.

2. The Praetor's Edict. As Justinian suggests, the Roman praetor probably just recognized a pre-existing social institution. *Peculia* are well attested at Rome by the early second century B.C., and indeed such funds are characteristic of virtually all known slaveholding systems. The praetor permitted third parties who had entered into dealings with the holder of a *peculium* to sue the person responsible for setting it up but limited his liability "to the value of the *peculium.*" The same action also established an exception to this limited liability where the contents of the *peculium* had been "turned to the benefit" of the *pater familias* (Cases 122–123). Case 135 illustrates how the two causes of action worked together.

3. Explaining the Liability. Why does Justinian think that it is "fair" that masters or fathers have limited liability on *peculium* transactions? In this context, how is it relevant that a *peculium* can be described as the constructive "property" of children or slaves, even though they cannot own anything in the legal sense? The jurists also occasionally seem to regard *peculia* as belonging to their holders; a good example is Florentinus, D. 15.1.39, who defines the *peculium* as consisting of "what a person has earned by his own thrift or has been given by a third party in return for services, plus that which he (the owner) wished his slave to have as his own property (*proprium patrimonium*)."

Some legal rules follow this logic; for example, if a slave is freed by a living master, the slave keeps his or her *peculium* unless the master expressly states otherwise (Papinian, *Frag. Vat.* 261). Within Roman law, what prevented further extensions of the idea?

CASE 126: The Contents of a *Peculium*

D. 15.1.7.4–7 (Ulpianus libro vicensimo nono ad edictum)

(4) In peculio autem res esse possunt omnes et mobiles et soli: vicarios quoque in peculium potest habere et vicariorum peculium: hoc amplius et nomina debitorum. (5) Sed et si quid furti actione servo deberetur vel alia actione, in peculium computabitur: hereditas quoque et legatum, ut Labeo ait. (6) Sed et id quod dominus sibi debet in peculium habebit, si forte in domini rationem impendit et dominus ei debitor manere voluit aut si debitorem eius dominus convenit. quare si forte ex servi emptione evictionis nomine duplum dominus exegit, in peculium servi erit conversum. . . . (7) Sed et si quid ei conservus debet, erit peculii, si modo ille habeat peculium vel prout habebit.

(Ulpian in the twenty-ninth book on the Edict)

(4) A *peculium* can contain all sorts of property, both movables and land. A *peculium* can also contain "underslaves" (*vicarii*) and the *peculium* of underslaves, as well as accounts receivable from debtors. (5) But also if anything is owed to the slave from the action on theft or some other action, this is assigned to the *peculium*; and likewise an inheritance or legacy, as Labeo says.

(6) But the *peculium* will also have what the master owes to it, for example, if he (a slave) spends to the master's benefit and the master wished to remain his debtor, or if the master sues his (the slave's) debtor. Therefore, if, after the slave made a purchase, the master happened to sue for double damages owing to eviction, this is turned to the benefit of the slave's *peculium*. . . .

(7) But also if a fellow slave owes something to him, this belongs to the *peculium* if he (the fellow slave) has a *peculium* or to the extent he will have one.

1. The Assets of a *Peculium*. In relation to a slave (although the Case would also apply to a child-in-power), Ulpian lists the assets of a typical large *peculium*: movable and immovable property, including on occasion slaves who might have *peculia* of their own (see below); debts owed to the *peculium* by third parties, including not only transactional debts but also judicial judgments and bequests; and debts owed to the *peculium* by the master as well as by fellow slaves who have *peculia* of their own. The total value of the assets may usually not be calculated unless the master is sued on a debt owed by the slave in connection with the *peculium*. Then the master's liability is limited to the value of the *peculium*; but that value is calculated only after making important deductions that are discussed in Case 135. The *peculium* is therefore not an object in itself (e.g., it cannot be claimed by a lawsuit over ownership: Julian, D. 6.1.56) but rather only an amalgam of tangible and intangible property. The jurists often think of it primarily as an accounting entity; thus, a late Republican jurist (Tubero, cited by Celsus and Ulpian, D. 15.1.5.4) describes it as "what a slave, with his master's permission, holds separate from

the master's accounts, with debts to the master deducted." How close is this to a modern corporation? See also Case 127 on forming a *peculium*.

2. Ownership of the *Peculium*. The jurists are unequivocal: the master retains full ownership of the property in a *peculium* (see Case 113); the child or slave is described only as "holding" it (*tenere*), a word indicating the absence of property rights. (See also Marcian, D. 50.17.93.) Further, the owner is in principle free at any time, except with fraudulent purpose, to withdraw assets or to dissolve the *peculium* entirely (Case 127); the effect of this is simply to re-merge the *peculium*'s assets with his other property. In this connection, consider the following problem, based on Paul, D. 18.1.40.5 (of a slave): A father allowed his son to operate a farm through his *peculium*. The father then sold the farm to a third party, and in the bill of sale specified that all storage vessels on the farm would go to the buyer. The son had used his *peculium* to buy some storage vessels that he placed on the farm. Can the buyer claim them? Yes, says Paul, adding that this claim is not limited by the value of the *peculium*. Do you see why?

3. Underslaves (*Vicarii*). One of the most startling aspects of Roman slavery is that the *peculium* of a privileged slave often contained other slaves, called *vicarii* (loosely, "underslaves"), to whom the principal slave (*ordinarius*) might grant sub-*peculia* of their own (see Celsus, D. 15.1.6). These *vicarii* could then enter debt relationships not only with third parties but also with their master, their principal slave, other *vicarii*, and other slaves held by the master. The resulting relationships were potentially very complex, of course. Third parties who entered into contracts with a *vicarius* could sue the master on the basis of the sub-*peculium* of the *vicarius* (master's liability limited to its value) and, if they failed to get full satisfaction, next on the basis of the *peculium* of the *ordinarius* (master's liability limited to the value of this *peculium*) (Ulpian, D. 15.1.19 pr.).

4. Slaves and Sons. In several of the Cases in this section, the emphasis is on slaves rather than on sons. Does this suggest that Roman fathers frequently looked to their slaves rather than their sons for entrepreneurship? If so, what impact might this have had on the development of free entrepreneurship at Rome? One small piece of evidence in this matter is that a son was allowed to entrust management of his *peculium* to a *procurator*, who presumably might handle it more professionally (Ulpian, D. 3.3.33 pr.).

CASE 127: Constituting a *Peculium*

D. 15.1.4 pr. (Pomponius libro septimo ad Sabinum)

Peculii est non id, cuius servus seorsum a domino rationem habuerit, sed quid dominus ipse separaverit suam a servi rationem discernens: nam cum servi peculium totum adimere vel augere vel minuere dominus possit, animadvertendum est non quid servus, sed quid dominus constituendi servilis peculii gratia fecerit.

D. 15.1.7.2–3 (Ulpianus libro vicensimo nono ad edictum)

(2) Scire autem non utique singulas res debet, sed *pachumeresteron*, et in hanc sententiam Pomponius inclinat. (3) Pupillum autem tam filium quam servum peculium habere posse Pedius libro quinto decimo scribit, cum in hoc, inquit, totum ex domini constitutione pendeat. ergo et si furere coeperit servus vel filius, retinebunt peculium.

(Pomponius in the seventh book on Sabinus)

Property in a *peculium* is not what a slave keeps in a separate account from the master but what the master himself detaches by dividing his account from the slave's. For since the master is able to remove a *peculium* entirely, or increase or diminish it, we must observe not what the slave (does) but what his master does by way of establishing the slave's *peculium*.

(Ulpian in the twenty-ninth book on the Edict)

(2) But he (the master) should be aware not of each and every object (in the *peculium*) but of it *en bloc,* a view that Pomponius tended to favor. (3) Pedius, in his fifteenth book (on the Edict), writes that a minor, no matter whether a son or a slave, can have a *peculium,* since, he says, in this case everything depends on what the master establishes. Likewise, if a slave or son goes insane, he will retain the *peculium*.

1. The Father's Will. The issue in this Case is important: to what extent is the initial existence of a *peculium* (as well as its continuation and eventual dissolution) dependent on the will of the *pater familias?* Many jurists, like Pomponius and Ulpian in this Case, appear to regard this dependence as absolute. But problems arose. For instance, what if the *pater* went insane? The *peculium* simply continued if the *pater* granted it before going insane (Ulpian, D. 15.1.7.1). But could it arise thereafter? Obviously, a madman cannot grant it himself, but his legal guardian could do so (see Ulpian, D. 15.1.3.4, 7.1; on the *curator,* see Chapter V.A.3). Both passages give the same justification: "the madman's slave can have a *peculium,* not in the sense that he was permitted to have one, but that he was not forbidden to have one." Is this just a commonsensical solution to the problem (as with marriage by the children of the in-

sane, Case 101), or is a deeper issue at stake? Compare Ulpian, D. 15.1.24 (the *peculium* of a madman's child).

2. How Formal? If the *pater* must consent, does he have to do so formally? No special ceremony is known, though Paul (D. 15.1.8) says that the *pater's* intent alone is not enough; at least in the case of tangible property, he must either hand over property to the holder of the *peculium* or, if the holder already has it, treat it as handed over. What seems to be crucial is that the *pater* confers on the holder actual day-to-day control of the property; and this initial conferral is in fact apparently enough, in itself, to create a *peculium*. However, once the property was in the holder's hands, further acquisitions remain with him. But Pomponius (D. 15.1.49 pr.) adds one proviso: "if, had he (the *pater* or owner) known, he would have allowed them to be in the *peculium*." This suggests that the giver of the *peculium* must be interpreted as wishing the acquisitions to remain in the *peculium*, a test that must usually have been met by evaluating common practice.

3. A Test Case: Clothing. A *pater* gives his son clothing to wear. Use the principles of this Case to determine whether the clothing is in the son's *peculium*. See Pomponius, D. 15.1.25 (of a slave; only if given for his permanent use, but not if only for special occasions such as processions; does this seem right?).

4. The Profits of Crime. Pomponius, D. 15.1.4.2: "It follows that a *peculium* contains, not what a slave has without his master's knowledge, but (what he has) with his master's assent. Otherwise, the *peculium* will also contain what a slave stole from his master; but this is untrue." Does this result in fact follow from more general principles? The *peculium* also did not contain property obtained illegally from third parties (see Javolenus, D. 41.2.24).

5. The Holder's Will. As Ulpian stresses, it is not essential that the holder of a *peculium* enjoy full legal capacity; even a minor or a lunatic can have a *peculium*. But there's a catch, of course: by nature, minors and lunatics are incapable of becoming legally obligated to third parties and so cannot obligate the *pater*.

CASE 128: Slave Women and Daughters

D. 15.1.27 pr. (Gaius libro nono ad edictum provinciale)

Et ancillarum nomine et filiarum familias in peculio actio datur: maxime si qua sarcinatrix aut textrix erit aut aliquod artificium vulgare exerceat, datur propter eam actio. depositi quoque et commodati actionem dandam earum nomine Iulianus ait: sed et tributoriam actionem, si peculiari merce sciente patre dominove negotientur, dandam esse. longe magis non dubitatur, et si in rem versum est, quod iussu patris dominive contractum sit.

(Gaius in the ninth book on the Provincial Edict)

An action on the *peculium* lies regarding slave women and daughters-in-power. Especially if a woman acts as a seamstress or weaver or practices some common trade, an action is given for this reason.

Julian holds that an action should lie in respect of these women also for deposit and loan-for-use, as well as the *actio tributoria* if they conduct business with the property in the *peculium* with the knowledge of their *pater (familias)* or owner. This is particularly true if something has been turned to his benefit or if a contract was made on the father's or owner's order.

1. Nature of the Trade. The contracts of a daughter-in-power, like those of slaves of both sexes, were invalid at law (see Case 118) but were enforceable against a *pater familias* through the *peculium*. What does Gaius mean by specifying certain trades as "especially" relevant to women? If the slave woman or daughter-in-power does not practice such a trade, does the action fail? Suppose she works as a prostitute or procuress.

2. Julian's Extension. The contracts of deposit and loan-for-use are both gratuitous contracts, meaning that no money changes hands. In the former, one person receives property from another and promises to safeguard it and to return it on demand; in the latter, one person lends property to another for that person's use, with the borrower similarly promising return on demand. Why does Julian regard these contracts as ones that are suitable for enforcement by means of the woman's *peculium*? Does he seem more reluctant to permit liability when a woman transacts business with her *peculium* property? Why is it "particularly true" in the case where the *pater* ordered a transaction or took benefit from it (see Cases 121–123)? On the *actio tributoria,* see the Discussion on Case 137; on the general legal status of women, see Chapter V.B.1–2.

CASE 129: Acquiring Property

D. 41.2.3.12 (Paulus libro quinquagensimo quarto ad edictum)

Ceterum animo nostro, corpore etiam alieno possidemus, sicut diximus per colonum et servum, nec movere nos debet, quod quasdam <res> etiam ignorantes possidemus, id est quas servi peculiariter paraverunt: nam videmur eas eorundem et animo et corpore possidere.

D. 41.2.44.1 (Papinianus libro vicensimo tertio Quaestionum)

Quaesitum est, cur ex peculii causa per servum ignorantibus possessio quaereretur. dixi utilitatis causa iure singulari receptum, ne cogerentur domini per momenta species et causas peculiorum inquirere. nec tamen eo pertinere speciem istam, ut animo videatur adquiri possessio: nam si non ex causa peculiari quaeratur aliquid, scientiam quidem domini esse necessariam, sed corpore servi quaeri possessionem.

(Paul in the fifty-fourth book on the Edict)

But we take possession also by our own intent but through another's physical act, as for instance through a tenant farmer and a slave. Nor should it influence us that we possess some property even though unaware of it, that is, what slaves have acquired through a *peculium;* for we are held to possess this property through their intent and physical act.

(Papinian in the twenty-third book of *Questions of Law*)

Question has arisen as to why, on the basis of a *peculium,* possession is acquired through a slave for those unaware of it. I answered that this exceptional rule was introduced for the common good, so that owners not be compelled constantly to examine the content and circumstances of *peculia.* Nor is this an example of our being held to acquire possession by intent (alone). For if something is not acquired on the basis of the *peculium,* the owner's knowledge is required but possession is taken through the slave's physical act.

1. Different Explanations. Paul (see also Case 116) and Papinian agree that, although a slave or child-in-power ordinarily can acquire property for a *pater* only if he knows of their act, his knowledge is not required when they take possession through their *peculia.* The two jurists disagree, however, on how this rule should be explained. In Case 116, Paul argues that the rule results from the legal nature of a *peculium:* children and slaves "are understood to possess by our will since we allowed them to have a *peculium.*" What does this mean? Is Paul suggesting that the *peculium* includes a general authorization to acquire property in the *pater's* name, and that a general authorization removes the need for knowledge of individual acquisitions? Would he be willing to extend this legal theory to other persons not subject to another's power, such as a *procurator* (see Case 115)? Should Papinian's emphasis on the peculiar na-

ture of "this exceptional rule" be interpreted as indicating that he is cautious about such extensions? The underlying problem here is the extent to which the jurists were willing to encourage development of commercial relationships outside the *familia*. Why should it matter exactly how a legal rule is explained?

CASE 130: Free Administration

D. 15.1.46 (Paulus libro sexagensimo <secundo> ad edictum)

Qui peculii administrationem concedit, videtur permittere generaliter, quod et specialiter permissurus est.

D. 6.1.41.1 (Ulpianus libro septimo decimo ad edictum)

Si servus mihi vel filius familias fundum vendidit et tradidit habens liberam peculii administrationem, in rem actione uti potero. sed et si domini voluntate domini rem tradat, idem erit dicendum: quemadmodum cum procurator voluntate domini vendidit vel tradidit, in rem actionem mihi praestabit.

(Paul in the sixty-second book on the Edict)

A person who grants administration of the *peculium* is understood to give blanket authorization for everything he would have permitted in particular cases.

(Ulpian in the seventeenth book on the Edict)

If a (third party's) slave or son-in-power has free administration of his *peculium*, and he sells a farm and hands it over to me, I will be able to use an action *in rem* (to assert ownership of the farm). Likewise, if he hands over the master's property by the master's will (*domini voluntate*), the same holds true. In like manner, when a *procurator* sells or hands over (property to me) with the owner's consent, he will provide me with the action *in rem*.

1. Free Administration. A child or slave who was given a *peculium* was not thereby automatically entitled to deal with the property in it. The right to deal required a separate grant, the requirements for which were more rigorous than those for establishing the *peculium* itself; as Ulpian says (D. 15.1.7.1): "It is otherwise with the free administration of a *peculium*, since this must be expressly granted." Ulpian here refers to what is usually the most generous form of authorization, called "free" or "full administration" (*libera* or *plena administratio*); for adult children or slaves, this was also probably the most common grant. What does Paul mean by "everything he would have permitted in particular cases"? Suppose, for instance, that a son-in-power enters a losing contract that his father, had he known, certainly would not have permitted; is the contract nonetheless authorized (and hence binding) because the father had granted free administration? Is there a better way to understand Paul's words?

2. Conveying Title. In the fragment from Ulpian, a child or slave sold a farm in the *peculium* and handed it over to the buyer. The issue is whether the buyer thereby acquires title. What conditions does Ulpian set for the validity of the buyer's title? How does free administration differ from a specific authorization

of the sale (see Case 121)? In general, a *peculium* holder needed free administration not only in order to transfer title (Venuleius, D. 44.3.15.3; Paul, D. 41.2.14 pr.) but also to encumber the property, for instance, by using it as security for a debt (Paul, D. 12.6.13 pr., 13.7.18.4). Granted the risks that are involved, why would a *pater* have been willing to allow a child or slave to alienate property in a *peculium*?

3. Paying *Peculium* Debts. A son-in-power has free administration of his *peculium*. He buys and receives a horse, and he promises to pay the price of the horse in a month; a friend of his guarantees the payment (as a surety). If the son then pays the seller, is the surety thereby released from liability? Why? Would it make a difference if the seller had instead received the price from the *pater familias*? See Proculus, D. 46.3.84. Note that in order to pay the seller successfully, the son had to have had the legal capacity to transfer ownership of the money paid.

4. Restricted Authorization. A *pater* could also limit the authorization given to a child or slave, and the determination of how far the authorization went is treated as a matter of fact (Marcian, D. 20.3.1.1). One restriction might be to forbid alienation of property. What would the consequence be if the *peculium* holder nonetheless tried to transfer ownership of something to a third party? See Diocletian, C. 4.26.10.1 (A.D. 294; the transaction is void), and Proculus, D. 12.6.53 (the *pater* can reclaim the property or its value). Are third parties adequately protected if they mistakenly assume that the *peculium* holder has free administration?

5. Prohibited Transactions. A son-in-power runs a shop. In the shop his father posts a sign saying: "I forbid transactions with my son." The son purchases and receives goods from someone who is aware of the sign, and he promises to pay for them in a month. The sign is effective in barring a managerial action (*actio institoria*; see Case 124); but can the seller at least sue on the *peculium*? See Gaius, D. 15.1.29.1, and Paul, D. 15.1.47 pr. (yes; both of a slave). This holding seems to conflict with the rule above on restricted authorization; how might the conflict be resolved?

6. Limits on Free Administration. Although the grant of free administration is fairly extensive, it is not unlimited. Some of the restrictions arise from how the jurists conceived of free administration in its ordinary operation; these limits are discussed in the next two Cases. Others derive from more general considerations of public policy. Marcellus (D. 42.8.12) discusses one of these limits: "When a *pater* gave a son-in-power free administration of a *peculium*, he is not held to have granted him the power to alienate in fraud of creditors." Suppose that the son sold off *peculium* assets at a below-market price, thereby

lowering the value of the *peculium* and endangering the position of creditors; would such sales be void? Marcellus goes on to note that if the *pater* granted his child the extraordinary power to alienate in fraud of creditors, the *pater* would make himself liable for such alienations. Does this suggest the policy background of the rule?

CASE 131: Gifts from a *Peculium*

D. 39.5.7 pr.–3 (Ulpianus libro quadragensimo quarto ad Sabinum)

(pr.) Filius familias donare non potest, neque si liberam peculii administrationem habeat: non enim ad hoc ei conceditur libera peculii administratio, ut perdat. (1) Quid ergo, si iusta ratione motus donet, numquid possit dici locum esse donationi? quod magis probabitur. (2) Item videamus, si quis filio familias liberam peculii administrationem concesserit, ut nominatim adiceret sic se ei concedere, ut donare quoque possit, an locum habeat donatio: et non dubito donare quoque eum posse. (3) Nonnumquam etiam ex persona poterit hoc colligi: pone enim filium esse senatoriae vel cuius alterius dignitatis: quare non dicas videri patrem, nisi ei specialiter donandi facultatem ademit, hoc quoque concessisse, dum liberam dat peculii administrationem?

(Ulpian in the forty-fourth book on Sabinus)

(pr.) A son-in-power cannot make a gift, not even if he has free administration of a *peculium*. For the reason that he is granted free administration of the *peculium* is not that he squander it.

(1) What then if in making a gift he is motivated by a good reason? Can it be said that there is any room for a gift? The better view is that it is valid. (2) Likewise, let us examine whether a gift is valid if someone has granted free administration of the *peculium* to a son-in-power, but he specifically adds that he is doing this so that he also will have the right to make gifts. I do not doubt that he (the son) can also make a gift.

(3) Sometimes this result can be inferred from the type of person concerned. Take the son of someone of senatorial or some other (high) rank: why would you not say that the *pater* (*familias*), unless he specifically takes away the power of making gifts, seems to have granted this as well, provided that he has given him free administration of his *peculium*?

1. Good Reason. In Ulpian's opinion, what might a "good reason" be for making a gift? In section 1, his reference to the "better view" strongly suggests that some jurists disagreed. Presumably they held that a gift from a *peculium* is void, even if motivated by a good reason. What justification might they have offered for this position? From the following Case, would you judge it likely that Julian held the "better view"?

2. Elite Gifting. Why should the social status of the person concerned affect the legal rule? Does Ulpian recognize that gift giving was widely practiced to the point of constituting a norm in such circles?

3. Manumitting Slaves. Can a son-in-power successfully manumit slaves in his *peculium?* The Emperor Alexander held that he could not (C. 7.11.2; A.D. 222–235). What might Alexander's reasoning have been?

CASE 132: Lending Money

D. 14.6.3.2 (Ulpianus libro vicensimo nono ad edictum)

. . . quemadmodum ipse dicit Iulianus libro duodecimo, si filius familias crediderit, cessare senatus consultum, quod mutua pecunia non fit, quamvis liberam
peculii administrationem habuit: non enim perdere ei peculium pater concedit,
cum peculii administrationem permittit: et ideo vindicationem nummorum patri
superesse ait.

D. 12.1.2.4 (Paulus libro vicensimo octavo ad edictum)

In mutui datione oportet dominum esse dantem, nec obest, quod filius familias et
servus dantes peculiares nummos obligant: id enim tale est, quale si voluntate mea
tu des pecuniam: nam mihi actio adquiritur, licet mei nummi non fuerint.

(Ulpian in the twenty-ninth book on the Edict)

. . . As Julian himself says in the twelfth book (of his *Digests*), if a son-in-power
makes a loan (to another son-in-power), the decree of the Senate (SC Macedonianum) does not apply, the reason being that the money is not (effectively)
loaned even if he (the lender) had free administration of his *peculium*. For his father, when he granted him administration of the *peculium,* was not authorizing
him to squander it. Accordingly, he says the father can sue to recover the coins.

(Paul in the twenty-eighth book on the Edict)

In giving a loan (of money), the giver must be the owner (of the money that is
lent). It is not a contradiction that a son-in-power and a slave create an obligation by giving (in loan) cash from their *peculia*. For this situation resembles one
in which you give (your) money (as a loan) on my authorization; I acquire the
action (for repayment), although the coins were not mine.

> 1. Two Opinions. A son-in-power who has free administration of his *peculium*
> lends money to a third party. Is the loan effective? This turns on whether the
> son had the capacity to transfer ownership of the money as part of making the
> loan. If he did, the loan is effective (and so his father can sue for repayment);
> but if not, it is ineffective (and so his father can sue to recover the coins them-
> selves or their value). What might explain the sharply different views of Julian
> and Paul? Does Julian assume that all loans are wasteful, or that they cannot
> serve legitimate business purposes? Would it matter to him if the loan bore
> interest? Ulpian, in any case, agreed with Paul (see D. 12.1.11.2). On the SC
> Macedonianum, which made loans of money to sons-in-power irrecoverable,
> see the Discussion on Case 119. If a son uses *peculium* cash to repay a money-
> lender, can his father recover the payment? See Ulpian, D. 14.6.9.1 (citing Ju-

lian; yes). Is Julian too vigilant in protecting the father? Compare Gaius, D. 2.14.28.2 (citing Julian).

2. **Hush Money.** If a son pays off someone who threatens to reveal a crime the son has committed, can his *pater* recover the payment? See Julian, D. 12.5.5 (yes; of a slave).

CASE 133: Defending the *Peculium*

D. 15.1.21.3 (Ulpianus, libro vicensimo nono ad edictum)

Si dominus vel pater recuset de peculio actionem, non est audiendus, sed cogendus est quasi aliam quamvis personalem actionem suscipere.

(Ulpian in the twenty-ninth book on the Edict)

If a master or *pater* (*familias*) declines to defend an action on the *peculium,* he is not to be accorded a hearing (by the judge); rather, he must be compelled to take up the defense as though it were any other lawsuit, despite its personal character.

1. Who (Or What) Is Being Sued? This disarmingly modest little Case raises a very important legal issue. As we have seen, when a *pater* permits a son or slave to have a *peculium,* he opens himself to being sued on their authorized transactions; but his liability is ordinarily limited to the value of the *peculium.* In a sense, therefore, the liability attaches not to the *pater* but to the *peculium;* and certainly, if there is no *peculium,* in the absence of fraud this form of liability does not exist (Paul, D. 21.1.57.1). On the other hand, the plaintiff does not actually sue the *peculium* but rather proceeds directly against the *pater,* who, as Ulpian says, is "compelled to take up the defense." What this means is that the defendant *pater's* liability is not confined to the actual property in the *peculium;* rather, the current value of the *peculium* only determines the maximum amount of his personal liability, but a judgment for the plaintiff can be satisfied from any of his assets. What argument might a *pater familias* have used to deny his liability?

2. A Slave Sold with His *Peculium.* Test your understanding of the principle in this Case by considering the following problem. Sempronius gives his slave a *peculium,* on the basis of which the slave incurs a debt to a third party. Sempronius then sells to Titius the slave together with his *peculium.* If the third-party creditor now decides to sue, who is the proper defendant, Sempronius or Titius? Does the defendant's liability include any increase in the *peculium's* value after the date of the sale? See Ulpian, D. 15.1.32.1–2.

3. A Useful Year. A son-in-power incurs a debt on the basis of his *peculium* but then dies before paying the debt. Since by definition the son has no assets, the debtor seems to be left in the lurch, with no one to sue. To prevent the injustice that would result, the praetor allowed debtors to bring suit against the *pater* for up to one "effective year" (*annus utilis*) after the son's death or emancipation; see Ulpian, D. 15.2.1 pr. (and similarly for a slave).

4. Double Liability? A son-in-power is liable on his contracts, even if he has no assets of his own with which to pay his debts (Cases 118–119); but often he

can be effectively sued after he becomes *sui iuris* (see Ulpian, D. 14.5.2). Suppose that a creditor sues the father on his son's *peculium* and wins, but the value of the *peculium* is insufficient to pay off the debt. After the son becomes *sui iuris,* can the creditor bring a second lawsuit against the son for the remainder?

CASE 134: Computing the Balance

Gaius, *Institutiones* 4.72a

Est etiam de peculio et de in rem verso actio a praetore constituta. licet enim ne-gotium ita gestum sit cum filio servove, ut neque voluntas neque consensus patris dominive intervenerit, si quid tamen ex ea re, quae cum illis gesta est, in rem patris dominive versum sit, quatenus in rem eius versum fuerit, eatenus datur actio. Ver-sum autem quid sit, eget plena interpretatione. At si nihil sit versum, praetor dat ac-tionem, dumtaxat de peculio, et edictum utitur his verbis. quod edictum loquitur et de eo, qui dolo malo peculium ademerit. si igitur verbi gratia ex HS X, quae servus tuus a me mutua accepit, creditori tuo HS V soluerit, aut rem necessariam, puta fa-miliae cibaria, HS V emerit et reliqua V quolibet modo consumpserit, pro V quidem in solidum damnari debes, pro ceteris V eatenus, quatenus in peculio sit. Ex quo scilicet apparet, si tota HS X in rem tuam versa fuerit, tota me HS X consequi posse; licet enim una est formula, qua de peculio deque eo, quod in rem <patris> do-mini<ve> versum sit, agitur, tamen duas habet condemnationes. itaque iudex, apud quem ea formula agitur, ante dispicere solet, an in rem <patris> domini<ve> versum sit, nec aliter ad peculii aestimationem transit, quam si aut nihil in rem <patris> do-mini<ve> versum intellegatur aut non totum.

(Gaius in the fourth book of his *Institutes*)

An action is also given by the praetor concerning the *peculium* and for benefit re-ceived. For although a business transaction may be arranged with a son-in-power or a slave without the wish or consent of the *pater* (*familias*) or master coming into play, if, all the same, something of substance from that transaction should be turned to the benefit of the *pater* (*familias*) or master, an action will be given for the full amount turned to his benefit.

The meaning of "turned to the benefit" requires detailed interpretation. But if there is no benefit, the praetor grants an action (only) for "as much as the *pe-culium* contains," and the Edict uses these very words. But the Edict also applies to a person who diminishes the *peculium* (of his slave or son) in deliberate bad faith (*dolo malo*).

So if, for example, out of the 10,000 (sesterces) which your slave accepts from me as a loan, he pays 5,000 to your creditor or purchases necessities, say food for the household, and he uses up the other 5,000 in some other way, you should be found liable for the entirety of the first 5,000, and for the second only for as much as the *peculium* contains.

From this it is clear that if all 10,000 were turned to your benefit, I can be awarded the full amount upon suit. For although there is one formula for (both) the action on the *peculium* and that for benefit received by the *pater* (*familias*) or master, nevertheless there are two condemnations. Thus the *iudex*, before whom the formula is raised, typically examines first whether anything has been turned to the benefit of the *pater* (*familias*) or master, and does not move to valuing the *peculium* before it is clear that nothing has been turned to the benefit of the *pater* (*familias*) or master, or not (at any rate) the whole claim.

1. The Calculating Plaintiff. This Case (which is very heavily reconstructed after the first two sentences, mainly from Justinian, *Inst.* 4.7.4) is wonderful because it vividly illustrates the practical perils that plaintiffs faced in bringing lawsuits on *peculium* debts. Although the benefit received by the *pater* (see Cases 122–123) involves a different theory of liability than an action on the *peculium,* the Roman praetor, in his Edict, bundled the two together in a single action, presumably because the exact accounting boundaries between *peculium* assets and those of the *pater* were often difficult to know in advance of fact-finding in a trial. Follow Gaius's explanation of how a *iudex* usually calculates damages in these lawsuits. As a plaintiff, what strategy would you pursue in presenting your case to the *iudex?* Are you in a better position if you can prove that your extension of credit has ended up benefiting the *pater familias?*

2. When Can a Plaintiff Claim? Liability on the *peculium* must stem from a "transaction" with the slave or child-in-power (Ulpian, D. 15.1.1.2: *negotium*). This transaction will usually be a contract that the plaintiff had entered into with the holder of the *peculium;* by this contract the holder undertook a debt that has not yet been paid. But the jurists give some examples that are hard to think of as transactions. Suppose, for instance, that a third party who is insolvent gives a son-in-power property in order to conceal it from a creditor; if the text is to be believed, Ulpian, D.42.8.6.12 (of a slave), makes the son's *pater* liable to the creditor for benefit received by him or up to the value of the son's *peculium.* In what sense had the creditor entered into a transaction with the son? In any case, generally a son's liability arising from his delicts did not give rise to an action on the son's *peculium;* see Cases 139–141.

3. At What Point in Time Is the *Peculium* Evaluated? Suppose that a *peculium* has no assets at the present time. Can a plaintiff nonetheless sue a *pater* on a *peculium* debt, in the hope that the *peculium* will have some value when the judgment is eventually made? See Ulpian, D. 15.1.30 pr. (yes).

4. Plaintiff Protection. Gaius notes situations in which those who do business with a *peculium* are protected: first, if a *pater* materially benefits, even innocently or even without wishing this, from *peculium* assets that are traceable to the customer (liability for benefit received); second, if the *pater* acts in bad faith to reduce the value of the *peculium,* for instance, by stripping it of assets in anticipation of bankruptcy (see Case 136). To which of the two protections do the examples given by Gaius refer?

5. Limited Liability. It is worth considering, at this point, exactly why it is that a *pater* should enjoy a limited liability in relation to a *peculium* managed by a child or slave. Is this related to the fact that he (or she, in the case of a *sui iuris* woman with a slave) does not consent to particular business dealings with the *peculium* holder? What is the logic here? Is the legal institution of the *peculium* in fact well designed to unleash some of the entrepreneurial capacity of those in another's power?

CASE 135: Deductions from the *Peculium*

D. 15.1.9.2–4 (Ulpianus libro vicensimo nono ad edictum)

(2) Peculium autem deducto quod domino debetur computandum esse, quia praevenisse dominus et cum servo suo egisse creditur. (3) Huic definitioni Servius adiecit et si quid his debeatur qui sunt in eius potestate, quoniam hoc quoque domino deberi nemo ambigit. (4) Praeterea id etiam deducetur, quod his personis debetur, quae sunt in tutela vel cura domini vel patris vel quorum negotia administrant, dummodo dolo careant, quoniam et si per dolum peculium vel ademerint vel minuerint, tenentur: nam si semper praevenire dominus et agere videtur, cur non dicatur etiam hoc nomine eum secum egisse, quo nomine vel tutelae vel negotiorum gestorum vel utili actione tenebitur? nam ut eleganter Pedius ait, ideo hoc minus in peculio est, quod domino vel patri debetur, quoniam non est verisimile dominum id concedere servo in peculium habere, quod sibi debetur. sane cum ex ceteris causis ipsum a semet ipso exegisse dicimus qui negotia vel tutelam geret, cur non etiam in specie peculiari exegerit, quod exigi debuit? defendendum igitur erit quasi sibi eum solvere, cum quis agere de peculio conabitur.

(Ulpian in the twenty-ninth book on the Edict)

(2) But (the value of) the *peculium* should be assessed after deducting what is owed to the master, since the master is regarded as having preceded (any third party) in suing his own slave.

(3) To this rule, Servius added (that deduction should first be made) also if something is owed to those in his (the master's) power, since nobody doubts that this too is owed to the master.

(4) Further, also deducted is what is owed to those persons who are in the tutelage or care of the master or father, or whose affairs they administer; (but this is the rule) provided they are free from *dolus* (intentional deceit), since they are likewise liable if through *dolus* they either reclaim or diminish the *peculium*. For if the owner is always held to precede (a third party) in suing (on a claim against the *peculium*), why should it not be held that he also "sued himself" on behalf of those to whom he is liable for tutelage or administration of affairs or by an analogous action?

For, as Pedius convincingly observed, what is owed to the master or father is for this reason no longer in the *peculium,* since it is unlikely that the master would let a slave keep in his *peculium* something that is owed to himself (the master).

Since in other cases we say that a person who administers (another's) affairs or a tutelage has "collected from himself" (by deducting debts owed to him), why in the case of a *peculium* should he not also collect what should be collected?

So the view is defensible that he (the father or master) in a sense pays himself whenever someone tries to sue on the *peculium*.

1. What Can the *Pater* Deduct? As we saw in Case 126, the value of a *peculium* includes debts "owed" to it by the *pater familias* and by other slaves belonging to him (apart from those in the *peculium* itself). However, as this Case shows, when suit is brought on the *peculium,* its value is reduced by the debts that the *peculium* owes to these same persons. Indeed, even if the *pater* has only an indirect interest in the debt (e.g., where he is the guardian of a *sui iuris* minor to whom the *peculium* owes money; how might that happen?), he can also deduct this debt. And most debts can be deducted, particularly if a debt results from a contract open to slaves. Try to discover the pattern that underlies the following examples:

   - The *pater* has paid a debt owed by the *peculium* or has been found liable for the debt in a trial; this is deductible from the *peculium;* see Ulpian, D. 15.1.9.8 (of a slave).
   - The *pater* has formally promised to pay a debt owed by the *peculium;* this is deductible even before payment; see Ulpian, D. 15.1.11.1 (of a slave).
   - The *pater* has paid medical expenses for his son or slave; this is not deductible; see Ulpian, D. 15.1.9.7 (of a slave). Why not? Ulpian reasons that the master is looking after his own interests. Convinced?
   - The *peculium* holder damaged property that belonged to the *pater* but that was not in the *peculium;* the loss is deductible; see Pomponius, D. 15.1.4.3 (of a slave).
   - The *peculium* holder stole property belonging to a third party; if the *pater* paid its owner for the property, its value is deductible, but not any additional penalty; see Ulpian, D. 15.1.9.6, and Africanus, D. 19.1.30 pr. (both of a slave).

2. Why Can the *Pater* Deduct? This is a far more difficult issue. Before the value of a *peculium* is assessed for judicial purposes, the *pater* can deduct debts owed to him or his other slaves. However, debts owed to third parties not in the *familia* cannot be deducted. This makes the *pater* a preferred creditor, since in effect the *peculium* assets are used to satisfy him before other creditors such as the plaintiff. Accordingly, these third parties need to take care in extending credit to a *peculium,* since (even in the absence of fraud; see the following Case) there is always a possibility that a *peculium* is or may become valueless because of debts to the *pater.* (For this reason, a modern corporation cannot prefer its ordinary stockholders to its unsecured creditors.) What explains the Roman rule? Ulpian gives two justifications:

   - In section 4, he cites the jurist Pedius to the effect that "it is unlikely that the master would let a slave keep in his *peculium* something that is owed to himself (the master)." Is the issue, then, simply what the *pater* wants? Why should his desires be preferred to those of other creditors? One answer may be that the practice has a customary (prelegal) origin: masters were initially willing to satisfy other creditors only after they had satisfied themselves.

- Also in section 4, Ulpian says that "the owner is always held to precede (a third party) in suing," and that he has, in effect, "collected from himself" by deducting debts owed to him. Does this do any more than restate the problem?

Can you think of a more convincing explanation than these?

CASE 136: The Deceitful *Pater*

D. 15.1.36 (Ulpianus libro secundo Disputationum)

In bonae fidei contractibus quaestionis est, [an] de peculio an in solidum pater vel dominus tenerentur: ut est in actione de dote agitatum, si filio dos data sit, an pater dumtaxat de peculio conveniretur. ego autem arbitror non solum de peculio, sed et si quid praeterea dolo malo patris capta fraudataque est mulier, competere actionem: nam si habeat res nec restituere sit paratus, aequum est eum quanti ea res est condemnari. . . .

(Ulpian in the second book of *Disputations*)

For good-faith contracts, it is questionable whether a *pater* (*familias*) or master is liable for the entirety (of a *peculium* debt) or only up to the limit of the *peculium*. Similarly, the issue has arisen in the action on dowry as to whether, if a dowry is given to a son (who is in his father's power), the *pater* (*familias*) is liable only up to the limit of the *peculium*.

For my part, I think that an action lies not only on the *peculium* but also for anything in addition out of which the wife has been cheated and deceived through the intentional deceit (*dolus malus*) of the *pater* (*familias*); for if he possesses the property and is not prepared to surrender it, it is fair that he be found liable for its full value. . . .

1. Fraud (*Dolus Malus*). The general rule is discussed by Ulpian (D. 15.1.21 pr.): "With full justification the praetor included in the *peculium* anything that was not in it because of a master's *dolus malus*. We should consider it *dolus malus* if he takes away the *peculium*. But likewise if, to the harm of creditors, he allowed him (the holder of the *peculium*) to entangle the *peculium*'s affairs, Mela writes that this was done with *dolus malus*. Again, if he thought that one (creditor) was about to sue him and diverted the *peculium* to another one, he is not free of *dolus malus*. But if he (simply) paid off one (creditor), I do not doubt that he is not liable, since payment was to a creditor and the (other) creditor could have been alert in protecting his own interests." What does this passage suggest about the degree of care the *pater* must exercise in order to avoid liability for deceit? Note that the effect of *dolus* is to negate what the *pater* did in lowering the value of the *peculium*.

2. Good-Faith Contracts and Dowries. Both these relationships impose a high standard of conduct on the parties to them, in the sense that dishonest behavior gave grounds for liability. If a son-in-power entered into a good-faith contract (such as a sale), why is the *pater*'s liability in full a matter for discussion? As to the right of a wife to recover a dowry after a marriage's dissolution, see Chapter II.D.2. How might her position be prejudiced by the fact that her ex-husband was a son-in-power?

CASE 137: Alternative Remedies

Gaius, *Institutiones* 4.74

Ceterum dubium non est, quin et is, qui iussu patris dominive contraxit cuique exercitoria vel institoria formula competit, de peculio aut de in rem verso agere possit.
sed nemo tam stultus erit, ut qui aliqua illarum actionum sine dubio solidum consequi possit, in difficultatem se deducat probandi <vel> habere peculium eum cum
quo contraxerit, exque eo peculio posse sibi satisfieri, vel id quod persequitur in
rem patris dominive versum esse.

(Gaius in the fourth book of his *Institutes*)

All the same, it is beyond doubt that a person who has made a contract in reliance on the order of the *pater* or master, or who has standing as plaintiff in the
actio exercitoria or the *actio institoria,* can (also) bring a suit on the *peculium* or
for benefit received.

But no one will be so stupid that, if he can undoubtedly recover the entire
amount by raising either of the former actions, he will subject himself to the
hardship of proving either that the person with whom he contracted had a *peculium* and that he can be paid in full out of this *peculium* or that the amount he
seeks was turned to the benefit of the *pater* or owner.

1. Diverse Remedies. This Case reveals something of the realities of Roman litigation. The same transaction can often give rise to multiple theories of liability; Gaius is advising plaintiffs to pick the theory that makes it easiest for them
   to prove liability. The *actio institoria* lies against the owner who places another
   person in charge of a business and concerns that person's transactions with
   third parties (see Case 124; the *actio exercitoria* is similar but involves the
   command of ships); but this manager might be a son or slave with a *peculium,*
   and if so, the customer could also sue on this basis. Why are problems of
   proof likely to be easier in the former case?

2. Another Alternative. Creditors of a *peculium* had yet another possibility, the
   actio tributoria (action on division), which we will not consider in detail here.
   In brief, when a son or slave was doing business with all or a portion of his *peculium,* and he contracted debts with the *pater's* knowledge, creditors could
   sue the *pater* if the *peculium* then became insolvent. This liability effectively
   forced the *pater* to share out the business portion of the *peculium* among all its
   creditors, including himself (i.e., unlike in the action on the *peculium,* the
   pater was not given preference as a debtor); any creditor dissatisfied with the
   allocation could bring the *actio tributoria.* See D. 14.4. Gaius (*Inst.* 4.74a) remarks that creditors generally prefer the action on the *peculium* and on benefit received: "The *tributoria* takes account only of that part of the *peculium*
   with which the son or slave was transacting, plus what was earned from it;
   but the action on the *peculium* (takes account) of it all." Can you imagine circumstances in which creditors might nonetheless prefer a division?

CASE 138: The Camp *Peculium*

Tituli ex Corpore Ulpiani 20.10

Filius familiae testamentum facere non potest, quoniam nihil suum habet, ut testari de eo possit. Sed divus Augustus [Marcus] constituit, ut filius familiae miles de eo peculio quod in castris adquisivit testamentum facere possit.

D. 14.6.1.3 (Ulpianus libro vicensimo nono ad edictum)

In filio familias nihil dignitas facit, quo minus senatus consultum Macedonianum locum habeat: nam etiamsi Consul sit vel cuiusvis dignitatis, senatus consulto locus est: nisi forte castrense peculium habeat: tunc enim senatus consultum cessabit

D. 14.6.2 (Ulpianus libro sexagensimo quarto ad edictum)

usque ad quantitatem castrensis peculii, cum filii familias in castrensi peculio vice patrum familiarum fungantur.

(Excerpts from *Ulpian's Writings*)

A son-in-power cannot make a will since he has nothing of his own that he can make a will for. But the deified Augustus established that a son-in-power who is a soldier can make a will for the *peculium* he has acquired in the (military) camp.

(Ulpian in the twenty-ninth book on the Edict)

The social position of a son-in-power is irrelevant to application of the SC Macedonianum, for it is applied even if he is a consul or of whatever position. But if he happens to have a camp *peculium*, then the decree of the Senate is not applied

(Ulpian in the sixty-fourth book on the Edict)

up to the amount of the camp *peculium*, since, with respect to a camp *peculium*, sons-in-power function as *patres familiarum*.

1. An Exceptional Fund. The camp *peculium* (*peculium castrense*) starts out as a narrow exception to usual rules, whereby soldiers, although still in a father's power, are allowed to control their military earnings. The Emperor Augustus (reign: 31 B.C. to A.D. 14) presumably created the exception to attract recruits. Does this exception suggest that adult children-in-power may have resented their legal inability to own and dispose of property? Gradually emperors and jurists expanded a soldier's control over this separate fund; under Hadrian, he remained in charge of it even after retirement (Justinian, *Inst.* 2.12 pr.). The inapplicability of the SC Macedonianum (see the Discussion on Case 119) means that loans to soldiers were valid and enforceable directly against the borrower. In the postclassical period the exception was expanded still further to earnings from various other professions.

So far in this part we have considered the limited power of household subordinates in holding and dealing with property. But the *familia* organization caused similar problems when children-in-power or slaves committed wrongs against others.

Roman law is fairly well developed as to delicts, private wrongs that broadly resemble torts in Anglo-American Common Law. The three main delicts were all rooted in archaic statute but remained central in classical Roman law: theft (*furtum*), the appropriation of property belonging to someone else against that person's will; affront (*iniuria*), an antisocial attack on the dignity of another person; and wrongful infliction of loss (*damnum iniuria datum*), harm to another's property. Each of these delicts enabled the victim to sue the miscreant for what the jurists thought of as a "penalty," a sum of money intended to repair the social breach the defendant's act had opened. Theft and affront were sources of liability only if the miscreant had acted with the intent to commit them (*dolus*); but for wrongful damage to property a defendant was also liable for unintentional fault (*culpa*).

When children-in-power or slaves committed delicts, they were in theory personally responsible for them (on children, see Gaius, D. 44.7.39). But the obvious hurdle was that they had no assets with which to satisfy their victims. From a very early time, the Romans solved this problem by allowing the victim to sue the *pater* over his subordinate's act. But this liability may have seemed unfair in the case of a *pater* who may not even have known of the delict. Therefore, in a curious sort of compromise, the *pater* as defendant was allowed to choose either to pay the legally prescribed penalty in full or to surrender to the plaintiff the subordinate who had committed the delict. This form of surrender is called "noxal liability" after the Latin phrase *noxae deditio*, "handing over an offender."

In the case of a slave, ownership of the offender was permanently conveyed to the plaintiff. A child-in-power occasions more difficulty. The offender, after being surrendered, did not cease to be a free citizen (nor, e.g., did his marriage end), but he did enter into a form of civil bondage called *mancipium*. Effectively, *mancipium* put him in the position of his victim's slave, *servi loco*, where he remained until he had worked off the debt (Papinian, *Coll.* 2.3.1). The law offered some minimal protection for the offender's personal dignity while in *mancipium* (Gaius, *Inst.* 1.141).

This somewhat rough-and-ready arrangement was used only for private wrongs. In the classical period, noxal surrender was probably far more commonly used for sons-in-power than for daughters; and Justinian (*Inst.* 4.8.7) later abolished the practice for both sexes. Crimes are treated differently: children-in-power are fully liable for their own criminal offenses.

Children-in-power have no property of their own and so cannot be the victims of theft or wrongful damage; but they do have independent legal personalities that third parties might offend against. Somewhat oddly, it may seem, an affront (*iniuria*) directed against a child-in-power was also often considered an affront against the child's *pater familias*, who was then entitled to bring his own lawsuit, in addition to that of his child.

CASE 139: Noxal Actions

Gaius, *Institutiones* 4.75–76

(75) Ex maleficio filiorum familias servorumque, veluti si furtum fecerint aut iniuriam commiserint, noxales actiones proditae sunt, uti liceret patri dominove aut litis aestimationem sufferre aut noxae dedere. erat enim iniquum nequitiam eorum ultra ipsorum corpora parentibus dominisve damnosam esse. (76) Constitutae sunt autem noxales actiones aut legibus aut edicto praetoris: legibus, velut furti lege XII tabularum, damni iniuriae lege Aquilia; edicto praetoris, velut iniuriarum et vi bonorum raptorum.

(Gaius in the fourth book of his *Institutes*)

(75) Noxal actions are given for the wrongful acts of sons-in-power and slaves, for example, if they commit theft or inflict affront. These actions allow the *pater* (*familias*) or owner either to pay the damages arising from a lawsuit or to make noxal surrender (of the miscreant). For it was unfair that beyond the value of their own bodies, their depravity cause loss to their fathers or owners. (76) Noxal actions have been established both by statutes and by the praetor's Edict: by statutes, for instance, by the Twelve Tables for theft and by the *lex Aquilia* for loss wrongfully inflicted; by the praetor's Edict, for instance, for affront and robbery.

1. Choice of Liability. How is it "fair" that the *pater familias* or owner be allowed a choice that limits his (or her, in that women could own slaves) liability in this way? Does the aim of noxal surrender appear to be to punish the true wrongdoer or to limit the liability of the *pater familias*? Can both occur simultaneously? Which receives greater emphasis?

2. Bad Behavior. Gaius uses strong language to characterize the supposed depravity (*nequitia*) of the offending sons-in-power and slaves. This seems appropriate for intentional fault (*dolus*), which is required for affront and theft. But wrongful infliction of loss to property (*damnum iniuria datum*) can also involve liability for fault (*culpa*), most commonly unintentional carelessness. Does this suggest that the true aim of noxal surrender is to limit the liability of the *pater familias* or owner rather than to punish or deter wrongdoing?

3. The Father's Liability. The *pater* has the option of noxal surrender if he did not "know" of the offender's act, that is, if he could not have prevented it. Where he did "know" of the act, he was considered to have committed the act himself and held fully liable. See, for example, Ulpian and Paul, D. 9.4.2–4 pr. Does this suggest that the *pater* is supposed to exercise at least a modicum of oversight in relation to his subordinates? In general, to what extent do you

think that parents should be liable for the acts of their children? Which of the following should be taken into account in answering this question: the child's age; the child's general intellectual capacity; the nature of the act; the foreseeability of the act or of its harm to others; the relationship of the victim to the parents?

CASE 140: Liability and Status

Gaius, *Institutiones* 4.77

Omnes autem noxales actiones caput sequuntur. nam si filius tuus servusve noxam commiserit, quamdiu in tua potestate est, tecum est actio; si in alterius potestatem pervenerit, cum illo incipit actio esse; si sui iuris coeperit esse, directa actio cum ipso est, et noxae deditio extinguitur. ex diverso quoque directa actio noxalis esse incipit. nam si pater familias noxam commiserit et is se in adrogationem tibi dederit aut servus tuus esse coeperit, <quod> quibusdam casibus accidere primo commentario tradidimus, incipit tecum noxalis actio esse, quae ante directa fuit.

(Gaius in the fourth book of his *Institutes*)

Moreover, all noxal actions attach to the wrongdoer. For if your son or slave commits a wrong, the action lies against you as long as he is in your power. If he passes into the power of another person, the action begins to lie against that person; if he becomes *sui iuris,* he is liable in a direct action, and noxal surrender is no longer available.

   Conversely, a direct action can also become noxal. For if a *pater familias* commits a wrong and (then) allows himself to be adopted by you or becomes your slave—something, as we indicated in the first book (at 1.160), that happens in certain cases—the noxal action begins to lie against you, though it had previously been direct.

Hypothetical Situation

Titius, a son-in-power, publishes a tract defaming Sempronia, an eminent person. Before she can sue, Titius's father, who is unaware of the tract, frees him from *patria potestas* (through emancipation). Whom should Sempronia sue?

1. The Wrongdoer's Head. Literally, the actions "follow the head" of the wrongdoer (*caput sequuntur*). This means that the noxal action is available against the person who currently holds the wrongdoer in his or her power. If the person is no longer in power, then suit can be brought directly against the wrongdoer, but the *pater* no longer is answerable for the delict. What does this suggest about the nature of noxal liability?

2. Emancipation and Adoption. Could the plaintiff's interest be injured through release of the wrongdoer from someone's power? Is the same true of passage into someone else's power?

3. Own Goal. Gaius (*Inst.* 4.78) also notes that if a son-in-power or slave commits a wrongful act against his *pater familias* or owner, there is no action. Is this consistent with the rules for other obligations?

CASE 141: Defending the Son

D. 9.4.33 (Pomponius libro <nono> decimo ad Sabinum)

Noxali iudicio invitus nemo cogitur alium defendere, sed carere debet eo quem non defendit, si servus est: quod si liber est qui in potestate sit, indistincte ipsi sui defensio danda est:

D. 9.4.34 (Iulianus libro quarto ad Urseium Ferocem)

quotiens enim nemo filium familias ex causa delicti defendit, in eum iudicium datur

D. 9.4.35 (Ulpianus libro quadragensimo primo ad Sabinum)

et si condemnatus fuerit, filius iudicatum facere debet: tenet enim condemnatio. quin immo etiam illud dicendum est patrem quoque post condemnationem filii dumtaxat de peculio posse conveniri.

(Pomponius in the nineteenth book on Sabinus)

No one can be forced against his will to defend another person in a noxal action, but if it is his slave, he ought to lose him if he makes no defense. But if it is a free person-in-power, he (the child) should be given the unqualified right to conduct his own defense,

(Julian in the fourth book on Urseius Ferox)

for whenever no one defends a son-in-power in a suit for delict, the action is granted against the latter

(Ulpian in the forty-first book on Sabinus)

and if judgment is given against him, the son must discharge it himself, since he is liable for the judgment. In fact, this too must be said, that the father can also be sued after the adverse judgment against the son, but only up to the limit of the *peculium*.

1. Refusal to Defend. Why would a *pater familias* simply refuse to defend a son-in-power instead of performing noxal surrender? Why would the praetor permit this?

2. Automatic Surrender. Why does a refusal to defend a slave in a noxal action result in automatic surrender to the plaintiff, while the child-in-power is allowed to conduct a legal defense?

3. Suing the Father. Why allow the *pater familias* to be sued after adverse judgment against the son? One possibility is that the son might have died before satisfying the judgment (see Case 120, which also specifies that liability is limited to the value of the *peculium* or for benefit received).

CASE 142: Wrongs against Children-in-Power

D. 47.10.30.1 (Ulpianus libro quadragensimo secundo ad Sabinum)

Si filio iniuria facta sit, cum utrique tam filio quam patri adquisita actio sit, non eadem utique facienda aestimatio est,

D. 47.10.31 (Paulus libro decimo ad Sabinum)

cum possit propter filii dignitatem maior ipsi quam patri iniuria facta esse.

(Ulpian in the forty-second book on Sabinus)

If an affront is inflicted on a son, although both father and son are allowed to bring suit, the estimate of damages should not be precisely the same,

(Paul in the tenth book on Sabinus)

since it is possible that because of the son's social position a greater affront was inflicted on him than on his father.

1. Wrongs Done to Sons. How does a man suffer affront (*iniuria*) when his son is insulted? Does the rule in this Case apply to daughters or wives as well? See Case 44 (yes). As Gaius notes, an affront to a woman might result in three lawsuits: her own, her *pater's*, and her husband's. In Ulpian's view, a man could also sue on an affront inflicted through his betrothed bride-to-be (Case 27). What justifies this proliferation of lawsuits from a single act? Note that an insult to a *pater familias* is not normally an insult to his wife and children as well (Justinian, *Inst.* 4.4.2; for an exceptional case, see Ulpian, D. 47.10.1.6–7). Why is this so? Paul (D. 47.10.2) says, with regard to wives, that "it is right that wives be defended by their husbands, not husbands by their wives." Pure sexism?

2. Assessing Damages. Where multiple lawsuits were brought on the basis of a single act, this Case indicates that damages were assessed independently in each, depending on the relative social position of each plaintiff. Although this Case indicates that a son might occasionally have higher social position than his father (what sort of a situation would result in this?), the reverse would be more usual.

3. Intent. The offender must have *dolus,* that is, he must intend to affront his victim. Are Ulpian and Paul assuming that the offender was intentionally seeking to affront the son's *pater*? What if the offender didn't know the son was in another person's power? What if he was mistaken about whose power the son was in? See Paul, D. 47.10.18.3–5.

PART C

Creation and Termination

Given the potentially enormous consequences for an individual's status, creation and termination of *patria potestas* were far from minor matters. Most Romans entered directly into *patria potestas* at their birth, when, indeed, a *pater familias* exercised his power by determining whether to raise the child or instead to expose or kill it. But this initial exercise of power only symbolized his more general authority, which could last for life; further, that authority was intimately bound up with his conferral of free citizen status on his offspring. The main constraints on his power were, as we have seen, social; but the marriage legislation of Augustus had transformed the raising of children into a matter of public policy, so that he was obliged to consider this aspect as well.

A *pater familias* was also free to bring an outsider under his *potestas*, through adrogation and adoption. Adrogation (*adrogatio*) is the adoption of one *pater familias* by another, a particularly delicate process, as the Cases suggest, that is permitted only as a last resort, since it involved extinguishing one family line in order to sustain another. Not surprisingly, adrogation can be accomplished only by direct state intervention. By contrast, the more usual process of adoption involves the transfer of a child-in-power from one household to another; here public policy issues are regarded as less pressing, and the procedure is accordingly more informal. What is perhaps most surprising, in any case, about both adrogation and adoption is that the Romans typically tend to adopt adults rather than small children. These procedures are therefore not mainly used to deal with the problem of orphans, nor is the welfare of the child a primary consideration. The interests of the *pater familias* are considerably more salient, and it is his personal perspective that dominates, leading to what we might regard as oddities: even a bachelor can adopt.

Release from *potestas*, or emancipation, is a procedure whereby a child-in-power is freed from the power of a *pater familias*. (The word "emancipation" is usually reserved, in Roman legal texts, for the release of free persons from power; "manumission" is used for freeing slaves.) Emancipation often formed part of a larger strategy for the settlement of family property and succession after the death of the *pater familias*; indeed, the same is true, of course, of adrogation and adoption, especially when this is practiced within the family. It is therefore important to bear in mind that emancipation was not necessarily a punishment, above all since an emancipated child could and often did benefit from it.

Patria potestas could also terminate through the death of a *pater familias* if the child-in-power thereby became *sui iuris*, or by a change in legal status (e.g., through loss of citizenship or capture by the enemy) of the *pater* or the child.

This area of Roman law has been considerably clarified in Jane F. Gardner's *Family and Familia in Roman Law and Life* (1998), which we also recommend for further information on the social background.

SECTION 1. Birth

CASE 143: Paternal Power and Status

D. 1.6.4 (Ulpianus libro primo Institutionum)

Nam civium Romanorum quidam sunt patres familiarum, alii filii familiarum, quaedam matres familiarum, quaedam filiae familiarum. patres familiarum sunt, qui sunt suae potestatis sive puberes sive impuberes: simili modo matres familiarum: filii familiarum et filiae, quae sunt in aliena potestate. nam qui ex me et ex uxore mea nascitur, in mea potestate est: item qui ex filio meo et uxore eius nascitur, id est nepos meus et neptis, aeque in mea sunt potestate, et pronepos et proneptis et deinceps ceteri.

(Ulpian in the first book of his *Institutes*)

Some Roman citizens are *patres familiarum,* others are sons-in-power; some women are *matres familiarum,* others are daughters-in-power. *Patres familiarum* are males who are of independent legal status (*suae potestatis*), whether they have reached the age of legal majority or not. The same holds for *matres familiarum.*

    Sons- and daughters-in-power are those (Roman citizens) in someone else's power. For a person born to myself and my wife is in my power. Likewise, a person born to my son and his wife, that is, my grandson and granddaughter, is just as much in my power as are my great-grandson and great-granddaughter, and so on.

1. Offspring from a Legitimate Marriage. This point is central. As Gaius (*Inst.* 1.55) says: "In our power are our children who are the offspring of a legitimate marriage (*iustae nuptiae*)." On the requirements for legitimate marriage, see Chapter II.A. A marriage is legitimate if it involves a union between two citizens or one between a male citizen and a woman, such as a Latin, possessed of *conubium,* the right of intermarriage with Roman citizens (Case 9). In the latter form of marriage, children follow their father's status and are in his power. Why is this not true when a female citizen marries a man who is not a citizen but has *conubium?*

2. *Mater Familias.* In what sense is the status of a *mater familias,* as described in this Case, analogous to that of a *pater familias?* In what ways is it not? *Mater familias* is not a technical term (unlike *pater familias*); it is used sometimes as a synonym for "wife" (*uxor*), sometimes to mean an upright woman, sometimes to mean a *sui iuris* woman. Which sense does Ulpian use?

3. Grant of Citizenship. A grant of citizenship to a veteran who had a noncitizen wife had to be accompanied by the award of *conubium* if the marriage was to be legitimate and so give him *patria potestas* over their children (Gaius, *Inst.* 1.57). In the same way, a grant of citizenship to a foreign family had to be augmented by a separate grant of *potestas* over their children (ibid. 1.93). Do you see why?

CASE 144: Presuming a Father

D. 2.4.4.3 (Ulpianus libro quinto ad edictum)

Parentes etiam eos accipi Labeo existimat, qui in servitute susceperunt: nec <tantum>, ut Severus dicebat, ad solos iustos liberos, sed et si volgo quaesitus sit filius, matrem in ius non vocabit,

D. 2.4.5 (Paulus libro quarto ad edictum)

quia semper certa est, etiam si volgo conceperit: pater vero is est, quem nuptiae demonstrant.

(Ulpian in the fifth book on the Edict)

Labeo thinks that persons who have produced children while in slavery are also considered "parents." Nor (does the term apply) only in the case of legitimate children, as (the jurist Valerius) Severus used to claim; but even when a child is illegitimate, he will not (be able to) summon his mother into court (i.e., sue her),

(Paul in the fourth book on the Edict)

since even if she conceives a child illegitimately, her identity (at least) is always known. But it is a legitimate marriage that shows who the father is.

1. Summoning the Father. These decisions were made in a discussion of the rules for summoning persons to court. The praetor's Edict forbade children to sue their parents. As Ulpian and Paul say, an illegitimate child cannot sue his mother. Does this mean the father is unknown or unknowable? If he is known, can a child sue him? Does Labeo's point about slave parents clarify the issue? See also, for example, Paul, D. 2.4.6: "No one can summon his natural (biological) parents into court; for the same reverence (*reverentia*) is owed to all parents."

2. Paternity Problems. Is the last part of the Case convincing? In a society without DNA testing, can we be that certain of paternity? What does Paul seem to be getting at? Is he primarily concerned with the welfare of the child? Should modern courts resort to DNA to settle such questions rather than relying on the presumption that Paul makes?

3. The SC Plancianum. This decree of the Senate, passed, it is thought, during the reign of Vespasian (A.D. 69–79), contained a provision requiring a woman who believed herself to be pregnant to notify her ex-husband within thirty days of a divorce; he could then either send attendants to protect his interest in the child's birth or declare himself not to be the father (see Case 47). If he neglected to do either, he could be compelled to accept the child as his own (Ulpian, D. 25.3.1.4). Is the law consistent with Paul's assertion that "it is a legitimate marriage that shows who the father is"?

CASE 145: Periods of Gestation

Aulus Gellius, *Noctes Atticae* 3.16.12

Praeterea ego de partu humano, praeterquam quae scripta in libris legi, hoc quoque usu venisse Romae comperi: feminam bonis atque honestis moribus, non ambigua pudicitia, in undecimo mense post mariti mortem peperisse factumque esse negotium propter rationem temporis, quasi marito mortuo postea concepisset, quoniam decemviri in decem mensibus gigni hominem, non in undecimo scripsissent; sed divum Hadrianum, causa cognita, decrevisse in undecimo quoque mense partum edi posse; idque ipsum eius rei decretum nos legimus. In eo decreto Hadrianus id statuere se dicit requisitis veterum philosophorum et medicorum sententiis.

(Aulus Gellius in the third book of his *Attic Nights*)

Moreover, on the subject of human gestation, besides what I have read in books, I have discovered that the following situation actually took place at Rome. A woman of good and honorable character, and of unquestioned sexual virtue, gave birth to a child in the eleventh month after the death of her husband. Because of the time involved, she was accused of having conceived after her husband was already dead, since the decemvirs had written that a person is born within ten months and not in the eleventh month.

The deified Hadrian, however, after hearing the case, gave his decision that birth can also take place in the eleventh month. I have read the actual decision of this case. In it, Hadrian states that he delivers his opinion after having consulted the views of ancient philosophers and doctors.

1. Woman Accused. What accusation was leveled against the woman? Given the apparent absence of sexual wrongdoing, she was probably not charged under Augustus's adultery law (see Cases 50–55). Gellius is notably unclear; but if a posthumous child, as a "privileged heir" (*suus heres*), was not mentioned in a father's will, the will was void (see Case 182) and recourse was had to the rules for intestate succession. Perhaps, therefore, the dead husband's will was compromised by the birth of a child he could not have foreseen, leading one or more of the beneficiaries of that will to question the child's legitimacy. The Emperor Hadrian probably heard the case on appeal from a lower court.

2. Intestacy. The regulation of the decemvirs upon which the accusers relied was a part of the Twelve Tables, the semicodification of private law dating to 449 B.C. Ulpian (D. 38.16.3.11) gives us something of its content: "a child born ten months after the death (of its father) shall not be admitted to intestate succession." This statute seems to presuppose that there is no will. In the present Case, Gellius does not mention a will, and possibly there was none. But it is somewhat more probable that there was a will (do you see why?), and the heirs under the will were accusing the widow of misconduct.

3. Ten Months. Does the tenth-month rule make sense? Does it seem fair? Whose interests does it consider? Keep in mind that the Romans strictly prohibited remarriage by a widow for a mourning period, originally, it seems, of ten months, and later a year; see the Discussion to Case 23.

4. Brief Gestation. Other texts show that the Romans admitted full-term gestations of less than seven months (Paul. D.1.5.12, citing the eminent Greek physician Hippocrates), to as few as 182 days (Ulpian, D. 38.16.3.12, also citing Hippocrates, as well as a rescript of Antoninus Pius). Why might it have been necessary to know the lower limits of a pregnancy?

5. Imperial Standard. Hadrian claims to have consulted the appropriate moral and medical authorities in formulating his decision. Given this emperor's reputation for learning, there is no reason to doubt that he did. But how likely is it that the woman's reputation played a more decisive role in the outcome of this particular case? What if her reputation had been more questionable? In the final analysis, is Hadrian's standard moral, medical, or legal in nature? The antiquarian Pliny the Elder (*Naturalis Historia* 7.5.40) mentions a Roman praetor who awarded an inheritance to a posthumous child allegedly born after thirteen months of pregnancy (i.e., thirteen months after the testator's death). Do you think that Hadrian would have been willing to accept this result?

CASE 146: Strange Bedfellows?

D. 1.6.6 (Ulpianus libro nono ad Sabinum)

Filium eum definimus, qui ex viro et uxore eius nascitur. sed si fingamus afuisse maritum verbi gratia per decennium, reversum anniculum invenisse in domo sua, placet nobis Iuliani sententia hunc non esse mariti filium. non tamen ferendum Iulianus ait eum, qui cum uxore sua adsidue moratus nolit filium adgnoscere quasi non suum. sed mihi videtur, quod et Scaevola probat, si constet maritum aliquamdiu cum uxore non concubuisse infirmitate interveniente vel alia causa, vel si ea valetudine pater familias fuit, ut generare non possit, hunc, qui in domo natus est, licet vicinis scientibus, filium non esse.

(Ulpian in the ninth book on Sabinus)

We define a child as someone born from a man and his wife. But if we hypothesize that a husband has been away, for example, for a decade, and upon his return he finds a year-old child in his house, I agree with Julian that (as a matter of law) this is not the husband's child. All the same, Julian says that we should not put up with a man who, having lived with his wife without interruption, refuses to accept a child on the ground that it is not his.

On the other hand, I am persuaded, and Scaevola too was of this view, that if it is determined that for some time a husband has not slept with his wife because of the onset of an infirmity or for some other reason, or if the *pater familias* had a disease rendering him impotent, a child born in his home, even if the neighbors were completely in the know, is not his own.

1. Suspicious Minds. In the first hypothetical situation, where the husband, away for ten years, returns to find a one-year-old presented as his own, do Julian and Ulpian assume there is no other evidence of the wife's adultery? Would the facts have to be this extreme? Would being away for only two years suffice?

2. Absence of Evidence. In the second situation, where the husband has been living with his wife without interruption, do Julian and Ulpian assume there is no evidence that the wife had an extramarital affair?

3. Neighbors in the Know. Is the third situation essentially the same as the first? What does Ulpian mean by "even if the neighbors were completely in the know"? What do the neighbors have to do with proving paternity? Is there any similarity with proving the existence of a legitimate marriage? See Case 16, which also mentions informed (or nosy?) neighbors.

4. Benefit of Doubt. How does the outcome of this case differ from that of Case 145? Is it that the standard is objective here and subjective there? Who receives the benefit of the doubt when paternity is in question?

CASE 147: A Divorced Wife Takes Vengeance

D. 22.3.29.1 (Scaevola libro nono Digestorum)

Mulier gravida repudiata, filium enixa, absente marito ut spurium in actis professa est. quaesitum est an is in potestate patris sit et matre intestata mortua iussu eius hereditatem matris adire possit nec obsit professio a matre irata facta. respondit, veritati locum superfore.

(Scaevola in the ninth book of his *Digests*)

A man divorced a pregnant woman; she (then) gave birth to a son, whom she, in her ex-husband's absence, recorded as illegitimate in the public register. The question was raised as to whether he is in his father's power, and (as a result), should his mother die without a will, whether he can upon his father's order enter upon this inheritance, the record made by his mother while angry not being held against him.

He (Scaevola) responded that there will still be room for the truth.

1. Separate Statuses. This passage assumes a point implicit in earlier cases and raised explicitly by Gaius (*Inst.* 1.94): paternal power, unlike both citizen status and freeborn status, depends strictly upon the status and marital relationship of the parents at the moment of conception. That is why the child of a deceased or divorced father can still be fully legitimate and in his or her father's *potestas*. Compare Case 46.

2. Messy Divorce. As the issue was put to Scaevola, the ex-wife was motivated by a desire to embarrass her husband by declaring her son illegitimate, even at the expense of her own reputation. But is this her only possible motive? Note that a divorced woman could not abort without her ex-husband's permission (Case 48). Do you see why? Can you draw a connection with this case?

3. Son's Advantage. Under the SC Orphitianum of A.D. 178, the son had an enhanced right to the intestate succession of his mother, whether he was legitimate or not; see Cases 169–170. If he was in someone else's power, however, he needed permission to enter upon the inheritance and the property went to the *pater familias* in actual fact. How, then, does the inheritance benefit the son, as the questioner in this Case appears to imply it will?

4. Problem of Proof. Scaevola's laconic response (which is typical of his juristic style) shows that what mattered to him was not the official record but whether the ex-husband was actually the boy's father. How realistic is his holding? In the text immediately preceding this one (D. 22.3.29 pr.), Scaevola quotes a rescript of Marcus Aurelius and Lucius Verus (joint reign: A.D. 161–169) affirming the evidentiary value not just of witness testimony but also of letters sent by husbands to wives, provided they are genuine. Does this suggest that the problem of proof was great? Or does it merely confirm that the stakes could be high?

SECTION 2. Adrogation and Adoption

Case 148. Adrogation

D. 1.7.15 pr., 2–3 (Ulpianus libro vicensimo sexto ad Sabinum)

(pr.) Si pater familias adoptatus sit, omnia quae eius fuerunt et adquiri possunt tacito iure ad eum transeunt qui adoptavit: hoc amplius liberi eius qui in potestate sunt eum sequuntur: sed et hi, qui postliminio redeunt, vel qui in utero fuerunt cum adrogaretur, simili modo in potestatem adrogatoris rediguntur. . . . (2) In adrogationibus cognitio vertitur, num forte minor sexaginta annis sit qui adrogat, quia magis liberorum creationi studere debeat, nisi forte morbus aut valetudo in causa sit aut alia iusta causa adrogandi, veluti si coniunctam sibi personam velit adoptare. (3) Item non debet quis plures adrogare nisi ex iusta causa, sed nec libertum alienum, nec maiorem minor.

(Ulpian in the twenty-sixth book on Sabinus)

(pr.) If a *pater familias* is adopted (through adrogation), all property that belongs to him or that accrues to him passes by tacit operation of law into the ownership of the person adopting him. Further, the children who were in his power follow him; and those who return from enemy captivity or who were *in utero* at the time he was adrogated are likewise transferred into the power of the adrogator. . . .

    (2) In cases of adrogation, official enquiry turns on whether the adrogator happens to be under sixty years old, because (in that case) he should rather be attempting to procreate (and not to adopt), unless perhaps disease or ill-health is a factor, or there is some other appropriate reason for adrogating, for example, if he wants to adopt someone related to him. (3) Likewise, no one ought to adrogate more than one person except for just cause; nor (should anyone adrogate) someone else's freedman; nor (should) a younger person (adrogate) an older one.

> 1. Adopting Romans. The Roman practice of adoption was radically different from our own. We tend to adopt orphans and prefer babies at that; the Romans usually adopted adults and actually put legal roadblocks in the way of adopting orphans, as you can see with the rules for adrogation. What do you think explains these differences?
>
> 2. Adrogating a *Pater Familias*. Adoption of a *pater familias,* that is, a male of *sui iuris* status, was regarded with special sensitivity since it involved the extinction of an independent household (see Gaius, *Inst.* 1.98–107). Both parties had to give explicit permission. Since in the process one family's cult practices (its *sacra*) were extinguished, the priestly board of pontiffs had to be consulted. Then adrogation had to be ratified through an archaic assembly known as the *comitia curiata* or, later, as this became inconvenient, by means of an imperial rescript: a high level of governmental involvement. What are the implications of the fact that the adrogator receives not only the property but all the persons in the adrogated person's power? How would,

for example, their rights of inheritance from their erstwhile *pater familias* be guaranteed?

3. Age Limit. Why insist that the adrogator be over sixty or, if younger, at least incapable of begetting children? Is there a connection between this rule and that only one person be adrogated? Do these requirements give a clue as to the motive that a Roman usually had in deciding to adrogate: affection between the parties or continuation of the family line? Gaius (*Inst.* 1.102) tells us that adrogation of a minor was not permitted until the reign of Antoninus Pius (A.D. 138–161), and then only upon a showing of good cause. Why were the Romans so reluctant to permit adrogation of *sui iuris* juveniles?

4. Excepting Relatives. Why make an exception for a relative? Why not allow adrogation of someone else's freedman?

5. Seniority. What is the rationale for requiring that the adrogator be older than the person adrogated?

CASE 149: The Adoption Process

Gaius, *Institutiones* 1.134

<Praeterea parentes eos liberos in potestate habere desinunt, quos aliis in adoptionem dederunt. et in filio quidem si in adoptionem datur, tres mancipationes> et duae intercedentes manumissiones proinde fiunt, ac fieri solent, cum ita eum pater de potestate dimittit, ut sui iuris efficiatur. deinde aut patri remancipatur, et ab eo is qui adoptat, vindicat apud praetorem filium suum esse, et illo contra non vindicante <a> praetore vindicanti filius addicitur: aut non remancipatur patri, sed ab eo vindicat is qui adoptat, apud quem in tertia mancipatione est: sed sane commodius est patri remancipari. in ceteris vero liberorum personis seu masculini seu feminini sexus una scilicet mancipatio sufficit, et aut remancipantur parenti aut non remancipantur. eadem et in provinciis apud praesidem provinciae solent fieri.

(Gaius in the first book of his *Institutes*)

Further, parents no longer have in their power those children whom they have given in adoption to others. In the case of a son given in adoption, three mancipations and two intervening manumissions are made, just as occurs when his *pater* releases him from power in order to make him *sui iuris*. Then he is remancipated to his father, from whom the adopting person claims him (the son) as his own before the praetor; and when he (the father) does not counterclaim, the praetor awards the son to the claimant. Alternatively, he is not remancipated to the father; instead, the adopting person claims him from the man with whom he is during the third mancipation. Still, the more convenient course is remancipation to the father.

But for all other children of either sex, one mancipation suffices, and they are either remancipated or not to their parent. In the provinces the same things take place before the provincial governor.

1. Mancipation and Manumission. This Case gives a brief description of the procedure for adoption when a child passes from one *familia* to another. The procedure exhibits many archaic formalities, but the core of it involves a series of three fictional sales (called mancipations) in which the father "sells" his son to a third party. After the first two sales, the "buyer" manumits the son (rather as if he were a slave) and the son reverts to his father's *potestas*. But the third sale permanently breaks the father's *potestas*, according to a rule in the archaic Law of the Twelve Tables that Gaius quotes earlier (*Inst.* 1.132: "If the father gives a son up for sale three times, the son shall be free from the father"). So far the process has occurred entirely in private, among a limited number of individuals: the father, his son, the adopting person, possibly a third party as the intermediate "buyer," five adult Roman citizen witnesses, and another adult Roman citizen who holds the scales for the mancipation ceremony (described by Gaius, 1.119). What is the function of these wit-

nesses? Why require such a formal and complicated procedure, with its elaborate fictions? What advantages and disadvantages does such an insistence on formality entail? You might want to consider this problem in light of the absence of formal requirements for marriage (Cases 13–23).

2. The Proceedings before the Praetor. Up to this point, the procedure for adoption and that for emancipation of a child (see section 3 below) were identical. The last stage in the adoption procedure involves a remancipation of the son (now freed from his father's *potestas*) usually to the father, followed, in Rome, by a collusive trial before the praetor. The person adopting claims the son as his own, rather as if he were property, by an action called vindication; the father puts up no defense, and so the praetor, who was surely aware of what was happening, awards the son to the claimant. With this award the adoption is complete. Why was it important to the Romans that a magistrate play some role at least in the final stages of this procedure? The Cases below provide evidence of at least some official supervision of adoptions, though little of it seems directed toward the welfare of the child. In any case, why is the role of government so much smaller in the case of adoption than in adrogation?

3. Other Children. The archaic Twelve Tables, quoted above, prescribed that a "son" (*filius*) be released from parental power after three sales. The exact meaning of the original provision is not certain, but it seems to have been reinterpreted for use in adoptions and emancipations. For purposes of this reinterpretation, *filius* was interpreted narrowly to mean the son of a *pater familias;* this excludes daughters, grandchildren of both sexes, and so on, who, it was held (on no statutory authority) were released after only one mancipation. Assess this as an example of archaic legal interpretation.

4. Defects in Procedure. What if the parties made an innocent mistake in executing the formalities? See Marcellus, D. 1.7.38: "An adoption that is not legally made can be confirmed by the emperor." Does this necessarily prove that "the sales were empty forms" (W. W. Buckland)? The ceremony of adoption was finally abolished by Justinian (*Inst.* 1.12.8), who substituted official registration of the adoption.

5. Consent? The adoption process is plainly controlled by the two *patres*. But were the child's wishes given any legal weight? Probably not. Justinian (C. 8.47.10 pr. and 11; both from A.D. 530) mentions an "old rule" that a son is not "forced" to pass to another household, by which is meant that he must not openly object. (Does this resemble the rule in marriage? See Case 99.) A tortured text of Celsus (D. 1.7.5), which the compilers of the *Digest* undoubtedly altered or badly abbreviated, may give the same rule. Absent some clear legal empowerment, how bold would a child be in resisting a father's plans?

6. The Children. Unlike with adrogation (Case 148), a son can be given in adoption while his *pater* retains the son's children in his power; see Gaius, *Inst.* 1.135. (The same is true for emancipation; Case 155.) Is this just another illustration of the force of *patria potestas*?

7. Do Adopted Children Count as Children? The marriage legislation of Augustus gave privileges to those with a stipulated number of children (Case 12). These laws, which created false incentives to adopt, were later amended (Tacitus, *Annales* 15.19); for purposes of the count, adopted children did not benefit the adopter, nor did the natural father lose them. See Justinian, *Inst.* 1.25 pr.

CASE 150: Age Requirements

D. 1.7.16 (Iavolenus libro sexto ex Cassio)

Adoptio enim in his personis locum habet, in quibus etiam natura potest habere.

D. 1.7.40.1 (Modestinus libro primo Differentiarum)

Non tantum cum quis adoptat, sed et cum adrogat, maior esse debet eo, quem sibi per adrogationem vel per adoptionem filium facit, et utique plenae pubertatis: id est decem et octo annis eum praecedere debet.

(Javolenus in the sixth book from Cassius)

Adoption is appropriate in the case of those persons between whom a natural relationship can also exist as well.

(Modestinus in the first book of *Distinctions*)

Not only when someone adopts, but also when he adrogates, he ought to be older than the person whom he makes his son either through adrogation or adoption, and certainly he should be of full legal majority; that is, he ought to be older than the other by (at least) eighteen years.

1. Adoption of Minors. Unlike in adrogation, adoption of minors was always permitted. What explains this difference? Why require a minimum age difference of eighteen years in either case? Does Javolenus's remark about biological relationship (he uses the word *natura,* "nature") help explain this rule?

2. Forbidden Marriage. Persons adrogated or adopted could not marry persons whom they would be forbidden to marry if related biologically (Gaius, *Inst.* 1.59–63; Paul. D. 23.2.14.4; Gaius, D. 23.2.17). Is the rule explained by concern that adoption should mimic biological relationships? Does the rule remain even after an adoption is dissolved? Should it?

3. Biology. As the previous Case shows, persons incapable of bearing children were preferred as adrogators. The jurists point out that persons absolutely incapable of producing children, such as eunuchs (*spadones*), can both adrogate and adopt (Gaius, *Inst.* 1.103; Modestinus, D. 1.7.40.2). How does this square with Javolenus's comment about "persons between whom a natural relationship can also exist"? But Justinian (*Inst.* 1.11.9) draws a distinction: *spadones* who are unable to beget children can adopt, but *castrati* cannot (compare Cases 8, 184). Would Javolenus accept this distinction?

4. Unmarried Men. Can unmarried men adopt? See Paul, D. 1.7.30 (yes). Is this logical in light of the present Case?

CASE 151: Family Ties

D. 1.7.23 (Paulus libro trigensimo quinto ad edictum)

Qui in adoptionem datur, his quibus adgnascitur et cognatus fit, quibus vero non adgnascitur nec cognatus fit: adoptio enim non ius sanguinis, sed ius adgnationis adfert. et ideo si filium adoptavero, uxor mea illi matris loco non est, neque enim adgnascitur ei, propter quod nec cognata eius fit: item nec mater mea aviae loco illi est, quoniam his, qui extra familiam meam sunt, non adgnascitur: sed filiae meae is quem adoptavi frater fit, quoniam in familia mea est filia: nuptiis tamen etiam eorum prohibitis.

(Paul in the thirty-fifth book on the Edict)

A person given in adoption becomes a relative (*cognatus*) of those to whom he is (now) related agnatically; but he does not become a relative (*cognatus*) of those to whom he is not related agnatically. The reason is that adoption does not confer a legal blood connection, but only an agnatic one.

And for this reason, if I adopt a son, my wife is not in position of a mother to him, since she is not agnatically related to him, and for this reason she is not his relative (*cognata*) either. Likewise, my mother is not in position of a grandmother to him, because he has no agnatic relationship to those outside my household (*familia*). But the person I adopt does become a brother to my daughter, since my daughter is in my household (*familia*). All the same, marriage between such (nonrelated) persons is prohibited.

1. Agnates. Agnates are relatives traced only through males; cognates are all relatives, including those related through females (see Case 3). Because adoption and adrogation depend upon passing into someone's *potestas,* they create kinship only through the holder of that *potestas,* and therefore only agnatic ties count. Do you see why an adopted son is not related to his adoptive "mother" or "grandmother"? Do you see why he does, however, become the brother of his adoptive sister? What does this suggest about the purpose behind adoption?

2. Forbidden Marriage. If a *pater familias* dies, his adopted son is not permitted to marry the *pater's* widow even though she is not technically his mother; why is this so? Why is he not permitted to marry the *pater's* mother, when by law she is not his grandmother? Is this rule founded on any consistent understanding of incestuous marriage?

3. Why Does It Matter? The main issue underlying this Case is the inheritance rights an adoptive child acquires with respect to the estates of those in the adopted family. According to Ulpian (D. 38.8.1.4), the adopted child also remains a "relative" (*cognatus*) to all those in his former household. On the inheritance rights of *cognati,* see Chapter IV.A.1–2.

CASE 152: Adoption and Adrogation of Women

Gaius, *Institutiones* 1.101

Item per populum feminae non adoptantur, nam id magis placuit; apud praetorem vero vel in provinciis apud proconsulem legatumve etiam feminae solent adoptari.

(Gaius in the first book of his *Institutes*)

Likewise, women are not adopted through the comitial procedure (i.e., they are not adrogated), since this is the majority opinion. By contrast, women too are typically adopted in the procedure held before the praetor (at Rome) or in the provinces before the governor or his representative.

1. Adopting Women. As the text suggests, adoption of women was legally unproblematic, though attested cases are rare. Were there any disincentives to adopting women?

2. Adrogation. Adrogation was a different matter, as Gaius demonstrates. Since the extinction of a line of descent was not an issue (legally speaking, this was going to happen anyway), what was the difficulty here? Aulus Gellius (*Noctes Atticae* 5.19.10) explains their exclusion on the ground that they could not participate in any voting assembly. Given the demise of such institutions under the Principate, the reason seems anachronistic at best. What other reason(s), specific to the regime for adrogation, might have influenced the majority view in Gaius's day? Is adrogation's function of continuing the male line and family name relevant?

3. Dissenting View. Gaius indicates that there was a minority view concerning adrogation of women; what would that view be, and how could it be justified? At D. 1.7.21, Gaius says: "For women as well can be adrogated by a rescript of the emperor." Is he necessarily contradicting himself?

CASE 153: Adoption by Women

Gaius, *Institutiones* 1.104

Feminae vero nullo modo adoptare possunt, quia ne quidem naturales liberos in potestate habent.

(Gaius in the first book of his *Institutes*)

Women, to be sure, cannot adopt by any method, since they do not even have power over their natural (biological) offspring.

1. Biology versus *Potestas*. Does this text suggest that the real concern of the jurists was that the rules on adoption mimic those for biological relationships? Or was it that they adhere to the regime for *patria potestas*? If the latter, was their concern exclusively legal, or could there be a sociological angle as well?

2. Women Adopting. A text of Ulpian (D. 5.2.29.3) begins "Because a woman cannot adopt a child without an order from the emperor," suggesting that emperors occasionally gave permission for adoption by women; see, for instance, Diocletian, C. 8.47.5 (A.D. 291). How can this be reconciled with the requirement that the adopter hold *potestas* over the adoptee? Does it suggest a possible redefinition of adoption, at least concerning female adopters, so that, for example, certain legal aspects of the mother-son relationship (such as rights to succession) might be created between them?

3. Adoption by the Husband Alone. Jane F. Gardner (in *Family and Familia*) observes: "Children were not adopted by married couples, but by the husband alone, and his adoptive children were not related to his wife even as cognates." Is this view approximately right, at least as a general description? If so, what strains would you anticipate as a result on ordinary family life?

CASE 154: The Imitation of Nature

D. 28.2.23 pr. (Papinianus libro duodecimo Quaestionum) (= Ulpianus, D. 37.4.8.7)

Filio, quem pater post emancipationem a se factam iterum adrogavit, exheredationem antea scriptam nocere dixi: nam in omni fere iure sic observari convenit, ut veri patris adoptivus filius numquam intellegatur, ne imagine naturae veritas obumbretur, videlicet quod non translatus, sed redditus videretur: nec multum puto referre, quod ad propositum attinet, quod loco nepotis filium exheredatum pater adrogavit.

(Papinian in the twelfth book of his *Questions of Law*)

A father emancipated his son and subsequently adrogated him again. I gave my opinion that his previously executed disinheritance (of his son) remained effective (now) against the son. For in nearly every area of the law the accepted rule is that a son should never be regarded as having been adopted by his true (biological) father. The point is that the truth not be obscured through the imitation of nature, for the obvious reason that he seems to have been, not transferred, but restored (to his father's power).

Nor do I believe that it makes much difference, as far as the present case is concerned, that the father adrogated his disinherited son as a grandson.

1. New Will Needed. Normally an adrogation or adoption made a new will necessary because it added a new *suus heres,* as did birth. In this Case, a father first emancipated his son and then, after the son was *sui iuris,* adrogated him. Is it likely that the father's adrogation of the emancipated son, even if in legal terms apparently inadequate, was probably meant to supersede his earlier disinheritance? That is, can we assume that the father disinherited and emancipated the son to show his displeasure but then relented and tried to undo the damage by adrogation, though without changing his will? Compare Ulpian, D. 1.7.12: "After a person is freed from *patria potestas,* he can later be honorably returned into (his natural father's) *potestas* only by adoption." But is it also possible that some fraudulent motive might underlie Papinian's case?

2. Too Clever? Does Papinian's comment suggest he believes that the father in this case has been overly clever? How precisely can the truth be "obscured through the imitation of nature"?

3. Adopting Grandchildren. Persons might be adrogated or adopted as grandchildren by using as an intermediary a son-in-power (whose consent was needed: Paul, D. 1.7.6, citing Julian). In this way, for purposes of law the emancipated and adrogated son becomes his biological father's grandson! A motive for doing this might be the childlessness of an older son, for example. Here, to judge from Paul, D. 1.7.10, it does not seem to have been necessary

to redo the will in most circumstances. Does Papinian seem to stress the element of "imitation" over that of "nature"?

4. Too Much of a Good Thing? Paul, D. 1.7.37.1: "One cannot adopt for a second time a person one has (previously) adopted and then emancipated or given in adoption." Why?

SECTION 3. Emancipation

CASE 155: The Decision to Emancipate

D. 1.7.28 (Gaius, *Institutiones* 1.133)

Liberum arbitrium est ei, qui filium et ex eo nepotem in potestate habebit, filium quidem potestate demittere, nepotem vero in potestate retinere: vel ex diverso filium quidem in potestate retinere, nepotem vero manumittere: vel omnes sui iuris efficere. eadem et de pronepote dicta esse intellegemus.

(Gaius in the first book of his *Institutes*)

When a person has in his power a son and through him a grandson, it is his free choice whether to release the son from power while retaining the grandson in power; or, conversely, to retain the son in power but free the grandson; or to make all of them *sui iuris*. And we understand the same rules to apply to a great-grandson.

1. The Process. Emancipation begins in the same way as the ordinary adoption process (Case 149): for a son, three fictional sales are used to break *patria potestas;* and for all other children-in-power, one sale (Gaius, *Inst.* 1.132; *Tit. Ulp.* 10.1). Unfortunately, the text of Gaius breaks off just before describing the next step, but it can be restored: the child is remancipated to the *pater,* who carries out a third manumission that makes the child a free *sui iuris* Roman. For emancipation, there seems to be no participation by any government official. Was that wise?

2. Who Decides? Does this Case (restored as Gaius, *Inst.* 1.133) suggest that a *pater familias* had total freedom to decide about emancipating a child in his power? It is clear that a child could not force his father to emancipate him (Marcian, D. 1.7.31). But what if the child was opposed to being emancipated? Our sources are poor on this point, although a late imperial text (Paul, *Sent.* 2.25.5) says unequivocally: "A son-in-power is not forced to be emancipated against his will." But this text may reflect postclassical law; a rescript of Anastasius, for instance, requires that a child clearly consent to emancipation (C. 8.48.5; A.D. 502). By contrast, at least in relation to adoption, Justinian asks only that the child not be openly opposed to it; see the Discussion on Case 149.

3. Was Emancipation a Privilege or a Punishment? Unfortunately, there is no easy answer to this question. We do know that it was not unusual for fathers to provide their emancipated children with some means of support, perhaps most commonly their *peculia*. For example, Papinian (D. 39.5.31.2 = *Frag. Vat.* 255; compare 260) mentions a man who gave his daughter-in-power some slaves and then did not take away her *peculium* when he emancipated her; this ex post facto gift is irrevocable. But was this an act of kindness or just a minimal provision to make emancipation viable for the child? In any case,

do you think that many Roman children-in-power would have welcomed the chance to escape from *patria potestas?* We do have numerous legal and literary texts mentioning fathers who were induced by the terms of a will to emancipate children ("I leave a legacy of 100,000 sesterces to Sempronius if he frees his son from his power"); most frequently, the testators are ex-wives who are the children's mothers. Why might they have sought this?

4. The Effects of Emancipation. The principal result is that the child is no longer in a father's power (Case 154) and the agnatic tie connecting him with other members of his former family is broken; for example, if a *pater* emancipates one of his two sons, thereafter neither of them has the agnatic right to be appointed as guardian to the other (Gaius, *Inst.* 1.163). Originally, the emancipated child was, as it seems, legally estranged from his former family. However, in classical law this harshness was gradually eased, particularly as concerns the right of the emancipated person and his former family to inherit from each other; this development is discussed at length in Chapter IV, see especially Case 162. The result, for emancipated children, was a family regime that somewhat resembles our own: usually by their late teens or early twenties, children become legally and financially independent of their parents in modern Western societies, but reciprocal rights of inheritance remain, often accompanied by continuing strong affective relationships. Be alert, however, to important differences in detail.

CASE 156: Study Abroad

D. 10.2.50 (Ulpianus libro sexto Opinionum)

Quae pater filio emancipato studiorum causa peregre agenti subministravit, si non credendi animo pater misisse fuerit comprobatus, sed pietate debita ductus: in rationem portionis, quae ex defuncti bonis ad eundem filium pertinuit, computari aequitas non patitur.

(Ulpian in the sixth book of *Opinions*)

When a father provides financial aid to his emancipated son who is living abroad while pursuing his studies, if it is proved that the father sent this support not with the intent of making a loan but motivated by the usual *pietas,* considerations of equity (in this case) do not permit such (aid) to be reckoned as part of the share that has passed from decedent's property to the son.

1. Division of an Estate. The Case arises in the context of discussing how to divide an estate that was inherited in common. It assumes that an emancipated child might have a claim. What does this fact suggest about the child's relationship with his former *pater familias?* If the father had strong feelings of affection for his son, why did he emancipate him? If the father's motive for sending the money was *pietas,* why should this help determine the outcome?

2. Loan. If the father had made a loan to the emancipated son, the latter would owe this amount to the estate. Note that unless specifically revoked by a *pater familias* upon emancipation, a *peculium* became the property of the child at that point (Papinian, *Frag. Vat.* 260). Is there any connection between this rule and the holding in the principal Case? Here of course the payment is made after emancipation. Is that relevant?

3. Social Practice. Do the circumstances of the payment influence the jurist's decision? We know that upper-class Roman fathers often sent their teenage sons to study in the Greek East, at no small expense. Could the relative youth of the son, as well as his probable financial vulnerability and the evident usefulness of the expenditure, have played a role in influencing Ulpian's decision?

4. Punishment or Family Strategy? "Such evidence as there is is finely balanced. Some makes it sound as if emancipation was a punishment: it broke the family tie, a fact which may have been of great consequence in a society as obsessed as Rome was with family pedigree and ancestors. . . . But there are also signs that emancipation was used as part of a strategy of planning for the future of the family as a whole, by making separate provision for, rather than punishing, emancipated family members. . . . [I]t might be called into service for any of a variety of purposes, positive or negative" (David Johnston). Does this seem about right? Which motive appears to prevail?

CASE 157: Emancipated versus Freed

D. 37.12.4 (Marcellus libro nono Digestorum)

Patri qui filium emancipavit de his, quae libertatis causa imposita fuerint, praetor nihil edicit, et ideo frustra pater operas stipulabitur de filio.

(Marcellus in the ninth book of his *Digests*)

The praetor says nothing in his Edict about (the possibility of) obligations imposed in return for freedom when a father has emancipated his son, and for this reason a father's stipulation for services from his son will have no legal validity.

1. No Claim. The jurist Tryphoninus (D. 37.15.10) holds that a father has no claim to payment in return for emancipation. Is the principle the same here?

2. Like a Patron. The emancipating *pater familias* had rights over the estate of a child similar to those that a patron had over the estate of a freedman (Ulpian, D. 37.12.1 pr.). It was common practice to manumit a slave in return for a promise of future services (*operae*) that might involve a wide variety of commercial and domestic duties, depending on the needs of the patron and the talents of the freedperson. Why is this not allowed from an emancipated son?

3. Not Like a Patron. If a freedperson attempted to defraud a patron of an interest in his or her estate, the patron could claim the property through an *actio Fabiana* or an *actio Calvisiana*. Gaius (D. 37.12.2) denies this recourse to an emancipating *pater familias*, on the ground that a freeborn person should have full power to alienate property. Do you find this logic convincing?

4. Recall into Power? In classical Roman law, emancipation was irrevocable (Paul, D. 1.7.34); the emancipated child could return into his father's power only through adrogation (Case 154), which obviously required his consent. But in the fourth century A.D. laws began allowing recall if emancipated children displayed manifest ingratitude: Constantine, *Frag. Vat.* 248 (330); Valentinian, Valens, and Gratian, *C.Th.* 8.14.1 = C. 8.49.1 (367). Is this a radical innovation?

CASE 158: The State Intervenes

D. 37.12.5 (Papinianus libro undecimo Quaestionum)

Divus Traianus filium, quem pater male contra pietatem adficiebat, coegit emancipare. quo postea defuncto, pater ut manumissor bonorum possessionem sibi competere dicebat: sed consilio Neratii Prisci et Aristonis ei propter necessitatem solvendae <potestatis> denegata est.

(Papinian in the eleventh book of *Questions of Law*)

The deified Emperor Trajan forced a father to emancipate a son whom he was mistreating, in contravention of *pietas*. When the son later died, his father claimed that possession of the estate accrued to him as the (son's) emancipator. On the advice of Neratius Priscus and Aristo, however, this (action) was denied to him on the ground that the emancipation had to be compelled.

1. Benefit. Does this text support the view that emancipation was thought to benefit a child?

2. *Bonorum Possessio.* Normally a father had a right, as a quasi patron, to the estate of his emancipated child (see Case 161). In this Case, is the father's claim justified in formal legal terms? It should be noted that the emperor's intervention is unusual and presumably motivated by a particularly callous instance of child abuse.

3. *Pietas.* Does *pietas* play a role here similar to that in other texts concerning *potestas?* See Cases 92, 94, and 156.

CHAPTER IV

Succession

As we have seen, Roman law concentrated extensive legal power in the hands of *patres familiae,* who constituted a relatively small portion of the citizen population. For this reason, the death of a *pater familias* was frequently an event of singular importance, above all to the survivors within his household: a moment they anticipated and experienced with hope, dread, or a dozen other emotions, but at the very least with anxiety about how the division of his estate would affect them. In such tense circumstances, Romans became astonishingly litigious.

It comes as no surprise, then, that the law of succession (which governs the process whereby heirs "succeed into the position" of a decedent) had an importance in Roman law considerably greater than in ours. Whether succession was regulated by a will or through the rules for intestacy, it was always a primary means whereby members of the elite acquired wealth and social position. Testamentary bequests, above all from relatives but also from friends, enabled upper-class Romans to maintain or enhance the status enjoyed by previous generations, as well as to prepare to transmit this status to future ones. This process of intergenerational transmission soon acquired a moral aspect as well, as an expression of familial affection and duty (*pietas*) that transcended individuals and implicated broader social opinions.

The amount of space devoted to succession in surviving Roman juristic writings suggests its actual importance in life: as much as 40 percent of Justinian's *Digest.* Therefore this chapter only samples relevant case law illustrating fundamental themes related to the family.

Technical complexity, a hallmark of the Roman law of succession, should be appreciated and enjoyed for its own sake. Even a glance at its most basic features shows that the Romans had no use for Occam's razor. Entity is piled on entity, in a fashion that today may seem extravagantly hyperdeveloped. For intestate succession, the complicated rules of the civil law (*ius civile*) were joined by the even more intricate rules of praetorian law (*ius honorarium*). Much the same is true for wills, where a series of will forms and bequest types developed at an amazing pace.

This multiplication of entities is partially explained by a cultural conservatism keyed to precise interests that the legal system struggled to define. The story of the Roman law of succession is that of a continuously unstable compromise between the freedom of a testator to dispose of property and the sense of responsibility that the Romans saw as integral to the exercise of this freedom—or, if you will, a compromise between the desires of the dead and those of the living. The elements of the Roman compromise came to be articulated in more than one way: for example, in terms of the need for legal certainty or for the orderly and equitable transmission of property, as well as other, more concrete social goals enshrined in positive legislation, such as the marriage laws of Augustus.

For readers who want a quicker survey of the law of succession, we have constructed a fast track, consisting of Cases 159–161, 165, 167–169, 171–174, 177–179, 182–184, 186–187, 192–193, 195, 198–199, 201, 203–204, and 206. These twenty-eight Cases are marked below with an asterisk.

PART A

Intestate Succession

In classical Roman law, intestacy is the default position: what happens when a *sui iuris* Roman dies without a will that results in an appointed heir or heirs. Doubtless, as is also true today, many Romans simply never wrote a will; often their estates were insufficiently great to be worth the effort, or they simply forgot to do so. Others, even though of *sui iuris* status, were legally incapable of writing wills: all children of minor age, the deaf and mute, the prodigal and the insane (if they had guardians), and others. Until the reign of Hadrian (A.D. 117–138), women who had not undergone a legal change of status known as *capitis deminutio* (see Case 1) could not write a will; and both before and after Hadrian, women without the Augustan "right of children" (*ius liberorum*) needed the permission of a guardian (*tutor*) to make a will (Case 228).

But even when Romans both desired and had the legal capacity to write wills, their wills often could fail because they did not meet some formal requirement. Such failures also led to the default scenario of intestacy, the law that dictated who would receive the estate.

From the start, the law on intestacy is confusing because we are confronted with the dual system of the civil and praetorian law. The relationship between the two is summarized by a famous statement of the jurist Papinian, who observed that the praetor aimed to "support, supplement, and correct" the older *ius civile* (D. 1.1.7.1). In fact, Papinian's summary applies only to details; the civil law was in no general sense invalidated, superseded, or set aside by the praetorian system. We should thus be cautious of generalizations about an evolutionary process whereby the claims of a wider circle of blood kin prevailed over the older regime's recognition of the rights of the agnatic *familia*. In the law of succession, the tug-of-war between the agnatic and cognatic conceptions of the family reaches back to the mid-Republic at minimum, and it was never fully resolved in classical Roman law.

Indeed, even after the praetorian reforms, the law of intestate succession remained largely bound to the viewpoint of the *pater familias*. Only in the second century A.D. did two statutes, the Senatusconsulta (SCC) Tertullianum and Orphitianum, finally privilege the reciprocal interests of mothers and children, and then only on a limited basis.

The complex rules on intestacy allowed the jurists considerable room for maneuver. Their efforts reveal an aim similar to that of most testators: a concern to protect the interests of the offspring of the decedent as the preferred ultimate recipients of a decedent's property.

CASE 159: Rules of the *Ius Civile**

Collatio 16.2.1–4 (Gaius, *Institutiones* 3.1–4)

(1) Intestatorum hereditates ex lege duodecim tabularum primum ad suos heredes pertinent. (2) Sui autem heredes existimantur liberi, qui in potestate morientis fuerunt, veluti filius filiave, nepos neptisve <ex filio>, pronepos proneptisve ex nepote filio nato prognatus prognatave. nec interest, <utrum> naturales <sint> liberi an adoptivi. ita demum tamen nepos neptisve et pronepos proneptisve suorum heredum numero sunt, si praecedens persona desierit <in potestate parentis esse, sive morte id acciderit>, sive alia ratione, veluti emancipatione. nam si per id tempus, quo quisque moriatur, filius in potestate eius sit, nepos ex eo suus heres esse non potest. idem et in ceteris deinceps liberorum personis dictum intellegemus. (3) Uxor quoque, quae in manu est, <ei cuius in manu est> sua heres est, quia filiae loco est. . . . (4) Postumi quoque, <qui> si vivo parente nati essent, in potestate eius futuri forent, sui heredes sunt.

(Gaius in the third book of his *Institutes*)

(1) By the Law of the Twelve Tables, the inheritances of those who die intestate fall first to their *sui heredes* (privileged heirs).

(2) By *sui heredes* are meant descendants who are in the dying man's *potestas*, for example, a son or daughter, grandson or granddaughter through a son, (or) a great-grandson or great-granddaughter through a grandson born of a son. Nor does it matter whether the children are natural (i.e., biological) or adopted. All the same, grandchildren or great-grandchildren only count as *sui heredes* if the person above them in the family line has ceased to be in the power of a parent, whether this occurs through death or for some other reason, like emancipation. So if at the point someone dies he has a son-in-power, for this reason his grandson (by that son) cannot be a *suus heres*. And we understand the same rule to hold for other descendants.

(3) A wife in *manus* is also a *sua heres* to the man in whose *manus* she is, since she is in the position of a daughter (*filiae loco*). . . . (4) Posthumous children are also *sui heredes* if they would be in their father's power had they been born while he was still alive.

1. Privileged Heirs. Intestate succession occurs when a *sui iuris* person dies either with no legally valid will or with a will that does not result in acceptance by an eligible heir. The *sui heredes* are those persons-in-power who become *sui iuris*, legally independent, as a result of the testator's death. Civil law gave great importance to the *sui heredes* mainly because its rules were intended to encourage passage of an estate to the immediate members of the household, if any survived. Therefore, for the will to be valid, all such privileged intestate heirs had to be disinherited (by name, if they were sons) in the will; however, they also could not refuse an inheritance (they are *necessarii*; Gaius, *Inst.*

2.157). Are "privileged heirs" defined as a matter of biology or law? In answering that question, is it relevant that adopted children are treated as equal to natural children? Note, finally, that only males can have *sui heredes,* for the reason stated at the end of Case 4.

2. Exclusion of Descendants. Why is it that the existence of a son-in-power excludes the son-in-power's own son or daughter from the circle of *sui heredes*? For more on section 3, see Case 37, which establishes that when a woman enters an archaic *manus* marriage, she becomes her husband's *sua heres* if he is *sui iuris;* but if she is married to a son-in-power, for these purposes she is in the position of the son's daughter, hence not a *sua heres* to the *pater.* The general principle is that free persons who will remain in power despite the death of their *pater familias* are not *sui heredes.*

3. Share and Share Alike? Succession among *sui heredes* operated through a distribution system that was "stirpital" in the sense that primary importance was accorded to "stems" (*stirpes*) traced back to the dead *pater familias.* Gaius (*Inst.* 3.7–8) explains how this works:

- A *pater familias* is survived by his son, his daughter, and a grandson by a son who had died previously. Upon intestacy, each takes a third of the estate because each represents an independent "stem."
- Survivors are a grandson by one son and a great-granddaughter by the son of another son, the intermediate generations having died earlier. Each takes half.
- Survivors are a son, a daughter, and the son and daughter of a deceased son. The son and daughter each take a third; the two grandchildren each take a sixth.
- Survivors are two children from one deceased son and three children from another deceased son. The first two each take a quarter; the other three each take a sixth.

In each case, figure out the math and the principle that underlies it. Note that no distinction is made among *sui heredes* on the basis of their sex or their relative age. From a social perspective, what possible defects can you spot in this system? Is it as fair as it seems?

4. Next in Line. If there are no privileged heirs, the estate passes to the closest agnate (*proximus agnatus*), a relative connected to the decedent through males (Gaius, *Inst.* 3.9). (This is the rule for freeborn Romans; the estates of freedmen, who had no agnates because as a matter of law they had no fathers, passed to their patrons.) Unlike the *sui heredes,* this person could refuse the inheritance (ibid. 12), in which case the estate originally passed to the third class of intestate successors, the *gentiles* (persons believed to share the same

agnatic lineage though the tie is distant); but this class was entirely obsolete in Gaius's day. What rule do you think held for the estates of freeborn women who died without a will? For freedwomen?

5. Intestate Succession and the *Familia*. To what extent do the original rules for intestate succession reflect what might be thought of as the "ancient" form of the *familia*?

CASE 160: An Unwilling Heir*

D. 38.16.1.8 (Ulpianus libro duodecimo ad Sabinum)

Sciendum est autem nepotes et deinceps interdum, etiamsi parentes eos mortis tempore praecesserunt, tamen posse suos heredes existere, quamvis successio in suis heredibus non sit. quod ita procedit. si pater familias testamento facto decesserit exheredato filio, mox deliberante herede instituto filius decessit, postea deinde repudiavit heres institutus: nepos poterit suus heres esse, ut et Marcellus libro decimo scripsit, quoniam nec delata est filio hereditas. idem erit dicendum et si filius ex asse sub condicione, quae fuit in arbitrio ipsius, vel nepos sub omni institutus non impleta condicione decesserint: nam dicendum erit suos posse succedere, si modo mortis testatoris tempore vel in rebus humanis vel saltem concepti fuerint: idque et Iuliano et Marcello placet.

(Ulpian in the twelfth book on Sabinus)

Further, one should recognize that sometimes grandsons and their descendants can count as *sui heredes* even if their fathers take precedence over them at the time of (their grandfather's) death although no succession has yet occurred among the *sui*.

This is how it comes about. A *pater familias* died after having made a will disinheriting his son; then, while the heir he appointed in his will was deliberating (whether to accept the inheritance), the (disinherited) son (also) died. The appointed heir subsequently declined to accept. Since the estate was not offered to the son, the grandson can be a *suus heres* (under these circumstances), as Marcellus also wrote in the tenth book (of his *Digests*).

The same rule will also hold true if the son is appointed sole heir under a condition it was in his power to fulfill, or a grandson under any condition, and he died before fulfillment (of the condition). For it will have to be held that their *sui* can succeed, provided that at the time of the testator's death they were alive or at least conceived. And this was the view of both Julian and Marcellus.

1. Express Disinheritance. In Ulpian's first hypothetical case, note the precise series of events: the *pater* died; his will disinherited his son; then, while the heir named in the will dithered about acceptance, the disinherited son died; the testamentary heir finally declined the estate, thus rendering the will ineffective. In this precise sequence of events, a grandson by the disinherited son would be a *suus heres* even though he was not one at the time of his grandfather's death. Would the result have been the same if the son had died, not after, but before his father died? If he had died after the appointed heir declined the inheritance?

2. Explaining the Paradox. Ulpian and his predecessors are arguing a paradox, namely that the son's ineligibility for the estate makes the grandson eligible. Do you see how this is so? Does the paradox in turn help you to understand

the rationale in the second hypothetical situation, involving nonfulfillment of conditions? In this instance, a will appointed the son or grandson heir, but under a condition that had not been fulfilled at the time of the would-be heir's death; accordingly, his *sui* became eligible. (On the distinction between the son and the grandson, see Tryphoninus, D. 28.2 28 pr.: if sons were instituted heirs under a condition, it had to be within their power to fulfill the condition.)

3. Policy behind the Paradox. Why do you think the jurists construct such an intricate argument here? Whose interests are they ultimately trying to protect?

4. Limits to (Il)logic. Why does Ulpian insist that the *suus heres* of the son or grandson must at least have been conceived at the time of the testator's death?

5. Another Opinion? As often, Ulpian's citation of his predecessors may suggest that the jurists disagreed about the issue he is discussing. The compilers of the *Digest* may have suppressed another view. Can you reconstruct it?

CASE 161: The Praetor's Rules*

D. 38.6.1.1–2 (Ulpianus libro quadragensimo <sexto> ad edictum)

(1) Sed successionem ab intestato in plures partes divisit: fecit enim gradus varios, primum liberorum, secundum legitimorum, tertium cognatorum, deinde viri et uxoris. (2) Ita autem ab intestato potest competere bonorum possessio, si neque secundum tabulas neque contra tabulas bonorum posssessio agnita sit.

(Ulpian in the forty-sixth book on the Edict)

(1) But he (the praetor) split succession on intestacy into several parts by constructing different classes: the first is that of children; the second, of statutory heirs; the third, of cognate relatives; and finally, that of husband and wife.

(2) Moreover, *bonorum possessio* on intestacy is made available if possession has not been claimed (by a third party) either in accordance with the terms of a will or contrary to them.

1. Emancipation and Adoption. To a large extent, the urban praetor built on the system of the *ius civile* in constructing his own. For example, his first class of "children" (*liberi*) contained the *sui heredes* of the Twelve Tables, who could be adopted, as well as biological, children; but it also included children who had been emancipated, and even the children of an emancipated son who had previously died (*Tit. Ulp.* 28.7–8).However, children who had been adopted by another *pater familias* were not included. Why not?

2. Children Preferred over Parents? The effect of the praetor's innovation was to give first priority, in the law governing intestacy, to those children who were not irrevocably committed (as a result of their adoption) to some other household. Papinian (D. 38.6.7.1) justifies this preference as resulting from "nature, together with the common wish of parents." By contrast, the right of parents to their children's estates is less favored (a father of an emancipated child takes under the second praetorian class, a mother only in the third class until the late classical period; see Cases 164–165, 168); Papinian explains that their claim is based only on "compassion" (*miseratio*), evidently a desire to console them for their loss. Is Papinian's contrast compelling? In any case, both parents and children were allowed a generous period of one year for claiming on intestacy, while other intestate heirs were allowed 100 days (Ulpian, D. 38.9.1.8, 12). Why was there a distinction?

3. The Statutory Heirs. After the *liberi*, the next group to be called are the statutory heirs (*legitimi*): the traditional *sui heredes* (already entitled in the first praetorian class) and the nearest agnate, plus some additional persons who became entitled under imperial legislation (see Section 2 below). The remaining praetorian classes are examined in subsequent Cases. If no heir

emerges either by testate or by intestate succession, the estate falls to the public treasury (Gaius, *Inst.* 2.150; *Tit. Ulp.* 28.7).

4. **Multiple Claims.** Suppose that a man dies without a will and with only one child, a son-in-power. The son can claim in the first praetorian class (*unde liberi*); but if he misses the deadline, can he also claim as the closest agnate (*proximus agnatus*) in the second class (*unde legitimi*), and then, if necessary, also as a cognate relative in the third class (*unde cognati*)? Sure; Ulpian (D. 38.9.1.11) notes "the better view" that it would not matter even if he had refused the inheritance. (Remember that agnates are also cognates; see Case 3.) Is the praetor just being indulgent to procrastinators? An emancipated child, by contrast, can claim only under the first and the third rubrics. The reason is that emancipation breaks the agnatic tie; see the Discussion on Case 155.

5. **Civil versus Praetorian Law.** Oddly, at least to anyone unfamiliar with the quirks of the Roman legal tradition, the praetorian system did not in itself invalidate that of the *ius civile*. The praetor did not claim legal primacy for his system. Indeed, he did not pretend to make anyone heir, offering instead only possession of the estate (*bonorum possessio*) that might eventually ripen into ownership (Gaius, *Inst.* 3.32). When succession was intestate, however, his grant of possession, if it contradicted the older *ius civile* entitlements, tended to prevail because the praetor's court was the only available mechanism for enforcement. The praetor also granted *bonorum possessio* in order to enforce wills or to provide equitable exceptions to their terms. Do you see how, in Ulpian's section 2, *bonorum possessio* on intestacy is effectively worked into, and subordinated to, the magistrate's grant of possession in case of a will? In fact, however, the system that underlay these grants is extremely complex; we just skim the surface.

CASE 162: Emancipated and Disinherited

D. 38.6.1.9 (Ulpianus libro quadragensimo <sexto> ad edictum)

Si emancipatus filius exheres fuerit, is autem qui in potestate fuerat praeteritus, emancipatum petentem ab intestato bonorum possessionem unde liberi tueri debet praetor usque ad partem dimidiam, perinde atque si nullas tabulas pater reliquisset.

(Ulpian in the forty-sixth book on the Edict)

An emancipated son was expressly disinherited (in a testator's will), while his son-in-power was passed over in silence. If the emancipated child seeks *bonorum possessio* upon intestacy in the class for children (*unde liberi*), the praetor ought to protect his interests up to the limit of one-half the estate, just as if his father had left no will.

Hypothetical Situation

A *pater familias* had one child, a son whom he emancipated; he also disinherited this son in his will and left his estate to a distant relative. Subsequently, his wife bore him another son, but through inadvertence he did not then change his original will. On his death, does the emancipated son have a claim to the estate?

1. Exploiting a Loophole. Why did the father's will fail? A will is invalid if it does not either institute a *suus heres* as heir or disinherit him (Case 178). Therefore, the rules for intestate succession came into play. The emancipated son advances his claim for *bonorum possessio* under the praetorian rubric *unde liberi*. Did he have a claim under the older *ius civile*? Why is he entitled to one-half of his father's property?

2. The Testator's Interest. In this Case, the testator's wishes are thwarted: the son takes half despite having been expressly disinherited. Did those who made law at Rome suppose that, on the whole, the rules of intestacy did a better job of distributing private estates than did testators themselves? Or is this just a penalty that a testator may have to pay for failing to follow correct procedure? If so, why might lawmakers have insisted that wills follow a prescribed form? This issue will resurface constantly throughout the present chapter.

3. The Grandchildren's Interest. A man dies without a valid will, and his emancipated son fails to claim *bonorum possessio* on intestacy. Do the son's children have a claim? See Pomponius, D. 38.6.5.2 (yes). How can this be explained?

CASE 163: A Legal Puzzler

D. 38.6.5 pr. (Pomponius libro quarto ad Sabinum = Ulpian, D. 37.8.1 pr.)

Si quis ex his, quibus bonorum possesionem praetor pollicetur, in potestate parentis, de cuius bonis agitur, cum is moritur, non fuerit, ei liberisque, quos in eiusdem
familia habebit, si ad eos hereditas suo nomine pertinebit neque nominatim exhere-
des scripti erunt, bonorum possessio eius partis datur, quae ad eum pertineret, si in
potestate permansisset, ita, ut ex ea parte dimidiam habeat, reliquum liberi eius,
hisque dumtaxat bona sua conferat.

(Pomponius in the fourth book on Sabinus)

If any of those persons to whom the praetor promises *bonorum possessio* is not in
the power of the parent whose estate is in question at the time of his death, to this
person and to any children whom he will have in the decedent's *familia*, provided
that the inheritance will go to them in their own names and they will not have
been expressly disinherited, *bonorum possessio* is given of that share which
would go to him had he remained in (the decedent's) power, on the following
terms: he has half of that share, the children the remainder, and he brings his
own property into contribution with them.

Hypothetical Situation

A *pater familias* has two sons in power, Gaius and Titus. He emancipates Titus but
retains in his power Titus's two daughters (see Case 155). The *pater familias* then
dies intestate. Can Titus successfully sue for a portion of the estate?

1. The Statutory Solution. In the statutory (prepraetorian) law of intestate succession, the emancipated son had no claim. The estate would have been divided on a stirpital basis: the son-in-power would take half, and the two
   granddaughters would each take a quarter.

2. The Praetorian Dilemma. As Cases 161–162 showed, the praetor's reform
   permitted the emancipated son to sue for *bonorum possessio,* a share in the estate. But where should his share come from and how much is it? If the portion
   of the son-in-power is reduced, this would unfairly benefit the emancipated
   son's side of the family; but this son's two daughters, as *sui heredes,* are independently entitled to the estate, so it might also seem unfair that their father
   profit at their expense. A further potential inequity is that the emancipated
   son may in the meantime have accumulated wealth of his own; should this be
   taken into consideration in determining his share?

3. Julian's Solution. The dense legislative language in this Case stems from the
   eminent jurist Julian (Marcellus, D. 37.8.3), who prepared the final version of
   the praetor's Edict; Julian seems to have come up with the solution. It goes as

follows: The son who was in power receives his half share. The other son and his daughters get the rest, but the son must first contribute his own estate to their "pot," of which he then receives half and the daughters divide the other half. Is this outcome "eminently fair" (so Ulpian, D. 37.8.1.1) or entirely artificial? See also Discussion 3 on Case 186.

CASE 164: The Third Praetorian Class (*Unde Cognati*)

D. 38.8.1.3 (Ulpianus libro quadragensimo sexto ad edictum)

Haec autem bonorum possessio, quae ex hac parte edicti datur, cognatorum gradus sex complectitur et ex septimo duas personas sobrino et sobrina natum et natam.

(Ulpian in the forty-sixth book on the Edict)

The *bonorum possessio* that is given in this part of the Edict includes six degrees of cognates, as well as, in the seventh degree, the son and daughter of a male or female second cousin.

1. Seven Degrees of Separation. On calculating degrees of kinship, see the Discussion on Case 11. First cousins (*consobrini*) were in the fourth degree of relationship; second cousins (*sobrini*) were in the sixth, thus placing their children in the seventh. Do you think it likely that persons beyond the third degree of relationship would be close acquaintances, close enough to have been remembered in a will?

2. Praetorian Invention. Unlike the first two praetorian classes, the third class was entirely the creation of the praetor and replaced the old civil-law category of the *gentiles*. What motive can you supply for this move? Would you regard this innovation as a decisive strike against the previous legal preference for agnate relationship?

3. An Anomaly. According to Papinian (D. 38.8.9 pr.), an agnate in the eighth degree can claim possession under the *unde legitimi* rubric, even though he was not appointed heir in a will (that had presumably failed); but he is not eligible as a cognate even if he was named an heir. Should the same rules have been enforced for both groups? Another difference is that under the *unde legitimi* rubric, only the "nearest" agnate was called, and if he or she refused, that category was closed (Justinian, *Inst.* 3.2.7). By contrast, under the *unde cognati* rubric, if the nearest cognates declined, then the next nearest were eligible (Ulpian, D. 38.9.1.6, 10). What happened if two or more persons were related to the decedent in the same degree (e.g., two first cousins) and were each willing to take the estate? They divide it equally (Ulpian, D. 38.8.1.10; compare Gaius, *Inst.* 3.16).

CASE 165: Illegitimate Children*

D. 38.8.2 (Gaius libro sexto decimo ad edictum provinciale)

Hac parte proconsul naturali aequitate motus omnibus cognatis promittit bonorum possessionem, quos sanguinis ratio vocat ad hereditatem, licet iure civili deficiant. itaque etiam vulgo quaesiti liberi matris et mater talium liberorum, item ipsi fratres inter se ex hac parte bonorum possessionem petere possunt, quia sunt invicem sibi cognati, usque adeo, ut, praegnas quoque manumissa si pepererit, et is qui natus est matri et mater ipsi et inter se quoque qui nascuntur cognati sint.

(Gaius in the sixteenth book on the Provincial Edict)

In this part (of his Edict), the governor, motivated by considerations of natural fairness, promises *bonorum possessio* to all cognates who are called to the inheritance by reason of blood relationship, even though they are not entitled under civil law.

So even illegitimate children can ask for *bonorum possessio* with respect to their mother, and a mother with respect to such children; and likewise brothers with respect to each other under this section of the Edict, because each of these is respectively cognate to the other; and (this is true) to the extent that also if a pregnant (slave) woman is manumitted and then gives birth, her child will also be a cognate to its mother, and the mother to it, and likewise her children to each other.

1. Praetor and Proconsul. The model provincial governor's Edict, on which Gaius comments, was largely drawn from that of the urban praetor, whose motives are therefore more pertinent. Does Gaius's justification of the rubric *unde cognati* in terms of natural fairness (*naturalis aequitas*) make sense? Is it entirely convincing to see this as an assertion of the claims of blood relationship against those of the *ius civile*? Which receives preference under the Edict?

2. Illegitimate Children. Does it make sense to recognize the cognate relationship of a mother with her illegitimate children? Why not also recognize such a tie with their father, assuming that he can be conclusively identified? ·

3. Freedwomen. Slaves had neither agnates nor cognates. Because of their origin, freedwomen had no agnates. But this Case shows that a freedwoman could at least have cognates in her children, provided they were born after manumission (otherwise, they would be slaves unless separately freed). Could a freedwoman's children be agnates as well as cognates to each other? Does the answer depend on whether she entered a legitimate marriage?

4. Grandchildren. Modestinus (D. 38.8.8) held that illegitimate children could inherit from their maternal grandmother on intestacy. Could they succeed to a paternal grandmother whose will had failed?

CASE 166: Son-in-Power as Cognate

D. 38.6.8 (Papinianus libro sexto Responsorum)

Filius familias ut proximus cognatus patre consentiente possessionem adgnovit: quamvis per condicionem testamento datam, quod in patris potestate manserit, ab hereditate sit exclusus, tamen utiliter possessionem adgnovisse videbitur nec in edicti sententiam incidet, quoniam possessionem secundum tabulas non adgnovit, cum inde rem habere non potuerit nec in filii potestate condicio fuerit nec facile pater emancipare filium cogi poterit.

(Papinian in the sixth book of *Responses*)

With his father's permission, a son-in-power claimed *bonorum possessio* as the closest cognate. Although a condition in the will excluded him from inheritance because he remained in his father's power, nevertheless he may successfully claim *bonorum possessio* (upon intestacy); and (in doing so) he will not run up against the force of the Edict because he did not (earlier) claim *bonorum possessio* in accordance with the will (*secundum tabulas*) since he has no valid claim on this score. The condition is not in the son's power (to fulfill), and the father cannot easily be compelled to emancipate his son.

1. Father's Permission. The testator, probably a relative through the son's mother (but see Papinian, D. 29.4.27.1), was willing to leave the son an inheritance only if the son was no longer in his father's power (see the Discussion on Case 155). The will named the son heir on the condition that he be *sui iuris*; but his father failed to emancipate his son, who therefore did not claim the inheritance. Why might the father have been reluctant? For this or some other reason, the will failed and resort was had to the rules for intestacy. Why does a son-in-power require the permission of his *pater familias* to claim *bonorum possessio*? Who effectively receives title to the estate? See Case 114. Note that the father himself would not have a claim upon intestacy to inheritance from his relatives by marriage.

2. The Testator's Wishes. Why should the son-in-power take the inheritance through intestate succession when this flies directly in the face of the testator's wishes? What could the testator have done to avoid this result? (See below, Part C.2.)

3. The Praetor and Wills. This Case indicates the complex role played by the praetor in the law of succession. Even though the son-in-power was named an heir, he did not apply for praetorian *bonorum possessio* in accordance with the will (*secundum tabulas*) because he did not meet the will's condition; that is, the praetor can enforce wills by awarding possession of the estate to the heirs named in them. But if the will is manifestly inequitable in certain ways,

the praetor can also award possession contrary to the will (*contra tabulas*), a legal recourse that leaves some provisions of the will intact while invalidating others. Finally, the praetor also awards possession to heirs on intestacy (*ab intestato*) when there is no will or the will fails, as in this Case. As you read other Cases, keep this complexity in mind.

CASE 167: Husbands and Wives*

D. 38.11.1 (Ulpianus libro quadragensimo septimo ad edictum)

(pr.) Ut bonorum possessio peti possit unde vir et uxor, iustum esse matrimonium oportet. ceterum si iniustum fuerit matrimonium, nequaquam bonorum possessio peti poterit, quemadmodum nec ex testamento adiri hereditas vel secundum tabulas peti bonorum possessio potest: nihil enim capi propter iniustum matrimonium potest. (1) Ut autem haec bonorum possessio locum habeat, uxorem esse oportet mortis tempore. sed si divortium quidem secutum sit, verumtamen iure durat matrimonium, haec successio locum non habet. hoc autem in huiusmodi speciebus procedit. liberta ab invito patrono divortit: lex Iulia de maritandis ordinibus retinet istam in matrimonio, dum eam prohibet alii nubere invito patrono. item Iulia de adulteriis, nisi certo modo divortium factum sit, pro infecto habet.

(Ulpian in the forty-seventh book on the Edict)

(pr.) A legitimate marriage is necessary to claim *bonorum possessio* in the class for husband and wife (*unde vir et uxor*). But if the marriage is illegitimate, *bonorum possessio* cannot be successfully claimed, and similarly the inheritance cannot be entered on the basis of the will nor can *bonorum possessio* be sought in accord with the will (*secundum tabulas*). In sum, nothing can be taken on the basis of an illegitimate marriage.

  (1) Moreover, for *bonorum possessio* to be available, she must be a wife at the time of death. But if a divorce has transpired, but the marriage still legally exists, this rule of succession is inoperative. That occurs in situations of the following kind. When a freedwoman divorces her unwilling patron, the *lex Iulia* on status-appropriate marriage keeps her in the married state (at least) to the extent that it prevents her from marrying someone else against her patron's will. Likewise, the *lex Iulia* on adultery treats a divorce as invalid unless it has been carried out in a prescribed way.

  1. Legitimate Marriage. Ulpian privileges fully legitimate marriage over unions that are not completely legally valid (though they may be viewed by the participants and others as marriage). What reasons justify this? And why deny persons in illegitimate marriages the capacity to receive under a will? Note that the Augustan marriage legislation (the *lex Iulia et Papia*) banned them from receiving bequests from each other. Should this rule carry over into intestate succession?

  2. Marriage after Divorce. Ulpian notes two anomalous instances in which marriage continues after divorce. Augustus, in an effort to encourage nonsenatorial Romans to marry freedwomen, allowed patrons who had manumitted slaves for this purpose to have an effective veto over unilateral divorce by the woman (see the Discussion on Case 14). His law on adultery also provided a formal procedure for divorce, which was probably required (though this is far

from clear) in cases of manifest adultery (see Case 54 and the Discussion on Case 78). Why does Ulpian rule out intestate succession in such cases?

3. The Precarious Position of Spouses. Under praetorian rules, upon intestacy, a wife inherits from her husband, or he from her, only in the fourth class, if no other intestate heir is forthcoming. From a modern perspective, this is extremely odd. Should this rule be understood as a carryover from the fairly rigid rules separating the property of the two spouses during their marriage? See Case 56. Plainly, in many circumstances the economic position of a surviving spouse might be tenuous unless provision had been made in advance; and this insecurity is likely to have affected women more than men. Are you now better prepared to understand why questions such as the return of dowry (Chapter II.D.2) were so important in Roman law? But many husbands, dissatisfied with mere return of dowry, made separate provision for their wives in their wills by giving them a bequest of a usufruct (usually a life estate) in all or part of their property (Case 203). What is interesting here is how deficiencies in the law of intestate succession may have impelled many Romans, particularly in the upper classes, to write wills. Is that a desirable legal outcome? All things considered, is it a good or a bad thing if as many decedents as possible die with a will?

SECTION 2. The Senatusconsulta Tertullianum et Orphitianum

CASE 168: Mothers Inherit from Children*

Tituli ex Corpore Ulpiani 26.8

Intestati filii hereditas ad matrem ex lege duodecim tabularum non pertinet: sed si ius liberorum habeat, ingenua trium, libertina quattuor, legitima heres fit ex senatus consulto Tertulliano, si tamen ei filio neque suus heres sit quive inter suos heredes ad bonorum possessionem a praetore vocatur, neque pater, ad quem lege hereditas bonorumve possessio cum re pertinet, neque frater consanguineus: quod si soror consanguinea sit, ad utrasque pertinere iubetur hereditas.

(Excerpts from Ulpian's Writings)

By the Law of the Twelve Tables, a mother does not receive an inheritance from an intestate child. But if she has the "right of children" (*ius liberorum*)—(if she has borne) three (children) in the case of a freeborn woman, four for a freed-woman—she becomes a statutory heir because of the SC Tertullianum, provided that there is no *suus heres* to her son, nor anyone whom the praetor summons to *bonorum possessio* together with the *sui heredes* (i.e., the *liberi*), nor a father to whom by statute the inheritance or *bonorum possessio* comes, nor a blood brother (of the decedent; a brother from the same father). But if there is a blood sister, the statute orders that the inheritance go to both women.

1. The SC Tertullianum. This statute, from the reign of Hadrian (A.D. 117–138), promoted mothers who possessed the "right of children" to the rank of statutory heirs (*legitimi*), the second praetorian class; other mothers remained in the third class (*cognati*). Still, even a woman who was so privileged inherited only if an intestate heir could not be located among the decedent's children, father, and brothers. How big a privilege was this, in reality? Why was it given only to women who had borne several children? On the marriage legislation of Augustus, see Case 12.

2. The Position of Mothers. It was, as it seems, the statute itself that preferred a decedent's children to his mother (Paul, D. 38.17.5 pr.–1). These children are preferred whether they are *sui heredes* or emancipated, whether male or female, and whether natural or adopted. Paul describes the statutory preference as "eminently fair" (*aequissimum*); why so? Is it equally fair that her son's father and brother be preferred to her? Is this pure sexism?

3. Births Out of Wedlock. Is the statutory privilege available even if the child was illegitimate? Ulpian (D. 38.17.2.1) says yes; why is this so, do you think? Is the privilege available even if the woman is "of ill repute" (*famosa*), for example, a prostitute or a procuress? See Ulpian, ibid. 4 (yes). What is the argument for including such women? Would the same argument hold for adulteresses? Bear in mind that adultery was against the law, while prostitution was not.

CASE 169: Children Inherit from Mothers*

Tituli ex Corpore Ulpiani 26.7

Ad liberos matris intestatae hereditas ex lege duodecim tabularum non pertinebat, quia feminae suos heredes non habent: sed postea imperatorum Antonini et Commodi oratione in senatu recitata id actum est, ut sine in manum conventione matrum legitimae hereditates ad filios pertineant, exclusis consanguineis et reliquis agnatis.

(Excerpts from Ulpian's Writings)

By the Law of the Twelve Tables the inheritance of an intestate mother did not go to her children, because women do not have *sui heredes*. But later, through a proposal of the Emperors Marcus Aurelius and Commodus that was delivered in the Senate, it was enacted that, without their entering into *manus*, the statutory inheritance from mothers goes to their children, while their blood relatives and other agnates are excluded.

1. The Senatusconsultum Orphitianum. This statute, enacted by the Senate in A.D. 178 (though the Case refers to the speech from the throne proposing it), raised children from the third praetorian class (*unde cognati*) into the second (*unde legitimi*), but on a far more generous basis than the SC Tertullianum: children were given priority over all members of their mother's family. The concrete result was that if a woman died intestate and was survived only by a brother and a daughter, her brother (as nearest agnate) took her entire estate before the SC Orphitianum, and her daughter took the entire estate after it. The mother did not have to possess the *ius liberorum;* further, the same privilege was extended also to freedwomen (see Ulpian, D. 38.17.1 pr.). Why was this statute more liberal than the SC Tertullianum? Does it necessarily reflect a sea change in attitudes about the Roman family?

2. Different Marriages. Modestinus (D. 38.17.4) observes: "The rule is that all her children are eligible for a deceased mother's estate on intestacy, even if they are the product of different marriages." What are the implications of this statement? Paul (D. 38.17.6 pr.) says that even a child in someone else's *potestas* is eligible. Because a mother, like any woman, cannot wield *patria potestas,* what does Paul seem to mean? Do you see the relation to Modestinus's opinion? What problems might arise here?

3. Illegitimate Children. Ulpian (D. 38.17.1.2) extends eligibility to illegitimate children, but without giving an explanation. Is it likely that he is simply reasoning from the general irrelevance of *patria potestas* under this statute? Is the rationale here the same as that which permitted a mother to succeed to her illegitimate children under the SC Tertullianum?

CASE 170: Disqualifications

D. 38.17.1.6 (Ulpianus libro duodecimo ad Sabinum)

Qui operas suas ut cum bestiis pugnaret locavit quive rei capitalis damnatus neque restitutus est, ex senatus consulto Orphitiano ad matris hereditatem non admittebatur: sed humana interpretatione placuit eum admitti. idem erit dicendum et si hic filius in eius sit potestate, qui in causa supra scripta sit, posse eum ex Orphitiano admitti.

(Ulpian in the twelfth book on Sabinus)

A person who has hired out his services to fight wild beasts or who has been condemned on a capital charge and not been restored to his former status used to be barred from succession to his mother's estate under the SC Orphitianum, but through a generous interpretation, it was decided to allow him to succeed.

The same principle must hold even in the case of a son who is in the *potestas* of a man who falls into one of these categories; namely that he is eligible for his mother's estate under the Orphitianum.

1. A Harsher Rule. This statute was enacted in A.D. 178 (Justinian, *Inst.* 3.4 pr.). Evidently it contained certain disqualifications that are not in evidence for the SC Tertullianum (which, at least as interpreted by the jurists, allowed even prostitutes to benefit from its provisions). Why the harsher rule in this statute?

2. Relaxing the Rule. Ulpian's language (*humana interpretatione placuit*) suggests that an imperial decision lay behind the relaxation of the statutory prohibitions, an idea supported by the fact that this "interpretation" directly invalidates legislative provisions. Why would an emperor allow such persons to succeed to an intestate mother's estate? Note that the state confiscated the property of those convicted of a capital offense.

3. Other Professions. Does it seem likely that other professional types besides wild-beast fighters were included in the ban? What about prostitutes? Why would they not benefit from the relaxation in the same way?

4. A Disgraced Father. A son-in-power who receives an estate will see ownership of it pass to his *pater familias* (Case 114). Does Ulpian's holding make sense in light of the Discussion in the previous Case?

PART B

Heirs and the Will

As we have seen in Part A, although intestate succession was the default position in Roman law, its rules were such that many Romans were understandably uncomfortable with them. Two features were especially cumbersome: shares were allocated to children in a potentially undesirable way (no discrimination between males and females or between older and younger children); and widowed spouses, especially wives, were poorly protected. For this reason, many Romans preferred to write wills that departed from intestate principles.

Older Roman law set significant obstacles in their way, however. In order to make a will, Romans were obliged to perform a prescribed ceremony, and even innocent mistakes in execution could be fatal; but eventually the Roman praetor intervened to provide more flexibility. Still more difficulty was caused by the intestate preference for *sui heredes,* those family members who became *sui iuris* upon the death of a *pater familias*. A will that ignored a *suus heres* was in principle void, even if the testator was unaware of the heir's existence (see Case 46). Therefore, in drafting their wills, testators were obliged to exercise great care, though legislation and juristic interpretation found ways to circumvent some of the difficulties.

Once the formal requirements were met, Roman testators enjoyed considerable freedom to dispose of their estates as they wished. This freedom, to be sure, was hedged about by limits intended to serve the interests of clarity and good form, limits that if not observed might even compromise the effectiveness of the will. Further, the praetor provided some remedy when wills departed grossly from acceptable social standards. But juristic discussion of wills is characterized in general by a concern to implement the testator's actual desires: what did the testator want, and are his or her wishes better located in the letter or the spirit of the will?

As it seems, Roman testators fairly seldom used their freedom in order to depart radically from the felt obligations of family and class; indeed, wills usually fit into the broader strategies of property devolution pursued by the Roman elite. As a study by Edward Champlin has shown, in our sources the typical Roman testator is an upper-class male, a *pater familias* who is seeking to control the transfer of property into the next generation. In 90 percent of the cases known to us, the property left in wills goes to relatives in the third degree or closer: children, grandchildren, parents, siblings, nephews, and nieces. Children are favored above all others, including spouses. The overwhelming majority of Roman testators make all or some of their children either heirs or major legatees. Even where nonfamily heirs are known, it is often possible that close family members were coheirs. A central concern of a Roman testator, in other words, was to sustain the economic viability and social status of his family.

But this was far from the only concern. Succession had a moral aspect as well. The Greek satirist Lucian gets at this when he has a philosopher declare that the Romans tell the truth only once in their lives: in their wills (*Nigrinus* 30). Makers of wills often made use of their freedom to express their true opinion of others, in language that to outsiders might seem at times excessive and unseemly. In short, moral judgments were made both in the will and about the will, and writing a will was considered a moral duty in itself.

SECTION 1. Freedom of Testation and Substitution

CASE 171: The Mancipatory Will*

Gaius, *Institutiones* 2.104

Eaque res ita agitur: qui facit <testamentum>, adhibitis, sicut in ceteris mancipa-tionibus, V testibus civibus Romanis puberibus et libripende, postquam tabulas tes-tamenti scripserit, mancipat alicui dicis gratia familiam suam; in qua re his verbis familiae emptor utitur: "familiam pecuniamque tuam endo mandatela tua custode-laque mea <esse aio, eaque>, quo tu iure testamentum facere possis secundum legem publicam, hoc aere," et ut quidam adiciunt, "aeneaque libra, esto mihi empta"; deinde aere percutit libram idque aes dat testatori velut pretii loco; deinde testator tabulas testamenti <manu> tenens ita dicit: "haec ita ut in his tabulis cerisque scripta sunt, ita do, ita lego, ita testor, itaque vos, Quirites, testimonium mihi perhibetote"; et hoc dicitur nuncupatio: nuncupare est enim palam nominare, et sane quae testator specialiter in tabulis testamenti scripserit, ea videtur generali sermone nominare atque confirmare.

(Gaius in the second book of his *Institutes*)

This procedure (for making a mancipatory will) goes as follows: The person making the will, after collecting, as with other forms of mancipation, five adult Roman citizens as witnesses plus a person to hold a scale, and after writing out the text of the will, mancipates his estate to someone only as a matter of form.

In this procedure the "purchaser" of the estate uses the following formula: "I declare that your household and resources are entrusted by you to my care, and that these things, under that right by which you are empowered to make a will according to the public statute, are purchased by me with this piece of bronze," and, as some add, "and this bronze scale." Next, he strikes the scale with the piece of bronze and gives it to the testator as though in payment.

At that point the testator, holding the text of the will in his hand, makes the following declaration: "Just as these things are written on the wax tablets, thus I convey, thus I bequeath, thus I declare; and thus shall you, fellow citizens, bear witness for me." And this is called the attestation; for to attest is to proclaim openly, and in fact he is deemed by his blanket pronouncement to proclaim and affirm those particulars which he has written in the text of the will.

1. Fictive Sale. Gaius makes clear that the validity of the will (as a document) depends on its ratification through a ceremony of pretended sale with a no-tional payment by a "purchaser of the estate" (*familiae emptor*). The "piece of bronze" became a small bronze coin after coinage was introduced in the third century B.C. Why rely on this fictive sale as a means of ratifying a will? Gaius points out that the procedure is the same as for other types of *mancipatio,* a form primarily used to convey ownership of certain types of property known as *res mancipi* (a category that included slaves, most farm animals, and land in Italy). *Mancipatio* was also used for many other purposes, such as manumit-

ting slaves, constituting a dowry, and emancipating children or giving them in adoption (Case 149). Why was the same ceremony employed for making a will? Why were so many witnesses summoned, in this as in other types of *mancipatio*?

2. Archaic Form. Does the *familiae emptor* actually acquire the property in exchange for his notional payment? Might this have been possible at a very early stage in the history of the mancipatory will? Suppose that, as some scholars think, the making of the will tended to precede the testator's death by only a brief time. Would that suggest that actual transfer of the property in some form took place? Gaius (*Inst.* 2.105; cf. 103) even says that the *familiae emptor* stood "in place of an heir" (*heredis loco*); but in classical law there is no sign that the fictive purchaser took the role of an executor. Why would this have changed? What do you make of Gaius's odd comment about "attestation," that the blanket statement confirms the particulars in the will? Does this suggest that originally those particulars might have been stated openly in the attestation itself, so that the will was once entirely oral? If so, why do you think that the Romans stopped giving the particulars openly? And once the written will became customary, why did they continue with the entire, rather awkward ritual of the mancipatory will?

3. Form over Function. Suppose some legal defect in the fictive sale was later discovered, for example, that one or more of the witnesses were not Roman citizens (for other rules regarding the witnesses, see Gaius 2.105–108). Would this render the will invalid? Yes; but eventually the praetor was prepared to grant *bonorum possessio* in accordance with the terms of the will (*secundum tabulas*) to the heir named in the will, provided it had the seals of seven witnesses (ibid. 2.119–120). All the same, at least until the reign of Antoninus Pius (A.D. 138–161), this grant would not withstand a challenge from an intestate heir entitled under the *ius civile*. Does this seem like formalism run amok?

4. The Written Will. Roman wills were customarily written out on tablets that were then sealed by the witnesses and only opened after the testator's death. Why is it helpful if testators write out their wishes? What problems can arise from writing? The written will had a required form, and failure to observe the rules could render the entire will invalid, even when the testator's wishes were easily discernible. For example, the heirs usually had to be named at or very near the start of the will. If this was postponed, the entire will could fail. Why insist on such formalism?

5. A Specimen Will. The Appendix to this chapter gives a specimen will illustrating the draftsmanship of Roman wills. You should note especially that the will provides for a division of the entire inheritance (the heirs receive frac-

tions adding up to the entire estate), but that the inheritance is then diminished by various legacies going either to the heirs or to third parties. The will also provides for the validity of subsequent addenda, called "codicils," if the testator wishes to make changes in his will; codicils became legally acceptable during the reign of Augustus (31 B.C. to A.D. 14; see Justinian, *Inst.* 2.25 pr.).

CASE 172: Common Substitution*

Gaius, *Institutiones* 2.174–175

(174) Interdum duos pluresve gradus heredum facimus, hoc modo: "L. Titius heres esto cernitoque in diebus centum proximis, quibus scies poterisque. quod ni ita creveris, exheres esto. tum Maevius heres esto cernitoque in diebus centum et reliqua"; et deinceps in quantum velimus, substituere possumus. (175) Et licet nobis vel unum in unius locum substituere pluresve, et contra in plurium locum vel unum vel plures substituere.

(Gaius in the second book of his *Institutes*)

(174) Sometimes we make two or more ranks of heirs, as follows: "Let Lucius Titius be heir and let him formally declare acceptance within the next one hundred days once you (i.e., Lucius Titius) know and are able. But if you do not make a formal declaration, you are disinherited. At that point let Maevius be heir and let him formally declare acceptance within the next one hundred days, etc."; and from that point onward, as far as we like, we can make substitutions. (175) We are also permitted to substitute one person or several for one person, and conversely either one or several persons for several persons.

1. No Limits? These two passages suggest that a broad discretion was allowed the testator. In case one of his primary heirs predeceased him or refused the inheritance, a testator could name substitutes. Are any limits implied by Gaius's words? What would happen if the primary heir died a day after accepting the inheritance?

2. Wording of the Substitution. The testator was not bound to the precise formula laid out by Gaius. What were the consequences if he or she omitted the time period for acceptance? If the primary heir is not expressly disinherited when the time limit expires? In the latter case, Gaius, *Inst.* 2.177, holds that both the primary and the secondary heirs share the estate equally unless the primary heir either disavows the inheritance or takes no action to assume control of the property.

3. Reciprocal Substitution. Some testators fine-tuned their wills by making the coheirs reciprocal substitutes. Suppose a will appoints three heirs to unequal shares: A to a twelfth of the estate, B to eight-twelfths, and C to a quarter. And suppose that C declines the inheritance. If A and B had both accepted, and all three were also appointed as substitutes for one another, would each receive an additional one-eighth, or would their respective shares depend on the mathematical proportions they originally received? The latter is true; see Ulpian, D. 28.6.24. So A ends up with a total of one-ninth of the entire estate, and B gets eight-ninths. Follow the math?

CASE 173: Pupillary Substitution*

Gaius, *Institutiones* 2.179

Liberis nostris impuberibus, quos in potestate habemus, non solum ita, ut supra diximus, substituere possumus, id est, ut si heredes non extiterint, alius nobis heres sit; sed eo amplius ut, etiamsi heredes nobis extiterint et adhuc impuberes mortui fuerint, sit iis aliquis heres, velut hoc modo: "Titius filius meus mihi heres esto. si filius meus mihi <heres non erit, sive heres mihi> erit et is prius moriatur quam in suam tutelam venerit, tunc Seius heres esto."

(Gaius in the second book of his *Institutes*)

For our children whom we have in power and who are not yet adult (*impuberes*), we can make a substitution not only in the way we just described—that is, if there are no heirs, that someone else be our heir—but in addition as follows, that even if they become our heirs and then die while still minors, someone else is heir to them.

This is done as follows: "Let my son Titius be my heir. If my son does not become my heir, or if he becomes my heir and dies before reaching the age of legal majority, then let Seius be my heir."

1. Genus and Species. Is it more correct to view pupillary substitution (from *pupillus*, Latin for minor-age child) as a subtype of common substitution, or is it something entirely different? As Gaius later observes (2.181), pupillary substitutions were often made, not in the primary will, but in separate documents annexed to it and opened only if the minor died, "in order to prevent the minor from being exposed to foul play after his father's death." What sort of dangers did the father fear?

2. How Many Wills? Pupillary substitution is the only instance in Roman law where one person is allowed to make testamentary dispositions for another. Gaius (*Inst.* 2.180) says: "For this reason there are, in a sense, two wills, one the father's and one the son's, as if the son named an heir for himself; or at any rate there is one will for two inheritances." Which of these two descriptions more accurately represents pupillary substitution? In Gaius's model wording, is the substitute heir an heir to the testator or an heir to the *pupillus*?

3. Minor-Age Children. The age of legal majority was fourteen for boys and twelve for girls, and these were the legal minimums for marriage (Cases 6–7). Children under these ages who were legally independent (*sui iuris*) had a *tutor* or guardian to supervise their property (Chapter V.A.1), and also, by law, they could not make a will for themselves. Could a testator grant them that power? That is, could a testator alter the general legal rule for his own children?

4. Heir in Suspension? Is there a sense in which the *pupillus* becomes a true heir only upon reaching the age of legal majority?

CASE 174: The *Causa Curiana**

Cicero, *De Oratore* 1.180

Quid vero? clarissima M'. Curii causa Marcique Coponii nuper apud centumviros, quo concursu hominum, qua exspectatione defensa est! cum Q. Scaevola, aequalis et collega meus, homo omnium et disciplina iuris civilis eruditissimus, et ingenio prudentiaque acutissimus, et oratione maxime limatus atque subtilis, atque, ut ego soleo dicere, iuris peritorum eloquentissimus, eloquentium iuris peritissimus, ex scripto testamentorum iura defenderet, negaretque, nisi postumus et natus, et, antequam in suam tutelam venisset, mortuus esset, heredem eum esse posse, qui esset secundum postumum, et natum, et mortuum, heres institutus: ego autem defenderem, hac eum tum mente fuisse, qui testamentum fecisset, ut, si filius non esset, qui in tutelam veniret, M'. Curius esset heres. Num destitit uterque nostrum in ea causa, in auctoritatibus, in exemplis, in testamentorum formulis, hoc est, in medio iure civili, versari?

(Cicero in the first book *On the Public Speaker*)

"Finally, there is the illustrious case of Manius Curius and Marcus Coponius, which was recently heard before the Court of One Hundred—what a crowd of people, what anticipation!

"Quintus (Mucius) Scaevola, my contemporary and colleague, a man who knows more than anyone about the *ius civile,* whose talent and judgment are very keen, whose speaking style is especially refined and exquisite, and who is, as I often say, the best public speaker among jurists and the best jurist among public speakers, defended interpreting wills in accordance with their words and claimed that if a man was appointed as substitute heir to a posthumous child who is born and then dies, he cannot inherit unless the posthumous child was (actually) born and then died before reaching the age of legal majority.

"I, on the other hand, argued that the testator, when he made the will, had intended that if he had no child who reached the age of legal majority, Manius Curius would be his heir. During this case, did either one of us cease being immersed in jurists' decisions, precedents, testamentary formulas, that is, in the heart of the *ius civile*?"

Hypothetical Situation

Marcus Coponius makes a will in which he names his posthumous child as his heir and then names Manius Curius as a substitute heir to this child. Coponius then dies, but his wife miscarries before giving birth to the child. Can Curius claim the estate, or does the will fail and the estate go to the intestate heirs?

1. *Postumi.* Posthumous children (*postumi*), that is, children conceived before but born after the testator's death, were protected under the rules for both testate and intestate succession in much the same way as other *sui heredes.* Thus, for instance, failure to disinherit a posthumous child would invalidate the entire will (Case 182). In this Case, Coponius, evidently aware that his wife was pregnant, instituted his posthumous child as his heir. Granted the very high levels of infant mortality that prevailed in the Roman world, does it make sense that Roman law allowed him also to make pupillary substitution for the *postumus*? What legal problem arose when Coponius's wife failed to give birth to the anticipated posthumous child?

2. Words versus Will. In this dialogue of Cicero, the speaker is M. Licinius Crassus, a renowned orator of the early first century B.C. and one of Cicero's teachers. Crassus is here speaking about an actual trial in the late 90s B.C., in which he had represented Curius against the intestate heirs, who in their turn had retained Q. Mucius Scaevola, a famous and exceptionally talented Roman jurist of the time. One reason this trial is so notable is that it seems to pose a classic contrast between the claims of the literal sense of the testamentary document, the will, and those of the testator's intent. Reconstruct the arguments for both sides. Which seems stronger? Is the jurist right to place on the testator the heavy burden of expressing his intent in language that is both clear and legally proper? On the other hand, if we incline to look beyond the plain meaning of the words, how certain can we then be that we have correctly grasped a writer's intent? What are the larger implications of this dispute for the law of testamentary succession?

3. Common Substitution within Pupillary? The victorious Curius, represented by Crassus, in essence made the argument that a pupillary substitution necessarily implies a common one, at least in this particular case. Scaevola was evidently unpersuaded. Are you? The issue remained controversial until the Emperor Marcus Aurelius finally settled it in the second century A.D. (Modestinus, D. 28.6.4 pr.). Guess which side won.

CASE 175: Who's on First?

D. 28.6.2.4 (Ulpianus libro sexto ad Sabinum)

Prius autem sibi quis debet heredem scribere, deinde filio substituere et non convertere ordinem scripturae: et hoc Iulianus putat prius sibi debere, deinde filio heredem scribere: ceterum si ante filio, deinde sibi testamentum faciat, non valere. quae sententia rescripto imperatoris nostri ad Virium Lupum Britanniae praesidem comprobata est, et merito: constat enim unum esse testamentum, licet duae sint hereditates, usque adeo, ut quos quis sibi facit necessarios, eosdem etiam filio faciat et postumum suum filio impuberi possit quis substituere.

(Ulpian in the sixth book on Sabinus)

Moreover, a person ought to put down an heir for himself first and then name a substitute for his child, and not reverse the order of writing. Julian also thinks that he (the testator) ought first to name an heir for himself, then a substitute for his child; but if he makes a will for his child first, then one for himself, they are (both) invalid.

This opinion was approved by a rescript of our emperor (Caracalla) to Virius Lupus, the governor of Britain; and rightly so, since the consensus is that there is one will even though there are two inheritances, to the point that someone who creates necessary heirs for himself creates them also for his child, and someone can substitute a posthumous *suus heres* for a prepubescent child.

1. Disinheriting the *Pupillus*. As this Case makes clear, the testator can name a substitute for a *pupillus* even if he disinherited the child. Does this seem fair? Do the same justifications apply here as for pupillary substitution where the *pupillus* is primary heir?

2. The Last Shall Be First. Why do Julian and Ulpian insist that the primary heir be placed first, that is, before the pupillary substitution? The penalty for failure to do so is invalidation of the will, as the text makes clear. Are the jurists being too fussy? Note that, as a general principle, a pupillary substitution is invalid unless a primary will is made.

3. Necessary Heirs. A necessary heir is a special type of heir, a slave who is manumitted and named heir. As a *necessarius,* he or she is compelled to accept the inheritance, even if it is burdened by debt. Elsewhere, Ulpian (D. 28.6.10.1) indicates that making the testator's *necessarius* the substitute for the *pupillus* as well was an option, not an automatic consequence. Do provisions such as this, or making the *postumus* a substitute for the minor child, tie the "two inheritances" together into one will?

4. How Many Wills? Ulpian, against Gaius, cites a consensus that in this instance there is just one will in the case of pupillary substitution, not two. In light of the arguments he makes, do you find this view persuasive?

CASE 176: Two Wills

D. 28.6.16.1 (Pomponius libro tertio ad Sabinum)

Si suo testamento perfecto alia rursus hora pater filio testamentum fecerit adhibitis legitimis testibus, nihilo minus id valebit et tamen patris testamentum ratum manebit. nam et si sibi et filio pater testamentum fecisset, deinde sibi tantum, utrumque superius rumpetur. sed si secundum testamentum ita fecerit pater, ut sibi heredem instituat, si vivo se filius decedat, potest dici non rumpi superius testamentum, quia secundum non valet, in quo filius praeteritus sit.

(Pomponius in the third book on Sabinus)

If a father makes a will for himself and subsequently makes a will for his son with the legally appropriate witnesses, this (the son's will) is still valid even though the father's will remains in force.

For also, if the father had made a (single) will for (both) himself and for his son, and later (he made a will) only for himself, both the earlier provisions are broken.

But if a father makes a second will so as to institute an heir to himself if his son dies during his (the father's) life, it can be held that the earlier will is not broken, because the second one, in which the son was passed over in silence, is invalid.

1. Dueling Wills. It is a fixed rule of Roman law that when someone makes a legally valid will, this automatically cancels all previous wills (see Case 178). In the first hypothetical situation, why doesn't that happen when the father makes a subsequent will for his son? Does Pomponius seem to agree with Gaius (Discussion to Case 173) that pupillary substitution involves two distinct wills, or with Ulpian (Case 175) that it involves only one?

2. The Dependency of Pupillary Substitution. In the second hypothetical situation, the father's second will named an heir and a substitute for himself but (unlike the first) did not include a pupillary substitution. Do you think that the father supposed his earlier pupillary substitution would remain in force? The problem is that his second will effectively canceled his first will, and a pupillary substitution is always dependent on the existence of a valid father's will. See *Tit. Ulp.* 23.9: "No one can substitute an heir for a minor son unless he names an heir for himself, either the son himself or a third party." Why this rule?

3. Invalidity of a Subsequent Will. However, if the subsequent will is not legally valid, the prior will remains in force. As it seems, the *pater* in the third hypothetical situation simply wrote: "Let X be my heir if my son predeceases me." Does it seem likely that he simply wanted to supplement his earlier will? What should he have done to make the supplement effective? Since the son is mentioned in the condition, why does Pomponius say that he was passed over in silence?

SECTION 2. The *Sui Heredes*

CASE 177: Privileged Heirs*

D. 28.2.11 (Paulus libro secundo ad Sabinum)

In suis heredibus evidentius apparet continuationem dominii eo rem perducere, ut nulla videatur hereditas fuisse, quasi olim hi domini essent, qui etiam vivo patre quodammodo domini existimantur. unde etiam filius familias appellatur sicut pater familias, sola nota hac adiecta, per quam distinguitur genitor ab eo qui genitus sit. itaque post mortem patris non hereditatem percipere videntur, sed magis liberam bonorum administrationem consequuntur. hac ex causa licet non sint heredes instituti, domini sunt: nec obstat, quod licet eos exheredare, quod et occidere licebat.

(Paul in the second book on Sabinus)

In the case of privileged heirs (*sui heredes*), continuity of ownership has the rather obvious consequence that there appears to be no actual inheritance, rather as if they were long since owners. In a sense, they are regarded as having owned while the father was still alive. For this reason a son-in-power (*filius familias*) is even named like a *pater familias,* a qualification being added only to distinguish parent from offspring.

Therefore, after the death of the father, they (the *sui heredes*) are not regarded as acquiring an inheritance; instead, they (just) attain unobstructed power to dispose over their property. For this reason, even though they have not been instituted as heirs, they are owners. Nor is it an objection that it is permitted to disinherit them, for it was also (once) permitted to kill them.

1. *Sui Heredes.* The "privileged heirs" (*sui heredes*) are those who became legally independent (*sui iuris*) at a testator's death. One way these heirs were privileged was that, for a will to be valid, such persons had to be made heirs or expressly disinherited. How does Paul attempt to justify this? In light of what you know about the property rights of children-in-power, are you convinced by his argument that the *sui heredes* were quasi owners of the estate even before the testator's death? Is it any more persuasive to observe that a son and father share the same name?

2. Heirs and Owners. What does Paul mean when he describes the *sui* as owners rather than heirs? Is he saying that they are not just the presumptive but the default owners of the decedent's property, and that they remain so unless and until they are disinherited and a more qualified heir—more qualified because duly instituted by the testator—takes the inheritance?

3. The *Vitae Necisque Potestas.* What is Paul getting at in the last sentence? Is he saying that a right or privilege that is not exercised has no weight? Is this sentence reconcilable with Cases 90–93 on a father's right to kill his children? Note Paul's careful use of the past tense.

CASE 178: Defective Wills*

Tituli ex Corpore Ulpiani 23.1–4

(1) Testamentum iure factum infirmatur duobus modis, si ruptum aut inritum factum sit. (2) Rumpitur testamentum mutatione, id est si postea aliud testamentum iure factum sit. item agnatione, id est, si suus heres agnascatur, qui neque heres institutus neque ut oportet exheredatus sit. (3) Agnascitur suus heres aut agnascendo aut adoptando aut in manum conveniendo aut in locum sui heredis succedendo, velut nepos mortuo filio vel emancipato, aut manumissione, id est si filius ex prima secundave mancipatione manumissus reversus sit in patris potestatem. (4) Inritum fit testamentum, si testator capite deminutus fuerit, aut si iure facto testamento nemo extiterit heres.

(Excerpts from Ulpian's Writings)

(1) A will that was legally made is invalidated in two ways: if it is broken or rendered ineffectual.

   (2) A will is broken by (subsequent) change, that is, if another will is legally made; and also by accession (of subsequent *sui heredes*), that is, if a *suus heres* accedes who is neither instituted an heir nor disinherited as is required. (3) A *suus heres* accedes either by birth or by adoption or by entry into *manus* (a *manus* marriage) or by succeeding into the place of a *suus heres,* like a grandson when a son dies or is emancipated, or by manumission, that is, if a son has been manumitted after the first or second mancipation and has returned to his father's power.

   (4) A will is rendered ineffectual if the testator undergoes loss of status (*capitis deminutio*) or if there is no heir under a legally made will.

1. Accession of Subsequent *Sui Heredes*. This postclassical source summarizes classical Roman law (compare Gaius, *Inst.* 2.130–134, which, unfortunately, is defectively preserved). The crucial rule is stated in section 2: a will is "broken" (*ruptum*), that is, entirely void, if it does not either institute or disinherit a *suus heres,* including a person who becomes a *suus heres* after the writing of the will. Accession of a *suus heres* can occur in several ways: birth of a new *suus* (including posthumous children); adoption; *manus* marriage; and succession into the place of a *suus*. In each case, the addition of a new *suus* seems to require a new will. The rule seems to be the starting point for classical law, although, as we shall see, it was somewhat modified by legislation and juristic interpretation. Why might the rule ever have come into existence? That is, what are its purposes?

2. Birth. This includes cesarean section, says Ulpian (D. 28.2.12), who adds that the will is broken even "if a defective creature is born, so long as it breathes." Ghoulish excess?

3. Subsequent Death. A child who would be a *suus* is born after a will is made but then dies before the testator's death. Is the will, which ignores the child, broken? No, says Ulpian (D. 28.3.12 pr.); but it took imperial rescripts to thwart "the strict observance of law."

CASE 179: Name Games*

D. 28.2.2 (Ulpianus libro sexto Regularum)

Nominatim exheredatus filius et ita videtur "filius meus exheres esto," si nec nomen eius expressum sit, si modo unicus sit: nam si plures sunt filii, benigna interpretatione potius a plerisque respondetur nullum exheredatum esse.

(Ulpian in the sixth book of his *Rules of Law*)

A son is held to have been disinherited by name even in the following way: "Let my son be disinherited." This works even though his name is not expressly stated, provided he is an only son; for if there is more than one son, most jurists, using a generous interpretation, respond that no one has been disinherited (by such a phrase).

1. More Equal. Some of the *sui heredes* are more privileged than others; a will failed unless a testator's sons were disinherited by name, whereas the rest could be disinherited generically ("Let all others be disinherited"). Why are sons singled out for this privilege? Granted the privilege, is it fair to uphold disinheritance when a son is referred to but not expressly named?

2. "My Son, the Bastard." Always assuming that it is clear to whom he refers, can a testator use more elaborate circumlocutions in disinheriting a son? What if the testator referred to his son as "Seia's boy" (using his mother's name)? What if he used an abusive description: "the unspeakable one," "the bandit," "the gladiator," "the bastard"? Ulpian (D. 28.2.3 pr.–1) permits disinheritance in all these cases. But Africanus (D. 28.2.14.2) cites Julian's dissenting view with regard to "he who is not my son": the father is not disinheriting his son as his son but as someone else's son, and for this reason the wording fails. (See also Ulpian, D. 37.10.1.9.) Do you agree?

3. False Accusations. When a testator gives a reason, especially an abusive reason, for disinheriting a son, what if the allegation is untrue? Can the son overthrow the will by disproving the allegation? Africanus, in the passage cited above, says yes; Ulpian (D. 28.2.15) says the same, and some other sources are to the same effect. If the testator's charges can be contested, would he have been better advised to hold his tongue? But there are also dangers to this course, as we shall see in Section 4 below.

4. Improper Reasons. Does a son have recourse if he is disinherited because he disobeyed his father's command to divorce his wife? See Cases 104–107 and also Diocletian and Maximian, C. 3.28.18 and 20 (A.D. 286, 294), which allow a lawsuit for an "undutiful will" (Section 4 below).

5. Generosity to a Fault. Who benefits from the "generous" interpretation in the last sentence of this Case? Suppose the testator had actually wanted to disinherit all of his sons. Was he obliged to name them all? In interpreting ambiguous wills, should law favor the living over the dead?

CASE 180: Disinheritance as an Advantage

D. 28.2.18 (Ulpianus libro quinquagesimo septimo ad edictum)

Multi non notae causa exheredant filios nec ut eis obsint, sed ut eis consulant, ut puta impuberibus, eisque fideicommissam hereditatem dant.

(Ulpian in the fifty-seventh book on the Edict)

Many persons disinherit their children, not to defame them nor to put them at a disadvantage, but in order to serve their interests. An example is prepubescent children (*impuberes*), to whom they give the inheritance in the form of a trust (*fideicommissum*).

1. The Trust (*Fideicommissum*). The trust was a common form of bequest among the Romans; it is discussed in Part C below. The form of will that Ulpian is discussing might take the following form: the testator disinherits his minor child and then appoints a third party, usually a close friend or relative, as his heir. The heir is then requested, on the basis of "trust" (*fides*), to convey the estate to the minor child. This method held advantages over instituting the minor directly, in that it avoided imposing on the minor many technical requirements and burdens in executing a will. Keep in mind also that an inheritance perhaps typically came with debts as well as assets, and the debts might be rather high; some estates were in the red.

2. Minor-Age Children. Why was the position of a minor-age child (*impubes*) considered particularly delicate? Who would handle the estate settlement for a minor? Might similar reasons motivate the disinheritance of an insane child? See also Ulpian, D. 38.2.12.2: in this situation, a child is not disinherited "with malice" (*mala mente*).

3. Who Benefits? In the other Cases you have read, do the jurists always take into account that disinheritance may be intended to benefit the *suus heres*?

CASE 181: Partial Disinheritance

D. 28.2.19 (Paulus libro primo ad Vitellium)

Cum quidam filiam ex asse heredem scripsisset filioque, quem in potestate habebat, decem legasset, adiecto "et in cetera parte exheres mihi erit," et quaereretur, an recte exheredatus videretur, Scaevola respondit non videri, et in disputando adiciebat ideo non valere, quoniam nec fundi exheres esse iussus recte exheredaretur, aliamque causam esse institutionis, quae benigne acciperetur: exheredationes autem non essent adiuvandae.

(Paul in the first book on Vitellius)

A certain man had written (in his will) that his daughter was to be heir to his entire estate. To his son he had left a legacy of ten, but he had added "and as to the rest (of my estate) let him be disinherited." Question was raised as to whether he (the son) seemed to have been correctly disinherited.

    Scaevola responded that he did not think so, and in a discussion he also added that the disinheritance was invalid because a person cannot be correctly disinherited with regard to a farm. He distinguished the situation where an heir was instituted, which would be construed generously. Disinheritance, however, should not be promoted (through interpretation).

1. An Ambiguous Will? Try to reconstruct the relevant terms of the will as Paul gives them. Is the phrase at issue ambiguous? Is the testator's intent unclear? What should he have written?

2. Disinheritance from a Farm. What point is Scaevola, cited by Paul, making about the farm? Is it that no one can be appointed heir to specific items in an estate, so that, logically, no one can be disinherited from such items? What does this have to do with the case under discussion?

3. Policy and Logic. With this Case, compare Ulpian, D. 28.5.1.4: "If someone was instituted sole heir 'to a farm,' the institution is valid; the mention of the farm is excised" (i.e., effectively ignored). This is a "generous" interpretation because, as a rule, a person must be named sole or partial heir to an entire inheritance, not to discrete property within it. (The property can be separately left as legacies; see below Part C; but first there must be an heir.) Why does Scaevola (and evidently Paul) believe that juristic interpretation should be generous in support of instituting heirs but neutral, or perhaps even restrictive, with regard to disinheritance? Does such a policy do violence to the operation of legal logic in this Case?

CASE 182: Providing for *Postumi**

D. 28.2.10 (Pomponius libro primo ad Sabinum)

Commodissime is qui nondum natus est ita heres instituitur: "sive vivo me sive mortuo natus fuerit, heres esto," aut etiam pure neutrius temporis habita mentione. si alteruter casus omissus fuerit, eo casu, qui omissus sit, natus rumpit testamentum, quia hic filius nec sub condicione quidem scriptus heres intellegitur, qui in hunc casum nascitur, qui non est testamento adprehensus.

(Pomponius in the first book on Sabinus)

A person who is not yet born is quite conveniently instituted an heir in the following way: "whether he be born when I am alive or after I am dead, let him be heir." Or even unconditionally, with no mention of either time period.

If one or the other of these situations (the testator being either still alive or dead) is omitted, and a child is born in the situation that was omitted, he breaks the will. For the son is not understood to have been even conditionally instituted heir if he was born in a situation that was not embraced in the will.

1. The Unborn Child and the Will. Any child born after the writing of a will still counts as a *suus* (unless subsequently deceased, emancipated, adopted, or given in marriage with *manus*). Thus, if in a will such a child is not named heir or disinherited, the will is rendered invalid. Given that abortion was not illegal, and that the *pater familias* might decide to abandon or even kill his newborn child, what do you make of this protection extended to the unborn child?

2. The *Postumus* Problem. As Pomponius says, the new child might break the will regardless of whether it was born before the testator's death or afterward. What is the most obvious way to deal with the first scenario, if the child had not been accounted for in the will? Do you see why the posthumous child (*postumus*) posed special problems?

3. Draftsmanship. The jurists are deeply concerned with drafting wills to avoid problems that stem from subsequently born *sui heredes*. One common situation was when a *pater* had in his power a married son; if that son should die while his father was still alive, any grandchildren (including *postumi*) would immediately become *sui heredes* to their grandfather. As to posthumous grandchildren, the late Republican jurist Aquilius Gallus (cited by Scaevola, D. 28.2.29 pr.) suggested the following wording: "If my son dies during my lifetime, then if my grandson or granddaughter through him is born after my death and within ten months of my son's death, let them be heirs." Is this wording fussy enough? For instance, what if a *pater* is predeceased by both his son and grandson, but after the testator's death his grandson's wife gives birth to his great-grandchild? Unless that child is either instituted or disinherited, the will is void.

CASE 183: *Postumi* and the (Un)married Man*

D. 28.2.4 (Ulpianus libro tertio ad Sabinum)

Placet omnem masculum posse postumum heredem scribere, sive iam maritus sit sive nondum uxorem duxerit: nam et maritus repudiare uxorem potest et qui non duxit uxorem, postea maritus effici. nam et cum maritus postumum heredem scribit, non utique is solus postumus scriptus videtur, qui ex ea quam habet uxorem ei natus est, vel is qui tunc in utero est, verum is quoque, qui ex quacumque uxore nascatur,

D. 28.2.5 (Iavolenus libro primo ex Cassio)

ideoque qui postumum heredem instituit si post testamentum factum mutavit matrimonium, is institutus videtur, qui ex posteriore matrimonio natus est.

(Ulpian in the third book on Sabinus)

It is generally accepted that any male, whether he is already married or has not yet married, can institute a *postumus* as heir. This is because a married man can divorce his wife, while an unmarried man can later become a married one. For even when a husband institutes a *postumus* as heir, the *postumus* who is instituted is not necessarily held to be one born from the woman to whom he is then married, or a *postumus* who is then still in the womb, but also one who is born from any wife whatsoever,

(Javolenus in the first book from Cassius)

and therefore, if someone who institutes a *postumus* as heir should later remarry, the person born from the later marriage is held to be instituted.

Hypothetical Situation

Titius's girlfriend has just informed him that she is pregnant with his child. Titius does not intend to marry her but is writing his will. What should he do?

1. **Adversity to Risk.** Ulpian is quite clear: an unmarried male writing a will should be concerned about a prospective *postumus*. What if, as in the hypothetical situation, he has no plans to marry his pregnant girlfriend? Should the testator wait until he learns his partner is pregnant before instituting a *postumus*? Suppose he is not currently in a relationship: what result then? What if he is at present married to someone else?

2. **Obscurity Helps.** Do Ulpian and Javolenus recommend that the institution of the *postumus* be made without any indication of who the mother is or, for that matter, the identity of the child? The jurists usually demand precision in the writing of wills. Why not here?

3. An Impermissible *Postumus*? Can you institute as your heir your posthumous child from a woman, such as your sister, to whom legal marriage is impossible? See Paul, D. 28.2.9.3, citing Pomponius: yes, you can. Why? The text suggests that the point was disputed.

CASE 184: Subfecundity*

D. 28.2.6 (Ulpianus libro tertio ad Sabinum)

(pr.) Sed est quaesitum, an is, qui generare facile non possit, postumum heredem facere possit, et scribit Cassius et Iavolenus posse: nam et uxorem ducere et adoptare potest. spadonem quoque posse postumum heredem scribere et Labeo et Cassius scribunt: quoniam nec aetas nec sterilitas ei rei impedimento est. (1) Sed si castratus sit, Iulianus Proculi opinionem secutus non putat postumum heredem posse instituere, quo iure utimur. (2) Hermaphroditus plane, si in eo virilia prae-valebunt, postumum heredem instituere poterit.

(Ulpian in the third book on Sabinus)

(pr.) But a question has been raised as to whether a person who cannot readily procreate can institute a *postumus* as heir. Both Cassius and Javolenus write that he can, for he is capable of both marrying and adopting. That a eunuch (*spado*) too can institute a *postumus* as heir both Labeo and Cassius agree, because nei-ther age nor procreative incapacity is an obstacle to doing this.

(1) But if he was castrated, Julian, following the view of Proculus, thinks that he cannot institute a *postumus* as heir, and this is the rule we follow. (2) A hermaphrodite, to be sure, if his male characteristics predominate, can institute a *postumus* as heir.

1. Difficult Procreation. Ulpian first gives the view of Cassius and Javolenus that "a person who cannot readily procreate" can still institute a *postumus* as heir. Is this because there is still a chance that he could produce a *postumus*? Why do the jurists not explicitly use this rationale? Why should it matter that he can marry and adopt? (On marriage and adoption, see Cases 8, 150.)

2. The Eunuch. Ulpian then reports Labeo and Cassius to the effect that a eu-nuch (*spado*) can institute a *postumus* as heir, since "neither age nor procreative incapacity is an obstacle to doing this." What do they mean? Are they suggest-ing that complete certainty about the inability to procreate is impossible?

3. Controversy. The presence of so many jurists' names in this passage suggests a controversy, which you should try to reconstruct. The Latin word for "eu-nuch," *spado,* sometimes includes male sterility no matter how it arises. Is it clear that Cassius and Labeo disagree with Proculus, Julian, and Ulpian as to the castrated man? Why does Ulpian support the negative position on the castrated eunuch? Does the case of the hermaphrodite help at all to explain his decision?

4. An Objective View? With this Case, compare Paul, D. 28.2.9 pr.: "If anyone institutes as his heirs *postumi* whom he happens to be unable to have because

of age or ill health, his prior will is rendered invalid, for the nature and practice of human procreation should be considered more significant than a temporary defect or illness whereby a person is deprived of the capacity to procreate." Is Paul's standard different from Ulpian's?

CASE 185: Twins

D. 28.2.13 pr. (Iulianus libro vicesimo nono Digestorum)

Si ita scriptum sit: "si filius mihi natus fuerit, ex besse heres esto: ex reliqua parte uxor mea heres esto. si vero filia mihi nata fuerit, ex triente heres esto: ex reliqua parte uxor heres esto," et filius et filia nati essent, dicendum est assem distribuendum esse in septem partes, ut ex his filius quattuor, uxor duas, filia unam partem habeat: ita enim secundum voluntatem testantis filius altero tanto amplius habebit quam uxor, item uxor altero tanto amplius quam filia: licet enim suptili iuris regulae conveniebat ruptum fieri testamentum, attamen cum ex utroque nato testator voluerit uxorem aliquid habere, ideo ad huiusmodi sententiam humanitate suggerente decursum est, quod etiam Iuventio Celso apertissime placuit.

(Julian in the twenty-ninth book of his *Digests*)

It (a will) was written in this way: "If a son is born to me, let him be my heir to two-thirds; let my wife be heir to the remainder. If a daughter is born to me, let her be my heir to one-third; let my wife be heir to the rest." Both a son and a daughter were born (after the testator's death).

The holding should be to divide the whole (estate) into seven parts, in such a way that the son receives four of these, the wife two, and the daughter one part. For thus, in accord with the testator's wishes, his son will receive twice as much as his wife, and his wife will receive twice as much as his daughter.

For although it was consistent with a strict rule of law that the will was rendered invalid, nevertheless, since the testator wanted the wife to have something in the case of either child, for this reason, consonant with considerations of humanity, recourse was had to this sort of holding, which also was quite clearly endorsed by Juventius Celsus.

1. Reading the Design of the Testator. Julian claims that his seven-part division is supported by the intentions of the testator. Is this persuasive? How can he divine the man's wishes under these circumstances?

2. Strict Law. What is the "strict rule of law" to which Julian refers? Did the testator not adequately take his *postumi* into account? How could anyone in antiquity accurately predict the birth of twins? Does the situation described here seem a likely occurrence? How should the testator have written his will to conform exactly with the strict rule?

3. Oh, the Humanity! How did "humanity" persuade Julian and Celsus that this solution was the correct one? What would the wife receive if the will were broken (see Cases 159, 167)? Are the jurists perhaps influenced by the fact

that provision for a widow in a husband's will was customary? Are they short-changing the interests of the children, especially the daughter?

4. Other Hypotheses. Would the outcome have been the same if the wife had borne two boys or two girls or triplets?

CASE 186: The Challenge of the *Emancipatus**

D. 37.4.8.14 (Ulpianus libro quadragesimo ad edictum)

Non est novum, ut emancipatus praeteritus plus iuris scriptis heredibus fratribus suis tribuat, quam habituri essent, si soli fuissent: quippe si filius qui in potestate patris est ex duodecima parte heres scribatur emancipato praeterito, dimidiam partem beneficio emancipati occupat, qui, si emancipatum fratrem non haberet, duodecimam partem habiturus esset. sed si ex parte minima sit heres institutus, non pro ea parte, qua institutus est, tuendus est commisso edicto, sed amplius per bonorum possessionem habere potest. praetori enim propositum est, cum contra tabulas bonorum possessionem dat, eas partes unicuique liberorum tribuere, quas intestato patre mortuo in hereditate habiturus esset, si in potestate mansisset: et ideo sive emancipatus sive is qui in potestatem mansit sive in adoptionem datus ex minima parte heres scriptus sit, non redigitur ad eam portionem, ex qua institutus est, sed virilem accipit.

(Ulpian in the fortieth book on the Edict)

It comes as no surprise that an emancipated child, if he is passed over (in his father's will) when his siblings were named heirs, may confer more rights on them than they would have had on their own (with no emancipated brother or sister). For if a son-in-power is instituted heir with respect to a twelfth (of the estate) and his emancipated brother is passed over, he takes a half share because of the *emancipatus;* but if he did not have an emancipated brother, he would receive (only) a twelfth share.

　　And if he were instituted heir with respect to a very small portion of the estate, once the Edict has been invoked, he should be protected not (only) with respect to the share to which he was appointed heir; he can receive more through *bonorum possessio.*

　　The praetor's policy, when he grants *bonorum possessio* against the terms of a will, is to distribute to each of the children (*liberi*) those portions they would receive if their father had died without a will and they had remained in his power. For this reason whether a child was emancipated or has remained in *potestas* or has been given in adoption, if he is instituted heir for a very small share, he is not limited to that part of the estate for which he or she was appointed heir but receives a full share.

　　1. The Praetor Upsets the Will. By creating a preferred class called *liberi,* the praetor permitted children emancipated from their father's power to enjoy rights similar to those of *sui heredes* (see Cases 162–163). That is, he required that an emancipated child either be instituted heir or disinherited, in the same manner as the *sui;* thus, a male descendant had to be disinherited by name, and a female at least through a general clause (Gaius, *Inst.* 2.135). If a testator passed over a son-in-power, the praetor invalidated the will and gave

possession to the heirs upon intestacy (Ulpian, D. 38.6.1.9). In the case of all others (whether *sui heredes* or not), the praetor upheld the will in part: he enforced disinheritances, pupillary substitutions, and some legacies. But apart from these exceptions, he ignored the heirs who were instituted in the will; instead, to those intestate heirs who had not been disinherited he granted possession of their intestate shares. See Gaius, *Inst.* 2.125–126 (also noting an exception to this distribution).

2. Applying the Rules. In Ulpian's hypothetical situation, the testator had two heirs upon intestacy: his son-in-power and an emancipated son. In his will, the testator passed over the emancipated son, left only a twelfth to his son-in-power, and directed the rest of his estate elsewhere (e.g., to his widow). What happened next? Who won and who lost from the praetor's intervention? As Ulpian remarks, in this situation the son-in-power's share would increase from a twelfth to a half as a result of the emancipated son's claiming his share. In another situation, however, the son-in-power might lose: for example, if the will named him heir to the entire inheritance but passed over his emancipated brother. Could it be, though, that Ulpian uses his hypothetical situation to make a subtler point? Who is likely to have been the first person to object to the distribution in the will?

3. Collation. Though Ulpian does not mention this, his hypothetical situation raises another problem. Suppose that the son had been emancipated ten years before the testator's death; during that time, unlike his brother who was still in power, he would have been able to amass property of his own. Should he profit from his early independence? In order to prevent this possible unfairness, the praetor required him to combine his own property (or its value) with his father's estate, through a process called collation (*collatio*). The two sons would then divide the total. The resulting legal problems are discussed at length in D. 37.6. See also Case 163.

4. Collation of Dowry. Suppose that the father in Ulpian's hypothetical situation had also left a married daughter-in-power to whom he had given a dowry; if she wishes to claim her intestate share in the estate, should she be first required to contribute the value of her dowry? See D. 37.7 (yes). Is this situation entirely equivalent to the one discussed in the previous paragraph? Remember that the daughter does not have control of her dowry during the marriage.

5. Adoptees. The rights created for adopted children who are instituted heirs under the will of their biological father are discussed in the next case.

CASE 187: Adopted Children*

D. 37.4.8.11 (Ulpianus libro quadragesimo ad edictum)

In adoptionem datos filios non summoveri praetor voluit, modo heredes instituti sint, et hoc iustissime eum fecisse Labeo ait: nec enim in totum extranei sunt. ergo si fuerunt heredes scripti, accipient contra tabulas bonorum possessionem, sed ipsi soli non committent edictum, nisi fuerit alius praeteritus ex liberis qui solent committere edictum. sed si ipse scriptus non sit, sed alius, qui ei adquirere hereditatem potest, non est in ea causa, ut eum ad bonorum possessionem contra tabulas admittamus.

(Ulpian in the fortieth book on the Edict)

The praetor did not want the exclusion of children given in adoption, provided that they were instituted heirs. Labeo states that he acted very justly; for they are not entirely outsiders. Therefore, they will receive *bonorum possessio* against the terms of the will if they were named heirs in the will. But they themselves will not invoke the Edict unless someone else has been passed over from among the category of *liberi* who are accustomed to invoke the Edict. But if he himself has not been instituted heir, and someone else has been who can obtain the inheritance for him, he is not eligible for our grant of *bonorum possessio* against the terms of a will.

1. Adoptees in the Will. This Case illustrates how *bonorum possessio* against the terms of the will differed from *bonorum possessio* on intestacy. Children given in adoption have no intestate claim to the estate of their biological father. The same is not true for *bonorum possessio* against the terms of the will, provided that the biological father's will appointed them heirs at least to a small fraction of the estate. In that case, if the will is challenged because it omits one or more *liberi,* an adopted child is raised to the position enjoyed by children-in-power and *emancipati.* Why should adopted children have this privilege? What does Ulpian (perhaps quoting Labeo) mean when he says that they are not entirely outsiders? How is it relevant that they were named heirs?

2. Entitlement to a Claim. Besides the requirement that the adoptee be named in the biological father's will, Ulpian imposes another condition. The adoptee cannot make a claim to *bonorum possessio* against the terms of a will unless one of the *liberi* has been passed over, making his position even more derivative. If this happens, can the adoptee take action, or does he or she have to wait until the person passed over applies to the praetor?

3. Strict Requirements. The last sentence of this Case states that the adoptee, to be eligible for *bonorum possessio* against the terms of a will, must be named as an heir in the will in question, not just as the beneficiary of a trust (*fideicommissum*). What is the reason for this requirement? Will only biological children benefit from this privilege of being eligible to take possession against the will? See Ulpian, D. 37.4.8.12 (yes).

CASE 188: Passing over *Sui Heredes*

D. 37.4.13.2 (Iulianus libro vicesimo tertio Digestorum)

Si pater emancipato filio praeterito heredes duos scripserit, filium quem in potestate habebat et alterum quem in adoptionem dederat, ex quo duos nepotes in familia retinuerat, qui et ipsi testamento praeteriti sint: bonorum possessionem pro parte tertia emancipatus, pro parte tertia is qui in potestate remansit, pro parte tertia qui in adoptionem datus est et filii eius simul habebunt, ita ut sextans patri, sextans nepotibus cedat.

(Julian in the twenty-third book of his *Digests*)

A father (in his will) passed over his emancipated son and instituted, as his two heirs, his son-in-power along with another son he had given in adoption, from whom he had kept two grandsons in his *familia;* but they themselves were also passed over.

    The emancipated son will receive *bonorum possessio* (against the terms of the will) of a third share; the son-in-power will receive a third share; and the son given in adoption and his children will receive a third share all together, with a sixth going to the father and a sixth to the grandchildren.

Hypothetical Situation

Titius has three sons, Aulus, Gaius, and Marcus. He keeps Aulus in power, emancipates Gaius, and gives Marcus away in adoption. In his will, Titius institutes Aulus and Marcus as heirs but passes over Gaius and Marcus's two children, who remained in their grandfather's power. After Titius's death, the praetor throws out the will. Why?

1. Grandchildren Cut Out of the Will. As we saw in the previous two Cases, the praetor granted *bonorum possessio* against the terms of a will not only if any *sui heredes* were passed over but also if an emancipated child was ignored. In this Case, even if the emancipated son had been either disinherited or made an heir, the will would have been invalid because the two grandchildren whom the testator passed over were *sui heredes*. Do you see why?

2. A Smaller Slice of the Pie. On the rules for intestate succession, see Part A above. Normally, if a son is no longer in a father's power because of death or adoption, the son's share is split by his children still in their grandfather's power. In this Case, why do the two grandchildren, who had remained in their grandfather's power but became *sui iuris* upon his death, have to be content with only a sixth of the estate instead of a full third? Or why does the fact that their father is alive not exclude them entirely? See Case 163, along with its Discussion.

3. Matching Wits with the Jurists. This Case and the next three illustrate some of the many complex situations considered by the jurists. Try to isolate the principles that determine their decisions in these (often rather bizarre) cases.

CASE 189: The Son of an Adopted Child

D. 37.4.21 pr. (Modestinus libro sexto Pandectarum)

Si is, qui filium et ex eo nepotem in potestatem habebat, filium in adoptionem dedit nepote retento in potestate, postea filius emancipatus a patre adoptivo decessit extraneis heredibus institutis: filius huius, qui in potestate avi remansit, contra tabulas patris sui bonorum possessionem petere poterit, quamvis numquam in potestate huius fuerit. ideo nec debuisse in potestate esse videtur. nam, si aliter observatur, nec si emancipatus filius fuerit, nepos ex eo, qui in potestate avi remansit, bonorum possessionem contra tabulas petere poterit.

(Modestinus in the sixth book of his *Pandects*)

A man had in his power a son and through him a grandson. He gave the son in adoption, while keeping the grandson in his power. Later this son, after having been emancipated by his adoptive father, died, with non–family members named as his heirs.

His son, who remained in his grandfather's power, can apply for *bonorum possessio* against the terms of his father's will, even though he was never in his father's power. And so it does not seem necessary to have been in power. For, if any other rule is observed, and if the son had been emancipated, the grandson through him, who remained in the power of his grandfather, will not be able to request *bonorum possessio* against the terms of a will.

Hypothetical Situation

Titius gives his son in adoption to Maevius, while keeping in his power his grandson through this son. Maevius later emancipates the son, who dies leaving a will that institutes heirs only from outside his family of birth. Is this will invalid, and if so, why? What can the grandson claim from his father's estate?

1. A Disputed Will. All we are told about the will is that the son instituted non–family members (*extranei*) as heirs. Is it likelier that he passed over his biological son or that he explicitly disinherited him? Would the testator have assumed it was necessary to disinherit his son expressly? Is it fair to hold him to a requirement not found in the law?

2. Never in Power. The grandson was never in his biological father's power, so that he was in no position to be either emancipated or given away by him in adoption. What basis is there for recognizing the grandson's claim to *bonorum possessio*? Is he being analogized to an *emancipatus* or in some way considered an *emancipatus* in reverse?

3. A Problem. Suppose that a *pater familias* emancipated a son but kept in power a grandson by him; later he gave the grandson in adoption to the

emancipated son. The *pater* dies and his will passes over his grandson; can the grandson claim *bonorum possessio* against the will? Modestinus (D. 37.4.21.1–2) says that he can since he was not "in another's *familia*" (meaning what?). The outcome, says Modestinus, would be different if the emancipated son had adopted a child from an outsider, since that child would have no relationship to the grandfather.

CASE 190: Adopting a Son as a Grandson

D. 37.4.1.7 (Ulpianus libro trigesimo nono ad edictum)

Qui habebat filium, habebat et nepotem ex eo, filium emancipavit et adoptavit in locum nepotis, deinde emancipavit: quaeritur an nepoti obstet. et mihi magis videtur hunc nepotem non excludi, sive pater eius in adoptione mansisset quasi nepos sive emancipatus est: puto enim et emancipato patre nepotem quoque cum patre suo ex edicto admitti.

(Ulpian in the thirty-ninth book on the Edict)

A man had a son and through him a grandson. He emancipated the son and adopted him as a grandson; then he emancipated him (again). The question arises as to whether he (the biological son) prejudices (the claim of) the grandson (to *bonorum possessio* against the will).

What seems preferable to me is that the grandson in question is not excluded, no matter whether his father had remained as an adopted grandson or was emancipated (for the second time). For I believe that even if the father were emancipated (again), the grandson is admitted together with his father, in accord with the Edict.

1. Context. What does Ulpian presume has already happened in order for these questions to be raised? Has the grandfather's will already been successfully contested?

2. Rationale for Adoption. Why would a man adopt his son as his grandson, and why would he subsequently reemancipate him? Cases such as this one may suggest to you that some Roman householders pursued a restless strategy of shaping and reshaping the structure of their families, with repeated adoptions and emancipations of the persons subject to their power. What reasons might have impelled this sort of manipulation? Is it likely to have been largely the result of momentary pique, or could some more rational motive underlie their conduct?

3. Holding. Ulpian appears to hold that the son and grandson are entitled to equal shares of the inheritance under the rules for *bonorum possessio* against the terms of a will. How do you explain this?

4. Capital Exile. In the following text (D. 37.4.1.8), Ulpian considers a situation in which a *pater familias* has a son and through him a grandson; the son was convicted of a crime and deported, with loss of civil rights. Ulpian holds that whether this son was exiled after being emancipated or while still in his father's power, he does not prejudice the claim of the grandson to the grandfather's estate. Ulpian's rationale is that someone deported is treated like a dead person. Why is the rule the same both when the father is emancipated and when he is still in power?

CASE 191: Adopting a Grandson as a Son

D. 37.4.3.1–2 (Ulpianus libro trigesimo nono ad edictum)

(1) Si duos habens nepotes alterum emancipatum loco filii adoptaverit, videndum, an solus ille quasi filius admittatur: quod ita scilicet procedit, si quasi patrem eius nepotis, quem retinuerat, sic adoptaverit: melius est autem dicere posse eum solum ad bonorum possessionem pervenire. (2) Sed si sit hic nepos emancipatus, verum est dicere non admitti eum quasi filium: hic enim quasi filius non est ex liberis, cum iura adoptionis emancipatione finita sint.

(Ulpian in the thirty-ninth book on the Edict)

(1) If someone with two grandsons emancipates one and (then) adopts him as a son, it must be determined whether only that quasi son is admitted (to *bonorum possessio*). This is the result, to be sure, if the grandfather had adopted him as the father of the grandson whom he had retained (as a grandson). But the better result (also in the earlier case) is that he alone can receive *bonorum possessio*.

    (2) But if the grandson in question has been emancipated (a second time), the correct holding is that he is not admitted as a son. For this quasi son does not rank as one of the praetorian *liberi,* since the rights created by adoption were extinguished by emancipation.

Hypothetical Situation

Titius emancipates one of his two grandsons and then adopts him as a son. Titius dies and his will is successfully challenged. Can the grandson who was adopted as a son claim *bonorum possessio* against the terms of the will? Does the other grandson also have a claim?

1. The Grandson as Son. Is it clear why the grandson adopted as a son would unambiguously exclude the other one if he were adopted as his father? Is it equally clear why the same result should obtain when the emancipated grandson was not adopted as the father of the grandson still in his father's power? Ulpian's language is a bit odd, and one phrase (*melius est*) suggests not all jurists would agree with him. What are the arguments on either side?

2. Emancipation Cancels Adoption. Why should the grandson who was emancipated, adopted as a son, and then reemancipated not enjoy the same rights as a son who has been emancipated? What does Ulpian mean when he says that such a grandson does not rank as one of the praetorian *liberi*? Why wouldn't he revert to being a grandson?

SECTION 4. The Undutiful Will

CASE 192: Complaints about the Will*

D. 5.2.1 (Ulpianus libro quarto decimo ad edictum)

Sciendum est frequentes esse inofficiosi querellas: omnibus enim tam parentibus quam liberis de inofficioso licet disputare. cognati enim proprii qui sunt ultra fratrem melius facerent, si se sumptibus inanibus non vexarent, cum optinere spem non haberent.

(Ulpian in the fourteenth book on the Edict)

It should be realized that complaints about the undutifulness (of a will) are common, since it is open to parents as well as to children to argue over undutifulness. One's relatives (*cognati*) more distant than a brother would do better not to trouble themselves with futile expense, since they have no hope of succeeding (in such a lawsuit).

1. Duty and the Will. Only persons entitled to succeed on intestacy could bring an action (called the *querella inofficiosi,* "complaint of undutifulness") charging that a will treated close family members inappropriately. To qualify, a plaintiff's bequest under the will had to be less than a quarter of what he or she would have received on intestacy (Ulpian, D. 5.2.8.8). Success normally meant that the will was overturned entirely, and the regime on intestacy went into effect (Ulpian, D. 5.2.6.1, 8.16); but if there were multiple heirs, each had to be sued individually and split decisions were not unknown (see Pliny, *Epistulae* 6.33.2–6; Papinian, D. 5.2.15.2; Ulpian, D. 5.2.24). Thus, the successful plaintiff could receive at least four times the amount required to exclude his suit in the first place but had to bear the cost and risk of bringing one or more lawsuits. Does this seem reasonable? How are the interests of the various parties balanced against one another? For instance, what incentives are provided to testators to give their close family members at least a pittance?

2. Chances of Success. Ulpian concedes that a broad circle of relations might bring a suit against an undutiful will but notes that relatives beyond the degree of brother have no chance of success. Why should this be so? Why didn't the praetor simply exclude such suits as a matter of law? Does Ulpian mean to suggest that suits by close relatives were usually worth the expense? In any case, it is worth noting that the complaint was available not only to agnates but to relatives by females as well (Marcellus, D. 5.2.5).

3. Disrespecting the Emperor. Imperial rescripts, says Ulpian (D. 5.2.8.2), have often held that a suit on an undutiful will can be brought even when the emperor has been named as an heir. Why might this have been a concern? Would the legal admissibility of such lawsuits be the only worry that might deter potential plaintiffs?

CASE 193: Duty and Sanity*

D. 5.2.2 (Marcianus libro quarto Institutionum)

Hoc colore <de> inofficioso testamento agitur, quasi non sanae mentis fuerunt, ut testamentum ordinarent. et hoc dicitur non quasi vere furiosus vel demens testatus sit, sed recte quidem fecit testamentum, sed non ex officio pietatis: nam si vere furiosus esset vel demens, nullum est testamentum.

(Marcian in the fourth book of his *Institutes*)

An action on an undutiful will is brought on the argumentative premise that they (the testators) were of unsound mind for composing a will. And this claim is made on the basis, not that the testator was actually insane or demented, but that he or she made a will that is, to be sure, legally valid but inconsistent with the duty imposed by *pietas*. For if he or she were truly insane or demented, the will is invalid.

1. Madmen and the Will. The praetor officially recognized some persons as insane (*furiosi*) and granted guardians (*curatores*) to look after their property (see Case 223). The insane lacked legal capacity to make a valid will, although a will made prior to the onset of insanity or during intermittent lucidity remained valid (Paul, *Sent.* 3.4a.5; *Tit. Ulp.* 20.13). Some sources hint that a will's validity could also be attacked on the ground that the testator was actually insane though not declared so (e.g., Paul, *Sent.* 3.4a.11). According to Marcian, how does such an attack differ from the complaint on undutifulness? In this action is actual insanity an issue at all?

2. Degrees of Madness. If the result is the same no matter whether the testator was insane or undutiful, what is the point of Marcian's distinction? Is it that proving madness is more difficult than proving lack of duty? Or that failure to observe a basic social responsibility can be regarded as madness per se? In other words, does Roman law consider highly inappropriate social behavior as akin to madness? What arguments might be available to a defender of the will as written?

3. Pietas. This word means roughly "family affection," "the love and respect owed by close family members to one another." Does the concept help explain Marcian's argument about quasi insanity? A text of Marcellus (D. 5.2.5) appears to equate this state of mind with unfairness: a testator "seems to have been of unsound mind when he unfairly (*inique*) drew up his will." Unfairness by whose standard? In order to upset a will, should it be enough to say of it that the testator "unfairly" allocated his estate among his near relatives?

CASE 194: Evil Stepmothers

D. 5.2.3 (Marcellus libro tertio Digestorum)

Inofficiosum testamentum dicere hoc est allegare, quare exheredari vel praeteriri non debuerit: quod plerumque accidit, cum falso parentes instimulati liberos suos vel exheredant vel praetereunt.

D. 5.2.4 (Gaius libro singulari ad legem Glitiam)

Non est enim consentiendum parentibus, qui iniuriam adversus liberos suos testamento inducunt: quod plerumque faciunt, maligne circa sanguinem suum inferentes iudicium, novercalibus delenimentis instigationibusve corrupti.

(Marcellus in the third book of his *Digests*)

To state that a will is undutiful is to make a claim as to why one ought not to have been disinherited or passed over. This generally occurs when parents are spurred by falsehoods to disinherit or pass over their children.

(Gaius in his monograph on the *lex Glitia*)

For we must not condone parents' inflicting an injustice on their children in their wills. They (the fathers) generally do this by making a negative judgment on their own flesh and blood after they have been misled by flattery and provocations from stepmothers.

1. Mistake. Marcellus says that a parent who composes an undutiful will is typically induced by a mistake. Is this a simple factual error or an error of judgment, or does Marcellus wish to leave the question open? Is there a hint in his language that someone else is usually responsible for the misinformation? Is his view different from that of Marcian in Case 193?

2. Erroneous Reports. A mother thinks her son is dead and institutes someone else as her heir. Can the son sue on the ground of an undutiful will? Yes, according to Ulpian (D. 5.2.27.4). Why should this be so? Has the mother acted in a manner that can be characterized as insane or lacking in *pietas*? Was she unfair? Paul (D. 5.2.28) relates a case in which a mother, acting on a false report that her soldier-son had perished, appointed others as her heirs. The Emperor Hadrian (reign: A.D. 117–138) granted the inheritance to the son but allowed the other arrangements in the will (the legacies and manumissions of slaves) to stand. The jurist reports that this decision was controversial, since the usual practice for undutiful wills was to invalidate all of their provisions. Do you agree with Hadrian? His critics? Should the will have been upheld, at any rate against an attack on this ground?

3. The Stepmother. Gaius justifies treating the testator's will as "undutiful" when it is inspired by the machinations of a wicked stepmother. What, aside from popular prejudice, makes the stepmother a likely candidate for this role? Must her "undue influence" be actually proven?

CASE 195: A Mother's Mistake*

C. 3.28.3 (Impp. Severus et Antoninus AA. Ianuario)

(pr.) Si mater filiis duobus institutis tertio post testamentum suscepto, cum mutare idem testamentum potuisset, hoc facere neglexisset, merito utpote non iustis rationibus neglectus de inofficioso querellam instituere poterat. (1) Sed cum eam in puerperio vita cessisse proponas, repentini casus iniquitas per coniecturam maternae pietatis emendanda est. quare filio tuo, cui nihil praeter maternum fatum imputari potest, perinde virilem portionem tribuendam esse censemus, ac si omnes filios heredes instituisset. (2) Sin autem heredes scripti extranei erant, tunc de inofficioso testamento actionem instituere non prohibetur.

(The Emperors Septimius Severus and Caracalla to Januarius; A.D. 197)

(pr.) If a mother instituted her two children as her heirs and (then) gave birth to a third after making her will, and at a time when she was in a position to make changes to this very will, she neglected to do so, the child, insofar as he was omitted for no good reason, can justly bring a complaint of undutifulness.
    (1) But when you mention the (additional) fact that (the mother) died in childbirth, the unfairness that this unexpected mischance generated ought to be corrected by inferring the mother's *pietas*. For this reason, we ordain that your son, to whom no blame can be imputed beyond his mother's ill luck, ought to be assigned his full share of the inheritance, just as if his mother had appointed all of her children as heirs. (2) If, on the other hand, non–family members were appointed as heirs, then he is not prevented from bringing suit against an undutiful will.

1. Imperial Rescript. Severus and Caracalla (joint reign: A.D. 197–211) respond to an inquiry evidently put by the father of a child omitted from his mother's will; her other two children may be from a prior marriage. What facts are assumed? Has a suit actually been filed yet?

2. The Neglectful Mother. On the first set of facts, what precisely did the mother do wrong? Was this an oversight, or is she actually at fault for not changing her will after giving birth?

3. Death in Childbirth. Why is it that the "unexpected mischance" of death in childbirth ought to be corrected by inferring the mother's *pietas*? Is it correct to assume that the mother, had she survived giving birth, would have written her son into her will for an equal portion of her inheritance? Does the decision essentially rewrite her will to conform to social expectations?

4. Outside Heirs. If the mother had instituted non–family members, why would that open up a suit against an undutiful will? Who would be entitled to bring the claim?

5. Illegitimate Children. If a mother's will ignores her illegitimate child, can her child bring this action? See Ulpian, D. 5.2.29.1 (yes). Is this consistent with other law on the subject?

CASE 196: Multiple Claims

D. 5.2.14 (Papinianus libro quinto Quaestionum)

Pater filium emancipavit et nepotem ex eo retinuit: emancipatus suscepto postea filio, duobus exheredatis patre praeterito vita decessit. in quaestione de inofficiosi testamenti praecedente causa filiorum patris intentio adhuc pendet. quod si contra filios iudicetur, pater ad querellam vocatur et suam intentionem implere potest.

D. 5.2.15 pr. (Papinianus libro quarto decimo Quaestionum)

Nam etsi parentibus non debetur filiorum hereditas propter votum parentium et naturalem erga filios caritatem: turbato tamen ordine mortalitatis non minus parentibus quam liberis pie relinqui debet.

(Papinian in the fifth book of his *Questions of Law*)

A father emancipated his son while keeping in his power a grandson by that son. The emancipated son, after having another son, died (with a will) disinheriting both sons and passing over his father. In a hearing over an undutiful will, because the sons' cause takes precedence, the father's claim remains in suspense. But if judgment is against the sons, the father is summoned to bring a complaint (against an undutiful will) and can pursue his case.

(Papinian in the fourteenth book of his *Questions of Law*)

For although the parents' claim to inheritance from their children is not based upon the parents' desires and their natural affection for their children, still, when the usual pattern of mortality is upset, *pietas* should characterize no less bequests made to parents than those to children.

1. Three Claimants. All three parties had a claim to the intestate succession of this *emancipatus,* which in turn justifies their suit against an undutiful will. Why does the sons' suit take precedence over that of their grandfather? What hope does he have if their suit fails? How will disposition of the property be affected by which plaintiffs win?

2. Multiple Remedies. Can the father also claim *bonorum possessio* against the terms of a will? Would the result be any different?

3. A Fine Distinction. What Papinian says in the second text is not altogether clear, but he seems to make the following distinction: when a child claims inheritance from a parent, this claim is founded on what parents are likely to have wanted and on their emotional attachment to their child; but when a parent claims inheritance from a child, the claim is founded only on a more general and hence vaguer consideration of familial affection (*pietas*). Does this explain why the sons in this Case take precedence over their father? Compare Cases 193–194.

CASE 197: Procedural Alternatives

D. 5.2.8.12 (Ulpianus libro quarto decimo ad edictum)

Si quis et irritum dicat testamentum vel ruptum et inofficiosum, condicio ei deferri debet, utrum prius movere volet.

D. 37.4.8 pr. (Ulpianus libro quadragesimo ad edictum)

Non putavit praetor exheredatione notatos et remotos ad contra tabulas bonorum possessionem admittendos, sicuti nec iure civili testamenta parentium turbant: sane si velint inofficiosi querellam institutere, est in ipsorum arbitrio.

(Ulpian in the fourteenth book on the Edict)

If someone should claim that a will is not only ineffective or broken but undutiful as well, he or she should be permitted to choose which action to bring first.

(Ulpian in the fortieth book on the Edict)

The praetor did not think that persons who were singled out and disinherited should be allowed to claim *bonorum possessio* against the terms of a will, just as they also do not overturn their parents' wills under the *ius civile*. To be sure, if they should wish to bring a complaint about undutifulness, this is up to them.

1. Choice of Remedies. Under what circumstances can a prospective litigant choose whether to claim *bonorum possessio* against the terms of a will or instead sue on an undutiful will? Paul (D. 5.2.23 pr.) discusses a case in which a father's will passes over his emancipated son and institutes as heir a grandson by him; the grandfather had retained the boy in his power. As Paul decides, the son can seek *bonorum possessio* but cannot sue on undutifulness; however, if the son had been disinherited, then he could raise the issue of undutifulness. How is Paul's decision to be explained, and can it be entirely reconciled with this Case?

2. The Better Remedy. Do the two suits, if successful, have the same result? Which might a litigant prefer? If one case is lost, can the other remedy still be sought?

3. Not My Son. In another text (D. 5.2.27.1) Ulpian says that if, in his will, a testator denies that someone is his son but nonetheless disinherits him, the putative son can still attack the will as undutiful. Why is this true? Why can he not bring a claim for *bonorum possessio* against the terms of a will?

4. Why Permit the *Querella*? "There were perfectly good reasons for disinheriting relatives, but it is rather interesting that the jurists do not appear to dis-

cuss them. It may be that they took the high-minded view that this was a matter for the rhetoricians" (David Johnston). Would Roman law have been better off to approach the problem more directly? What reasons might the Romans have had for such caution?

PART C

Bequests to Nonheirs

The primary function of a will in classical Roman law was to appoint an heir or heirs, who would then succeed into the position of the testator according to their shares of the inheritance. The testator's estate may therefore be thought of as a sort of pie that is apportioned by the will. The ultimate size of the pie, however, can be strongly affected by legacies and other bequests, which can substantially reduce the assets of an estate. As Florentinus puts it (D. 30.116 pr.): "A legacy is a deduction from the inheritance by which a testator wishes there to be transferred to someone property out of that which would (otherwise) be entirely the heir's."

Strategies of property devolution become ever more complex as we move to consider nonheir bequests. These must be examined in light of the testator's plan regarding the heirs to the estate. For example, a child might be disinherited only so that he or she might be spared the obligations of inheritance and advantaged by a legacy or trust; the jurist Ulpian tells us explicitly that trusts were used in this way (D. 28.2.18 = Case 180). While reading the Cases below, ask yourself precisely how these bequests are being used to supplement the testator's goals in instituting heirs.

Multiplying the testator's options could support a variety of ends. If the children were deemed the main beneficiaries of the estate, how would a widow be provided for? A legacy of personal belongings, as well as the obligatory return of the dowry, was one answer. A life interest in a share of the property, to revert to the heirs upon her death, was another possibility. Many scholars think usufruct was invented to serve precisely such a purpose.

The three main forms of bequest—legacy, trust, and gift on account of death (*mortis causa*)—each display a similar process of transformation at work. Each was introduced to provide testators with greater freedom and flexibility; and each was then gradually domesticated by subjecting it to the broader rules that governed the law of succession. This begins with legacies, which together with inheritance itself were regulated by positive legislation such as the *lex Falcidia* and the Augustan marriage law. The jurists, in close consultation with the Roman government, next extended these regulations to trust, and then to gift *mortis causa*. This process may be viewed as one more example of the tension between personal freedom and social responsibility that stands out as a defining characteristic of the Roman law of succession.

Even the present chapter's very short introduction to the law of succession should be sufficient to persuade you of the extraordinary complexity of this area of Roman law. One may well come away with mixed feelings. As Fritz Schulz once observed, "The classical lawyers have studied the law of legacies (*legata* and *fideicommissa*) with unconcealed predilection. The classical writings . . . are full of subtle and detailed inquiries concerning legacies. . . . However, this achievement of the classical lawyers reveals their limitations as well as their greatness. Studying these discussions in full detail, one cannot help wondering whether it was really justifiable to spend so much time and labour on these difficult and tortuous questions, the practical importance of which was so slight." As you read this part, see if you agree.

CASE 198: The *Lex Falcidia**

D. 35.2.1 pr. (Paulus libro singulari ad legem Falcidiam)

Lex Falcidia lata est, quae primo capite liberam legandi facultatem dedit usque ad dodrantem his verbis: "qui cives Romani sunt, qui eorum post hanc legem rogatam testamentum facere volet, ut eam pecuniam easque res quibusque dare legare volet, ius potestasque esto, ut hac lege [sequenti] licebit." secundo capite modum legatorum constituit his verbis: "quicumque civis Romanus post hanc legem rogatam testamentum faciet, is quantam cuique civi Romano pecuniam iure publico dare legare volet, ius potestasque esto, dum ita detur legatum ne minus quam partem quartam hereditatis eo testamento heredes capiant, <itaque> eis, quibus quid ita datum legatumve erit eam pecuniam sine fraude sua capere liceto isque heres, qui eam pecuniam dare iussus damnatus erit, eam pecuniam debeto dare, quam <dare> damnatus est."

(Paul in his monograph on the *lex Falcidia*)

There was enacted the *lex Falcidia,* which in its first chapter granted freedom to make legacies up to three quarters (of one's estate), using these words: "Let any Roman citizen who, after this statute becomes law, wishes to make a will have the right and power to give or legate his or her money to whomever he or she wishes, so far as it is permitted by this law."

In the second chapter it sets a limit to legacies with the following words: "Let any Roman citizen who, after this statute becomes law, makes a will have the right and power to give and legate under our law as much money to any Roman citizen as he or she wishes, so long as what is given and bequeathed does not leave less than a quarter of the estate for the heirs to take under that will. Therefore, those to whom something is given and legated under these conditions will be permitted to take that money lawfully, and the heir in this case, who is obliged to make over the money, ought to give that money that he is obliged to give."

1. Law on Legacies. The *lex Falcidia,* passed in 40 B.C., superseded the provisions of earlier statutes that attempted to place limits on legacy giving. These statutes were defectively drafted and proved insufficient, but the *lex Falcidia* was much more enduring. All these laws sought to protect the interests of the heirs. Why might this have been considered desirable? What was the consequence if no one accepted an inheritance?

2. The Falcidian *Quarta*. Much of the juristic discussion on this law centers on calculating the one-fourth portion (*quarta*) that was reserved for the heir or heirs. For example, the *quarta* was assessed on the basis of the estate's value at the time of the testator's death; and only assets counted; that is, debts were excluded, as were funeral expenses and the value of slaves freed under the will. (See Paul, *Sent.* 4.3.3; Gaius, D. 35.2.73.) Some types of legacies to close family members were, as we shall see, also exempted from inclusion in the calcu-

lation of the Falcidian *quarta*. Did these rules favor the heirs or the legatees? What would happen, for instance, if the decedent's debts exceeded one quarter of the estate?

3. Sanctions. If legacies did not leave heirs with their Falcidian *quarta,* the will was not rendered invalid; all that happened was that either the legacies were reduced proportionately (Paul, *Sent.* 3.8.1) or the legatee was required to refund the excess (Gaius, D. 35.2.80.1). Testators were not permitted to circumvent the statute (Scaevola, D. 35.2.27), but they could place the burden of it on some legatees more than others (Africanus, D. 35.2.88.2).

4. Why Did the Problem Arise? Of course, since in writing their wills testators could seldom be even approximately certain what their estates would be worth at their death, some may have inadvertently legated too much. Still, legal sources suggest that many testators deliberately piled on the legacies, thereby diminishing the value of the inheritance for the named heirs. As you read the Cases that follow, consider what their motives might have been.

5. The Problem of Form, Revisited. The law of legacies was highly complicated, mainly because there were four different forms of legacy, each of which had a particular wording and could be used only with specific effects and subject to specific rules; see, for a reasonably detailed description, Gaius, *Inst.* 2.192–223. Is it reasonable to assume that, just as formal requirements operate to favor intestate heirs over the heirs in the will, so legacy rules favor heirs over legatees? Does the *lex Falcidia* tend to support this assumption?

CASE 199: Legacy of a Dowry*

D. 33.4.1 pr., 2 (Ulpianus libro nono decimo ad Sabinum)

(pr.) Cum dos relegatur, verum est id dotis legato inesse, quod actione de dote inerat. . . . (2) Et verum est commodum in dote relegata esse repraesentationis, quamvis annua die dos praestaretur.

(Ulpian in the nineteenth book on Sabinus)

(pr.) When a dowry is returned by legacy, the correct rule is that what is obtained through an action on dowry (*actio de dote*) is (also) obtained through legacy of a dowry. . . .

(2) And the correct rule is that the advantage in restoring a dowry through a legacy consists in immediate payment, while a dowry would be paid in annual installments.

1. Return of the Dowry. While a marriage lasted, the dowry remained in the husband's ownership, but if he predeceased his wife, the dowry usually had to be returned to her. A wife could reclaim what she was owed through a suit called the *actio rei uxoriae* (see Chapter II.D.2). The legacy allowed the husband to return the dowry in his will. Why was this preferable to recovery through the *actio rei uxoriae*?

2. The Falcidian *Quarta*. Does the fact that the dowry is actionable suggest that it should be treated as a debt and excluded from the calculation of the Falcidian *quarta*? Note that Ulpian in this text speaks of "restoring" the dowry. Gaius (D. 35.2.81.1) observes that legacy of a dowry falls outside the calculation "because the wife is held to recover her own property." Does it make sense to speak of a legacy when the estate already is under an obligation to return the dowry?

3. Immediate Payment. The standard schedule for repayment of a cash dowry was three annual installments (*Tit. Ulp.* 6.8). As this Case points out, legacy of a dowry bypassed that schedule by requiring one immediate payment. Why might the testator have desired this, despite the difficulties it could cause the heir in raising cash?

4. *Bonorum Possessio.* The successful claimant to *bonorum possessio* against the terms of a will was obliged by the praetor to pay legacies to close family members of the decedent, including the legacy of return of a dowry; see Ulpian, D. 37.5.1 pr.

CASE 200: Legacy in Place of a Dowry

D. 33.4.6 (Labeo libro secundo Posteriorum a Iavoleno Epitomatorum)

(pr.) Cum scriptum esset: "quae pecunia propter uxorem meam ad me venit quinquaginta, tantundem pro ea dote heres meus dato," quamvis quadraginta dotis fuissent, tamen quinquaginta debere Alfenus Varus Servium respondisse scribit, quia proposita summa quinquaginta adiecta sit. (1) Item ei, quae dotem nullam habebat, vir sic legaverat: "quanta pecunia dotis nomine" et reliqua, "pro ea quinquaginta heres dato." deberi ei legatum Ofilius Cascellius, item et Servii auditores rettulerunt: perinde habendum esse ac si servus alicui mortuus aut pro eo centum legata essent. quod verum est, quia his verbis non dos ipsa, sed pro dote pecunia legata videtur.

(Labeo in the second book of his *Posthumous Works as Epitomized by Javolenus*)

(pr.) The terms (of a will) said: "As to the 50 (thousand sesterces) in cash that came to me on account of my wife, let my heir give (her) the same amount in place of this dowry." Although the (actual) dowry amounted to 40, nevertheless Alfenus Varus records Servius's response that he (the heir) owes 50, since the amount intended was set at 50.

(1) Likewise, if a woman had no dowry and her husband made a legacy to her in the following manner: "As much money as is in the dowry account, etc., in place of that let my heir give 50," Ofilius, Cascellius, and the students of Servius held that the legacy was due to her, the same rule being applied as when a legacy was made of a slave who (subsequently) died or of 100 in place of him. This view is correct because by these words it is not the dowry itself but money in place of a dowry that was legated.

1. *Pro Dote*. The husband might frame a legacy in terms of a monetary amount instead of the actual items of property in the dowry. This device possessed all the advantages of the *legatum dotis* over the *actio rei uxoriae*. In addition, the usual expenses associated with the dowry were not deducted from its value (compare Cases 84–88). Nor was the value lowered by loss of an item such as the death of a slave. Finally, the amount did not have to be linked to the actual value of the dowry. Indeed, as this Case shows, where the testator provided a cash estimate (see Justinian, *Inst.* 2.20.15), there did not have to be an actual dowry at all. Why is this so? Where the legacy exceeds the actual dowry, should the excess still be regarded as a debt?

2. The Amount Intended. Servius holds that if the amount stipulated in the legacy exceeds the value of a dowry, it is valid, because, in the hypothetical case given, "the amount intended was set at 50." Does this refer to the intention of the testator? Why should this intent be decisive? Would it matter if the amount intended was less than the value of the dowry?

3. Old and New Reasoning. How convincing is the analogy to the situation where the legacy is of a slave (worth 50, say) or of 100, where the slave dies before the legacy is conveyed? Is Labeo's justification, that the wording indicates the legacy was not of the actual dowry, any better? For instance, could the wife theoretically claim both the legacy and her dowry?

CASE 201: Generic Legacies*

D. 32.100.2 (Iavolenus libro secundo ex Posterioribus Labeonis)

"Uxori meae vestem, mundum muliebrem, ornamenta omnia, aurum argentum quod eius causa factum paratumque esset omne do lego." Trebatius haec verba "quod eius causa factum paratumque est," ad aurum et argentum dumtaxat referri putat, Proculus ad omnia, quod et verum est.

(Javolenus in the second book from the *Posthumous Works* of Labeo)

"To my wife, I give and legate the clothing, women's toiletries, all the jewelry, gold and silver, that has been made and acquired for her, all of it." Trebatius believes that the words "that has been made and acquired for her" refer only to the gold and silver; Proculus (believes they refer) to everything, which is also the correct view.

1. Testator's Intent. Which of the two opinions, that of Trebatius or that of Proculus, is better supported by the text of the will given in this passage? Are the jurists deciding intent on the basis of the wording, or do they rely instead on what they take to be common usage in such legacies? Does the ban on gifts to spouses (Cases 61–65) help explain the ruling here?

2. Categorical Bequests. The jurists elaborated complex categories for the individual rubrics of clothing, lady's personal-hygiene items, and jewelry named in such bequests to wives. "Clothing," for instance, was defined not only in terms of fabric or material but also by its purpose and use (Ulpian and Paul, D. 34.2.23–25). Does this building of categories suggest that social convention was decisive in construing an individual testator's intent? Note that Paul (D. 34.2.26) distinguishes clothing from jewelry on the basis of custom, even though some clothing is used for ornament rather than covering the body, and some jewelry for covering the body rather than ornament. Suppose a testator specified an item as jewelry that most people would consider to be an article of clothing. What would be the result at law? See also Case 58.

3. Who Wears Women's Clothing? Pomponius (D. 34.2.33) discusses the following problem: A testator, who was "accustomed to wear certain clothing that is also appropriate to women," legates to someone "my women's clothing"; does the legacy include the women's clothing he kept for his own use? According to Ulpian (D. 34.2.23.2), women's clothing was defined as that which a male could not wear "without incurring criticism"; and we can safely assume that the testator, in his personal life, violated that criterion. The issue in Pomponius's problem is this: should the words of the will be interpreted in their plain meaning, or should evidence for the specific intention of the testator be examined? Pomponius concludes: "the legacy is what the testator

meant, not what is actually male or female." This ought to mean that evidence of a testator's specific intent is relevant to interpreting a will. Is this result a good one? Note that if, during his life, the testator had promised by contract to convey to someone "all my women's clothing," his own ball gowns would have been included (Pomponius, D. 45.1.110.1). Inconsistent?

CASE 202: Things Acquired for a Wife

D. 34.2.10 (Pomponius libro quinto ad Quintum Mucium)

Quintus Mucius ait: si pater familias uxori vas aut vestimentum aut quippam aliud ita legavit "quod eius causa emptum paratumve esset," id videtur legasse, quod magis illius quam communis usus causa paratum esset. Pomponius: sed hoc verum est non solum, si ipsius viri et uxoris communis usus, sed etiam si liberorum eius aut alterius alicuius communis usus fuerit: id enim videtur demonstrasse, quod proprio usui uxoris comparatum sit. sed quod Quintus Mucius demonstrat "vas aut vestimentum aut quid aliud," efficit, ut falsa sint quae subiecimus: multum enim interest, generaliter an specialiter legentur haec. nam si generaliter, veluti ita "quae uxoris causa comparata sunt," vera est illius definitio: si vero ita scriptum fuerit "vestem illam purpuram," ut certa demonstraret, licet adiectum sit "quae eius causa empta paratave essent," licet neque empta neque parata neque in usum ei data sint, legatum omnimodo valet, quia certo corpore legato demonstratio falsa posita non peremit legatum. veluti si ita sit scriptum, "Stichum, quem ex venditione Titii emi": nam si neque emit aut ex alia venditione emit, legatum nihilo minus valet. plane si ita legatum fuerit "vas, aut vestimenta, aut quae uxoris causa parata sunt," tunc aeque erit vera Quinti Muci sententia: quo casu sciendum est, etiam si alienae res hae fuerint, quas putavit testator suas esse, heredem teneri, ut eas det.

(Pomponius in the fifth book on Quintus Mucius)

Quintus Mucius says: If a *pater familias* legates to his wife a vessel or clothing or anything else in the following way: "what has been bought or acquired for my wife," he appears to have legated that which was acquired more for her than for common use.

Pomponius (adds): This is the case not only where the use has been common to the husband himself and his wife but also where the use has been common to their children or any other person, for he seems to have indicated (with this phrase) that which was acquired for the particular use of the wife.

However, as Quintus Mucius suggests: (the wording) "a vessel or clothing or something else" casts doubt on our argument; for it makes a great deal of difference whether these things are legated generically or specifically. For if given generically, as for example, "the things that have been acquired for my wife," his holding is correct.

If, to be sure, the wording was "that purple clothing" so as to indicate particular objects, even though the phrase was added "which have been bought or acquired for her," the legacy will be absolutely valid even if these had been neither bought nor acquired nor given to her to use; for when a certain item has been given as a legacy, an ancillary erroneous identification does not invalidate it. For example, if the wording was "Stichus, whom I purchased at Titius's sale," the legacy is still valid if he (the testator) had either not bought him at all or bought him at another sale.

Clearly, if a legacy were framed as follows: "the vessel or garments or what has been acquired for my wife," then Quintus Mucius's opinion will be just as correct. In this case it must be made known that even if these things were someone else's property, which the testator (falsely) thought were his, the heir is obligated to give them.

1. **Acquired Objects and Sex.** The jurists construe "things acquired for a wife" as a broad category embracing clothing, jewelry, and other objects purchased for a wife (Ulpian, D. 32.45). Does this suggest a core definition that encompasses things only a woman would use? What about a litter, a sedan chair, or the slaves that would carry the wife in one of these? See Ulpian, D. 32.49 pr. (yes). Might things intended for use by men be included in such a legacy if the husband had in fact given them to his wife for her use? See Ulpian, D. 32.49.1 (yes).

2. **Mucius's Holding.** What precise distinction does Quintus Mucius draw in the first part of this case? Does he mean that the inclusion in the legacy depends in the final analysis on its exclusive use by the wife, rather than on the nature of the object itself? Ulpian elsewhere says (D. 32.49.2) that if an object was used by husband and wife in common, but he had made a practice of lending it, so to speak, for her use, it is included in the category of things acquired for a wife. Is this consistent with Mucius's holding?

3. **Generic versus Specific.** Quintus Mucius points out that his holding applies only when the legacy has been made generically through a phrase such as "the things acquired for my wife," but not when specific items are named. Why is this so? Pomponius adds that if the legacy reads "the vessel or garments or things that have been acquired for my wife," the same principle holds. Why? Is the latter wording easier to rule on than the wording "the things acquired for my wife"?

4. **Generic and/or Specific.** Does it matter whether the testator places "and" between a list of specific legated items and the catchall category "what has been acquired for my wife" or leaves this out? See Paul. D. 32.46 (yes). What is the difference? Is this an application of the plain-meaning rule?

5. **Mistake.** What rule does Mucius apply if the testator specified certain items described as "acquired for my wife" when in fact one or more of these items was not so acquired? Is his rule consistent with his other holdings in this Case? Suppose the testator legated something he erroneously thought belonged to him? Does the Case suggest the heir must seek to acquire this for the legatee or, if it cannot be acquired, pay its value? (The answer is yes.)

6. **Presumption of Innocence.** Consider the famous presumption of Quintus Mucius, as reported by Pomponius in Case 59. Does this seem to concern the

inclusion of the items of disputed origin in a generic legacy of "things acquired for a wife"? Quintus Mucius evidently wants to avoid encouraging challenges to the will based on allegations about the wife's infidelity. Does this seem to privilege such property excessively?

7. The Falcidian Exception. The *lex Falcidia* specifically exempted "things acquired for a wife" from the calculation of the *quarta*. Was such property perhaps regarded as informally "owed" to the wife, to be repaid in a manner analogous to that of the dowry?

CASE 203: Legacy of a Usufruct*

D. 33.2.32.2–4 (Scaevola libro quinto decimo Digestorum)

(2) Uxori usum fructum domuum et omnium rerum, quae in his domibus erant, excepto argento legaverat, item usum fructum fundorum et salinarum: quaesitum est, an lanae cuiusque coloris mercis causa paratae, item purpurae, quae in domibus erat, usus fructus ei deberetur. respondit excepto argento et his, quae mercis causa [com]parata sunt, ceterorum omnium usum fructum legatariam habere. (3) Idem quaesiit, cum in salinis, quarum usus fructus legatus esset, salis inventus sit non minimus modus, an ad uxorem ex causa fideicommissi usus fructus pertineat. respondit de his legandis, quae venalia ibi essent, non sensisse testatorem. (4) Idem quaesiit, cum eodem testamento ita caverit: "a te peto, uxor, uti ex usu fructu, quem tibi praestari volo in annum quintum decimum, contenta sis annuis quadringentis, quod amplius fuerit, rationibus heredis heredumve meorum inferatur," an recessum videatur a superiore capite ideoque uxor non amplius habeat ex usu fructu, quam annuos quadringentos. respondit satis id, quod quaereretur, aperte verba quae proponerentur declarare.

(Scaevola in the fifteenth book of his *Digests*)

(2) A man legated to his wife the usufruct of (certain) houses as well as of everything inside the houses except for the silver, and also the usufruct of farms and saltpans. It was asked whether she was owed the usufruct of the wool of various colors that was readied for sale, and also the purple dye, which were in the houses. He (Scaevola) responded that the legatee had the usufruct of everything except the silver and the things readied for sale.

(3) When no small quantity of salt was discovered in the saltpans, the usufruct of which was legated, the same questioner asked whether its usufruct went to the wife because of the *fideicommissum*. He responded that the testator had not intended to legate those things that were for sale there.

(4) The same questioner asked about a clause in the same will that provided: "I ask of you, my wife, that from the usufruct that I wish to be provided to you for fifteen years, you be content with 400 (gold coins) per year, and that the excess be transferred to the accounts of my heir or heirs." Does he seem to retract the earlier clause, so that the wife takes no more than 400 per year from the usufruct? He responded that the quoted words quite clearly answer the question.

1. Usufruct. This is a property right that usually arises through a will: the ownership of specified property (typically land, but most other types of property are also possible) is vested in one person, usually an heir; but the right to exploit the property—to enjoy its use (*usus*) and fruits (*fructus*)—is given to another person either for that person's life or, as with this will, for a term of years. While a usufruct lasts, the usufructuary enjoys many of the practical rights of an owner, but the usufruct ends when the usufructuary dies, even if

the term has not expired. Many scholars believe that the legal device of usufruct was originally created in order to benefit wives and other persons whom a testator wished to support for their lives while keeping title to the property within the family. Is it well suited to that purpose? The relationship of the questioner in this Case to the usufruct is not specified, but the questioner is male—perhaps the testator's son and heir, who wants clarification as to his mother's rights. What kind of tensions does a usufruct create between the owner and the usufructuary? Are they somewhat similar to the tensions between a wife and her husband as holder of her dowry (Cases 84–88)?

2. A Persistent Questioner. In this Case, the testator's wife received a usufruct over extensive properties both urban and agricultural. Why did the usufruct cause so many problems for the questioner? How can these problems be classified?

- When he died, the houses contained cloth and dye that the testator had presumably intended to sell. Why does Scaevola hold that the widow cannot sell and profit from these commercial goods? If the houses contain cloth shops along their street frontage, will she be able to receive rents from them? Can she profit from future cloth manufacture within the shops?

- Saltpans are used to collect salt from evaporated sea water. Normally a usufructuary is allowed to continue exploiting a commercial operation, but major new discoveries raise some problems (see, e.g., Ulpian, D. 7.1.9.2–3). Does Scaevola answer the question he was asked, and if so, how? Would the result be the same if the property contained a coal mine, and a major new vein of coal was then discovered? What interests are being balanced here?

- In the original text of this Case, the will asked the widow to be content with a total annual income from the usufruct of 400,000 sesterces, an enormous income by Roman standards. Why does Scaevola think the interpretation of the will is so obvious? If the usufruct income fell below this figure, would the heir be obliged to make up the difference? (Scaevola's exasperation with his questioner is fairly typical; he is often impatient, and sometimes rather hostile.)

The jurists discuss such questions at great length in D. 7.1; but their rulings are not easy to systematize. Why might this subject have been difficult for them?

3. Improvements. The general rule was that the usufructuary was responsible for the upkeep of the property and could make some changes to it but could not make changes that would alter the property's essential character or lower its value; see, for instance, Ulpian, D. 7.1.7 pr.–9.3. Could the usufructuary uproot a vineyard in order to mine for gold? Convert a residential home into

a lodging house, or into a business such as a dry-cleaner's shop or a public bath? Turn an existing private bath into a public facility? Erect a new building on an empty lot? Whose interests are being protected, and do these interests conflict?

4. Legacies and *Fideicommissa*. In (3) Scaevola describes the legacy as a *fideicommissum*. In his day these two forms of bequest were still distinct (Gaius, *Inst.* 2.268–289), but the divergence was gradually eroding; Scaevola often ignores it. See the following section.

CASE 204: Legacy of a *Peculium**

D. 33.8.26 (Scaevola libro tertio Responsorum)

"Tit<e> fili, e medio praecipito sumito tibique habeto domum illam, item aureos centum"; alio deinde capite peculia filiis praelegavit. quaesitum est, an peculio praelegato et centum aurei et usurae eorum debentur, cum rationibus breviariis in aero alieno et sortem et usuras inter ceteros creditores complexus sit. respondit, si id faenus nomine filii exercuisset et usuras ita, ut proponeretur, filio adscripsisset, id quoque peculio legato deberi.

(Scaevola in the third book of his *Responses*)

(In his will, a testator provided:) "Titus, my son, take by preference and have for yourself that (particular) house, plus 100 gold coins." In another clause, he left his sons an advance legacy (*praelegatum*) of their *peculia*. It was asked whether, under the advance legacy of the *peculium,* both the 100 gold coins and the interest (earned) on them are owed; for in his account books, both the principal and the interest were listed by him (the testator) under debts, together with his other creditors.

He (Scaevola) responded that if, in the manner stated, he had loaned out the money in his son's name and had credited the interest to the son, this too was owed under the legacy of a *peculium*.

Hypothetical Situation

A testator had an estate worth 1,000 gold coins at the time of his death. In his will, he left his estate in equal shares to his two sons; but he also made two legacies in favor of the sons Titus and Marcus. First, he legated to his son Titus a house and 100 gold coins, which Titus was to take "by preference." Second, he made an "advance legacy" of their *peculia* to both sons. During his lifetime, the testator had kept a separate account of 100 gold coins under Titus's name; he had lent out this money and credited the interest as well to Titus, with the result that the account is now worth 200 gold coins. How is this account to be handled in relation to the two legacies?

1. Preferential Legacy and Advance Legacy. These are two special forms of legacy, the technical details of which need not detain us. Both allow a testator to assign particular pieces of property to a legatee, who may also be an heir. The testator's will in this Case made two legacies to his son Titus. The first is a preferential legacy (*legatum per praeceptionem*) under which Titus's half share of the estate will include a house plus 100 gold coins, both of which he takes by preference when the inheritance is divided with his brother; so this legacy does not increase Titus's share of the value of the inheritance, though he does get the house and money. The second is an advance legacy (*praelegatum*) to Titus and his brother of their *peculia*, which they will be allowed to remove

from the inheritance before its division; this legacy therefore can possibly increase the value of what Titus receives. Testators often used these forms of legacy to direct a particular object to a family member, usually when the item had sentimental value; a nice example is Paul, D. 34.2.32.4 (a business woman leaves her daughter a preferential legacy of her "women's jewelry"; this does not include jewelry that she traded as part of her business). Was the testator in the present Case motivated by sentimental concerns, do you think?

2. **Which Legacy?** If the inheritance is divided equally between Titus and Marcus, his brother, each will receive (in the hypothetical situation outlined above) 500. The legacy by preference to Titus just means that the house and the coins will be allocated to his half. It therefore makes an enormous difference to Titus (and also to Marcus) if the special account, now worth 200, can be considered part of Titus's *peculium,* since he will acquire this *peculium* before the division. That is, if (for instance) the brothers have no other assets in their *peculia,* Titus will ultimately receive the 200 in the special account and 400 as half of the remaining estate, or a value of 600 in all; while his brother will receive only 400. One issue that therefore arises in this Case is whether the money in the account should be counted as part of the son's *peculium.* Does it seem to meet the technical requirements for *peculium* property in Cases 125–127? Is there any indication that Titus was administering this fund himself? What do you think it likely that the testator was actually trying to do, and why did he fail: because of carelessness or inattention? Why does Scaevola decide as he does?

3. **Calculating the *Peculium*.** A legacy of a *peculium* had to be expressly left in a will; it was not presumed. (Why not?) In interpreting the legacy, some of the same problems arise as with the action on a *peculium* (Cases 134–135). The child or slave who is legated a *peculium* receives it as it existed when the testator died. However, any debts owed to the testator or to the heir are deducted (Ulpian, D. 33.8.6 pr., 5), while anything they owed to the *peculium* is added (Ulpian, D. 33.8.6.4, who notes that this rule was reversed by Septimius Severus and Caracalla for slaves who were freed with their *peculia*). Is it possible that Scaevola regards the account administered by the testator for Titus as, in effect, a loan by Titus to his father? Before the father's death, does it seem that Titus ever had the money in his *peculium*? Did he even know of the account?

4. **A Problem.** A son manumitted a slave in his *peculium* without his father's permission. Later the father died and in his will left the *peculium* to his son. Does the slave become free retrospectively? See Papinian, D. 33.8.19.2 (no); why not? Would it matter if the slave was manumitted after the father wrote his will? No again, says Marcian (D. 33.8.20).

CASE 205: Release from Liability

D. 34.3.28.3 (Scaevola libro sexto decimo Digestorum)

Titius testamento facto et filiis heredibus institutis de patre tutore suo quondam facto ita locutus est: "Seium patrem meum liberatum esse volo ab actione tutelae." quaero, haec verba quatenus accipi debent, id est an pecunias, quas vel ex venditionibus rerum factis aut ex nominibus exactis in suos usus convertit vel nomine suo faeneravit, filiis et heredibus testatoris nepotibus suis debeat reddere. respondit eum, cuius notio est, aestimaturum. praesumptio enim propter naturalem affectum facit omnia patri videri concessa, nisi aliud sensisse testatorem ab heredibus eius approbetur.

(Scaevola in the sixteenth book of his *Digests*)

Titius, after making his will and instituting his children as heirs, said (in his will) the following about his father, who had formerly been his guardian (*tutor*): "I want my father Seius to be released from an action on guardianship."

I ask how widely these words should be applied? That is, would he (the father) be obligated to return to the children and heirs of the testator (his own grandchildren) the proceeds that he collected from sales of property or foreclosure of loans and has converted to his own use or lent out under his own name?

He (Scaevola) responded that the finder of fact will have to weigh (both sides of the case). A presumption based on natural affection makes it appear that the father was granted everything, unless the heirs show that the testator intended another result.

1. Release by Will. The *legatum liberationis* was a means of releasing someone from an obligation owed to the estate: a debt or some form of liability, in this Case the action on guardianship, which otherwise could be raised by the testator's heirs (see Discussion 5 on Case 218). Why might a problem have arisen in this Case? Is it that the release seems breathtaking in scope? What sort of evidence could the heirs produce to overturn Scaevola's presumption about the testator's intent?

2. Natural Affection and Fraud. Why does Scaevola invoke "natural affection"? In what respect are the testator's words insufficiently clear? Usually a testamentary release from liability is ineffective if the beneficiary had engaged in fraud that was unknown to the testator (see, e.g., Pomponius, D. 34.3.8.6). Are the father's actions likely to have been fraudulent? If so, is this Case an exception to the general rule? Why might an exception be appropriate?

3. Whose Children? In his will, a man legates a farm to his wife "whenever she has children." They divorce, she remarries, has children by her second hus-

band, divorces him, and returns to her first. After his death, can she claim the legacy? Julian (D. 35.1.25) says no, since it is unlikely that the testator contemplated his wife's giving birth to children by another man during his lifetime. Does Julian presume that "natural affection" is wanting?

CASE 206: Inheritance by Another Name?*

D. 31.77.12 (Papinianus libro octavo Responsorum)

"Fidei tuae committo, uxor, ut restituas filiae meae, cum morieris, quidquid ad te quoquo nomine de bonis meis pervenerit." etiam ea, quae postea codicillis uxori dedit, fideicommisso continebuntur, nam ordo scripturae non impedit causam iuris ac voluntatis: sed dos praelegata retinebitur, quoniam reddi potius videtur, quam dari.

(Papinian in the eighth book of his *Responses*)

(A testator provided in his will:) "I charge it to your trust (*fidei tuae committo*), my wife, that you restore to my daughter, when you die, whatever of my property comes to you under whatever title."

Even those things that he afterward gave to his wife in codicils are included in the *fideicommissum*, since the order of composition does not get in the way of applying the legal rule and the testator's intent. A dowry given by *praelegatum*, however, will be held back, because it is deemed to be returned, not given.

1. The Trust. A *fideicommissum*, or testamentary trust, has the following form: the testator confers a benefit on a trustee but accompanies the benefit with a request that the trustee transfer all or some of this benefit to another person, the true beneficiary of the trust. Trusts have a long and complicated history. During the Roman Republic, because of the rigidity of traditional legacies, Roman testators began asking favors of their heirs and legatees. At first only the recipient's trustworthiness (*fides*) guaranteed performance; but beginning in the early Empire many such *fideicommissa* became enforceable through imperial courts (Justinian, *Inst.* 2.23.1), thus greatly easing the formalism of the Roman law of succession. Unlike legacies, trusts could be charged on legatees as well as heirs and could be made for all or part of the estate (though in time they too were made subject to the requirements of the *lex Falcidia* [see Case 198], as well as to those of the Augustan marriage legislation [see Case 212]). A trust could even function upon intestacy, not only where a will failed but even in the absence of a will (see Discussion 6 below). Thus, it made sense to many testators to insert a trust clause in their wills as a safeguard in case some or all of their dispositions failed. In time the trust came to be viewed as inhering in the property itself rather than in the trustee. Though not subjected to the same formalities, *fideicommissa* in practice often mimicked the function of wills and legacies.

2. Transmitting an Inheritance. In this Case, which illustrates the freedom of the new form of bequest, a husband apparently made his wife a partial heir and then left her further property through legacy in codicils. All of this property effectively reverts to the daughter upon the wife's death, according to the terms of the *fideicommissum*. By contrast, a testator had only very limited abil-

ity to restrict a legatee's power over a legacy. Is it a good idea to allow a testator to control the disposition of property long after his or her death? What limits should there be on this control? What are the potential social and economic advantages or disadvantages?

3. **Dowry.** Why isn't the wife's dowry included in the *fideicommissum*? Does the wife not receive this from the estate of her former husband? Suppose a wife names her husband heir, subject to a *fideicommissum* that when he dies, he should restore all he received from her inheritance to their common son. Is the property in her dowry that had been returned to her after their divorce included in the *fideicommissum*? See Scaevola, D. 36.1.80.9 (yes). Why the difference?

4. **Comparative Law.** A *fideicommissum* resembles a trust in Common Law, but they differ in many details. Above all, a *fideicommissum* does not involve a divided ownership (legal as opposed to equitable ownership); instead, the recipient is full and sole owner, but the beneficiary is entitled to sue the recipient for enforcement of the *fideicommissum*. What risks does this involve? What if the recipient sold the property and conveyed title to a third party?

5. **Malleable Procedure.** Flexibility of form was matched by flexibility of procedure. Lawsuits on *fideicommissa* were heard at Rome, not by the praetor under the formulary procedure, but by other magistrates under the *cognitio extra ordinem,* an imperial form of procedure that gave them considerable discretion on how to proceed. While under the praetorian system judgment was routinely given in monetary terms, under *cognitio* the magistrate could compel performance. This meant that if a testator really wanted a beneficiary to have an item left as a bequest rather than its value in money, he was well advised to employ a trust rather than a legacy as a means of leaving the property.

6. **Imposing Trusts on Intestate Heirs.** Much the oddest result of the flexible *fideicommissum* was that it could be imposed on anybody receiving a benefit from the deceased, even an intestate heir. As Paul says (D. 29.7.8.1): "Trusts can be charged on intestate successors, since the *pater familias* is considered to have voluntarily left them an inheritance based on statute." Is this pure fiction? Does it make any sense to permit a person to die without a will but still with the ability to determine where some or all of the estate will go? What if intestacy results only because a will has been broken, perhaps through a technicality?

CASE 207: *Fideicommissum* or Not?

D. 31.77.21 (Papinianus libro octavo Responsorum)

Pater pluribus filiis heredibus institutis moriens claves et anulum custodiae causa maiori natu filiae tradidit et libertum eidem filiae, qui praesens erat, res quas sub cura sua habuit adsignare iussit. commune filiorum negotium gestum intellegebatur nec ob eam rem apud arbitrum divisionis praecipuam causam filiae fore.

(Papinian in the eighth book of his *Responses*)

As his heirs, a father appointed several of his children. On his deathbed, he handed over his keys and his signet ring to his oldest daughter for safekeeping, and he ordered that a freedman who was present make over to her the things he had in his care. This was interpreted as a measure taken for all of his children in common, and for this reason the daughter's position with the arbitrator for the division (of the estate) would not be enhanced.

1. Formlessness. *Fideicommissa* are in theory form free; they did not have to be written down or even stated orally. See, for instance, Paul, *Sent.* 4.1.6a (= D. 32.21 pr.): "A *fideicommissum* is also left by a nod, so long as the person who so leaves it can speak, unless a supervening disease prevents him." Under what circumstances do you suppose that a person might use a nod of the head in order to leave an inheritance or a bequest? What possibilities for misunderstanding could arise from such extreme informality? *Tit. Ulp.* 25.1 states that the validity of a *fideicommissum* derives "from the will of the person leaving it" (*ex voluntate relinquentis*). Suppose that a dying woman says to an heir at her bedside: "I commend my cousin to your care." Is that sufficient to create a *fideicommissum*? See Ulpian, D. 32.11.2 (no); why not? What problems are likely to result from the fact that witnesses to such scenes may be highly emotional? That they may sometimes have ulterior motives for shading the truth? That the "nod" might be a mere spasm?

2. Keys and a Signet Ring. What is it that the dying father was trying to accomplish by handing over his keys and signet ring to his oldest daughter? Reconstruct the arguments on both sides of this Case. Is it entirely unreasonable to believe that the father intended to repudiate the other heirs in favor of his oldest daughter? Or that he intended to leave her the property (including the property to which the keys belonged) that was handed over to her or that the freedman was ordered to make over? Is Papinian's alternative explanation clearly preferable? Does his view involve a tacit placement of the burden of proof? What precisely would have been required in this Case in order to convert the dying person's gesture into a true *fideicommissum*?

3. Dividing an Estate. When there are several heirs to fractions of an inheritance, they will usually arrange to divide the assets. If the heirs cannot agree on a division or at least on a private arbitrator, one of them can apply to the praetor, who will appoint one for them, through the action for dividing an inheritance (*familiae erciscundae*; D. 10.2).

CASE 208: The Gargilian Farm

D. 32.41.3 (Scaevola libro vicesimo secundo Digestorum)

Felicissimo et Felicissimae, quibus libertatem dederat, fundum Gargilianum legavit cum casa, et alio capite Titio filio, quem ex parte quarta heredem scripserat, praelegaverat in haec verba: Titi fili, hoc amplius de medio sumito legata mea, quae mihi tam pater tuus Praesens quam Coelius Iustus frater patris reliquerunt'. quaesitum est, cum fundus Gargilianus testatrici a marito eius, id est a patre Titii filii legatus sit, cui fundus ex causa fideicommissi debeatur, utrum Titio filio tantum an Felicissimo et Felicissimae an tribus. respondit non esse verisimile eam, quae nihil aliud Felicissimo et Felicissimae nisi haec quae specialiter legavit, ad filium, cui et hereditatis suae partem reliquit, legatum generali sermone transferre voluisse.

(Scaevola in the twenty-second book of his *Digests*)

To Felicissimus and Felicissima, whom she had manumitted, a woman legated the Gargilian farm and its farmhouse. In another clause, she gave to her son Titius, whom she had instituted heir for a quarter of her estate, an advance legacy in these words: "Titius, my son, take from the estate, in addition, the legacies that your father Praesens as well as your father's brother Coelius Justus left to me." The Gargilian farm had been left as a legacy to the testator by her husband, that is, the father of her son Titius. Question was raised as to whom the farm was due on the basis of a *fideicommissum,* whether to Titius or to Felicissimus and Felicissima or to all three.

  He (Scaevola) responded that it was unlikely that she, who had legated nothing to Felicissimus and Felicissima except what she specified, had intended by a general proviso to transfer this as a legacy to her son, to whom she had also left a share of her estate.

1. Pension Plan. When testators manumitted slaves in their wills, they often provided material support through an annuity or, as here, a piece of property. Why should it matter that the testator left nothing else to Felicissimus and Felicissima?

2. Advance Legacy. The wording of the case shows that the testator granted her son Titius a legacy that he was to take from the estate before it was divided among the heirs (a *praelegatum*). Does this not give him precedence over the claim of the two freedpersons? Compare Case 204. Try to reconstruct Titius's argument; why did he think that his mother's bequest had nullified the legacy to her freedmen? He seems to have referred to a *fideicommissum* whereby her husband had obliged the testator to transfer the Gargilian farm to her son. Why does the jurist seem to dismiss its relevance to the immediate question?

Does his position seem reasonable? Note that Scaevola may be confusing the category of legacy with that of *fideicommissum*.

3. Generalizing Proviso. What does Scaevola imply in his response? Does he imply that the testator had probably just forgotten or overlooked the source of the Gargilian farm?

CASE 209: Legacy and *Fideicommissum*

D. 33.2.32.6 (Scaevola libro quinto decimo Digestorum)

Duas filias et filium mente captum heredes scripsit, filii portionis mente capti [datae] usum fructum legavit in haec verba: "hoc amplius Publia Clementiana praecipiet sibi quartae partis hereditatis meae, ex qua Iulium Iustum filium meum heredem institui <usum fructum>: petoque a te, Publia Clementiana, uti fratrem tuum Iulium Iustum alas tuearis dependas pro eo: pro quo tibi usum fructum portionis eius reliqui, donec mentis compos fiat et convalescat." quaesitum est, cum filius in eodem furore in diem mortis suae perseverans decesserit, an usus fructus interciderit. respondit verbis quae proponerentur perseverare legatum, nisi manifestissime probetur aliud testatorem sensisse.

(Scaevola in the fifteenth book of his *Digests*)

As heirs, a testator appointed two daughters and a mentally ill son, and legated the usufruct of the mentally ill son's share in the following words: "In addition to this (her share of the inheritance), Publia Clementiana will take as a preferential legacy the usufruct of the quarter share of my estate that I gave as an inheritance to my son, Julius Justus; and I ask you, Publia Clementiana, to provide maintenance for your brother, Julius Justus, to look out for him, and to pay off his creditors. In return, I have left you the usufruct of his share of the inheritance until such time as he recovers his senses and becomes well." The son died after continuing in the same madness until the day of his death. Question was raised whether the usufruct (then) terminated.

He (Scaevola) responded that, on the basis of the words given, the legacy continues, unless it is unambiguously shown that the testator intended something else.

1. Legacy or *Fideicommissum*? The bequest to Publia Clementiana is described by the testator as a preferential legacy (*per praeceptionem*); see Case 204. This means that, as part of her share, Publia Clementiana receives the usufruct from her brother's share. To what extent is the bequest to her different from the legacy of a usufruct in Case 203? In particular, does the legacy here come with strings attached, and, if so, what are those strings? Is Publia Clementiana obliged, for instance, to use all the income from her brother's share in order to maintain him and pay his debts? Can she keep any excess? What if his expenses exceed the income? Are these strings sufficient to justify treating the "legacy" as a *fideicommissum*? Note Gaius, *Inst.* 2.271: "A legacy cannot be imposed on a legatee, but a *fideicommissum* can be."

2. The Testator's Intent. What did the testator probably intend with the final sentence of the legacy? Is Scaevola right to interpret the language as indicat-

ing that the usufruct continues beyond Julius Justus's death, unless the opposite can be proven? Would Scaevola have reached the same result if Julius Justus had recovered his sanity during his lifetime? Who is likely to own this property after the death of Julius Justus?

CASE 210: Bad Blood

D. 31.88.16 (Scaevola libro tertio Responsorum)

Matre et uxore heredibus institutis ita cavit: "a te, uxor carissima, peto, ne quid post mortem tuam fratribus tuis relinquas: habes filios sororum tuarum, quibus relinquas. scis unum fratrem tuum filium nostrum occidisse, dum ei rapinam facit: sed et alius mihi deteriora fecit." quaero, cum uxor intestata decessit et legitima eius hereditas ad fratrem pertineat, an sororis filii fideicommissum ab eo petere possunt. respondi posse defendi fideicommissum deberi.

(Scaevola in the third book of his *Responses*)

After instituting his mother and his wife as his heirs, a testator provided the following: "I ask, dearest wife, that after your death you leave nothing to your brothers. You have the children of your sisters to whom you may leave (it). You know that one of your brothers killed our son during a robbery, while the other has done even worse things to me." The wife died intestate and her estate goes to her brother as intestate heir. I ask whether her sister's children can claim a *fideicommissum* from him.

I responded that it can be maintained that the *fideicommissum* is owed.

1. In-Laws as Outlaws. A truly dysfunctional family! In his will, the husband made serious accusations against his brothers-in-law but apparently provided no evidence; nor does it appear that the two brothers had been convicted for their crimes. Would it matter if the husband's charges could be proven false? Does Scaevola simply assume that they are true? Or does he rather think that the wife believed them to be true when she accepted a share of her husband's estate, or at least that such a belief can be imputed to her on the basis of her acceptance? Is it likely that the charges influenced the jurist in his decision? In any case, should they have?

2. Content of the *Fideicommissum*. What was the precise content of the testator's request to his wife? That she leave nothing to her brothers, or as well that she leave her estate, or some portion of it, to her nephews and nieces? How is his request different from giving advice ("Live a rich and happy life!" or "Don't do drugs!")? If the *fideicommissum* is owed, the sister's children will be able to claim it. Would you judge that they have a sufficient basis for a claim?

3. Trust and Intestacy. Why should a *fideicommissum* be allowed to override the rules on intestacy? In a strict sense, didn't his widow comply with her deceased husband's request by dying intestate and so leaving nothing to her brothers? How far should the *fideicommissum* run: just to what she inherited from her husband or to her entire estate?

SECTION 3: Gifts *Mortis Causa*

CASE 211: Motives and Reasons

D. 39.6.35.2 (Paulus libro sexto ad legem Iuliam et Papiam)

Sed mortis causa donatio longe differt ab illa vera et absoluta donatione, quae ita proficiscitur, ut nullo casu revocetur. et ibi qui donat illum potius quam se habere mavult: at is, qui mortis causa donat, se cogitat atque amore vitae recepisse potius quam dedisse mavult: et hoc est, quare vulgo dicatur: "se potius habere vult, quam eum cui donat, illum deinde potius quam heredem suum."

D. 39.6.2 (Ulpianus libro trigensimo secundo ad Sabinum)

Iulianus libro septimo decimo digestorum tres esse species mortis causa donationum ait, unam, cum quis nullo praesentis periculi metu conterritus, sed sola cogitatione mortalitatis donat. aliam esse speciem mortis causa donationum ait, cum quis imminente periculo commotus ita donat, ut statim fiat accipientis. tertium genus esse donationis ait, si quis periculo motus non sic det, ut statim faciat accipientis, sed tunc demum, cum mors fuerit insecuta.

(Paul in the sixth book on the *lex Julia et Papia*)

But a gift on account of death (*mortis causa*) is far different from a true and absolute gift, which occurs in such a way that in no circumstances is it revoked. In the latter case, the donor prefers that something be owned by him (the donee) rather than by himself. But one who gives *mortis causa* considers his own interests and, from love of life, prefers to have received something (back) rather than to have given it. This is why it is commonly said: "He wanted himself to have it rather than the donee, and this person (the donee) to have it rather than his heir."

(Ulpian in the thirty-second book on Sabinus)

Julian, in the seventeenth book of his *Digests*, says that there are three types of gifts *mortis causa*. One occurs when someone gives a gift, not because he is frightened by fear of an immediate danger, but simply out of contemplation of his own mortality. He says that the second type of gifts *mortis causa* occurs when someone, stirred by an imminent danger, makes a gift in such a manner that it immediately becomes the property of the receiver. He says that a third kind of gifts *mortis causa* is when someone, motivated by danger, makes a gift in such a way that it becomes the property of the recipient, not immediately, but only when the donor dies.

> 1. Legalese. Paul gets to the essence of the Roman distinction between ordinary gifts and gifts *mortis causa*: the former become irrevocable once the gift is conveyed to the donee, while gifts *mortis causa* are regarded as somehow contingent on the donor's actual death after the gift is conveyed. Paul tries to trace

this distinction back to the donor's intention: the giver of a "true and absolute" gift is spurred by altruism, while the giver of a gift *mortis causa* actually prefers to keep the gift but consigns it to a donee only because if he must die, he prefers that the donee rather than the heir have the object. Does this distinction seem plausible? How easy would it be, in practice, to recognize the difference?

2. Why Recognize Gifts *Mortis Causa*? Roman law anticipates that persons who wish to dispose of property after their deaths will do so through a will; "gifts" will thus take the form of a share in the inheritance or a bequest of some type. Why recognize a separate category for gifts in contemplation of death? Is this just being realistic—because many people will realize, on their deathbeds, that their wills are outdated and no longer reflect their desires? If gifts *mortis causa* had not been recognized, would this have stimulated Romans to keep their wills up to date? What other problems result from recognition of such gifts? For instance, what happens when the donor unexpectedly recovers?

3. When Is Death Imminent? Ulpian, citing Julian, writes of gifts made in consideration of one's "imminent death." At D. 39.6.3–6, Gaius, Ulpian, and Paul list a series of circumstances that might impel us to fear that death is near: declining health; an attack by foreign enemies or robbers; "the cruelty or hatred of a powerful man"; an upcoming sea voyage or travel through dangerous places; and weariness brought on by old age. "All these," says Paul (ibid. 6), "establish impending danger." Is it to be presumed that any gift given close in time to one of these circumstances is motivated by fear of death? Are these various circumstances all functionally equivalent?

4. Contemplating Mortality. Whatever impels legal recognition of gifts *mortis causa*, is that same rationale applicable to gifts made "simply out of contemplation of (the donor's) own mortality"? As Paul (D. 39.6.35.4) says: "Sometimes, with no anticipated danger, a person who is well and in good health thinks of death as resulting from the human condition." What problems of proof does this criterion raise? Could the jurists be thinking, perhaps, of a healthy hypochondriac who irrationally fears death and gives away all her property to friends? Should she be able then to reclaim it?

5. Forms and Revocability. Usually a gift *mortis causa* is simply handed over to the donee. If the donor survives the imminent danger, the gift can be recovered by suing for it or its value. Would it always be clear that the anticipated circumstances had passed? Can the donor recover if she simply changes her

mind? See Ulpian, D. 39.6.30 (yes); how can this holding be explained? As to the two main types of gifts *mortis causa* described in this Case (the first subject to a condition that the gift is revoked if the donor survives; the second subject to a condition that the gift becomes valid only when the donor dies), which is likely to be more common? Which presents greater legal difficulties?

CASE 212: Just Like a Legacy

D. 39.6.17 (Iulianus libro quadragensimo septimo Digestorum)

Etsi debitor consilium creditorum fraudandorum non habuisset, avelli res mortis causa ab eo donata debet. nam cum legata ex testamento eius, qui solvendo non fuit, omnimodo inutilia sint, possunt videri etiam donationes mortis causa factae rescindi debere, quia legatorum instar optinent.

D. 39.6.35 pr. (Paulus libro sexto ad legem Iuliam et Papiam)

Senatus censuit placere mortis causa donationes factas in eos, quos lex prohibet capere, in eadem causa haberi, in qua essent, quae testamento his legata essent, quibus capere per legem non liceret. . . .

D. 39.6.37 pr. (Ulpianus libro quinto decimo ad legem Iuliam et Papiam)

Illud generaliter meminisse oportebit donationes mortis causa factas legatis comparatas: quodcumque igitur in legatis iuris est, id in mortis causa donationibus erit accipiendum.

(Julian in the forty-seventh book of his *Digests*)

Even if a debtor did not intend to defraud his creditors, property that he gave *mortis causa* should be taken away. Since legacies in the will of an insolvent person are entirely void, it can be held that gifts made *mortis causa* should also be rescinded, for they resemble legacies.

(Paul in the sixth book on the *lex Iulia et Papia*)

The Senate decreed that gifts made *mortis causa* to those whom the statute prohibited from taking bequests had the same status as property legated to those whom the law prohibited from taking bequests. . . .

(Ulpian in the fifteenth book on the *lex Iulia et Papia*)

One should keep in mind that general principle whereby gifts made *mortis causa* are analogized to legacies. Therefore, any rule that holds for legacies must be accepted for gifts *mortis causa*.

1. Defrauding Creditors. As might have been anticipated, Roman law contains a fairly rich body of legal rules designed to protect creditors from debtors who endanger repayment by dissipating their assets. For example, the *lex Aelia Sentia* (A.D. 4) established that slaves manumitted in fraud of creditors did not become free (Gaius, *Inst.* 1.37, 47); the "fraud" occurs when the debtor acts with knowledge of insolvency and to the detriment of creditors. In the case of wills, usually the heir is not obligated to perform beyond the resources of the estate (see, e.g., Papinian, D. 35.2.11.5), which means that, as Julian says, legacies from an insolvent inheritance are absolutely void; the creditors get

first crack at the assets. How does it follow that gifts *mortis causa* should also be revocable?

2. **The Augustan Marriage Law.** Under the *lex Iulia et Papia* (two laws are here cited as one), adults who did not marry or who married but failed to bear children were penalized chiefly by losing eligibility for testamentary bequests in whole or in part, according to a complex series of rules. The *senatusconsultum* mentioned by Paul is of unknown date, though most scholars think it followed a decree passed in the reign of Vespasian (A.D. 69–79) that assimilated *fideicommissa* to legacies for the purpose of the marriage law. Why treat gifts *mortis causa* in the same way? Could this statute have preceded the rule given by Julian in the first text?

3. **The General Principle.** Why didn't Julian and Paul simply cite the general rule given by Ulpian? Does it seem practical to equate *donatio mortis causa* with legacy for all intents and purposes? For example, does the rule regarding the Falcidian *quarta* apply here as well? See Papinian, D. 31.77.1 (yes, by a statute of Septimius Severus; but this enactment seems very late in coming). Can we safely assume that the general principle took a long time to develop?

4. **Applications.** Here are some more instances in which the analogy between legacies and gifts *mortis causa* is discussed; you should be able to work out the solutions.

   • Usually, if a husband gives a gift to his wife (or vice versa), the gift is voidable; see Cases 61–65. Does this rule apply also to gifts *mortis causa*? See Ulpian and Gaius, D. 24.1.9.2–11 pr.
   • Can a *fideicommissum* be imposed on a gift *mortis causa*? See, for example, Papinian, D. 31.77.1.
   • If a person is incapable of taking under a will, can he or she receive a gift *mortis causa*? See Javolenus, D. 35.1.55.

Still, some significant differences remain. Above all, unlike with legacies (but like trusts), the validity of gifts *mortis causa* did not depend on the existence of a valid will (Marcian, D. 39.6.25).

APPENDIX

A Specimen Roman Will

This Roman will, though fictitious, illustrates what a real Roman will could have looked like. It is indebted to the specimen offered by F. H. Lawson, *The Roman Law Reader* (Dobbs Ferry, N.Y., 1969) 83–85, as well as to the real and fictional wills discussed by E. Champlin, *Final Judgements: Duty and Emotion in Roman Wills, 200 B.C.–A.D. 250* (Berkeley, 1991).

Let my elder son, Marcus, be my heir as to one-half.[1] Let him make a formal declaration of acceptance within one hundred days of my death; if he does not, let him be disinherited and let his children take equal portions of his share, on condition that he emancipate them if they are still in his power at the time of my death.[2]

Let my elder daughter, Sempronia, because she has never failed to show me the greatest affection, nor has she omitted to heed my counsels, be my heir as to one-quarter. Let her make a formal declaration of acceptance within one hundred days of my death; if she, my most dutiful daughter, does not, let her be disinherited and my nephew Publius Sempronius be my heir as to her share.

Let my loyal and devoted wife, Claudia, be my heir as to one-twelfth. Let her make a formal declaration of acceptance within one hundred days of my death; if she does not, let her be disinherited and my brother, Gaius Sempronius, be my heir as to her share.

Let my younger daughter be disinherited; she knows the reasons why and must be content with the legacies I leave her, which are generous under the circumstances.[3]

Let my son Lucius, who shows so little promise, be my heir as to one-sixth. Let him make a formal declaration of acceptance within two hundred days of my death; if he does not, or if he does and, having taken his share, dies before reaching the age of legal majority, let that person be my heir as to his share who is named in the separate, sealed tablets accompanying this will.[4]

If a child is born to me after the making of this will, whether he be born when I am alive or after I am dead, let him be my heir as to one-sixth, with the shares of the other heirs reduced in proportion.[5] Let him make a formal declaration of acceptance within three hundred days of my death; if he does not, or if he does and, having taken his share, dies before reaching the age of legal majority, let the same person be my heir as nominated to substitute for Lucius. If that person or Publius Sempronius or Gaius Sempronius or any of the children of my son Marcus do not make a formal declaration of acceptance within one hundred days of the date when his share is offered to him, let each of the other heirs take a part of that share in proportion to the amount I have granted them in this will.[6]

If none of my heirs or substitute heirs makes a formal declaration of acceptance within the time periods set forth, let my slave Auctus, who is now forty years old, be free and my heir.[7] If Auctus is no longer alive, let my slave Rufio, who is at least thirty-five years old, be free and my heir. If Rufio is no longer alive, let the oldest slave who is in my *familia* at the time of my death and is over thirty years old be free and my heir, except for Cordax and Glycera, whom I absolutely forbid any of my heirs ever to manumit.

I appoint my brother, Gaius, as *tutor* to my son Lucius and my nephew Publius as *tutor* to the one I have not named; perhaps he will have better fortune than I in reigning in her unacceptable behavior. Let my excellent elder daughter, Sempronia, have her choice as *tutor*, anyone but that unreliable Regulus fellow.

Whoever shall be my heir or heirs shall be liable to give and bequeath the following as legacies:

- To my beloved wife, Claudia, the usufruct of the Cornelian farm for as long as she lives.[8]
- To my beloved wife, Claudia, as to the 50,000 sesterces in cash that came to me on account of my wife, the same amount in place of this dowry.[9]
- Again to my dearest, Claudia, the clothing, women's toiletries, all the jewelry, of gold and of silver, that has been made, bought, and acquired for her, all of it.[10]
- To my sons, as advance legacies, their *peculia*.[11]
- To my eldest daughter, Sempronia, the apple of my eye, the preferential legacy of the house in which she lived as a child.[12]
- To that other daughter, the usufruct of the farm in Dacia, as long as she lives; it is more than she deserves.
- To that same daughter, a life-size marble, togate statue of myself, that she should forever contemplate the father whom she has so deeply wronged.
- To my friends and business associates, the worthy Cn. Salvius, L. Porcius Grunnus, and M. Fufidius Sempiternus, as well as to my excellent freedmen M. Sempronius Calator and M. Sempronius Glyco, I grant release from their debts to me.[13]
- Again to my excellent and most dutiful elder daughter, Sempronia, I ratify the gift I made to her, in contemplation of my impending demise, of her grandmother Marcia's jewelry.[14]
- To my best friend, T. Inebrius Bibulus, enjoyment for his life of the contents of my wine cellar.
- To my most devoted friends [a list of ten names follows], ten pounds of gold each.
- To my most loyal freedmen and freedwomen (a list of eight names) five pounds of gold each.

I impose on my son Marcus the *fideicommissum* of passing on 500,000 sesterces to his younger brother, Lucius, when Lucius reaches the age of twenty-five.

I order the following to be free, all of whom are older than thirty years of age: Coactus, the accountant, on condition that he render his accounts; Fortunata, the nurse; Lycas, the ship captain, on condition that he render his accounts, with his *peculium* as a legacy.

[Instructions for funeral and monument.]

If any of my heirs, except for Lucius, fails to obtain one quarter of what he would be entitled to if I had died intestate, let his share be made up to that amount at the discretion of a good man.[15]

If I shall have left anything written and sealed in codicils or by any other kind of disposition, I desire it to be as valid as if it were written and sealed in this my will.

All that I have above ordered to be written and done, I wish to be given and done by any heir or possessor of my estate I shall have, even upon intestacy; and I similarly entrust to him that the things I shall order to be given shall be given and done.[16]

C. Petronius bought the household and its resources with a single sesterce for the purpose of making this will.[17] L. Annaeus Seneca held the scales. C. Lucilius, Q. Horatius Flaccus, A. Persius Flaccus, M. Valerius Martialis, and D. Junius Juvenalis were witnesses.

[Date and place of the witnessing of the will.]

NOTES

1. The first paragraphs are devoted to instituting heirs. *Sui heredes* had to be expressly disinherited, sons by name and others, including daughters, by unambiguous reference: see Cases 178–179.

2. The grants to the sons of Marcus and others in default of acceptance by the primary heirs are "common substitutions"; see Case 172. If the substitute heirs accept their shares, they are also liable to pay the legacies that are laid out later in the will.

3. On the wisdom of giving an explanation for disinheritance, see the Discussion in Case 179 and also Case 194. Should the testator have been more forthcoming?

4. The grant in substitution to Lucius is both a "common" and a "pupillary" substitution; see Cases 172–174. In the latter case, why is the identity of the heir kept a secret, only to be revealed upon Lucius's death?

5. Any child born after the writing of a will could count as a *suus heres*. On providing for *postumi*, see Cases 182–185.

6. This clause is an example of reciprocal substitution; see the Discussion in Case 172. What is the testator getting at here?

7. If the inheritance was vested in a slave through substitution, it was usually because all free persons mentioned in the will had refused to accept the inheritance on the ground that it was insolvent. The slave was instituted because he could not refuse; see the Discussion on Case 175. The slave became free and could keep any property acquired subsequently. Note that under the Augustan legislation regulating manumission of slaves, thirty years was the standard minimum age at which a slave could be freed.

8. This is a very common type of usufruct; in fact, usufruct may have been developed initially as a support for widows; see Case 203.

9. On the "return of the dowry" *pro dote*, see Case 200.

10. On generic legacies and things acquired for a wife, see Cases 201–202.

11. On advance legacies (*praelegata*), especially of *peculia*, see Case 204.

12. On preferential legacies (*legata per praeceptionem*), see Case 204. How does this legacy differ in its practical effects from that to the sons?

13. On the legacy of a release from liability, see Case 205.

14. On gifts *mortis causa*, see Cases 211–212.

15. This clause is designed to avoid difficulty with the *querella inofficiosi testamenti*; see Cases 192–197. It excludes Lucius and does not mention the daughter who has been disinherited. Does this wording adequately protect the will from attack?

16. This clause effectively converts the entire will into a *fideicommissum*, valid even upon intestacy. Do you see how?

17. This is a mancipatory will; on the procedure, see Case 171.

CHAPTER V

Tutelage and the Status of Children and Women

PART A

Children, Young Adults, Lunatics, and Spendthrifts

Roman law, like other legal systems, recognized that some individuals, although they have become *sui iuris*, continue to require supervision, especially (in the Roman view) with regard to their property. From this recognition there derived a rather haphazardly concocted law of guardianship whereby a *sui iuris* person could be subject to the control of a *tutor* or *curator*; the extent of this control, however, varied widely from case to case.

Young children presented a particular challenge. The harsh Roman demographic regime meant that many children became orphans before reaching adulthood. The Roman Empire offered only limited public assistance in handling orphans; and, as we have seen (Cases 148–154), adoption of *sui iuris* persons was actually discouraged, obviously because the Romans disliked eliminating independent households. Therefore, they instead relied heavily on tutelage. Archaic statute required the child's nearest male agnate to become *tutor*, but this system had a clear potential for abuse since the agnate would often be an heir if the child died intestate. As a result, from an early date it became common for a child's *pater familias* to name a *tutor* in his will; the power to name a testamentary *tutor* went hand in hand with the *pater's* right to dispose of the child's inheritance if the child died before reaching adulthood (Cases 173–176). When both these possibilities failed, by the late third century B.C. the praetor, in concert with other magistrates, could name a *tutor*; serving as *tutor* was conceived as a public duty.

The powers and responsibilities of these *tutores* were extensive. Managing the ward's estate meant maintaining not only its financial well-being but also, indirectly, the welfare of the ward. In principle, the *tutor* enjoyed the status of an owner of the property in question, though this still left some room for action on the part of the child in tutelage. But for the *tutor* there was a palpable downside to wielding so much authority. *Tutores* could be compelled to take up their role by a magistrate and were liable if they failed to do so. Acting as the guardian of a minor-age child might itself entail liability under one or more headings if the *tutor* acted fraudulently or simply without due care.

Tutelage ended with adulthood, which came quite early: twelve for girls, fourteen or so for boys (Case 6). The Romans quickly realized that this was too early, since children so young often lacked sufficient judgment about their own welfare. Legal protections for young adults eventually resulted in creation of *curatores,* optional guardians who exercised no regular control over wards but could give them trustworthy advice particularly on business matters.

A different type of *curator* was used for adult *sui iuris* persons who were considered to be insane (*furiosi*) or who displayed chronic tendencies to squander their own property (*prodigi*). The roots of this institution are very old and clearly centered first on the protection of the ward's property, mainly in the interest of potential heirs. But by the classical period, particularly in the case of the insane, the ward's welfare was also closely supervised by the *curator*.

SECTION 1. The Tutelage of Children

CASE 213: Defining Tutelage

D. 26.1.1 pr.–1 (Paulus libro trigesimo octavo ad edictum)

(pr.) Tutela est, ut Servius definit, vis ac potestas in capite libero ad tuendum eum, qui propter aetatem sua sponte se defendere nequit, iure civili data ac permissa. (1) Tutores autem sunt qui eam vim et potestatem habent, exque re ipsa nomen ceperunt: itaque appellantur tutores quasi tuitores atque defensores, sicut aeditui dicuntur qui aedes tuentur.

(Paul in the thirty-eighth book on the Edict)

(pr.) Tutelage, as Servius defines it, is a force and power over a free person, granted and allowed by the *ius civile* in order to protect someone who because of (young) age is incapable of self-protection if left on his own.

(1) *Tutores* are those who possess this force and power, deriving their name from their function. And so they are called *tutores* on the basis that they are "protectors" (*tuitores*) and "defenders," just as persons who look after temples are called "temple wardens."

1. Power and Trust. In the definition of tutelage that Paul takes from Servius, which element is dominant: the power held by a *tutor* or its legal function in safeguarding the interest of a minor-age child? Does the balance change in section 1? Paul, writing in the early third century A.D., takes the definition from his first-century B.C. predecessor; does this suggest that the juristic position on the purpose of tutelage had not undergone fundamental change over the period that separated the two jurists? Does Paul, or Servius for that matter, recognize an independent interest for the *tutor*, perhaps as one who stands in for the family, especially with regard to the estate of the minor-age child, should, for instance, that child die before reaching adulthood?

2. Etymology and Analogy. Paul's derivation of *tutores* from *tuitores* (protectors) is a rare example of a Roman etymology that is halfway convincing. How does it assist understanding of the *tutor's* role? What of its amplification through *defensores* (defenders)? And what do you make of the analogy to the etymology of *aeditui* (temple wardens)?

CASE 214: Appointing a *Tutor*

D. 26.7.1 pr.–1 (Ulpianus libro trigesimo quinto ad edictum)

(pr.) Gerere atque administrare tutelam extra ordinem tutor cogi solet. (1) Ex quo scit se tutorem datum si cesset tutor, suo periculo cessat: id enim a divo Marco constitutum est, ut, qui scit se tutorem datum nec excusationem si quam habet allegat intra tempora praestituta, suo periculo cesset.

(Ulpian in the thirty-fifth book on the Edict)

(pr.) It is common for a *tutor* to be compelled, *extra ordinem,* to take up and administer a tutelage. (1) So if a *tutor* who knows that he has been appointed *tutor* fails to fulfill his duty, he does so at his own risk; for the deified Emperor Marcus Aurelius laid down the rule that a person who knows he has been appointed *tutor* and who within the prescribed time limit does not offer a legitimate excuse if he has one (for not performing) fails to fulfill his duty at his own risk.

1. *Extra Ordinem.* When minor children became *sui iuris* through the death of their *pater familias,* they usually received a *tutor* through his will, and this was the preferred method. In the absence of such a testamentary appointment, "statutory *tutores*" (*tutores legitimi*) were named automatically through legislative provisions; for freeborn Romans, the *tutor* was usually the child's nearest male agnate. If both these mechanisms failed, the only Roman fail-safe was to have a magistrate name a *tutor.* Over the centuries the Romans often changed the forum for doing this; Justinian, *Inst.* 1.20, has an overview. During the classical period of Roman law, *tutores* were appointed *extra ordinem,* "outside the usual judicial order" of the urban praetor's court: through consuls from the reign of Claudius (A.D. 41–54), and through a special praetor from that of Marcus Aurelius (A.D. 161–180). In this Case, is Ulpian saying that resort to compulsion was "common" in an absolute sense or only "common" *extra ordinem?* In legal principle, tutelage was meant to be universal for *sui iuris* minors, but the reality was probably different except for the wealthy.

2. Demanding a Tutor. The request that a magistrate appoint a *tutor* normally came from the relatives of the minor, but it might also be made by family friends or foster parents (Modestinus, D. 26.6.2 pr.). Where no such request was forthcoming, a creditor could also ask for one (ibid. 3).

3. A Public Duty. Members of the upper class were expected to serve when named. Paul (D. 4.5.5.2 and 7 pr.) describes tutelage as a public duty, somewhat like being a magistrate or a senator or a *iudex.* Still, it is quite clear that many Romans tried to avoid tutelage by offering an acceptable excuse, and in time an elaborate repertory of excuses developed; see *Frag. Vat.* 123–247 and D. 27.1. Among the alleged excuses were that one was too old, too young, too physically weak (e.g., permanently deaf or mute; temporarily but acutely ill),

too poor, too illiterate or ignorant, living too far away, and so on. Further, the incumbents of high offices were excused, as were persons already exercising three guardianships. Prior hostility between the parties also provided an excuse. In late classical law it was even possible to escape a tutelage by naming someone who was better qualified (*Frag. Vat.* 157–167a).

4. Neglect of Duty. How serious were the Romans about enforcing this "public duty"? Ulpian says that if a person whom a magistrate ordered to be a *tutor* knew of the nomination and failed to allege an excuse or exercise the tutelage, he did so "at his own risk" (*suo periculo*). This apparently means that he would be liable for any harm that the *pupillus* suffered as a result, and the liability would run from when the original order was given (see Pomponius, D. 26.7.17). Would this be enough to prevent slacking?

5. Security. A *tutor* was frequently obliged to provide security (*satisdatio*) as a performance bond. Gaius (*Inst.* 1.199–200) explains the basic rules, which were designed "so that the estates of *pupilli* and those under the supervision of *curatores* not be exhausted or diminished." But the requirement is not universal; "*tutores* appointed in a will are not compelled to give security, since their honesty and dedication (*fides et diligentia*) have been approved by the testator." Does this exception offer adequate protection for the ward? Could some testators actually be deterred from naming a *tutor* for their children?

6. Dangers. Guardians present a legal situation that we have encountered before in relation to dowry (Chapter II.C.5, D.2) and the *peculium* (Chapter III.B.3): one person has effective control of property in which another person has a strong and legally protected financial interest. The problem is how to get the controlling person (loosely, the "agent") to manage the asset in such a way as to benefit the other person (loosely, the "principal"). There is no easy answer to this problem, but two broad dangers can be identified: that the "agent" will inappropriately exploit the property to his own advantage rather than to that of the "principal" (opportunism), and that the "agent" will be insufficiently attentive to the long-term economic exploitation of the property (shirking). In the following Cases we will look more closely at the Roman solutions to this problem as it concerns the *tutor*; but it is worth thinking about the broader issues now. The *tutor* was not directly compensated for his efforts on the ward's estate; does this leave him with inadequate incentive to perform diligently? What does Gaius (*Inst.* 1.200; cited in the previous paragraph) imply about the standard of conduct that *tutores* had to display? Are they liable if they are lacking in the "honesty and dedication" (*fides et diligentia*) that are postulated for the ideal testamentary *tutor*? That is, under what circumstances should a *tutor* forfeit his security?

CASE 215: The *Tutor* as Owner

D. 26.7.27 (Paulus libro septimo ad Plautium)

Tutor, qui tutelam gerit, quantum ad providentiam pupillarem domini loco haberi debet.

D. 41.4.7.3 (Iulianus libro quadragensimo quarto Digestorum)

Si tutor rem pupilli subripuerit et vendiderit, usucapio non contingit, priusquam res in potestatem pupilli redeat: nam tutor in re pupilli tunc domini loco habetur, cum tutelam administrat, non cum pupillum spoliat.

(Paul in the seventh book on Plautius)

A *tutor,* who manages a tutelage, should be deemed the owner (of the ward's estate) insofar as he cares for the interests of the ward (*pupillus*).

(Julian in the forty-fourth book of his *Digests*)

If a *tutor* appropriates and sells the ward's property, usucapion does not take place until it returns to the ward's control. For with regard to the ward's property, a *tutor* is deemed the owner when he administers the tutelage, not when he robs the ward.

1. Power and Care. How is the *tutor's* authority qualified by the phrase "insofar as he cares for the interests of the ward"? Is Paul interested in the *tutor's* intentions or in the results he achieves? Does he mean that the *tutor* is the actual owner of the property or that he is only so for some purposes, in a technical sense?

2. Misappropriation of a Ward's Property. Usucapion is a process whereby a person who takes possession of property in the good-faith belief that he or she is becoming owner can become owner through the passage of time. In Roman law, this process has rather severe limits, however. One limit, imposed by an early statute, is that stolen property cannot be usucapted until it returns into the control of the property's owner (Paul, D. 41.3.4.6: the *lex Atinia*). How does Julian's ruling illustrate the limits of the "ownership" exercised by a *tutor*? Suppose that a third party stole the property; would it return "to the ward's control" if the *tutor* received it back from the thief? See Julian, D. 47.2.57.4 (yes, "since the *tutor* is deemed the owner"); is this consistent with the ruling in this Case?

3. Is the *Tutor* a Thief? Does this Case indicate that a *tutor* who misappropriates a ward's property is also guilty of stealing it? Tryphoninus (D. 26.7.55.1) says no, since "*tutores,* because of the supervision that they undertake, are held less to handle it against the owner's will than to betray a

trust." But Ulpian (D. 47.2.33) thinks differently, reasoning that the *tutor* has no power to pillage the ward's property. Which is the better legal position? Which is more likely to deter the *tutor* from opportunistic behavior? Note that, in case of misappropriation, the ward can also sue the *tutor* by the action on tutelage.

CASE 216: Authorization

D. 26.8.9 pr.–1 (Gaius libro duodecimo ad edictum provinciale)

(pr.) Obligari ex omni contractu pupillus sine tutoris auctoritate non potest: adquirere autem sibi stipulando et per traditionem accipiendo etiam sine tutoris auctoritate potest: sed credendo obligare sibi non potest, quia sine tutoris auctoritate nihil alienare potest. (1) Ex hoc autem, quod pupillus nullam rem sine tutoris auctoritate alienare potest, apparet nec manumittere eum sine tutoris auctoritate posse. hoc amplius licet tutoris auctoritate manumittat, debet e lege Aelia Sentia apud consilium causam probare.

(Gaius in the twelfth book on the Provincial Edict)

(pr.) A ward (*pupillus*) cannot become obligated on any contract without a *tutor*'s authorization; however, he can acquire for himself through stipulation and by informal handover even without a *tutor*'s authorization.

But he cannot make someone obligated to himself by a loan, since he is incapable of alienating (transferring title of) anything without a *tutor*'s authorization. (1) Further, from the fact that a *pupillus* cannot alienate anything without a *tutor*'s authorization derives the rule that he cannot manumit slaves without his *tutor*'s authorization. What is more, although with his *tutor*'s authorization he can *manumit*, the *lex Aelia Sentia* requires him to show cause before a judicial commission (*consilium*).

1. Giving and Receiving. Compare the legal position of a *pupillus* with that of a child-in-power (Chapter III.B.1–2). The *pupillus* needs no authorization to acquire both property and obligations from third parties but without a *tutor*'s authorization cannot become obligated on a contract and cannot alienate property. A child-in-power acquires for his or her *pater*; but that aside, is the ward similarly positioned? Note that a *pupillus,* as a *sui iuris* person, would not have a *peculium* (contrast Chapter III.B.3).

2. Manumission. Why does Gaius believe that it follows, from the inability of a *pupillus* to alienate property without authorization, that he or she also cannot manumit slaves? The *lex Aelia Sentia* (A.D. 4), which placed limits on nontestamentary manumission, established a minimum age for the manumissor of twenty years, which would obviously apply to all *pupilli*. Exceptions needed approval from a judicial commission composed of prominent members of the community (*consilium*). Why might the legislator have been uneasy about manumissions by young masters?

3. Presence and Authority. Gaius (D. 26.8.9.5 = Justinian, *Inst.* 1.21.2) states that the *tutor* must be present to authorize the transaction; authorization by letter is ineffective, as also ratification *post factum*. (See also Marcian, D.

41.1.11.) What is the reason for this requirement? If the *tutor* did not give the required authorization, the transaction by the *pupillus* is null, although the *pupillus* is required to surrender any enrichment that he or she receives (see Ulpian, D. 26.8.5 pr.–1). Justinian (*Inst.* 2.8.2) points out that a creditor's position may therefore be quite risky.

CASE 217: Welfare of the Child

D. 26.7.12.3 (Paulus libro trigesimo octavo ad edictum)

Cum tutor non rebus dumtaxat, sed etiam moribus pupilli praeponatur, imprimis mercedes praeceptoribus, non quas minimas poterit, sed pro facultate patrimonii, pro dignitate natalium constituet, alimenta servis libertisque, nonnumquam etiam exteris, si hoc pupillo expediet, praestabit, sollemnia munera parentibus cognatisque mittet. sed non dabit dotem sorori alio patre natae, etiamsi aliter ea nubere non potuit: nam etsi honeste, ex liberalitate tamen fit, quae servanda arbitrio pupilli est.

(Paul in the thirty-eighth book on the Edict)

Since a *tutor* is placed in charge of not only the property but also the character of the ward (*pupillus*), he will, to begin with, determine the wages of the teachers, not the lowest possible but consistent with the resources of the estate and the social rank (*dignitas*) of the child's family. He will furnish maintenance for the slaves and freedmen, sometimes even for those outside (the household) if this will be advantageous for the *pupillus*; and he will send the traditional gifts to parents and (other) relatives.

All the same, he will not provide a dowry to a half sister (of the ward) born of a different father, even if otherwise she is unable to marry; for this act, although upright, is still an act of generosity, which is something that should be reserved for the discretion of the *pupillus*.

1. Tutorial Oversight. Unlike in modern law, the *tutor* is not a true custodian of a child (on custody, see Cases 49, 108–111). But because he controlled the child's resources, the *tutor* acquired great discretionary authority in determining the ward's day-to-day life. According to Paul, how broad is his authority? Although this Case suggests that the decision was his alone, Ulpian (D. 27.2.2–3) indicates that the praetor often played a decisive role in determining the amount that should be spent on maintenance, including the allocation for slaves and the amount for clothing and housing; and even in the case of very large estates, frugality is commended (ibid. 3.3). Is Paul saying that the *tutor* should actually select the ward's teachers himself?

2. Limits to Generosity. Does the qualification "traditional" imply an upper or a lower limit on the cost of family gifts? Could you apply the same standard that is given for teachers' salaries? As to the dowry, why does this fall into a category within the ward's discretion? Could the *tutor* refuse to approve it? Could he provide a dowry for the ward's half sister by the same father, as the text seems to imply? Why is this so? On the familial duty to provide dowries,

see Cases 32–33, 103. Ordinarily, a *tutor* is not allowed to make gifts from a ward's property; see Paul, D. 26.7.22, 46.7.

3. Educating Sisters. Is it a legitimate expense if a *tutor* pays for the education of the ward's full sister? See Julian, D. 27.2.4 (yes, if ordered to do so by a magistrate).

CASE 218: Pitfalls of Tutelage

D. 26.7.7 pr., 2–3 (Ulpianus libro trigesimo quinto ad edictum)

(pr.) Tutor, qui repertorium non fecit, quod vulgo inventarium appellatur, dolo fecisse videtur, nisi forte aliqua necessaria et iustissima causa allegari possit, cur id factum non sit. si quis igitur dolo inventarium non fecerit, in ea condicione est, ut teneatur in id quod pupilli interest, quod ex iureiurando in litem aestimatur. nihil itaque gerere ante inventarium factum eum oportet, nisi id quod dilationem nec modicam exspectare possit. . . . (2) Competet adversus tutores tutelae actio, si male contraxerint, hoc est si praedia comparaverint non idonea per sordes aut gratiam. quid ergo si neque sordide neque gratiose, sed non bonam condicionem elegerint? recte quis dixerit solam latam neglegentiam eos praestare in hac parte debere. (3) Si post depositionem pecuniae comparare praedia tutores neglexerunt, incipient in usuras conveniri: quamquam enim a praetore cogi eos oportet ad comparandum, tamen, si cessent, etiam usuris plectendi sunt tarditatis gratia, nisi si per eos factum non est quo minus compararent.

(Ulpian in the thirty-fifth book on the Edict)

(pr.) If a *tutor* did not make the list that is commonly termed an inventory, he is held to have acted with deceit (*dolus*), unless, as it happens, some necessary and very suitable reason can be set forth as to why this has not been done. If therefore through *dolus* someone has not made an inventory, he is in a position where he is liable for the amount of loss suffered by the *pupillus,* which is reckoned through an oath as to the value at stake. So he (a *tutor*) ought not to take any action (regarding the tutelage) before the inventory is complete, except one that can tolerate no delay, not even a minor one. . . .

(2) *Tutores* are liable under the action on tutelage (*actio tutelae*) if they made a bad contract; for example, if through greed or favor (to another) they purchased properties that are unsuitable. But what if they acted not out of greed or favor but (simply) made a bad choice? It will be correctly claimed that in this situation they ought to be responsible only for gross negligence (*neglegentia lata*).

(3) If, after money was deposited (with them), *tutores* neglected to buy property, they begin to be liable for interest (on the money). For although the praetor should compel them to buy, still, if they fail to do so, they should also be punished by (paying) interest because of their indolence, unless it was not their fault that they did not buy.

1. The Inventory. Postclassical sources also stress the necessity of taking an inventory at once after being named *tutor:* C. 5.37.24 (= C.Th. 3.30.6; Arcadius and Honorius, A.D. 396), 5.51.13.2 (Justinian, A.D. 530). What is the purpose of this inventory, and who is protected? What "loss" is feared? Should the failure to carry out an inventory necessarily be construed as deliberate misconduct? What might serve as an acceptable excuse not to conduct one?

2. Administration. In sections 2 and 3, this Case provides a good introduction to the usual activities of a *tutor*. These two sections both deal with transactions in land, the return from which was the major source of income for upper-class Romans. The *tutor* is expected to invest the ward's money promptly and in a productive manner. Failure to invest can make the *tutor* liable for interest on the money (as a substitute for the lost investment); imprudent investment can lead to liability for the ward's losses. Does Ulpian give adequate guidance as to how the *tutor* should proceed? The *tutor* was also required, for instance, to collect the ward's debts; see Paul, D. 26.7.15, noting that the *tutor* becomes liable for the loss if he fails to sue debtors in a timely fashion and a debtor becomes less able to pay. Paul also requires investment of cash within six months. Is a *tutor* encouraged to make only very cautious investments? If not, how much risk would be legally tolerable?

3. Degree of Care. The jurists vary in establishing the standard of conduct for a *tutor*. The absolute minimum standard is always *dolus*, that the *tutor* not deliberately harm the ward's estate. Very closely connected with this standard is the view, expressed in section 2, that the *tutor* be also liable for "gross negligence" (*neglegentia lata* or *culpa lata*), defined as "not understanding what everyone understands" (Ulpian, D. 50.16.213.2). But beginning in the second century A.D. the jurists often impose even higher standards: a level of care at least equal to that the *tutor* displays toward his own property (Celsus, D. 16.3.32; Ulpian, D. 27.3.1 pr.), or simply "fault" (*culpa*), failure to observe the standards of a careful Roman (Modestinus, *Coll.* 10.2.3; Ulpian, D. 26.7.10). Should the standard vary according to the situation? For instance, what standard underlies the discussion in section 3 of this Case? Papinian (D. 26.7.39.2–3, 7, 11–16) discusses a number of instances in which a *tutor* is held liable for ordinary fault; but most or all of these concern omissions, not positive acts that turned out to be misguided. Do you see why it may be appropriate to use a more lenient standard for some acts? In section 2, what if the *tutor* makes a choice that is honest but wrong? Suppose he buys property advertised as prime beachfront that turns out to be under water? Or makes a wrong guess about soil quality, access to public roads, or development trends? Who should bear the resulting loss: the *tutor* or the ward?

4. Greed. It is easy to see why favor (*gratia*) might count as *dolus* if, for instance, the *tutor* colluded with a seller who wanted to unload some undesirable properties at the expense of the *pupillus*. But why should greed count as such? Is this a willful refusal to manage the ward's estate properly? Is an objective standard involved, one not tied to the *tutor*'s personal avarice?

5. Suits against the Tutor. The most general and flexible remedy was to sue the *tutor* through an action on tutelage (*actio tutelae*), which amounted to a full

settling of accounts between the *tutor* and ward. Where it was suspected that a *tutor* was guilty of malfeasance, there was also a criminal charge to that effect (*accusatio suspecti tutoris*); and, obviously, a misbehaving *tutor* also risked losing any security (see the Discussion on Case 214). On the other hand, the *tutor* could also countersue to receive compensation for legitimate expenses; see Ulpian, D. 27.4.1 pr.

6. Who Guards the Guardians? If an infant's *tutor* misbehaves, can his mother sue to protect the child? Yes, says Ulpian (D. 26.10.1.7; or also another interested female, such as a grandmother, sister, or nurse); but they do not have to intervene, see Tryphoninus, D. 26.6.4.4.

CASE 219: Liability for Alienating Property

D. 26.7.12.1. (Paulus libro trigesimo octavo ad edictum)

Quae bona fide a tutore gesta sunt, rata habentur etiam ex rescriptis Traiani et Hadriani: et ideo pupillus rem a tutore legitime distractam vindicare non potest: nam et inutile est pupillis, si administratio eorum non servatur, nemine scilicet emente. nec interest, tutor solvendo fuerit nec ne, cum, si bona fide res gesta sit, servanda sit, si mala fide, alienatio non valet.

(Paul in the thirty-eighth book on the Edict)

What a *tutor* has done in good faith is deemed valid, a point also supported by rescripts of Trajan and Hadrian. And for this reason a *pupillus* cannot claim title to something that was lawfully alienated by the *tutor*. For it is also disadvantageous to *pupilli* if the management of their property is not confirmed, because, obviously, no one would buy (from them). Nor does it matter whether the *tutor* was solvent or not, since if the act was done in good faith, it must be upheld; (and) if in bad faith, the alienation is invalid.

1. Alienating Property. This Case raises concerns about which, as we have seen in earlier chapters, the Romans were very sensitive; see, for example, Cases 72 and 132. By the late classical period, a *tutor's* powers were severely restricted in relation to rural or suburban land belonging to his ward; a law of Septimius Severus (A.D. 195) prevented him from alienating such land or using it as security for a debt except in special circumstances (Ulpian, D. 27.9.1.2, quoting the law). Probably in the same law, however, a *tutor* was specifically obligated to dispose of unproductive movables, houses, and nonagricultural slaves (C. 5.37.22 pr.; Constantine, A.D. 326). This law may simply enact preexisting custom. Even before the law, how free was the *tutor* in managing the ward's property? Does it seem excessive to invalidate a transfer of title if it can be shown, after the fact, that a *tutor* was acting in bad faith?

2. Good Faith versus Bad. Paul points out that permitting recovery of property where the *tutor* has acted in good faith would prejudice the interests of *pupilli* as a class, since it would create uncertainty and scare off potential buyers. Why would rescission for bad faith not already have this effect? Does Paul's scenario permit invalidation if a *tutor* is merely negligent? Would negligence count as "bad faith"? Can you see why the jurists might be reluctant to impose liability for negligence in the case of positive acts such as the sale of a ward's property?

3. The Insolvent *Tutor*. What is Paul's point concerning the *tutor's* possible insolvency? Is he suggesting that the ward wanted to recover the alienated object because he feared that the tutor was judgment-proof in an action on tutelage? In any event, in the wake of this ruling, how will the ward structure his lawsuit, especially if the *tutor* is insolvent?

SECTION 2. Curatorship of Young Adults

CASE 220: Making Whole: *Restitutio in Integrum*

D. 4.4.1 (Ulpianus libro undecimo ad edictum)

(pr.) Hoc edictum praetor naturalem aequitatem secutus proposuit, quo tutelam minorum suscepit. nam cum inter omnes constet fragile esse et infirmum huiusmodi aetatium consilium et multis captionibus suppositum, multorum insidiis expositum: auxilium eis praetor hoc edicto pollicitus est et adversus captiones opitulationem. (1) Praetor edicit: "Quod cum minore quam viginti quinque annis natu gestum esse dicetur, uti quaeque res erit, animadvertam."(2) Apparet minoribus annis viginti quinque eum opem polliceri: nam post hoc tempus compleri virilem vigorem constat. (3) Et ideo hodie in hanc usque aetatem adulescentes curatorum auxilio reguntur, nec ante rei suae administratio eis committi debebit, quamvis bene rem suam gerentibus.

(Ulpian in the eleventh book on the Edict)

(pr.) In accord with natural fairness, the praetor published this edict whereby he undertook to protect minors (persons under twenty-five years of age). For since everyone agrees that judgment, at this age above all, is delicate and weak, exposed to numerous deceptions and vulnerable to the treachery of many, the Praetor has in this edict promised such persons aid and assistance against deceit.

(1) The praetor states in his Edict: "When, in the future, some business is said to have been conducted with a person less than twenty-five years of age, I will examine the situation." (2) It is clear that he offers help to those less than twenty-five years old. For after this time, it is agreed that full male adulthood is reached.

(3) And for this reason, young adults are today guided by the assistance of *curatores* up to this age limit. Prior to this age, management of their own property ought not to be entrusted to them, even those who handle their own property well.

    1. Restoration to the *Status Quo Ante*. This Case describes the principal remedy that was available to persons who, even if they were in principle capable of "handl[ing] their own property well," were still minors (*minores*), regarded as too young to exercise mature judgment, especially in their business transactions. The Edict's wording is oblique ("I will examine"), but what the praetor is in fact promising is that if, after investigation, he believes that a transaction has adversely affected a minor, he will undo the transaction and order the minor restored "to wholeness" (*in integrum*). Though his open-ended wording is wide enough to include all minors, even those still in tutelage or under a father's power, the praetor sought mainly to protect *sui iuris* males between the age of legal majority (Case 6; about fourteen) and twenty-five. What indications are there in the Case that young adult males were in fact the praetor's chief concern?

2. When to Intervene? According to Ulpian, the praetor "promised . . . aid and assistance against deceit." Does this mean that the minor must actually be the victim of deceptive conduct? Consider the following situations:

- The transaction results in neither loss nor gain to the minor. See Ulpian, D. 4.4.7.6 (restitution is still possible). Would this be true if the minor profited?
- The minor sells his property at a "considerable loss." See Ulpian, D. 4.4.49: restitution is possible, "even if there is no collusion". This is true also if the minor purchases property at what turns out to be an excessive price (Gaius, D. 4.4.27.1).
- In an auction, the minor sells property to the highest bidder, but subsequently a still higher bidder emerges. See Ulpian, D. 4.4.7.8: "Praetors daily restore them by reopening the bidding."
- The minor without cause grants a formal release from a debt that is owed to him. See Gaius, D. 4.4.27.2 (restitution available).
- The minor accepts an inheritance, which shortly thereafter becomes a financial loss as a result of an act of God. See Ulpian, D. 4.4.11.4–5 (controversy).
- The minor enters a transaction with fraudulent intent. See Ulpian, D. 4.4.9.2 (no restitution); compare Paul, *Sent.* 1.9.1.

What do these examples suggest about the praetor's aims in granting *restitutio?*

3. Unintended Consequences. The jurists occasionally express concern that if *restitutio* is easily available, no one will do business with minors. For example, as to reopening auction bidding, Ulpian (D. 4.4.7.8) observes that intervention "should be cautious; otherwise, no one will enter upon purchase of a ward's property even if it is sold in good faith." Similarly, Paul insists that relief be given only in cases of manifest fraud on the part of others or extreme carelessness on the part of the young adult (D. 4.4.24.1). See also Ulpian, D. 4.4.44. Do such reservations make sense? Are they consistent with the case law surveyed in the previous paragraph?

4. Natural Fairness. What do you suppose Ulpian means by "natural fairness" (*naturalis aequitas*) as the praetor's motive for creating *restitutio in integrum?* Is this motive related to what "everyone agrees"? Is such agreement persuasive, either in the sense that young persons' judgment tends "naturally" to be weak or in the sense that many, even most, cultures tend to grant special protection of this kind to young adults? How does our own society evaluate the capacity for sound judgment of ten-year-olds? Twenty-year-olds? Twenty-four-year-olds? Is it fair to suggest that Roman law moved from setting adulthood too early to setting it too late?

5. *Restitutio* and the *Curator*. How does Ulpian link *restitutio* to the appointment of a *curator* for minors? A *curator* is plainly supposed to assist a minor with good advice; does he also provide a measure of cover for the minor's creditors?

CASE 221: The Appointment of a *Curator*

Iustinianus, *Institutiones* 1.23 pr.–2

(pr.) Masculi puberes et feminae viripotentes usque ad vicesimum quintum annum completum curatores accipiunt: qui, licet puberes sint, adhuc tamen huius aetatis sunt, ut negotia sua tueri non possint. (1) Dantur autem curatores ab isdem magistratibus a quibus et tutores. sed curator testamento non datur, sed datus confirmatur decreto praetoris vel praesidis. (2) Item inviti adulescentes curatores non accipiunt praeterquam in litem: curator enim et ad certam causam dari potest.

(Justinian in the first book of his *Institutes*)

(pr.) Males over puberty and females capable of bearing children have *curatores* until the end of their twenty-fifth year. Although they are over puberty, they are still of such an age that they cannot safeguard their affairs. (1) *Curatores* are given by the same magistrates as are *tutores*. A *curator* is not appointed by will, but one who is appointed is confirmed by decree of the praetor or governor. (2) Again, unwilling youths do not have *curatores* except for litigating, for a *curator* can also be given for a specific purpose.

1. A Little History. Justinian stands at the end of a long development in this area. By the late third century B.C., Romans already recognized that puberty was too early to mark the transition into full adulthood. About 200 B.C., the *lex Laetoria* established a quasi-criminal penalty for those who (apparently deliberately) had cheated persons younger than twenty-five years of age. By the classical period this action was gone, but there survived a praetorian defense that the minor could use if sued over an unfavorable contract. The praetor then went on to provide a generalized procedure for *restitutio;* and this procedure led, in turn, to the creation of *curatores* for particular transactions, especially lawsuits. At some point in his reign (A.D. 161–180), Marcus Aurelius is said to have established that "all adults" receive *curatores* (*Historia Augusta, Marcus,* 10.12: *omnes adulti*); this source is clearly inaccurate, but probably the process for appointing *curatores* was regularized at this date, so that young adults could now have a *curator* continuously from the end of tutelage (see Callistratus, D. 26.7.33.1). Thereafter, in the postclassical period, there is a tendency to assimilate *curatores* to *tutores*. Still, even in Justinian's day, the two survive as distinct institutions, above all in that having a *curator* continues to be largely voluntary.

2. Appointment. As this Case indicates, *curatores* are appointed by magistrates; see also Gaius, *Inst.* 1.198. A rescript of Caracalla (C. 5.31.1; A.D. 214) shows that the minor normally requested a *curator,* but that if the minor was recalcitrant, someone who wished to sue him or her could also ask that a *curator* be appointed; see also Alexander Severus, C. 5.31.6 (A.D. 224).

3. Function. The *curator* did not authorize transactions but merely consented to them; nor did his agreement automatically validate a transaction. See, for example, Alexander Severus, C. 2.24.2 (A.D. 222–235): the presence of *curatores* does not preclude later restitution. So what did the *curator* do?

CASE 222: Paying a Debt

D. 4.4.7.1–2 (Ulpianus libro undecimo ad edictum)

(1) Proinde si emit aliquid, si vendidit, si societatem coiit, si mutuam pecuniam accepit, et captus est, ei succurretur. (2) Sed et si ei pecunia a debitore paterno soluta sit vel proprio et hanc perdidit, dicendum est ei subveniri, quasi gestum sit cum eo. et ideo si minor conveniat debitorem, adhibere debet curatores, ut ei solvatur pecunia: ceterum non ei compelletur solvere. sed hodie solet pecunia in aedem deponi, ut Pomponius libro vicensimo octavo scribit, ne vel debitor ultra usuris oneretur vel creditor minor perdat pecuniam, aut curatoribus solvi, si sunt. permittitur etiam ex constitutione principum debitori compellere adulescentem ad petendos sibi curatores. quid tamen: si praetor decernat solvendam pecuniam minori sine curatoribus et solverit, an possit esse securus? dubitari potest: puto autem, si allegans minorem esse compulsus sit ad solutionem, nihil ei imputandum: nisi forte adversus iniuriam appellandum quis ei putet. sed credo praetorem hunc minorem in integrum restitui volentem auditurum non esse.

(Ulpian in the eleventh book on the Edict)

(1) Accordingly, if he (a minor) buys or sells something, enters a partnership, or borrows money, and he is disadvantaged, he will get relief.

(2) But also if money was paid to him by his father's debtor or his own, and he (then) lost this, it must be held that he gets relief, on the theory that business was conducted with him. And so if a minor sues the debtor, he should summon his *curatores* so that the money is paid to him; otherwise, there is no compulsion to pay him.

But today the money is usually deposited in a temple, as Pomponius writes in the twenty-eighth book (on the Edict), both to free the debtor of further interest payments and to prevent the minor creditor losing money; or it is paid to the *curatores,* if there are any. Also, by an imperial constitution, a debtor can force a youth to obtain *curatores* for himself.

So then, what if the praetor decides that money should be paid to a minor who has no *curatores;* if he (the creditor) pays, would he be safe? This can be doubted. But I think that if he was forced to pay (despite) alleging that this was a minor, he should bear no further liability, unless perhaps someone thinks that he must appeal against the wrong (of this judgment). But in my opinion the praetor would not hear such a minor if he sought *restitutio in integrum.*

1. Paying Can Be Difficult. Here the debtor wishes to repay money to a minor but wants to be sure that the payment will release him from the debt; among the dangers is that the minor might "lose" the money (what is meant?). How should the debtor proceed? What role does Ulpian envision for the *curatores?*

Payment into a temple escrow account is one option; is this preferable to paying the ward directly?

2. Suing the *Curator*. There is no special lawsuit, but the *curator* can be sued if he takes an active role in administering the minor's affairs (see, e.g., Paul, D. 26.7.26).

SECTION 3. Curatorship of Lunatics and Prodigals

CASE 223: Parting Lunatics and Prodigals from Their Property

Gaius, *Institutiones* 3.106

Furiosus nullum negotium gerere potest, quia non intellegit, quid agat.

D. 27.10.1 (Ulpianus libro primo ad Sabinum)

(pr.) Lege duodecim tabularum prodigo interdicitur bonorum suorum administratio, quod moribus quidem ab initio introductum est. sed solent hodie praetores vel praesides, si talem hominem invenerint, qui neque tempus neque finem expensarum habet, sed bona sua dilacerando et dissipando profundit, curatorem ei dare exemplo furiosi: et tamdiu erunt ambo in curatione, quamdiu vel furiosus sanitatem vel ille sanos mores receperit: quod si evenerit, ipso iure desinunt esse in potestate curatorum. (1) Curatio autem eius, cui bonis interdicitur, filio negabatur permittenda: sed extat divi Pii rescriptum filio potius curationem permittendam in patre furioso, si tam probus sit.

(Gaius in the third book of his *Institutes*)

An insane person (*furiosus*) is incapable of performing any legal transaction because he does not understand what he is doing.

(Ulpian in the first book on Sabinus)

(pr.) The Law of the Twelve Tables prohibits a prodigal (*prodigus*) from managing his own property, a rule that, to be sure, was originally introduced by custom. These days, however, if praetors and governors come across persons who limit their expenses neither by time nor space but squander their property through wastefulness and extravagance, they make a practice of appointing a *curator* for them on the analogy of an insane person.

And both of these will remain under a *curator,* the insane person until he recovers his senses, and the other (the prodigal) until he returns to sane behavior. If this happens, by operation of law they cease to be in the power of their *curatores.* (1) The curatorship, however, of the person prohibited from managing his property has been traditionally denied to his son; but there is a rescript of the deified Emperor Pius to the effect that preference should be given to the son of an insane father, provided he is suitable.

1. Lack of Intent. As seen in Case 13 (Discussion) and Case 101, an insane person could not marry and could not, as *pater familias,* grant or withhold consent for a son- or daughter-in-power to marry, because he was not able to form the requisite intent. Is this the point Gaius is making in the first fragment? The Latin in this passage is gender inclusive: both for the insane and for prodigals, women as well as men are meant.

2. Prodigals Too. Spendthrifts (*prodigi*) are persons whose reckless behavior with their own property endangers not only their economic position but that

of their families. Though the restriction on prodigals is very old, Ulpian derives contemporary procedure for assigning guardians through analogy with the insane. Does this make logical sense to you? Is the behavior of prodigals analogous to that of the insane? Why not simply use one category of persons prone to socially unacceptable behavior? How do you suppose that praetors might "come across" persons in need of care?

3. Exclusions. Could a lunatic

   - make a will? See Paul, D. 28.1.17 (no).
   - act as a witness? See Ulpian, D. 28.1.20.4 (no, except in lucid intervals).
   - bear criminal liability? See Macer, D. 1.18.14 (no, except perhaps in lucid intervals).

   Would any of these prohibitions apply to prodigals? (They could not make a will.)

4. Lucid Intervals. What does the mention of the possibility of "lucid intervals" suggest about the Roman conception of madness?

5. Operation of Law. The rights of the insane and prodigals are recovered by operation of law, that is, automatically, upon cessation of the condition or behavior that led to the appointment of a *curator*. Does this make sense to you? Why not require approval by the praetor or governor first?

6. Son as *Curator*. The Twelve Tables stipulated that *curatores* should be appointed from among the civil-law heirs, though the praetor could choose someone else if the heirs were unsuitable (Gaius, D. 27.10.13). Why were sons, at least before the reign of Pius (A.D. 138–161), routinely excluded from this responsibility? Ulpian (D. 26.5.12.1) says that many earlier jurists, including Celsus, had held it unbecoming (*indecorum*) for a father to be managed by his own son. What does this mean and why should it matter? Why did Pius change the law, and do so only for the sons of the insane?

CASE 224: A Worried Mother

D. 26.5.12.2 (Ulpianus libro tertio de Officio Proconsulis)

Divus Pius matris querellam de filiis prodigis admisit, ut curatorem accipiant, in haec verba: "non est novum quosdam, etsi mentis suae videbuntur ex sermonibus compotes esse, tamen sic tractare bona ad se pertinentia ut, nisi subveniatur is, deducantur in egestatem. eligendus itaque erit, qui eos consilio regat: nam aequum est prospicere nos etiam eis, qui quod ad bona ipsorum pertinet, furiosum faciunt exitum."

(Ulpian in the third book of his *On the Duties of a Proconsul*)

The deified Emperor Pius accepted the complaint of a woman (who sought) that her wastrel sons be assigned a *curator,* in the following words: "It is no novelty that certain persons, even if they seem of sound mind in their speech, nevertheless manage the property at their disposal in such a manner that unless help is given to them, they will be reduced to poverty. Therefore, someone must be appointed to guide them with advice. For it is fair that we take heed for those who, with respect to their property, bring things to an insane conclusion."

1. No Novelty? Some scholars think that this text marks a departure from previous practice, since in earlier law prodigals were apparently not deprived of management of their property. Is this necessarily true? Wasn't this the role of a *curator*? Or does the fact that the *mother's* request is heard mark this text as distinctive? Would she have an interest in her children's property?

2. Insanely Prodigal. Does Pius (reign: A.D. 138–161) appear to rely on a model of wasteful behavior based on insanity? Could his point about appearing to be of sound mind apply to a lunatic as well?

3. Welfare of the Spendthrift. Julian (D. 27.10.7 pr.) notes that the care and concern of the *curator* should extend beyond the property to the health and well-being of the lunatic. Does this principle also apply to prodigals? Why or why not? At any rate, what is the emphasis in these texts: safeguarding property or maintaining people?

PART B

The Status of Women

By ancient standards, adult Roman women, when no longer under the control of a *pater familias*, enjoyed considerable freedom. Greek writers often remark upon Roman women's social and economic power, although it seems still rather constricted to modern eyes. The decline of *manus* marriage (Cases 37–40) and the rise of free divorce (Cases 75–80) meant that women were also not legally subjected to the authority of husbands. Elsewhere in the law, there is a detectable drift toward recognizing the importance of blood relationship between women and, in particular, their children (see Cases 112, 168–170). At this early date it would plainly be anachronistic to speak of female emancipation, but in most respects adult women were more independent in Roman law than in most subsequent legal systems before the modern period.

Still, classical Roman private law retained from its archaic period some restrictions on women's freedom; as Papinian dryly observes (D. 1.5.9): "In many areas of our law the condition of women is inferior to that of men." The most striking restriction is that women were subject to permanent tutelage even after they reached adulthood. An adult *sui iuris* woman's *tutor* was originally intended mainly to safeguard her property, especially in the interests of near relatives who could expect to inherit after her death; the intrusion on her autonomy was popularly justified by insisting on her "weakness of judgment," which rendered her susceptible to double-dealing by the unscrupulous.

Already by the late Republic, however, the *tutor's* role had been reduced to what was usually little more than a petty hindrance. Cicero, clearly tapping into a wellspring of popular resentment, describes this development as the consequence of misapplied juristic ingenuity (*Pro Murena* 27). And in fact, as we shall see, there is good evidence that some jurists were skeptical of the traditional arguments for tutelage of women. Although the institution was never abolished, ways were found to render it fairly innocuous, although it may go too far to describe it as "pure formality" (David Johnston).

Rather more serious are the restrictions that, in Rome as in other premodern societies, were placed on women's participation in the public domain. Women were excluded altogether from such civic responsibilities as voting, holding magistracies, and so on; and this is justified by positing certain "male duties" (*officia virilia*), a conventional sphere of male civic privilege. As the "weakness of judgment" argument declined in effectiveness, the strength of the "male duties" argument seems to have increased during the classical period; the most notable instance is its use in a decree of the Senate barring women from using their credit on behalf of third parties.

In the end, the Roman legal sources on this subject are not especially consistent, but they do tacitly imply an image of adult women as somehow "too pure" for the rigors of this world, hence as requiring shelter from at least the more forceful stresses of social and political life. This image, which we have good reason to believe many upper-class Roman women would have found either quaint or fantastic, is perhaps most clearly perceptible in the curious Roman approach to sexual harassment.

SECTION 1. The Permanent Tutelage of Women

CASE 225: The Weaker Sex?

Gaius, *Institutiones* 1.190–191

(190) Feminas vero perfectae aetatis in tutela esse fere nulla pretiosa ratio suasisse videtur; nam quae vulgo creditur, quia levitate animi plerumque decipiuntur et aequum erat eas tutorum auctoritate regi, magis speciosa videtur quam vera; mulieres enim, quae perfectae aetatis sunt, ipsae sibi negotia tractant, et in quibusdam causis dicis gratia tutor interponit auctoritatem suam; saepe etiam invitus auctor fieri a praetore cogitur. (191) Unde cum tutore nullum ex tutela iudicium mulieri datur; at ubi pupillorum pupillarumve negotia tutores tractant eis post pubertatem tutelae iudicio rationem reddunt.

(Gaius in the first book of his *Institutes*)

(190) There is, to be sure, no very good reason for adult women being in tutelage. The reason that is commonly given, namely that since they are frequently deceived through their weak judgment (*levitas animi*), they are rightly controlled by the authority of *tutores,* seems more specious than true, since adult women handle their business matters for themselves, and in certain situations the *tutor* grants his authorization (merely) as a matter of form. Often he is compelled by the praetor to give authorization even against his will.

(191) For this reason a woman with a *tutor* has no action on tutelage. By contrast, *tutores* who manage the affairs of male or female minors give an accounting of their tutelage under the *actio tutelae* when those children reach the age of majority.

1. *Levitas Animi.* This phrase, translated "weak judgment" (other possibilities are "unreliability, inconstancy, fickleness, shallowness of mind"), was used by laypersons to justify the permanent tutelage of adult women; sentiment to this effect is common in ancient authors (almost all male, of course). Is this simply a misogynistic slur? What other justification can be given for women's tutelage? Could one argue, for example, that their exclusion from public life (see Section 2 below) left them vulnerable to the predatory behavior of others? *Tit. Ulp.* 11.1 justifies the tutelage of women on the basis of "the weakness of their sex and their ignorance of judicial business."

2. The "Good Old Days." At *Inst.* 1.144, Gaius explains women's tutelage in more historical terms: "For the ancestors (*veteres*) wanted women, even adult women, to be in tutelage because of their *levitas animi.*" (Compare Cicero, *Pro Murena* 27: "Our ancestors wanted all women to be under a *tutor's* power because of the weakness of their judgment.") For Gaius, the "ancestors" (*veteres*) are probably Republican jurists, perhaps also prejuristic political and legal authorities. Is Gaius hinting that the institution was an archaic holdover? If so, why didn't later jurists move to end it? As Gaius also points out (ibid.

145), even the *veteres* conceded freedom from tutelage to the women chosen as Vestal Virgins, an exemption confirmed by the Twelve Tables. Was this a reward or a punishment?

3. The Weaker *Tutor*. Gaius, evidently drawing on personal observation, refutes the thesis of *levitas animi* by pointing out that in certain situations the *tutor's* authorization is only a matter of form and that often the praetor compels it to be given. Does his language ("in certain situations," "often") suggest that there were instances where a *tutor's* authorization still meant something? Keep in mind that female Romans were deemed adults from the age of twelve years. Do these considerations support resort to a modified form of female tutelage or one limited in scope? Were there viable alternatives to *tutela mulierum*? Many young women between the ages of twelve and twenty-five had both a *tutor* and a *curator*; see above, Part A.2.

4. Exemptions. As Gaius also observes (*Inst.* 1.145, 194), under Augustus's law on marriage women with (depending on the case) three or four children were exempt from tutelage. Were such women presumptively less likely to be deceived? If not, what does the exemption indicate about how seriously the requirement of tutelage was taken during the early Roman Empire?

5. No Marriage? A *tutor* was almost invariably male (Case 231). A *senatusconsultum* passed under Marcus Aurelius and Commodus (coreign: A.D. 175–180) prohibited marriage between a *tutor* and a woman who had been his minor-age ward (*pupilla*). What was the reason for this ban? Does it seem likely to have been applied to marriage between adult women and their guardians? Why or why not?

6. No Accounting. As Gaius says, a woman, unlike a juvenile ward, cannot sue her *tutor* for malfeasance. Does this seriously compromise her legal protection? If, beyond his usual duties, a woman's *tutor* undertook at her request to manage all or part of her affairs, he would be liable for his acts like any other manager.

7. Compelling Authorization. What sorts of situations would provoke the praetor to force a *tutor* to lend his authority to a transaction by his female ward? The Augustan marriage legislation prohibited a *pater familias* from wrongfully preventing children in his power from marrying or from wrongfully refusing to constitute a dowry for a daughter-in-power (Marcian, D. 23.2.19); evidently, enforcement was extended to the provinces through a *senatusconsultum* sponsored by Severus and Caracalla (coreign: A.D. 197–211). Likewise, it provided for praetorian appointment of a replacement *tutor* to establish a dowry for a woman whose *tutor* was a minor (Gaius, *Inst.* 1.179). (Compare Case 33.) An undated *senatusconsultum* provided the same

for a woman whose guardian was insane or incapable of speech (ibid. 1.180). Would the praetor customarily intervene when a *tutor* refused to approve constitution of a dowry or the contraction of the odd marriage with *manus?* If the woman and the *tutor* were at complete loggerheads, she could also apply to have him replaced; see Case 227.

CASE 226: The *Tutor's* Authorization

Tituli ex Corpore Ulpiani 11.27

Tutoris auctoritas necessaria est mulieribus quidem in his rebus: si lege aut legitimo iudicio agant, si se obligent, si civile negotium gerant, si libertae suae permittant in contubernio alieni servi morari, si rem mancipii alienent. pupillis autem hoc amplius etiam in rerum nec mancipii alienatione tutoris auctoritate opus est.

(Excerpts from Ulpian's Writings)

Women require the authorization of a *tutor* in these situations: if they bring suit by statute or in a statutory trial; if they obligate themselves; if they conduct a transaction in the *ius civile;* if they allow their freedwoman to remain in cohabitation with another person's slave; if they alienate a *res mancipi.*

For minor wards (*pupilli*), the *tutor's* authorization is additionally required also in the alienation of *res nec mancipi.*

1. When Was a *Tutor's* Authorization Required? Basically, the *tutor's* authorization was required in two circumstances: conduct of most formal legal acts (including bringing certain lawsuits that require the use of ceremonial language but also *ius civile* transactions such as the mancipation of property and the execution of a will; see Case 228); and conduct of acts that obligated her, thus endangering the size of her estate. Is the rationale behind these two circumstances the same? Women have considerably broader powers than do minor wards, in any case; without a *tutor's* authorization they can alienate *res nec mancipi* (property except for certain types, especially land, slaves, and draft animals), receive payment of debts, engage in some litigation, and name a *procurator* to manage their property (see Gaius, *Inst.* 2.80–81, 85; *Tit. Ulp.* 11.25; *Frag. Vat.* 325, 327). How much are women really inhibited? As to marriage, see Paul, D. 23.2.20, quoting a rescript of Septimius Severus and Caracalla: "A female ward (*pupilla*) can marry as she pleases."

2. Letting Your Freedwoman Sleep with Another Person's Slave. Why is a *tutor's* authorization required for this? Under a decree of the Senate of A.D. 52, severe penalties were assessed against free women who cohabited with the slaves of other persons. A freedwoman who, with the knowledge of her former owner and patron, cohabited with another's slave was made the slave of the person who informed on her (Paul, *Sent.* 2.21a.6). The patron who consented to such a union therefore risked losing rights of succession to the freedwoman.

CASE 227: Escaping a *Tutor*

Gaius, *Institutiones* 1.173

Praeterea senatus consulto mulieribus permissum est in absentis tutoris locum alium petere; quo petito prior desinit; nec interest quam longe absit is tutor.

(Gaius in the first book of his *Institutes*)

What is more, women are allowed by a *senatusconsultum* to request a *tutor* in place of one who is absent. Once the request is made, the first one ceases to be *tutor*. It does not matter how far away the *tutor* is.

Hypothetical Situation

Titius, the *tutor*, packs his bags for a weekend at the seashore. To his dismay, he becomes entangled in business concerns before he makes it out of the suburbs, and he is forced to return to Rome later that same day. In the meantime, his ward, a sixteen-year-old named Seia, has approached a magistrate and asked for a new *tutor* in order to approve a will that Titius has long opposed her making. Will Seia prevail?

1. Time versus Distance. Does brevity of distance imply brevity of time as well?

2. Senatorial Intervention. What do you think motivated the Senate to act? Is there a risk that the authority of *tutores* will be undermined as a result?

3. Where There's a Will . . . Gaius (*Inst.* 1.114–115) also reports an older and far more complex method for getting rid of a *tutor*. The woman undergoes a formal and entirely fictitious "sale" (*coemptio*) in which she sells herself to third party, who then remancipates her to another person, who "manumits" her and thereafter becomes her "fiduciary guardian" (*tutor fiduciarius*); that is, he replaces her original *tutor*. This extraordinarily contrived ceremony derives from an archaic procedure for marrying with *manus* (see Discussion on Case 19). Another variant of the same ceremony had once been used to allow a woman to write a will; see the following Case.

4. Exceptions. In two situations in classical law, a woman was not allowed to change her statutory *tutor*: if he was the ex-master and patron of a freedwoman, and if he was an emancipating *pater familias* (Gaius, *Inst.* 1.174–175). What is the reasoning behind these exceptions? One situation when an absent patron could be substituted even in these circumstances was when there was an opportunity to accept an inheritance. What does this exception to the exception tell us about the intended scope of the *senatusconsultum* for women who were neither freed nor emancipated?

CASE 228: Women's Wills

Gaius, *Institutiones* 1.115a

Olim etiam testamenti faciendi gratia fiduciaria fiebat coemptio: tunc enim non aliter feminae testamenti faciendi ius habebant, exceptis quibusdam personis, quam si coemptionem fecissent remancipataeque et manumissae fuissent: sed hanc necessitatem coemptionis faciendae ex auctoritate divi Hadriani senatus remisit.

Gaius, *Institutiones* 2.112

Ex auctoritate divi Hadriani senatus consultum factum est, quo permissum est <sui iuris> feminis etiam sine coemptione testamentum facere, si modo non minores essent annorum XII; scilicet ut quae tutela liberatae non essent, tutore auctore testari deberent.

(Gaius in the first book of his *Institutes*)

At one time a "fiduciary sale" (*coemptio fiduciaria*) was made in order to execute a will. For at that time, with certain exceptions, women had the right to execute a will only if they had made a "sale" and had been remancipated and manumitted. But on the authority of the deified Hadrian, the Senate remitted the requirement of making the "sale."

(Gaius in the second book of his *Institutes*)

On the authority of the deified Hadrian, a *senatusconsultum* was enacted that permitted *sui iuris* women to execute a will even without a "sale," so long as they were at least twelve years old. Obviously, those women who have not been released from tutelage need their *tutor's* authorization to make a will.

1. Selling Yourself. This archaic form of "sale" is described in the Discussion to the previous Case. In the early Republic, the core of the problem was that the household of a *sui iuris* woman perished with her (see Case 4 at the end), and accordingly her property would normally return to her agnate family. As older principles of family organization declined, women sought ways to leave their property to people other than those of their family of birth; surviving husbands and children were likely candidates. This ceremony was contrived to meet that need. How frequently women made use of it we have no way of telling, but we often hear of women's wills from the late Republic on.

2. Hadrian's Reform. Hadrian (reign: A.D. 117–138) had enacted a decree of the Senate that abolished the need for the "sale" but preserved other conditions. The woman had to be of adult age (see Cases 6–7; as Gaius, *Inst.* 2.113, notes, women became adults and could write wills sooner than men), and her *tutor* had to authorize the will. Why might this latter requirement be a problem for

a woman who wished to write a will? A woman's *tutor* often came from her family of birth, so the *tutor* might have a venal reason to resist her writing a will; see Cases 159 and 169 on intestate succession. Is the woman adequately protected against such pressures? Does it appear that he authorized the actual contents of her will?

SECTION 2. Women's Public Position

CASE 229: Where the Boys Are

D. 50.17.2 pr. (Ulpianus libro primo ad Sabinum)

Feminae ab omnibus officiis civilibus vel publicis remotae sunt et ideo nec iudices esse possunt nec magistratum gerere nec postulare nec pro alio intervenire nec procuratores existere.

D. 5.1.12.2 (Paulus libro septimo decimo ad edictum)

Non autem omnes iudices dari possunt ab his qui iudicis dandi ius habent: quidam enim lege impediuntur ne iudices sint, quidam natura, quidam moribus. natura, ut surdus mutus: et perpetuo furiosus et impubes, quia iudicio carent. lege impeditur, qui senatus motus est. moribus feminae et servi, non quia non habent iudicium, sed quia receptum est, ut civilibus officiis non fungantur.

(Ulpian in the first book on Sabinus)

Women are excluded from all civic and public duties (*officia civilia vel publica*), and so they cannot be judges (*iudices*), hold magistracies, bring legal claims for others (*postulare*), represent others in court, or act as *procuratores* (for others in lawsuits).

(Paul in the seventeenth book on the Edict)

Moreover, not everyone can be appointed a judge (*iudex*) by those who have the right to appoint judges. Certain kinds of persons are prevented from acting as judges by statute, by nature, or by convention. By nature, there are the deaf and the mute; and also a permanent lunatic and a prepubescent child, since they lack judgment. By statute, a person who has been removed from the Senate is prevented (from serving as a judge). By convention, there are women and slaves, not because they do not possess judgment, but because it is traditional that they do not perform civic duties (*civilia officia*).

1. Semicitizens? In the early Roman Empire, as in most Western societies until the success of the women's suffrage movement in the early twentieth century, women were citizens but were nonetheless legally barred from voting, holding magistracies, serving as jurors, and generally performing what were thought of as public duties. This view is repugnant today, but it is worth trying to see why it once prevailed. If it is conceded that women are free citizens who "possess judgment," what justifications can possibly be offered for excluding them from public duties, beyond Paul's half-hearted point that this is "traditional" (*receptum*)? The Latin word *mores,* here translated "convention," has strong overtones of what is acceptable as decent and civilized behavior. What exactly were Roman men afraid of? Just sharing power?

2. Judges. Being a judge (*iudex*) in a Roman criminal or civil trial does not mean being a legal professional; most judges were laypersons specifically appointed

to hear and decide particular trials. But this was a public duty that was often imposed on, especially, the elite. Ordinarily, if both parties to a civil lawsuit agreed on who they wanted to judge their case, the praetor would name that person. So, for instance, Pomponius, D. 5.1.80: If a *iudex* is named on the basis of the agreement of the two parties, the *iudex* is the person they intend even if they make a mistake on the person's exact name. However, the praetor enforces certain broad requirements for naming judges, one of which, as Paul notes, is that a *iudex* cannot be a child (*impubes*). What if the parties nonetheless settled on a child? Ulpian (D. 42.1.57) says that so long as they did so knowing the boy's age, his decision is binding. Although dispute continues as to whether this decision gives classical law, it raises an interesting point: what would the outcome be if the parties agreed on a woman as *iudex*?

3. Appearance in Court. The praetor, in an effort "to take account of his own position and to preserve his dignity and social position" (Ulpian, D. 3.1.1 pr.), issued rules on the sort of persons who could appear in his court and apply for actions or defenses. Certain persons (e.g., minors and the deaf) could not appear at all and therefore always had to be represented by others (ibid. 3). Others could appear for themselves but could not represent others; in addition to women, also included in this class (ibid. 5–6) were the blind, passive homosexuals, those who had been condemned on a capital charge or for bringing a malicious criminal charge against others, gladiators, and those who had fought wild beasts in the arena. Is there any common thread to these prohibitions? Representation can take several closely related forms: bringing or defending a claim on behalf of someone else (*postulare;* see ibid. 2); intervening as a representative of one party (*intervenire*); or acting as a *procurator* for the lawsuit, particularly when a litigant is physically unable to be present in court. A woman is forbidden to act in any of these functions; for possible reasons, see the following Case.

4. Criminal Law. Rome had no public prosecutor as such, so that the criminal-law system depended heavily on the initiative of private persons indicting wrongdoers before the authorities. Women were excluded from bringing criminal charges except in cases involving their parents, children, patrons, patron's children, or patron's grandchildren (Pomponius, D. 48.2.1; Papinian, D. 48.2.2 pr.; Ulpian, D. 49.5.1.1). What do you think the rationale for this exclusion might be? Is it similar to the one for *postulatio?* Certain exceptions were permitted in situations involving false wills and interference with the grain supply (Papinian, D. 48.2.2 pr.; Marcian, D. 48.2.13). What explains these exceptions?

5. Witnesses. Women were not allowed to witness a will, but they were permitted to give evidence in criminal (and civil) cases, a rule that Ulpian (D. 28.1.20.6) infers from the prohibition in the adultery law on convicted adulteresses doing so; see also Paul, D. 22.5.18. Was it the statute's intent to allow women to bear witness, or was this just an inadvertent outcome? Does the jurist's reasoning suggest that they did not appear as witnesses very often?

CASE 230: Order in the Court

D. 3.1.1.5 (Ulpianus libro sexto ed edictum)

Secundo loco edictum proponitur in eos, qui pro aliis ne postulent: in quo edicto excepit praetor sexum et casum, item notavit personas in turpitudine notabiles. sexum: dum feminas prohibet pro aliis postulare. et ratio quidem prohibendi, ne contra pudicitiam sexui congruentem alienis causis se immisceant, ne virilibus officiis fungantur mulieres: origo vero introducta est a Carfania, improbissima femina, quae inverecunde postulans et magistratum inquietans causam dedit edicto. . . .

(Ulpian in the sixth book on the Edict)

In the second category a provision of the (praetor's) Edict is laid down against those who are forbidden to make claims (*postulare*) on behalf of others. In this part of the Edict the praetor framed specifications on the basis of sex and disability; further, he blacklisted those who merit this because of their depravity.

On the basis of sex: he bars women from making claims on behalf of others. And, indeed, the basis for this exclusion is to prevent women from entangling themselves in the lawsuits of others and performing male duties (*virilia officia*), contrary to the modesty that is becoming to their sex. The origin (of the ban) came in fact from Carfania, a very disreputable woman, who by shamelessly making claims and disturbing the praetor furnished the reason for this provision of the Edict. . . .

1. Carfania's Offense. Carfania, the wife of a Roman senator (Valerius Maximus, 8.3.2), tried to practice law sometime during the last decades of the Roman Republic. What is it that seems to have upset the praetor: that a woman was taking an active role in his court, or that this particular woman was performing badly in the role? Why did the praetor ban all women from representing others? Was the ban punitive or protective?

2. Mind Your Own Business. What does Ulpian mean by "entangling themselves in the lawsuits of others" as a motive for women's exclusion as representatives? Why, for example, should a mother not be allowed to represent her children?

3. Male Stuff. The other justification expresses a concern with women "performing male duties." Why is *postulare* so conceived? Is it that the private-law system operates in a public forum? Why did the Romans decide that women can make claims for themselves but not for others? What does the exclusion say about women's status as Roman citizens?

CASE 231: Male Jobs

D. 26.1.16 pr. (Gaius libro duodecimo ad edictum provinciale)

Tutela plerumque virile officium est.

D. 26.1.18 (Neratius libro tertio Regularum)

Feminae tutores dari non possunt, quia id munus masculorum est, nisi a principe filiorum tutelam specialiter postulent.

D. 2.13.12 (Callistratus libro primo Edicti Monitorii)

Feminae remotae videntur ab officio argentarii, cum ea opera virilis sit.

(Gaius in the twelfth book on the Provincial Edict)

Tutelage is generally a male duty (*virile officium*).

(Neratius in the third book of his *Rules of Law*)

Women cannot be appointed *tutores* since this is a responsibility of males (*munus masculorum*), unless they specifically request the tutelage of their children from the emperor.

(Callistratus in the first book *On the Monitory Edict*)

Women are held to be excluded from the position of banker, since this is a male job (*opera virilis*).

1. Public Duty. As the wording of Case 214 suggests, tutelage was thought of as a kind of civic responsibility. How is the ineligibility of women to act as *tutores* of minor-age children related to their exclusion from public duties? Is it that tutelage is conceived of as also a public trust? Or is it that women themselves were usually required to have *tutores?* In a late classical rescript, Alexander Severus (C. 5.35.1; A.D. 224) justifies the ban by referring to women as the "gender of female weakness" (*sexum femineae infirmitatis*). Is this rationale persuasive in light of Gaius's observations in Case 225 above, especially that many women managed their own affairs?

2. Private Duty. A number of texts suggest that the tutelage of minor-age children was regarded as a private family matter, best entrusted to their mother. Papinian (D. 3.5.30.6) denies that a mother can act as a guardian to her son as requested in her husband's will insofar as she is unable to engage in lawsuits at her own risk: she cannot sue in her son's name, alienate his property, or grant formal release to his debtors. Does this amount to saying that a woman cannot be a *tutor* because she cannot be a *tutor?* The same jurist implies that if a provincial governor wrongly upheld a will making such an arrangement, his successor should quash it (D. 26.2.26 pr.). How could a provincial governor make such an error? Finally, Ulpian, citing Papinian,

seems to record an attempt by a father to dodge this rule in his will by entrusting the management of his children's estate to their mother and releasing the *tutores* from responsibility for it (D. 26.7.5.8). Why not allow this?

3. Exceptions. In the principal Case, Gaius implies (see "generally") and Neratius states outright that some women could obtain leave from the emperor to act as *tutores* for their own children. Why was this exception allowed? Ulpian (D. 5.2.29.3; cited in the Discussion to Case 153) allows some women to adopt with the permission of the emperor. Is the rationale in both instances similar?

4. Quasi Exceptions. Though not permitted to act as *tutores,* women could and evidently did manage the estates of minor-age descendants. See Paul, D. 3.5.33, for a case involving a grandmother and grandson. Did this entail reducing the real *tutor* to the status of a figurehead? Ulpian (D. 26.7.5.8; citing Papinian) indicates that the responsible *tutor* can appropriately accept the mother's beneficial advice, though this in no way diminishes his authority. Does this ruling strike you more as the statement of an ideal rather than a reflection of reality?

5. Legal Protection. Pomponius (D. 27.5.4) says that someone who administers property in place of a *tutor* should display the same good faith and care that a *tutor* does. Was a mother, to the Roman mind, capable of showing these qualities? Persons who, although not guardians, managed the affairs of others were still liable under contractual or quasi-contractual actions. Does this protection of the ward's interests seem adequate to you?

6. Why Banking? Women were not legally barred from entering most professions, but banking was an exception. Although ancient banks, minuscule by modern standards, were owned and operated by private individuals, they were loosely supervised and regulated by the government. Further, the records of bankers had privileged status as evidence of financial transactions, and bankers could therefore often be obliged to appear in court to provide this evidence (Ulpian, D. 2.13.4 pr.). Is all this enough to explain the exclusion of women? Is it likely that women would also be excluded from other professions with a public nature, such as surveying or the keeping of weights and measures? Could a woman be a jurist if she avoided court appearances?

CASE 232: Ignorance of the Law

D. 22.6.9 pr. (Paulus libro singulari de Iuris et Fach Ignorantia)

Regula est iuris quidem ignorantiam cuique nocere, facti vero ignorantiam non nocere. videamus igitur, in quibus speciebus locum habere possit, ante praemisso quod minoribus viginti quinque annis ius ignorare permissum est. quod et in feminis in quibusdam causis propter sexus infirmitatem dicitur: et ideo sicubi non est delictum, sed iuris ignorantia, non laeduntur. hac ratione si minor viginti quinque annis filio familias crediderit, subvenitur ei, ut non videatur filio familias credidisse.

(Paul in his monograph *On Ignorance of Fact and Law*)

It is a legal rule, to be sure, that ignorance of the law harms everyone, but ignorance of fact does not. Let us examine, then, to what situations this rule applies, granting first of all that persons under age twenty-five are allowed to be ignorant of the law.

In certain cases this is also true for women, because of the weakness of their sex (*sexus infirmitas*); and so, whenever it is a matter not of their wrongdoing but of their ignorance of the law, they are not harmed. On this principle, if someone less than twenty-five loans (money) to a son-in-power, he is aided to the effect that he is not held to have loaned to a son-in-power.

1. Four Types of "Ignoramus". Four types of persons were on occasion permitted to plead that they had been disadvantaged because they were unaware of legal rules: those under twenty-five, soldiers, women, and "rustics," this last group evidently being uneducated peasants. Why would these particular groups be thought to require protection? Do such exceptions erode the principle that "ignorance of the law is no excuse"?

2. Loans to Minors. The SC Macedonianum held that a person who lent money to a son-in-power could not subsequently sue to recover the loan; see the Discussion on Case 119. Is this a technical rule that we would expect highly skilled professional moneylenders to know? If one teenager loans money to another and the lender is unaware of the decree, Paul says that the money can be recovered. Would the same be true if an adult woman, also unaware of the decree, loaned the money?

3. No Profit. What does Paul mean by "whenever it is a matter not of their wrongdoing . . ."? Is there a hint here that not all women might be disadvantaged by ignorance of the law and so entitled to the benefit of the exemption?

4. The Imperial Revenue Service. If you are unaware of your rights and so inadvertently incriminate yourself to the imperial treasury, can you hope that your blunder will be excused? Only in the case of women and "rustics," according to Callistratus, who relies on an imperial rescript (D. 49.14.2.7). Regarding women, is that holding consistent with this Case?

CASE 233: The Credit of Women

D. 16.1.1 (Paulus libro trigensimo ad edictum)

(pr.) Vell<ae>ano senatus consulto plenissime comprehensum est, ne pro ullo feminae intercederent. (1) Nam sicut moribus civilia officia adempta sunt feminis et pleraque ipso iure non valent, ita multo magis adimendum eis fuit id officium, in quo non sola opera nudumque ministerium earum versaretur, sed etiam periculum rei familiaris. (2) Aequum autem visum est ita mulieri succurri, ut in veterem debitorem aut in eum, qui pro se constituisset mulierem ream, actio daretur: magis enim ille quam creditor mulierem decepit.

(Paul in the thirtieth book on the Edict)

(pr.) A prohibition against women interceding on behalf of another person was very fully prescribed in the SC Vellaeanum. (1) For since by convention public duties (*civilia officia*) have been denied to women and by operation of law they are generally rendered invalid (in their effects), it seemed for this reason all the more necessary to deny them this responsibility (as well), in which not (only) their mere effort and bare assistance were at stake but also a risk to their family property.

  (2) Moreover, it seemed fair to help out a woman by making available (to her) an action against the prior debtor or against the person who had made the woman liable on his behalf, for it is he and not the creditor who more probably deceived the woman.

  1. Intercession. "Intercession" is a technical term that includes many instances in which one person assumes another person's debt or liability. A typical instance is suretyship, when a debtor owes money to a creditor, and a third party promises the creditor that he or she will pay the debt if the debtor does not. But there are many other ways in which such assumption can occur; for example, the third party, the creditor, and the debtor come to an arrangement whereby the debtor's debt is extinguished and an equivalent debt from the third party arises in its place (novation); or the third party gives property to the creditor as security for the debt (pledge); or the third party borrows money from the creditor and then immediately hands it over to the debtor as a loan (a loan to the interest of a third party); and so on. In some instances such an intercession might occur without the creditor's knowledge (Paul, D. 16.1.11, gives an example), but the SC Vellaeanum, which dates from the mid–first century A.D., is concerned only with situations where the creditor is aware that a woman is interposing her credit on behalf of a debtor; see Ulpian, D. 16.1.4 pr.

  2. Why Did the Senate Act? Paul gives three explanations, which somewhat overlap:

- Woman cannot perform "public duties" and so should not be permitted to intercede for others. This takes up the thought in Cases 229–231; and this explanation was mentioned in the wording of the SC Vellaeanum: Ulpian, D. 16.1.2.1. How might interposition of credit be regarded as a public or civic act?
- If women intercede for others, they risk their family property (*res familiaris*). This reason is doubtless related to the *levitas animi* theory that justifies permanent female tutelage (Case 225); Ulpian (D. 16.1.2.2) specifically mentions "the weakness of a woman's sex" in this connection. But women can freely engage in other transactions that may be very risky; for example, they can buy and sell their property. Why does intercession seem to present more problems? What is the real underlying fear here, do you think?
- In section 2, Paul makes a subtle point: it is the debtor, and not the creditor, who is likely to "deceive" a woman into interceding. Paul may have a particular situation in mind. What sort of debtor might be particularly likely to pressure a woman into interceding? What sort of deception might Paul be thinking of?

Ulpian (D. 16.1.2 pr.) indicates that, even before this decree, imperial edicts had forbidden women from interceding on behalf of their own husbands. Does this help to clarify the problem that the Senate may have been addressing? At ibid. 5, Ulpian mentions a woman's husband, son, and father as typifying the beneficiaries of intercession. Could it be that a woman might require more protection from her husband and his relatives than from her own relatives?

3. What about the *Tutor*? The prohibition is absolute, so even a *tutor's* authorization will not help the woman. Why not? It was also usually ineffective for a woman to promise that she would not make use of the defenses provided by the statute (Paul and Pomponius, D. 16.1.31 and 32.4).

4. Generosity. Callistratus (D. 16.1.21.1) holds that a woman cannot use the *senatusconsultum* as a defense if she acts "out of generosity" (*liberaliter*), for example, if she has been emancipated and promises to pay her father's debts so that his creditors will not foreclose; "for the Senate helps out (only) when women are burdened." Why is she not burdened in this situation? How easy is this situation to distinguish from those that the *senatusconsultum* covers? In any case, says Ulpian (D. 16.1.4.1), the *senatusconsultum* was not meant to discourage a woman from giving gifts, even if they take an unusual form (e.g., a woman borrows money and gives it to Titius as a gift, or she uses her own money to pay off his creditors).

5. Self-Interest. According to Africanus (D. 16.1.17.2) a woman may intercede on behalf of a partner in a business enterprise when her own interest is at stake. Suppose a woman makes a profit from a deal where she incurred an obligation on behalf of someone else; would the *senatusconsultum* apply? See Callistratus, D. 16.1.21 pr. (no). Why not?

6. Deceit. Is the *senatusconsultum* of any help to a woman if she intercedes in order to deceive a creditor? See Paul, D. 16.1.30 pr. (= *Sent.* 2.11.3) (no). Does this ruling suggest any trial strategies for plaintiff creditors?

CASE 234: Protecting Women in Financial Matters

D. 12.6.40 pr. (Marcianus libro tertio Regularum)

Qui exceptionem perpetuam habet, solutum per errorem repetere potest: sed hoc non est perpetuum. nam si quidem eius causa exceptio datur cum quo agitur, solutum repetere potest, ut accidit in senatus consulto de intercessionibus: ubi vero in odium eius cui debetur exceptio datur, perperam solutum non repetitur, veluti si filius familias contra Macedonianum mutuam pecuniam acceperit et pater familias factus solverit, non repetit.

(Marcian in the third book of his *Rules of Law*)

Whoever has a permanent defense (*exceptio*) can reclaim what was paid by mistake. But this is not always true. For if the defense is provided to benefit the (potential) defendant, it is possible to reclaim what is paid, as occurs with the *senatusconsultum* (Vellaeanum) on intercessions.

But when the defense is provided as a sanction against the person to whom it (the debt) is owed, the mistaken payment is not (able to be) reclaimed. For example, if, contrary to the (SC) Macedonianum, a son-in-power receives money on loan and (then), on becoming a *pater familias,* pays (this debt), he does not reclaim it.

1. Defenses. In a Roman trial, a defense (*exceptio*) is a legal mechanism that a defendant can use to render a plaintiff's claim ineffective; see Gaius, *Inst.* 4.115–125. The SC Vellaeanum provided a woman with such a defense when, contrary to the provisions of the statute, she had interceded on behalf of another person. If the creditor subsequently sued her, she could interpose the defense and thereby defeat the creditor. Her defense is "permanent," meaning that it does not expire with the passage of time. Further, even if a woman neglects to use it at the trial and is condemned to pay the creditor, she can still use the *senatusconsultum* to resist execution of the trial judgment. The SC Macedonianum provided a similar defense at trial when a third party loaned money to a son-in-power (see the Discussion on Case 119).

2. Reasons Have Consequences. Suppose that a woman interceded contrary to the statute, and she then paid the creditor; can she recover the payment? This Case says that she can, but that a son-in-power cannot if he received a loan and then repaid it upon becoming *sui iuris*. On what legal distinction is this difference in outcomes based? How does this distinction reflect the various explanations for the statute in Case 233?

CASE 235: Sexual Harassment

D. 47.10.15.15, 20–22 (Ulpianus <quinquagesimo> septimo ad edictum)

(15) Si quis virgines appellasset, si tamen ancillari veste vestitas, minus peccare videtur, multo minus, si meretricia veste feminae, non matrum familiarum vestitae fuissent. si igitur non matronali habitu femina fuerit et quis eam appellavit vel ei comitem abduxit, iniuriarum <non> tenetur. . . . (20) Appellare est blanda oratione alterius pudicitiam adtemptare: hoc enim non est convicium sed adversus bonos mores adtemptare. (21) Qui turpibus verbis utitur, non temptat pudicitiam, sed iniuriarum tenetur. (22) Aliud est appellare, aliud adsectari: appellat enim, qui sermone pudicitiam adtemptat, adsectatur, qui tacitus frequenter sequitur: adsidua enim frequentia quasi praebet nonnullam infamiam.

(Ulpian in the fifty-seventh book on the Edict)

(15) If someone accosted respectable young girls, but they were dressed in slaves' clothing, he is understood to commit a lesser offense; and a much lesser offense if the women were dressed as prostitutes and not as respectable women. Therefore, if a woman has not been wearing respectable clothing and someone has accosted her or abducted her attendant, he is not liable to the action on outrage (*iniuria*). . . .

(20) To accost is to assault another's chastity with smooth talk. This is not clamor (*convicium*) but to make an assault contrary to good morals. (21) One who uses foul language does not make an assault on chastity but is liable for *iniuria*. (22) It is one thing to accost, another to stalk. For one accosts by using speech to assault chastity; one stalks by silently, persistently pursuing. For (a pursuer's) ceaseless presence virtually ensures appreciable disrepute.

1. *Iniuria*. The delict of outrage (*iniuria*) by Ulpian's day had come to include almost any intentional affront to another's social personality. Ulpian is discussing a type of *iniuria* that dealt with the sexual harassment of women. The three well-defined instances of harassment were accosting (*appellare*), stalking (*adsectari*), or abducting an attendant (*comitem abducere*). The first two gave rise to liability only if performed "contrary to good morals." What is the precise nature of this offense? Is it a defense to claim that the victim was already unchaste? Paul (D. 47.10.10) implies yes. Do you see why?

2. Accosting. How is accosting—that is, harassment through attempted seduction—distinguished from obscene speech, dirty jokes, and the like? Ulpian makes a defendant liable for "foul language" (*turpia verba*), but he regards this, not as accosting, but as a more general form of *iniuria*. Does this make sense? Was a Roman woman's reputation and social profile threatened more by attempted seduction than by other types of coarse behavior? What do you make of the requirement that the accosting be done "contrary to good

morals"? Does this exclude all nonamorous encounters? Some amorous ones? Is the woman's consent to the approach relevant?

3. Stalking and Abducting. Is there a potential difference between these two behaviors and accosting, in terms of the harasser's intent? Could either stalking or abducting an attendant be construed as a prelude to rape? Why else would such actions be treated under this subrubric? What is the point of requiring that stalking be "contrary to good morals"? Why in particular is it an offense to abduct an attendant? Ulpian (D. 47.10.15.16), following Labeo, defines an attendant as one "who is appointed to follow someone as a companion." He adds that this includes slaves who take children to school (*paedagogi*). "Abducting" means successfully forcing or persuading the attendant to leave the side of the intended target.

4. Clothing. Does Ulpian assume distinct types of clothing for slaves, prostitutes, and respectable women? At any rate, does he take for granted that the clothing of these types will be readily distinguishable? Does this detail, together with the offense of abducting an attendant, suggest that the delict primarily aims to protect women of a certain social rank?

5. Sex and Status. In general terms, what does the Case tell us about the status of women in the Roman world? What is the apparent social function of extending such protection to women, and what social image of women does the law presuppose? The delict protects not only women of any age but also adolescent males against homosexual advances; why doesn't it also protect adult men? Is it fair to argue that whereas our law of harassment is chiefly based on the policy goal of equality between the sexes (where harassment is seen as a barrier to this equality), Roman law was based on a policy goal of difference between the sexes (where harassment undermines the "privileged status" of women)?

APPENDIX

Biographies of the Major Roman Jurists

Jurists who are cited or referred to more than once in the Cases are marked by an asterisk.

*AFRICANUS. Sextus Caecilius Africanus was a student of Julian; in his nine books of *Questions* he generally seems to follow and comment on Julian's decisions. The *Digest* contains 130 fragments or citations of his writings.

*ALFENUS. Publius Alfenus Varus, consul in 39 B.C. and a student of Servius, wrote forty books of *Digests* that were excerpted and commented on by Paul in the late classical period. He is the only preclassical jurist whose writings are represented by numerous excerpts (eighty-one fragments) in the *Digest;* they frequently report views of Servius.

BRUTUS. Marcus Junius Brutus, praetor in 142 B.C., is counted among the three founders of Roman legal science.

*CALLISTRATUS. Callistratus was a late classical jurist whose writings are mainly concerned with extraordinary cognition and administrative law. The *Digest* contains 108 fragments of his writings.

CAPITO. Gaius Ateius Capito was suffect consul in A.D. 5. From an undistinguished family, he enjoyed the favor of Augustus (reign: 31 B.C. to A.D. 14), in sharp contrast to Marcus Antistius Labeo, who did not attain the consulate. Capito wrote a treatise on pontifical law and a collection called *Miscellanies (Coniectanea)*.

CASCELLIUS. Aulus Cascellius was a contemporary, if not a student, of Servius in the first century B.C. He was evidently an expert in the law of real estate.

*CASSIUS. Gaius Cassius Longinus, descended from an eminent Republican family, was consul in A.D. 30, later proconsul and legate in Asia and Syria, but in 65 he was banished to Sardinia by Nero (reign: A.D. 54–68). A pupil of Sabinus, he helped found the school of jurists that is also called Cassian. His major work, a commentary on the *ius civile,* is known from excerpts reworked by Javolenus.

*CELSUS. Publius Juventius Celsus (praetor in A.D. 108, consul for the second time in 128, governor of Thrace and Asia, a member of Hadrian's Council) is one of the most prominent juristic personalities of the high classical period. His acuteness and originality were accompanied, at times, by aggressive polemics. Along with Neratius, he headed the Proculian school and appears to have contributed to overcoming school controversies. Of special note are his abstract statements on the sources of law and the methods of legal interpretation.

Celsus's major work, the *Digests* in thirty-nine books, follows the order of the Edict (Books 1–27) and a standard list of statutes and decrees of the Senate (279 fragments).

CINNA. Cinna was a student of Servius Sulpicius Rufus and thus is datable to the second half of the first century B.C. Nothing else is known about him.

FLORENTINUS. He wrote the *Institutes*, a fairly comprehensive introductory work in twelve books, apparently no earlier than the reign of Marcus Aurelius (A.D. 161–180).

FULCINIUS. Fulcinius Priscus is cited by Neratius and so dates at the latest to the late first century A.D. Nothing more is known about him.

FURIUS ANTHIANUS. He is an obscure jurist, possibly of late classical date, who wrote a commentary on the Edict.

*GAIUS. Gaius (his family name and origin are unknown) was an outsider in classical jurisprudence; he was a teacher of law, probably without the *ius respondendi*. His writings (some twenty in number, dating from A.D. 150–180) were intended mainly to instruct (e.g., the material is carefully organized) and also show an interest in legal history (e.g., his commentary on the Twelve Tables); but they avoid casuistic discussion of legal problems. Perhaps for this reason, Gaius was not considered worthy of citation by his contemporaries, but he came to be recognized as a major jurist in the postclassical period and is frequently cited in the *Digest* (521 fragments). His main significance lies in the area of abstract doctrine and system building.

Gaius's thirty books on the Provincial Edict are an extended commentary on the model Edict for the provinces; the Emperor Hadrian (reign: A.D. 117–138) had ordered the Provincial Edict to be edited along with the urban praetor's Edict, and the two closely resembled each other. Governors were required to proclaim the Provincial Edict unchanged. Gaius's commentary was perhaps written as a basis for law courses in a provincial city.

Gaius's *Institutes*, a beginner's text in four books, was used as the basis for Justinian's *Institutes,* which have profoundly influenced Continental legal education and codification down to modern times. Gaius's *Institutes* is the only work of classical jurisprudence that survives in approximately its original form. The single manuscript (a palimpsest, in which the text of Gaius was overwritten with the letters of Saint Jerome) was rediscovered by the historian B. G. Niebuhr in Verona in 1816 and identified by the legal historian F. C. von Savigny soon thereafter.

Gaius also prepared an expanded seven-book edition of the *Institutes,* which he called the *Res Cottidianae* or *Aurea.* Scholars today believe that the preserved fragments from this work contain some postclassical additions.

GALLUS. Gaius Aquilius Gallus, a student of Quintus Mucius Scaevola, was praetor in 66 B.C. and one of the major jurists of his day. He apparently wrote nothing, and his opinions are mainly transmitted through Servius.

*HERMOGENIANUS. He was an early postclassical jurist who wrote six books of *Legal Excerpts* under Diocletian (reign: A.D. 284–305); he probably also compiled the Hermogenian Code, a collection of Diocletian's rescripts between 291 and 294.

*JAVOLENUS. Lucius Javolenus Priscus, head of the Sabinian school and Julian's teacher, wrote during the late first and early second centuries A.D.; he was consul in A.D. 86 and later governor in Upper Germany, Syria, and Africa, as well as a member of Trajan's Council (reign: A.D. 98–117). The *Digest* contains seventy-two excerpts from his most important work, the *Letters* (fourteen books), the longer fragments of which preserve the response format. He also prepared critical editions of several earlier jurists (Labeo, Cassius, Plautius).

*JULIAN. Publius Salvius Julianus, a student of Javolenus, enjoyed a brilliant career during the reigns of Hadrian (A.D. 117–138), Antoninus Pius (A.D. 138–161), and Marcus Aurelius (A.D. 161–180), to whose Council he belonged. "Because of his extraordinary learning" (so an honorary inscription tells us) the young Julian's pay as quaestor was doubled by Hadrian, who later entrusted to him the final edition of the praetor's Edict. Julian reached the consulate in 148 and served as governor in Lower Germany, Nearer Spain, and Africa.

Besides his major juristic work, the *Digests* (ninety books), he also wrote four books commenting on Urseius Ferox and six books of excerpts from Minicius (an otherwise unknown jurist of the late first century A.D.). Julian is praised especially for his clarity, elegance, and intuition and for the concrete vividness and realistic persuasiveness of his decisions. He seldom cites other jurists, basing his decisions instead on virtuosic reasoning from case to case; nor does he hesitate to overstep doctrinal boundaries in order to obtain fair results. The late classical jurists, especially Ulpian, cite him as a towering authority. In the *Digest* the compilers include more than 900 direct excerpts or citations from Julian's work.

*LABEO. Marcus Antistius Labeo was a student of Trebatius; because of his creative originality, he is considered the preeminent figure in early classical jurisprudence. He allegedly declined the consulate because of his opposition to the Emperor Augustus (reign: 31 B.C. to A.D. 14). Labeo taught law extensively—the Proculian juristic school is traced back to him—and also wrote at length. Labeo's voluminous works (over 400 books) are known to us only through two abbreviated versions: the jurist Javolenus epitomized and commented on Labeo's posthumous writings (in ten books), and Paul later did the same for the *Arguments* (*Pithana*), in eight books).

LICINIUS RUFINUS. Marcus Gnaeus Licinius Rufinus, very likely a student of the jurist Paul, wrote a work in twelve books: *Rules* (*Regulae*).

MACER. Aemilius Macer was from a senatorial family prominent in the late second and early third centuries A.D. and was himself active in the reigns of Caracalla (211–217) and Alexander Severus (222–235), when he composed monographs on procedure, military law, and the provincial governorship.

*MARCELLUS. Ulpius Marcellus, a high classical jurist, belonged to the Councils of Antoninus Pius (reign: A.D. 138–161) and Marcus Aurelius (reign: A.D. 161–180). His major work is thirty-one books of *Digests,* a collection of problems influenced by Julian's *Digests.* Justinian's *Digest* contains 292 fragments of his writings.

*MARCIAN. Aelius Marcianus, one of the last of the late classical jurists, wrote a lengthy *Institutes,* in sixteen books, as well as a collection of *Rules* (*Regulae*) and some monographs, mainly on criminal procedure, most likely in the reigns of Elagabalus (218–222) and Alexander Severus (222–235).

MAURICIANUS. Junius Mauricianus wrote an extensive commentary on the *lex Iulia et Papia,* the Augustan marriage legislation, under Antoninus Pius (reign: 138–161).

MELA. Fabius Mela is thought to have written during the reign of Augustus (31 B.C. to A.D. 14).

*MODESTINUS. Herennius Modestinus, a student of Ulpian, is the last securely datable late classical jurist. Modestinus was Prefect of the Watch under Alexander Severus (reign: 222–235) and/or one of his successors. He composed *Responsa* in nineteen books, as well as *Controversial Questions* (*Differentiae*), *Rules* (*Regulae,* and—in Greek— *Excusationes,* a work dealing with grounds for exemption from guardianship.

P. MUCIUS. Publius Mucius Scaevola, consul in 133 B.C., and pontifex maximus, himself the son of a consul, was a founder of Roman legal science and the father of Quintus Mucius Scaevola.

*Q. MUCIUS. Quintus Mucius Scaevola (the pontifex), consul in 95 B.C., is considered the most important preclassical jurist. He came from an aristocratic family that boasted many jurists, and his father, Publius Mucius Scaevola, was one of the founders of Roman legal science. According to Pomponius, Quintus Mucius was the first jurist to present the *ius civile* in systematic classifications. His eighteen books on the *ius civile* were still commented on by Pomponius in the second century A.D.

*NERATIUS. Lucius Neratius Priscus (consul in A.D. 98, later legate in Pannonia) headed the Proculian school after the elder Celsus; he belonged to the Imperial Council of Trajan (reign: A.D. 98–117) and of Hadrian (A.D. 117–138). His major works are collections of case law (*Responses, Letters, Rules of Law, Parchments*). He is well represented by 188 fragments or citations in the *Digest*.

NERVA. Marcus Cocceius Nerva (consul in A.D. 21 or 22) was a close advisor of the Emperor Tiberius (reign: A.D. 14–37). Along with Proculus, he led what was later called the Proculian school of jurists. Although later jurists often cite him, the titles of his writings are unknown. His son was also a jurist, and his grandson was Emperor Nerva (reign: A.D. 96–98).

OCTAVENUS. He appears to have written at the beginning of the second century A.D.; his work is cited fairly frequently by later authors.

OFILIUS. Aulus Ofilius was a student of Servius and a friend of Julius Caesar; no excerpts from his work survive in the *Digest*, but he is cited by other jurists more than fifty times.

*PAPINIAN. Aemilius Papinianus rose to the summit of the imperial bureaucracy. In A.D. 198 Papinian appears to have headed the Office of Petitions (*a libellis*), which drafted rescripts for the Emperor Septimius Severus (reign: A.D. 193–211) and his son, coruler, and successor, Caracalla (A.D. 198–217). Ulpian, who served as Papinian's clerk (*adsessor*), often refers to Severus's rescripts in his writings. From 203 to 211 Papinian served as praetorian prefect, with Paul and Ulpian probably acting as his clerks (*adsessores*) during part of this period. Papinian was executed in 211 or 212, allegedly because he objected to Caracalla's murder of his brother and coruler Geta.

Papinian's works (especially his thirty-seven books of *Questions* and nineteen books of *Responses*) preserve casuistry in its highest form. Despite their difficult style and their frequent extreme brevity of expression, Papinian's works are fascinating because of the richness of his thought and the sureness of his handling. The compilers of the *Digest* regarded him highly and made numerous excerpts from his writings (only Ulpian and Paul are used more frequently); and still today he is rightly regarded as one of the greatest Roman jurists.

PAPIRIUS JUSTUS. He may have held an equestrian post in the imperial bureaucracy; he collected the constitutions of Marcus Aurelius and Lucius Verus (joint reign: A.D. 161–169) and those of Marcus from his sole reign (A.D. 169–176). He is the only jurist known to have edited imperial constitutions in their original text, without commentary.

*PAUL. The late classical jurist Julius Paulus was a student of Cervidius Scaevola. Like Ulpian, he began his bureaucratic career as a clerk (*adsessor*) to the praetorian prefect Papinian. Along with Ulpian, he then served on the Council of Septimius

Severus (reign: A.D. 193–211); and under Alexander Severus (A.D. 222–235) he may have become praetorian prefect, the highest imperial office. Paul is considered more original than his slightly younger contemporary Ulpian, who seems to have inclined more strongly toward consolidating legal conceptions through dogma, thereby obscuring their original elasticity.

Despite his undoubtedly difficult and time-consuming official duties, Paul was astonishingly productive (notes on Neratius, Julian, Marcellus, and Scaevola; sixteen books on Sabinus; twenty-six books on *Questions*; twenty-three books on *Responses*; dozens of monographs on specialized topics). Paul's commentary on the praetor's Edict is a monumental work in eighty books, in which classical case law is critically assembled, examined, and presented from a relatively systematic viewpoint. The compilers of the *Digest* made numerous excerpts from his writings, amounting to about one-sixth of the entire *Digest*; but in the process they usually struck out Paul's extensive citation of earlier jurists and his reports of controversies.

The *Sentences*, attributed to Paul, is a collection of excerpts from the writings of Paul and (perhaps) other jurists; the collection was assembled in the late third century A.D. Until fairly recently the *Sentences* was considered a genuine and important work of Paul; as such, it had a major influence on postclassical and medieval law. Today the work is valued mainly because it preserves many texts of Paul in pre-Justinianic form.

PEDIUS. See SEX. PEDIUS.

PEGASUS. Pegasus succeeded Proculus as head of the Proculian school, served as prefect of the city under Vespasian (reign: A.D. 69–79) and under Domitian (reign: A.D. 81–96), and also became consul. His great reputation for learning led contemporaries to describe him as "a book, not a man"; but he is rarely cited by other jurists.

PLAUTIUS. Plautius was an adherent of the Proculian school and wrote during the Flavian period (A.D. 69–96). His writings were regarded as highly as Sabinus's *Civil Law*; they were annotated by Neratius and Javolenus. Pomponius (seven books) and especially Paul (eighteen books) wrote commentaries on his work.

*POMPONIUS. Sextus Pomponius, a contemporary of Gaius, like him represents an academic tendency in Roman jurisprudence. Nonetheless, he had great influence as the author of wide-ranging commentaries (39 books on Quintus Mucius; an exhaustive commentary on Sabinus in 35 books; his commentary on the praetor's Edict may have reached the impressive length of 150 books). Pomponius is frequently cited, especially by Ulpian, and there are numerous excerpts from him in the *Digest* (861 fragments or citations).

*PROCULUS. The early classical jurist Proculus wrote in the first half of the first century A.D. Probably in A.D. 33 he took over direction of the school that was later named for him. The *Digest* contains thirty-three fragments from his main work, the *Letters*. This work discusses legal problems in the question-and-answer format of responses; but the actual cases are less prominent than their theoretical extensions. Proculus's numerous distinctions give the work a didactic schematism.

*SABINUS. Masurius Sabinus was an early classical jurist to whom the Emperor Tiberius (reign: A.D. 14–37) gave the *ius respondendi*. Sabinus was the first member of the equestrian order to have that right. The Sabinian school of jurists was founded by him. His most significant work, three books on the *ius civile*, was widely used throughout the classical period. Pomponius, Paul, and Ulpian wrote enormous commentaries on them.

SATURNINUS. Of uncertain date, though most likely from the mid– to late second century A.D., Claudius Saturninus wrote a treatise on criminal-law penalties.

*SCAEVOLA. Quintus Cervidius Scaevola was Paul's teacher and an advisor of Marcus Aurelius (reign: A.D. 161–180). His casuistic writings (six books of *Responses*, twenty of *Questions*, forty of *Digests*) contain brief, precise descriptions of cases, often without justifications. His writings are well represented by 344 excerpts or citations in the *Digest*.

*SERVIUS. Servius Sulpicius Rufus, consul in 51 B.C., was one of the most prominent and versatile jurists of the later Republic. He taught many students; Cicero praised his eloquence as an advocate. Servius wrote, among other things, the first commentary on the praetor's Edict. After his death a comprehensive collection of his responses was published by his students Aufidius and Alfenus.

SEX. PEDIUS. Sextus Pedius is known only through citations by Paul and Ulpian. He wrote a wide-ranging commentary on the praetor's Edict and was probably a contemporary of Julian.

TERENTIUS CLEMENS. He is thought to have been a student of Julian; under Antoninus Pius (reign: A.D. 138–161) he wrote an extensive twenty-book commentary on the *lex Iulia et Papia*, the Augustan marriage legislation.

TREBATIUS. Gaius Trebatius Testa, a friend and protégé of Cicero, also served as a legal advisor to Julius Caesar and Augustus. His opinions are known mainly through his student Labeo.

TRYPHONINUS. Claudius Tryphoninus was a member, along with Papinian, of the Council of Septimius Severus (reign: 193–211). He wrote a lengthy (twenty-one books) casuistic work, *Disputationes,* and is credited with a collection of *Annotations* (*Notae*) to the work of Cervidius Scaevola.

TUBERO. Quintus Aelius Tubero. There were two jurists by this name. The elder is said to have been praetor in 129 B.C. and wrote on constitutional law and the duties of a judge. The younger was a student of A. Ofilius. Of an old senatorial family (his father was an associate of Cicero), his son was evidently the first to reach the consulate, in 11 B.C.

*ULPIAN. The late classical jurist Domitius Ulpianus was a student of Papinian; like Paul, Ulpian served as clerk (*adsessor*) when Papinian was praetorian prefect. Ulpian later became a member of the Imperial Council; under Alexander Severus (reign: A.D. 222–235) he finally reached the office of praetorian prefect. In 223 he was murdered during a riot of the Praetorian Guard.

Ulpian's eighty-three-book commentary on the praetor's Edict had virtually the same breadth as Paul's; it contained extensive discussion of the views of earlier jurists. Ulpian's commentary on the *ius civile* (fifty-one books on Sabinus) breaks off at the discussion of vindication; we do not know whether it was left incomplete at his death or a part has been lost. He also wrote numerous monographs and collections of legal opinions.

The compilers of the *Digest* drew more extensively on Ulpian's writings than on those of any other classical jurist; more than 40 percent of the *Digest* comes from his work. Although Ulpian is often considered less brilliant than his slightly older contemporary Paul, the compilers were evidently attracted by the comprehensive character of Ulpian's writing, as well as by his open-minded willingness to entertain divergent views of earlier jurists.

URSEIUS FEROX. Apparently, he wrote in the second half of the first century A.D.; Julian commented on his writings.

VALERIUS SEVERUS. He is first cited by Julian and may have written during the early second century A.D.

*VENULEIUS. Venuleius Saturninus wrote extensive monographs on private and public law during the reigns of Antoninus Pius (A.D. 138–161) and Marcus Aurelius (A.D. 161–180).

VITELLIUS. He most likely worked in the reign of Augustus (31 B.C. to A.D. 14); he was commented upon by Sabinus and Paul.

VIVIANUS. He seems to have written a commentary on the Edict during the first century A.D.; later jurists cite him occasionally.

Glossary of Technical Terms

References are to Cases or sections of the Casebook. Definitions for Roman law terms rely heavily on A. Berger, *Encyclopedic Dictionary of Roman Law,* Transactions of the American Philosophical Society, n.s., 43.2 (Philadelphia, 1953).

action (*actio*): a "lawsuit" or the claim upon which it is based. A "cause of action" is a recognized legal basis for a lawsuit. In Roman private law, the praetor's Edict listed the available causes of action; see "Edict" and "*formula.*" Among the main actions referred to in this book are the *actio rei uxoriae* or *de dote* for recovery of a dowry (see Chapter II.D.2); the *actio de peculio* on the *peculium* of a son or slave (Case 128), which is amalgamated with the *actio de in rem verso* when a *pater familias* receives benefit from *peculium* transactions (Cases 122, 137); and the *actio tutelae* on guardianship (Chapter V.A.1). Of less direct significance are the *actio quod iussu* for business conducted on the order of a *pater familias* (Case 121); the *actio institoria* and *exercitoria* on management of a business or a ship (Cases 124, 137); the *actio tributoria* to force the breakup of a *peculium* business (Cases 128, 137); and the *actio familiae erciscundae* for division of an estate (Case 207). An *actio in rem* is a property claim. For *actio noxalis*, see "*noxae deditio.*"

administratio, administratio libera: the "administration" (or "free administration") of private affairs; more specifically, the right, given by a master to a slave, to administer the *peculium* as the slave sees fit (Case 130).

adrogatio (adrogation): the adoption of one *sui iuris* person by another, with the result that the adopted person's independent *familia* ceases to exist; see Case 148 for the procedure.

adulterium (adultery): a criminal offense made punishable by, especially, the *lex Iulia de adulteriis* (see Cases 50–55 and 95–97).

aestimatio: "appraisal," the money valuation of property. This device is widely used in Roman law, notably in dowry (see Case 36). When the bride's side gives dowry property that is appraised, the husband may be obliged to restore its appraised value even if the property is now worth less.

affectio maritalis (marital affection): treating one's partner as a spouse; this is used as one touchstone in establishing the existence of marriage (see Cases 17–18).

affront: see *iniuria*.

agnate relationship: kinship traced solely through males (see Case 3); the relationship between persons who are subject to the same *pater familias*, or who would be if all their ancestors in the male line survived. The *proximus agnatus* (nearest agnate) is the closest relative among the *agnati*.

alienation of property (*alienatio*): the transfer of the ownership of property through or as a result of a transaction such as a sale or a gift. This generalized term is useful when legal discussion centers on the transfer itself rather than on the reasons for a particular transfer.

alieni iuris: subject to another's legal power. This term describes all free persons who are within the power of a *pater familias*. (The term itself, however, is not technical and was not used by the Romans; it was formed by analogy with *sui iuris*.) See Case 5.

annus utilis: an "effective year" in which a party can sue after the occurrence of an event; in essence, a statute of limitation on lawsuits. See Case 133 for an example.

benefit, father's benefit: see "*actio de in rem verso,*" under "action."

betrothal (*sponsalia*): engagement to marry or the process whereby a couple become engaged (see Chapter II.B.1). Betrothal has some incidental legal effects; for an example, see Case 7.

bonitary owner (Case 115): a person who holds legally effective title to property but, usually because of some technical flaw in its transfer from someone else, is not the actual owner. The bonitary owner will normally acquire full title in time, through usucapion.

bonorum possessio: in the law of succession, the possession of an estate that is granted by the praetor to someone whose claim to the estate the praetor recognizes; see especially Case 166. Depending on the circumstances, the praetor can enforce a will by granting possession in accordance with its terms (*secundum tabulas*), he can upset the will by granting possession to someone not entitled under the will (*contra tabulas*), or he can grant possession when there is no will (*sine tabulis*). The praetorian possessor, though not an actual heir, is treated as an effective heir.

burdens of marriage (*onera matrimonii*): expenses connected with the common life of a married couple. They are usually borne by the husband or his *pater familias* (see Case 35).

coemptio: "sale." Usually, reference is to a symbolic sale, as in the archaic ritual by which a woman is "purchased" as a wife (see Case 19). In classical law, a fictitious sale (*coemptio fiduciaria*) could be used to help a woman escape the control of her *tutor* (see Cases 227–228).

cognate relationship: blood kinship, contrasted with agnate relationship (see Case 3). The praetor gave rights to cognates (*cognati*) in succession to their blood relatives (see Cases 164–165 and 192).

cognitio (*extra ordinem*): literally, "extraordinary examination." This is an imperial form of judicial procedure that was originally thought of as "extraordinary" because it did not involve the praetor's court but instead relied directly on the emperor's authority and was administered by judges subject to him; it was also generally much more modern in its form. During the early Empire, this judicial procedure gradually supplanted the older praetorian court, until finally, in the postclassical period, the "extraordinary" became the norm. See Cases 206, 214.

collatio: a "contribution." Case 186 mentions one instance: an emancipated child whom the praetor entitles to a share in a father's estate must first combine his own independent estate with the father's, in order to avoid unfairness to other heirs.

commodatum: loan-for-use, the gratuitous loan of property that the borrower is to use and then return in accordance with the agreed terms.

concubine (*concubina*): a woman who lives in a permanent, monogamous union with a man to whom she is not legally married. Concubinage has few legal consequences. See Case 18.

condictio: a form of action in Roman law by which a plaintiff claims something from the defendant. Although the *condictio* had a generalized form, the jurists note many specific types. Two examples are the *condictio indebiti*, an action for the recovery of a payment that is erroneous because no debt actually exists; and the *condictio furtiva*, an action for recovery of stolen property or its value.

consilium: an advisory group, used by magistrates and private citizens. Although a *pater familias* was not legally obliged to use a *consilium,* this was customary (see Cases 90–91).

constitutio: a general term that embraces all types of enactments by an emperor. The *constitutio Antoniniana* is a decree of the Emperor Caracalla (A.D. 212) granting Roman citizenship to most free residents of the Roman Empire.

contract (*contractus*): a promissory agreement that creates liability if a promise is not fulfilled. Contracts based on good faith (*bona fides*), referred to in Case 136, require that both sides exercise fairness in performing their duties; most informal Roman contracts are in this category. A stipulation (*stipulatio*), by contrast, is a formal oral contract consisting of a question ("Do you promise to pay me 100?") and an answer ("I promise"); this promise is valid because of its form and, in principle, strictly enforced (see Case 117).

conubium: the legal capacity of a man and a woman to conclude a valid marriage (see Case 9).

culpa: "fault," particularly nondeliberate carelessness (by contrast with *dolus*, intentional infliction of harm). *Culpa* is used in a wide variety of contexts in Roman law, but it often refers to the legal duty of one individual to exercise reasonable care in protecting someone else or that person's property. Examples are a husband's duty with respect to dowry property (Case 70) and the duty of a *tutor* with respect to a ward's property (Case 218). Some texts speak of particular types of *culpa,* although it is sometimes disputed whether these texts are classical; an example is *culpa lata* ("wide" *culpa,* or gross negligence), in Cases 218–219.

cura: the "care" of a ward, a form of guardianship exercised by a *curator.* Roman law knows several types of *cura* for young adults, lunatics, and prodigals; see Chapter V.A.2–3.

damnum iniuria datum: "loss wrongfully inflicted," which gives rise to an action under the *lex Aquilia* of the third century B.C. This statute established liability when one person wrongfully damages property belonging to another person.

daughter-in-power (*filia familias*): a daughter who is under the paternal power of her father or of a paternal ascendant.

decemvirs (*decemviri*): members of a Board of Ten. Case 145 refers to the decemvirs who were commissioned in 451 B.C. to create the important archaic law code called the Twelve Tables.

deductio: the solemn introduction of a bride into her husband's house, usually accompanied by religious ceremonies; it is often treated as marking the beginning of marriage. See Case 20.

deposit (*depositum*): a contract whereby one person gives property into the physical control of another, who assumes the duty to watch over it without being paid.

diligentia: carefulness, a legal duty to exercise cautious conduct when another's interest is involved. A husband is required to exercise *diligentia* toward dowry property (see Case 70).

dolus or *dolus malus*: the "intent" to inflict loss or hurt on another person. Some actions require that a defendant have exhibited *dolus;* but more usually (as in Cases 70 and 218), *dolus* is used with *culpa* to indicate a more general liability for both intentional and unintentional fault.

dowry (*dos*): property given to a bridegroom by the bride or by someone else (usually her father) on her behalf, as part of the marriage process. During the marriage, the husband exercised effective control of the dowry, but he (or his heirs) might be obliged to return all or part of the dowry when the marriage ended. See especially Chapter II.B.2, C.5, D.2. A will could also leave a dowry in the form of a legacy (Cases 199–200). The rules for returning dowries vary somewhat depending on its source. A *dos profecticia* is a dowry given by a woman's paternal ascendant (usually her *pater familias*); a *dos adventicia* comes from any other source, including from the woman if she was *sui iuris*. See Cases 30 and 81–82.

Edict (*edictum*): the proclamation of the urban praetor at the beginning of his year in office in which he specified the forms of action that he accepted. The praetor's Edict contained numerous special edicts on particular causes of action. The jurists often organize their legal writings as commentaries on the Edict. During the early Empire, the contents of the Edict gradually became fixed, and a final "permanent" version (the Edictum Perpetuum) was issued under the Emperor Hadrian (reign: A.D. 117–138). The "Provincial Edict" was issued by governors in Roman provinces.

emancipation (*emancipatio*): the voluntary release of a son or daughter from the power of a *pater familias*. See especially Chapter III.C.3.

equestrian: a high social standing, held by *equites* (roughly, "knights"). In the Empire, equestrians ranked just below those of senatorial status. Many of the later classical jurists were equestrians.

exceptio: a defense that the defendant opposes to the plaintiff's claim. If the defense is proven, the plaintiff's claim is ineffective. See Case 234 for an example of a defense based upon a statute.

extra ordinem: see "*cognitio.*"

familia: the "household," including especially the free persons who are subject to the power of a *pater familias*. This is one of the fundamental concepts in Roman family law (see Case 4). The concept also extends to the household property. The "purchaser of the estate" (*familiae emptor*) is the person who fictitiously buys the estate in the ordinary form of Roman will (Case 171).

favor matrimonii: a legal policy that favors marriage in situations of legal uncertainty; for examples, see Cases 99, 102.

fideicommissum: a form of bequest in which the testator asks an heir or legatee to carry out a performance (such as a payment of money) that benefits a third party; a trust. See Chapter IV.C.2.

filiae loco: "as a daughter" or "in the position of a daughter." In the archaic *manus* marriage, the wife is treated as her husband's daughter for some purposes (see Case 36).

filius or *filia familias*: see "son-in-power" and "daughter-in-power."

formula: a written document by which, in a civil trial, the praetor appoints a *iudex* (judge) and authorizes him to condemn the defendant if certain factual or legal circumstances are proven or to absolve the defendant if this is not the case. The *formula* is settled upon during the initial portion of a trial (*in iure*), and it defines the basic issues, including especially the plaintiff's cause of action, that the parties will argue about in the second portion of the trial (*apud iudicem*). "Formulary procedure" was the normal method of bringing private lawsuits during the classical period of Roman law.

fraud (*fraus* or *dolus*): any act or transaction accomplished with the intent to swindle another or to deprive him of a legitimate advantage (see Case 220).

freedman (*libertus*), freedwoman (*liberta*): a person who has been manumitted from slavery.

fruits (*fructus*): the products or proceeds deriving from property. The term refers mainly to the natural produce of fields and gardens, the offspring of animals, and the output of mines, but also to profits obtained through legal transactions (such as rent from a lease).

furiosus (lunatic): an insane person, who by legal definition lacks the will to perform valid legal acts. Lunatics were often in the charge of a *curator* (see Case 223).

furtum: "theft," the unauthorized appropriation of another person's property. On theft of children, see Case 108.

gentiles: persons belonging to the same *gens* (clan) and sharing the same family name.

gift (*donatio*): an act of generosity in which a donor hands over something to a donee, without clearly expecting anything in return. In classical law, husbands and wives were restricted in their ability to make gifts to one another (Cases 61–65). One important form of gift is that made "in contemplation of death" (*mortis causa*), where the donor acts on the assumption that he will die in the immediate future; this gift resembles a legacy and does not become fully effective until the donor actually dies (see Chapter IV.C.3).

good-faith contract: see "contract."

guardian: see "*tutor*."

heres: the "heir," the person who enters into the rights and the place of the deceased. See also "*sui heredes*."

impubes (plural: *impuberes*): a person below the age of puberty; one who has not yet attained legal majority (see Case 6). Minors who were *sui iuris* had restricted legal rights and were usually subject to the guardianship of a *tutor* (see Chapter 5.A.1).

infamia: evil reputation or disgrace, usually as a result of having committed some act deemed publicly offensive. *Infamia* carries with it not only loss of public esteem but also some legal disabilities.

infirmitas sexus: the weakness of an individual because of his or her sex. In the case of women, this weakness is used to explain certain legal disabilities, including guardianship (see Case 225).

iniuria: a deliberate "affront" to another's personal dignity, giving rise to an action for damages. More generally, "lack of right" or "wrongfulness."

interdict (*interdictum*): an administrative order issued by the praetor at the request of a claimant and addressed to a third party, who is required to do or not to do something. The interdict *de liberis ducendis* (on leading away children) allowed a *pater familias* to reestablish physical control over his children (see Cases 49, 107–111).

iudex: a "judge" in a private trial (*iudicium*), appointed by the praetor to listen to the parties to a specific lawsuit and then to decide the case on the basis of the formula.

ius: "law" or "a right," depending on the context. The *ius civile* is the "civil law," the private law peculiar to the Roman people, especially those parts of the law that are not of praetorian origin (the *ius honorarium*); but the term *ius civile* is also used to designate private law in general.

ius liberorum: a set of privileges enjoyed by parents of several children; these privileges were first introduced by the Augustan marriage legislation.

ius occidendi: the right of a *pater familias* to kill free persons who are subject to his power (see Chapter III.A.1).

ius respondendi: the right to give authoritative legal responses. Although the nature of this right is debated, it was probably a privilege that emperors from Augustus on granted to certain jurists in recognition of their skill in interpreting the law; these jurists then had the emperor's official backing for their decisions.

iussum: an "order," including especially an order or authorization given by a *pater familias* to his son or slave to conclude a transaction or commit an act (see Case 121).

jurist (*iuris consultus, peritus*): an expert in private law.

law of persons (*ius personarum*): the body of private law pertaining to personal status. This area of law, defined in Case 1, embraces all institutions that have an influence on the legal condition of a person and his or her capacity to have rights and assume obligations.

legacy (*legatum*): a bequest made by a testator to third party and paid by the heir (see Chapter IV.C.1). Legacies are commonly of money or of property, including dowries (Cases 199–200); they may also order release from a debt owed by a third party (*legatum liberationis*, Case 205). Legacies come in many different forms. Among those discussed in this book are the legacy *per praeceptionem* (preferential legacy), ordering an heir to take specified property as part of his or her share in the estate; and the *praelegatum* (advance legacy), ordering a legatee to take a legacy before the estate is divided up among the heirs. On both these forms, see Case 204.

legitimi: a class of praetorian heirs who inherit under the *ius civile* (Case 161).

lex (plural: *leges*): a "statute" passed by an assembly of the Roman people. Statutes play a large role in Roman family law. The most important for this book are the marriage laws of Augustus: the *lex Iulia de maritandis ordinibus* of 18 B.C., the *lex Iulia de adulteriis coercendis* of 18 or 17 B.C., and the *lex Papia Poppaea* of A.D. 9. The first and third of these statutes, commonly treated together by the jurists as the *lex Iulia et Papia*, established incentives to marriage and childbirth (Cases 10, 12); the adultery law protected marriage (Cases 50–55, 95–97). Among the other statutes mentioned in this book are the *lex Aelia Sentia* of A.D. 4, which restricted the right to manumit slaves (Cases 212, 216); the *lex Aquilia* of 287 B.C., which granted redress against the wrongful infliction of harm to property (Case 139); the *lex Atinia*, which forbade usucapion of stolen property (Case 215); the *lex Cornelia de veneficis et sicariis*, the fundamental murder statute of 81 or 80 B.C. (Cases 52 and 96); the *lex Falcidia* of 40 B.C., which established that legacies could not exceed three-quarters of a testator's estate (Cases 198, 202); the *lex Glitia*, of unknown date, which dealt with undutiful wills (Case 194); the *lex Laetoria* of 192/191 B.C., which protected minors aged less than twenty-five (Case 221); *lex Minicia* of ca. 90 B.C., whereby a child whose parents had different citizenship status received the lower status (Case 9); and the *lex Pompeia de parricidiis* of 55 or 52 B.C., which repressed homicide of family members (Case 92). In the Roman Empire, *leges* were gradually superseded by *senatusconsulta* (decrees of the Senate) and imperial enactments (*constitutiones*), both of which acquired the effect of statutes.

libera administratio: see "*administratio*."

liberi: children or, more generally, descendants. This is a preferred class of heirs under the praetorian rules for intestate succession (Case 161).

litis contestatio: joinder of issue; the point at which the first phase of a Roman civil trial ends with the establishment of a *formula* appointing a *iudex* who is ordered to decide the case.

mancipatio: "mancipation," a solemn ceremony that was originally used to convey ownership of property from one person to another. This ceremony was subsequently (but at a very early date) adapted to many other purposes. For instance, it could be used to create a *manus* marriage (through *coemptio*, see Case 19; obsolete in classical times), to adopt a child in someone else's power (Case 149), to emancipate a child in one's own power (Case 155), or to create a valid will (Case 171).

mancipium: roughly, "charge." This word is used in numerous ways in Roman law, but important to family law is *mancipium* describing the legal status of a free person who has been conveyed by *mancipatio* to another, especially in an adoption or emancipation or in a noxal surrender. See Case 114.

manumission (*manumissio*): the release of a slave from the power of his or her master.

manus: literally, "hand," but the word usually means "control." In Roman law, *manus* is most commonly used to describe a husband's power over his wife in an archaic *manus* marriage (see Chapter II.C.1).

mater familias: "mother of the household," usually a wife (*uxor*) (see Case 143).

matrimonium: see "*nuptiae*."

mortis causa: "in contemplation of death"; see "gift."

necessarius: a "necessary" or "compulsory" heir. If a son or daughter under a father's power (but not a grandchild) was named an heir in the father's will or succeeded upon intestacy, this person was a *heres suus et necessarius*; he or she had no power to refuse the inheritance, though the praetor often granted an exception. Case 175 refers to another type of *heres necessarius*, in which a slave is manumitted and instituted as an heir in his master's will.

neglegentia: "carelessness," usually synonymous with "fault" (*culpa*). In Case 218, *neglegentia lata* means "gross carelessness."

noxae deditio: noxal liability. A form of liability in which a *pater familias* or master is held responsible for the acts of a son-in-power or a slave but can escape this liability by surrendering the son or slave to the plaintiff. The plaintiff acquires ownership of the slave, but the son is held in a status called *mancipium* until the debt is worked off, after which he returns to his father's power (Cases 139–140).

nuptiae or *matrimonium*: "marriage," or the marriage ceremony. *Nuptiae iustae* (or *matrimonium iustum*) refers to a marriage that is valid in Roman law.

obligatio: "obligation," a duty to pay or act that derives, in most instances, either from a contract or a delict (a civil wrong). An *obligatio naturalis* (natural obligation) is an obligation that cannot be enforced by an action but that is irreversible if carried out (see Case 118).

onera matrimonii: see "burdens of marriage."

oratio principis: the speech of the emperor in the Senate in which he proposes a *senatus-consultum*. Although the text of the Senate's decree became law, by the second century A.D. the jurists recognize the real source of the legislation by citing the *oratio* as decisive.

parricidium: the murder of one's *pater familias* or, later, other close relatives.

pater familias: the "head of a household," irrespective of whether he is married or has children; a *sui iuris* person not under the power of another. The *pater familias* was the head of his family; his power lasted, in principle, as long as he lived, without regard to the age or official position of the persons under his paternal power (*patria potestas*). He alone had the ultimate right to dispose of family property.

patria potestas: "paternal power," the power of a *pater familias* over the members of his household, including his natural and adopted children but also his wife and the wives of his sons-in-power (in an archaic *manus* marriage).

peculium: a fund of property or cash set aside by a *pater familias* for the exclusive use of a child-in-power or a slave (see Chapter III.B.3). A *peculium castrense* is a special fund comprising everything that a son-in-power earns or otherwise acquires during military service (Case 138).

pietas: "respect," the moral and legal duty that one owes, especially, to near relatives.

peregrinus: a foreigner, a non-Roman citizen. The term usually refers to the many aliens residing within the Roman Empire, until Caracalla's extension of the citizenship in A.D. 212 virtually eliminated the category. Peregrines did not enjoy the political rights of Romans and Roman private law often did not apply to them. A peregrine could not contract a valid Roman marriage (unless possessed of *conubium*, Case 9), could neither make nor witness a valid Roman will, and could not be instituted heir or receive a legacy under one, except in a soldier's testament.

postliminium: the recovery of civil rights that are held in suspension during a person's exile or capture by enemies, upon that person's return (see Cases 102–103).

postumus: a "posthumous child" born after the death of a testator or after his will is made (see Cases 182–185).

potestas: "power." In Roman family law, this term usually refers to the power of a *pater familias* over his offspring (*patria potestas*). One aspect of power is the power of life and death (*vitae necisque potestas*) (see Chapter III.A.1).

praelegatum: see "legacy."

praetor: an annually elected Roman magistrate, ranking below the consul among the traditional magistrates. The urban praetor presided at the first stage of private lawsuits between Roman citizens. His Edict listed the causes of action that he accepted; the praetor used the Edict to enforce existing law and create new causes of action.

procurator: a person who administers another's affairs with his authorization; a sort of general manager. The scope of a *procurator's* action is set by the authorization. For instance, a *procurator ad litem* is appointed by a litigant to represent his or her interests during a lawsuit (see Case 229).

prodigus: a "prodigal," a spendthrift or wastrel. Roman law permits appointment of a *curator* to manage the affairs of a *prodigus* (see Chapter V.A.3).

proximus agnatus: see "agnate relationship."

pupillus, pupilla: "ward," a child below the age of majority who is not under the power of a *pater familias* and so is under the guardianship of a *tutor* (see Chapter V.A.1).

querella inofficiosi testamenti: the "complaint that a will is undutiful" because a person who would be a legitimate heir upon intestacy has been either omitted from a will or unjustly disinherited (see Chapter IV.B.4).

repudiation (*repudium*): the unilateral dissolution of a betrothal or a marriage by one of the parties.

res: "property," applied to both corporeal and incorporeal things. Roman property law is complex, but one of its most fundamental categories, inherited from archaic law, is *res mancipi,* things the ownership of which is passed by mancipation or by other formal ceremony (see Cases 171, 226).

rescript (*rescriptum*): the written answer of the emperor to queries from officials or private individuals, expressing the emperor's authoritative opinion on a legal question. By the mid–second century A.D., this had become a major means for emperors to introduce new rules.

restitutio in integrum: "reinstatement into a former legal position." This was an extraordinary remedy used by the praetor to assist a person who had suffered an inequitable loss, especially because of that person's age (Cases 220, 222).

senatusconsultum: a decree of the Senate, which in the early Empire took on statutory force. Many of these decrees are important for family law; among them are the SC Macedonianum on cash loans to sons-in-power (Cases 119, 132, 138, 234), SC Orphitianum on the inheritance from women by their children (Cases 147, 169–170), SC Plancianum on a woman's pregnancy after divorce (Cases 47 and 144), SC Silanianum on the assassination of a master by slaves (Case 56), SC Tertullianum on the inheritance from children by their mother (Cases 168–170), and the SC Vellaeanum forbidding women to assume liability for others (Cases 233–234). See also "*oratio principis*."

senator: a member of the Roman Senate. Roman senators and their immediate families hold the rank of *clarissimi,* "most eminent persons."

son-in-power (*filius familias*): a son (or, more generally, any descendant in the male line) who is in the power of a *pater familias.*

spado: a "eunuch" (see Case 8).

sponsalia: see "betrothal."

stipulation (*stipulatio*): see "contract."

stuprum: sexual "depravity," an illicit sexual act; especially, sex with a woman who was respectable but not married. See also "*adulterium*."

substitution (*substitutio*): in a will, the appointment of another heir in the event that the heir who was first instituted does not take the inheritance. A particular form is pupillary substitution, the appointment of a substitute by the father for his child (a minor, *pupillus*) who was instituted as heir in the father's will (see Cases 172–173).

succession: the body of law governing the process whereby an heir takes the place of a deceased person.

sui heredes: the "privileged heirs," those who become *sui iuris* upon the death of a *pater familias.* They hold a privileged position in the law of succession (see Cases 159 and 177).

sui iuris: "in one's own legal power," that is, legally independent, not under a *pater familias* (see Case 5).

testamentum: "will." The formal act whereby a testator institutes one or more heirs to succeed to his estate after his death. A *testamentum inofficiosum* is an "undutiful will," which fails to take adequate account of near family members; see "*querella inofficiosi testamenti.*"

trust: see "fideicommissum."

tutor: a "guardian," a person appointed to look after another person, who is in a legal state of *tutela* (guardianship). Roman law knows two basic types: the *tutor* for a *sui iuris* child below the age of majority (Chapter V.A.1) and the *tutor* for adult *sui iuris* women (Chapter V.B.1).

Twelve Tables (Duodecim Tabulae): the earliest Roman collection of the fundamental rules of Roman customary law, published in 449 B.C. on twelve "tables" (probably wooden boards). This codification had major influence on the subsequent development of Roman law.

unde liberi, unde legitimi, unde cognati, unde vir et uxor: classes of heirs under the praetorian rules for intestate succession ("children, statutory heirs, cognate relatives, husband and wife"; see Cases 161–167).

usucapion (*usucapio*): acquisition of ownership of property belonging to another through possession of the property for a prescribed period of time.

usufruct (*ususfructus*): the right to use another's property and to take produce from it without impairing its substance.

uxor: "wife"; see "*vir et uxor.*"

vicarius: a slave who is within the *peculium* of another slave and who often exercises a *peculium* of his own (see Case 126).

vir et uxor: "man and wife." This is also a class of heirs under the praetorian rules for intestate succession (see Case 167).

vitae necisque potestas: see "*potestas.*"

Suggested Further Reading

The most important primary source for Roman law is Justinian's *Digest*, which has in recent years been translated into English: *The Digest of Justinian*, 4 vols., ed. A. Watson (Philadelphia, 1985). Besides the *Digest*, Gaius's *Institutes*, available in more than one English translation, is also essential. F. de Zulueta, *The Institutes of Gaius*, 2 vols. (Oxford, 1946–1953), has a fine commentary and is preferable on that basis to W. M. Gordon and O. F. Robinson, *The Institutes of Gaius* (Ithaca, 1988). As for Justinian's *Institutes*, J. A. C. Thomas's *The Institutes of Justinian* (Cape Town, 1975) is the best English version, though several others are available; P. Birks and G. McLeod's *Justinian's Institutes* (Ithaca, 1987) may be more accessible. Justinian's *Institutes* presents Roman law in a somewhat "modernized" Byzantine version. For commentary see now E. Metzger, ed., *A Companion to Justinian's Institutes* (Ithaca, 1998). Most other primary sources on classical law have not received good English translations or good translations that are reasonably accessible, though M. H. Crawford, ed., *Roman Statutes*, 2 vols. (London, 1996), has a critical edition of the text, translation, and commentary (with good bibliography) of some Roman statutes, that is, sixty-five *leges* and *rogationes* (and no *senatusconsulta* or magisterial and imperial edicts).

On works relevant to Roman family law as well as history, see the "Bibliography on the Roman Family" below.

For a short general summary of Roman law, B. Nicholas's *An Introduction to Roman Law* (Oxford, 1962) is hard to beat for brevity and clearness; Nicholas is particularly good at expounding Roman law for readers in the common-law tradition. Among other available introductions, probably the fullest is M. Kaser, *Roman Private Law*, 4th ed., trans. R. Dannenbring (Pretoria 1984); Kaser looks at Roman law from a distinctively European perspective, and he is not always easy to read. W. W. Buckland's *A Textbook of Roman Law*, 3d ed., ed. P. Stein (Cambridge, 1963), is intended, despite its name, mainly for advanced readers. A. Borkowski's *Textbook on Roman Law*, 2d ed. (Oxford, 2002), on the other hand, is well organized and accessible to the beginner, featuring plenty of cases in translation. More extensive, better documented, and at the same time more formidable is J. A. C. Thomas, *Textbook of Roman Law* (Amsterdam, 1976).

On the historical background of Roman law, W. Kunkel's *An Introduction to Roman Legal and Constitutional History*, 2d ed., trans. J. M. Kelly (Oxford, 1973), is brief and well organized. H. F. Jolowicz and B. Nicholas's *Historical Introduction to the Study of Roman Law*, 3d ed. (Cambridge, 1972), is fuller, though some may find it hard to follow. A. A. Schiller, *Roman Law: Mechanisms of Development* (The Hague, 1978), offers a more institutional approach; the book also has an excellent bibliography. E. Metzger, *A New Outline of the Roman Civil Trial* (Oxford, 1997), presents new arguments and recently discovered evidence regarding the law of civil procedure. Two recent books are designed particularly for those with an interest in ancient history. O. F. Robinson, *The Sources of Roman Law: Problems and Methods for Ancient Historians* (London, 1997), has three short expository chapters setting forth various aspects of the legal sources in clear and concise fashion, followed by two, more innovative chapters, one exploring problems in the law of civil procedure and the second discussing difficulties ancient historians can expect to encounter in treating the sources for Roman law. D. Johnston, *Roman Law in Context* (Cambridge, 1999), examines some of the same topics, though from a somewhat different perspective; the bulk of the book is devoted to a clear, concise, and engaging treatment of some major aspects of substantive law and procedure in light of the Roman economy and society. One particularly useful feature is the brief analytical bibliography.

J. A. Crook, *Law and Life of Rome* (Ithaca, 1967), looks at Roman law from the perspective of Roman social history; Crook discusses numerous surviving private documents that reflect Roman law in practice. Among the many other books discussing particular aspects of Roman law from a social perspective, readers may enjoy B. W. Frier, *Landlords and Tenants in Imperial Rome* (Princeton, 1980). B. W. Frier, *The Rise of the Roman Jurists* (Princeton, 1985), recounts the emergence of the legal profession in the later Roman Republic and the effect of "legal science" on Roman society. On other topics, see S. D. Martin, *The Roman Jurists and the Organization of Private Building in the Late Republic and Early Empire* (Brussels, 1989); D. P. Kehoe, *Investment, Profit, and Tenancy: The Jurists and the Roman Agrarian Economy* (Ann Arbor, 1997); T. A. J. McGinn, *Prostitution, Sexuality, and the Law in Ancient Rome* (Oxford, 1998), which has extensive discussions of the marriage and adultery legislation of Augustus.

For a lively account of the main social values expressed in Roman private law, F. Schulz, *Principles of Roman Law*, trans. M. Wolff (Oxford, 1936), can be recommended.

On the historical influence of Roman law, O. F. Robinson, T. D. Fergus, and W. M. Gordon, *An Introduction to European Legal History*, 2d rev. ed. (London, 1994), present a good overview. W. W. Buckland and A. McNair, *Roman Law and Common Law*, 2d ed., ed. F. H. Lawson, rev. J. C. Hall (Cambridge, 1965), survey the basic differences between the two systems. J. H. Merryman's *The Civil Law Tradition*, 2d ed. (Stanford, 1985), is a good summary of the basic characteristics of modern civil law.

Finally, those interested in the case-law approach applied to Roman law should consult B. W. Frier, *A Casebook on the Roman Law of Delict* (Atlanta, 1989).

Bibliography on the Roman Family

The bibliography provides a selection of books and articles representing modern scholarly approaches to the Roman family. The actual bibliography on these subjects is vast, so what follows is only what is essential, relatively recent, and (for the most part) in English. Some collections listed here contain a number of items of interest that are not listed separately. Abbreviations for philological and historical works generally follow those given by *L'Année Philologique;* for Roman legal literature, those given by M. Kaser, *Das römische Privatrecht,* vols. 1–2, 2d ed. (Munich, 1971–1975). An asterisk designates books recommended for persons new to the field.

Andreau, J., and H. Bruhns, eds. *Parenté et strategies familiales dans l'antiquité romaine.* Coll. Éc. Franç. 129. Rome, 1990.

Ariès, P. *L'Enfant et la vie familiale sous l'ancien regime.* Paris, 1960. Trans. R. Baldick under the title *Centuries of Childhood: A Social History of Family Life* (New York, 1962).

Astolfi, R. *La Lex Iulia et Papia.* 4th ed. Padua, 1996.

Badian, E. "A Phantom Marriage Law." *Philologus* 129 (1985) 82–98.

Bagnall, R. S. "Church, State, and Divorce in Late Roman Egypt." In K.-L. Selig and R. Somerville, eds., *Essays in Honor of Paul Oskar Kristeller,* 41–61. New York, 1987.

Bagnall, R. S., and B. W. Frier. *The Demography of Roman Egypt.* Cambridge, 1994.

Bannon, C. J. *The Brothers of Romulus: Fraternal Pietas in Roman Law, Literature, and Society.* Princeton, 1997.

Bauman, R. A. *Women and Politics in Ancient Rome.* London, 1992.

Beaucamp, J. *Le statut de la femme à Byzance (4ᵉ–7ᵉ siècle).* Vol. 1, *Le droit impérial.* Vol. 2, *Les pratiques sociales.* Paris, 1990–1992.

Beck, M. "Properzens Elegie 2,7 und die augusteische Ehegesetzgebung." *Philologus* 144.2 (2000) 303–324.

Boswell, J. *The Kindness of Strangers: The Abandonment of Children in Western Europe from Late Antiquity to the Renaissance.* New York, 1988.

Boulvert, G., and M. Morabito. "Le droit de l'esclavage sous le Haut-Empire." *ANRW* (Berlin) 2.14 (1982) 98–182.

Bradley, K. R. *Slaves and Masters in the Roman Empire: A Study in Social Control.* Oxford, 1987.

*———. *Discovering the Roman Family: Studies in Roman Social History.* Oxford, 1991.

———. *Slavery and Society at Rome.* Cambridge, 1994.

Brown, P. *The Body and Society: Men, Women, and Sexual Renunciation in Early Christianity.* New York, 1988.

Buckland, W. W. *The Roman Law of Slavery from Augustus to Justinian.* Cambridge, 1908. Reprint, New York, 1969.

Cantarella, E. "Famiglia romana e demografia sociale: Spunti di riflessione critica e metodologica." *Iura* 43 (1992) 99–111.

*Champlin, E. *Final Judgements: Duty and Emotion in Roman Wills, 200 B.C.–A.D. 250.* Berkeley, 1991.

*Corbett, P. E. *The Roman Law of Marriage.* Oxford, 1930.

Daube, D. *The Duty of Procreation.* Edinburgh, 1977.

Dixon, S. "*Infirmitas Sexus:* Womanly Weakness in Roman Law." *TR* 52 (1984) 343–371.

———. "Breaking the Law to Do the Right Thing: The Gradual Erosion of the Voconian Law in Ancient Rome." *Adelaide L.R.* 9 (1985) 519–534.

———. *The Roman Mother.* Norman, Okla., 1988.

*———. *The Roman Family.* Baltimore, 1992.

Evans, J. K. *War, Women and Children in Ancient Rome.* London and New York, 1991.

Evans-Grubbs, J. *Law and the Family in Late Antiquity: The Emperor Constantine's Legislation on Marriage and the Family.* Oxford, 1995.

Fantham, E. "*Stuprum*: Public Attitudes and Penalties for Sexual Offences in Republican Rome." *EMC/CV* n.s. 10 (1991) 267–291.

Finley, M. I. *Ancient Slavery and Modern Ideology.* London, 1980.

Frier, B. W. "Natural Fertility and Family Limitation in Roman Marriage." *CPh* 89 (1994) 318–333.

———. "The Demography of the Early Roman Empire." In *CAH,* vol. 11, *A.D. 70–192,* 787–816. Cambridge, 2000.

*Gardner, J. F. *Women in Roman Law and Roman Society.* London and Sydney, 1986.

———. *Being a Roman Citizen.* New York, 1993.

*———. *Family and Familia in Roman Law and Life.* Oxford, 1998.

*Gardner, J. F., and T. Wiedemann. *The Roman Household: A Sourcebook.* London, 1991.

*Johnston, D. *The Roman Law of Trusts.* Oxford, 1988.

Kertzer, D. I., and R. P. Saller, eds. *The Family in Italy from Antiquity to the Present.* New Haven and London, 1991.

Lefkowitz, M. R., and M. B. Fant. *Women's Life in Greece and Rome: A Source Book in Translation.* 2d ed. Baltimore, 1992.

Martin, D. B. "The Construction of the Roman Family: Methodological Considerations." *JRS* 86 (1996) 40–60.

McGinn, T. A. J. "Concubinage and the *Lex Iulia* on Adultery." *TAPA* 121 (1991) 335–375.

———. "The *SC* from Larinum and the Repression of Adultery at Rome." *ZPE* 93 (1992) 273–295.

———. "The Legal Definition of Prostitute in Late Antiquity." *MAAR* 42 (1997 [1998]) 73–116.

———. *Prostitution, Sexuality, and the Law in Ancient Rome.* Oxford, 1998.

———. "The Social Policy of Emperor Constantine in *Codex Theodosianus* 4.6.3." *TR* 67 (1999) 57–73.

———. "Widows, Orphans, and Social History." *JRA* 12.2 (1999) 617–632.

———. "The Augustan Marriage Legislation and Social Practice: Elite Endogamy vs. Male 'Marrying Down.'" In J.-J. Aubert and A. J. B. Sirks, eds., *Speculum Iuris: Roman Law as a Reflection of Economic and Social Life,* 46–93. Ann Arbor, 2002.

———. "Missing Females? Augustus' Encouragement of Marriage between Freeborn Males and Freedwomen." *Historia.* In press.

Meinhart, M. *Die Senatusconsulta Tertullianum und Orfitianum in ihrer Bedeutung für das klassische römische Erbrecht.* Graz, 1967.

Ozment, S. *Ancestors: The Loving Family in Old Europe.* Cambridge, 2001.

Parkin, T. G. *Demography and Roman Society.* Baltimore, 1992.

Peppe, L. *Posizione giuridica e ruolo sociale della donna romana in età repubblicana.* Milan, 1984.

*Rawson, B., ed. *The Family in Ancient Rome: New Perspectives.* Ithaca, 1986.

———. "*Spurii* and the Roman View of Illegitimacy." *Antichthon* 23 (1989) 10–41.

———. *Marriage, Divorce and Children in Ancient Rome.* Oxford, 1991.

————. "'The Family' in the Ancient Mediterranean: Past, Present, Future." *ZPE* 117 (1997) 294–296.

Rawson, B., and P. Weaver, eds. *The Roman Family in Italy: Status, Sentiment, Space.* Oxford, 1997.

Rizzelli, G. *Lex Iulia de adulteriis: Studi sulla disciplina di adulterium, lenocinium, stuprum.* Lecce, 1997.

————. *Le donne nell'esperienza giuridica di Roma antica: Il controllo dei comportamenti sessuali (una raccolta di testi).* Lecce, 2000.

Robinson, O. F. "Women and the Criminal Law." In B. Carpino, ed., *Raccolta di scritti in memoria di Raffaele Moschella,* 527–560. Perugia, 1985.

————. "The Status of Women in Roman Private Law." *JR* Part 2 (1987) 143–162.

Saller, R. P. "Slavery and the Roman Family." *Slavery and Abolition* 8 (1987) 65–87. Also in M. I. Finley, ed., *Classical Slavery* (1987).

*————. *Patriarchy, Property and Death in the Roman Family.* Cambridge, 1994.

*————. "The Family and Society." In J. Bodel, ed., *Epigraphic Evidence: History from Inscriptions,* 95–117. London and New York, 2001.

Saller, R. P., and B. D. Shaw. "Tombstones and Roman Family Relations in the Principate: Civilians, Soldiers and Slaves." *JRS* 74 (1984) 124–156.

Scheidel, W., ed. *Debating Roman Demography.* Mnemosyne Supplements 211. Leiden, 2000.

Selb, W. "Vom Ius Vitae Necisque zum Beschraenkten Zuechtigungsrecht und zur Magistratischen Zuechtigungshilfe." *Irish Jurist* 1 (1966) 136–150.

Shaw, B. D. "Latin Funerary Epigraphy and Family Relations in the Later Empire." *Historia* 33 (1984) 457–497.

————. "The Age of Roman Girls at Marriage: Some Reconsiderations." *JRS* 77 (1987) 30–46.

————. "The Family in Late Antiquity: The Experience of Augustine." *P & P* 15 (1987) 3–51.

————. "The Cultural Meaning of Death: Age and Gender in the Roman Family." In D. I. Kertzer and R. P. Saller, eds., *The Family in Italy from Antiquity to the Present,* 66–90. New Haven and London, 1991.

————. "Raising and Killing Children: Two Roman Myths." *Mnemosyne* 54.1 (2001) 31–77.

Treggiari, S. *Roman Freedmen during the Late Republic.* Oxford, 1969.

————. "*Concubinae.*" *PBSR* 49 (1981) 59–81.

————. "Women as Property in the Early Roman Empire." In D. K. Weisberg, ed., *Women and the Law: A Social Historical Perspective,* 2:7–33. Cambridge, 1982.

*————. *Roman Marriage: Iusti Coniuges from the Time of Cicero to the Time of Ulpian.* Oxford, 1991.

Voci, P. *Diritto ereditario romano* 1² (Milan 1967), 2² (Milan, 1963).

Wallace-Hadrill, A. *Houses and Society in Pompeii and Herculaneum.* Princeton, 1994.

Watson, A. *The Law of Persons in the Later Roman Republic.* Oxford, 1967.

————. *Roman Slave Law.* Baltimore, 1987.

Weaver, P. R. C. *Familia Caesaris: A Social Study of the Emperor's Freedmen and Slaves.* Cambridge, 1972.

Index of Sources

The following list includes all ancient sources cited in this Casebook. Case numbers in bold are to the Cases themselves; other Case numbers refer to the Case Discussions.

Gaius, *Institutiones* (*continued*)

1.136: 19
1.137–137a: 40
1.144–145: 225
1.156: 3, 151, 161
1.163: 155
1.173: 225, 227
1.174–175: 227
1.179: 225
1.180: 225
1.190–191: 225, 231, 233
1.194: 225
1.196: 1, 6, 7, 8, 110, 173, 228
1.199–200: 214
2.62–63: 66, 72, 219
2.79: 63
2.80–81: 226
2.85: 226
2.86–87: 114, 115, 116, 166, 170
2.89: 115, 116, 129
2.95: 115, 116, 129
2.96: 39
2.98: 38
2.103: 171
2.104: 171
2.105–108: 171
2.105: 171
2.112: 226, 228
2.113: 228
2.119–120: 171
2.125–126: 186
2.130–134: 178
2.135: 186
2.157: 159
2.174–175: 172
2.177: 172
2.179: 173, 176
2.180–181: 173
2.192–223: 198
2.268–269: 203
2.271: 209
3.1–4: 37, 159, 185, 228
3.1–3: 4, 37, 108
3.7–9: 159
3.12: 159
3.14: 37
3.16: 164
3.32: 161
3.83–84: 38
3.92–109: 117

3.104: 39, 118, 121, 128, 133
3.105–106: 117
3.106: 12, 223
3.114: 39
3.125: 36
3.151: 17
3.199: 39, 108
3.221: 27, 44
4.38: 38
4.62–63: 81
4.70: 121, 122, 128, 130
4.71: 124, 130, 137, 204
4.72a: 134
4.74: 124, 137
4.74a: 137
4.75–76: 139
4.77: 140
4.78: 140
4.115–125: 234

Gai. Augustod.

86: 90

Gellius, *Noctes Atticae*

3.16.12: 145, 146
4.3.2: 38
5.19.10: 152

Historia Augusta, Marcus

10.12: 221

Orosius

4.13.8: 90
5.16.8: 90

Paulus, *Sententiae* (Paul, *Sent.*)

1.9.1: 220
1.21.11: 84
2.8.1–2: 124
2.11.3: 233
2.19.1: 25
2.19.2: 104
2.19.6: 9
2.19.8: 20
2.20.1: 18
2.21a.6: 226
2.23.2: 61
2.23.4: 62
2.24.1–3: 9
2.25.5: 155

2.26.10: 54
2.26.12: 55
2.26.15: 11
3.4a.5: 193
3.4a.11: 193
3.8.1: 193
4.1.1: 66
4.1.6a: 207
4.3.3: 198
5.1.1: 93
5.6.15: 24, 104, 105, 107

Plinius (the Elder), *Naturalis Historia*

7.5.40: 145

Plinius (the Younger), *Epistulae*

1.14: 100
6.33.2–6: 192

Quintilianus, *Institutio Oratoria*

5.11.32: 15

[Quintilianus], *Declamationes Maiores*

3.17: 90

Sallustius, *Bellum Catilinae*

39.5: 90

Scholia Sinaitica

6: 41

Seneca, *De Clementia*

1.15.1–6, 16.1: **91**, 177

Tacitus, *Annales*

4.16: 19
15.19: 149

Tituli ex Corpore Ulpiani (*Tit. Ulp.*)

5.2: 7, **13**, **14**, 98
5.3–5: **9**, 143
5.6–7: 9, **11**, 98
5.8–10: **9**, 143
6.2: **30**, **69**, **81**, 104
6.4–5: 30, 69, **81**, 83
6.6–7: 30, 38, 66, 79, **82**, **99**
6.8: 29, 81, 199
6.9–10: 34, 61, 69, 73, 80, 83
6.12–13: 34, 61, 69, 73, 80, 83
6.15: 71

6.16: 86
6.17: 88
10.1: 155
11.1: 225
11.20: 103
11.25: 226
11.27: **226**
13.2: 1, 9, **10**, 18, 42
15.1–2: 12
16.1–1a: 7, 8, 10, **12**, **15**, **103**, **149**, **168**
16.2: 10
19.18–19: 39
19.19: 114
20.10: 113, **138**
20.13: 193
23.1–4: 46, **162**, 178
23.3: 37
23.9: 176
25.1: 207
26.7: 151, **169**, **228**
26.8: 147, 151, 161, **168**
28.7–8: 161

Valerius Maximus

5.4.5: 97
5.8.5: 90
5.9.1: **90**, 177
6.1.5–6: 90
8.3.2: 230

Justinianic Sources

Codex Justinianus (C.)

2.24.2: 221
3.28.3: **195**
3.28.18: 179
3.28.20: 179
4.26.10.1: 130
5.1.1: **28**, 78
5.1.6: 24
5.3.1: 26
5.3.6: 20, **21**, **22**
5.4.1–2: 100
5.4.5: 100
5.4.9: **16**, 146
5.4.10: 42
5.4.11: 108
5.4.12: 100
5.4.14: **41**, 75
5.4.18: 100

Printed in the United States
141501LV00006B/1/A